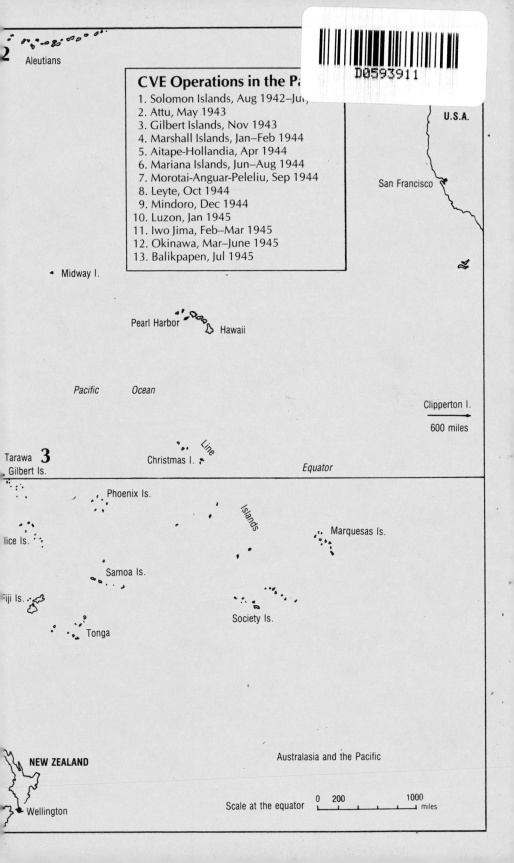

2 Aleutians

U.S.A.

CVE Operations in the P...

1. Solomon Islands, Aug 1942–Ju...
2. Attu, May 1943
3. Gilbert Islands, Nov 1943
4. Marshall Islands, Jan–Feb 1944
5. Aitape-Hollandia, Apr 1944
6. Mariana Islands, Jun–Aug 1944
7. Morotai-Anguar-Peleliu, Sep 1944
8. Leyte, Oct 1944
9. Mindoro, Dec 1944
10. Luzon, Jan 1945
11. Iwo Jima, Feb–Mar 1945
12. Okinawa, Mar–June 1945
13. Balikpapen, Jul 1945

San Francisco

Midway I.

Pearl Harbor   Hawaii

Pacific   Ocean

Clipperton I.

600 miles

Tarawa **3**
Gilbert Is.

Christmas I.   Line

Equator

Phoenix Is.

Islands

lice Is.

Marquesas Is.

Samoa Is.

Fiji Is.

Society Is.

Tonga

NEW ZEALAND

Australasia and the Pacific

Wellington

Scale at the equator   0   200   1000
miles

THE LITTLE GIANTS

THE
LITTLE
GIANTS

U.S. Escort Carriers Against Japan

William T. Y'Blood

NAVAL INSTITUTE PRESS   *Annapolis, Maryland*

Library of Congress Cataloging-in-Publication Data

Y'Blood, William T., 1937–
    The little giants.

    Bibliography: p.
    Includes index.
    1. World War, 1939–1945—Aerial operations, American.
    2. World War, 1939–1945—Naval operations, American.
    3. World War, 1939–1945—Campaigns—Pacific Area.
    4. Aircraft carriers—United States. I. Title.
    D790.Y42   1987   940.54′26   87-7866
    ISBN 0-87021-275-3

Printed in the United States of America

CONTENTS

INTRODUCTION

THEY WERE CALLED "jeeps," "baby flattops," "two-torpedo ships," "combustible, vulnerable, expendable," and other, unprintable, names. They were the CVEs—the U.S. Navy's designation for aircraft carrier, escort.

These ships, envisioned as hardly more than convoy escorts in the beginning, evolved into remarkably versatile vessels. Yes, they were used to escort convoys, but they also hunted submarines, provided air support for invasion forces, ferried men and planes to far-flung bases, delivered replacement aircraft and pilots to the fast carriers of Task Forces 58 and 38, and worked as troop transports. Despite the great activity of the eighty-six vessels built (some finished after the war) to serve all around the world for the United States Navy, their accomplishments, except for one glorious action in October 1944, have never received the publicity and credit that they deserve.

Too often the CVE sailors heard comments like the one from a new officer on the *Saginaw Bay* who had just come from one of the fast carriers: "I don't know how you take care of that routine here, but I know how it's done on a carrier!" Too often they saw the headline "Fast Carriers Winning the War"—a headline hard for them to stomach after sending their planes out day after day to pound the enemy defenses in front of the ground forces or to attack skulking submarines. Too often they saw their own deserving shipmates passed over for awards while sailors and airmen on the fast carriers seemed to be raking them in.

This lack of recognition may have frustrated or even angered the "jeep" sailors, but it didn't stop them from doing their jobs and doing them well. History has shown that the fast carriers didn't win World War II; neither did the Army Air Forces nor army or marine troops. It was a team effort that won the war, and a vital part of this team effort was the escort carriers. Until now, little has been written about their accomplishments, and this book is intended to give the CVEs and their sailors their long-overdue attention.

The sources consulted include action reports, war diaries, ships' histories, air action reports, and so forth. I am greatly indebted to those men, listed in the bibliography, who contributed their personal accounts of service on the "jeeps." In addition, this book would not have been possible without the help of several people: Henry "Hank" Pyzdrowski of the *Gambier Bay*/VC-10 Association (a real go-getting organization), Herb Faulkner of the *Natoma Bay* Association, Bob Zubik and Hank Henderson of the *Ommaney Bay* Association, and James Dresser. Many, many thanks to these men, who provided me with material and leads to track down, saving me hours of possibly fruitless digging for information. My thanks also to Dr. Dean Allard and his staff, particularly Mike Walker, at the Naval Historical Center's Operational Archives Branch. A special thanks goes to my editor, Laurie Stearns, who cleared away much of the underbrush. Finally, I must thank my wife, Carolyn, and children, Kent and Laura. They'd been through this rat race before but still gave me much-needed and much-appreciated support.

GLOSSARY

AA	Antiaircraft
ACI	Air combat intelligence
ACV	Auxiliary aircraft carrier
airedale	Flight deck crewman
AO	Oiler
APV	Transport and aircraft ferry
ASP	Antisubmarine patrol
ASW	Antisubmarine warfare
AVG	Aircraft tender, general purpose
black gang	Engine-room crew
bogey	Unidentified aircraft
CAG	Air group commander
CAP	Combat air patrol
CarDiv	Carrier Division
CarTransRonPac	Carrier Transport Squadron Pacific
CASD	Carrier aircraft service detachment
CASU	Carrier aircraft service unit
CIC	Combat Information Center
CinCPac	Commander in Chief Pacific Fleet
CO	Commanding officer
CortDiv	Escort Division
CruDiv	Cruiser Division
CSA	Commander Support Aircraft
CTG	Commander of task group
CVE	Aircraft carrier, escort
CVEG	Escort carrier air group
DD	Destroyer
DE	Destroyer escort

"deck"	Sea level
DesRon	Destroyer Squadron
F	Flagship
FDO	Fighter director officer
FF	Force or task group flagship
flak	Antiaircraft fire
GP	General-purpose bomb
GPM	Gallons per minute
hedgehog	Type of throw-ahead missile launcher
HF/DF	High frequency direction finding
IFF	Identification, friend or foe
JASCO	Joint Assault Signal Company
JCS	Joint Chiefs of Staff
jink	To take evasive action in an aircraft
KIA	Killed in action
LCI(G)	Landing craft, infantry (gunboat)
LCI(R)	Landing craft, infantry (rocket)
LCT	Landing craft, tank
LSM	Landing ship, medium
LSO	Landing signal officer
LST	Landing ship, tank
MAG	Marine Air Group
Magic	Code name for U.S. efforts to break the Japanese codes
MASG	Marine Air Support Group
MCVG	Marine Carrier Air Group
NAS	Naval air station
OTC	Officer in tactical command
RAMP	Recovery of allied military personnel
SAP	Semi-armor-piercing
scramble	Immediate launch of aircraft
SFCP	Shoreline Fire Control Party
SOPA	Senior officer present afloat
TASP	Target antisubmarine patrol
TBS	Talk-Between-Ships
TCAP	Target combat air patrol
TF	Task Force
TG	Task Group
TU	Task Unit
USN	United States Navy
USS	United States Ship
VC	Navy composite squadron (both fighters and bombers)

VF	Navy fighter squadron
VGF	ACV-based fighter squadron
VGS	ACV-based scout squadron
VMF	Marine fighter squadron
VMO	Marine observation squadron
VMSB	Marine scout-bomber squadron
VMTB	Marine torpedo bomber squadron
VOC	Navy composite observation squadron
VOF	Navy fighter observation squadron
VS	Navy scout squadron
VT	Navy torpedo bomber squadron
WP	White phosphorus

United States Aircraft Types

Avenger	Grumman/General Motors TBF/TBM torpedo plane
Corsair	Vought F4U fighter
Dauntless	Douglas SBD dive bomber
Dumbo	Search and rescue aircraft, usually a PBY
Hellcat	Grumman F6F fighter
Helldiver	Curtiss SB2C dive bomber
Seagull	Curtiss SOC float scout plane
Thunderbolt	Republic P-47 army fighter-bomber
Wildcat	Grumman/General Motors F4F/FM fighter

Japanese Aircraft Types

Betty	Mitsubishi G4M attack bomber
Frances	Yokosuka P1Y night fighter
Hamp	Mitsubishi A6M3 fighter; later called Zeke 32
Irving	Nakajima J1N1 reconnaissance plane or night fighter
Jake	Aichi E13A reconnaissance floatplane
Jill	Nakajima B6N torpedo bomber
Judy	Yokosuka D4Y dive bomber
Kate	Nakajima B5N torpedo bomber
Lily	Kawasaki Ki-48 light bomber
Mavis	Kawanishi H6K flying boat
Myrt	Nakajima C6N reconnaissance plane
Nell	Mitsubishi G3M attack bomber or Yokosuka L3Y transport
Nick	Kawasaki Ki-45 fighter
Oscar	Nakajima Ki-43 fighter
Pete	Mitsubishi F1M observation seaplane

Rufe   Nakajima A6M2-N fighter seaplane
Sally   Mitsubishi Ki-21 heavy bomber
Sonia   Mitsubishi Ki-51 assault plane
Tabby   Douglas L2D transport
Tojo   Nakajima Ki-44 fighter
Tony   Kawasaki Ki-61 fighter
Val   Aichi D3A dive bomber
Zeke   Mitsubishi A6M fighter

Flight Maneuvers

chandelle   An abrupt, steep climbing turn to gain altitude
                        and change direction.
flipper turn   A sharp, steeply banked turn.
Immelmann turn   A half loop with a rollout, from which the air-
                        craft emerges heading in the opposite direction
                        at a higher altitude.
Lufbery circle   A formation of two or more aircraft in a nose-
                        to-tail circle to protect one another and be in
                        position to face attacking planes.
split S   A half roll on the aircraft's back followed by a
                        descending loop.
Thach Weave   A maneuver in which two fighters or two sec-
                        tions weave or scissor toward each other, en-
                        abling the planes to cover their tails.

Doug MacArthur's Navy

Oh, we're the boys in the CVEs,
A little bit shaky in the knees.
Our engines knock and cough and wheeze
In Doug MacArthur's Navy.

We operate where it's hot as hell,
Move in close to ring the bell,
Prime targets for a Zeke or Nell
In Doug MacArthur's Navy.

While Jeeps are not dependable,
Their actions are commendable,
But gosh, they are expendable
In Doug MacArthur's Navy.

They sent us out to the Philippines,
Shuffled supplies behind the scenes,
And all that was left for us was beans
In Doug MacArthur's Navy.

To make the Leyte show complete
They let us tackle the whole Jap Fleet,
While the big shots sat in a grandstand seat
In Doug MacArthur's Navy.

Next they sent us to the Inland Seas,
Screened by cruisers and old BB's,
Giving cover by CAP's
In Doug MacArthur's Navy.

For the biggest show of the whole campaign
We entered the Sulu Sea again
And the Jap attacks were thick as rain
In Doug MacArthur's Navy.

We survived the trip intact (almost).
Near to Lingayen took up our posts,
Our fannies exposed to the China Coast
In Doug MacArthur's Navy.

Said Halsey to his big CVs,
This time we'll trap those Japanese.
We'll bait the trap with CVEs
In Doug MacArthur's Navy.

Oh, we'll bait the trap with CVEs.
Those ships sure look like a lot of cheese.
And all that we could say was "Jees"
In Doug MacArthur's Navy.

When the war is over I'll tell it true.
We took whatever the enemy threw.
Weathered it—and MacArthur, too,
In Doug MacArthur's Navy.

HAM LOKEY

THE LITTLE GIANTS

PROLOGUE

A LIGHT BREEZE ruffled the surface of the water, a breeze more felt than seen because night had fallen. Against a starlit sky darker shapes were silhouetted. The shapes, resolving into the outlines of warships, constituted Task Group 52.13, a unit of a U.S. Navy task force steaming off Makin Island on 24 November 1943, Thanksgiving eve.

Included in the task group were the battleships *New Mexico* and *Mississippi*, the cruiser *Baltimore*, the escort carriers *Liscome Bay*, *Coral Sea*, and *Corregidor*, and seven destroyers. These vessels had been supporting the operations of the Army's 27th Infantry Division on Makin (one of the Gilbert Islands) since the twentieth. Because the 27th Division had been slow in conquering the island, the ships had been steaming in the same general area since the invasion began. If the assault had gone as planned, most of the ships (including the thin-skinned escort carriers) would have been on their way back to Hawaii. Instead, the U.S. ships were still hanging around while enemy submarines began congregating about the Gilberts. A tragedy was in the making.

The *Liscome Bay*, one of the new *Casablanca*-class carriers being mass-produced in the Kaiser shipyards, was on her first operation. Captain Irving D. Wiltsie's ship had been launched on 19 April 1943 and commissioned on 7 August 1943. Flying his flag in the *Liscome Bay* was Rear Admiral Henry M. Mullinnix, commander of the escort carrier group.

For the carrier's crew and her squadron, VC-39, the preceding days had been hectic, and they fully expected that the twenty-fourth would be more of the same. At 0450 flight quarters was sounded. The deck crew began manhandling thirteen planes into position on the flight deck in preparation for a dawn launch, while another seven planes roosted on the hangar deck, armed but not fueled. Stowed in the carrier's magazine were over 200,000 pounds of bombs.[1]

At 0505 the *Liscome Bay*'s crew was called to general quarters. Dawn was only about thirty minutes away as pilots and aircrewmen began to climb into their planes. Five minutes later the *Liscome Bay*, as guide of the formation, started a turn to the northeast. At this time the formation was a bit ragged because of the absence of a pair of destroyers. The *Hull*, which had been operating off the carrier's starboard rear quarter, had been detached at 0400 to proceed to Makin. Her departure had not altered the task group's disposition. At 0435, however, the *Franks,* also operating off the *Liscome Bay*'s starboard side, reported a dim light on the surface in the distance and was directed to investigate. With the *Hull* and *Franks* gone, the task group commander, Rear Admiral Robert M. Griffin, ordered the remaining destroyers to reorient toward the gap left by the two ships. This shifting of position was taking place while the task group was in its turn to the northeast.

Not far away an unwelcome intruder was surveying the scene with interest. Hidden by the blackness of night and water, Lieutenant Commander Sunao Tabata found that his submarine, the *I-175,* was perfectly positioned to make an attack through the hole left by the *Hull* and *Franks.* Tabata gave the order and a spread of torpedoes streaked from the *I-175*'s tubes. Then he took his submarine deep to escape the inevitable depth charges.[2]

At 0510 an officer at the 40-mm director located on the starboard quarter screamed into his telephone, "Christ, here comes a torpedo!"[3] Hardly had "torpedo" been uttered than the deadly missile struck the carrier's starboard side.

A violent explosion rocked the *Liscome Bay.* A huge column of bright orange flame, flecked with white-hot pieces of metal, shot a thousand feet into the air, the intensity of the explosion stunning lookouts on the other vessels. Immediately following this blast came another large explosion, hurling fragments of the ship and clearly discernible planes 200 feet in the air. In an instant, the interior of the after portion of the carrier blazed with flames as in a blast furnace. Thrown into the sea, a large mass of wreckage drifted slowly away, still burning fiercely.[4]

Debris from the *Liscome Bay* rained down on the other ships. Fifteen hundred yards away, the *New Mexico* was showered from forecastle to quarterdeck with particles of oil, fragments of decking up to three feet long (some still burning), molten drops of metal, bits of clothing, and pieces of human flesh. Even the *Maury*, 5,000 yards distant, was splattered by pieces of the carrier.[5]

The *Liscome Bay* had been hit in the worst possible spot—the bomb stowage area. This most combustible area had no protection against a torpedo hit or fragment damage. When the torpedo struck, the bombs stored there detonated en masse.[6] The resulting explosion virtually disintegrated half the ship. No one aft of the forward bulkhead of the after engine room survived.

Few survived on the flight deck. The blast caught most of them; flying shrapnel scythed down the others. Flaming material was flung the length of the hangar deck and into the forward elevator well, and the hangar itself became a roaring world of fire. Because all water pressure was lost in the fire main, fighting the blaze was impossible.

The initial explosion knocked the men in the forward engine and boiler room off their feet. Lights went out, and as lines ruptured, scalding steam and hissing air filled the space. Nine men scrambled to their feet, only to find their normal exit blocked. Through the escape trunk they reached the second deck near the chaplain's office. Clambering over the mounds of debris clogging the passages, they first tried to reach the hangar deck via a nearby ladder, but gashes and holes in the overhead showed fires raging there. As they returned to the escape trunk, they heard others trying to get out of the engine room through the normal access trunk. The distorted door of the trunk would open only twelve inches. With great exertion on both sides, two men were able to squeeze through the narrow opening; a third had to be left behind.

Now numbering eleven men, the party headed aft to find a way out. In the vicinity of the after engine room forward bulkhead they saw that the second deck was gone and that they could step directly onto the fresh water tank tops, normally thirty inches below the level of the second deck.[7]

Here they met ten men from the auxiliary machinery spaces, who had faced similar problems. Using flashlights and battle lanterns to find their way, they had climbed over piles of debris and up bent and distorted ladders to reach the second deck. Along the way they saw a thirty-inch-wide athwartship passageway crushed to only twelve inches.

As the two groups of men gathered, they could see in the lurid glow of the flames that the hangar and flight decks above them and aft had disappeared; toward the after part of the ship, they saw nothing above the waterline except a few fragments of frames and some strips of plating along the port side. Most of the sailors aban-

doned ship at this point, having only to climb over the remnants of
the hull and drop a few feet into the water.[8]

Three of the group decided to take a longer route. Using dangling cables as ropes, they pulled themselves up to the gallery level
and jumped from a 20-mm gun platform. Cables weren't the only
connection with the upper decks. One man, unable to make his way
up a crowded ladder, used a superheated steam line, burning both
of his hands severely in the process. Another sailor climbed forty
feet up some electric wires to reach a gun plot.[9]

When the torpedo hit, several pilots scheduled for later flights
had still been asleep. The explosion collapsed their bunks, throwing
most men out but temporarily trapping some. Like most of the other
survivors, the escaping pilots had to crawl over or dig through the
jumble of wreckage scattered throughout the ship. Eventually fifteen
of the VC-39 officers abandoned ship and were picked up by the
destroyers, but fourteen other pilots died, most caught in their
planes when the after flight deck disappeared in a fireball.[10]

The blast had sent the ship's bullhorn and radar antenna crashing
down on the bridge, killing two men. As the rest of the personnel in
the island structure regained their senses, they felt tremendous
waves of heat engulfing the island from below. From the *Corregidor* it
looked as if the *Liscome Bay*'s bridge was glowing a "cherry red."[11] For
a moment the heat abated, and the men threw knotted lines over the
bridge railing on the island's inboard side and scrambled down to
the flight deck.

VC-39's skipper, Lieutenant Commander Marshall U. Beebe, had
been in the head when the torpedo hit. Lifted off his feet by the
explosion, he found himself in total darkness, unable to locate an
exit, and almost panicked. After another, lesser, explosion, light
from a fire on the hangar deck illuminated the scene; he could see
that several bulkheads had been blown down. Over the forward
bulkhead he struggled into the neighboring compartment and out
into the passageway, finally reaching the flight deck, although later
unable to explain how.[12]

The flight deck was ablaze in several places, burning oil floated on
the water near the bow, and ammunition was beginning to explode.
Captain Wiltsie ordered all hands to go aft as far as possible and
then go over the side. On his way aft he met Beebe, and the two
officers proceeded along what was left of the catwalk. Seeing that it
was time to leave the ship, Beebe called to Captain Wiltsie to jump,
but Wiltsie didn't answer. He continued walking aft into the choking
mass of smoke and flame and disappeared, never to be seen again.

Finding a line from the catwalk to the water, Beebe used it to

descend, holding an uninflated life raft he had managed to extri-
cate. His left arm had been injured and he couldn't maintain his
grip; clutching his raft, he fell heavily into the water and surfaced,
sputtering and blowing, next to the raft, where two of his pilots soon
joined him. Not wishing to be pulled down as the ship sank, they
pushed the raft almost 200 yards before stopping to inflate it.[13]

The fate of Admiral Mullinnix is unknown. In air plot when the
torpedo struck, he had apparently been severely injured. Several
men recalled last seeing him there seated at a desk, his head cradled
on his folded arms; others reported seeing him swimming away
from the ship. In any event, Admiral Mullinnix, an outstanding
officer with a promising career ahead of him, did not survive.[14]

Admiral Mullinnix's chief of staff was Captain John G. Crommelin, Jr., one of five famous brothers who were all navy officers.
Crommelin had just stepped out of the shower when the *Liscome Bay*
exploded. Naked as a baby, he was badly burned. Nevertheless, he
took charge of the men in his area and directed the abandonment of
the ship there. After leaving the carrier himself, he swam for almost
an hour and a half before being rescued, still stark naked.[15]

Like Beebe, the ship's chaplain, Lieutenant (jg) Robert H. Carley,
had been in the head when the blast came. Picking himself up from
the jumble of smashed sinks, toilets, and urinals, he staggered out
into the passageway, where someone rushed by him. It was Frank
Sistrunk, a pilot who had had an appendectomy only six days before
but was making pretty good time as he headed topside. Reaching the
flight deck, Sistrunk jumped overboard and, though not a swimmer,
managed to make it to a raft several hundred yards away with the
help of friends and a small piece of floating debris. Upon reaching
the *Morris,* he scrambled up the life net the destroyer had draped
over her side and begged for a rubber boat to use in assisting others
still in the water. Sistrunk had not been the only patient in sick bay.
One other man, also recovering from an appendectomy, was able to
walk out of sick bay and get into the water, but, unlike Sistrunk, he
was not recovered.[16]

Meanwhile, Carley met the *Liscome Bay*'s senior medical officer,
Lieutenant Commander John B. Rowe, who had been in the sick bay
with four other men. A "yellow flash and a roar" had knocked Rowe
off his feet. Staggering back up, he was dumped on the deck again
by a second explosion. Rowe rushed into the operating room to get
his patients ready for evacuation but they were already long gone, so
Rowe and Carley began searching for a way out. The port passageway appeared to be usable for at least a short distance. Their group
had grown to about fifteen men, including the ship's first lieutenant

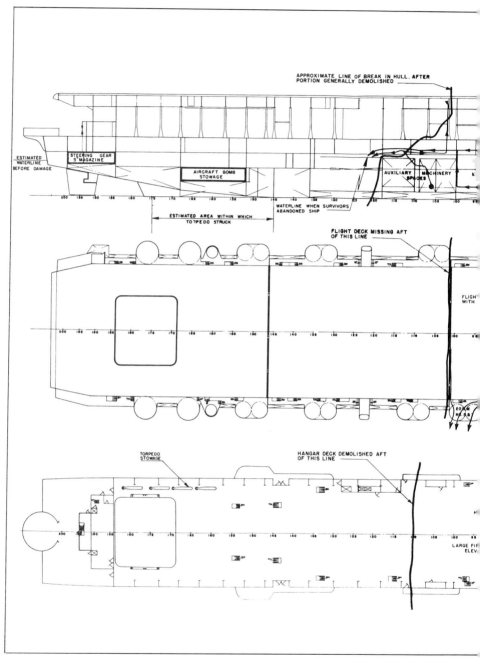

Liscome Bay *Damage and Paths of Survivors, 24 November 1943*

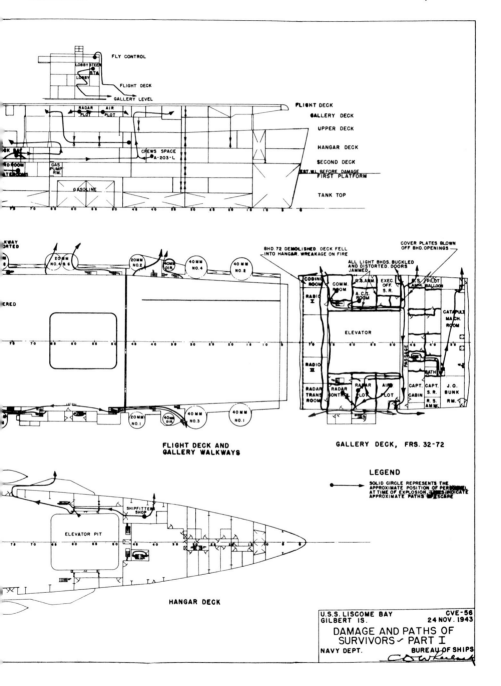

FLY CONTROL
LOBBY STEER
STA
LOBBY
FLIGHT DECK
GALLERY LEVEL
RADAR PLOT   AIR PLOT
CREWS SPACE
A-203-L
GAS PUMP RM.
GASOLINE

FLIGHT DECK
GALLERY DECK
UPPER DECK
HANGAR DECK
SECOND DECK
BEFORE DAMAGE
FIRST PLATFORM
TANK TOP

KWAY
ORTED
20MM NO.4 & 6
20MM NO.2
40MM DIR.
40MM NO.4
40MM NO.2
BHD 72 DEMOLISHED DECK FELL INTO HANGAR. WRECKAGE ON FIRE
COVER PLATES BLOWN OFF BHD. OPENINGS
ALL LIGHT BHDS. BUCKLED AND DISTORTED. DOORS JAMMED

CODING ROOM   COMM. ROOM   R.S. AMM   EXEC OFF. S.R.   R.S. PILOT AMM. BALLOON
RADIO I   A.C/L ROOM
ELEVATOR
CATAPULT MACH. ROOM
RADIO II
BATH
PASSAGE
RADAR TRANS ROOM   RADAR CONTROL   RADAR PLOT   AIR PLOT   CAPT. CABIN   CAPT. S.R.   J.O. BUNK RM.
R.S. AMM.

20MM NO.1
40MM DIR.
40MM NO.3
40MM NO.1

FLIGHT DECK AND
GALLERY WALKWAYS

GALLERY DECK, FRS. 32-72

LEGEND

SOLID CIRCLE REPRESENTS THE APPROXIMATE POSITION OF PERSONNEL AT TIME OF EXPLOSION LINES INDICATE APPROXIMATE PATHS OF ESCAPE

SHIPFITTERS SHOP
ELEVATOR PIT

HANGAR DECK

U.S.S. LISCOME BAY	CVE-56
GILBERT IS.	24 NOV. 1943
DAMAGE AND PATHS OF SURVIVORS - PART I	
NAVY DEPT.	BUREAU OF SHIPS

and damage control officer, Lieutenant Commander W. W. Carroll, who refused Rowe's offer to dress his wounds.[17]

Carroll, with three others, had been in his small office when the explosion ripped from his hands the book he had been reading and the lights went out. One man had his life jacket, shirt, and shoes blown off but was otherwise fine. Commander Carroll was not fine: something had hit him in the face and chest and he was covered with blood, although able to move. The men made an attempt to fight the fires they saw flickering through holes in the overhead but were unable to get any pressure in the fire main. Giving that up, they groped their way through smoke-filled passages to join Rowe and Carley's party.

The group clambered slowly over piles of debris and squeezed through passageways crushed inward like tin cans until they reached the forward elevator well, where a sailor named Hunt was trying to extinguish the blaze with portable CO_2 bottles. Seeing from several spent bottles lying around him that Hunt's efforts were useless, Carroll told him to get out before he was trapped, but Hunt motioned him away and returned to his firefighting.

Carroll climbed painfully to the flight deck with his party. To them the scene there was Dante's *Inferno* come to life. Flickering and wavering in great sheets of flame, the fire was roaring so loudly that men had to shout to be heard. The flames and the dense smoke made the spectacle undulate eerily. Small explosions resounded constantly as ammunition went off, adding to the tumult. Three men who were huddled around a 20-mm gun made no reply when Carley told them to abandon ship—they were dead. Three others standing numbly nearby woke up when they received Carley's order and slid down a rope into the water, followed by Carley.

Though weakening, Carroll paced up and down the flight deck, ordering and helping men to abandon ship. He refused the urging of Hunt (who had finally given up his firefighting efforts and come topside) to leave the ship until Hunt declared his own determination not to leave without him. After the men leaped, Hunt swam off to find a raft. The doctor supported Carroll until Hunt returned and asked how the commander was. Looking down at the man he was holding, Rowe replied, "He's dead," and let Carroll's body slip beneath the waves.[18]

Just twenty-three minutes after the torpedo hit the *Liscome Bay*, the carrier sank, stern first, still burning furiously, hissing and gurgling, her bow enveloped by a cloud of steam. By the time the cloud evaporated, she had disappeared.

The casualties were terribly high. Only 55 officers and 217 men were rescued, primarily by the destroyers *Morris* and *Hughes*. Besides Admiral Mullinnix and Captain Wiltsie, 51 other officers and 591 enlisted men went down with the ship.[19] Many survivors were badly injured. Shattered limbs, frightful burns, and severe concussions from the enormous blast were common. The men on the *Morris*, who had rescued survivors from the *Lexington, Yorktown,* and *Hornet,* felt unanimously that the "condition of the comparatively few survivors constituted the most heart-rending disaster yet seen." For that matter, they thought "it was a miracle that *anyone* managed to escape such a roaring inferno."[20]

Silently watching the hideous death of the *Liscome Bay* and the abrupt snuffing-out of the lives of many men they had known and worked with were the crews of the *Coral Sea* and *Corregidor*. Suddenly and forcibly, the horror of war had been brought to their attention, and they thought about their own ships, sisters to the *Liscome Bay*. If the *Liscome Bay* could blow up like that . . . They remembered with dread the mocking words that other sailors had hurled at the escort carrier men (and that they had often used themselves)—"combustible, vulnerable, expendable."

LEARNING THE ROPES

On 7 December 1941 the U.S. Navy didn't know what an escort carrier was, though in the *Long Island* it had the embryo of the type. Before World War II was over, the navy would know the escort carriers well and be very glad to have them.

In October 1940 President Franklin D. Roosevelt, concerned with the growing intensity of the war in the Atlantic, had directed the Chief of Naval Operations to obtain a merchant vessel for conversion to an aircraft carrier. Displacing 6,000 to 8,000 tons, this ship would carry eight to twelve helicopters (or autogiros) or ten short takeoff and landing aircraft at a speed of not less than 15 knots. She would therefore be much smaller and slower than the fast carriers, and her primary mission would be convoy escort and submarine detection.

At almost the same time Rear Admiral William F. Halsey, then Commander Aircraft, Battle Force, proposed building new auxiliary carriers for use in pilot training and aircraft transport. Halsey's carriers differed from those envisioned by the president in being a bit larger and faster.[1] Neither the president nor Halsey saw these ships as much more than auxiliaries; their combat role and their related designation would come later.

Initial studies indicated that this new carrier would need a full-length landing deck with arresting gear. This ship would have no island, being conned from a bridge underneath the flight deck, the bridge extending outward from the sides of the ship. For the ship's engineering plant, diesel power was favored.

The main stumbling block to this proposal was the length of time it would take to accomplish, about a year and a half. This was not what the president wanted to hear. In no uncertain terms he told the navy he would not tolerate any plan that would take longer than three months.

With Roosevelt adamant, the navy quickly decided to obtain two diesel-powered C-3 merchant ships, the *Mormacland* and *Mormacmail*, from the Maritime Commission. These vessels would require the least conversion. Late in January the navy was told that the *Mormacmail* would be available around the first of March. Available at the same time, the *Mormacland* eventually became the HMS *Archer*.

The *Mormacmail* was acquired by the Maritime Commission on 6 March 1941 and turned over to the navy. Entering the Newport News yards on 18 March, she began her conversion almost immediately. Probably because of the president's interest in the project, the ship had a priority equal to that of the fleet carrier *Hornet*, then also building at Newport News.[2]

As shipyard workers swarmed over the ship, her merchant vessel profile took on the appearance of a flattop. A 362-by-70-foot flight deck, supported by a girder framework, lay atop the original amidships superstructure, no island breaking the flatness of her silhouette; the pilothouse was under the forward end of the flight deck. Her overall length was 492 feet and she had a full load displacement of 13,500 tons. Part of this tonnage came from the addition of 1,650 tons of ballast to maintain a sufficient metacentric height. One catapult was fitted; oddly enough, it ran thirty degrees diagonally from starboard to port. One elevator aft led to the small hangar deck, which was limited in size by the original amidships superstructure. Her armament was nothing to rave about—one 5-inch/.51-caliber single-purpose gun on the fantail, two 3-inch/.50-caliber antiaircraft guns on the forecastle deck, and .50-caliber machine guns at each corner of the flight deck. (Sometime later her carpenter's mates fashioned a yoke that cradled four .50-calibers.)[3]

Finally, after some $1.5 million had been spent on the conversion, the ex-*Mormacmail* was commissioned as the *Long Island* on 2 June 1941. Taking command of the ship was Commander Donald B. Duncan. Earlier the *Long Island*'s designation had been APV-1 (Transport and Aircraft Ferry), but this was changed to AVG-1 (Aircraft Tender, General Purpose) just prior to being commissioned.[4]

The *Long Island*, with the F2A-2s and fixed-wheel SOC-3A Seagulls of VS-201 aboard, was assigned to Carrier Division 3 of the Atlantic Fleet.[5] Much of her time would be spent operating in an experimental capacity off the East Coast. Nonetheless, she was involved in several important maneuvers over the next few months.

An early one foretold one of the escort carriers' most important missions in the coming war. At the beginning of August the *Long*

Island took part in maneuvers involving air support of landings on a "hostile" shore. The VS-201 planes provided gunfire spotting for an ex-battleship doing the prelanding bombardment, provided a combat air patrol over the transports while they unloaded, and also covered the troops as they moved from the transports to the beach.

Reviews of the *Long Island*'s performance in this exercise were mixed. Several senior officers complained about "inadequate" air support, somehow never grasping the point that one small carrier with only about ten planes obviously could never provide proper air support. Nevertheless, "Wu" Duncan saw the need for air cover for assault landings and knew that ships such as his *Long Island* would be well suited for this job.[6]

Following the conclusion of this exercise, the *Long Island* set course for a rendezvous in the North Atlantic. On 14 August 1941 the little carrier joined several other warships, among them the heavy cruiser *Augusta,* off Nova Scotia. Aboard the cruiser was President Roosevelt, returning from the Atlantic Charter meeting with Winston Churchill.

Roosevelt wished to see how "his" carrier was doing. The *Long Island* provided him with a spectacular, albeit unplanned, display. While she was launching aircraft, there was a catapult malfunction and one of the F2A-2 fighters dribbled off the flight deck. With great finesse and a lot of luck, the pilot was able to keep his fighter airborne, though his propwash left a large wake on the surface of the sea. Deck launches were made by the remaining planes, with all making normal landings to complete the demonstration.[7]

After a routine "Neutrality Patrol" of the mid-Atlantic almost to the Cape Verde Islands (a group of islands that would figure prominently in the exploits of a later class of escort carriers), the *Long Island* put back in to Norfolk on 12 September for some major alterations. The early operations had shown that the carrier needed a longer flight deck, so seventy-seven feet were added, extending the flight deck forward over the pilot house. To improve her "damaged stability" and floodable length, two additional transverse bulkheads were installed. These additions and various other improvements caused her full load displacement to rise to 14,953 tons. But she still had the same diesel engines, which Commander Duncan had hoped to have replaced because of inadequate performance.[8]

Upon her return to the high seas, the *Long Island* began conducting pilot carrier qualifications. Among the squadrons the ship qualified was VT-8, its date with history at Midway less than a year away.

While the carrier went about her business, serious discussions concerning her future were being held. Admiral Harold Stark, Chief of

Naval Operations, was not enthusiastic about the ship, complaining that her lack of speed (which had long been known to be a limiting factor) made her useless as a carrier. On the other hand, Admiral Ernest J. King, then Commander, Atlantic Fleet, believed that his force could use seven escort carriers and had even included in the Atlantic Fleet's "Escort-of-Convoy" instructions a section on escort carrier convoy operations.[9]

When 7 December 1941 came, the *Long Island* was anchored at Bermuda, still operating in a training and experimental role. While she was anchored her planes were flown aboard, this difficult task accomplished with some sweating and praying by those involved. As Captain Richard S. Rogers, USN (Ret.), then a young "jaygee," recalls, "Even the SOCs snubbed up in unladylike fashion after hitting the arresting gear that day. As for the F2As, we took a few extra wave-offs, snugged up shoulder harnesses and kept our teeth off our tongues and succeeded in getting all aboard in sound condition just as Captain D. and a good Landing Signals Officer willed it."[10]

On 22 December the carrier sailed for Norfolk, where she got a new skipper, Commander John J. Ballentine. The same day Ballentine took command—26 December—the ship left port for Placentia Bay, Newfoundland. Her operations there were not particularly useful, poor weather being the major factor, though her crew gained some valuable experience in North Atlantic operations. The only excitement encountered by VS-201 during this period was an attack by three depth-charge-carrying SOCs on a reported "submarine." The whale didn't appreciate the depth-charging. By 28 January the carrier was back in Norfolk.

For the next few months the *Long Island* was again used for carrier qualifications, but in April she saw some changes. VS-201 was redesignated VGS-1 on 2 April, trading in its F2As for F4F-4 Wildcats at the same time, and on the thirteenth Commander James D. Barner took command of the ship. Then on 10 May she left for the Pacific and a more active part in the war.

By the time she reached San Diego a major battle was looming. Near an insignificant piece of real estate named Midway Atoll were gathering two opposing fleets, one powerful and up until then almost all-conquering, the other much smaller but possessing information that could turn the tide. During the epic battle that took place between 4 and 6 June, no battleships took part because they could not keep up with the fast-stepping carriers. Nevertheless, Vice Admiral William S. Pye took a force of seven battleships out of San Francisco on 5 June to backstop the U.S. forces at Midway and also to protect the San Francisco Bay area. Included in Pye's TF (Task

The Long Island *at Pearl Harbor, 3 July 1942. (National Archives)*

Force) 1 was the *Long Island,* carrying a meager twenty aircraft (of which only twelve were Wildcats) to cover the force—not much of a deterrent if the Japanese had been able to come east.[11]

After Midway the *Long Island* returned to San Diego to conduct more carrier qualifications. In July she ferried a load of planes to Pearl Harbor, continuing on to Palmyra with another load of fighters. She probably would have remained in obscurity, plodding the waters of the Pacific carrying passengers, cargo, and aircraft, if not for a clash of titans over a hitherto little-known island in the South Pacific: Guadalcanal.

Landing on Guadalcanal on 7 August 1942, the 1st Marine Division soon found they were going to need air support and fast, particularly after the fearsome drubbing U.S. naval forces had taken at the Battle of Savo Island and the retirement of the fleet carriers covering the landings.

Help was already on the way, courtesy of the little *Long Island.* In company with the destroyer *Aylwin,* she sailed from Pearl Harbor on 2 August bound for Guadalcanal. On board her were two marine squadrons inexperienced in carrier operations—Captain John L. Smith's VMF-223 and Major Richard C. Mangrum's VMSB-232, both squadrons part of Marine Air Group 23.[12] The ground echelon of MAG-23 was embarked in the transport *William Ward Burroughs.*

Originally the plans had been to send the two squadrons directly to Guadalcanal, but the Savo Island disaster dictated a change. On the thirteenth Commander Barner brought his ship into Suva, in the Fijis, to await further orders. Concerned about his marine wards, Barner reported to Rear Admiral John S. McCain (Commander Air Force, South Pacific) that they needed at least six more weeks of training before they could be considered combat-ready. But there was no time for additional training. The fliers were needed at Guadalcanal!

As a partial remedy to this problem, the carrier was sent to Efate, in the New Hebrides. There Captain Smith was able to trade some of his less experienced pilots for more seasoned fliers from the Efate-based VMF-212. Finally, escorted by the cruiser *Helena* and two destroyers, the flattop sailed for a point about 200 miles southeast of Guadalcanal. From that spot on the afternoon of 20 August she catapulted from her small deck nineteen Wildcats of VMF-223 and twelve SBD Dauntlesses of VMSB-232. Despite Barner's worries, the launch came off smoothly.[13] The arrival of these planes on Guadalcanal elated the beleaguered ground forces, and before long they were showing their worth.

Before their relief in October, the VMF-223 pilots claimed 111½ enemy planes downed against the loss of six pilots killed and another six wounded. Few of the squadron's survivors were in good health, though. The same was true of VMSB-232. Only one pilot was able to walk away when that squadron was relieved; seven had been killed, four wounded, and the rest were hospitalized. Four gunners had also been killed and one wounded. But at a time when they were desperately needed, the men of VMF-223 and VMSB-232 had done all that was asked of them and more.[14]

For a little while longer the *Long Island* remained in the South Pacific. Returning to Efate, she picked up nineteen VMF-224 Wildcats and twelve VMSB-231 Dauntlesses for delivery to Guadalcanal. This time, however, she didn't take them all the way. Instead, it was decided that the carrier would take the planes to Espiritu Santo, the aircraft flying on to Guadalcanal from there. So on 28 and 29 August she catapulted off her load of aircraft and then set course for home.[15]

On 19 September 1942 the *Long Island* returned to San Diego, her brief time in the limelight over. She fell back into obscurity as a training carrier on the West Coast and as a ferry carrier. Her original squadron, VGS-1 (né VS-201), was redesignated VC-1 and assigned to the *Card* for Atlantic antisubmarine duty. (VC-1 would do quite well in the Atlantic, being credited with sinking five U-boats.)

By the time the *Long Island* went back to the training and ferry role, she was not the only escort carrier in the Pacific. There were some newcomers, also based on the Maritime Commission C-3 hulls but much improved. The *Long Island*'s early trials and tribulations were bearing fruit.

These new escort carriers, now designated ACVs (Auxiliary Air-

A Wildcat is loaded onto the Long Island *from the aircraft ferry* Kittyhawk *at Vila on 28 August 1942. Later that day the carrier catapulted most of the planes for Guadalcanal. (National Archives)*

craft Carriers), reflected lessons learned from the *Long Island*'s operational experience. The initial recipient of this knowledge, however, was Great Britain. Her first U.S.-built escort carrier, the *Archer*, had been converted from the second of the C-3 hulls acquired by the

Maritime Commission in January 1941, the *Mormacland*. A further five C-3s were converted based on the improved *Long Island* plan. One of these, the *Charger,* was returned to the U.S. Navy in March 1942 and spent most of her career as a training carrier.

It was obvious to the navy that these early carriers could be improved on. Thus was born the *Bogue* class of carriers. In late December 1941 twenty-four C-3-S-A1 hulls were approved for conversion. Steam turbines would be the propulsion plant of choice, with single screws to drive the vessels. As built, the ships had a flight deck 436 feet 8 inches by 80 feet, slightly larger than the *Long Island*'s deck. Instead of one elevator, two were installed, and a much larger hangar deck extended 240 feet between them. Unfortunately, the camber and sheer of the original C-3 hull were retained in the hangar deck, which made plane handling difficult, if not impossible, in bad weather. On top of this, the after elevator was installed with its long side athwartship, which also hampered plane handling considerably.

While not very well endowed with armament, these new flattops seemed so, in contrast with the *Long Island*. Two 5-inch/.51s (later 5-inch/.38s) were located on the port and starboard quarters. Rounding out this armament were approximately ten 40-mm mounts and twenty-seven 20-mm mounts. Plans to upgrade this armament existed throughout the war, but only when the kamikazes appeared were the *Bogue*-class vessels recognized as being seriously undergunned.

These new carriers had greater stability than the *Long Island*, primarily because of a lower flight deck, and were better compartmented and stronger, with more transverse bulkheads. Finally, the addition of a small island to starboard greatly enhanced these vessels' navigational capabilities.[16]

Many times before the Pacific War ended, the names of such *Bogue*-class ships as the *Copahee, Barnes, Altamaha,* and *Breton* would appear over and over again in the official reports.

In December 1942 an increase in carrier power in the South Pacific came with the assignment of the "big" escort carriers *Sangamon, Suwannee,* and *Chenango* to the area. These flattops had been converted from *Cimarron*- or "River"-class oilers.

Bigger (553 feet long, with flight decks 502 by 85 feet) than the *Bogue*s, the *Sangamon*s had about the same maximum speed. Geared-turbine engines in a single engine room aft drove twin screws. This arrangement made them vulnerable to a single torpedo hit. These carriers were more stable than the previous escort carriers because of a still lower flight deck. Their hangars were quite a bit shorter than those of the other flattops, but increased width and no sheer on the hangar deck made plane handling a much easier chore. As befitted their increased size, their armament was also increased. Two 5-inch/.38-caliber guns were on the port and starboard quarters, and twenty-two 40-mm guns in twin and quad mounts and about twenty-one 20-mm mounts were eventually installed.[17]

These three carriers, plus their sister ship, the *Santee*, had taken part in the invasion of North Africa in November 1942. The *Santee* would remain in the Atlantic until early 1944, but because of losses sustained by the fast carriers during the Guadalcanal campaign, the other three flattops were urgently needed in the South Pacific. Initially, the *Bogue*-class vessels *Nassau*, *Altamaha*, and *Copahee* had been considered for use in the South Pacific to help support the fast carriers still present in that arena. However, with their services no longer needed off North Africa, the *Sangamon*s became available more quickly than had been planned. They would be suitable for operations in the South Pacific, being combat ready, whereas the other escort carriers needed much more training to reach that stage.

So after a short "availability period" for maintenance at Norfolk following the North African invasion, the *Sangamon*, *Suwannee*, cruisers *Wichita* and *Cleveland*, and several destroyers left Norfolk on 5 December 1942. Rear Admiral Robert C. "Ike" Giffen's force was organized as TF 32, and it was bound for Noumea. The voyage was relatively uneventful but there were a few fireworks (primarily verbal) when the *Suwannee*'s signal yardarm tangled with a Panama Canal control tower.[18]

Leaving Norfolk about two weeks after her sisters, the *Chenango* transited the Panama Canal on Christmas Day. The carrier then joined TF 13, composed of several cargo vessels, destroyers, and the cruisers *Columbia*, *Montpelier*, and (late of TF 32) *Cleveland*. This force arrived at Noumea on 18 January 1943.[19]

After a short stay at Noumea, the three carriers moved up to Efate, where Havannah Harbor would be their primary anchorage for the next several months. It was not long before the "jeeps" saw some action. The general American opinion, noting the ever-increasing number of enemy transports and combat vessels known to be gathering north of Guadalcanal, was that the Guadalcanal campaign wouldn't be over until about 1 April. What the Americans did not yet know was that the campaign was winding down, and these ships had gathered to evacuate the remnants of the Japanese forces on the island.

Also sending transports to Guadalcanal in January was Vice Admiral Halsey, now Commander, South Pacific. Mindful of the enemy shipping north of Guadalcanal, Halsey had five separate task forces

An Avenger is pushed onto the elevator to join others on the deck of the Suwannee, *January 1943. (National Archives)*

available to cover a four-transport convoy and to meet any enemy force that might be coming south. Unfortunately, these five task forces were widely scattered. Of the five, it was TF 18 that ran into a hornet's nest.

Task Force 18 was commanded by Admiral Giffen and was composed of three heavy and three light cruisers, eight destroyers, and

A formation of Wildcats flies over the Chenango, *January 1943. (National Archives)*

two escort carriers. Commanding TF 18's air unit, TG (Task Group) 18.2, was the *Chenango*'s skipper, Captain Ben H. Wyatt. The *Chenango* was carrying the eleven Wildcats of VGF-28 and the eight Dauntlesses and nine TBF Avengers of VGS-28. The other carrier was the *Suwannee*. Just a few days earlier Captain Frederick W. McMahon had assumed command of the ship from the legendary Captain J. J. "Jocko" Clark. The *Suwannee*'s air complement consisted of VGF-27's eighteen F4F-4s and VGS-27's fifteen TBFs.[20]

It was the task of TF 18 to escort the four transports for a short period on 29 January. Upon completion of this assignment, Giffen was to rendezvous with a destroyer force near Guadalcanal at 2100 on the thirtieth. Preoccupied with this rendezvous, Giffen was not going to let anything stop or slow him from making it, and the two escort carriers were slowing him down. Their slow speeds and the constant necessity for them to turn back into a southeast wind to launch and recover aircraft was causing Giffen's timetable to go awry. Giffen decided to detach the escort carriers and proceed on his way.[21]

Admiral Nimitz later commented somewhat unfavorably on Giffen's fixation on making the rendezvous and his poor use of the planes from the carriers. "[Giffen's] inadequate use of planes from ACVs attached to his task force on 29 January," Nimitz said, "was based in part on the tight operating schedule to which he was committed. Subsequent movements of his task force indicate that such a close schedule may not have been necessary and that his orders might have been more flexible."[22]

At 1400 on the twenty-ninth Giffen authorized flights to search for possible snoopers (reconnaissance aircraft) in the Indispensable Reef–San Cristobal areas. An hour later the carriers were detached to retire to the southeast. They would still provide air cover, albeit at a distance, for TF 18 throughout the rest of the day and on the following morning, when the carriers would rejoin TF 18 some ninety miles from Guadalcanal. Shortly after 1400 the *Chenango* launched two radar-equipped Avengers and four F4F-4s to scour the Indispensable Reef–San Cristobal areas. More planes were launched for task group cover while four fighters and three TBFs from the *Suwannee* were sent to cover the cruiser force.[23] However, the cruisers and carriers were gradually moving apart as they went their separate ways, and the planes soon had to return to their ships.

Many bogeys—unidentified aircraft—had been discovered sniffing around Admiral Giffen's force, but none were shot down. The presence of the enemy planes didn't seem to bother Giffen.[24] Fresh from the North African landings and the numerous submarine attacks there, he was more concerned with possible submarine encounters than with air attacks, and the disposition of his force reflected this concern. It was poorly aligned to combat air attacks, and the heavy cruiser *Chicago* would wind up the loser of the impending battle.

As afternoon slid toward evening, the bogeys became bolder. At dusk the first group of Bettys attacked Giffen's force. They were beaten off rather handily, but the battle was just beginning. Still attempting to make his rendezvous, Giffen stubbornly remained on his previous course and even stopped zigzagging, perhaps believing the darkness would protect his ships.[25] He quickly learned that nighttime was one of the Japanese fliers' favorite times for attack. Flares and float lights suddenly surrounded the task force as more Bettys darted in to deliver their deadly "fish."

One dud torpedo hit the cruiser *Louisville* and another slammed into the cruiser *Wichita,* but the *Chicago* was the unfortunate recipient of two very effective torpedoes. The cruiser's damage control parties had their hands full trying to save their ship as the remaining enemy planes scooted out of the area. It soon became evident that the only way to save the *Chicago* was to tow her. In the blackness the *Louisville* closed with the *Chicago* and passed over a towline. Early on the thirtieth the tow was begun toward Espiritu Santo at a painful 4 knots.

Shortly after the *Louisville* moved in to pass over the towline, at 2115, Giffen directed Captain Wyatt to provide air cover over TF 18 at dawn, but to remain 150 miles from the *Chicago.* Two hours later, Admiral Halsey countermanded this, stating that 150 miles was too far for effective air support and ordering Wyatt to close as necessary for proper air coverage. The two "jeeps" proceeded back toward the rest of TF 18 at a speed of 17 knots. This speed would put them about sixty miles southeast of the *Chicago* and some ninety miles from Guadalcanal the next morning.

Upon receiving word of the attack on the cruiser force, Captain Wyatt decided that following the first dawn launches, the two escort carriers would rendezvous with TF 16 (the *Enterprise* and her screen), which Halsey had also sent to help. At 0600, while it was still dark and raining slightly, the *Chenango* launched a seven-fighter CAP (combat air patrol) and three search planes. The CAP arrived over the *Chicago* about an hour later, when the sky was just becoming light. Over the "jeeps" themselves the *Suwannee* provided the CAP, while the *Enterprise* supplied another six-plane CAP for TF 18.[26]

At noon the *Chenango* and *Suwannee* joined TF 16, coming under the command of Rear Admiral Frederick C. Sherman. Sherman decided to keep his force about fifty miles southeast of the *Chicago*— close enough to help, but far enough removed from the scene to avoid attacks on his ships. But now communications problems between the various forces would conspire against the *Chicago*'s survival. By this time TF 18 had split up, the *Chicago* being left behind with five destroyers while the remaining vessels headed for Efate. At 1534 Admiral Giffen directed the two escort carriers to provide air cover into Espiritu Santo for the stricken cruiser. Unfortunately, by the time this message was received by the carriers, the *Chicago* had gone down.

In the meantime, coastwatchers had reported eleven or twelve twin-engined planes heading south, and a hot reception was planned. Ten additional fighters were launched from the "Big E" to reinforce the six already over the cruiser and the four over TF

16. Because the two escort carriers did not receive orders to provide any air cover until the action was over, their planes did not take part in the fight. On their own, the *Chenango* and *Suwannee* had launched nineteen fighters and four TBFs in anticipation of a dusk attack. But without orders, they were effectively out of the battle.

Shortly before 1700 the enemy planes were picked up on the *Enterprise's* radar, heading directly for the carrier. When these planes, identified as Bettys, were intercepted by the CAP, they turned back northwest toward the *Chicago.* Despite losing several bombers to the fighters and antiaircraft fire, the attackers bored in to plant four more torpedoes into the virtually immobile *Chicago* and one more into the destroyer *La Vallette.* All but two of the Bettys were shot down, but the enemy fliers had accomplished their mission. The *Chicago* soon sank stern-first and the *La Vallette* had to be towed to Espiritu Santo.

More enemy aircraft were reported by the coastwatchers at 1915, estimated to arrive over the escort carriers at 2030. Since it would be dark at that time and the "jeep" fliers had limited night flying experience, the two flattops beat a hasty retreat into the cover of a rainstorm. When it became evident that the enemy planes were not coming, TG 18.2 began its retirement to Espiritu Santo.[27]

The Battle of Rennell Island was over. For the Americans it had not been well run. The various forces covering the transports had been too widely separated to provide assistance when trouble broke out; Giffen's tactics were not particularly well thought out; and U.S. carrier forces evidently were woefully deficient in night air operations, a deficiency not overcome for some time.

The escort carriers had been little more than bystanders. They almost seemed to have been forgotten by the top commanders. Their planes had not seen any enemy aircraft, and the only damage suffered had been when two *Chenango* planes closed with the injured *La Vallette.* Though proper recognition signals were given, the "tin can's" nervous gunners opened fire, ventilating one plane and slightly wounding its pilot. For the remainder of the mission, planes gave the destroyer a wide berth.[28]

The two escort carriers returned to Efate to rejoin the *Sangamon.* Soon these three vessels were operating together as a carrier division, the first such unit for escort carriers. On 25 February 1943 CarDiv 22 was "temporarily" constituted under the command of Captain Wyatt. Taking command of the division on 7 March was Rear Admiral A. C. McFall. The "temporary" status of CarDiv 22 lasted until 8 November 1945, when it was finally dissolved.[29]

The Suwannee *anchored in Havannah Harbor on 22 April 1943. (National Archives)*

For the rest of their stay in the South Pacific, the three carriers spent much of their time swinging around the hook in Havannah Harbor. There were occasional sorties to escort troop convoys to Guadalcanal, but the carriers themselves saw little action.

It was another story for the flattops' air groups. Between 10 March and 25 April, Air Groups 26, 27, and 28 operated from the Guadalcanal airfields. CVEG-27 now had only Wildcats and Avengers, and its squadrons were designated VF and VT; the other CVEGs still had Dauntlesses as part of their equipment, and the bombing squadrons were designated VC. Generally, the TBFs and SBDs were used to attack enemy positions on Kolombangara, Bougainville, New Georgia, and Rendova, many of these missions being night attacks. Additionally, the CVE planes flew several minelaying missions, often together with marine aircraft.

Usually the attacks by the "jeep" fliers were against airfield and supply installations, but beginning on 16 April the Avengers began making masthead bombing attacks on enemy shipping. The pilots had practiced on a Japanese hulk beached at Tassafaronga before trying their hand at the real thing on the night of the sixteenth.

While seven Avengers from VT-26 and one from VT-28, as well as fifteen Army B-17s and B-24s, hit the Kahili area of southern Bougainville, VC-27's skipper, Lieutenant Commander R. E. C. Jones, led two TBFs against a pair of large cargo ships anchored offshore nearby. In the darkness, the night illuminated only by green flares, searchlights, and tracers, the two planes darted in to lob their 500-pounders at the two ships. Although it was dark and the TBFs altimeters were not the most accurate, Jones and his wing-man made several individual runs on the vessels at less than 300 feet. A couple of hits were scored by the intrepid pair, but whether these were enough to sink either ship is unknown. All the planes on this mission returned safely to Guadalcanal.[30] Before the squadrons returned to their carriers, they made several more attacks of this nature against other enemy ships with good results.

Meanwhile, the Wildcats from the three escort carriers were also busy in the Solomons. The fighters were used primarily for CAPs over Guadalcanal and the Russell Islands, which had been taken unopposed on 21 February. While operating from shore, the fighters were involved in one big scramble, a prelude to the imple-mentation of Admiral Yamamoto's planned crushing air offensive against Allied positions in New Guinea and the Solomons—the "I" Operation.

The first of April saw a scramble over the Russells as at least seventy Japanese fighters roared down the Slot to tangle with the defenders. In the thick of the fighting were the CVE pilots. The action quickly turned into one huge, whirling dogfight as Wildcats, F4U Corsairs, and a few army P-38s cavorted madly about the sky with the agile Zekes.

One of the CVE pilots who scored was VF-27's Lieutenant (jg) George Seel. One of twelve defenders who tore into a group of forty enemy fighters, Seel picked out one Zeke at 23,000 feet and began chasing him. It wasn't long before Seel discovered he was, in turn, being chased by another Zeke. Tracers flashed past his cockpit and Seel could feel his plane shudder as other shells struck home. Glanc-ing back, he saw a Zeke closing in, its cowl and wing guns twinkling. He did a quick pushover, followed by a gut-wrenching pullout, and the Zeke overshot. In a flash Seel was on his adversary's tail, and he needed only one burst to blow the lightly armored Zeke to pieces. Before he had to dive away from the battle, out of ammunition, Seel scored one more kill and two probables.

Two other VF-27 pilots were not quite as lucky as Seel. One claimed a definite and a probable before being shot up and having to crash-land at Guadalcanal. The other, Lieutenant (jg) William

Sweetman, had an even closer call. Having already shot down one plane, Sweetman was looking around for others when a Zeke tagged him with several 20-mm shells into the cockpit. Sweetman was badly wounded, his plane no less so. Constantly fighting to remain conscious, Sweetman nursed his Wildcat back to Guadalcanal, where he crash-landed. As his plane shuddered to a halt, Sweetman fell unconscious, awakening in the hospital several hours later.[31]

When the Japanese scooted back north to their bases, they left behind eighteen of their fighters against the loss of only six of the defenders, one of those being a VF-27 pilot, Lieutenant (jg) D. O. Lebow. A week later the Japanese were back with one of the biggest enemy armadas seen since Pearl Harbor—some 67 Vals and 110 Zekes. In the ensuing 'battle twenty-seven Zekes and twelve Vals were credited to the Americans, the defenders losing only seven fighters. This fierce action on 7 April did not see the CVE fighters taking part, as they were back on their carriers for a brief stay. Eventually the "I" Operation petered out, leaving the Japanese with the loss of skilled fliers they were ill equipped to replace.[32]

Losses for the CVE air groups while land-based were not excessive, the *Chenango*'s CVEG-28 having the most—two Avengers and four Wildcats.[33] On 24–25 April the air groups returned to their carriers, seeing little action while aboard except for one convoy operation between 15 and 24 June. A number of enemy aircraft did try to attack the ships of this convoy, but were beaten off. Only one aircraft, a Betty shot down by VF-26's exec, Lieutenant Commander F. L. Palmer, Jr., was credited to the "jeep" fliers. Lack of altitude, inability to drop wing tanks, and a simple lack of speed contributed to allowing most of the snoopers to escape.[34]

Guadalcanal was revisited by the three air groups between 26 June and 5 August. It would be the "last hurrah" for the air groups and their carriers in the Solomons. Targets were still plentiful, and the fliers had more good shooting on this tour.

The biggest, and costliest, mission took place on 18 July. Twenty-eight CarDiv 22 Wildcats were to escort eighteen SBDs to Kahili, rendezvousing with eighteen TBFs and their escorts en route. As it turned out, the other fighters never showed up, and the CVE aircraft took over the entire escort mission.

As the formation neared the Shortlands, the Wildcats were stacked in three groups—eight planes providing low cover, six in the middle, and fourteen as high cover. Just before reaching the Shortlands, some twenty-five to thirty Zekes and Hamps bounced the Americans, the low cover taking the brunt of the attack. In a wild, tumbling battle in and out of the "cotton basket" clouds that dotted the area, the Wildcat pilots claimed fourteen Zekes shot down with one more as a probable. And they kept the enemy off the backs of the SBDs and TBFs. But it had been a costly victory. Although only two were known to have been shot down, six of the "jeep" pilots were listed as missing in action.

There was one more large air battle before the three groups returned to their carriers. Following a bomber escort mission to New Georgia on 21 July, eight F4F-4s flew CAP over Rendova. Shortly after they took station, a large formation of Vals and Zekes was reported coming in. Two of the Wildcats had to drop out of the fight because of mechanical problems, but the other six tore into the enemy. The Zekes were able to keep the CVE fliers away from the vulnerable Vals but suffered in the process. Three of the Japanese fighters fell to the Wildcats' guns with another three claimed as probables. The CarDiv 22 pilots suffered no losses.[35]

At last the fighting in the Solomons was over for the three escort carriers and their squadrons. The Wildcats, Avengers, and Dauntlesses returned to their ships, and the carriers began preparations to leave for a welcome period of rest and yard availability in the United States. The fliers especially needed the rest, the strain of combat having taken its toll. Among the fliers and their maintenance crews malaria was rampant, and a fifteen-pound weight loss per man was not considered too bad. One after another during August the flattops left Havannah Harbor for the United States. Before the *Sangamon*, *Suwannee*, and *Chenango* steamed west again, they would once more be in top fighting trim.

(Three other squadrons with escort carrier ties were also active in the Solomons during this time. VGS-11, VGS-12, and VGS-16, all ostensibly assigned to the *Altamaha*, *Copahee*, and *Nassau*, respectively, played important roles in the Solomons. Actually, the three squadrons had really only been on board for the ride, being transported to the South Pacific by their carriers and seeing little duty from those ships. All three units were later redesignated: VGS-11 to VF-21, VGS-12 to VT-21, and VGS-16 to VF-33.)

Meanwhile, as fighting continued in the Solomons, the *Nassau* was experiencing action in an arena far removed from the tropical waters of the South Pacific. One of the new *Bogue*-class vessels, she had been commissioned on 20 August 1942. Among her crew were over 100 survivors of the *Lexington*. Most of these were not pleased to have come to the smaller ship from a carrier the size of the *Lexington*, but they were eager to get on with the war and repay the Japanese for sinking their ship. The *Nassau*'s shakedown period had

Close call on the Suwannee. *Out of control, the Wildcat is about to go over the side, taking pilot and plane handler with it. Luckily, in this 14 June 1943 accident, neither man was seriously hurt. (National Archives)*

been short, and in October Captain Austin K. Doyle had brought his ship south to the Guadalcanal area on a transport mission.

The *Nassau* remained in the South Pacific until February, using a couple of "pick-up" squadrons (VF-72 and VT-6 from the sunken *Hornet*) to replace the squadron she had brought south, VGS-16, which had since been sent on to Guadalcanal. As she sat waiting at Espiritu Santo or Noumea, Vice Admiral John H. Towers, as Commander Air Force, Pacific Fleet, was debating the feasibility of using the *Nassau, Altamaha,* and *Copahee* in a combat role in the South Pacific. The arrival of the *Sangamon*'s rendered Towers's idea moot, and the *Bogue*-class vessels (except for the *Nassau*) would see little combat action in the Pacific. Only one event of note broke the doldrums for the *Nassau* as she waited. For several weeks in December and January she was the flagship of Rear Admiral Charles F. Mason, commander of TF 65, thus becoming the first escort carrier to carry a flag officer.[36]

Finally, after disembarking VF-72 and VT-6, the *Nassau* headed back to Pearl Harbor on 6 February for a short availability period. Then it was back to Espiritu Santo with the aircraft and personnel of MAG-21.

This trip was wearing on the nerves of the flattop's crew. On 24 February, the destroyer *Sterett* picked up a sound contact astern of the carrier, attacked, and then lost the contact. Of course, the *Nassau* went to general quarters and began radical maneuvers until the threat was over. This sequence of events—the *Sterett* attacking and then losing a contact astern of the carrier and the *Nassau* going to general quarters—was repeated seven times before the carrier anchored safely at Espiritu Santo. Sighs of relief came from the *Nassau*'s crew, grateful that they had escaped the mystery submarine.

While anchored at Espiritu Santo, the carrier's aerology officer came to the executive officer with a complaint. It seemed that while en route from Pearl Harbor, every time he had dropped his bathythermograph into the water and attempted to take some readings, the carrier had gone to general quarters and he had had to retrieve his equipment. This upset him greatly, for he was trying to do a good job.

Questioning him closely, the exec found out that the times of the *Sterett*'s sound contacts and the times the bathythermograph had been dropped into the water coincided exactly. The *Nassau*'s mystery submarine had been her own scientific equipment.[37]

Her return trip was noticeably devoid of submarine contacts, and the *Nassau* arrived in San Francisco on 27 March to begin a seventeen-day yard period. Following this, she sailed for San Diego to prepare for her part in the Attu landings.

In June 1942 the islands of Attu and Kiska in the Aleutians had been taken by the Japanese. The Americans eventually decided to eliminate these Japanese outposts, and chose Attu, believed to be more lightly garrisoned than Kiska, as the initial target. In addition, since Attu is at the western tip of the Aleutians, while Kiska is farther east, they believed that leapfrogging Kiska would force the Japanese on that island to either evacuate or starve.

The *Nassau* was added, relatively late, to the Attu attack force because Rear Admiral Francis W. Rockwell, Commander Amphibious Force, North Pacific, who would be in overall command of the landings, felt that land-based aircraft would not always be available because of the fog and wind that seemed to be a constant in the Aleutians and that a carrier would be a valuable adjunct to the operation.

The flattop didn't have much time to prepare because the landings were to take place on 7 May and she didn't get her new squadron until 16 April. VC-21 was composed of thirty pilots, one air combat intelligence (ACI) officer, twenty-eight enlisted men, and twenty-six F4F-4s. Also aboard were the ship's utility plane, an SOC-3A nicknamed "Jeepers Creepers," and three F4F-3P photo planes. These latter three aircraft were part of VMO-155, which also had reported aboard on the sixteenth. Originally organized in the South Pacific, this marine unit had been broken up into two parts. A new VMO-155 was reorganized stateside, and a detachment of six pilots, one enlisted pilot, and eight enlisted men was sent to the *Nassau*.[38]

The *Nassau*'s planes were to be used primarily for air cover and observation, but were to be available for close air support as needed. Thus, the *Nassau* became the first carrier in the Pacific to be used for close air support. VC-21's training in this art was conducted by Lieutenant Colonel Peter P. Schrider, USMC, who sailed on the carrier as air support operations officer.[39]

On 23 April the carrier sailed from San Diego bound for the Aleutians. Less than one week of training had been afforded the pilots of VC-21. More, but not much more, training was conducted on the way north. After a short stay at Cold Bay, Alaska, the *Nassau* sailed for Attu on 4 May. The Attu landings were to have taken place on 7 May but a tremendous storm swept along the Aleutians chain, bringing high winds and boiling seas with it. Huge waves swept over the *Nassau*'s flight deck and the little flattop pitched and bobbed like a cork in the chaotic seas, but she was able to weather the blow, though with a bit of discomfort to her crew. Because of the weather, which was not much worse than usual for the Aleutians, the landings were postponed until the eleventh. On that day dense fog was present but the landings went off without too much difficulty.

At 0623, in the fog, the *Nassau* began launching the first of three flights. The first two flights consisted of eight and seven Wildcats, respectively, while a mixed quartet of photo and fighter Wildcats made up a reconnaissance and photo flight. Some of these planes inadvertently caused some tense moments for one landing party. A few hours prior to the main landings, an advance force had paddled ashore in rubber boats from the big submarines *Narwhal* and *Nautilus*. Moving inland, the soldiers left their rafts on the rocky shore. As the rising sun began to burn away the fog, several VC-21 fighters spotted the beached rafts. Frustrated by the weather and the apparent lack of targets on this mountainous island, the pilots were quick to take advantage of this opportunity to attack the "enemy." Several strafing runs rendered the rafts useless, leaving the infantrymen in a spot, since the rafts were their only means of escape if they ran into trouble. Luck was with the soldiers, though; their rafts weren't needed.[40]

These strafing attacks were almost the only activity by VC-21 planes on the eleventh, as fog and low clouds prevented much flying. Though there had been no opposition, there had been losses. Two planes were ditched, but both pilots were plucked from the icy waters. Several more planes were damaged in landing incidents, including one F4F-3P that was so extensively damaged it had to be jettisoned later. Another photo plane created some excitement during its landing when a parachute flare it was carrying dropped onto the flight deck and burst into flames. The small fire was quickly extinguished.[41]

The next day the weather cleared just before noon, and the Wildcats were able to strafe and drop hundred-pound bombs in the Holtz Bay area. They encountered heavy antiaircraft fire, but this only "plinked" a few planes. Because of the capricious fog, not until 1715 was the *Nassau* able to send off a major strike—nine planes—against some enemy barges in Holtz Bay reported to be firing into the American lines. In addition, a number of machine-gun positions holding up the advance were silenced.[42]

For attacks such as these, the ship and squadron had jury-rigged the 100-pounders, or "centuries," to be "daisy-cutters" (explode just above the ground) by adding twenty-inch extensions to the bombs' nose fuzes. This worked just fine. Also working pretty well were the "oil bombs" (a forerunner of the napalm bomb), which were used to good effect against trenches and dug-in positions.[43]

Tragedy struck VC-21 on the fourteenth. Already airborne to support the ground troops were four Wildcats when, at 1232, a group of bogeys was reported closing. To ward off the possible intruders, eight more fighters were launched, one of these crashing shortly after takeoff. The pilot, wet and shivering, was picked up by the *Aylwin*. When the bogeys were reported as friendlies, all the F4Fs were directed to attack positions on Attu.

Four of the planes flew up Massacre Bay valley to drop their bombs ahead of the advancing troops. Suddenly a williwaw, that violent and treacherous wind common to the Aleutians, swept through a pass, blowing the leading two planes thousands of feet into the air. Then, with the perverseness the williwaw was known for, the wind suddenly reversed direction to drive the last two fighters into the island's craggy slopes. There was one more loss for VC-21. While strafing positions in the Sarana Bay area, the squadron's leader, Lieutenant Commander L. K. Greenamyer, disappeared. Neither he nor his plane was ever found.[44]

Weather on the fifteenth was the usual sort—bad—and no missions were flown, but on the following day the VC-21 planes were

The Nassau *off Attu on 13 May 1943. The smoke, issuing from her uptake vent (another was on the opposite side), could be a problem for the men manning the guns aft of the vent. The sheer of the hangar deck is delineated by the galleries built onto the sides. (National Archives)*

airborne again. During the day fifteen planes were launched on missions. Two didn't return. One pilot was killed when his plane crashed into Holtz Bay following a strafing run. The other pilot killed was VMO-155's Second Lieutenant Waldo P. Breeden (just commissioned from technical sergeant), who spun into the sea near the carrier.[45]

Attacks on the sixteenth caused not only Japanese casualties but some American ones as well. Not advised that the ground troops had seized an important ridge, the VC-21 pilots took the dots of brown moving across the rocky terrain to be Japanese soldiers. Several infantrymen were wounded by the strafing and bombing runs before they could be stopped.[46]

Again, weather was the cause of a suspension of flying on the seventeenth and the eighteenth. Several strikes were flown the next two days, and then the battle was over for the *Nassau*. Fighting on the island would continue until the thirtieth, however, the remaining Japanese troops sacrificing themselves in a bloody attack on the twenty-ninth or committing suicide. The next day, after mopping-up operations, Attu was declared secure.

The Attu operation had not been particularly well executed on either the army's or the navy's part. The army troops, of the 7th Division, had not shown much offensive élan. (That division would improve, becoming one of the best in the Pacific.) On the navy's side,

naval gunfire vessels had a lot to learn, as did the cargo and transport ships. This was only the third U.S. amphibious assault of the
war, and the learning curve was still on the rise.

One bright spot of this battle was the performance of the *Nassau*
and her planes. For both ship and squadron it had been a tiring,
frustrating operation. "Very rarely could more than four planes operate efficiently against an enemy position," the navy commented
later. "It was not considered advisable to risk having a total of more
than eight planes in the air at once lest a shift of weather prevent
recovery."[47] Still, despite the wretched weather, the VC-21 planes
succeeded more often than not in providing the necessary support
to the ground forces.

At Attu the *Nassau* seldom operated more than forty miles from
the island and often was within ten miles of Holtz Bay. Because of
the lack of wind around Attu, notwithstanding the williwaws, almost
all of the sorties were launched by catapult.[48] Considering VC-21's
lack of training, the nature of the operation, and, of course, the
treacherous Aleutian weather, the loss of five pilots was thought to
be low.[49]

The one big deficiency of the *Nassau*'s operations was the lack of
TBFs for real bombing attacks. Nevertheless, Rear Admiral Rockwell was impressed by the carrier's accomplishments, recommending
that "an adequate number of ACV's of the *Nassau* type should be
earmarked for amphibious operations and should train with Amphibious forces."[50]

Rockwell felt that three escort carriers, one carrying bombers and
two with fighters, would be desirable for operations such as Attu.
Also, these "jeeps" could provide advance or emergency landing
decks for the big fast carriers supporting landing operations.[51] His
ideas would not be followed completely by the navy. But the operational experience of escort carriers at North Africa and Attu was
showing how they might be used most profitably in the Pacific—for
close air support. This plan would grow in importance with the
influx of the newer escort carriers to the Pacific Fleet.

THE QUICKENING PACE

THE ATTU BATTLE pretty much put an end to the combat activities of the *Nassau*. She would put in cameo appearances in the Gilberts and Marshalls, but for all intents she would no longer be a "combat" carrier.

Her skipper, Captain Doyle, knew that she was to revert to a ferry and transport, but he was hoping, somehow, to change her fate. "The invaluable experience of the *Nassau* in amphibious operations has been wasted due to her pending conversion for use as airplane cargo transport," he lamented. "It is recommended that, whenever possible, the high morale of a ship with a 'fighting reputation' be balanced against repairable deficiencies in evaluation of her military efficiency. The Commanding Officer respectfully invites attention to the value of tradition in a new class and recommends that the honor of being designated as a combatant ACV be given this ACV which, from the beginning, has consistently, despite many contrary opinions, advocated combatant use of her class."[1]

It was no use. Along with the other *Bogue*-class ships, the *Nassau* was relegated in the Pacific to the task of transporting aircraft and personnel. This was not a denigration of the type; it was because a newer escort carrier, better suited to the task, was appearing on the scene. This was the Kaiser- or *Casablanca*-class vessel.

This class had been the brainchild of shipyard magnate Henry J. Kaiser, who had gotten the ear of President Roosevelt. After much haggling among the president, Kaiser, the Maritime Commission, and the navy, fifty ships of this class were ordered. Based on a design by the naval architectural firm of Gibbs & Cox, these vessels were the first all-welded carriers, and much of their construction was by mass production methods using prefabricated sections.

In many ways their design and construction were superior to

those of the earlier escort carrier classes. Their 257-foot-long hangar decks, with no sheer or camber, were longer than those of both the *Bogue* and *Sangamon* classes. Because of the way the propeller race acted on the large balanced rudder, the new ships were extremely maneuverable. Twin screws and separated machinery spaces were a plus. Though lighter by some 3,000 tons, they had a longer flight deck (477 feet) than the *Bogue*s. And especially important for a flat-top, they were faster.

Not everything about the Kaiser carriers was better. Continual troubles plagued the Uniflow reciprocating steam engines. These old-fashioned engines used superheated steam, which presented several problems in cylinder lubrication and the filtering system. The engines were never quite up to the task of day in, day out, hard-charging operations. Exorbitant piston ring wear was a malady of these engines that drove many a chief engineer to near despair. Designed and rated to run at 4,500 IHP and 161 RPM, too often they had to be run at speeds of 178 to 182 RPM or higher. These speeds were not good for the brick walls and decks of the boilers, as well as the auxiliary machinery, which also had to be operated at full throttle. Also, many of the fittings used were not "navy quality" and tended to break or give way under stress. And the fast-paced construction of these ships sometimes meant that the welding was not of high quality.

Protection for these carriers was sparse, a point driven home by the sinking of the *Liscome Bay,* but the very design of the ships militated against substantial improvements in this area. Armament was on a par with that of the other escort carrier classes. One 5-inch/.38-caliber gun was located at the stern; its only useful purpose, as far as one sailor on these Kaiser carriers could see, was "to keep the rudder in the water."[2] Sixteen 40-mm guns in twin mounts and twenty 20-mm guns comprised the antiaircraft armament.[3]

Several of these new carriers joined the three *Sangamon*s in Operation Galvanic, the assault on the Gilbert Islands. The taking of these islands had been proposed at the Casablanca Conference in February 1943, along with the seizure and consolidation of positions in the Solomons, New Guinea, and the Aleutians. By May of that year, at the Trident Conference, the main effort in the Pacific was set to go through the Central Pacific. This was not to the liking of General Douglas MacArthur, down in the South Pacific, but it was the desire of the Joint Chiefs of Staff.

Next came the choice of targets and a timetable. After the Trident Conference, the Joint War Plans Committee suggested the taking of the Marshall Islands in October. MacArthur would have to be content with little more than a holding action. Of course this brought about an outburst from MacArthur, who had his supporters in Washington, too.

MacArthur's very vocal disagreement with the planners was one consideration that caused the Joint War Plans Committee to reevaluate the Marshalls proposal. An assault on the Gilberts, instead, appeared to be a promising scenario and would not divert as many troops from the Southwest Pacific as would the Marshalls operation. Finally the planners decided that the invasion of the Gilberts would open the Central Pacific offensive, and they set a target date of 15 November 1943. Seizure of the Marshalls would follow about 1 February 1944.[4] In recognition that the offensive in the Central Pacific would be a navy show, a formidable naval force was organized.

On 5 August 1943 Vice Admiral Raymond A. Spruance became commander of the Fifth Fleet. This force would contain the majority of the combatant ships and would be used as the navy's striking force in the Pacific, making long-range strikes on enemy-held islands and also supporting landings on these islands.

Actually conducting the landings would be Rear Admiral Richmond K. Turner's V Amphibious Force. Constituted on 15 August 1943, "V 'Phib" was the force assigned the job of taking the Gilberts. The escort carriers to be used in this operation were part of Turner's force. For Galvanic, Turner's command was divided into two parts. Fresh from extensive overhauls, the three *Sangamon*s were assigned to Rear Admiral Harry W. Hill's Southern Attack Force— TF 53. Staging out of the New Hebrides, Hill's ships would support the 2nd Marine Division, which would be landing on the then little-known island of Betio in Tarawa Atoll. The composition of the escort carrier group for Tarawa was:

TASK GROUP 53.6   AIR SUPPORT GROUP
R. Adm. Van H. Ragsdale (ComCarDiv 22)

Sangamon (F)	Capt. E. P. Moore
Air Group 37	Lt. Cdr. B. E. Day
VF-37 12 F6F-3	Lt. Cdr. F. L. Bates
VC-37 6 TBF-1, 3 TBF-1C, 9 SBD-5	Lt. Cdr. Day
Suwannee	Capt. F. W. McMahon
Air Group 60	Lt. Cdr. A. C. Edmonds
VF-60 12 F6F-3	Lt. Cdr. H. O. Harvey
VC-60 9 TBF-1, 9 SBD-5	Lt. Cdr. Edmonds
Chenango	Capt. D. Ketcham
Air Group 35	Lt. Cdr. S. Mandarich
VF-35 12 F6F-3	Lt. Cdr. Mandarich
VC-35 6 TBF-1, 3 TBF-1C, 9 SBD-5	Lt. Cdr. R. L. Flint

Screen: Destroyers *Aylwin, Farragut, Monaghan, Cotten, Cowell*

In addition, the *Barnes* and *Nassau* would join TG 53.6 on the eighteenth, each carrying twenty-two Hellcats of VF-1, the Tarawa garrison squadron.[5]

Gathering at Pearl Harbor for the Gilberts operation were more escort carriers. Since 15 July, escort carriers had been classified as combatant vessels, CVEs (Aircraft Carrier, Escort), and three new CVEs would be making their first combat appearances during Galvanic. They were the *Liscome Bay, Coral Sea,* and *Corregidor,* all three having been commissioned within three weeks of each other in August. Commissioning ceremonies had been held at Astoria, Oregon, at the mouth of the Columbia River, the site of the navy's escort carrier precommissioning detail. At this time the commanding officer of the Astoria Naval Station was Captain James Barner, former skipper of the *Long Island.*

After being launched at the Kaiser shipyards in Vancouver, Washington, just across the Columbia from Portland, Oregon, the brand-new carriers were sailed down down the river to Astoria by a skeleton crew of some of that ship's officers and a few shipyard workers. The carrier got its final outfitting at Astoria, and it was there that both officers and seamen got their first look at those who would turn an inanimate object, the ship, into a living, breathing, fighting weapon. They also got their first look at the ship they would be manning—an ungainly-looking, flattopped thing squatting alongside an Astoria pier. When someone didn't like what he saw, a little sales pitch was required to get that person to realize how important it was to be a part of an escort carrier's crew. And if that didn't work, the salesman pointed out that there were far less attractive assignments than being on a CVE. On the whole, though, most sailors looked on an escort carrier with equanimity, and in the future would come to believe that their ship was the best, the fightingest, the prettiest of any ship, CVE or not.

Astoria in the summertime can be beautiful; in the winter sailors have less enthusiasm for the cold, wet winds sweeping in off the Pacific and the dark, dank fogs that shroud the area on too many days. Some of the men who were there waiting for their ships came back after the war to live, while others vowed never to return to such a wet, miserable place. But it was at Astoria, with its Jekyll and Hyde climatic personality, that all the disparate personalities that made up a CVE crew came together.

Though most of the officers and men had undergone training in their specialties at other places, especially at Bremerton, Washington, where a Pre-Commissioning School was established, it was at Astoria that they were assigned to the various departments and divi-

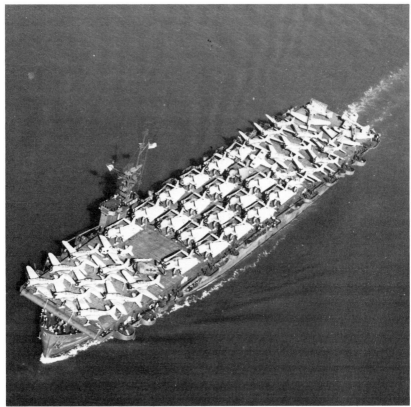

The Liscome Bay *as seen on 20 September 1943 carrying a load of SBDs, TBFs, and a couple of F4Fs. (National Archives)*

sions of the carrier. Also first meeting their ships at Astoria were the squadrons. At the Clatsop County Airport (not much of a field, but it would have to do) the squadrons usually began their intensive training in carrier operations and combat tactics. The squadrons would fly from other fields (notably Holtville, California, and the training carriers off San Diego where the men became carrier qualified), but at Astoria the pilots, aircrewmen, and maintenance personnel gained the first impressions of the ship from which they would do the bulk of their flying and fighting.

And so the escort carriers and the men who manned them met at Astoria to prepare for war. Then, when the equipment had been installed and the men had been trained and fitted into their positions as well as could be in the short time allotted, the carriers sailed from Astoria, out across the Columbia bar where the swells of the

Pacific met the surge of the river and the waters were never still, and turned south for San Francisco and, finally, San Diego. Though heading south, not west, these carriers were inexorably being drawn closer and closer to the shooting war.

Having been commissioned only since August, the *Liscome Bay, Coral Sea,* and *Corregidor* had had little time for proper shakedown cruises because they were greatly needed for the next offensive in the Pacific: the attack on the Gilbert Islands. In early November they found themselves in Pearl Harbor. The next time they sailed, it would be for the real thing. As part of Rear Admiral Turner's Northern Attack Force—TF 52—they would operate off Makin Atoll in support of the army's 27th Infantry Division fighting on Butari-tari Island. The carrier group was organized as follows:

TASK GROUP 52.3   AIR SUPPORT GROUP
R. Adm. Henry M. Mullinnix (ComCarDiv 24)

Liscome Bay (F)		Capt. I. D. Wiltsie
VC-39	11 FM-1, 5 F4F-4, 9 TBM-1, 3 TBM-1C	Lt. Cdr. M. U. Beebe
Coral Sea		Capt. H. W. Taylor
VC-33	12 F4F-4, 10 TBF-1C	Lt. Cdr. J. J. Lynch
Corregidor		Capt. R. L. Bowman
VC-41	12 FM-1, 9 TBF-1	Lt. Cdr. G. M. Clifford

Screen: Destroyers *Morris, Hoel, Franks, Hughes*[6]

(Because the Grumman plant was needed for production of the new F6F Hellcat, construction of all Wildcats was turned over to General Motors' Eastern Aircraft Division. These Eastern Aircraft–built planes were designated FM-1s and were virtually identical to F4F-4s except for having two fewer wing guns and a slight increase in weight. Also, to assist Grumman in the production of Avengers, Eastern Aircraft built the torpedo bomber as the TBM.)

No one on the carriers, of course, yet knew where they were headed, but they were pretty sure they would see action soon. On the *Corregidor,* shortly after leaving Pearl Harbor, the crew became certain of this when Captain Bowman announced, "We have just changed course to 270 . . . and that's not in the direction of Chicago!"[7]

Every sailor publicly proclaimed that the invasion forces wouldn't be discovered, but privately feared that there was no way forces of this size could get close to the Gilberts without being detected. And there was a good chance they would be discovered because, sensing something in the air, the Japanese were out looking for the Americans.

On 18 November Japanese reconnaissance planes found the LST (Landing Ship, Tank) group bound for Makin, and the next day a

prowling Mavis (a four-engine flying boat) came across TF 53 as it
headed northwestward for Tarawa. The Mavis didn't remain airborne very long. Led by VF-60's executive officer, Lieutenant Edward L. Dashiell, a division of *Suwannee* F6F Hellcats made short
work of the Mavis. Not until too late did the enemy crew realize that
the four planes charging in were American. Set ablaze, the big flying
boat spiraled into the ocean.[8]

D day for the Gilberts was 20 November. On Betio the 2nd Marine Division met stiff resistance, and a bloody battle began that
lasted until the twenty-third. To the men of the *Sangamon*, miles
away from the bloodbath occurring on Betio, the twentieth would be
remembered more for the fact that "Sangy," the ship's mascot, gave
birth to a litter of pups than for the excitement of D day itself.[9]

Although the planes from the three CVEs in TG 53.6 were also
kept busy, it was the aircraft from the fast carriers that provided
most of the air support for the marines on Betio. Many of the initial
attacks were poorly executed: not on time when they should have
been, or right on time when there should have been a delay. The
bombs that were dropped were often off-target and the strafing
runs were done haphazardly.[10] The fast carriers were doing most of
the close support work, and most of the criticism was directed at
them.

The aviators learned quickly, especially those from the escort carriers. Air support operations improved considerably over the next
few days; nevertheless, there was still a great amount of room left
for improvement. Luckily, antiaircraft fire was not a big concern,
though at least three Hellcats were lost to the flak. Several other
planes were lost operationally.

During Galvanic the fighting was not always between enemies. At
one point the destroyer *Ringgold* tried to sink the submarine *Nautilus,* happily without success. On the twenty-second a *Suwannee* plane
and the destroyer *Meade* were involved in a minor civil war.

That afternoon the *Meade* and fellow destroyer *Frazier* caught the
Japanese submarine *I-35.* A series of depth charge attacks brought
the submarine to the surface, where she was rammed by the *Frazier.*
As the destroyer backed away, the sub sank, chased down by depth
bombs from some *Suwannee* Avengers. Both destroyers launched
whaleboats to recover four survivors from the *I-35* who were seen in
the water. One Japanese resisted capture and was killed, but the
other three were picked up by the *Meade*'s boat. While this was going
on, a *Suwannee* pilot overhead mistook the boat for a sub's conning
tower and dropped a bomb just a few feet from it. The boat was
flung into the air, but no one was seriously hurt. Seeing the attack

on her boat and unable to positively identify the attacker, the *Meade* quickly filled the sky around the Avenger with black puffs of flak. She scored two hits, but again, no one was seriously hurt. When plane and destroyer saw that they were on the same side, they called the fight a draw and went their separate ways.[11]

Also getting into the act at Tarawa had been the *Nassau* and *Barnes*. Although their planes had not been intended to undertake combat operations, the progress of the battle forced Admiral Hill to request that the two flattops use the VF-1 aircraft they were ferrying in a combat role. Thus, the VF-1 pilots put in a number of CAP, bombing, and strafing missions without a loss before they flew ashore.[12]

If Admiral Ragsdale's carriers had a relatively easy time off Tarawa, the same could not be said for the new "jeeps" operating off Makin. From the start the three CVEs were kept busy with numerous ground support missions. Though many of these were designated strike missions, many more were improvised attacks by planes returning from patrol missions, striking such targets as directed by the Support Aircraft Commander.

As a new kind of mission for the escort carriers, every flight was an experiment. One ship's history noted, "Frequent changes in types of bombs and fuses were made, various methods of target designation were tried and air to ground communications received particular attention."[13] But as in Tarawa, the end result of these operations was disappointing to the ground forces. Poor communications, poor coordination, and poor training all combined to reduce the effectiveness of the support missions.[14] Finally, operational accidents, especially afflicting the *Corregidor*, kept the number of available aircraft down.

Butaritari was finally secured on the morning of the twenty-third, with other islands in the atoll being inspected over the next several days. Though no more ground support missions were needed, the planes for the CVEs (the air support group now operating as part of TG 52.13 under the command of Rear Admiral Robert M. Griffin) kept busy on the twenty-third flying antisubmarine and CAP missions.

One of these missions came close to disaster that evening. Five Wildcats from the *Liscome Bay* had been on a late afternoon patrol. Upon returning to the spot where the carrier should have been, they couldn't find her. Bad weather and growing darkness compounded their problem. Finally they called for help and were directed to land on the big carriers of Rear Admiral C. A. Pownall's TG 50.1, then operating about sixty miles south of the escort carriers. Four planes made night landings on the *Yorktown,* while Lieutenant Maurice E.

Wells (a VC-41 pilot temporarily assigned to VC-39) landed on the *Lexington*.[15] The "Lex's" crew took Wells and his little (in comparison to the *Lexington*'s new Hellcats) FM-1 to their hearts, lovingly tending his fighter and making sure Wells was cared for.

As Wells and the other pilots in the flight hit the sack that night, they had no idea how lucky they were. Creeping in on the escort carriers steaming off Butaritari was Lieutenant Commander Tabata's *I-175*. As dawn neared, Tabata fired a spread of torpedoes. One struck the *Liscome Bay*, ravaging her. Her magazines exploded and her after third virtually disintegrated; a column of flame shot into the air and pieces of the carrier showered on nearby vessels. Miles away on the *Lexington*, the glow of the *Liscome Bay*'s funeral pyre could be seen. The glow did not last long. In twenty-three minutes the shattered hulk of the *Liscome Bay* sank beneath the surface of the Pacific. Immediately following the attack, the ships of TG 52.13 began evasive action and started a search for the *I-175*, but the sub escaped unscathed.

To the crews of the other carriers, the loss of the *Liscome Bay* was a terrible shock. Bitterly they complained that the Kaiser flattops were "two-torpedo ships—one in the side and one over the flight deck." For some time the quality of workmanship and materials had been a topic of conversation by the crews. Now that they believed the carriers were poorly built, the crews' morale plummeted, and the prevailing mood became restrained and introspective.[16]

Later that morning Lieutenant Wells was eagerly preparing to return to the *Liscome Bay* when he heard the *Lexington*'s skipper, Felix B. Stump (who himself would become intimately involved with CVEs in the not-too-distant future), announcing the sinking of the carrier. Blanching, Wells returned to his quarters without a word. The following day, though, looking relieved and happy, Wells took off for Tarawa. Gaily emblazoned on his fighter were the names "Baby Airedale" and "Orphan Annie," with VF-16's insignia completing the decorations.[17]

For the new carriers this introduction into combat had been sobering, particularly in light of the loss of the *Liscome Bay*. Aircraft losses had been heavy also, most being the result of operational accidents. Only one, a *Coral Sea* Avenger caught in the explosion of an ammunition dump, was a combat loss. Twenty planes went down with the *Liscome Bay*, while operational accidents took a toll of four pilots and crewmen and six deck personnel killed, and sixteen aircraft washed out.[18]

"The cost of inexperience was high," as the CarDiv 24 history later put it.[19] The shocking losses during Galvanic caused recommendations of varying quality but vast quantity to pour forth from all commands involved in the operation. Intensive studies were conducted to bring about measures to eliminate or, at the least, minimize the deficiencies and problem areas encountered during Galvanic.

Like the other commands, CarDiv 24 made its share of recommendations. The majority were of the usual kind found in many sources—better training, more firepower, increased communications facilities, and so forth. But there was one that was very unusual. In CarDiv 24's action report, Captain Crommelin, the chief of staff, proposed the development of carrier-based gas attack units. This surprising idea was quickly quashed at Nimitz's headquarters as "not in accordance with national policy."[20] Why Crommelin should have even considered this idea is unknown, but perhaps it was due to the shocking loss of the *Liscome Bay* and the terrible price the marines were paying at Tarawa, with a consequent desire for revenge.

Taking over as commanding officer of CarDiv 24 was the *Corregidor*'s Bowman. His tenure in this job would be short, as there was little left for the escort carriers to do in the Gilberts. After delivering VF-1 to Tarawa on the twenty-fifth, the *Barnes* and *Nassau* joined the *Coral Sea* and *Corregidor* on 28 November for the return to Pearl Harbor. The trip back was made at the pretty good clip, for the CVEs, of 18 knots, even in the face of heavy seas that caused violent pitching. Not one to let heavy seas ruin the occasion, Captain Taylor held a full-dress personnel inspection on the *Coral Sea*'s flight deck. While the crew, clad in immaculate white, stood at attention for the inspection, the forward ranks got thoroughly drenched from the sea spray.[21]

Remaining in the Gilbert's a bit longer were the three *Sangamon*s, which finally returned to Pearl Harbor on 14 December, thence on to San Diego. The work of these three flattops had shown that they were very versatile and useful ships. Low winds in the Gilberts had been a problem, but the carriers could safely operate their planes in winds as low as 5 knots. Of great use during Galvanic had been the large fuel capacity of these ex-oilers. During the operation the three CVEs fueled forty-five destroyers (twenty-one by the *Chenango* alone) and two cruisers and still had enough fuel to operate for another two weeks.[22]

Returning to the Gilberts on 14 December was the *Nassau*. This time she was carrying a load of thirty-seven P-39s and thirteen A-24s for delivery to Makin. Much to the consternation of the army pilots, who had no experience on carriers, their planes would have to be catapulted off. Many of them "could be seen on the flight deck, standing around the catapult and scratching their heads."[23]

Nevertheless, all the army pilots launched safely, to their great relief, on the fourteenth. To celebrate the successful catapultings, "they came back to zoom around the ship with such gusto and enthusiastic abandon that the *Nassau*'s skipper, Captain [Stanley J.] Michael, warned them to stay clear of the ship."[24]

Two other escort carriers made ferry trips to the Gilberts shortly after their capture. On 14 January 1944 the *White Plains* first appeared in the combat zone to deliver the thirty-nine Corsairs of VMF-532 and VMF-113 to Tarawa. Three days later thirty-four VF-1 Hellcats came aboard for return to Pearl Harbor. She then headed west again to supply planes to the carriers covering the Marshalls invasion.

These ferrying missions were far from cut-and-dried. Upon her departure from San Diego, the *White Plains* was missing a landing signal officer (LSO) and numerous other important members of her crew. When she was sent to the Marshalls to deliver aircraft, she was not given an operation plan and found her task group only by luck. Then when sent to an island known to her merely as "Burlesque" (actually the island of Roi), she had to find it by falling in with a vessel that did know the island's location.[25] These problems would play a big part in the formation of a Carrier Transport Squadron.

Also ferrying aircraft back and forth to the Gilberts was the *Kalinin Bay*, commissioned just since 27 November. Following her first delivery of planes to Pearl Harbor on 9 January, she was ordered to deliver a further batch—twenty-four Corsairs, thirty-one Hellcats, twelve Avengers, five Helldivers, and one lonely Stinson spotter plane—to Tarawa and the various task groups in the area.[26]

For the men of VMF-422 who flew the Corsairs, tragedy flew with them. On the morning of 24 January the Corsairs were catapulted for Tarawa. VMF-422 remained there that day, then left as a group for Nanomea (about 460 miles south of Tarawa). From there they were to proceed on to Funafuti in the Ellice Islands. In one of the more unfortunate incidents of the war, the squadron encountered severe weather en route and, one by one, the planes went into the ocean. VMF-422 was wiped out, with six pilots and twenty-two planes lost.[27]

After the VMF-422 planes were catapulted, the *Kalinin Bay* headed toward the Marshalls to supply aircraft replacements to the fast carriers covering the Marshalls invasion and then returned to Pearl Harbor, picking up the remaining F6Fs of VF-1 on the way.[28]

The mission had not been particularly exciting for the *Kalinin Bay,* just a typical operation for a typical escort carrier.

Occurring just a little over two months after the fall of the Gilberts, Flintlock, the invasion of the Marshalls, had the makings of a very risky undertaking. Instead of assaulting the eastern portion of the islands, Nimitz planned on bypassing the strongly held atolls of Wotje, Maloelap, Mili, and Jaluit to strike at the center of the Marshalls—Kwajalein.

Again in command of the entire operation would be Vice Admiral Spruance, with Rear Admiral Turner in charge of the Joint Expeditionary Force (TF 51). As in Galvanic, Major General Holland M. Smith, USMC, would command the ground troops. Two attack forces would make the assault: the Northern Attack Force (TF 53) under Rear Admiral Richard L. Conolly was to capture Roi-Namur, and the islands in the northern half of the atoll; the Southern Attack Force (TF 52) was under Admiral Turner and would undertake the mission of seizing Kwajalein and the islands in the atoll's southern half. The principal ground troops assigned were the 4th Marine Division for Roi-Namur and the 7th Infantry Division for Kwajalein.

In addition, a third force under the command of Rear Admiral Harry W. Hill was assigned the task of taking Majuro Atoll, an excellent anchorage on the eastern edge of the Marshalls, as a preliminary to the main assault on Kwajalein, scheduled for 31 January. Two escort carriers would be part of Admiral Hill's force. One, the *Nassau* with VC-66 aboard, had already seen action at Attu and Tarawa. The other, Captain Harold L. Meadows's *Natoma Bay,* carrying VC-63, was brand-new to combat operations.

Meadows was tough and had already melded his ship and men into a first-class fighting team. Not necessarily loved by his men, but definitely respected, Meadows was a strict disciplinarian who preferred to do things by the book.

His crew found this out early. One day while landing the VC-63 planes during the shakedown cruise, one of the Wildcats came a cropper. On a waveoff the fighter caught its left wing on a signal bridge stanchion and cartwheeled into the water. The pilot got out safely and was soon rescued, but a large portion of the plane's left wing still hung on the stanchion. Every time the ship rolled, the wing section would flap crazily about the stanchion. Where it would fall or how much damage it would cause was anybody's guess. A veteran warrant officer named Perkins decided to do something about it. Obtaining some rope, he climbed above the bridge and began inching his way out the narrow stanchion.

The Coral Sea, Corregidor, Natoma Bay, *and* Nassau *(as seen from the* Manila Bay*) head for action in the Marshalls, 13 January 1944. (National Archives)*

Just as he was about to secure the flapping wing, Captain Meadows stepped onto the bridge and looked up. "Perkins, come down from there at once!" an aghast Meadows roared.

"Yes, sir," Perkins replied. "Just as soon as I secure the wing section with this rope."

"I said come down *now!* You're out of uniform!"

"I'm what?" was the surprised response.

"You're out of uniform," shouted Meadows, his face beet red. "You're wearing white socks!"

Shortly after his ship had been commissioned, Captain Meadows had ordered that no white socks were to be worn on the *Natoma Bay*. Now one of his men was flouting his order right in his face. Wearily, Perkins clambered down, put on black socks, then climbed back up to the swaying and unsteady stanchion to finish the job. The men on the *Natoma Bay* got the picture; the skipper wanted things done his way. One thing was sure, there wasn't a white sock on the carrier from then on.[29]

The occupation of Majuro turned out to be unopposed, only a handful of enemy soldiers being in the entire atoll. There was still work for the CVE planes. While the *Natoma Bay* planes maintained a

CAP and ASP (antisubmarine patrol) at Majuro, VC-66 patrolled the enemy-held atolls of Wotje, Maloelap, and Taroa. One Wildcat was shot down into Taroa lagoon, but in a daring rescue a *Salt Lake City* floatplane plucked the flier from under the noses of the Japanese.[30]

No VC-63 planes were lost in combat, but there was the usual attrition through operational accidents, including a rare one on 1 February. On takeoff a Wildcat was just passing over the *Natoma Bay*'s bow when she ran into a heavy swell. As her bow pitched up, it hit the tail of the fighter, flipping it into the water. The pilot was picked up, dripping but unhurt.

For most of February the two "jeeps" provided protection for the ships using Majuro as an anchorage. Late in the month the *Nassau* left for Pearl Harbor, while the *Natoma Bay* didn't leave until 7 March, and then, instead of heading east, sailed south for Espiritu Santo.[31]

The occupation of Majuro had been bloodless. Kwajalein would be a different story. Helping to cover the landings on Roi-Namur were the three "Old Indispensables" of Rear Admiral Van H. Ragsdale's TG 53.6:

TASK GROUP 53.6   NORTHERN CARRIER GROUP
R. Adm. Ragsdale (ComCarDiv 22)

Sangamon (F)		Capt. E. P. Moore
Air Group 37		Lt. Cdr. B. E. Day
VF-37	12 F6F-3	Lt. Cdr. F. L. Bates
VC-37	6 TBF-1, 4 TBM-1C, 9 SBD-5	Lt. Cdr. Day
Suwannee		Capt. W. D. Johnson
Air Group 60		Lt. Cdr. H. O. Feilbach
VF-60	12 F6F-3	Lt. Cdr. Feilbach
VC-60	2 TBF-1, 7 TBM-1C, 9 SBD-5	Lt. W. C. Vincent
Chenango		Capt. D. Ketcham
Air Group 35		Lt. Cdr. S. Mandarich
VF-35	12 F6F-3	Lt. F. T. Moore
VC-35	4 TBF-1, 5 TBM-1C, 9 SBD-5	Lt. T. Carr

Screen: Destroyers *Farragut, Monaghan, Dale*[32]

Even before nearing the Marshalls, TG 53.6 had a series of misadventures, most of them involving the *Sangamon*. On the afternoon of 25 January a VF-37 Hellcat was landing on the flattop. After getting his "cut" (landing signal) from the LSO, the pilot let his plane float up the deck. Slicing through two barriers, the fighter plowed into the planes parked at the forward end of the flight deck and knocked an SBD over the side. The Hellcat's belly tank, full of gasoline, was ripped off and flaming fuel scattered among the parked aircraft.

Caught in the cockpit of his parked plane, a pilot was incinerated, as were six "airedales" (flight deck crewmen) trapped by the raging blaze. Flames ran aft ninety feet along the starboard side and up the bridge. An ugly column of black smoke soared into the sky. Faced with being roasted, a number of men leapt overboard. Fortunately, damage control parties soon had the fire under control and the *Sangamon* was able to resume operations, but the accident had been costly. Besides the Dauntless over the side, four Hellcats had been destroyed. Seven men had been killed in the fire and nine others injured. Of those men forced into the water, two were not picked up.

The *Sangamon*'s misfortunes continued. Later that afternoon, while the debris from the accident was still being cleaned up, an Avenger crashed through the remaining barrier and smashed into parked aircraft. Three SBDs and a TBM were damaged beyond repair, and three more Dauntlesses were slightly damaged. This time, however, there were no serious injuries.[33]

A potentially more serious accident was narrowly averted the next day. Fueling of the carriers had just ended and they were resuming a standard zigzag pattern. However, for air operations the CVEs were free to maneuver individually. So shortly before 1600 the *Suwannee* began a turn to the right to recover aircraft, while the *Sangamon* turned left in accordance with the zigzag plan. At this time both vessels were about 1,800 yards apart.

The *Sangamon*'s skipper, Captain Edward P. Moore, was not on her bridge, being ill and confined to his bed at the time. Neither was the executive officer, who could only be reached by messenger. But Admiral Ragsdale was on the bridge.

As the two ships continued their turns, it became obvious that they were on a collision course. The weak steam whistles on both ships bleated out their collision signals. One of the few who heard these signals was Green Peyton, the noted novelist then serving on the *Suwannee* as an air combat intelligence officer. Peyton was in the ACI room located near the carrier's forecastle when he heard the signals. They didn't mean anything to him, but there was an urgency about the sound that bothered him.

Stepping out on a catwalk, Peyton looked down on the forecastle. An unusual scene lay before him. A group of men who had been sunning themselves there were now trying to crowd through a door all at the same time. They were glancing fearfully over their shoulders. Because the flight deck overhang obstructed his view, Peyton couldn't see what the others were staring at. Suddenly the traffic jam below melted away and the men raced up a ladder past Peyton and bolted aft.

A few words also raced past Peyton's ears—"Collision!" "We're going into the water!" By the time he digested these tidbits and realized what they meant, a loud rumbling followed by a splintering sound rent the air and the *Suwannee* rocked sharply.

When the threat of a collision became clear, Admiral Ragsdale ordered his flagship to turn hard right and back full. He also ordered the *Suwannee* to do the same thing. It was too late. The two flattops scraped bow to bow, with the *Suwannee* getting the worst of the encounter. The first twenty feet of her flight deck was buckled inboard four feet, the port catwalk back to the No. 2 40-mm platform was carried away, and her hull was pierced down to the main deck. There were no personnel casualties, but when the *Sangamon* sliced into the *Suwannee*, the executive officer's quarters were right in the way. As the two ships disentangled, the *Sangamon* took the exec's private head and shower and dumped them into the sea.

Luckily, the damage to both ships turned out to be minor and they were able to continue operating throughout Flintlock. Eventually the *Suwannee*'s commanding officer, Captain William D. Johnson, was held responsible for the collision, though it apparently didn't affect his career too much—he retained his command and was later promoted.[34] Of course, the *Suwannee*'s crew didn't agree with this assessment, blaming the whole affair on the *Sangamon*. Shortly after this incident a notation appeared next to the 26 January position on the pilot's ready room track chart—"Attacked by *Sangamon*."[35]

While Admiral Ragsdale's carriers moved into position north of Roi-Namur, another escort carrier force was closing in to support landings on the atoll's southernmost island, Kwajalein:

TASK GROUP 52.9   SOUTHERN CARRIER GROUP
R. Adm. Ralph E. Davison (ComCarDiv 24)

Manila Bay (F)		Capt. B. L. Braun
VC-7	16 FM-2, 9 TBF-1, 3 TBF-1C	Lt. Cdr. W. R. Bartlett
Coral Sea		Capt. H. W. Taylor
VC-33	5 FM-1, 9 F4F-4, 6 TBF-1C, 4 TBF-1, 2 TBM-1	Lt. Cdr. J. J. Lynch
Corregidor		Capt. R. L. Bowman
VC-41	6 FM-1, 3 F4F-4, 3 TBF-1C, 8 TBM-1	Lt. Cdr. G. M. Clifford

Screen: Destroyers *Bancroft, Coghlan, Caldwell, Halligan*[36]

This was Ralph Davison's first operation as a carrier division commander. He had formerly been assistant chief of the Bureau of Aeronautics, and had taken command of CarDiv 24 on 9 December.

Tough and intelligent, with an impish streak, he would remain with the escort carriers only a relatively short time before moving to command of a fast carrier division.

Flintlock saw an innovation for TG 52.9 that met the approval of all concerned. In the previous operation, Galvanic, tactical command of a CVE group had rested with a nonaviator based in a battleship. This time tactical command was held by Admiral Davison, who flew his flag from an escort carrier. A command setup of this type would remain standard throughout the war.

Making their first appearance in combat were the *Manila Bay* and the FM-2. The "Manila Maru" ("Maru" being the Japanese name for a cargo vessel) would remain in the thick of the action through Okinawa. An improved version of the Wildcat, with a more powerful engine and a lighter airframe, the FM-2 was armed with four .50-caliber guns and was specifically intended for use from CVE decks. The "Wilder Wildcat," as Barrett Tillman described it, would be a very successful addition to the "jeeps' " arsenals.

On the afternoon of the thirtieth, as TG 52.9 eased into position about sixty miles southwest of Kwajalein Island, a *Manila Bay* Avenger joined forces with the destroyer *Haggard* to hunt down a suspected sub a few miles from the task group. This hunt was unsuccessful, and in the contortions of the search, the Avenger pilot became lost. When he finally regained his bearings, he was very low on fuel. He ran out of gas while approaching the *Manila Bay* and, in attempting to ditch, spun in. The plane exploded when it hit the water; only the pilot was rescued, by one of the screening vessels.[37]

There was almost another tragedy when a *Corregidor* pilot also became lost while on patrol. However, he was able to find the *Belleau Wood*, then over a hundred miles away, and land on the light carrier. The pilot's navigational ability did not impress Admiral Davison, who stated, "This stupid incident caused considerable confusion and necessitated launching of search aircraft."[38]

Things improved for TG 52.9 during the rest of the operation, D day, 31 January 1944, saw planes from all the CVEs making numerous attacks on Roi-Namur, Kwajalein, and many of the lesser islands in the atoll. Off to a rough start were the air groups from the *Suwannee* and *Chenango*. A mixed group of VC-60 and VC-35 Dauntlesses were to bomb Ennumennett, a small island near Namur. As he approached the pushover point, at which the bombers were to begin their dive, the flight leader ordered a change of formation from a stepped-up echelon of V's to a simple echelon. Something happened.

One SBD drifted under another, causing the latter pilot to pull up

Kwajalein burns in the background on 2 February 1944 as the Coral Sea *operates offshore. (National Archives)*

slightly. Close behind—too close behind—a third plane rode up on the second bomber, its prop slicing into the other SBD's cockpit between the pilot and the gunner. Suddenly there was a tangle of aircraft and all three Dauntlesses whirled into the sea. A *Chenango* gunner was able to bail out, as did one of VC-60's gunners, but that was all.[39]

The thirty-first saw most of the minor islands in the atoll taken and artillery emplaced to take under fire the main islands of Roi-Namur and Kwajalein, which would be assaulted the next day. The escort carriers sent a host of planes out on D day plus one to cover these landings with good results.

One attack, in particular, is worthy of note. At 0925, prior to the landings on Roi-Namur, a panicky message came from a small boat beached on Ennugarret Island (taken the day before) that the island was being counterattacked from Namur. An air observer overhead could discern no such attack, but the decision was made to take some action. At the time, however, no planes were on station. Just then a flight of six VC-35 Avengers showed up, returning from antisubmarine patrol. (Planes returning from ASP were to drop unused depth bombs on assigned targets.)

The air observer pointed out the target, and within three minutes the Avengers were dropping their bombs on Namur's southeastern tip. The devastating power of these 325-pound depth bombs was quickly demonstrated as the bombs completely cleared away the dense underbrush and tree foliage. As for the counterattack, there had been none, just the figment of someone's vivid imagination.[40]

Roi and Namur, though bloody battles, were captured quickly. On Roi only mopping-up remained at the end of the day, and Namur was secured on the afternoon of the second.

Kwajalein Island took a bit longer. Helping in this conquest were the planes from Davison's TG 52.9 VC-7, from the *Manila Bay*, was the first Pacific squadron to be equipped with forward-firing rockets, and these quickly showed their effectiveness. On 1 February a pair of VC-7 Avengers strafed and made rocket attacks against installations on Bigej, an island north of Kwajalein Island. As rockets tore into it, a hidden ammunition dump blew up with devastating force, the shock wave bouncing the Avengers about. On a later mission a pilot fired his rockets at what appeared to be a camouflaged building. It was not a building but a fuel dump, and it disappeared in a huge fireball.[41] Attacks such as these resulted in numerous commendations for the fliers, though Admiral Turner, never satisfied with less than perfection, would complain, "It is considered that this new weapon was not employed to its best advantage, either through misunderstanding of its capabilities or lack of practice in its use."[42] Still, the "jeep" pilots obviously were learning their trade well.

Less air support was flown for the Kwajalein landings than for those to the north. Continuing rainstorms, which hampered flying, and extensive and accurate ship's gunnery prompted Admiral Turner to assign the main task of beating down the defenders to the gunnery ships. As it turned out, the planes weren't needed that much at Kwajalein anyway.

The atoll was finally secured on 8 February. Three days before this, Admiral Davison sent his carriers into Kwajalein Lagoon to refuel and rearm in its sheltered waters. On board the first CVE to enter the lagoon, the *Coral Sea*'s crew was quick to boast of being the first American carrier to anchor in formerly Japanese waters. The experience was an interesting one for the flattop's crew. Fighting was still under way on a few of the islands, and the *Coral Sea*'s men had a front-row seat for the action.

"During the afternoon," the carrier's history recalls, "the crew aired their bedding on the flight deck beneath a glaring sun while watchers with binoculars could observe Marines [actually troops of the Army's 7th Infantry Division] with fixed bayonets carrying on more war-like actions on the beach. During the evening movies on the hangar deck, those who preferred other entertainment could go

A rocket-armed TBM from VC-7 flies over the Marshalls on 7 February 1944. The rocket rails are British-style. (National Archives)

topside and watch the bombardment of the objective that was continuing, and the glow of the resulting fires."[43]

On the night of the twelfth there was more excitement when an enemy air attack struck the new U.S. base on Roi-Namur. Davison's ships were too far away to be affected by this raid, but Admiral Ragsdale's carriers, anchored just offshore, were too close for comfort. Luckily for the escort carriers, the enemy airmen were more intent on destroying the installations on the two islands. They did a good job of it, too, wrecking the main supply dump on Roi. Anchored helplessly in the lagoon, the men on the flattops could only watch the destruction and whisper to one another as if the Japanese buzzing around overhead could hear them. At last the Japanese flew away, not realizing they had missed some juicy targets in the lagoon.[44]

In the Central Pacific the American offensive was now on a roll. Hard on the heels of Flintlock came Catchpole, the invasion of Eniwetok. Lying 375 miles northwest of Kwajalein, this atoll would provide the U.S. with its best anchorage and staging area yet for the drive west. The surprisingly fast conquest of Kwajalein meant that D day for Eniwetok could be advanced from 19 March to 17 February. Although some consideration had been given to taking Eniwetok immediately after Kwajalein, the planners had not thought that this would really happen. Nevertheless, contingency plans had been drawn up and now were used.

Given overall amphibious command for Catchpole was Admiral Hill. His ground forces consisted primarily of the 22nd Marines and the 106th Regimental Combat Team from the Army's 27th Infantry Division, units that had initially been held in reserve for the Kwajalein operation. Not needed there, they were readily available for the landings in Eniwetok Atoll.

Once again the *Sangamon, Suwannee,* and *Chenango* would provide air support, along with the *Saratoga, Langley,* and *Princeton.* Close air support operations would be on a minor scale at Eniwetok, one reason being the army's lack of appreciation or knowledge of the effectiveness of this support.[45]

From the fifteenth through the twenty-fourth the CVEs plied their trade off Eniwetok Atoll, concentrating particularly on Engebi, the only island in the atoll with an airfield. Air support was also supplied for the landings on Parry, in the southern part of the atoll. Parry was a tough nut to crack but was "shelled" within a day.

With the end of resistance on Parry, the campaign in the Marshalls was over. Though many enemy-held islands still remained in the area, isolated and pounded by land-based aircraft until the end of the war, they were useless to the Japanese.

In the Marshalls the escort carriers had been busy, but not nearly as busy as they would be in the future. Only 12 percent of the CVE missions were for strike and ground support, as compared to 56 percent for the big carriers and 34 percent for the light carriers.[46] The total number of sorties flown off the three "big" CVEs is unavailable, but only 366 combat sorties were flown at Kwajalein and Eniwetok. For the other "jeeps" employed at Kwajalein, only 256 combat sorties were flown out of a total of 1,492 sorties. Like the scale of their operations, aircraft losses were reasonably low, fifteen planes being lost, and only two of those in combat.[47]

Both the Gilberts and Marshalls operations provided valuable experience for the escort carriers and their squadrons. These two operations led Admiral Davison to recommend that escort carriers operate as three-ship divisions, this disposition being "tactically more flexible and efficient than a four-ship division, both from the standpoint of control of air traffic and protection against submarines with a limited number of DDs."[48] Davison's three-ship division would not last long as a tactical disposition. Future operations would show that formations of up to six or seven ships offered greater flexibility.

Galvanic was a rough beginning, but the lessons learned there were of great value in the Marshalls. Several innovations that would become standard practice were tried out there: airborne rockets; the elevation of the Commander, Support Aircraft, to a more important role, with greater control over the support planes and in target selection; and increased, and better, ground-to-air communications, vital to this type of job. The biggest need of the escort carrier pilots was better proficiency, but after all, the only close support by a CVE prior to these attacks in the Central Pacific had been at Attu. Stronger emphasis on close support activities during training would turn out fliers much more highly qualified in that phase of combat operations.[49] They would be needed. There was still a lot of enemy territory to take.

MOVING WEST

THE ESCORT CARRIERS would not again see action in the Central Pacific until Operation Forager, the invasion of the Marianas, in June 1944. The CVEs were not inactive, however, in the months between the Marshalls and Marianas battles. In the Southwest Pacific they were very busy (see Chapter 4).

The escort carriers were also waging another war in the Pacific. This war was far from the shooting, and very much like the stifling boredom so richly described in *Mister Roberts*—the war of the transport and replenishment carriers.

For the "jeeps," their participation in this little-publicized but vital task had started back in August 1942, when the *Long Island* delivered two marine squadrons to Guadalcanal. From that time almost every escort carrier assigned to the Pacific was at some point used to transport men and equipment, to replenish the fast carrier forces at sea, or as a training ship. Only the *Sangamons* were rarely used for these tasks.

Among the first types available, the *Bogue*-class carriers were on the job the longest. Only the *Nassau*, in the Aleutians, was actively engaged in combat operations. The *Barnes* participated very briefly at Tarawa and the *Altamaha* made an unproductive antisubmarine warfare (ASW) cruise in April 1944. This cruise reflects a philosophical difference in the way the Atlantic and Pacific ASW commands looked at antisubmarine warfare. In the Atlantic the CVEs, their squadrons, and their escorts were "dedicated" to ASW; that is, it was basically their only task.

In the Pacific the story was different. By late 1943 Nimitz's command had downgraded Japanese submarines from a threat to a nuisance. Believing that submarines could be hunted down by regular task force units, the commander in chief of the Pacific Fleet considered dedicated ASW units to be a waste of ships and manpower.

The *Altamaha*'s cruise, along with some similar incidents, caused a rethinking of the place of hunter-killer forces in the Pacific. Apparently triggered by Magic intercepts of enemy radio traffic, the *Altamaha*'s trip was hurriedly organized. Neither the carrier nor her four escorts had operated together as a hunter-killer unit. For that matter, her squadron, VC-66, had received only rudimentary ASW training. Because of the hurry-up nature of this mission, VC-66 (then resting on Oahu after returning from the Marshalls) had no time to get in even a little practice.

Task Group 11.1, under the command of the *Altamaha*'s Captain A. C. Olney, sortied from Pearl on 30 March. The job of his force was to find some enemy submarines operating between Hawaii and the Marshalls. On 4 April VC-66 planes sighted and attacked a surfaced sub. These attacks were poorly timed and organized, and despite the use of rockets and the recently introduced homing torpedo known as Fido, the submarine escaped. Unfortunately, the same thing happened later in the day, when a second sub appeared.[1]

With the report of the failure of the *Altamaha*'s ASW cruise and with similar reports at hand, Nimitz's ASW experts took a hard look at the hunter-killer concept and what was needed in the way of training and ships. Before long, dedicated hunter-killer groups built around an escort carrier would be on the prowl in the Pacific, with great success.

The *Nassau*'s and *Altamaha*'s operations were atypical of the normal use of the *Bogue*-class vessels. More characteristic were the missions of the *Copahee*. Commissioned on 15 June 1942, in September of that year she made her first run to the South Pacific with a load of passengers, aircraft, and stores. For the rest of the war she traveled all over the Pacific performing the same chore. A similar course was followed by the *Barnes* and *Breton* after their commissionings in 1943. Another carrier, the *Prince William*, was in the Pacific from the summer of 1943 to the spring of 1944, when she was transferred to the Atlantic; returning to the Pacific in 1945, she resumed her ferry missions until the end of the war. Three Atlantic veterans, the *Bogue*, *Core*, and *Card*, came to the Pacific after V-E Day and made a few transport runs.

Other CVEs were also involved in this type of mission. The new Kaiser-class ships were now reporting to the Pacific Fleet at a rate of three or four a month. Their initial missions after shakedown, or

The Altamaha *leaves San Francisco on 16 July 1943 with a load of P-51s and a lone SOC. (National Archives)*

even as part of the shakedown, were often to ferry aircraft and personnel to various bases. However, because there was no one office to control and coordinate their movements or determine the disposition of the aircraft and equipment they were delivering, their efforts, as exemplified by the *White Plains* in the Marshalls (see Chapter 2), were often chaotic and unproductive.

In February 1944 Admiral Towers recommended that a carrier transport squadron be established. The commander of this unit (in the chain of command approximately equal to a task group commander) would exercise operational and administrative command of those ships assigned to the squadron and also arrange schedules for the supply of aircraft, parts, and personnel as needed.[2]

Finally, on 15 April 1944, Carrier Transport Squadron Pacific (CarTransRonPac) was established, with Rear Admiral Samuel P. Ginder assuming command on 1 June.[3] Initially thirteen escort carriers and two aircraft ferries (ex-Seatrains) were assigned to Ginder's command, but by the end of the war this number would grow to twenty-five CVEs and two aircraft ferries. In addition, other ships were temporarily assigned to CarTransRonPac—among them six British CVEs (all *Bogue*-class ships): the *Tracker, Rajah, Atheling, Patroller, Reaper,* and *Ranee.* These six flattops served with the squad-

With a load of almost 60 planes on deck, the Kwajalein *steams toward the combat zone, 19 July 1944. (National Archives)*

ron for various lengths of time between December 1944 and August 1945.[4]

The history of the squadron records its achievements:

> During the period between 1 June 1944 and 31 August 1945 the Squadron lifted: 31,701 airplanes of all types, exclusive of replenishment airplanes, 137,188 passengers including organized aviation squadrons, 7,528,224 cube of aviation cargo and steamed a total of 2,857,156 miles.[5] . . . Replenishment carriers, in air logistic support of the fast carrier task forces, delivered over 4,500 new aircraft and returned approximately 2,000 war-weary aircraft. An average of four to five

CVE(T)'s [a designation used only by the squadron] were normally employed on this duty.[6]

The carriers of CarTransRonPac came close to putting another, less tangible, mark in their record books. Following the occupation of the Marianas, the Civil Affairs Government inquired about using CVEs to ship cattle and hogs for use by the natives and the garrison forces. Admiral Nimitz requested Rear Admiral George D. Murray, the new Commander Air Force, Pacific Fleet, to study the matter. He warned Murray, however, that "the instinct of hogs to wander and cows to emit vocal noises which might be interpreted as whistle signals should be considered." Additionally, he suggested that it would be wise to select a "jeep" whose commanding officer and medical officer had farming backgrounds.[7]

Admiral Murray pondered the idea for a time before deciding that cows, pigs, and CVEs just didn't mix, and that was the end of the CVE farming experiment.

This, then, was the war of CarTransRonPac. This war was not glamorous nor exciting, but it was an extremely important part of the navy's march across the Pacific. The word "invaluable," often used inappropriately, is exactly right in speaking of CarTransRon-Pac. Without the planes delivered by the squadron, TF 58 would have been terribly ill-equipped; and without the replacement pilots delivered by the squadron, TF 58's flying units would have been woefully undermanned.

As Admiral Ginder took command of CarTransRonPac and its escort carriers on 1 June, other CVEs were gathering at widely scattered points in the Pacific. They would be taking part in the invasion of the Marianas, scheduled to begin on 15 June with landings on Saipan.

For Forager a Joint Expeditionary Force (TF 51) was organized under the command of Vice Admiral Turner, divided into two attack forces. Also commanded by Turner, the Northern Attack Force (TF 52) was forming on the West Coast and Hawaii to attack Saipan and Tinian. Being mounted from the Guadalcanal area was Rear Admiral Richard L. Conolly's Southern Attack Force (TF 53), scheduled to assault Guam a few days after the Saipan landings, although events would change this timing. A third force, the Floating Reserve (TG 51.1), mounting out of Hawaii, would be on hand if needed.

On 29 May the Northern Attack Force began leaving Pearl Harbor. Accompanying the slow transports en route to Eniwetok, the final staging point, were two groups of escort carriers. Upon arrival at the target the "jeeps" would also furnish close air support.

TASK GROUP 52.14
R. Adm. Gerald F. Bogan

Task Unit 52.14.1	R. Adm. Bogan (ComCarDiv 25)
Fanshaw Bay (FF)	Capt. D. P. Johnson
VC-68 16 FM-2, 12 TBM-1C	Lt. Cdr. R. S. Rogers
Midway	Capt. F. J. McKenna
VC-65 12 FM-2, 9 TBM-1C	Lt. Cdr. R. M. Jones

Screen: Destroyers *Cassin Young, Irwin, Ross*

Task Unit 52.14.2	Capt. Oscar A. Weller
White Plains (F)	Capt. Weller (to 16 July)
	Capt. D. J. Sullivan
VC-4 16 FM-2, 3 TBF-1C, 9 TBM-1C	Lt. Cdr. R. C. Evins
	(MIA 17 June)
	Lt. E. R. Fickenscher
Kalinin Bay	Capt. C. R. Brown
VC-3 14 FM-2, 9 TBM-1C	Lt. Cdr. W. H. Keighley

Screen: Destroyers *Porterfield, Callaghan, Longshaw*

TASK GROUP 52.11
R. Adm. Harold B. Sallada

Task Unit 52.11.1	R. Adm. Sallada (ComCarDiv 26)
Kitkun Bay (FF)	Capt. J. P. Whitney
VC-5 12 FM-2, 8 TBM-1C	Lt. Cdr. R. L. Fowler
Gambier Bay	Capt. H. H. Goodwin
VC-10 16 FM-2, 12 TBM-1C	Lt. Cdr. E. J. Huxtable

Screen: Destroyers *Laws, Morrison, Benham*

Task Unit 52.11.2	R. Adm. Felix B. Stump (ComCarDiv 24)
Corregidor (F)	Capt. R. L. Thomas
VC-41 15 FM-2, 12 TBM-1C	Lt. A. P. Kolonie
Coral Sea	Capt. P. W. Watson
VC-33 14 FM-2, 2 TBF-1,	Lt. Cdr. R. Gray
6 TBF-1C, 4 TBM-1C	

Screen: Destroyers *Bullard, Kidd, Chauncey*

(The ships of Task Unit 52.11.2 sortied from Espiritu Santo, joining Task Group 53.7 en route to Eniwetok.)[8]

Davison's three-ship division had only lasted a few months. The outpouring of carriers from the Kaiser yards, almost like a flood, made many of these new flattops available for the coming offensives in the Pacific, which were becoming larger and more powerful with every landing. With these new carriers came the need for more carrier division commanders with experience. In Sallada, Bogan, and Stump, all veteran aviators, the CVEs had the experience.

"Slats" Sallada had come up the ladder through the office of the

Chief of Naval Operations, where he had been director of the Aviator Planning Section for BuAer, then as Commander Support Aircraft at Kwajalein, where he had worked closely with the escort carriers. Bogan, a tough no-nonsense commander who loved to fight and an excellent teacher of carrier tactics, held several staff positions prior to this assignment. From the *Lexington,* where he had been her commanding officer through the exciting battles of 1943, came Felix Stump. Stump would remain with the escort carriers throughout the war, becoming a much-loved and -respected leader of the CVEs. Short-timers Sallada and Bogan would move on to fast carrier division command following this operation.

There were new ships, also. Making their first appearance in combat were the *Midway, White Plains, Kitkun Bay,* and *Gambier Bay.* All four of these ships had been ferrying replacement aircraft to various island bases, but this was to be their first taste of combat. In reality, this was the *Fanshaw Bay*'s baptism into combat, too, though the ship had made an unsuccessful ASW cruise in April–May.

All of the flattops were carrying FM-2s, most of these having the latest modifications. Modifications didn't always result in better aircraft. Recent experience had shown that these newer *Fox Mike Deuces* had some problems, one of the worst being a tailhook installation that, when extended, gave "the appearance of a happy dog wagging its tail as the plane entered its final approach."[9] The problem with this "tail-wagging" was that it often caused the hook to skip over the arresting gear, leading to some interesting (if not downright dangerous) situations. Many squadrons quickly made field modifications to rectify this problem.

The FM-2 itself was generally well liked by the pilots. With its narrow track, it could be a bear to handle on the ground or carrier deck, particularly with a crosswind, but during an approach and landing it was a relatively docile beast, though if a pilot came in too fast the plane had a tendency to float, and every now and then one would wind up in the barriers. It had good control responses and was very maneuverable, and with its powerful engine could get up and climb at a fair rate. It didn't have a very high top speed, only about 320 mph. This didn't stop the FM-2 from being a dangerous adversary to any enemy plane that decided to fight it out with the Wildcat.

Many pilots would have liked a landing gear that didn't have to be cranked up and down manually by the pilot, a chore carried over from the earlier Wildcats. To watch a Wildcat climbing out after takeoff was always somewhat amusing, its flight path taking a wobbling, undulating course as the pilot cranked up the gear. This took

about twenty-six to thirty turns of the gear handle located just behind the pilot's knee on the cockpit's right side. Every motion while
cranking the gear was transmitted through the pilot's body to his
arm on the control stick, resulting in an uneven flight path.

The simple task of cranking the gear could lead to some interesting situations. Mac McClendon, the *Gambier Bay*'s LSO, remembers
what happened to a friend of his, Johnny Thompson. While cranking the gear down prior to landing, the handle slipped out of
Thompson's hand and began whirling rapidly, threatening to break
his leg; his radio cord, caught by the handle, began wrapping itself
around it. Before Thompson could unplug the cord from his helmet, he found his head pulled down to the level of the handle—not
a good position for a landing. He was at last able to unplug the radio
cord, sit back upright, and make a normal landing. But he had had
an interesting few moments.[10]

Equally liked was the Avenger. A large plane for escort carrier
operations and being routinely overloaded, the TBF/TBM was still
not difficult to operate from CVEs. It was a relatively honest and
forgiving aircraft, despite a Wright R-2600 engine that was a bit
temperamental and that could have used a bit more power, and the
pilots found they were able to utilize almost all of the Avenger's
capabilities. The plane had been designed as a torpedo bomber, but
the CVE fliers had little chance to fly the plane in this manner. What
they did use the plane for was glide-bombing, and in this role it did
outstanding work. In the Marianas they would get many opportunities to hone their glide-bombing skills.

The new "jeep" sailors were quickly reminded that they were in a
war zone. Just one day out of Pearl en route to Eniwetok, the *Kalinin
Bay* was straddled by two torpedoes fired by an unseen and undis-
covered submarine.[11] (It is possible that these two "torpedoes" may
have been nothing more than a pair of playful dolphins misidenti-
fied by one of the "K.B.'s" still relatively green lookouts.)

As the invasion force plodded west, it received word of landings half
a world away. The news from Normandy was greeted with quiet satis-
faction by the sailors, but their thoughts were filled with a more immediate concern—the impending invasion of the Marianas. Did the Japanese have something up their sleeves? What did the future hold? For
some the future would be bleak, indeed. Saipan would be a tough nut
to crack, and many would fall in the taking of that island.

Meanwhile, leaving their bases about the same time as Turner's
force were the ships of Admiral Conolly's Southern Attack Force.
Part of this force was composed of three escort carriers and their
screen:

TASK GROUP 53.7
R. Adm. Van H. Ragsdale (to 27 July)
R. Adm. Thomas L. Sprague

Task Unit 53.7.1	R. Adm. Ragsdale (ComCarDiv 22)
	R. Adm. Sprague (ComCarDiv 22)
Sangamon (F)	Capt. M. E. Browder
Air Group 37	Lt. Cdr. S. E. Hindman
VF-37 22 F6F-3	Lt. Cdr. Hindman
VT-37 1 TBF-1C, 8 TBM-1C	Lt. Cdr. P. G. Farley
Suwannee	Capt. W. D. Johnson
Air Group 60	Lt. Cdr. H. O. Feilbach
VF-60 22 F6F-3	Lt. Cdr. Feilbach
VT-60 1 TBF-1, 8 TBM-1C	Lt. Cdr. W. C. Vincent
Chenango	Capt. D. Ketcham
Air Group 35	Lt. Cdr. F. T. Moore, Jr.
VF-35 22 F6F-3	Lt. Cdr. Moore
VT-35 1 TBF-1C, 8 TBM-1C	Lt. C. F. Morgan

Screen: Destroyers *Erben, Walker, Abbot, Hale*[12]

The venerable Dauntlesses had finally been put ashore, leaving only Avengers and Hellcats to operate from these flattops. Also, the fourth CarDiv 22 carrier, the *Santee,* which had finally arrived in the Pacific following ASW duty in the Atlantic, was given the more mundane task of ferrying the aircraft of MAG-21 to Guam after that island was taken.

On 7 June both invasion forces began arriving at Eniwetok and Kwajalein. Their stay would be short, the final leg to Saipan starting on the tenth. For the escort carriers their first few days of the voyage were relatively uneventful.

That changed on the thirteenth. That morning a *Kitkun Bay* Avenger spotted a periscope about six miles from the carrier and attacked it with no effect. A further search of the area by two destroyers and another plane was fruitless. Then about two hours later the carrier's CAP sighted a Betty twenty miles from the task group. The four VC-5 Wildcats made quick work of the hapless enemy bomber. That evening everyone on the *Kitkun Bay* celebrated the squadron's first triumph.[13]

Late on the thirteenth the CVEs and the bombardment vessels moved into position off Saipan. For the three days prior to the fourteenth, planes and ships of TF 58 had been bombarding Saipan, Tinian, and Guam. Now the old battleships had their turn to pound the Saipan landing beaches and surrounding terrain. Aircraft from the CVEs provided air cover, antisubmarine protection, and spotting for these vessels.

There were no losses to the fliers on the fourteenth, but a freak accident on the *Kitkun Bay* claimed the life of one of her plane handlers. The sailor was helping to push an Avenger into position when a rocket attached to the plane's wing suddenly fired. Directly in line with the rocket's fiery blast, the man was fatally burned. As it roared off, the rocket narrowly missed several planes. There were no easy, safe jobs on an escort carrier.[14]

D day for the Saipan landings was 15 June, a bright and clear day. For all concerned, not the least of whom were the escort carrier pilots, it would be an eventful one. As the landing craft surged in, CVE bombers and fighters strafed and bombed the beaches and the areas immediately behind. The Japanese were not taking this abuse lying down, and heavy antiaircraft fire greeted the attackers.

VC-10's fighter commander, Lieutenant John R. Stewart, was making his strafing run when he heard a "clang" and a small hole appeared in the Wildcat's cowling just in front of the windscreen. Glancing at his instruments, Stewart saw that his engine's oil pressure had dropped and the temperature had shot up. Then his engine began to sputter and smoke. Not wanting to ditch where the wind could carry his raft to enemy-held Tinian or near the landing beaches where he could easily be shot, Stewart nursed his plane toward a "friendly-looking destroyer," planning to set down next to it. However, as he said later, "I was somewhat excited since, when I reached the water and thought I should be stalling in, I continued to float for about a quarter of a mile, with the plane pouring black smoke in contrast to my white face, at which time the prop froze and I made a beautiful splash."[15]

Stewart would not return to the *Gambier Bay* for two weeks, having spent most of that time on the destroyer that rescued him doing odd jobs including aircraft identification for the gunners and running the decoding machine. Besides Stewart's fighter, several other planes had been lost on the fifteenth, including a VC-41 Wildcat shot down on a strafing run near Tinian Town.

Though air support missions had been the main order of the day, the fliers also found time to pick off some enemy planes. On an ASW patrol about twenty-five miles from the *Suwannee* were Ensign Harold Jedlund, in an Avenger, and Ensign Harold Lamb, in a Hellcat. No sub was found, but Jedlund sighted a Betty about 2,000 feet below him. Turning to close on the Betty, both planes were quickly on its tail. Jedlund opened fire with his wing guns at 1,000 yards, and the bomber's top and tail turrets returned it in kind. In an attempt to escape, the Japanese pilot jettisoned his bombs and racked his plane around in a series of violent S turns just off the deck. The Betty began to pull away slowly from the TBM, but Lamb was able to stay with it, making shallow beam runs.

Not wanting to be left out of the fight, though out of ammunition for his wing guns, Jedlund dumped his bombs and lumbered up in his portly Avenger. Flying his plane as if it were a fighter, Jedlund was able to get into a position for his gunner, AOM2c L. T. Bingham, to rake the Betty with some devastating fire. Lamb, in the meantime, had killed the bomber's tail gunner. On a third run Bingham hit the Betty's left engine, which immediately began to blaze. The wing suddenly broke off, cartwheeling the Betty into the water. It was Air Group 60's first kill since Tarawa, and only their second overall.[16]

Shortly before the sun went down at 1745, the ships of TG 52.14 got a close look at Japanese aircraft. Task group radars picked up a group of planes closing from the southeast, seventy-one miles distant. A division of *White Plains* fighters orbiting over the force at 10,000 feet was vectored to intercept. The four pilots found five torpedo-laden planes, either Kates or Jills, flying at 6,000 feet. In a running battle the VC-4 fliers shot down four of the attackers. The fifth plane was able to bull its way through the antiaircraft fire of the task group. Aiming at the *Fanshaw Bay*, the plane bored in from off her starboard bow. Perhaps the heavy flak threw the pilot off a little, because he dropped his torpedo while in a slight turn. With a hard right turn, the carrier easily evaded the torpedo.[17]

Just moments before this attack, nine Wildcats had been launched from the carriers. One of these pilots, Lieutenant (jg) C. C. Sanders, located the Kate by using the flak bursts surrounding it as his point of reference. Sanders pounced on the torpedo plane, his .50-caliber shells ripping into its right side. Suddenly its gas tank exploded, and fire enveloped the lower surface of the wing. There was another explosion, and the flames spread rapidly to the fuselage. Its landing gear drooping, the Kate began to turn left slowly; then, in a welter of foam, spray, and smoke, it smashed into the water.[18] Over the next few hours radar noted more bogeys near TG 52.14, but no attacks materialized and the rest of the night passed quietly.

Early on the sixteenth Admiral Stump took the CVEs and screen of TU 52.11.2 south to join in the pounding of Guam prior to the landings scheduled for 18 June. However, because of the imminent appearance of the Japanese fleet and the tougher-than-expected resistance on Saipan, these landings were postponed, not to take place until mid-July. The next afternoon the *Coral Sea* and *Corregidor* rejoined TG 52.11.[19]

Aside from the usual close support missions, the sixteenth was a generally calm day for the escort carriers operating east of Saipan. Off Guam planes from the *Suwannee*'s VF-60 picked off a couple of Bettys.[20] Other prowling enemy planes caused several alerts during the evening, but none closed with the escort carriers.

The next afternoon brought more action. Now heading east into that part of the Pacific between the Philippines and the Marianas known as the Philippine Sea was Vice Admiral Jisaburo Ozawa's Mobile Fleet, seeking decisive battle with the Americans. The fateful meeting of Japanese and American forces, to be known as the Battle of the Philippine Sea, would take place on 19–20 June. As part of their plan, Operation A-GO, the Japanese land-based aircraft were to destroy at least one third of the enemy carrier forces before the main Japanese naval units entered the fray.[21]

Attempting to comply with the provisions of A-GO, the enemy planes were active on the seventeenth, and they discovered that the escort carriers were very juicy targets. A group of thirty-one Zekes, seventeen Judys, and two Franceses (also known as Frans) had taken off from Yap intent on destroying the ships unloading at Saipan.[22] Their attacks were generally unsuccessful, but upon turning back toward Yap they ran across the CVEs.

About 1730 a large raid, estimated to be twenty to thirty aircraft, was picked up on task group radars some 110 miles away. When it became evident that the aircraft were closing, general quarters was sounded on all ships shortly before 1800. This was followed by a launch of more fighters to join the ones already on CAP. Eventually forty-four Wildcats would be in the air.

At 1850, as the sun dropped below the western horizon, TG 52.11 was hit. The sun's rays tinted the scattered cumulus clouds a roseate hue as the enemy planes darted in toward the twisting and turning ships. The *Gambier Bay* was the first target, two Judys zeroing in on her from dead ahead. At this time the flattop's airedales were hurrying to push a Wildcat, which had crashed into the barrier and fouled the deck, over the side. Another fighter was on the catapult, two officers perched on its wing, another in the cockpit.

Captain Goodwin had been watching the two Judys, waiting only until they released their deadly missiles before ordering a turn. Three black shapes separated from the Judys, and Goodwin ordered hard starboard. The *Gambier Bay* began to swing. Also watching the Judys was VC-10's skipper, "Hux" Huxtable. "As soon as I was sure the lead plane had us boresighted, I took for cover and ran for the door in the bridge structure . . . guys were stacked in there six deep, so I ran to the after corner of the island and hung out over the flag bag."[23]

The first bomb struck the sea fifty yards off the port bow, the second fifty yards off the port quarter, and the third twenty-five yards astern of the *Gambier Bay*. The ship shuddered and water drenched the men sitting on the Wildcat's wing. A bomb fin flew through the air to plop against the right wheel of the fighter. As the Judys skittered away, antiaircraft fire reached out for them, found them, and knocked the pair burning into the water.[24]

Almost immediately after these two planes splashed, another Judy dove on the *Coral Sea*. The enemy pilot's aim was off and his bomb hit just off the flattop's starboard quarter. Following close behind the bomb was the Judy, crashing about 300 yards from the carrier. Just two minutes later a wave-skimming Judy, trying to plant a torpedo into the carrier's thin skin, was hit by flak and cartwheeled into many small pieces.

Two other planes picked on the *Corregidor*, with fatal results for themselves. The first plane, a Judy, was hammered throughout its dive by accurate 20-mm and 40-mm fire. It never pulled out of its dive, plowing into the water some 200 yards off the *Corregidor's* starboard beam. Boring in low from the west came a Frances. Once again accurate antiaircraft fire found the target. Flames spurted from the plane's fuselage as the bomber neared the carrier; then it rolled over on its back. Curling in toward the *Corregidor*, the Frances crashed close aboard her starboard side.[25]

This attack on TG 52.11 had lasted about ten minutes. Following a short lull, there was another uncoordinated attack by several planes. Again the *Coral Sea* was the target. Picked up early in the fading light by the ship's gunners, one plane made it no closer than 2,000 yards before being shot down. By 1912 the attacks were over. Task Group 52.11 escaped virtually unscathed; a few planes had been holed by shrapnel and several men slightly injured. In trying to down the attackers, though, the Wildcat pilots had not had the best of luck. Few kills were registered.[26]

No TG 52.11 planes were lost during the battle, but a *Kitkun Bay* plane and pilot were lost afterwards. All but one fighter of the CAP had been landed. As this last plane approached the carrier, it was too low, and its tailhook hit the ship's rounddown with such force that it bent a handrail two inches in diameter into a sharp V. This sudden impact may have stunned the pilot, for the Wildcat staggered up the deck and over the side. Despite a prolonged search, the pilot was not recovered.[27]

Meanwhile, the Japanese had not left TG 52.14 alone. Though many Wildcats were in the air, the fading light and uncertain vectors by inexperienced fighter directors enabled most of the attackers to escape interception. One division of VC-65 planes managed to engage a few of the enemy aircraft. While climbing to 12,000 feet, the fliers saw a mass of planes between 18,000 and 20,000 feet. A bottom layer was made up of ten to twelve Judys, with another layer of seven to nine Judys above them. Sliding back and forth over these planes were twelve to eighteen Zekes. Zooming up, the VC-65 quartet tore into the enemy.

In the twisting, looping battle, one of the pilots smoked a Zeke. Then Lieutenant (jg) J. A. Hamman and Ensign L. E. Budnick trapped another Zeke between them. The two pilots fired simultaneously and the Zeke sprouted an orange glow just behind the cockpit, flipped over, and dove into the sea. Two other pilots, Lieutenant (jg)s C. H. Freer and V. D. Green, went after a Frances (which appeared out of nowhere). After a long chase down to sea level, where the bomber got so low it was leaving a wake, the pair sent it tumbling to its death.[28]

Other planes broke through to dive upon the carriers. Lookouts on the *White Plains* first spotted the enemy planes as they passed over TG 52.11 to the south. The attackers zeroed in on the *Fanshaw Bay* and *White Plains*. Two Judys glided in toward the *White Plains*. A series of violent evasive turns ordered by Captain Weller, as well as a heavy blanket of flak, kept the Judys at a distance, and they dropped their bombs over a thousand yards away.

Darkness was rapidly shrouding the scene as this attack petered out, but the Japanese were not yet finished. A short time later a second group of planes, estimated at five, was picked up on radar. Several *White Plains* fighters were vectored out by the fighter director officer (FDO), but in the growing darkness they missed the enemy.

A Judy zoomed out of the gloom to make a run on the *White Plains*. All guns on the starboard side took the plane under fire, and the pilot broke off his attack. Passing abeam the carrier, the Judy began to lose altitude and leave a trail of black smoke that ended only when the plane struck the water about 10,000 yards from the carrier.

While the Judy was making its final descent, the carrier's five-inch gun crew spotted another plane some 8,000 yards away. Three shots were fired at the plane as it disappeared into a small cloud, each shot sounding to the crew as if the flattop's entire rear end were falling off.[29] The members of the gun crew were sure they had bagged that aircraft.

There was a lull of twenty-two minutes before another group of planes was seen on the *White Plains* radar at a distance of fifty miles.

Shortly afterward a plane was seen only one hundred feet above the water, roaring in abaft the ship's starboard beam. Gunfire was begun immediately and had to be stopped almost as quickly because the glare of the tracers in the darkness blinded most of the gunners. The plane vanished, but a column of smoke darker than the surrounding blackness could be seen rising from the water. A probable was claimed.[30]

While the *White Plains* was fighting off her attackers, the *Fanshaw Bay* was undergoing a more successful assault. The Japanese planes had reached TG 52.14 at 1851, and within a minute the *Fanshaw Bay*'s guns had taken them under fire. Evading this fire, a Judy streaked in to drop a bomb (estimated at 250 pounds), which struck the carrier's aft elevator. The bomb ripped through the wooden decking of the elevator and detonated in the hangar about five feet below the flight deck.

Bomb fragments sliced through the air in the hangar. Virtually wiped out by the flying shards was Repair Party 3, which had just taken position forward of the elevator well. Eleven men were killed in the party; in addition, the dentist in charge of the after battle-dressing station was among those wounded.

In racks on both sides of the elevator well were stowed nine torpex-filled torpedoes. Three of these warheads were punctured by shrapnel but, luckily, did not explode. The explosion of the bomb was powerful enough, however, to jar depth bombs out of the bomb bays of several Avengers parked in the hangar. Though no fires were kindled in the parked planes, several began in various places on the hangar deck, but these were soon under control.

Besides the fires, another problem was the loss of steering from the bridge following the bomb hit. Steering control was transferred to after steering, but by 1958 all control was lost and the ship had to be maneuvered by her engines. Not until 0355 the next morning would steering control be regained by the bridge.

Of even greater concern to the "Fanny B's" men at this time was the flooding that was occurring. Almost immediately after the explosion, the carrier listed three degrees to port, and later in the evening the ship's stern had dropped six feet lower in the water. At first the ship's outer skin was thought to be broken, allowing seawater in. Also contributing to the problem was a ruptured fire main. Plugging the fire main gave the repair parties fits, and not until the aft engine room pumps were secured was any headway made on repairs to the fire main.

Not until the morning of the nineteenth did anyone realize that the fire main, not broken skinplates, had been the cause of most of the flooding.[31] Feisty Gerry Bogan, watching the repair efforts aboard his flagship, was not impressed, at one point sending his own chief of staff to take charge of these efforts. Later he complained that the *Fanshaw Bay*'s crew had been "unreasonably slow" in isolating the broken fire main and "did not have proper knowledge . . . of the ship nor of their job."[32] The crew eventually got everything under control, but fourteen of their comrades had been killed and another twenty-three wounded by the explosion and fires.

(Bogan apparently had it in for the *Fanshaw Bay*. Even years after the war he complained that the carrier was "the worst ship [he'd] ever seen in any Navy" and except for the air officer, "the entire complement was incompetent."[33] Granted, Bogan was a perfectionist and a hard man to please, but these are strong words twenty-five years after the fact. Bogan carried his "grudge"—if it can be called that—to an extreme, even later refusing to attend the awarding of the Presidential Unit Citation to the ships of Taffy 3, which included the *Fanshaw Bay,* because it would be "hypocritical."[34])

As the *Fanshaw Bay* fought her battle, the enemy planes were buzzing around the task group in swarms, darting in now and then to deliver an attack, then zooming away. Several of the planes didn't get to do much darting and zooming before being swatted from the sky by flak or fighters. During this action a *Fanshaw Bay* gunner had a close call. With the bolt only halfway forward on his 20-mm gun, a shell jammed, and as the gunner stepped forward to clear the jam, the shell went off. Fragments struck the gunner's helmet and bounced off, leaving the sailor with a headache but no injuries. With the breech cleared, the gun crew continued firing.[35]

At last the attack was over, the remaining Japanese planes scuttling back to Yap. But the task group's troubles were not over yet. Because of her list, the *Fanshaw Bay* had to send her airborne fighters to other carriers. Other fighters were also still in the air, and most of the pilots had little experience in night carrier landings. Then, to top it off, as two VC-4 Wildcats were returning to the *White Plains,* they were fired on by "friendly" ships and jumped by four other FM-2s.

Though neither fighter was shot down, one had its wing flaps knocked out. The *White Plains* began landing her own and some visiting aircraft. Not having seen many night landings, a large group of gawkers gathered at the forward end of the flight deck to watch. They didn't stay long. As one FM-2 from another carrier landed, its guns went off, sending several rounds zipping up the deck. No one was hurt, but the onlookers quickly disappeared, not to return.

The final plane to be landed was the damaged Wildcat, among its many problems the lack of flaps. The FM-2 was waved aboard. High and fast, it bounced over both the arresting gear and the first two barriers, hooked the third barrier, and careened into the parked planes. Pushed overboard by this collision were two planes, one carrying with it a sailor perched on its wing. A gasoline-fed fire broke out, burning several men before it was controlled. The tally of this costly accident was two men killed (one died of burns; the other was the man who had gone overboard), five men injured, two Wildcats lost overboard, and five more planes damaged beyond repair.[36]

It had not been a good action for TG 52.14. In addition to the *Fanshaw Bay*'s damage, several pilots were missing, including VC-4's skipper, Lieutenant Commander R. C. Evins, who was last heard complaining that his windscreen was coated with oil.

One of the missing pilots, Ensign J. T. Cuzzort, was very lucky. Following a run-in with several Japanese planes, Cuzzort found himself in the drink. Wet, cold, and rather lonely, Cuzzort was forced to be a spectator to the action going on around him. Because he had no light to attract rescuers, he resigned himself to spending a long, damp night in his raft. He knew he was on Saipan's windward side, so, not wishing to land on that unfriendly shore, he used his parachute (which he had luckily kept) to rig a sea anchor. When dawn came Cuzzort was hoping to see some friendly aircraft, but none came by. At last he saw a ship steaming over the horizon. Using his mirror (the seaplane tender *Pocomoke*'s crew at first taking it to be a drifting tin can), Cuzzort was able to attract their attention. After over seventeen hours in his raft, he was back on a U.S. Navy vessel, and within a few more hours he was aboard his carrier, the *Kalinin Bay*.[37]

On the eighteenth TG 52.14 retired temporarily from the Saipan area. The *Fanshaw Bay* had to return to Eniwetok for repairs and would not see action again until late July. A reorganization of the task group was needed, and for the time being Admiral Bogan and his staff transferred to the *White Plains*. Also leaving temporarily was the *Kalinin Bay*. Sending all her flyable FM-2s to the other carriers, in return she picked up a number of fighter pilots. As she left on the nineteenth for Eniwetok, where the extra pilots would be picking up new FM-2s, "Cat" Brown signaled Admiral Bogan, "Do not engage enemy until I return." Anxious to see more action, Brown made a speedy round trip and had his ship back off Saipan by the twenty-fourth.[38]

For TG 52.14, the next few days were quiet. Not so for TG 52.11. Having to pick up the slack left by TG 52.14's retirement, Admiral Sallada's planes were busy. Unfortunately, being busy meant losses.

Saipan's Aslito Airfield is in the background as VC-10 Avengers prepare for an attack on 18 June 1944. (National Archives)

One of those lost was a *Gambier Bay* Avenger shot down on the eighteenth.

Lieutenant (jg) Boyce "Jesse" Holleman was the pilot of the TBM, his plane set afire by antiaircraft fire as he attacked the town of Garapan. Though the flames licked about his cockpit, Holleman refused to jump until his aircrewmen had bailed out. He was able to nurse his burning plane out to Tanapag Harbor, where he ditched. Terribly burned, he was picked up by a landing craft and taken to a hospital ship. Holleman's two crewmen were never found, possibly having bailed out behind enemy lines where the probability of their survival was virtually nil.[39]

Another Avenger crew should have been a statistic, but instead survived a fracas. VC-33's Lieutenant R. S. Evarts was patrolling between Rota and Tinian when he was jumped by six planes identified as Tonys. Not aggressively flown, and making individual attacks, these planes shied away whenever Evarts turned into them. Their shooting was abysmal also, only putting two holes in the

Avenger. On the other hand, Evarts was able to send one of the fighters retreating with a heavily smoking engine. Sadly, Evarts didn't have much time to savor his victory, for he and his crew were shot down and killed at Tinian two days later.[40]

Active again on 18 June, Japanese reconnaissance planes pinpointed TG 52.11's position, and late that afternoon a force estimated to be thirty to fifty planes attacked. About 1615 a large bogey was painted on radar 121 miles to the south. General quarters was sounded fifteen minutes later, when it was evident that the bogey was closing. The CAP, with reinforcements being launched as fast as possible, kept most of the enemy planes away from the ships.

The pilots of VC-33 scored big in the ensuing battle. When first seen about fifty miles from the task group, six "Tonys" (more likely Judys) were flying a Lufbery circle, while six Zekes were below the Judys in a similar formation and three more fighters were "frolicking" above. Several bombers could be seen below the fighters. With the altitude advantage, the FM-2s screamed down onto the enemy fighters, surprising the Japanese. In quick succession several Judys were blown up or sent smoking into the sea like spent Roman candles.

Although the Japanese tried to hit back, surprise had been complete, and they were unable even to damage an FM-2. A short time later more enemy planes, this time some twelve to fifteen bombers covered by eighteen fighters, streaked toward TG 52.11. Once again the VC-33 Wildcats tore gaping holes in the enemy ranks. Pillars of smoke or burning pools of oil marked the end of the line for many of the Japanese planes. Before they were finished with this raid, the VC-33 fliers would claim eight "Tonys" (Judys) and two Frans shot down and another six planes damaged.

Scoring almost as well had been seven VC-5 pilots. In an initial encounter, three Zekes were found by four of the squadron's FM-2s. Caught completely by surprise, two of the Zekes were sent into the water, the third escaping but obviously in difficulty. A bit later the Wildcats were vectored toward a large bogey headed south.

Soon about twelve Zekes were sighted at 8,000 feet. In a wild melee that took place from 8,000 feet down to sea level, the seven FM-2s shot down an equal number of Zekes and damaged one more. Two of the Wildcats were badly damaged themselves and had to be ditched. VC-5's final score was nine Zekes destroyed and two damaged.[41]

At 1755 six planes (variously identified as Irvings or Bettys, but most likely Frans) broke through the CAP to make runs on the carriers. One of these planes dropped its torpedo just a hundred yards from the *Kitkun Bay*, and it bubbled by only twenty-five feet from the ship. The ship's guns caused the plane to burst into flames. Almost vertically the bomber climbed a thousand feet, then nosed over to plunge into the sea. A second plane didn't drop its torpedo, for some reason, and was quickly shot down.[42]

In the midst of this firing, the *Gambier Bay* was launching fighters, and two of them were damaged by the antiaircraft fire. Escaping this maelstrom was VC-10's Lieutenant Eugene W. Seitz. While still in his takeoff roll from the *Gambier Bay*, he charged his guns. When just clear of the ship and with his wheels and flaps still down, Seitz banked sharply left and caught a Frances in his sights. His four fifties tore into the bomber, which climbed steeply, stalled, and dove into the sea. (It is possible that this was the same plane claimed by the *Kitkun Bay* gunners.)[43]

A pair of planes attacking the *Gambier Bay* were sent blazing into the sea. The ship's LSO, "Mac" McClendon, had been watching the enemy planes darting in from the starboard side. A thought suddenly came to him: "If we're going to take a 'fish' from this side, perhaps I should be on the port side." Ducking down into the catwalk, he began to run through a passageway toward the other side. Halfway across he ran into Bill Cordner, VC-10's ordnance officer, running pell-mell the opposite way. McClendon yelled to Cordner, "They're coming from starboard! I'm going to port!"

"They're coming from port!" was Cordner's almost simultaneous reply. "I'm going to starboard!"

Both men came to a screeching halt, decided "what the hell," and climbed back up onto the flight deck to watch the rest of the raid.[44]

Yet another two planes went after the *Coral Sea* and *Corregidor* but were shot down before doing any damage. Returning from an ASW patrol, a VC-10 Avenger managed to finish off another Frances that had escaped from a Wildcat.[45] By the time the attack was over shortly after 1800, eight attackers (two more having joined the original six) had been claimed by the task group gunners. Fifteen to twenty planes were claimed by the CAP. Fighter direction appeared to be much better in this action than the day before, and the performance of the fighters was also very good. Several landing accidents, including a fatal one on the *Coral Sea*, marred the day's work, however.[46]

The rest of the night passed quietly, but things heated up the next morning as the sun rose. At 0615 enemy planes were detected on radar only twenty miles away and closing fast. These planes passed directly between two CAP flights hurrying to intercept. The four enemy planes that attacked the carriers were unable to score any hits, but the ships' gunners had no better luck. As the enemy planes scampered for home, though, the CAP caught up with them and sent two Zekes tumbling into the sea.[47]

To the men of the escort carriers it seemed that all the action was happening around them. But miles to the west a battle of epic proportions was beginning to unfold—the Battle of the Philippine Sea. This two-day battle, which took place on 19 and 20 June, would effectively end Japanese carrier power. The results of this tremendous carrier duel would not be known for some time, but its terrible consequences would be felt at Leyte Gulf, Lingayen, and Okinawa—the arrival of the kamikaze.

For the CVEs it was business as usual on the nineteenth and twentieth, with strikes again launched against Saipan and Tinian targets. VC-41 pilots bagged three Zekes in the air on the nineteenth, and a dozen more planes were claimed destroyed on the ground at Tinian the next day by *Corregidor* and *Coral Sea* aircraft. These victories were not without loss. The Tinian antiaircraft fire would down one fighter and three Avengers, including Evarts on the twentieth. One of the TBMs was able to limp to the recently captured Charan-Kanoa airstrip but ran into a parked truck and was demolished.[48]

Ensign James F. Lischer had teamed up with another pilot to down a Kate trying to land on Tinian. Upon his return to the *Gambier Bay*, Lischer, apparently still a little excited over his success, came in hot and wound up with his Wildcat upside down. Unhurt, with not even a scratch, Lischer dropped out of his cockpit and ambled across the flight deck. When his aircraft crashed, the barriers had been dropped and were now flush with the deck. Another plane was approaching and the barriers snapped up. Unfortunately, Lischer had just stepped on a barrier post when it came up, and he ended up airborne. A meeting with the deck brought his impromptu flight to an abrupt end, and he found himself in sick bay being stitched up. Because it was not a combat injury, he didn't get a Purple Heart.[49]

Standard operating procedure on the *Gambier Bay* had been for a drop tank to be hung on a Wildcat's starboard wing for the long CAP missions. The pilots had gotten used to this configuration, always trimming their aircraft for the increased weight on the right side. This day, when Lieutenant (jg) Dean Gilliatt walked to his FM-2, he found that the drop tank was hung on the plane's port wing. As he climbed into his cockpit, he gave no indication of concern with the placement of the tank.

Mac McClendon was concerned, however. Besides being the ship's highly respected LSO, McClendon had recently been given the job of flight deck officer by Captain Goodwin, who had dismissed the previous holder of the job. Having these two jobs put a lot of pressure on McClendon, who now had to land, spot, and respot planes and oversee other flight deck activities. Thus he was watching closely as the planes trundled into position for launch and saw the wing tank hung on the port wing of Gilliatt's Wildcat.

Climbing onto Gilliatt's wing, McClendon warned the pilot about the wing tank. Gilliatt nodded, but in the rush of the launch apparently did not retrim his plane. The FM-2 was waved off, and it started down the deck. Just as the fighter lifted off, it began a roll to the left. Gilliatt fought to right his plane, but before he succeeded, a wingtip struck a 40-mm mount and the fighter careened into the water.

The *Gambier Bay* couldn't stop, and as she swept by the Wildcat, onlookers could see Gilliatt slumped in the cockpit of his floating plane. Stunned, or perhaps dead from a broken neck, he remained motionless as the carrier drew away. When one of the plane guard destroyers rushed to the scene, there was no sign of plane or pilot. It had been an operational accident, not a combat loss, but Dean Gilliatt was just as dead.[50]

While the carriers of TGs 52.14 and 52.11 seemed to be attracting the most attention, TG 53.7 had not been idling the days away. Though the landings on Guam had been postponed, the planes from the three *Sangamon*s were kept busy flying patrols and searching for enemy aircraft.

On the nineteenth one of the patrols struck paydirt. Ensign Guy E. Sabin, from VT-60, was on an antisubmarine patrol that afternoon when he saw a surfaced sub just a mile away. Moments before, he had descended to 1,500 feet to get under a cloud. Suddenly the sub was there. In quick succession Sabin began a dive on the boat, ordered his radioman to arm the depth bombs, and told his gunner to man the turret. Sabin's attack would bring him right up the sub's wake.

Apparently the sub's crew sighted the Avenger about the same time, for it suddenly crash-dived, and instead of turning, continued straight ahead. A split second after the periscope disappeared, Sabin dropped his bombs in train from 150 feet. All exploded in line with the sub's course. The spray from the first two bombs was white, but that of the last two was black with oil spewing from a ruptured hull.

Soon an oil slick several hundred feet in diameter coated the water. For almost half an hour Sabin remained on the scene surveying the slick. Other planes relieved him and combed the area for another hour, but the only evidence of a submarine was the steadily expanding slick. Sabin's last two depth bombs had done the trick. His victim had been the *I-184*, returning from a transport mission to Jaluit.[51]

But for every win there is a loss, and VT-60 suffered theirs the next day. In the early morning hours of 20 June, before it was light, Lieutenant (jg) Paul Higginbotham eased his Avenger off the *Suwannee*'s deck. He was beginning a normal antisubmarine patrol around the transport group, then plodding northward. It should have been a routine mission. Instead, death brought this flight to a searing end.

Higginbotham was climbing slowly into the paling skies when a nervous gunner aboard one of the ships still hidden in the darkness below opened fire. A trail of flames suddenly erupted, ending in an explosion that colored the water for a few seconds. Finally, the darkness returned to cover the watery graves of Higginbotham and his crew.[52]

Late on the twentieth the *Sangamon* and *Suwannee* left TG 53.7 and headed north to relieve the *Corregidor* and *Coral Sea* off Saipan. Their presence would help beef up TG 52.11's striking power while TG 52.14's vessels were reorganizing. Joining the *Chenango* off Guam were Admiral Stump's carriers, the *Corregidor* and *Coral Sea*. Stump's ships, now designated TU 53.7.1, rendezvoused with the *Chenango* late on the twenty-first, Admiral Stump taking tactical command of the combined units. Shortly before midnight, orders were received from Admiral Turner, directing an air strike on Pagan. Chosen for this task was the *Chenango*, the other two flattops remaining behind to provide CAP and ASP over the Guam transport and bombardment forces.

Early the next morning the *Chenango* launched virtually her entire air group against Pagan, only two fighters being retained for CAP. This mission turned out to be relatively uneventful, with no enemy aircraft seen and with weak antiaircraft fire. After strafing and bombing a number of barges and luggers, all planes returned to the *Chenango*. Later in the day VF-35 Hellcats spotted a couple of Bettys sniffing around the edges of the task group. That action effectively concluded the *Chenango*'s participation in Forager for the time being.[53]

By 25 June the fight on Saipan was going well enough that Rear Admiral Conolly's Southern Attack Force could be relieved of any reserve duties for that island (the original reserve unit, the Army's 27th Division, having already been committed on Saipan). Also, the troops of the 3rd Marine Division and the 1st Provisional Marine

Brigade had been cooped up aboard the transports for some time now and were badly in need of relaxation and a break from the monotony of transport life. Thus, late on the twenty-fifth orders were received for the 3rd Marine Division to return to Eniwetok for restaging. The ships carrying the troops of the brigade would remain near Guam until the thirtieth, when they, also, would be released to return to Eniwetok.[54]

Also going back to Eniwetok were Rear Admiral Stump's three carriers. They would enjoy a short respite before sailing for Guam in July. During their involvement at Saipan the *Corregidor* had lost three fighters in combat, the *Coral Sea* one fighter and three bombers in combat and three fighters operationally. Four pilots and seven crewmen went down with these planes.[55]

Meanwhile, the fliers from the *Sangamon* and *Suwannee* had jumped into the Saipan fracas quickly, numerous strike and spotter missions being flown over Saipan and Tinian, while more missions were flown over Guam. A few enemy planes were encountered with generally fatal results to their crews. On the twenty-second a VF-37 pilot knocked down a Judy near the task unit, while VT-37's Lieutenant (jg) J. M. Murray tangled with a Betty north of Saipan. When Murray left the scene, the Betty was on its back in the water, one of its crew lying next to it in a pool of rapidly spreading blood, while another was swimming strongly toward Saipan.

Two days later, on the twenty-fourth, while covering a photo plane over Guam, Lieutenant (jg) James Ritchie encountered a Hamp. As Ritchie closed with the enemy plane, it waggled its wings and Ritchie obligingly returned the signal. The Hamp continued on, and Ritchie was able to get into firing position with no problems. His first burst splattered the Hamp's tail; his second set the fighter ablaze. After a few more bursts, the plane blew up, leaving Ritchie a souvenir, a large piece of the Hamp's fuselage lodged in the cowling of the Hellcat. The kill had been easy, so easy that the squadron ACI officer commented later, "This one chap evidently missed his rendezvous—and paid with his life for not being up on his identification of enemy aircraft."[56]

The airmen did not always have it their way. Three *Sangamon* and one *Suwannee* planes, but not their crews, were lost to the still-vicious flak on these missions.[57] Other pilots found that the recently captured Aslito airfield provided a welcome haven if they were unable to reach their carriers.

A few enemy planes continued to cause trouble off Saipan. On the evening of 26 June several attacked TG 52.11. One aircraft dropped a bomb on the *Suwannee* from only 500 yards away. The

bomb missed and the plane escaped. Another plane passed only 100
yards ahead of the *Sangamon,* circled back, and dropped a torpedo
that passed astern of her. For his trouble, the escorting destroyers
shot the plane down.[58]

Returning to action after their short rest were the carriers of TG
52.14. On the twenty-fourth planes from the task group recorded a
success. A medium-sized Japanese transport and several small craft
had been found in Rota's Sosanjaya Bay, and they had been bombed
and strafed since 12 June. Though damaged, the transport led a
charmed life until the twenty-fourth. That day VC-4's former executive officer and now its temporary commanding officer (CO), Lieutenant E. R. Fickenscher, planted a torpedo in the transport's side
and finally sent her to the bottom.[59]

That same day the *Kalinin Bay* returned from Eniwetok, where
she had picked up forty-two FM-2s and five Avengers. Upon her
return she was temporarily designated a "fighter carrier" by Admiral
Bogan. Her TBMs were sent to the other carriers, and a makeshift
squadron of VC-3 and VC-68 fighter pilots was assigned to her. The
squadron was commanded by VC-68's skipper, Lieutenant Commander R. S. Rogers. At the same time, because its CO had been
lost, VC-3's Bill Keighley temporarily took command of VC-4. This
continued until 13 July, when the *Kalinin Bay* returned to Eniwetok,
Keighley returned to command of VC-3, and Fickenscher took over
VC-4. As soon as the *Fanshaw Bay* was ready, the VC-68 fliers returned to her to prepare for the Palau operation. Though little
action was encountered by the combined squadron, what work they
did do was done with great vigor and earned the pilots a commenda-
tion from Admiral Bogan.[60]

About this time two more escort carriers made a brief appearance
off Saipan. The job of the *Manila Bay* and *Natoma Bay* was to deliver
the seventy-three P-47s of the 318th Fighter Group to Saipan. The
Thunderbolts had been scheduled to arrive earlier, but the Battle of
the Philippine Sea had delayed their delivery.

Only one of the army pilots had ever been catapulted off a carrier
(from the *Nassau* at Tarawa), and he had to continually assure his
fellow fliers that it would be a piece of cake. His buddies were not so
sure, one saying over and over that he wished he had learned to
swim. Others solemnly paced off the length of the catapult run,
shaking their heads when they finally came up with the distance.[61]

En route to Saipan, the *Natoma Bay*'s ACI officer, Lieutenant Ham
Lokey, began giving the army pilots a crash course on the application
of relative motion in case they needed to return to the ship. On the
morning of the first launches, 22 June, Lokey gave the pilots their

final briefing as to course and distance to Saipan along with the *Natoma Bay*'s course and speed after launch. The 19th Fighter Squadron's CO was to be launched first, and Lokey climbed up on the Thunderbolt's wing to ask him if he understood how to reach Saipan and, if necessary, return to the ship applying the principle of relative motion.

A bit puzzled, the pilot pointed to his right and said, "Isn't that it?" Lokey looked in the direction the pilot was pointing and there was Saipan, all greens and browns and almost close enough to touch. Abashed and a little disgusted that the army men wouldn't be able to derive the benefits of his lectures on relative motion, Lokey slunk off the P-47's wing.[62]

To the army fliers' relief, the catapultings went smoothly on the twenty-second, with a reasonable interval of two minutes before each of the twenty-five shots. The remaining planes would be launched over the next two days. An unwelcome intrusion by Japanese aircraft on the twenty-third complicated matters, however. At 0757 the *Natoma Bay* had finished catapulting the remaining twelve P-47s of the 19th Squadron. After this there was a break of several hours to allow the escorts to fuel, and then the *Manila Bay* was to send off her load of 73rd Fighter Squadron Thunderbolts. Before she could launch them, a quartet of enemy planes put in an appearance.

Shortly before noon the planes had been picked up on radar, closing fast. Four P-47s on the *Manila Bay* were readied for an immediate launch, but before they could be catapulted, four bomb-toting Zekes dove on the flattops out of some patchy clouds. The Zekes split up, with two to each carrier. Both carriers picked up speed and began evasive maneuvers while, belatedly, antiaircraft fire speckled the sky.

The two diving on the *Manila Bay* were not good bombers. Although they had caught the ships off guard, the four small bombs they dropped were off target to port. The pair attacking the *Natoma Bay* weren't any better, their bombs also falling wide to port. Retreating as fast as they had appeared, the Zekes raced to safety undamaged.

Watching the attack from the *Natoma Bay*'s signal bridge had been Herb Faulkner, a signalman. On a shelf by his elbow and held down by a paperweight was a pile of tear sheets, used to record various signals. As the carrier went through her gyrations, the paperweight slid off the tear sheets, and suddenly there was a blizzard of papers flying all around. Following the attack, an officer (fortunately unidentified) approached Faulkner. Quite seriously he asked Faulkner if he had been able to grab any of the "propaganda leaflets" the Japanese had dropped.[63]

Because of reports of additional Japanese planes in the vicinity,

Bombs explode near the Manila Bay *on 23 June 1944 as she prepares to launch the P-47s of the 73rd Fighter Squadron for Saipan. (National Archives)*

Glad to be off the carrier, a pair of 19th Fighter Squadron P-47s buzz the Natoma Bay *on 23 June 1944. (National Archives)*

the four P-47s being readied on the *Manila Bay* were launched a few
minutes after the attack to act as a CAP. When the bogeys disappeared off the radars, these P-47s were sent on to Saipan. There
were still thirty-two Thunderbolts left on the *Manila Bay*, but it was
decided to wait until the next day before launching them. Catapulting went according to plan on the twenty-fourth except for one
plane that was delayed a short time because of a damaged propeller.
Their job finished, the two CVEs took up a course for Eniwetok,
Pearl Harbor, and, finally, San Diego for some much-needed
repairs.[64]

The arrival of the P-47s meant that the escort carrier planes could
take it a bit easier. "Hux" Huxtable got a chance to see just how
effective these big fighter-bombers were. Acting as an air coordinator over Tinian one day, he led a flight of P-47s against a small
crossroads village. Hux showed the way, diving on the target with his
two .50-calibers popping away. Pulling up, he watched the P-47s dive
in, their eight fifties spewing out the lead. The Thunderbolts literally "ripped the place to pieces," greatly impressing Huxtable with
the P-47's firepower.[65]

With the Japanese being steadily forced toward Saipan's north tip,
there was less and less for the CVEs to do. Instead of close support
missions, their planes flew more and more antisubmarine patrols.
On one of these missions, Lieutenant Commander Huxtable came
close to not making it back to the *Gambier Bay*. Directed to join a
destroyer that had caught a sub west of Saipan, Huxtable arrived to
find that the "tin can" had apparently already destroyed the under-
seas intruder. After remaining over the scene for about an hour, he
returned to Aslito and landed.

The *Gambier Bay* would be landing aircraft on the hour, so Huxtable waited at Aslito until the time when he could reach the ship on
the hour. However, when he arrived over the carrier, he discovered
she wasn't landing planes and was busily involved in other operations. It was almost another hour before Huxtable was able to land,
his plane having only a few gallons of gas left.[66]

In early July the escort carriers remaining off Saipan proceeded
back to Eniwetok to prepare for the Tinian and Guam landings.
Saipan had been the most extensive air support operation yet for the
escort carriers. The CVE pilots had done much better than in the
Marshalls and Gilberts, but they were still far from being as good as
they could be.

At Saipan, control of air support missions was highly centralized.
The initial requests for close air support generally came from the

forty-one liaison parties assigned to battalions and regiments. Their requests moved up the ladder to division and corps headquarters, where they could be turned down, and finally to the commander support aircraft (CSA), Captain Richard F. Whitehead, USN, who was aboard Admiral Turner's flagship, the *Rocky Mount*. Once a mission had been approved, there were four methods for controlling it: by Captain Whitehead; by the support aircraft commander at the headquarters of Lieutenant General Holland M. Smith, USMC; by an air coordinator (usually a squadron commander) flying overhead; or by the flight leader assigned to the mission.

There were some real problems with this set-up. The air liaison parties had no direct communication with the planes, so they had to mark the target with white phosphorus (WP) shells and mark their own front lines with fluorescent panels. If targets couldn't be marked with WP, the planes would have to make dummy runs while the air liaison parties contacted the CSA, who then told the planes if they were on target or not. Naturally, this was time-consuming, and delays of over an hour between the requests for a strike and the actual strike were common. Most of the squadrons were less than enchanted by the requirement to work directly under the CSA, preferring to deal directly with the air liaison parties.[67]

To top if off, only one radio circuit, the support air request net, had been made available, and it was just not enough to get the job done. Along with a crowded radio net was the problem of radio discipline. Efforts to curb lax radio discipline continued throughout the war, but it was never eradicated.

As they had been doing since Tarawa, the marines once again pushed for their own airmen aboard escort carriers to be used in close support duty. And, once again they were turned down. A marine squadron would not fly combat off a CVE until Okinawa.

Saipan reconfirmed the trouble areas hampering close support operations; better communications, with a ground-to-air link between the air liaison parties and the planes overhead; control over the aircraft by the air liaison parties; increased training for the pilots; and better armament for the Wildcats, primarily incorporating rockets, which really came into their own at Saipan.[68]

Not all of the problems encountered on the close support missions could be attributed to the airmen. For example, on 26 June a 4th Marine Division colonel was riding in a *White Plains* TBM as an observer. In a "no-man's-land" area he saw three men run out of a small building and hop into a nearby depression. He made another pass and saw the three men run through a field to jump into a hole. Convinced they were enemy, the colonel ordered a strafing. After three of these passes, the men on the ground displayed yellow panels indicating friendly troops. Not until the Avenger had made at least seven low passes over the area were the fluorescent panels displayed.[69]

Following the departure of TGs 52.14 and 52.11 for Eniwetok, no escort carriers were in the area until the arrival of the *Hoggatt Bay*. This now-veteran CVE had been involved in a very successful hunter-killer cruise near the Admiralties in June (see Chapter 4). Now she and her screen of four destroyer escorts, designated TG 12.2, were assigned an area east of Guam and north of Truk. Entering the area on 7 July, for over a week TG 12.2 had little luck flushing out Japanese submarines. In a fortunate meeting, the task group came upon the oiler *Guadalupe,* and Captain W. V. Saunders, the *Hoggatt Bay*'s CO and task group commander, was able to finagle an unplanned fueling for his destroyer escorts. This enabled the group to remain in the area an additional eight days, during which time they struck paydirt.

Just before midnight on 18 July, the *Hoggatt Bay*'s SK radar painted a surface target 21,000 yards away. Sent to investigate were the destroyer escorts *Wyman* and *Reynolds*. When the two hunters closed to within 4,000 yards of the target it disappeared from the radar screens, but the *Wyman* was able to establish a sound contact at 1,600 yards. A full pattern of hedgehogs was fired, but these missed. Swinging around, the *Wyman* let fly with more of the projectiles. Fifteen seconds later came the unmistakable sound of five hits. Another five minutes passed, then a tremendous underwater explosion rattled the *Wyman,* followed by a similar blast thirty seconds later.

As dawn broke a two-and-a-half-mile-long oil slick could be seen, at its head oil continually bubbling to the surface. The *Wyman* lowered a small boat to recover debris from the slick. While the boat was scouring the slick, planes from the carrier, mistaking the boat for a sub's conning tower, strafed it. Before this deadly misunderstanding was resolved, two of the boat's crew were slightly wounded.

When TG 12.2 left the vicinity on the twentieth, oil was still bubbling to the surface, and the oil slick was now eight miles long and two miles wide. The oil was coming from what remained of the *Wyman*'s victim, the *RO-48*.[70]

Following a four-day stay at Eniwetok for supplies, TG 12.2 was back out on the prowl. On the afternoon of the twenty-eighth a submarine surfaced some eight miles away. Seeing the American ships himself, the sub commander quickly took his boat back down. Sent after the submarine, the *Reynolds* and *Wyman* soon established sound contact. At 1714 the *Wyman* fired a full hedgehog pattern; practically every one scored a hit. Five minutes later a violent explosion was felt on both DEs—the *I-55*'s death rattle.[71] This sinking was the last of the patrol for the *Hoggatt Bay*'s group. But the sinking of the two submarines showed that the Pacific CVE hunter-killer groups did not need to take a back seat to any of their colleagues in the Atlantic.

Before the Marianas could be considered secure, Guam and Tinian had to be taken, the remaining islands of the chain being of no threat. Although the landings on Guam took place a few days before those on Tinian, the latter operation ended much sooner. As at Saipan, the "jeeps" would provide convoy protection and close air support at Tinian.

The CVEs working Tinian were much the same group that had been at Saipan. However, there had been a few changes. Now in charge of TG 52.14 was Rear Admiral Sallada, with Rear Admiral C. A. F. Sprague in command of CarDiv 25. Ziggy Sprague had come from the *Wasp* to replace Gerry Bogan, who had moved up to command TG 58.4. Also, one new carrier had joined TG 52.14, this being Captain H. B. Butterfield's *Nehenta Bay*, with VC-11 aboard.[72]

Though Tinian had been under almost constant bombardment since 11 June, including attacks by CVE planes, for this phase the escort carriers didn't take part until the day before the 24 July landings. The majority of the air support missions would be flown by the P-47s based on Saipan, just a few miles from Tinian. On the twenty-third the escort carriers began their part in the assault on Tinian, with the *Kitkun Bay* sending sixteen fighters and eleven bombers and the *Gambier Bay* launching sixteen Wildcats and eight Avengers against various targets.

The day set for Jig Day, the landings on Tinian, was 24 July, and the escort carriers had eighty-nine planes in the air to help support the troops.[73] One of those airborne was "Hux" Huxtable, circling over the battleship *Colorado* as she supported a fake landing attempt at Tinian Town on the island's southwest shore. Three six-inch guns opened fire on the old battleship and the destroyer *Norman Scott*, pummeling them both with well-aimed shots. Six thousand feet above, Huxtable could see where this fire was coming from and led his aircraft in to rocket the site with telling effect. The rockets and the resulting pounding of the guns by the *Colorado* and other ships effectively ended their participation in the battle.[74]

During the Tinian operation, VC-10 lost one of its most popular pilots and his crew. One bright, sunny morning the antisubmarine patrol was preparing to launch: four new TBMs carrying 250-pound depth bombs. As usual, a fifth plane was being held in readiness in case of a problem with one of the assigned ASP aircraft. A problem did occur, and Lieutenant John B. "Sandy" Sanderson taxied the fifth plane into position on the catapult. It was obvious to the men on the bridge that Sanderson was feeling good, for he was grinning and waving to everyone while waiting for the catapult to be hooked up. Then it was down to business as he prepared for the launch.

Something went wrong. As Sanderson was catapulted, the nose of his big Avenger kept rising until it was at a sixty-degree angle; then the plane snapped to the left and dove into the water ahead of the *Gambier Bay*. A couple of seconds went by and the plane's depth bombs exploded, blowing both plane and crew to pieces. The carrier itself suffered some minor damage from the nearness of the explosions.

Launchings still had to proceed, however, and the pilots who took off after this tragic accident were much more grim-faced and tense than they had been just moments before. What had happened to Sanderson's plane—a trim problem, a broken control cable—would never be known. What was known was that three good men had died.[75]

Typical of the air support missions flown at Tinian were those of VC-11. On the twenty-fourth, squadron planes attacked a cave thought to be housing an artillery piece. Believing that a little overkill is better than no kill at all, the flight leader salvoed all twelve of his hundred-pounders on his first run. The bombs completely covered the area, with several actually entering the cave. There were a number of explosions, followed by a large secondary blast that flung chunks of coral and shrapnel high into the air. Four planes were splattered by this debris, and one gunner wounded slightly.

The following day three Avengers attacked emplacements north of Tinian Town. As the first bomber began its pullout, antiaircraft fire smashed into it, wounding the radioman and blowing away the right aileron and a main structural fuselage member. By very delicate flying, the pilot was able to get back to the *Nehenta Bay* for a safe landing. The Avenger, unable to be repaired, was deep-sixed.

A wooded area near the southwest tip of the island was the target on the thirtieth for five rocket-carrying Avengers. Rocket attacks, to be effective, were generally done in gliding runs. Being flatter and slower, these runs were dangerous to do. This day was no exception. Three Avengers had already braved extremely heavy antiaircraft fire before Lieutenant R. F. Stoner began his pass. At 1,500 feet, as Stoner was firing his rockets, the flak ripped into his plane. Its right wing was knocked off and the Avenger began to roll over and over to the right, the roll continuing until the Avenger slammed into the water. None of Stoner's crew got out.[76]

*A rocket-armed VC-11 Avenger flies over Tinian on 25 July 1944 as landing craft
stream back and forth from the beach. (National Archives)*

In general, air support at Tinian was fairly effective, the escort
carriers flying 534 support sorties with the loss of only two planes.
One problem area noted, though, was air-artillery coordination.
When aircraft were attacking positions, artillery fire often had to be
lifted for fear of hitting the planes. Sometimes the artillery people
refused to lift this fire. Commenting on one particular mission
where coordination had not been obtained, Rear Admiral Harry W.
Hill's air officer observed sarcastically, "The strike, strafing of enemy troops above northwest beach, was cancelled due to the refusal
of artillery to lift fire. They suggested that the planes fly up to the
area from the sea, strafe, and then turn away. Suggest flying lessons
for artillery personnel."[77]
     Again, as at Saipan, probably the one big weakness of close air
support at Tinian was the time between the request for a mission

and its execution. In one case, admittedly isolated, there was a delay of nineteen hours before aircraft could be obtained.[78] But there was a reluctance of the commanders to turn control of strikes over to the air liaison parties. Admiral Sallada explained this reluctance as being caused by "Uncertain air-ground communications, inadequately trained Air Liaison Parties and, frequently, pilots entirely inexperienced . . . in close air support."[79]

However, down at Guam most of the missions were being handled directly by the air liaison parties with good results. The techniques and procedures tested at Guam would become the norm for the rest of the war, not those used on Tinian.

On 1 August Tinian was declared secure. Construction on the airfields that would provide the runways for the B-29s that would drop the atomic bombs on Japan began shortly afterward.

Though the fighting was over on Tinian, one hundred miles to the south on Guam the fighting was still going on. And other escort carriers were in the thick of it. For Guam Rear Admiral Ragsdale's TG 53.7 was again present. This still included the *Sangamon, Suwannee,* and *Chenango,* but now also had Rear Admiral Stump's CarDiv 24 of the *Corregidor, Coral Sea,* and *Kalinin Bay.* After a short stay at Eniwetok, Stump's carriers (minus the *Kalinin Bay,* which had been operating at Tinian) arrived back off Guam on 9 July to renew the pounding of the island, which had been under way since early June. There was little excitement for the CVE fliers as they attacked numerous positions on the island, although the discovery of a beached and hastily camouflaged submarine provided a few moments' sport. With the rest of TG 53.7 arriving off Guam on the thirteenth, the *Corregidor* and *Coral Sea* returned to Eniwetok for replenishment.[80]

Because of problems with her "damnable" (spoken by more than one CVE engineering officer) and skittish uniflow engines, the *Coral Sea* was unable to participate further in the Guam operation, and she returned to San Diego for repairs. Taking her place, the *Kalinin Bay* joined with the *Corregidor* to escort the assault transports to Guam between 17 and 20 July.

Operations for all the escort carriers were quite routine from the day of the landings, 21 July, until the carriers left in early August. Two events of note during this period were the first landing on Orote airfield and Admiral Ragsdale's replacement as CTG 53.7. The airfield had only been taken the day before, and many Japanese troops were still hidden in the undergrowth west of the field when Lieutenant (jg) Edward F. Terrar, from the *Chenango,* showed up on the thirtieth. Engineering units had hardly started to clear the field, having only arrived six hours earlier, when Terrar came in, made a

touch-and-go landing, then circled back to make a full-fledged landing. Terrar's arrival disappointed some marines, who had been hoping that one of their planes would make the first landing. The second event was Rear Admiral Ragsdale's relief by Tommy Sprague
on the twenty-seventh. Ragsdale, who needed a rest, moved up to
Fleet Air Commander at Alameda.[81]

At Guam the air liaison parties were able to control many of the
strikes with varying degrees of success. There were the usual instances of carrier planes attacking friendly troops, but there were
also missions that were huge successes, such as the one where an
Avenger, using instantaneously fuzed 500-pounders, laid them
within one hundred yards of the front lines.[82] Also at Guam, delays
in the requests for and execution of strikes were cut somewhat.
Nonetheless, the marines still griped about the efficacy of these
strikes, seemingly wanting them flown immediately, if not sooner. It
was obvious the marines would never be satisfied until their own
airmen were supporting the ground troops.

Still, because of the lessons learned at Saipan, Tinian, and Guam,
close air support operations would become more effective during
the remainder of the war. One of the most important techniques
developed at Guam was that of limiting gunfire minimum ordinates
and also aircraft pullout levels so that air strikes and naval gunfire
could be done simultaneously.[83]

Of interest are Admiral Conolly's comments concerning CarDiv
22. "The importance of CarDiv 22 to this Force cannot be overemphasized," he stated.

> ... [Were] FM-2s to be substituted for the F6Fs they now carry, the
> loss to TF 53 would be enormous when the fighter-bomber feature of
> the latter airplane is considered in contrast with the FM-2's inability to
> carry any bombs. ... This class of carrier is very well suited for work
> with an amphibious group because, in contrast with the other type of
> CVEs, the *Sangamon, Suwannee, Santee* and *Chenango* (1) are able to
> carry a well balanced complement of Avengers and Hellcats (the latter
> aircraft being far superior to the FM-2 in its combined ability as a
> fighter, strafer and bomber), (2) are equipped with a thoroughly reli-
> able engineering plant, (3) have a larger oil and gasoline capacity, and
> (4) are most useful as refueling sources for smaller vessels of the attack
> force.[84]

Conolly was not the only one who saw the merits of the *Sangamon*'s
design. Already under construction and drawing much of the design
philosophy from the earlier class was the *Commencement Bay* class of
escort carrier, the first escort carrier class to be designed "CVE."

After the departure of TG 53.7, Admiral Sallada's carriers put in

Aboard the Santee *mechanics work on the planes of MAG-21 prior to launching them for Guam. (National Archives)*

a token appearance off Guam, but there was little for them to do and they, too, were soon on their way to other assignments. Also making a cameo appearance at Guam was CarDiv 22's fourth carrier, the *Santee*. She had been given the boring but necessary task of transporting MAG-21 from Espiritu Santo to Guam. On 4 August she launched the group's eighty-one planes for Orote, then rejoined CarDiv 22 at Eniwetok to prepare for a new assignment.[85]

That assignment was just a month away—Palau.

APPROACH TO THE PHILIPPINES

FROM THE TIME General MacArthur had arrived in Australia in March 1942, his earnest desire, almost his "destiny," had been to lead the U.S. forces back to the Philippines via a Southwest Pacific route. With great fervor and a veritable bombardment of messages to the Joint Chiefs of Staff (JCS), he pressed for the adoption of his plan of attack, the only one that would assure success in the Pacific (so he claimed). Despite MacArthur's heavily lobbied advocacy, the JCS were more inclined toward a two-pronged advance, one by MacArthur and one by Nimitz, and in mid-1943 ordered such an advance.

Outraged, MacArthur blustered, threatened, cajoled, and summoned up every bit of his celebrated oratorical skill to sway the JCS and the president, but it was no use. The decision had been made and it was final.

How to go about implementing the decision was another matter. Originally Rabaul had been the key target in MacArthur's move west. Realizing that Rabaul would be a difficult target to assault and would require more resources than were then on hand, the JCS in mid-1943 decided to bypass Rabaul and let it "wither on the vine." About the same time, MacArthur himself had come to a similar conclusion.

The isolation, or neutralization, of Rabaul really began in November 1943 with the landings on Bougainville and continued with the assault in December at Cape Gloucester, New Britain. The next step was the capture of the Admiralties, a task begun in February 1944 and completed in April.

There was one last step to complete Rabaul's isolation. Like Rabaul, Kavieng, at the northwest tip of New Ireland (a large island lying east and north of Rabaul), had been slated for capture. It soon became obvious that this attack would be unnecessary. Instead, the capture of Emirau, a small island a bit farther north, would be more useful and less costly. For this operation the fast carriers would not be needed, so the *Manila Bay* and *Natoma Bay* were sent south to provide the necessary air support. In addition, Rear Admiral Davison's TG 36.3 would help protect Rear Admiral Robert M. Griffin's bombardment group, which included the old battleships *New Mexico, Idaho, Mississippi,* and *Tennessee.*

There were no Japanese on Emirau, and the landings on 20 March went smoothly. Instead of bombarding Emirau, the battleships and carriers worked over Kavieng, where the flak was heavy but not particularly accurate. That same afternoon an enemy plane attempted to close with TG 36.3. Two divisions of Wildcats, one from each carrier, were sent to intercept. After a fifty-mile chase, the eight planes bracketed the enemy plane, a Tony. Two *Manila Bay* pilots and two from the *Natoma Bay* teamed up to make several runs on the hapless Japanese fighter and ventilated it well. Getting credit for finally shooting it down was VC-63's Lieutenant John H. Dineen.[1]

Upon his return to the *Natoma Bay,* Dineen was prevailed upon to recount his experience over the ship's loudspeaker system. While most of the crew enjoyed his talk, a few saw the whole incident through jaundiced eyes. One was the 5-inch gun's warrant gunner. Ham Lokey found him sitting rather glumly in the wardroom.

"What's the trouble, gunner? You don't seem happy over the ship drawing first blood," Lokey said.

"I ain't," came the gloomy reply. When pressed to explain, the gunner asked Lokey, "How many men do we have aboard?"

"About twelve hundred."

"And how many months have we been in commission?"

"About fourteen months."

"And how many miles do you think we've traveled?"

"I'd say fifteen thousand miles."

The gunner's face became glummer. "Twelve hundred men, fourteen months, and fifteen thousand miles to kill one Jap. It's going to be a long war."[2]

The crew of the *Natoma Bay* discovered that it could be an itchy war, too. The ship was operating so close to the equator that the flattop's quarters became stifling, with little, if any, air conditioning to relieve the situation, and thus heat rash became endemic aboard ship. But heat rash did not always explain the itching. One day Captain Meadows called the ship's service officer (in charge of the laundry, tailor shop, barber shop, and so forth) on the carpet. "Who put itching powder in my underwear?" he growled.

Airing the bunting on the Natoma Bay. *Notice the two large "squawk boxes," the searchlights, and the HF/DF loop antenna. (Via* Natoma Bay *Association)*

Flabbergasted, the officer replied that he doubted anyone on board had guts enough to do that.

"Well, it's there," Meadows uttered through clenched teeth, "and you'd better find out who did it, and on the double."

The obvious spot for something like this to have happened was the laundry, and that was where the officer headed. Assembling the men in the laundry, he roared, "All right, you men, who put the itching powder in the captain's underwear?" There was dead silence, and he was about to repeat the question when from the rear of the compartment a meek voice piped up. "Do you suppose that's where the fiberglass curtain went?"

On the *Natoma Bay* many of the doors had been replaced with fiberglass curtains. Somehow one of these curtains had found its way to the laundry, where it had been ground up. The captain was not the only one to start itching—he had just been the first to get his laundry. Before the day was over, practically the entire crew was scratching at the finely ground fiberglass particles embedded in their clothes. The crew's clothes had to be run through the entire laundering process not once, but twice, to get the offending particles out, and the laundry worked twenty-four hours a day for three days to finish the job. No more fiberglass curtains turned up in the laundry again.[3]

On 2 April the *Corregidor* and *Coral Sea* relieved the other two CVEs off Emirau, the *Manila Bay* and the *Natoma Bay* returning to Tulagi for supplies. For the two new carriers, their stay off Emirau was generally unexciting. The Japanese were hoarding what aircraft they could, and few planes were sent to snoop the U.S. forces.

Still, a pair of *Coral Sea* FM-2s did manage to bag a Betty. Sent to investigate a bogey, the two VC-33 pilots had trouble identifying the bogey, claiming it was either a B-24 or a B-17. Not satisfied with this identification, the *Corregidor*'s CO, Captain Bowman, ordered the two fighters to take a closer look. Only then did the duo see that the plane was a Betty. Jettisoning what appeared to be torpedoes, the bomber attempted to outrun the FM-2s. This was of no avail, and soon all that remained of the Betty was an oil slick on the water.[4]

While the Kaiser carriers were involved with the Emirau sideshow, the four *Sangamon* vessels (the *Santee* having just arrived from the Atlantic) were backstopping TF 58 during its attacks on Palau on 30–31 March. Protecting the fleet supply train, TG 50.15, was an unrewarding but necessary task for the four CVEs. The *Chenango* even got back into her old act as fleet oiler by fueling the light carriers *Langley* and *Princeton*. Following this tedious duty, the quartet headed back to Espiritu Santo to prepare for another operation.[5]

This new operation would entail bypassing the major Japanese base at Wewak on New Guinea's north shore to strike hundreds of miles farther west. The two targets of MacArthur's ambitious plan were Hollandia (where a large airfield complex was located) and Aitape, a bit over one hundred miles east of Hollandia. Reckless (an apt name) would be the code name for the Hollandia operation, and Persecution the name for Aitape.

Since Hollandia was beyond the effective range of his land-based fighters, General MacArthur sought to obtain the services of Admiral Nimitz's fast carriers. In early March the JCS instructed Nimitz to provide these carriers for Hollandia. Two task groups from TF 58 would be assigned to this operation. MacArthur wished to keep the fast carriers until D day plus eight, or until fields for land-based fighters had been constructed at Hollandia.

This proposal horrified Nimitz, who felt that this would leave his carriers open to attack from the many airfields still operational in the vicinity. He refused to leave the fast carriers any longer than necessary, setting D day plus three as the date they must retire from the area. Although not satisfied, MacArthur reluctantly accepted Nimitz's conditions.

Because the fast carriers would not be around for long, eight escort carriers were made available, which would be able to stay longer. (Perhaps they were considered to be more expendable than the fast carriers.) Initially the CVEs were to provide close support missions at both Hollandia and Aitape, but it was finally decided that the TF 58 carriers could handle everything at Hollandia. Therefore, the "jeeps" would support only the Aitape landings, remaining until one of the airfields could be rehabilitated. There was a time constraint on the escort carriers, however. They could stay no longer than D day plus nineteen, and the earlier their release, the better.[6]

The escort carriers assigned to this operation were divided into two task groups:

**TASK FORCE 78   ESCORT CARRIER GROUPS
R. Adm. Ralph E. Davison**

TASK GROUP 78.1
R. Adm. Van H. Ragsdale (ComCarDiv 22)

Sangamon (F)	Capt. M. E. Browder
Air Group 37	Lt. Cdr. S. E. Hindman
VF-37 22 F6F-3	Lt. Cdr. Hindman
VT-37 1 TBF-1, 8 TBM-1C	Lt. P. G. Farley
Suwannee	Capt. W. D. Johnson
Air Group 60	Lt. Cdr. H. O. Feilbach
VF-60 22 F6F-3	Lt. Cdr. Feilbach
VT-60 1 TBF-1, 8 TBM-1C	Lt. W. C. Vincent
Chenango	Capt. D. Ketcham
Air Group 35	Lt. Cdr. F. T. Moore
VF-35 18 F6F-3, 1 F6F-5P	Lt. Cdr. Moore
VT-35 9 TBM-1C	Lt. C. F. Morgan
Santee	Capt. H. F. Fick
Air Group 26	Lt. Cdr. H. N. Funk
VF-26 24 FM-2	Lt. Cdr. Funk
VT-26 9 TBF-1C	Lt. Cdr. T. M. Bennett

Screen: Destroyers *Morris, Hughes, Mustin, Ellet, Lansdowne, Lardner, Black*

(These carriers ceased using Dauntlesses on 10 March, and the squadron designation changed from VC to VT.)[7]

Task Group 78.2
R. Adm. Davison (ComCarDiv 24)

Natoma Bay (FF)		Capt. H. L. Meadows
VC-63	15 FM-2, 8 TBM-1, 4 TBM-1C	Lt. Cdr. S. S. Searcy
Coral Sea		Capt. H. W. Taylor
VC-33	14 FM-2, 7 TBF-1, 4 TBM-1C	Lt. Cdr. R. Gray
Corregidor		Capt. R. L. Bowman
VC-41	15 FM-2, 8 TBM-1, 1 TBM-1C	Lt. Cdr. G. M. Clifford
Manila Bay		Capt. B. L. Braun
VC-7	1 F4F-4, 15 FM-2, 5 TBF-1, 5 TBF-1C	Lt. Cdr. W. R. Bartlett

Screen: Destroyers *Erben, Walker, Hale, Abbot, Bullard, Kidd, Chauncey*[8]

Setting out from Purvis Bay and Tulagi, the carriers of TF 78 rendezvoused near Manus on 20 April with the transports of Rear Admiral Daniel E. Barbey's TF 77, the attack force. The next evening the carriers broke off from the main force to move into position off Aitape. Intelligence concerning the Hollandia-Aitape region was sorely lacking, which hampered the CVE pilots greatly. According to one source, the best map they had of the terrain was a reproduction of a chart drawn by a German trader in 1895. On the map the ship's ACI officer marked certain features with added notations such as "very mountainous and rough country. Cannibals too."[9]

Reconnaissance photos did show a large plantation-style house (obviously a prewar rubber or coconut planter's home) located on a hill overlooking the landing beaches. The house was to be destroyed so that the Japanese could not use it as an observation post. However, just a few hours before the first flights would have been launched to cover the landings, an urgent message was received on the carrier. It read,

DO NOT REPEAT DO NOT BOMB COLLETT'S HOUSE. IT WILL BE THE ARMY AIR CORPS OFFICERS CLUB.[10]

The house was not bombed.

Almost anticlimactic were the operations of the "jeeps" at Aitape, and later Hollandia. Though the lush, dense foliage (so different from what the fliers had become accustomed to in the Central Pacific) made finding targets difficult, there were few targets for the CVE airmen to attack anyway. Army planes and the fast carriers of TF 58 then pounding Hollandia had driven the Japanese from the skies and caused the ground forces to scuttle for cover.

Nonetheless, numerous missions were flown over Aitape on the next couple of days, with few results to show for the effort. With so little opposition encountered at Aitape, TG 78.2 was sent over to

The catapult crew rushes to reset the catapult as an Avenger leaps off the Manila Bay's *deck for Aitape, 22 April 1944. (National Archives)*

Hollandia to relieve the fast carriers. Admiral Ragdale's force went back to Manus for reprovisioning, returning to Hollandia on 27 April, at which time TG 78.2 took its turn at Manus.

As at Aitape, there was little for the "jeeps" to do at Hollandia. One of the few missions of interest during this period was a sweep of the Wakde-Sarmi area, the targets for MacArthur's next moves west. On 30 April twelve VF-37 and four VF-35 Hellcats plus a VT-37 TBM took off from the *Sangamon* to make the sweep. One of the VF-35 planes was a photo plane equipped to take oblique photos, while the Avenger was equipped to take vertical photos.

When this group arrived in the target area, it was met by an intense barrage of antiaircraft fire. Though heavy, this fire was inaccurate and no planes were hit. While the photo planes went about their work, the other Hellcats strafed several airstrips, also dropping their belly tanks and strafing these to start fires. All planes returned to the *Sangamon* by 1815. The mission hadn't been that exciting, but the photos that were taken were invaluable to the invasion force when the Wakde-Sarmi area was assaulted on 17 May.[11]

During their stay off New Guinea, the eight carriers suffered but four aircraft lost, all operational. Rain, which was quite prevalent during the course of the operation, was the cause of one of these losses, a VC-33 pilot who became disoriented in a squall and flew into the water. A lack of wind created the most problems, however. Lack of wind was a particular concern of the "big" CVEs because it hampered the use of their Hellcats. Instead of returning to Hollandia for a second tour, the *Santee* remained at Manus, where she traded all her Wildcats for the *Chenango*'s Hellcats. The smaller fighter worked out much better for the *Chenango* during the remainder of the operation.[12]

It was at Hollandia-Aitape that the men of the *Coral Sea* got a chance to see how their ship handled. "During this operation the full capabilities of the *Casablanca*-class CVEs were exploited fully for the first time," the carrier's historian related, "and their Polo-Pony characteristic of being able to 'Turn on a Dime' developed through exhaustive maneuvers. On one occasion Task Group 78.2 slipped neatly thru another group of four 'jeeps' [TG 78.1] with their respective courses at near right angles, passing bows across sterns in an exciting display of expert ship-handling."[13]

Also during this time, these carriers were discovered to be missing a vital piece of machinery—air conditioning. About the only air-conditioned sections were the Combat Information Center (CIC) compartment and the pilots' ready room. Numerous complaints were heard concerning this problem, particularly about the engineering spaces, where it was almost too hot for human endurance. Perhaps his office was air-conditioned, for CarDiv 24's historian was not especially sympathetic, saying, "Historically it might be noted that the great open spaces of the tropics are susceptible of the same complaint."[14]

The complaint about the lack of air conditioning on the "jeeps" would continue throughout the war, leading to many novel solutions—of which most didn't work. One of the more ingenious was the brainchild of the *Gambier Bay*'s Mac McClendon. On that ship the forward elevator was dropped down to the hangar deck, then a large piece of canvas was rigged over the elevator opening. The canvas was tied down at the rear of the opening and the sides, leaving the front open to scoop the wind down onto the hangar deck. It worked.[15]

By 5 May all the escort carriers were back at Manus, their job completed. At Manus the CVE sailors discovered reverse Lend-Lease. Among the supplies boarded there were Australian "cranberries, mutton, rather husky rabbits, and cream in 'tins' instead of cans."[16]

Most of the carriers that came through Manus found themselves also stocking up on Australian "goat meat." Generally the crews tried it only once because of its odor and taste. On the *Makin Island* the cooks tried to fry it, roast it, boil it, or mix it with other meat, to no avail—the men, including the captain, wouldn't touch it with a ten-foot pole. Finally, one dark night the captain had the whole load of meat, several hundred pounds of it, dumped overboard.[17] The most that can be said for many of these foods was that they added a little novelty to the normal fare.

Several of the Kaiser-class vessels were encountering problems with their reciprocating engine plants, problems that would never be completely eradicated in this class of carrier. One of these flattops was the *Natoma Bay*, which had to return to Pearl to obtain the necessary facilities to repair her boilers and engines. Though not in bad enough shape to be sent back to Pearl Harbor, the *Coral Sea* spent a full month at Espiritu Santo replacing many broken piston rings in her forward main engine. Not until 2 June was she ready for combat again.[18]

With the assault on the Marianas in the offing, many of the CVEs left the Southwest Pacific, returning to Pearl to prepare for the new operation. Remaining in the Guadalcanal area, however, were the four *Sangamon*s, and they would sortie from here in June. These movements left only one carrier, a new arrival, to be actively engaged in combat operations in the Southwest Pacific during this period.

The carrier was the *Hoggatt Bay*, commanded by Captain William V. Saunders and in commission only since 11 January. For her first combat mission she had been ordered to join a hunter-killer operation under way north of the Admiralties. The Japanese, certain that a major U.S. offensive was imminent, had stationed a number of submarines at various points in the Pacific. Believing that the main American thrust would be against the Palaus, the Japanese had set up a scouting line (the NA line) of seven submarines starting about 120 miles northeast of the Admiralties.

Unfortunately for the crews and vessels of the NA line, the Americans, through their codebreakers, knew about them, and a destroyer escort division, CortDiv 39, was assigned the task of destroying this line. In an outstanding display of antisubmarine tactics, the ships of the division (primarily the *England*) sank five submarines, including one unlucky one that was not part of the NA line. And the *England* was still not finished.

Following a short stay at Manus to pick up more projectiles for their deadly hedgehog throw-ahead launchers, the ships of CortDiv

39 sortied again. A fourth destroyer escort soon joined, and the unit split into two divisions, CortDivs 39 and 40. On 26 May they rendez-voused with the *Hoggatt Bay* and her screen of the destroyers *Hazel-wood, Hoel, McCord,* and *Heermann.* Together these vessels formed TG 30.4, a hunter-killer group.

The next few days were uneventful, but early on the thirtieth the *Hazelwood* got a strong sound contact. A pair of depth charge attacks by the destroyer were unsuccessful, and at 0435 the DEs (destroyer escorts) *Raby* and *George* took over. A series of attacks were made, wounding but not destroying the submarine. The skippers of the two destroyer escorts believed that their target was just a reef, but they were told to maintain contact. Time passed, and at 1945, just after the sun sank over the horizon, they both heard and felt several violent explosions. A few hours later a large submarine surfaced briefly, then disappeared.

More attacks were made by the destroyer escorts (except for the *England*—the OTC (officer in tactical command) wanted the other DEs to bag at least *one* sub), but they all missed. At last the *England* was given the green light. After only one hedgehog salvo, there was a thunderous blast and the *RO-105* was no more. It was 0735 on 31 May. This last sinking brought the *England*'s score to six subs sunk in thirteen days. Her performance earned her and her crew a well-deserved Presidential Unit Citation.[19]

Task Group 30.4 put in to Manus for more supplies, then sortied again to find more submarines. This time the group was made up of the *Hoggatt Bay* and the destroyers *Taylor, Nicholas, O'Bannon,* and *Hopewell.* On 8 June Captain Saunders received word of a navy patrol plane's attack on a surfaced sub north of the task group. Though the point of attack was considerably out of the *Hoggatt Bay*'s search area, Saunders received permission to investigate.

Two days later a patrolling fighter sighted an oil slick about eight miles west of the carrier. Sent to check it out, the *Taylor* soon had a sonar contact. Two depth charge patterns were laid with no discernible effect. However, at 1541, while the *Taylor* was stopped to get a better sonar reading, a submarine surfaced dead ahead and 2,500 yards distant. The destroyer's five-inchers began barking as she picked up speed and swung left to unmask her guns. Almost immediately the guns were on target, and in the few minutes the sub was on the surface, they hit it with at least ten 5-inch shells and innumerable 40-mm shells.

At 1546 the sub went under stern first at a 20-degree angle, leaving behind a considerable amount of oil and many pieces of planking. The *Taylor* charged in to drop another pattern of depth charges. These did the trick. There was a heavy underwater explosion at 1558, followed three minutes later by a lesser explosion. A huge bubble, ten feet high and thirty feet wide, came to the surface, marking the last resting place of the *RO-111*.[20]

It had not been a bad mission for the *Hoggatt Bay*'s force, two subs sunk by the carrier's screen in less than two weeks. And as related in Chapter 3, the successes continued in the Marianas.

With the principal focus of operations on the Marianas in midsummer, major naval forces, including CVEs, did not return to the Southwest Pacific until September. This time the "jeeps" would be covering two operations, one in the Halmahera region off western New Guinea and the other in the Palaus.

The invasion of these two island groups brought together the forces of MacArthur and Nimitz. MacArthur's troops, primarily the 31st Infantry Division, would assault Morotai, a forty-four-by-twenty-five-mile island about ten miles north of Halmahera. The job assigned Nimitz's forces was the capture of Peleliu and Anguar in the Palaus. For this mission the 1st Marine Division and the 81st Infantry Division would be the assault forces.

Morotai had been selected as a target for several reasons. It was almost halfway between New Guinea's western tip, the Vogelkop Peninsula, and Mindanao, where MacArthur was planning to return to the Philippines; it had adequate space for airfield development, necessary both to support a move into the Philippines and also to provide flank protection from any Japanese moves from Ambon, Ceram, and the Celebes; it was more lightly held than Halmahera; and it would provide a forward base from which PTs could operate.

The assault would be a Seventh Fleet job, with Rear Admiral Daniel E. Barbey handling the naval side of the operation. Helping to support the landings would be Rear Admiral Thomas L. Sprague's carrier group, TG 77.1. Another Sprague was present at Morotai, Rear Admiral Clifton A. F. Sprague. "Ziggy" Sprague, no relation to Thomas Sprague, had commanded the *Wasp* at the Battle of the Philippine Sea and was promoted to rear admiral in August. Now he was in command of an escort carrier division.

TASK GROUP 77.1
R. Adm. Thomas L. Sprague

Task Unit 77.1.1	**R. Adm. Sprague (ComCarDiv 22)**
Sangamon (FF)	Capt. M. E. Browder
Air Group 37	Lt. Cdr. S. E. Hindman
VF-37 22 F6F-3/5	Lt. Cdr. Hindman
VT-37 9 TBM-1C	Lt. Cdr. P. G. Farley

Suwannee	Capt. W. D. Johnson
Air Group 60	Lt. Cdr. H. O. Feilbach
VF-60 22 F6F-3	Lt. Cdr. Feilbach
VT-60 9 TBM-1C	Lt. Cdr. W. C. Vincent
Chenango	Capt. G. van Deurs
Air Group 35	Lt. Cdr. F. T. Moore
VF-35 18 F6F-3, 1 F6F-5P	Lt. Cdr. Moore
VT-35 1 TBF-1C, 7 TBM-1C	Lt. C. F. Morgan
Santee	Capt. R. E. Blick
Air Group 26	Lt. Cdr. H. N. Funk
VF-26 24 FM-2	Lt. Cdr. Funk
VT-26 7 TBF-1C, 2 TBM-1C	Lt. Cdr. T. M. Bennett

Screen: Destroyer escorts *Richard S. Bull, Dennis, J. C. Butler, Raymond*

Task Unit 77.1.2	**R. Adm. C. A. F. Sprague** **(ComCarDiv 25)**
Fanshaw Bay (F)	Capt. D. P. Johnson
VC-66 16 FM-2, 12 TBM-1C	Lt. G. O. Trapp
St. Lo	Capt. F. J. McKenna
VC-65 17 FM-2, 12 TBM-1C	Lt. Cdr. R. M. Jones

Screen: Destroyer escorts *Edmonds, Richard M. Rowell, Eversole, Shelton*[21]

(The *St. Lo* had previously been named the *Midway;* the name was changed on 15 September, when the name *Midway* was assigned to one of the new 45,000-ton carriers then building.)

Morotai turned out to be a relatively bloodless battle for the ground troops. Only seven GIs were wounded on D day, 15 September, and just thirty were killed up to 4 October, when the operation was declared over.[22] Within a week of the landings, work began on the airfields that would be so valuable in October when the Philippines were invaded. Because there was so little opposition and because land-based aircraft had already virtually destroyed enemy air power in the region, there was little for the "jeeps" to do except keep the airfields on nearby Halmahera neutralized.

At Halmahera one of the most daring rescues of the war took place. On 16 September seven VF-26 Wildcats had strafed enemy positions at Oba and were returning to the *Santee* when they saw three barges anchored off Wasile Bay's north shore. Ensign Harold A. Thompson was fourth to make a run, and was getting ready to fire when everything exploded around him. Antiaircraft fire disintegrated the FM-2, and the next thing Thompson remembered was being blown upward and out of his plane.

Automatically he pulled his ripcord, and his parachute opened soon enough to deposit him gently into the bay. Thompson was in trouble, with a badly torn left hand and a Mae West that would only

Framed by the barrels of some 40-mm guns, a VT-26 Avenger prepares to land on the Santee *after a mission over Halmahera, 29 September 1944. (National Archives)*

partially inflate. A PBY Dumbo arrived and threw out a five-man raft into which he was able to clamber. Though he had gotten out safely from his fighter, Thompson was still in a very precarious situation. Enemy guns were blasting away at him, and he soon discovered that his raft was drifting toward shore. His raft finally nudged up to a pier, which was not a good place to be.

Overhead the "jeep" pilots, in the face of the heavy flak, kept up a constant "ferris wheel" attack on the shoreline and the base of the pier. Under this cover Thompson was able to paddle to a barge about 200 yards out in the bay and tie his raft to its anchor chain, afforded the barge's dubious protection. A *Suwannee* fighter, making a strafing run, was hit by the flak and crashed just a hundred yards from where Thompson was crouched; its pilot, Ensign William P. Bannister, was killed instantly.

The PBY that had dropped the raft to Thompson attempted a rescue, but was driven off by the heavy fire. Meanwhile, a second PBY braved the flak to pull another *Suwannee* flier who had also been shot down but who had been able to ditch a bit farther out and get into his raft.

Word of Thompson's predicament had gone up the chain of command, and a pair of PT boats, just arrived at Morotai that day, were sent to try a rescue. Lieutenant A. Murray Preston, CO of PT Squadron 33, led the mission, riding in Lieutenant Wilfred B. Tatro's *PT 489*, which was accompanied by Lieutenant (jg) Hershel F. Boyd's *PT 363*. Every man on the two boats was a volunteer for this decidedly hazardous mission.

When the two PTs arrived at the entrance to Wasile Bay, they were met with a hail of gunfire and forced to retreat. For a while the boats appeared unable to get into the bay; then more fighters, accompanied by several Avengers, put in an appearance. The fighters began strafing both sides of the bay, dampening the enemy's enthusiasm, while several "smoker" Avengers laid smokescreens to cover the approach of the PTs. Towering waterspouts suddenly gushed near the plywood craft as they streaked down the middle of the bay. An Avenger swooped low over the shore to lay a dense smokescreen, an extra smoke pot being dropped on a particularly active gun position.

Under the smoke's cover, *PT 489* and *PT 363* eased in close to the barge where Thompson was precariously situated. The cacophonous din of fighters strafing, enemy guns firing, and explosions intensified as the PTs added their 40-mms and .50-calibers to the racket.

For five long minutes the two boats lay motionless as Lieutenant Donald F. Seaman and MoMM1c Charles D. Day swam to Thompson's raft and towed it back to the *PT 489*. With the downed flier finally aboard, it was time to get out of this extremely unhealthy place. As the two PTs retired, their gunners raked the shoreline and for good measure, set fire to the barge that had given Thompson protection.

The PT crews discovered quickly that getting out of the bay was going to be even harder than getting in. Because of low fuel, most of the planes had to return to their carriers, enabling the Japanese gunners to vent their full fury on the boats. For twenty minutes the PTs zigged and zagged out of the bay, at one point crossing a minefield. Enemy shells, some landing only ten yards away, chased the boats but never hit them. Finally, after some two and one-half hours of almost constant shellfire, the little PTs sped out of range. For Thompson the ordeal had lasted almost eleven hours.

"Sure was a wonderful show to watch," Thompson later remarked. For the PT crews some richly deserved medals were in the offing. Lieutenant Preston was awarded the Medal of Honor (one of only two received by a PT man); Tatro, Seaman, Boyd, and Day received Navy Crosses; and all other members of both crews were awarded Silver Stars. One of the more amazing things about this rescue was that no one was hurt on either boat, and the PTs themselves suffered only superficial damage.[23]

One more fighter was lost during this operation, though not to enemy action. En route to Wasile Bay, the Hellcat of Ensign Merville Knackstedt began leaking oil. Accompanied by his section leader, Knackstedt turned back toward the *Sangamon*. He hadn't gone far when his oil pressure dropped and oil coated his windscreen. Realizing it was time to leave, he climbed out of his cockpit, planning to make a nice flat dive off his fighter's wing. Instead, the oil coating the wing caused him to slip and tumble. Fortunately it wasn't his head that hit the Hellcat's horizontal stabilizer, but his legs.

This was enough to stun him, however, and he fell 2,000 feet before he was able to pull his ripcord. Still in pain from the impact, he made no effort to stop the swing of his chute and dropped heavily into the water. Sputtering his way back to the surface, Knackstedt chased his life raft down (attached to his chute, which he had released as soon as his feet entered the water), inflated it, and climbed in. The sea was rough and Knackstedt spent a very uncomfortable night before being rescued the next day.[24]

Carrier operations at Morotai continued until the first week of October. Few ground support missions were flown, and not many more attacks on the Halmahera airfields. A few grounded planes were claimed destroyed by the CVE fliers, and VC-66 pilots shot down a Hamp on the sixteenth, but that was the extent of their activities. Most of the losses incurred by the Americans were of the operational variety, though three planes, other than those shot down during the Wasile Bay free-for-all, were lost in combat.

One of these combat losses occurred on 21 September during a raid on the Kaoe airfield on Halmahera. The attack group had previously struck a storage area at Soebain and was now to drop its remaining bombs on the Kaoe strip. VT-35's Ensign James B. Gladney had already made one pass at the field and was circling at 5,000 feet when flak tore into his Avenger. Either killed or knocked unconscious, Gladney slumped over his controls, starting the plane into a dive. Riding with Gladney was Lieutenant Harold B. Thornburg, Air Group 35's flight surgeon. Seeing that Gladney was seriously hurt, Thornburg scrambled up to the pilot's cockpit and tried to revive him. He also told the other two crewmen to get ready to jump and began calling out their altitude. When 2,000 feet clicked by, the gunner parachuted, followed by the radioman at 1,500 feet. Before he left, the radioman yelled at Thornburg to get out and thought he saw him preparing to bail out. Only the two crewmen survived, however, Thornburg leaving the dying Avenger at too low an altitude for his chute to open fully.[25]

Task Unit 77.1.1 retired to Manus on 26 and 27 of September, leaving the *Fanshaw Bay* and *St. Lo* to finish the job. With the arrival of the permanent army squadrons at Morotai, these carriers left for Manus on the night of 3 October. Their last day off Morotai saw a lot of excitement that ultimately turned into tragedy.

On the third TU 77.1.2 was operating about thirty-five miles east of Morotai's northern tip. Unknown to the Americans, the *RO-41* was watching their movements. The first indication to the men of TU 77.1.2 that a submarine was near was the broaching of a torpedo ahead of the *St. Lo* and off the *Fanshaw Bay*'s port beam. Before the ships could maneuver, another torpedo sliced into the destroyer escort *Shelton*'s stern, killing thirteen men and wounding another twenty-two. Some well-placed depth charges from the *Richard M. Rowell* drove off the *RO-41* before it could do more damage. The *Rowell* then took off the *Shelton*'s crew. Unluckily, while under tow later the *Shelton* capsized and sank.

Planes from the carriers searched vengefully for the attacker. In one of the search sectors was a submarine safety lane that U.S. submarines were to use to safely transit possibly dangerous areas. All commands were to be notified of such safety lanes and the traffic in them, and no attacks were to be made in them. In fact, the *St. Lo* would report afterward that "the search for the enemy submarine was complicated by the fact that four friendly submarines were in the nearby safety lanes."[26] But despite this knowledge, not enough care was taken by those involved to ensure that any submarine attacked was actually Japanese. Tragic consequences would ensue.

The *Stingray* was returning from the Philippines in the safety lane when she was attacked by two Avengers from the *St. Lo*. One plane dropped a bomb that was wide of the mark and the other Avenger flew into the sea when its pilot became too intent on his attack.

Because of the poorly executed attacks, the *Stingray* escaped unscathed; not so lucky was the *Seawolf*. Running one day late, she was bound for Samar with a load of supplies for the guerrillas on that island plus seventeen army agents. At 1100 the surfaced sub was spotted by another *St. Lo* pilot, who, thinking the *Seawolf* was the enemy, dropped a brace of bombs (which missed). As the *Seawolf* dove, the pilot marked the spot with a dye marker. To help with the search, the *Rowell* was summoned to the scene.

Shortly after 1300 the *Rowell* picked up the *Seawolf* on sonar. The DE's skipper knew he was in a safety lane, but not knowing the

Seawolf was running late, believed there were no U.S. subs within seventy miles. He began an attack immediately. Not attempting to evade, the *Seawolf* sent Morse code signals over her sonar. The *Rowell*'s CO took these signals as a Japanese attempt to jam his own sonar and ordered another attack. This one-sided battle was over quickly. A large bubble broke the surface, followed by globs of oil and debris; the *Seawolf* was lost with all hands.[27]

While Morotai was a relatively easy battle for the Americans, Peleliu and Anguar, over four hundred miles north-northwest of Morotai, were a different story. Peleliu would become one of the bloodiest battles in Marine Corps history. Assaulting Peleliu was the veteran 1st Marine Division, while Anguar, just south of Peleliu, was the army's 81st Infantry Division's assignment. To many of the high brass it appeared that these assaults might only take a few days. Actually, it was almost two and a half months later, on 25 November, that the last organized resistance on Peleliu was beaten down, while it took almost a month to snuff out the last opposition on Anguar.

If Admiral Halsey had had his way, however, the invasion of Peleliu would never have taken place. In the summer of 1944 the Joint Chiefs of Staff were pondering where the Pacific offensives would head after the Marianas. Eventually, after much soul-searching and many arguments, with the two theater commanders, Nimitz and MacArthur, adding their two bits, they agreed on a timetable of operations. Morotai and the southern Palaus would be assaulted on 15 September, Yap and Ulithi following on 5 October, with landings on Mindanao on 15 November.

Enter Halsey. In August he had replaced Admiral Spruance in command of the Fifth Fleet, bringing with him a new name for the organization—the Third Fleet. This switching of leaders was akin to Pony Express riders switching horses, except in reverse—the horses stayed the same but the riders changed. While Spruance and his staff began planning the next operation, Halsey led the Third Fleet against Yap, the Palaus, and Mindanao.

When the TF 38 planes struck the Mindanao fields on 9 and 10 September, they were not even opposed. This surprising turn of events led Halsey to cancel more strikes on Mindanao and concentrate on the Visayas (the central Philippines) instead. Again there was hardly any opposition, and many enemy planes and other targets were destroyed. This lack of opposition gave Halsey an idea. On 13 September he sent a dispatch to Nimitz, who passed it on to MacArthur and King, recommending that the Morotai, Palau, Yap, and Mindanao landings be canceled. Instead, these forces would be used to strike immediately into the Philippines at Leyte.

Macarthur and Nimitz, while shocked, were quick to grasp the possibilities. When Halsey's dispatch arrived in the Southwest Pacific, MacArthur was en route to Morotai with ships operating under radio silence. Thus, Lieutenant General Richard K. Sutherland, MacArthur's chief of staff, actually made the decision to bypass Mindanao and go directly to Leyte on 20 October, two months earlier than planned. When apprised of the situation, MacArthur, to no one's surprise, gave his approval. Also approving of the Leyte operation was Nimitz, although he felt that the Palau landings had to go ahead as planned to secure forward airfields and another anchorage.

The Joint Chiefs of Staff were also quick to give their approval, and the landings on Yap, Mindanao, and the Talauds (a group of islands midway between Morotai and Mindanao) disappeared into the trash can of plans never used. The Yap assault force, then loading or already at sea, was assigned the task of landing on Leyte on 20 October. The fire support vessels and escort carriers at Palau were to be temporarily assigned to Admiral Thomas C. Kinkaid's Seventh Fleet for use at Leyte.

For Palau the largest contingent of escort carriers yet assembled in the Pacific was present:

TASK GROUP 32.7   WESTERN ESCORT CARRIER GROUP
R. Adm. Ralph A. Ofstie

Task Unit 32.7.1	R. Adm. William D. Sample (ComCarDiv 27)
Marcus Island (F)	Capt. C. F. Greber
VC-21 16 FM-2, 12 TBM-1C	Lt. Cdr. T. O. Murray
Ommaney Bay	Capt. H. L. Young
VC-75 16 FM-2, 11 TBM-1C	Lt. A. W. Smith
Savo Island	Capt. C. E. Ekstrom
VC-27 16 FM-2, 12 TBM-1C	Lt. Cdr. P. W. Jackson
Kadashan Bay	Capt. R. N. Hunter
VC-20 16 FM-2, 11 TBM-1C	Lt. Cdr. J. R. Dale

Screen: Destroyers *Thorn, McCord, Trathen, Heermann, Hoel*

Task Unit 32.7.2	R. Adm. George R. Henderson (ComCarDiv 28)
Saginaw Bay (F)	Capt. F. C. Sutton
VC-78 18 FM-2, 12 TBM-1C	Lt. Cdr. J. L. Hyde
Kalinin Bay	Capt. C. R. Brown
VC-3 16 FM-2, 1 TBF-1C, 11 TBM-1C	Lt. Cdr. W. H. Keighley
Petrof Bay	Capt. J. L. Kane
VC-76 16 FM-2, 10 TBM-1C	Cdr. J. W. McCauley

Screen: Destroyers *Haggard, Hailey, Johnston, Welles*

Task Unit 32.7.3   R. Adm. Ofstie
                                                        (ComCarDiv 26)
Kitkun Bay (FF)   Capt. J. P. Whitney
   VC-5   16 FM-2, 12 TBM-1C   Cdr. R. L. Fowler
White Plains   Capt. D. J. Sullivan
   VC-4   16 FM-2, 12 TBM-1C   Lt. E. R. Fickenscher
Gambier Bay   Capt. W. V. R. Vieweg
   VC-10   18 FM-2, 12 TBM-1C   Lt. Cdr. E. J. Huxtable

Screen: Destroyers *Claxton, Aulick, Cony, Sigourney*
(This task unit became TG 31.2 for the Ulithi occupation.)

TASK GROUP 30.7   HUNTER-KILLER GROUP
Capt. William V. Saunders

Hoggatt Bay   Capt. Saunders
   VC-14   16 FM-2, 12 TBM-1C   Lt. C. H. Obrist

Screen: Destroyer escorts *Steele, Bebas, Samuel S. Miles, Seid*

TASK GROUP 30.8   FLEET OILER AND TRANSPORT CARRIER GROUP
Capt. Jasper T. Acuff

7 CVEs (the *Barnes, Nassau, Nehenta Bay, Sargent Bay, Steamer Bay, Sitkoh Bay,* and *Rudyerd Bay*), 7 DD, 15 DE, 24 AO in eight task units.[28]

Task Group 30.8, the Fleet Oiler and Transport Carrier Group, also known as the At Sea Logistics Service Group, was a recent development that permitted the fast carriers to remain at sea much longer, putting more pressure on the enemy. As can be seen by the number of vessels assigned to it, TG 30.8 was really a fleet. Later, when it grew to full strength, the At Sea Logistics Service Group would comprise thirty-four fleet oilers, nineteen destroyers, twenty-six destroyer escorts, several sea-going tugs, and eleven escort carriers. These vessels were divided into a number of task units, which would operate near TFs 38 or 58, fueling and supplying the combat vessels every few days. Approximately every four days the empty oilers of that particular task unit would be replaced by fully laden oilers of another task unit. Each task unit had at least one CVE attached, which carried replacement aircraft and pilots from the replacement pools at Manus, Eniwetok, or Guam. Additionally, several other escort carriers provided CAP and ASP protection for the vulnerable oilers.[29]

Replacement of aircraft was generally not much of a problem, though there were exceptions. When the *Sitkoh Bay* was delivering aircraft to TF 38 from September to November, she occasionally received some "duds" for transfer to other carriers. "Planes received from damaged CVs for reissue and presumably combat ready were almost without exception in extremely poor condition," the ship's action report complained. "One Helldiver received for reissue was marked 'Do not dive this plane.' "[30]

Replacement of pilots was another story. These replacement pilots appear to be the lost souls, the nomads of the carrier war. They were reasonably well-trained when they were sent to the Pacific, but too often this training was allowed to deteriorate as they sat, and sat, and sat at the replacement pools. As Captain J. C. Cronin of the *Tulagi* characterized them, they were "the forgotten men of naval aviation."[31] Too often they were not allowed to fly, in some cases for as long as eight months, except for an occasional ferry flight.

If they did finally make it to a combat carrier, they were often rejected by the ship's squadron because they couldn't hack carrier operations. Again, the primary reason for this was a lack of re- fresher training at the replacement pools. But Captain Cronin saw other problems. "Even more alarming than the lack of refresher training," he would complain, "was their complete ignorance of such routine things as prescribed recognition signals, shackle code, carrier operating instructions, deck signals, to say nothing of operations briefing."[32]

In the same vein the *Sitkoh Bay* reported, "Pilots trained and des- ignated for specific types [of aircraft] were assumed fully qualified in these types until the ship was embarrassed by the ignorance of one fighter pilot as to the means of operating either his emergency hook or belly tank releases. This incident culminated in a minor barrier crash and a very pointed recommendation from Commander Task Group 38.4."[33]

VC-20's commanding officer, John Dale, was also not enthusiastic about the quality of some replacement pilots. "We received two op- erationally trained torpedo pilots the night before leaving Pearl," (for the Palaus), he said later. "For the preceding three weeks they had been languishing at Barbers Point and we had been operating. We unnecessarily lost a perfectly good TBM when one of them spun in on his first landing. Trying to use such green pilots (it would be a shame to have them sit around for three months without flying) puts a strain on everybody at a time when they should be reaping the benefits of the mutual confidence built up during training."[34]

As could be expected, the morale of these pilots was low. Again quoting Captain Cronin, "They are generally a pretty dismal lot, their spirit is naturally low, and their first question always 'what are the chances of hooking up with a squadron.' "[35] Notwithstanding Cronin's observations, occasionally the squadrons found some gold among the the dross the replacement pools sent them. In a group of replacement pilots boarded for the Lingayen operation, Cronin and VC-92's CO found an excellent exec for the squadron.

But the dross could be pretty bad. Most of the pilots the *Sitkoh Bay* delivered to TF 38 were considered eager and alert. Two of them, however, were not up to the stress of combat, one suffering from epilepsy and the other a psychiatric case. "The latter reported to the flight surgeon an overwhelming inclination to hurl himself into revolving propellers," the carrier commented drily. "There appeared to be some evidence that the strength of this inclination varied in direct proportion to the proximity of the combat area and was accompanied by an inclination of even greater intensity to return to Miami, Florida. It is considered that such cases should ordinarily be eliminated during some phase of training."[36]

Despite the barrage of similar comments from many CVE captains, the higher commands were very slow in taking remedial action, and not until the Okinawa campaign was this important problem area resolved, if only partially.

There were a lot of new faces for this operation. All of the carriers in TUs 32.7.1 and 32.7.2 except for the *Kalinin Bay* were making their first combat appearances. The *Gambier Bay* had a new captain, "Bowser" Vieweg, much to the relief of many of her crew and especially to the men of VC-10. Captain Goodwin, who had never gotten along very well with VC-10, had left the ship on 18 August to become chief of staff to Admiral Sallada, who was moving up to the fast carriers and command of CarDiv 6.

Vieweg quickly endeared himself to his crew and the squadron. When the *Gambier Bay* arrived in Espiritu Santo in August, the carrier needed some aircraft replacements. Sent ashore to obtain and guard the planes was VC-10's engineering officer, Hank Pyzdrowski. Being ashore at the time, Pyzdrowski did not know that Vieweg had taken command of the carrier.

Pyzdrowski was zealously guarding his charges when a large man with no rank showing on his collar climbed into the cockpit of one of the TBMs. In a flash Pyzdrowski was up on the plane's wing to fight for the aircraft. "Sir, these planes are set aside for VC-10 of the *Gambier Bay*," he said firmly. "If you want to check out in one of them I will have to have an order from the captain."

Looking down at Pyzdrowski, the man smiled and said, "I am 'Bowser' Vieweg, the new captain of the *Gambier Bay*."

"Oh," Pyzdrowski squeaked as he slunk off the wing, "that's fine."

Receiving no instruction in the TBM, Vieweg flew the big plane aboard the carrier later in the day with no problems, impressing the pilots of VC-10.[37]

There were other new faces with the escort carriers in the Palaus. Ralph Ofstie, TG 32.7's commander, had been the only aviator on Nimitz's staff in 1943. Moving to command of the *Essex* in late 1943, Ofstie made rear admiral in August 1944 and took command of CarDiv 26 that same month. Characterized by Samuel Eliot Morison as "one of the most expert aviator flag officers in the Navy," he would be an asset to the escort carriers.[38]

Other fast carrier COs climbing up the ladder of command were George Henderson, from the *Princeton,* and the *Hornet's* Bill Sample. Both men brought a great deal of combat carrier experience with them, and would expertly be leading escort divisions in the final battles of the war.

In late August the carriers of TG 32.7 gathered in the Guadalcanal vicinity to prepare for the upcoming invasion. On 4 September the various assault forces began moving out for the Palaus. One of the carriers, the *Hoggatt Bay,* had left a little earlier to conduct an antisubmarine sweep. For a short period the flattop joined forces with TF 38 as it swept in toward the Palaus for prelanding strikes on 6–8 September. When the *Hoggatt Bay* left TF 38, Captain Saunders sent a message to Admiral Mitscher's flagship, "Am proceeding in accordance with previous orders. You are now on your own."

The reply was quick. "Thank you very much for your protection."[39]

The first carriers to reach the Palaus were the four "jeeps" of Admiral Sample's TU 32.7.1, arriving on 12 September and commencing operations immediately. Task Units 32.7.2 and 32.7.3 joined Sample's force on D day for ground support of the troops on Peleliu and Anguar, and for strikes against other islands, particularly the big Japanese stronghold of Babelthaup (which was to be bypassed), to prevent reinforcement of the defenders of Peleliu and Anguar.[40]

D day was 15 September, a gorgeous day with only a few clouds to infringe on the blueness of the sky and with just the hint of a breeze. Despite the light wind, the CVE planes were up in force covering the landings. When the landing craft of the 1st Marine Division were about 800 yards off shore, forty-eight FM-2s (twelve each from VC-20, VC-21, VC-27, and VC-75) came roaring in to strafe the wooded area behind the landing beaches. This strafing was almost continuous until the first boats touched down.[41] Although it served to keep the defenders' heads down, when the first landing craft hit the beach they were back up and lashing the marines with artillery and machine-gun fire. Soon columns of black oily smoke marked the spots where landing craft were burning and men were dying. The planes returned to seek out the enemy, but too often the Japanese were cleverly hidden and extremely hard to find.

Shortly before 1700 a group of Japanese made their presence known. At about 1650 a counterattack by approximately thirteen small tanks (even smaller than light tanks) and infantry rumbled across the fire-swept airfield against the marine lines. This counterattack was doomed to failure, though, with U.S. 75-mm tank, 37-mm antitank, bazooka, and machine-gun fire hemming in the attackers.

Also contributing to the destruction of the enemy force were some CVE planes. An observer from the *Marcus Island* had first seen the tanks and infantry gathering east of the airfield and then charging across it. Because of his position relative to the tanks and friendly troops, he did not fire the rockets he was carrying. Instead, he called for help, and several Wildcats and Avengers answered. A *Petrof Bay* TBM laid a 500-pounder in the midst of three tanks, effectively ending their participation in the fight. Other planes joined in. Although having no bombs left, "Hux" Huxtable swept in to strafe. Totally engrossed with his run, Huxtable didn't realize how low he was until he saw, out of the corner of his eye, palm trees flashing by. He hauled back on the stick as hard as he could (his plane's G-meter registered 9) and just skimmed over some trees. His blood pressure took several minutes to return to normal. In the meantime, the remaining tanks and what troops chose to close with the marines were soon chopped to pieces.[42]

Though this counterattack had been crushed, it was only the first day of what would be a long, bloody battle. For the escort carriers and their fliers, the fight would not be particularly bloody, only one *Marcus Island* pilot and two planes being lost in combat and four other planes lost operationally. Flight operations at Peleliu were heavy the first couple of days, 366 sorties being flown against the island on the fifteenth and sixteenth, but operations tapered off rapidly after that.

Anguar was an even easier job. A total of 182 sorties were flown there on the seventeenth and eighteenth (D day and D plus one) and only 32 on the next two days. By the twentieth the 81st Division had no need of the CVE planes, and the "jeeps" ended their participation at Anguar.[43]

Captured the first day had been the Peleliu airfield, and construction began almost immediately. Even though the Japanese held commanding ground north of the field, they made little effort to interfere with operations there, content to save their bullets for the marines closing in. To the chagrin of the marines, a plane fron an escort carrier, instead of a marine aircraft, made the first landing on the field. Low on gas, an *Ommaney Bay* TBM landed on the eighteenth, returning to the ship the next day.[44] The Japanese took no notice of this occasion, but they should have. It meant that marine planes would soon be flying from the field to drop the hated napalm bombs on their hideouts.

With the arrival of marine planes in late September, there was no further need of naval air support, and the "jeeps" were relieved of this assignment on the twenty-eighth. The feeling of the fliers and the crews of the carriers was that they had done a good job, albeit a fairly routine one, in the Palaus.

They had been helped in this effort by a new organization, the Joint Assault Signal Company (JASCO). Each battalion was assigned a JASCO team, which consisted of a naval gunfire officer, an air liaison officer, a shore party officer, and the necessary communications personnel and equipment. With a JASCO team, a ground commander could have both naval gunfire and aircraft on call much sooner and with greater precision than previously because the frontline troops would actually be controlling the bombardments or air strikes. This does not mean that the commander support aircraft, Admiral Theodore S. Wilkinson in the Palaus, was just a figurehead. He still maintained overall control of the aircraft and could approve or deny any requests for air support.[45]

As usual, despite the navy fliers' belief that they had done a good job, the marines were not so quick with praise. Friendly troops had been bombed and strafed several times, particularly spooking the green troops of the 81st Division and greatly angering the infantry about the "stupidity" of the fliers. Bombing attacks had been effective, especially in the flat southern portion of Peleliu, but this effectiveness had dropped considerably when the fighting moved into the crags north of the airfield. The marines considered strafing attacks to be almost useless, complaining that the navy pilots too often pulled out at 1,800 feet or higher. This was not how the VC-21 pilots saw it, reporting strafing run pullouts of between 300 and 1,000 feet.[46]

One of the navy pilots who was not that impressed with the CVE planes' performance in the Palaus was VC-20's John Dale. "The results of our support missions," he said, "judging from the lack of observable destruction and from the subsequent difficulties of the ground troops, were disappointing. To us in the air our strafing and bombing seemed capable of jangling Jap nerves and of keeping the enemy under cover in his small, well-camouflaged, and heavily protected positions."[47]

Dale believed that use of the Wildcat as a fighter-bomber was a mistake. One reason was that the fighter pilots had little previous training in bombing tactics and now had to get on-the-job training. Another was that the plane was saddled with an unsatisfactory suspension and release mechanism. But Dale saw a silver lining in the cloud over the Wildcat's attack capabilities. This was the rocket armament now being fitted to the fighters. "Here is a flying five-inch gun which the powerful, highly maneuverable FM-2 can bring to bear quickly," he said, "which the pilot can fire accurately with a minimum of training . . . and which is the most effective aircraft weapon yet devised for accurately blasting small, tough targets close to our own lines."[48] As time would show, the rocket-toting FM-2s would more than carry their weight in the close support role in upcoming operations.

For the escort carriers, the Palau operation had been another step up the ladder of combat respectability. This operation was the first in which the "jeeps" were employed as a group, and with three-division strength. Later, Admiral Ofstie commented on his task group's operations:

> It is apparent that the escort carriers can handle completely the full support of a major operation once the beachhead has been established. Furthermore, if the Fast Carrier Task Forces have largely reduced enemy air strength within range, the escort carriers—given adequate numbers—are able to handle the preliminary softening-up process as well.
>
> The experience of the Palau Operation indicates the decided advantages from operating support escort carriers in a single Group Command. This practice should be continued.[49]

Ofstie also saw some serious limitations to the Kaiser-class vessels—the low speed of the type, resulting in marginal flight operations with no-wind conditions; their single catapult, with only FM-2s able to be used if it failed; because of the small aircraft complement of each carrier, their having to be used in groups of three to four to be effective; and the unsuitability of the type for night operations. Ofstie recommended that the *Sangamons* be adapted for this last task.[50]

The next operation, Leyte, would show that Ofstie's thoughts on CVE operations were valid. But that was still in the future. Before that there was one more small mission for TU 32.7.3. Ofstie's three carriers were to cover the Ulithi Attack Group in its assault on that atoll, with its marvelous deep-water lagoon. As it turned out, there was nothing to assault. Except for a few friendly Micronesians, the atoll was virtually deserted. This bloodless occupation provided the Pacific Fleet with an anchorage of inestimable value, which would see, seemingly, every U.S. naval vessel in the Pacific at one time or another before the end of the war. The only action of interest during this operation was a fighter sweep of Yap by VC-10 planes on the twenty-second, and even they couldn't find anything. After spending a couple of days at anchor at Ulithi, Ofstie's force returned to Manus.[51]

There is one other incident of note involving an escort carrier in the Palaus operation. After ending her protection of TF 38 in early September, the *Hoggatt Bay* found nothing for several weeks. Nothing, that is, until 3 October. At 0311 that morning the carrier's radar painted a "skunk" (unidentified surface target) 20,000 yards away. Sent by Captain Saunders to investigate was the *Samuel S. Miles,* commanded by Lieutenant Commander H. G. Brousseau.

As the *Miles* drew closer to the object, Brousseau realized that it was a submarine. When the *Miles* closed to within 5,000 yards of the sub, it dove, but thirteen minutes later sonar contact was made and the DE dashed in to deliver a hedgehog attack.

The first run was unsuccessful, but the second one brought better results. Timing the fall of the projectiles, the crew of the *Miles* was disappointed to hear only two small explosions. But twenty-five seconds later three tremendous blasts threw men off their feet on the destroyer escort and knocked out her radios, sonar, and radar. These explosions were not the result of a torpedo hit on the *Miles,* as some men thought, but were the death knell of the *I-364.* When dawn broke, the remains of the submarine—oil and debris—could be seen fouling the surface of the sea.[52]

Morotai, Anguar, and Peleliu were now history for the "jeeps." For them the operations had been pretty tame. However, Tommy Sprague was worried about the future. Noting the few radars fitted to escort carriers, he recommended that at least one of the CVEs in each CarDiv be fitted with additional radars. And in a most prescient comment, he stated, "In amphibious operations where operations are carried on in close proximity to land masses, it would be relatively easy for aircraft to follow land until opposite the formation and then close it without being detected."[53]

Leyte and the kamikaze were next.

THE RETURN

When General MacArthur reached Australia in March 1942 after having been ordered to leave the Philippines, he promised to return to those islands. On 20 October 1944 he kept that promise.

But the island where he kept his promise, Leyte, was not the original choice for MacArthur's triumphal return. In the summer of 1944 MacArthur and his planners had intended to invade Mindanao on 25 October, then Leyte on 15 November, and Luzon in January 1945, followed by other landings at various points in the Philippines through 1 April 1945. Less than enamored of this plan and its timetable was Admiral King. He saw it as not a plan but rather a vision of what MacArthur would like to do, and pointed out that because it was somewhat skimpy on air support, it was likely to result in a long and costly campaign. The proper strategy, he maintained, was a thrust through the Marianas to Formosa and mainland China.[1]

MacArthur needed some of his famed oratorical skills to sway those in the other camp, but in this he was greatly assisted by President Roosevelt. At a high-level conference at Pearl Harbor in July 1944 attended by Roosevelt, Nimitz, and other planners, MacArthur eloquently presented his case. Those present tended to agree with MacArthur, but the Joint Chiefs of Staff still had to approve the plan. After many internecine battles and after some pressure from Roosevelt, the JCS decided that Mindoro would be invaded on 15 November, with Leyte following on 20 December. King accepted Mindanao and Leyte but remained firmly opposed to any thought of Luzon, so whether Luzon or Formosa would be the next target was left for later debate.[2] In September, however, unforeseen events and an aggressive admiral completely changed these plans.

As noted in Chapter 4, when Halsey's Third Fleet struck Mindanao on 9–10 September, enemy opposition was surprisingly weak and great damage was inflicted on the Japanese. The same thing happened when Halsey switched his attacks to the Visayas. On 13 September Halsey recommended that the Palaus, Yap, Morotai, and Mindanao landings be canceled and that Leyte be seized immediately.

Halsey was wrong in believing that the Japanese were weak in the Philippines. They were only holding their forces back in anticipation of the landings they expected to come soon. But Halsey's recommendations fell on receptive ears. Finally the JCS agreed to a revision of their plans, although the Palaus and Morotai landings would still have to be held because of the late date and Nimitz's concern for airfields and anchorages. The ships and troops intended for Yap, already combat-loaded, were to be used for the Leyte landings, now targeted for 20 October.[3]

In the meantime, the Japanese had their own plans to counteract any American moves. Named SHO-GO (Victory Operation), these plans involved a go-for-broke "decisive battle." Unsure of where the enemy would strike, the Japanese developed four plans covering various parts of their holdings. SHO-1 dealt with an attack on the Philippines (considered the likeliest point by most planners), SHO-2 concerned Formosa and the Ryukyus, SHO-3 involved southern and central Japan, and SHO-4 was for the Kuriles and northern Japan.

SHO-GO involved a careful husbanding of resources to meet the American threat wherever and whenever it came. After the target area had been revealed, all the strength that could be mustered would be thrown against the invaders. First, Japanese air forces would strike the vulnerable transports and the carriers, but only when the landings were imminent. (This plan is similar to one used by the Japanese during the Battle of the Philippine Sea, a plan that was singularly ineffective and disastrous.) Next, Japanese naval forces would launch an all-out effort against the invasion forces in conjunction with the air attacks. Finally, the Japanese Army, using defense in depth tactics, would throw back into the sea whatever U.S. troops made it to shore. All that remained to put SHO-GO into effect was the target.

For the Americans, Leyte would involve one of the most complicated command setups in the entire war. There would not be one overall commander. Instead, the two top commanders in the Pacific, MacArthur and Nimitz, would share responsibility for this invasion— MacArthur for the ground forces and Nimitz for the fast carrier units. But under these two men would be the actual combat leaders, Vice Admiral Thomas C. Kinkaid with his Seventh Fleet and Halsey leading the Third Fleet (in reality TF 38).

The one real problem with this organization was that the right hand didn't know what the left hand was doing. Halsey reported to Nimitz and Kinkaid to MacArthur, with little communication between Halsey and Kinkaid. Kinkaid, of course, was more concerned with getting the troops ashore and protecting them, while Halsey's passion was the destruction of the enemy fleet. As became obvious later, this operation would have worked better if they had coordinated their plans and actions more closely.

For Leyte an imposing number of ships were gathered. Kinkaid's Seventh Fleet would number 738 ships, including eighteen CVEs loaned by Admiral Nimitz, and Halsey's Third Fleet would have eighteen carriers, six battleships, seventeen cruisers, and sixty-four destroyers.[4] The eighteen escort carriers assigned for support and the eleven "jeeps" bringing up replacement aircraft would compose the largest number of escort carriers yet assembled in the Pacific for one operation. As Admiral Ofstie had recommended earlier, the carriers would be operating in a single task group:

TASK GROUP 77.4   ESCORT CARRIER GROUP
R. Adm. Thomas L. Sprague

Task Unit 77.4.1 "Taffy 1"	**R. Adm. Sprague (ComCarDiv 22)**
Sangamon (FF)	Capt. M. E. Browder
Air Group 37	Lt. Cdr. S. E. Hindman
VF-37 16 F6F-3, 5 F6F-5	Lt. Cdr. Hindman
VT-37 9 TBM-1C	Lt. Cdr. P. G. Farley
Suwannee	Capt. W. D. Johnson
Air Group 60	Lt. Cdr. H. O. Feilbach
VF-60 22 F6F-3	Lt. Cdr. Feilbach
VT-60 9 TBM-1C	Lt. Cdr. W. C. Vincent
Chenango	Capt. G. van Deurs
Air Group 35	Lt. Cdr. F. T. Moore
VF-35 22 F6F-3	Lt. Cdr. Moore
VT-35 9 TBM-1C	Lt. C. F. Morgan
Santee	Capt. R. E. Blick
Air Group 26	Lt. Cdr. H. N. Funk
VF-26 24 FM-2	Lt. Cdr. Funk
VT-26 6 TBF-1C, 3 TBM-1C	Lt. Cdr. T. M. Bennett
	R. Adm. George R. Henderson (ComCarDiv 28)
Saginaw Bay (F)	Capt. F. C. Sutton
VC-78 15 FM-2, 12 TBM-1C	Lt. Cdr. J. L. Hyde, Jr.
Petrof Bay	Capt. J. L. Kane
VC-76 16 FM-2, 12 TBM-1C	Cdr. J. W. McCauley

Screen: Destroyers *McCord, Trathen, Hazelwood*, destroyer escorts *Edmonds, Richard S. Bull, Richard M. Rowell, Coolbaugh, Eversole* (sunk 28 October)

Task Unit 77.4.2   "Taffy 2"   **R. Adm. Felix B. Stump (ComCarDiv 24)**

Natoma Bay (F)   Capt. A. K. Morehouse
VC-81   16 FM-2, 12 TBM-1C   Lt. Cdr. R. C. Barnes
Manila Bay   Capt. Fitzhugh Lee
VC-80   16 FM-2, 12 TBM-1C   Lt. Cdr. H. K. Stubbs

                                       R. Adm. William D. Sample (ComCarDiv 27)

Marcus Island (F)   Capt. C. F. Greber
VC-21   17 FM-2, 12 TBM-1C   Lt. Cdr. T. O. Murray
Kadashan Bay   Capt. R. N. Hunter
VC-20   15 FM-2, 11 TBM-1C   Lt. Cdr. J. R. Dale
Savo Island   Capt. C. E. Ekstrom
VC-27   17 FM-2, 12 TBM-1C   Lt. Cdr. P. W. Jackson
Ommaney Bay   Capt. H. L. Young
VC-75   16 FM-2, 11 TBM-1C   Lt. A. W. Smith, Jr.

Screen: Destroyers *Haggard, Franks, Hailey,* destroyer escorts *Richard W. Suesens, Abercrombie, Oberrender, Leray Wilson, Walter C. Wann*

Task Unit 77.4.3   "Taffy 3"   **R. Adm. Clifton A. F. Sprague (ComCarDiv 25)**

Fanshaw Bay (F)   Capt. D. P. Johnson
VC-68   16 FM-2, 12 TBM-1C   Lt. Cdr. R. S. Rogers
St. Lo (Sunk 25 October)   Capt. F. J. McKenna
VC-65   17 FM-2, 12 TBM-1C   Lt. Cdr. R. M. Jones
White Plains   Capt. D. J. Sullivan
VC-4   16 FM-2, 12 TBM-1C   Lt. E. R. Fickenscher
Kalinin Bay   Capt. T. B. Williamson
VC-3   14 FM-2, 1 TBF-1C,   Lt. Cdr. W. H. Keighley
        11 TBM-1C

                                       R. Adm. Ralph A. Ofstie (ComCarDiv 26)

Kitkun Bay (F)   Capt. J. P. Whitney
VC-5   14 FM-2, 12 TBM-1C   Cdr. R. L. Fowler
Gambier Bay (Sunk 25 October)   Capt. W. V. R. Vieweg
VC-10   18 FM-2, 12 TBM-1C   Lt. Cdr. E. J. Huxtable

Screen: Destroyers *Hoel* (sunk 25 October), *Heermann, Johnston* (sunk 25 October), destroyer escorts *Dennis, John C. Butler, Raymond, Samuel B. Roberts* (sunk 25 October)

TASK GROUP 30.8   AT SEA LOGISTICS GROUP
Capt. J. T. Acuff

Escort carriers with replacement aircraft: *Altamaha, Barnes, Sitkoh Bay, Cape Esperance, Nassau, Kwajalein, Shipley Bay, Steamer Bay, Nehenta Bay, Sargent Bay, Rudyerd Bay*[5]

Manus and Hollandia were the main gathering points for Kinkaid's invasion fleet, with Manus being the escort carriers' anchorage. Most of the carriers and their crews would not get much rest between the Palaus and Leyte operations, many of the "jeeps" having only arrived at Manus the first week of October. The advancement of the date of the Leyte landings just didn't allow much time for a rest period.

Nevertheless, the ships tried to get most of the crews ashore to enjoy some beer, softball, or just plain relaxation. But even these relatively simple pleasures were not wanted by all. Aboard the *Chenango* Captain George van Deurs came across such a case, his own air group commander, Tom Moore.

Moore, with big protruding ears and a mashed-in nose, took delight in being called by some of the flattop's sailors "the ugliest man in the navy," but he wasn't delighted about taking his air group ashore. When van Deurs questioned him about this, Moore replied, "The fliers on some of these other ships are getting war fatigue, getting kind of low-spirited. My gang is in good shape. I don't want them to go over there and catch the disease."

Over his vehement objections, Tommy Sprague ordered Moore to go ashore and take his air group with him. Moore did as he was ordered, but made sure his men didn't associate with any other squadrons and brought them back aboard in good shape.[6]

Van Deurs was one of the few ship's captains who had a good idea where the *Chenango* was heading next and had already begun his plans. While at Morotai the ship had intercepted a dispatch along the lines of "Cancel KING ONE. Activate KING TWO. A-day 20 October." Van Deurs had a savvy ACI officer, Alexander Booth, and he figured that if anyone knew what KING TWO was, Booth would.

Booth did. Having cultivated several friends working on future projects at both MacArthur's and Kinkaid's headquarters, he knew that KING TWO meant Leyte. So when Captain van Deurs asked about it, Booth was able to tell the captain the code names applied to Mindanao and Leyte, and van Deurs got a jump on the other skippers in preparing for Leyte.[7]

At last the invasion force began to sortie for Leyte. Departing first were the *Gambier Bay* and *Kitkun Bay*. They would escort Rear Admiral William M. Fechteler's TG 78.2, carrying the troops of the 1st Cavalry Division, who would be landing at San Ricardo on the northern edge of the beachhead.

The main force of twelve CVEs left Manus in company with the Bombardment and Fire Support Group (TG 77.2) on 12 October. Two days later the *Petrof Bay, Saginaw Bay, Kadashan Bay,* and *Om-*

maney Bay set sail from Manus, the former two carriers escorting the transports of TG 79.3, which were carrying the troops of the 7th Infantry Division, destined to land near Dulag in the beachhead's southern half. The latter two flattops provided cover for TG 78.6, the Reinforcement Group, which arrived off Leyte on the twenty-second.[8]

For the first couple of days at sea things were tranquil, with sunny skies and calm seas, but the weather began to change on the fourteenth. That afternoon frequent squalls swept over the ships, bringing with them winds up to fifty knots. Then the sea began to kick up and pound the ships. The storm, which was actually the outer edge of a typhoon, grew in intensity, and a planned fueling rendezvous had to be postponed a day and then moved before it could take place.

The storm made everyone on the ships uncomfortable, but none more so than the *Natoma Bay*'s ACI officer, Ham Lokey. Just before leaving Pearl for the Southwest Pacific, the carrier had taken aboard six hundred cases of beer. Lokey was put in charge of making sure the beer was secure. Every day he had to check that no cases were missing, and he was checking them on the day of the storm.

When Lokey opened the door to the space where the beer was stored, out rushed a sea of foam that engulfed him. In the time since the beer had been purchased at Pearl Harbor, the cardboard cartons holding the bottles had absorbed so much moisture from the high humidity of the tropics that they were only as strong as tissue paper. Now, with the ship rolling and pitching in the storm, the cartons disintegrated, sending thousands of beer bottles flying around the storeroom. The space was awash with beer and foam, the resultant stench overwhelming. The next day Lokey saw that someone else took the inventory.[9]

Fueling took place on the sixteenth but the storm still didn't abate, so the force backtracked for a time to get some breathing room from the typhoon, which was finally moving away. The weather caused minor damage to many vessels, the most serious in the CVE force (besides the loss of the *Natoma Bay*'s beer) being the dismasting of the destroyer escort *Richard M. Rowell*.[10]

Initial bombardment and air strikes were to have begun on the seventeenth. Set back by the typhoon, not until the next day (A-2 day) were the first strikes launched. The operating area of Taffy 1 was to the southeast of Leyte Gulf, with the other two Taffies operating east-northeast of the entrance to Leyte Gulf and east-southeast of Samar's southern tip. Throughout their part in the campaign the "jeeps" would remain in the same general areas. TF 38 had origi-

Pilots of the Sangamon's *CVEG-37 are briefed on their targets on Leyte, 16 October 1944. (National Archives)*

nally planned to hit targets on Luzon and in the Visayas on 18–19 October, but Halsey held his carriers back in anticipation of a major Japanese effort against the invasion fleet. Thus the CVEs picked up another assignment.

Army Rangers had landed on Suluan and Dinagat Islands on the eastern and southeastern fringes of Leyte Gulf on the seventeenth. The following day the Rangers secured the last island, Homonhon, that blocked the entrance to Leyte Gulf. The next step would be the main landings on Leyte.

On the eighteenth numerous planes from the "jeeps" were out, the weather in the vicinity being much improved over that of the day before. Because of the new task assigned to the carriers—attacks on the Visayas airfields—many of the aircraft were not available to cover the underwater demolition teams reconnoitering the landing beaches, much to the swimmers' disgust.

The focus of the CVE planes' activities on the eighteenth was on the airfields on Negros, Cebu, Mindanao, and Luzon. The storm that had passed near the ships a few days earlier had continued through the Philippines, leaving the enemy's dirt airfields soggy and unusable. It had also left low clouds, particularly over Negros, which often forced the attackers to fly just under the clouds and only about 150 feet above the ground. Though the fighters were able to strafe under these conditions, the bombers were too low for safe bombing runs. Nevertheless, fourteen planes were claimed destroyed on the ground, a 5,000-ton oiler and several other ships sunk, and another 5,000-ton vessel and numerous other ships damaged. The planes on the ground may be a fairly accurate count, but the fliers' claims of ships sunk and damaged appear far out of line. The Japanese reported few, if any, ships sunk or damaged on the eighteenth.[11]

Not many Japanese planes were noted airborne, but a *Suwannee* pilot did catch a Val off Mactan and sent it spinning into the sea. A twin-engined bomber was also downed by VF-35 Hellcats.[12] There was one combat loss on the eighteenth. Ensign Radley E. Clemons, from the *Chenango*'s VF-35, was strafing Lahug airfield on Cebu when the belly tank on his Hellcat was hit by flak. Though there was little fuel in the tank, it exploded in a thunderous blast that jarred nearby planes.

Fire enveloped the aft fuselage for a brief time, then slowly died out, leaving the underside of the fuselage completely skinless behind where the tank had been located. Just as the fire burned itself out, Clemons's engine quit. Opening his canopy, Clemons crawled from his cockpit and bailed out. After landing in the water, he was picked up by natives in a canoe who took him ashore on Cebu and sheltered him from the Japanese until he could be returned to the Americans.[13]

Clemons was very lucky that friendly Filipinos had been close by when he was shot down, but throughout the day the fliers had seen many Filipinos waving and cheering the appearance of the blue-painted planes with the white stars and bars on their wings and fuselages.

Despite the fliers' optimistic claims, the results on the eighteenth were not particularly good. There were several reasons for this. One was that too much time was wasted by strike groups trying to rendezvous over water instead of using a visual point on land for the rendezvous. The consequent jockeying around used up fuel, leaving less time over the target. Another reason was that too often the rendezvous were made up of planes from different task units with resulting coordination problems. Finally, there were just too many aircraft for the types of targets attacked.

These problems may have been caused by the late change in plans in which the CVE planes assumed what had been a TF 38 task. The lateness of this change threw Tommy Sprague's plans out of kilter, forcing him to use his aircraft in whatever manner would not compromise his primary mission—close air support.[14]

Also, difficulties were encountered with the air coordinators. CAG-60's skipper complained about one air coordinator who

> merely told the pilots to go to certain areas to bomb and strafe, but did not tell the pilots what the targets were.
>
> Despite the air coordinator having been given the familiar "well done" for the part that he played, this was a typical, dull, exasperating and useless mission. All the bombs and bullets expended by the planes in this section, plus the loadings of other attack groups on this target, were utterly wasted. . . . There was nothing of a military nature to aim or shoot at, but three tons of bombs were "dumped" by this flight alone . . .
>
> At this time, the area inland and to the west of the island objective presented innumerable enemy targets such as trucks and troop concentrations and shipping.
>
> In order to eliminate unfortunate and inefficient employment of our offensive strength, more value must be placed on the opinion of the squadron commanders or strike leaders. There is too much evidence of selecting target areas from a chart and insisting that they be bombed, although pilots on the spot report nothing visible to aim at.[15]

One factor might have contributed to such somewhat disorganized missions as the one mentioned above. Leyte was the first operation in which this many CVEs had been working as one task group. There had been no training or exercises as a task group, and some on-the-job training was needed to work out the kinks. Later the kinks were indeed worked out, showing that a CVE group this size could be both efficient and effective.

Throughout 18 October Japanese air power had been conspicuous by its absence, leading Admiral Stump to say later, "From all appearances it looked as if the initial return to the Philippines would receive meager opposition."[16] How quickly this assessment would change. On this same day Admiral Soemu Toyoda, commander in chief of the Japanese Combined Fleet, ordered the activation of SHO-1 with a target date of 22 October. The date was quickly changed when Vice Admiral Takeo Kurita, leading the First Striking Force, the strongest Japanese naval unit to be involved in the battle, advised that his ships would need fuel and other items. Then 24 October was tentatively set as the target date.

The absence of air power that Stump noted meant, however, that SHO-1 had already misfired. The Japanese planes were to have destroyed the transports, but Halsey's raids on the Philippines in September had emasculated the ground-based air units. Another attack on Formosa by TF 38 in early October had accelerated the process, though not without retribution, which included the cruisers *Canberra* and *Houston* seriously damaged. Because of the losses suffered in these attacks, it would be some time before Japanese aircraft, not including kamikazes, would be a threat.

With the weather over the gulf again very good on the nineteenth, TG 77.4's planes were once more out in full force. Maintained on call over the beachhead region for most of the day was an air support group of twenty-eight fighters and fourteen bombers, these hitting various targets in the Tacloban-Dulag area as needed. In addition, a target CAP of thirty-six FM-2s was provided until 1730, a dusk TCAP of twelve planes taking over from 1700 to 1820.

Two strikes were launched during the day against Negros and Panay. The first, at 0630, consisted of forty-eight Wildcats and twenty-four Avengers, while the second, at 1230, had twenty-eight fighters and fifteen bombers. These strikes, being among the first to hit the western Visayas, were primarily meant to feel out the enemy, but as on the day before, enemy planes were hard to find in the air.[17] One Sally attempting to land at Fabrica was shot down by a VF-35 plane, and two fighters fell to the guns of other "jeep" fliers, though.

In one of these latter combats a group of TBMs was attacking positions near Dulag when a Zeke streaked past them heading west. Like hounds after the fox, the Avengers tore after the fighter, though all but one soon gave up the chase. Through towering clouds and rainshowers and up narrow ravines Lieutenant (jg) Richard G. Shiers kept on the Zeke's tail. The Zeke seemed to be trying to head west, so Shiers climbed out of the ravines to make better time and beat the fighter to Leyte's west coast.

When he reached the coast, Shiers began looking for the Zeke. Suddenly the fighter broke out of a cloud and dove on the TBM. Shiers's gunner, AOM2c James H. Korth, had been waiting for this. As soon as he opened up on the Zeke, he could see that his shells were hammering the plane. The Zeke shuddered, began to burn, rolled over, then dropped straight into the water, leaving a long trail of black smoke behind.[18]

In virtually a replay of the loss the day before, another *Chenango* Hellcat was lost. The belly tank of Ensign Jesse O. Kennedy's fighter was hit by flak during a strafing run over Negros. Although almost empty, it blew up with tremendous force. In less than thirty seconds the plane burned in two, Kennedy being unable to get out of the tumbling remains of his fighter before they plowed into the water at over 260 knots.[19]

The loss of two fighters in two days in virtually the same way caused great concern to the men of VF-35. Prior to these losses, the standard procedure had been to keep the belly tanks on for as long as possible because of the many long-distance strikes that had to be flown. After these two incidents the tanks were filled with only enough fuel to reach the target. Also, the pilots were directed to drop the tanks immediately "upon feeling concussion or any other indication of antiaircraft fire striking close." Finally, the commands particularly concerned with this problem were quickly notified to check into this situation and to come up with a solution as soon as possible.[20]

In the two days prior to the landings, the escort carrier planes flew 471 target sorties, dropped eighty-two tons of bombs, destroyed five enemy planes in the air and another fifty-seven on the ground. Many ground installations were also destroyed or damaged. The "jeeps" lost two fighters in combat, and two fighters and four bombers operationally.[21]

The twentieth was A day, the day of the landings on Leyte. Weather over the gulf was good, but low clouds and haze over the landing beaches caused a slight handicap in the early morning. These burned away about 1000, leaving excellent flying conditions. Earlier in the morning the *Saginaw Bay* and *Petrof Bay* had temporarily joined TU 77.4.2, having finished escorting the transports of TG 79.3. Joining TU 77.4.3 were the *Gambier Bay* and *Kitkun Bay*. Only the *Ommaney Bay* and *Kadashan Bay*, with the First Reinforcement Group, were not yet present. They would join the task group on the twenty-second.

Each Taffy would support one landing force: TU 77.4.1 with the Panaon Attack Group, landing on the small island of Panaon, which, along with Leyte, formed the western side of Surigao Strait; TU 77.4.2 covering the Southern Attack Force's landings near Dulag; and TU 77.4.3 supporting the Northern Attack Force at Tacloban.

A few enemy planes had been seen over the gulf the previous day, but these caused no great problems. More planes showed up on A day and selected Tommy Sprague's Taffy 1 as deserving of special attention. At 0755 radar picked up some bogeys closing in. The CAP was vectored out but recalled before contact was made. At 0820 the *Suwannee* began landing her planes, while the *Sangamon* started launching planes for the H hour strike. Four minutes later, lookouts saw three Zekes, landing gear extended, astern of the formation. The Japanese pilots were apparently trying to enter the landing pattern in hopes of attaining surprise.

Suddenly two of the planes dove on the *Santee*, strafing as they came. These Zekes were not kamikazes—they had yet to appear—and both dropped bombs, which missed the carrier, but not by much. At close to 300 knots all three planes scooted west, only to reappear a few minutes later racing back in about fifty feet above the water. Heavy antiaircraft fire greeted the onrushing planes.

This fire evidently spooked one of the enemy pilots, for he broke off his attack early and tried to escape. After a fifty-mile chase, a *Chenango* Hellcat caught the Zeke and blasted it into the sea. When only five hundred yards from the *Sangamon*, the second plane pulled out of its attack to fly close aboard the flattop's port side. It didn't fly for long. Lieutenant (jg) Herman Weiss had just been launched from the *Sangamon* and hardly gotten his gear retracted when he was on the Zeke's tail. This combat never got higher than fifty feet above the water before Weiss got in some good bursts, leaving the Zeke a blazing puddle of oil and gas floating in the ocean.[22]

The third Japanese pilot carried his attack home. Aboard the *Sangamon*, Captain Browder had been exhorting his men, roaring "Shoot the bastards down!"[23] His men tried to obey their captain's vividly phrased instructions but were unable to stop the Zeke before it had skipped a bomb into the carrier's port side from only fifty yards away. Upon impact the bomb did not explode, but ruptured. Bolts, pieces of the explosive charge, a small felt pad, and pieces of wadding were thrown onto a nearby sponson. The bomb sank, exploding fifteen seconds later.

Not a particularly large explosion, nevertheless it opened the carrier's main generator circuit breakers, causing a loss of electrical power to the auxiliaries, which then resulted in both main condensate pumps stopping. The final consequence of this chain of events was that the *Sangamon* lost her main engines temporarily, and she fell out of formation for a time. In studying this action later, the navy was very concerned about the great dependence on electrical auxiliaries in a combat vessel and their somewhat low resistance to shock damage.[24]

After releasing its bomb, the Zeke zoomed up right over the catapult crew then launching planes. The low-flying Zeke didn't faze the catapult crew one bit; they kept shooting off the planes. Just as the Zeke passed over the flattop's bow, it burst into flames and plunged into the sea. Surprisingly, the pilot of this plane, P/O1c Yashio Yamamoto, survived to be picked up by the *Trathen*. Transferred to the *Sangamon*, he was able to fill in some details of his attack on the carrier.[25]

Damage to the carrier turned out to be minor, with repairs made quickly and injuries few. For the ships, the rest of A day passed quietly. It was not so quiet for Rear Admiral Sample, however. Sample was commander of CarDiv 27 in Taffy 2, and he decided he had to see how his planes were doing over Leyte. This was a foolish decision for a senior officer to make. Positions in the Catmon Hill area, overlooking the landing beaches and obviously an important target, were the targets for the *Marcus Island* planes. Sample, however, wanted not just to observe but to participate. His pilot, Ensign William A. Balk, had already made one run, four rockets pummeling a possible machine-gun nest, and the TBM was now circling at five thousand feet as Sample watched the landing craft running in toward the beaches.

Suddenly a large-caliber shell sailed through the plane's right side. The shell destroyed the radio gear before it continued through the fuselage to explode near the left wing root. A huge hole was ripped in the Avenger's side, and Admiral Sample, who had been looking out the left tunnel window, was peppered with flying shards of metal. Though not life-threatening, the deep lacerations Sample received to his head, right hand, and right shoulder were very painful and debilitating.

Seeing the admiral bleeding and in great pain, ARM3c James C. Edinger scrambled out of his turret to give Sample immediate first aid. Edinger did such a good job that Sample promoted him to ARM2c as soon as they got back to the carrier. A safe landing was managed by Balk on the *Marcus Island,* but the TBM had been so seriously damaged that it was stripped and pushed over the side.[26]

Why Admiral Sample made a patently dangerous flight is unknown, but as Commodore Bates says, it was ill-advised. "This points up the battle lesson," Bates commented, "that it is unwise for a naval commander, who is conversant with the present and planned future operations of his command, and possibly of other commands as well, to expose himself in such a manner unnecessarily for, were he captured by the enemy, he might be forced to give away information of vital importance to the successful conduct of the operation."[27] Sample's flight is believed to be the only such mission by a senior CVE officer during the war.

As stated earlier, more enemy aircraft had been over the gulf on the twentieth, but not so many that they could be considered a real threat, though several ships (including the cruiser *Honolulu*) were damaged by enemy air attacks during the day. Still, because of the inability of radars to detect low-flying aircraft against the surrounding land masses, there was concern about large-scale air attacks. After a few more days the threat would become a reality.

The twentieth also saw Japanese plans for the decisive battle at

Leyte well under way. From Japan, Vice Admiral Jisaburo Ozawa's misnamed Main Body (or Northern Force, to the Americans) left the Inland Sea completely undetected that evening. This was not exactly what Ozawa wanted, because his ships were to be decoys to draw Halsey's ducks away from Leyte Gulf. But neither did he want to be discovered too early. Compared to what it once had been, Ozawa's force was anemic. Only one large carrier, the veteran *Zuikaku*, and three light carriers with a total of 116 planes (hardly more than what one *Essex*-class carrier had) composed the striking portion of this force. The other ships in this force were the two hermaphrodite battleship-carriers *Ise* and *Hyuga*, three light cruisers, and eight destroyers, plus a small supply unit.

Two days later, on 22 October, the real power of this enormously complicated plan departed Brunei Bay, Borneo, where it had been fueling, and set course for Leyte Gulf. This was Vice Admiral Takeo Kurita's First Striking Force (or Center Force). Kurita's force contained the firepower of what remained of the Combined Fleet's Mobile Force, which was also commanded by Admiral Ozawa. Present were the monster battleships *Yamato* and *Musashi* and three other battleships, the *Nagato*, *Kongo*, and *Haruna*, along with ten heavy cruisers, two light cruisers, and fifteen destroyers. The task of Kurita's ships would be to penetrate San Bernardino Strait north of Samar and fall upon the transports unloading in Leyte Gulf.

To assist Kurita in the destruction of the Americans, yet another force had been assembled, known to the Americans as the Southern Force. Actually, it was two separate units. The lead unit, Vice Admiral Shoji Nishimura's Force C (or Van Force), sortied from Brunei Bay several hours after the Center Force. It was composed of the battleships *Yamishiro* and *Fuso*, the heavy cruiser *Mogami*, and four destroyers. Bringing up the rear was Vice Admiral Kiyohide Shima's Second Striking Force (or Rear Force) with another ten ships composed of one light and two heavy cruisers and seven destroyers.

Shima's ships had come close to not being able to make it for this operation, having almost been suckered by Halsey during TF-38's Formosa attacks on 12–14 October. Believing that Halsey's ships had received a battering during the Formosa battle (at least that was what Japanese propagandists were proclaiming), Shima had sortied from the Inland Sea to pick off the cripples. Only at the last minute did the Japanese realize that the Americans were waiting for such a move. Putting in to Formosa, Shima received orders on the twenty-second to "support and cooperate" with Nishimura in Surigao Strait. In any event, Shima did not support or cooperate with Nishimura, which, in the end, didn't much matter.

The Japanese plan was extremely complex and required exquisite timing. If the American command setup at Leyte can be considered inadequate and susceptible to confusion, that of the Japanese was many times more so.

Not knowing of the plans the Japanese had for them, the men of the three Taffies went about their business on the twentieth. Aside from the attacks on the *Santee* and *Sangamon,* the day had been relatively routine. About 305 direct support sorties had been flown, along with 132 TCAP sorties and 20 TASP (target ASP) sorties. Two enemy planes had been shot down by the CAP. No planes had been lost in combat, but seven had been lost operationally, three of these from the *St. Lo,* reducing the number of planes on the escort carriers to 287 fighters and 170 Avengers.[28]

On 21 October the skies were cloudy, with intermittent showers cleansing the gulf in the afternoon. Over Leyte the weather was a bit better, though the clouds lowered in the afternoon. During the day a total of forty fighters and fourteen bombers were kept on call over the assault area, these planes flying 360 sorties in support of the troops pushing slowly inland. Particular emphasis was placed on knocking out enemy mortar batteries on Catmon Hill and Liberanan Head. In addition, fighters scouting farther inland claimed eight planes probably destroyed on several Leyte airfields.

At 1022 Tommy Sprague, concerned with the increasing activity of Japanese aircraft over Leyte Gulf that led to a kamikaze hitting the cruiser HMAS *Australia* that morning, recommended to Admiral Kinkaid that Sprague be authorized to send morning and afternoon sweeps over Cebu, Negros, Panay, and northern Mindanao. Sprague made this recommendation because the Japanese flier who had attacked the *Sangamon* revealed that the three planes had come from Cebu.

Though Sprague was as yet unaware of the threat, some of the first kamikaze attacks would come from the Cebu area. (The kamikaze that had hit the *Australia* had been a loner. The first organized suicide attacks would come on 25 October; for the evolution of the kamikaze units, see Chapter 7.) About an hour and a half after he made his recommendations, Sprague received a request from Kinkaid to send fighter sweeps over northern Mindanao and the Visayas. The two messages had passed each other, but obviously both commanders had the same thought.

In the afternoon aircraft from Taffy 1 swept in over Lahug field on Cebu, catching five Zekes (all of them kamikazes) warming up on the runway. In a short time the Zekes were burning hulks. Seventeen other planes were claimed by VF-26, but many of those might have been dummies. A few minutes after the attackers departed, three more Zekes, two of them kamikazes with an escort, were readied. Although they made an extensive search for U.S. naval units off Leyte, they found nothing, and two of them returned to Lahug that evening. The fate of the third plane, flown by one of the most aggressive pilots in the unit, Lieutenant (jg) Yoshiyasu Kuno, is unknown.[29]

In midafternoon Sprague received a disturbing dispatch that had come from Nimitz via Kinkaid. In the dispatch Nimitz stated that it was necessary to augment TF 38's destroyer screen and that DesRon (Destroyer Squadron) 47 had been chosen for this assignment. The DesRon 47 "tin cans" were the only destroyers in TG 77.4's screen, and their detachment would be a great blow to the task group, in both antiaircraft protection and antisubmarine defense. Fortunately, this move had not yet taken place when Kurita's ships appeared off Samar on the twenty-fifth.[30]

Aircraft losses were minimal on the twenty-first, only one *Manila Bay* Avenger being shot down. The Japanese couldn't claim credit for that TBM, though. The plane was shot down by friendly forces when it appeared to be acting in a hostile manner.[31]

The twenty-second saw Admiral Kurita's powerful force leave Brunei Bay and head north toward the Palawan Passage, the body of water that lies between the island of Palawan and the area known, because of its numerous reefs and shallows, as the Dangerous Ground. Kurita had chosen the Palawan Passage as the route for his ships because it lay outside the search sectors of U.S. land-based aircraft. He also knew that the passage had been used by enemy submarines, but the chance of meeting one was a chance he had to take.

So far the Americans were unaware that anything untoward was in the offing, yet there was an undercurrent running through both Seventh and Third Fleets that something was about to happen. For the escort carrier sailors and fliers the twenty-second was routine. Only one enemy plane was shot down during the day, a Val caught by *Chenango* fighters. At least nine other enemy planes were claimed destroyed on the ground at Lahug and Opon airfields on Cebu during an afternoon fighter sweep. Intense flak met the attackers at Lahug, knocking down one *Chenango* and two *Sangamon* fighters and a VT-35 TBM.

Back at the beachhead about 242 sorties were flown in support of the troops. Some of the best shooting of the operation took place in the morning, when a *Savo Island* Avenger crew spotted an enemy lookout in a tree. One pass was all it took: the lookout post and its occupants were blasted out of the branches.[32]

Losses on 22 October were quite a bit higher than the previous day. Five fighters and one bomber had been lost in combat, three fighters and one TBM operationally. These losses brought the number of aircraft available in TG 77.4 to 313 Wildcats and Hellcats and 190 Avengers, including those of the *Ommaney Bay* and *Kadashan Bay*, which had joined TU 77.4.2 that morning.

When the *Ommaney Bay* joined Taffy 2, the flattop's crew was in a high state of excitement. This had nothing to do with any anticipation of action, but rather with the score of the Navy–Georgia Tech game. On 21 October, back in the United States, the two football teams had squared off against each other, much to the interest of a couple of the "Big O's" officers. Captain H. L. Young was an Academy graduate, and VC-75's skipper, Lieutenant A. W. "Snuffy" Smith, Jr., was a graduate of Georgia Tech. Of course, this led to a bit of wagering over the winner of the game. The ship's crew chose to support Navy and the squadron backed Georgia Tech.

All through the evening of the twenty-second (the twenty-first back home because of the date line) a radioman tried to get the game's score, and finally it came through: Navy 17, Georgia Tech 15. Delighted with this, "Brigham" Young woke up his ship. It was hard to tell who were the winners and the losers on the carrier, as this announcement caused a near riot, with both sides being liberally doused by hoses brought out for the occasion. Actually, Young was not unhappy with his crew's shenanigans. For several days as the carrier drew nearer to the Philippines, he had sensed the tension growing on his ship, so he used the football game to relieve the tension. And it worked.

It worked twice, in fact. Young had only one day to savor Navy's "victory." The following day "Bowser" Vieweg signaled the *Ommaney Bay* his regrets over Navy losing the game 17–15. The radioman had gotten the score wrong! So there was a second riot as all bets changed hands. But again Young didn't mind. His crew was now loose and eager for action.[33]

A little before 1600 Tommy Sprague received word from Admiral Kinkaid that Kinkaid would be providing a couple of destroyer divisions to TG 77.4 to replace those destroyers going to the Third Fleet. The transfer would take place on the twenty-fifth or soon thereafter.[34] There would be a hitch in these plans, courtesy of the Japanese.

The night passed quietly for the Americans at Leyte Gulf. A bit farther east there had also been quiet for Kurita's force as it sliced through the sea at 16 knots. Confident that he could get through this stretch of water without encountering any submarines, Kurita had not stationed any destroyers ahead of his force to search for such intruders—a disastrous mistake.

Just inside the passage lay two submarines, the *Dace* and *Darter*. At 0116 the two boats were nestled close aboard each other on the surface, exchanging information by megaphone, when the *Darter* obtained a radar contact at 30,000 yards. Quickly the *Darter*'s CO, Commander David H. McClintock, yelled to the *Dace*'s Commander Bladen D. Claggett, "Let's go!" There was a rumbling and throbbing as the two subs' engines came up to flank speed. In a short time they made out what they took to be eleven heavy ships and six destroyers in two columns, but which were actually seventeen large ships and about twelve destroyers in several columns. A contact report was sent, a report that would be vital—the first to indicate where the Japanese were and where they were heading.

Because the Japanese vessels were steaming along at a leisurely 16 knots, the two submarines (both making 19 knots) were able to pull ahead on the surface. By 0600 they were about 20,000 yards ahead of the enemy force. The sky was still dark, but to the east a faint line of light rimmed the horizon; dawn was not far off. Submerging, the *Dace* and *Darter* waited for their quarry.

McClintock's targets were in the enemy's port column. Three heavy cruisers plus the battleship *Nagato* were in the lead. McClintock eyed the ships and chose the first one in line: the *Atago*, Admiral Kurita's flagship. At point-blank range, only 980 yards, six torpedoes leapt from the *Darter*'s forward tubes. Hardly had these left before McClintock was swinging around to bring his stern tubes to bear on the second cruiser in line, the *Takao*.

Just as he began firing four "fish" at the *Takao*, the first of four torpedoes slammed into the *Atago*. The cruiser was gutted by the torpedoes, huge billows of smoke accompanied by flashes of orange flame shooting into the sky. Meanwhile, two torpedoes hit the *Takao*, blasting off her rudder and two propellers and flooding three boiler rooms. As the *Darter* went deep to escape the inevitable depth-charging, a tremendous explosion shook the boat—the last of the *Atago*. She had taken only eighteen minutes to sink. Before that, Kurita was able to transfer to the destroyer *Kishinami* and thence to the *Yamato*. But there had been serious losses in communications personnel aboard the *Atago*, losses that would plague Kurita throughout the coming battle. Luckier was the *Takao*. She didn't sink, but she did have to return to Brunei.

So far two heavy cruisers had been knocked out of action. Over on the starboard column there would be one more. Claggett could see the results of the *Darter*'s activities and wanted to put his own two bits in. He soon had his chance. Trying to evade the attack from the port side, the vessels in the starboard column turned toward the *Dace*. Claggett picked out the first ship in line as his target, but changed his mind when the third ship appeared larger. (It is too bad that he didn't have time to take a look at the fourth ship in line, the mighty *Yamato*.)

At 0654 Claggett loosed six torpedoes from his forward tubes and took the *Dace* deep. Four of them hit the heavy cruiser *Maya*. Her end was even more violent than the *Atago*'s, a thunderous blast rattling the *Dace* so much that Claggett thought his own boat had been hit. The *Atago* had taken eighteen minutes to sink; the *Maya* took only four minutes to go under.

Under pressure to continue with their mission, the destroyers only desultorily depth-charged the two submarines, although a few patterns did come close to ending the subs' careers. After a while the destroyers departed, leaving only a pair of "tin cans" to screen the crippled *Takao*. In spite of the efforts of the subs to attack the cruiser, they were unable to carry it off. And while maneuvering, the *Darter* ran aground on Bombay Shoal, a particularly disagreeable coral reef on the China Sea side of the passage.

Dislodging the *Darter* proved impossible, and the *Dace* took off the sub's crew, then attempted to destroy the *Darter*. All that four torpedoes did was blow holes in the reef, but a number of 4-inch shells at the waterline made the submarine useless to anyone. A prowling Japanese aircraft aided in this task when it bombed the grounded sub, believing it still to be operational. Although conditions on the *Dace* were extremely cramped, the return to Fremantle, Australia, was generally harmonious—and why not? These two crews had put a big crimp in the enemy's plans for a decisive battle.

Shortly after dawn on the twenty-third Admiral Kinkaid was aware of the attacks on Kurita's Center Force. He also knew that another force had been attacked by the *Bream* near Luzon, an attack that resulted in the damaging of the cruiser *Aoba*. The cruiser was helping to screen a splinter unit of Admiral Shima's force, a transport unit, and would take no part in the Battle for Leyte Gulf, but the *Bream*'s contact report reinforced the thought that a major Japanese effort against the U.S. forces off Leyte Gulf was at hand.

Halsey was also aware of the coming threat and was preparing a hot reception. When informed of the *Darter*'s report, Halsey brought the Third Fleet closer to Leyte. Task Group 38.2 was stationed about fifty miles east of San Bernardino Strait; TG 38.3 was east of Luzon some sixty miles from Polillo Island; and TG 38.4 was operating sixty miles east of southern Samar. Unfortunately, TF 38's largest unit, TG 38.1, was then en route to Ulithi for replenishment and to pick up more aircraft. Instead of recalling TG 38.1 immediately, Halsey decided to wait until his planes had made contact with the enemy, in this case the Center Force, before recalling the task group.

For the escort carriers, 23 October would not be much different from previous days. Knowing that TF 38 was moving up behind him, Tommy Sprague felt that the presence of Japanese forces would not affect the CVEs' operations too much, the aircraft of TF 38 taking care of any major Japanese attacks.[35]

Several fighter sweeps were flown during the day, but once again airborne enemy planes were hard to find, though several were shot down. *Santee* pilots claimed two planes caught on the ground at Del Monte, while *Chenango* fliers reported destroying nine planes on the ground at Fabrica and four more at Carolina. A VF-26 Wildcat was lost in these attacks and a *Suwannee* Hellcat was shot down at Alicante, its pilot bailing out too low and hitting the ground before his parachute opened.[36]

These losses were among the eleven planes lost in combat by the CVEs between 18 and 23 October. During the same period six more planes were lost operationally. On the other side of the scoreboard, the "jeep" planes flew 1,326 combat sorties, dropped 268 tons of bombs, and claimed the destruction of 145 enemy planes in the air and on the ground.[37] (These figures do not include missions from the *St. Lo* or *Gambier Bay,* their records having been lost when they went down.)

Though few would admit to it, tension was building on the twenty-fourth among the men of the invasion fleet. At 0122 Kinkaid sent the following dispatch to Tommy Sprague: "Possibility large enemy air attack may be brewing. Until otherwise directed cancel western Visayas strike. Increase target CAP to 36 fighters with additional 16 fighters in Condition Eleven [ten-minute launch notice]."[38] A short time later this message was followed by reports that the submarines *Angler* and *Guitarro* had spotted the Center Force heading into the Mindoro Strait. If the enemy ships continued on their course, they would cross the Sibuyan Sea and enter San Bernardino Strait, the closest route to Leyte Gulf.

Most, but not all, of the day's action would occur in the Sibuyan Sea. Numerous enemy aircraft finally appeared over Leyte Gulf, giving the CVE fliers good hunting. In fact, 24 October would turn out to be their best day of the war for obtaining kills. Shortly before 0745 a large force of approximately eighty planes swept in over Leyte Gulf. These planes were from the Fourth Air Army, which

VC-4 FM-2s on CAP over Leyte Gulf on 23 October 1944. (National Archives)

had only just been able to concentrate its planes in the Visayas in support of the Japanese surface forces. In several swirling battles the Wildcats and Hellcats tore into the Japanese aircraft.

About 0830 the first group of attackers, primarily Sallys, was spotted by the CAP, which was orbiting at 8,000 to 12,000 feet over northeast Leyte. A quartet of VC-10 FM-2s went after a group of five Sallys. In the ensuing fight, the four pilots picked off three of the twin-engined bombers.[39] These combats showed that the Sallys had a marked tendency to shed wings easily.

Also in on this early action were pilots from "the Saints," VC-27. This battle would be the squadron's first contact with enemy planes, and they made the most of it. First they sighted four Oscars at 16,000 feet, about 4,000 feet above them. A steep climb brought the Wildcats up to the level of the Oscars, where they made an immediate attack. This first combat was inconclusive, the Oscars outrunning the Wildcats, which still retained their drop tanks.

This fight, however, had left the four FM-2s in great position to meet the main force of bombers. Lieutenant Ralph E. Elliott identified the bombers roaring in toward Leyte Gulf as Frans, but they were more likely Sallys. With an altitude advantage, the Wildcats swept in on the leading bombers from the side. Elliott and his wingman made three high-side passes on the Sallys, but the bombers did not burst into flames as expected. Instead, they continued to drone on. A bit nonplussed at the Sallys' apparent invulnerability, Elliott dropped back to come up behind another of the bombers. This time he was satisfied with his shooting. Smoke began to pour from the bomber's right engine; then the Sally spun lazily into the ocean.

As his first kill was going down, Elliott was already on the tail of another bomber. After a couple of bursts, the plane's left wing flew off and the plane dove into the sea. Although their numbers were diminishing rapidly, the remaining bombers pressed ahead doggedly. Again, Elliott got on a Sally's tail. Already in a dive toward the ships below, the Sally was hard for Elliott to catch. He was able to snap off a few shots that hit the bomber but did not deter it from its mission. The Sally continued on to smash into one of the ships (probably one of the LSTs damaged that day).

Puffs of exploding antiaircraft shells surrounded his Wildcat, and Elliott beat a hasty retreat. Out of range of the ships' guns, he began looking about for more targets and soon spotted yet another of the ubiquitous Sallys starting its dive. Racing in from ten o'clock, Elliott loosed a fusillade into the enemy cockpit. He noted no apparent damage, and Elliott racked his FM-2 into a tight turn to follow the bomber down. A few more shots sent the Sally into the sea.[40]

These three planes were Elliott's first kills but not his last. In fact, he would wind up as the navy's leading Wildcat ace, with a score of nine enemy planes shot down.

During this initial fracas VC-27's Lieutenant (jg) Frank M. Leighty also picked off three planes. The VC-10 and VC-27 planes had not been the only ones to jump the Sallys. Five fliers from the *Kitkun Bay*'s squadron, VC-5, joined in the battle, claiming seven enemy planes destroyed in the free-for-all.[41] That was good shooting, but a couple of other "jeep" pilots would each almost equal that score themselves.

Approximately twenty minutes after the initial clash, twenty-one Lilys (another of the separate groups that made up this first large onslaught) tried to break through the defensive screen. They didn't fare much better than their predecessors, one reason being the remarkable day that one VC-3 pilot had.

Leading a division patrolling over the gulf was Lieutenant Kenneth G. Hippe. Upon seeing the ships begin to lay a smokescreen, he took his fighters higher and picked up speed. He soon saw trails of smoke left by burning Japanese planes; then a Lily came his way. In position initially for a high-side run, he roared in for his attack, gradually swinging around behind the bomber. At last in firing range, Hippe squeezed the trigger on his control stick. Four times his .50-calibers roared. The bomber flamed at its wing roots, rolled over, and dove vertically into the water a few hundred yards from the Tacloban airstrip.

Following a fruitless chase of a fast-moving Jill, Hippe's division was vectored toward a large group of greenish-brown-painted Lilys stacked in a V of Vs. Still retaining their drop tanks, Hippe and his wingman, Ensign John E. Buchanan, maneuvered for another high-side attack on the slowly diving bombers. Hippe staked out one group of four planes as his prey, while Buchanan chose another formation of three.

Hippe's attack was deadly. Arcing in from astern, he picked off the four Lilys one by one, their rear gunners offering little resistance. The first, hit in the fuselage and engines, blossomed into flame and dove to its doom; the second was picked off from underneath and fell away out of control; the third and fourth went down like the first Lily, with engines and wings burning. This action had taken but seven minutes and made Hippe an "ace in a day."

Meanwhile, Buchanan was shooting down the three Lilys he had picked as his quarry. He brought the first two bombers down in overhead runs that flamed both. Buchanan splashed his third victim in a high stern attack, which apparently killed the crew members.

On the other side of the Japanese formation the other two pilots in the division, Lieutenant (jg) Ray A. Volpi and Ensign William McDaniel, were also having a field day. Volpi destroyed one of the Lilys with a head-on run that shattered the bomber's right engine and started a fatal fire. Scooting through the enemy formation, Volpi pulled up in a wingover and got on the tail of another bomber. The shattering impact of his four .50s sent the plane into a vertical dive from which it could not recover. Smoked by Volpi, a third Lily escaped only because he ran out of ammunition.

Volpi's wingman, McDaniel, was able to destroy two Lilys and claimed another as a probable, but the Japanese gunners finally got the range and drilled McDaniel's Wildcat. Although he was able to reach Tacloban, McDaniel crashed on landing and was seriously injured. Still, it had been an outstanding interception for the VC-3 fliers—twelve planes destroyed and two more claimed as probables.[42]

While Hippe had had an outstanding mission, the work of VF-26's skipper, Lieutenant Commander Harold N. Funk, was even better. Funk had taken off from the *Santee* at 0510 leading a division of FM-2s. The mission got off to a bad start when one of the planes crashed on takeoff, killing the pilot. The remaining fliers pressed on. During the rendezvous in the waning darkness, a lost VF-37 Hellcat with an inoperative radio tagged onto Funk's group.

With this unusual combination Funk began patrolling over the gulf. For a couple of hours things were quiet; then the fighter director vectored Funk toward the northern entrance of San Juanico Strait between Leyte and Samar, where a large group of bogeys was approaching. The VF-26 threesome's Wildcats headed for the incoming force, leaving the Hellcat pilot behind wondering what was going on.

Shortly Funk spotted four Sallys at 13,000 feet, 2,000 feet higher than his fighters. In a climb Funk made a head-on pass at the lead bomber. Seeing no apparent damage, Funk swung to the left while the other two pilots pulled out to the right. In a second run he sent the bomber down in a flaming spiral. This was number one for Funk.

Other fighters were now entering the fray, and with the fighter director calling out more planes coming in, Funk told his partners to rendezvous. After meeting, they began a climb to fifteen thousand feet. Funk saw many black specks ahead. "Thirteen bogey," he radioed, followed quickly by "Sixteen bogey," and almost immediately thereafter by "Many, many bogeys!" When he finished counting, Funk figured there were thirty-two bombers (which he identified as Sallys, though they may have been Lilys) plus some fighters.

The enemy aircraft were in waves of four abreast, with a good deal of distance between each wave, making it easy for the Wildcats to get behind a wave without interference from the following wave. A head-on pass by the VF-26 trio resulted in Funk downing his second bomber of the day. His wingman, Ensign H. V. Shultz, made an apparently unsuccessful pass and was coming around for another run when a ball of fire that had once been a Zeke tried to ram him. This attempt failed, but forced Shultz to take evasive action. Another Zeke pulled in on Shultz's tail but was blown out of the sky by the sharpshooting Funk: number three. Able to resume his own attacks, Shultz got one Sally with a low-side pass and followed that a couple of minutes later with another Sally that crashed into the mountains.

By now the bombers were starting to dive toward the ships, and Funk and his men were having trouble staying with them. Funk reformed his group and led them against a wave of bombers just appearing on the scene. Funk began an overhead run on a Sally, his pass turning into a stern attack. The bomber's wing began to blaze, then suddenly disintegrated, leaving the plane to flop wildly out of the sky. Still one more Sally came under Funk's sights, and he needed two passes to send it flaming into the gulf. These were numbers four and five.

Now out of ammunition, Funk (along with his partners) retired from the arena. On this mission alone Funk had shot down five aircraft, Shultz had added two more, and the third member of the flight, Lieutenant R. J. Thompson, had contributed one kill and a probable. And Funk was not yet finished. On a second flight the same day he added an Irving with a "roundhouse pass from above" to bring his score for the day to six planes shot down—not a bad day's work.[43]

Meanwhile, what had happened to the VF-37 Hellcat that had joined up earlier with Funk's FM-2s? Without a radio, Lieutenant (jg) Earl W. Kenyon didn't know where Funk was heading when he lit out toward San Juanico Strait. Deciding just to fly around for a while and see what developed, Kenyon remained over the gulf. With so many enemy aircraft around, he soon saw some Sallys.

In several attacks Kenyon downed three Sallys, the last one with guns so hot that his shells were tumbling and spiraling all around the bomber. Seeing no more interlopers, Kenyon turned back toward the *Sangamon*. He didn't make it. When he shifted to his reserve tank, the Hellcat's engine quit and couldn't be restarted. Hardly had he tightened his straps than his plane went into the water. Kenyon escaped his rapidly sinking fighter with little difficulty, and two hours later was safe on a destroyer escort.[44]

The slaughter of the hapless Sallys and Lilys in this later action was not confined to the work of VC-3, VF-26, or VF-37. Once again the fliers of VC-10 were in the thick of the fight. Lieutenant (jg) Joseph McGraw's first target proved to be sturdy, the .50-caliber shells peppering its fuselage but not stopping its steady droning toward the gulf. Looking for a more tender target, McGraw let fly at the next plane in formation. His shells hit the bomber's fuel tanks and it blew up, one wing falling off and the remains fluttering into the ocean. McGraw's next victim was another Lily flying below what was left of the formation. His .50s tore up the plane's left engine, causing the Lily to fall out of control to its death. Before it went into its final dive, however, the Lily's gunner holed McGraw's fighter with 7.7-mm fire, fortunately causing only minor damage.[45]

Few Japanese planes made it past the defending fighters and antiaircraft fire, but those who did managed to crash-dive on a few ships, including the ocean-going tug *Sonoma* and the *LCI-1065*. Both vessels sank, the first in a long line of kamikaze victims.

Later in the morning, after this attack petered out, the *Chenango* and *Saginaw Bay* completed the transfer of most of their planes to the other "jeeps," the two carriers then receiving the other vessels' flyable "duds." The *Chenango* and *Saginaw Bay* would leave in the afternoon for Morotai to pick up replacement aircraft. Thus, they would not be present the next day when the Center Force fell upon the escort carriers off Samar.

While the two flattops were preparing to leave Leyte Gulf, a second major attack, made up of several groups of planes, began. Like the first attack, this one had little success in penetrating the CAP, though it did cause the diversion of some planes from ground support missions. Also as at the first attack, the Japanese received a bloody nose, losing about sixteen planes to two U.S. aircraft.[46]

Three of the enemy planes shot down were bagged by two VC-27 pilots. The victor in two of these battles was Ensign R. A. Mayhew, but he had little time to savor his victories. Upon returning to the *Savo Island* Mayhew was entering the landing pattern when his engine quit and his Wildcat flipped onto its back. In this position the fighter slammed into the sea, killing Mayhew instantly.[47]

Also getting their share of enemy planes during this fight were some VC-68 fliers. Lieutenant C. C. Sanders's division was on a ground support mission when he was directed to join the CAP. Shortly after reaching sixteen thousand feet, Sanders saw eighteen Oscars coming in over southern Samar, eight of which were diving on his division. The leading Oscar overshot Lieutenant (jg) S. Legatos, who had begun maneuvering wildly, and Legatos was able to get on the enemy fighter's tail. What the Japanese pilot had intended as a split S turned into a burning spiral instead as four .50-calibers tore his Oscar apart.

Sanders sent a second fighter into the water, and he was in turn jumped by another Oscar. Before the fighter could do any damage, it was chased away by Sanders's wingman, Lieutenant (jg) R. T. Hoppe. Hoppe had to break off his chase of this plane when three more Oscars ganged up on him. They turned out to be poor shots, but Hoppe was not, riddling one of his assailants, which then tried to ram his Wildcat before diving into the sea. A fourth fighter was smoked by Lieutenant (jg) W. E. Dickey. Trying to stagger away over Samar, this Oscar flew only a short way before disappearing in a bright fireball. Sanders destroyed another of the flammable Oscars. Now low on fuel but with five enemy planes to their credit, the jubilant VC-68 pilots returned to the *Fanshaw Bay*.[48]

Despite the evident successes of the CVE pilots, the appearance of so many enemy planes worried Kinkaid and Sprague; thus, in midmorning Kinkaid ordered TG 77.4 to reinstitute strikes against the western Visayas airfields. At 1220 a strike group of thirty-two fighters and twelve bombers was launched to hit the western Visayan islands, in particular the airfield and harbor at Bacolod on Negros. This mission succeeded in destroying six planes on the ground at Bacolod and damaging one other.[49]

Throughout the day the Japanese sent small groups of planes out in vain attempts to break through to the ships in Leyte Gulf. Virtually all of these attempts were thrown back with heavy losses to the attackers. Among the victors during the afternoon activities was VC-21's Lieutenant G. D. Mickelwait. He was leading four FM-2s over Leyte when two Zekes flashed across in front of him. The VC-21 pilots gave chase, three of them dropping their wing tanks as they did and leaving the fourth to bring up the rear while he wondered what to do with the wing tank release handle that pulled off when he attempted to use it.

One of the Zeke pilots dove away into some clouds, leaving his buddy to face the Wildcats alone. All four pilots made runs on the wildly twisting Zeke, but it was Mickelwait who scored the telling hits. His first shells ripped into the cockpit, while his last ones started the Zeke burning. The Zeke tried a low altitude split S, which brought it face to face with a mountain; the mountain won. That night aboard the *Marcus Island* there was a raucous celebration for VC-21's first score of the war.[50]

When night fell, Admiral Sprague could finally assess what his planes had done during the day. His Wildcat and Hellcat pilots had turned in a good showing, claiming fifty-four planes destroyed and twenty probably destroyed. Later the Japanese reported that forty-seven of their aircraft had failed to return from these missions over Leyte Gulf.

Aircraft losses to TG 77.4 had been minimal. Five fighters had been lost in combat and four fighters and one Avenger lost operationally. The lost Avenger had been the plane of VC-10's Lieutenant (jg) Walter A. "Bucky" Dahlen. Along with five other pilots, he had been looking for enemy vessels to the southwest. Unfortunately, they missed both Shima's and Nishimura's forces as they converged on Surigao Strait. Coming back to the *Gambier Bay,* the other pilots jettisoned their loads of 500-pounders but Dahlen elected to keep his.

According to "Mac" McClendon, the carrier's LSO, Dahlen had a tendency to "cheat" on his landings, easing the throttle back when in the groove (lined up for landing) instead of making a power-on approach all the way. Usually this caused Dahlen's plane to settle, a situation McClendon had learned to recognize and anticipate. To-day, however, Dahlen was still carrying a full load of bombs, and when he eased off on the power, the big Avenger settled dramatically. McClendon frantically waved him off, but it was too late. The Avenger's engine sputtered at the wrong time and the "Turkey" hit the ship's rounddown. Into the water went the bomber, the crew able to escape before the TBM sank.[51]

Coming up to pull the crew from the water was Commander Amos T. Hathaway's *Heermann*. It appeared that Dahlen had had a lucky escape from death, but fate can be cruel. The next day Dahlen would be on the destroyer's bridge when she charged toward the enemy, and that time there would be no escape for him.

The losses suffered during the air action, together with the eleven Hellcats and four TBMs still aboard the *Chenango* and *Saginaw Bay*, reduced TG 77.4's air strength to 290 fighters and 183 bombers. This was still more than enough to meet almost any challenge, though in view of what transpired the next day, a few more aircraft would have been welcome.[52]

Although it appeared to the escort carrier fliers that most of the action was over Leyte Gulf, the real battles were elsewhere. A little after 0800 a search plane spotted Kurita's Center Force rounding Mindoro and apparently heading for San Bernardino Strait. Upon receipt of this sighting report, Halsey recalled TG 38.1, en route to Ulithi for replenishment, and ordered TF 38's other three task groups to concentrate off the strait.

Hardly had Halsey issued his orders than TG 38.3 was hit by a series of attacks by First Combined Base Air Force planes based on Luzon. Most of these aircraft met disastrous fates, but one Judy was able to elude the prowling Hellcats and dropped a bomb that hit the light carrier *Princeton* squarely on her flight deck. At first the crew expected that to clean up the damage would be a simple matter, but this rosy view swiftly faded as the hangar deck burst into flames and bombs, torpedoes, and aircraft began to explode.

A destroyer and the cruiser *Birmingham* came alongside to help fight the fires, and for a time the flames were being beaten down. Then, shortly after noon, planes from Ozawa's Northern Force (finally making their appearance and in the process drawing Halsey's attention northward—just what the Japanese wanted) made an unsuccessful raid on TG 38.3. This was followed by a sub scare. Because of these interruptions the *Birmingham* had to pull away from the burning carrier.

When the cruiser returned to take up her firefighting efforts again, the carrier's crew appeared to have made good progress in controlling the blaze except in one area where excess bombs had been stowed. Suddenly a tremendous blast blew off most of the *Princeton*'s stern. The *Birmingham,* in line with the blast, suffered terribly. Her casualties would be far in excess of those on the *Princeton.*

It was now obvious that the carrier could not be saved, and after several abortive tries by a destroyer to sink her, the cruiser *Reno* put two torpedoes into the *Princeton*'s gasoline storage area, disintegrating the carrier. The Japanese had drawn first blood this day, but throughout the rest of the day they would do most of the dying.

While the *Princeton* and *Birmingham* were undergoing their ordeal, aircraft from TG 38.2 were jumping all over the Center Force in the Sibuyan Sea. Just before 1030 a group of twenty-one Hellcats, twelve Helldivers, and twelve Avengers opened the attacks by lancing the huge *Musashi* with a torpedo and a bomb. The cruiser *Myoko* suffered a crippling torpedo hit near her propeller shafts and had to return to Brunei. Four more attacks by planes from all three task groups would fall on the Center Force during the day. Many of the attackers concentrated on the *Musashi*, fatally holing her, although it took nineteen torpedoes and seventeen bombs to finally put her under. That evening, at 1935, she capsized and sank.

The rest of the Center Force escaped relatively unscathed in what came to be known as the Battle of the Sibuyan Sea. The *Yamato* and *Nagato* had each received two bomb hits and the *Haruna* had had five near misses, but none of these were particularly damaging. Also not particularly damaging were the Center Force's antiaircraft guns. Out of over 250 aircraft that attacked, only eighteen were shot down.

There was one more raid, albeit a minor one, on another part of the Japanese units converging on Leyte Gulf. At 0905 a search/strike group from TG 38.4 sighted Admiral Nishimura's C Force (the van of the Southern Force) in the Sulu Sea heading east. They attacked immediately but were only able to score one hit on the battleship *Fuso* and another on the destroyer *Shigure.* This was a poor showing but served to worry Nishimura about the success of his mission.

Buoyed by enthusiastic and overoptimistic reports from his pilots of tremendous destruction rained on the Center Force, Halsey was ready to write off this force. He was aided in this decision by pilot reports that Kurita had turned back to the west. What the fliers had actually seen was the milling around of ships under attack and attempting to help damaged units. But if his fliers said the Japanese had been severely damaged and were retreating, Halsey was prepared to believe it.

Kurita, indeed, did turn back west for a time, afraid of receiving more air attacks, but by 1714 he was heading once more toward San Bernardino Strait. A little over two hours later the Center Force was spotted by a night-flying TBM from the *Independence*. The word was quickly passed to Halsey. Around 2030 another *Independence* plane discovered that the Japanese ships had moved nearer to the strait.

But Halsey really wasn't interested in what the Center Force was doing because he had already bitten on the hook dangled by Ozawa's decoy force. Ozawa's carriers had been seen at 1640, and at 2022 Halsey ordered TF 38's three concentrated groups to steam north to join battle, TG 38.1 to join when it could. When TF 38 headed north, so did the *Independence,* taking her night fliers with her. There was no one to watch San Bernardino Strait.

Without anyone to stop or report it, the Center Force passed through the strait, the sides of which were bright with navigation lights. This unusual fact, noted earlier by the *Independence* fliers, was brought to Halsey's attention but he chose to ignore it. Thus, unmolested and unobserved, the Center Force steamed out into the open sea and turned southeast for a fateful meeting off Samar.

Earlier in the day, before the Northern Force was sighted, Halsey issued a battle plan stating that TF 34, composed of four battleships, several cruisers, and escorting destroyers, would be formed to deal with the Center Force if it came through the strait. The carriers would remain clear of the action. This battle plan was intended to be just a preparatory indication of future possibilities. Unfortunately, Admiral Kinkaid intercepted the message (which was not addressed to him) and took it to mean that TF 34 was actually being formed. He was not the only one to believe this: back in Hawaii Admiral Nimitz, the recipient of an information copy of the message, interpreted it as an order to form TF 34. Farther east, in Washington, the message was interpreted similarly.

Neither Nimitz nor Kinkaid was near enough to the Third Fleet two hours later to intercept a short-range TBS message from Halsey to his commanders stating that TF 34 would only be formed on his direction. Thus, Kinkaid was left with the belief that TF 34 was off San Bernardino Strait, which to his mind was a logical, perfect plan.

Perhaps Kinkaid should have become concerned where TF 34 actually was when he received a message a little after 2000 that Halsey was heading north with three groups. Halsey meant that he was taking his entire force north, his fourth group, TG 38.1, not yet having rejoined. Kinkaid took this to mean that a fourth group, in his mind TF 34, was being left behind to guard San Bernardino

Strait. In war, words can sometimes mean as much as bullets, and in this case the misinterpretation of words had an impact far beyond what a mere recitation would indicate.

Satisfied that TF 34 could handle anything coming out of the strait, Kinkaid turned his attention to the Japanese force heading toward Surigao Strait. Shortly before noon, while the air battles were still raging over Leyte Gulf, Kinkaid had alerted his ships to prepare for a night engagement. It was obvious that a major naval force, called the Southern Force but actually two—Nishimura's C Force and Shima's Second Striking Force—would try to push its way through Surigao Strait that evening. Kinkaid prepared an extremely unfriendly reception.

Situated at the northern entrance to Surigao Strait was Rear Admiral Jesse B. Oldendorf's Bombardment and Fire Support Group, which now consisted of six old (but not feeble) battleships, four heavy cruisers, four light cruisers, twenty-eight destroyers, and thirty-nine PTs. Despite a shortage of armor-piercing shells, Oldendorf's ships had more than enough power to handle the seventeen ships of the Southern Force, of which only two were battleships.

Left to the PTs was the task of opening the action that became known as the Battle of Surigao Strait. At 2250 the first three boats sighted Nishimura's ships. From that time until about 0213 on 25 October, C Force was under observation or attack by the PTs. These attacks were made with great zeal and courage, but inflicted little damage. Nevertheless, they served to harass and worry the Japanese. For many of the enemy sailors, including Admiral Nishimura, their worries would be over, permanently, in just a few hours.

Next up in the ring were the U.S. "tin cans." Roaring down both sides of the strait (two ships on the west, three on the east), the destroyers of DesRon 54 caught sight of the Japanese ships a little before 0300. Half a minute after 0300 the three destroyers on the eastern side of the strait, the *Remey*, *McGowan*, and *Melvin*, began launching torpedoes. In less than two minutes twenty-seven torpedoes were streaking toward the enemy. At least one of these hit, that being one from the *Melvin* that tore open the battleship *Fuso* and caused her to fall out of line.

The Japanese were still recovering from that attack when a second torpedo onslaught struck from the opposite side. These torpedoes had come from the *McDermut* and *Monssen* and were devastatingly effective. The *Yamashiro* was hit by one of the *Monssen*'s "fish," while no less than three destroyers were hit by the *McDermut*'s torpedoes. The *Yamagumo* blew up and sank, the *Michisio* would not be around for much longer, and the *Asagumo* had her bow blown off, in some remarkable shooting.

Still more destroyer attacks plagued Nishimura as he doggedly plodded north. The unlucky *Michisio* took another torpedo, which put her under, and the *Yamashiro* was also the recipient of a pair of torpedoes. By now the big guns of the battleships and cruisers were joining in. Having performed the notable task of "capping the enemy's T," Oldendorf was ready to take advantage of the situation. Nine minutes before 0400 the cruisers' guns opened up, followed two minutes later by the throaty roar of the battleships' 16- and 14-inchers.

There was little left to shoot at. The *Fuso* had blown up at 0338, and several of the destroyers had been sunk or were trying to retire. Only the *Yamashiro, Mogami,* and *Shigure* were left to continue north. Hammered by the punishing gunfire of the battleships and cruisers, the *Mogami* and *Yamashiro* gamely returned the fire, but this one-sided battle was quickly over. The *Yamashiro*, burning brightly, began to turn back south and pick up speed to 15 knots. Her increased speed was misleading. At 0419 she capsized and sank. Few of her crew survived, and Admiral Nishimura was not among them.

Surprisingly, the battered *Mogami* was able to start south, as was the *Shigure,* which, amazingly, had received only one hit, from a shell that failed to explode. Though the two vessels were retiring, the battle was not over because Admiral Shima's force had yet to be heard from. Shima would not contribute much to the battle, however.

As Shima's ships entered the strait, the *Abukuma* was hit by a torpedo from the *PT-137,* causing the light cruiser to fall out of formation. As he continued north, Shima soon saw the remains of the *Fuso* burning on the water. That was not a good omen. Believing the situation was out of hand, Shima delivered a half-hearted torpedo attack at 0424, which accomplished nothing, and then turned south. As his ships began their retirement, the cruiser *Nachi,* mistaking the actual course of the crippled *Mogami,* collided with the other cruiser. Nevertheless, both ships were able to continue their retirement.

For all intents the Battle of Surigao Strait was over. All that was left now was pursuit and clean-up. Under gunfire from several destroyers and cruisers, the *Asagumo* finally sank at 0721. The *Mogami* was pasted again by cruiser fire but was still able to limp south. The Japanese Southern Force had been routed and almost completely obliterated. Of Nishimura's force only the *Shigure* would survive, and of Shima's ships only the cruisers *Nachi* and *Ashigara* and four destroyers would be able to sail away from this debacle. The *Nachi* would survive only until 4 November. American casualties were amazingly light, most of them on a destroyer caught between enemy and friendly fire.

While the Southern Force was being ripped to pieces, Kurita's Center Force passed through the restricted waters of San Bernardino Strait and by 0035 was into the open waters of the Philippine Sea. Pleasantly surprised but still wary at the ease in which his ships had reached the Philippine Sea, Kurita led his force eastward before he turned southeast at 0300 to make his run toward Leyte Gulf.

It is possible that the Center Force's movements were detected by at least one of the carriers of Taffy 3. Late the previous night a *White Plains* radar operator had reported a blip on the SG surface search radar. The object was only a short distance away, but its picture was very weak and soon faded off the scope. After midnight the blip reappeared, this time much farther out but with a stronger return. Duly reporting to Captain Sullivan, who was trying to catch a few winks after an eventful day, the watch was told to "keep an eye on things."

About 0300 the target was regained, and this time a course could be plotted. The target was moving southeast toward Taffy 3 at a speed indicating that it was a surface target. Again the contact was reported to Sullivan, who, having been awakened several times in the night, was not particularly receptive to this information.

A short time after the *White Plains* went to general quarters about 0430, the contact was once more reported to the captain. This time Sullivan called down to CIC to reprimand the radar operators for reporting "ghosts." After general quarters the crew went to breakfast, the contact forgotten. Breakfast would hardly be over before a hail of gunfire fell in the midst of Taffy 3.[53]

(Whether this contact was actually the Center Force will never be known. The SG surface search radar could be unreliable. Because the course and distance match fairly closely with the Center Force's actual track, though, the tantalizing possibility remains of a missed opportunity to do something about the Japanese force.)

A little over an hour after Kurita had turned southeast, Admiral Kinkaid, still concerned about the disposition of U.S. forces in the Leyte Gulf area, radioed Halsey to ask if TF 34 was guarding San Bernardino Strait. Halsey did not receive this query for over two and a half hours, and his reply, that it was not, was not sent until Taffy 3 was already under the fire of the Center Force. Thus, unknown to both sides, Kurita's ships had clear sailing toward the transports in Leyte Gulf; clear sailing, that is, except for some thin-skinned escort carriers and their screening vessels that stood in the way.

During the night, reports of the fight in Surigao Strait had filtered down to the escort carriers. Since it appeared that the old battleships were doing a bang-up job against the Japanese, no great concern manifested itself within TG 77.4. Nevertheless, Tommy Sprague directed his three task units to have aircraft loaded with torpedoes and semi-armor-piercing (SAP) bombs in case they were needed against the retreating enemy naval units. His decision was wise.

Several of the "jeep" captains began immediately readying their ships and planes; one of these was "Bowser" Vieweg of the *Gambier Bay*. Calling together his top officers, Vieweg wanted to make sure that his crew and the VC-10 fliers would be ready for almost any event. He asked the VC-10 skipper, "Hux" Huxtable, if his pilots were up on ship identification and also if they had been briefed on torpedo dropping tactics. (The VC-10 pilots had not dropped any torpedoes for a long time.) Huxtable assured Vieweg his men were ready. Finally, he wanted to make sure that his ordnance gang would be ready to load torpedoes on short notice. Two of the four Avengers on the hangar deck not scheduled for missions the next morning were loaded with torpedoes, and two more torpedoes were placed in a full ready position. However, when at 0530 the commander support aircraft made his requests known for the day's missions, the torpedoes were taken out of the two TBMs, although their bomb bays were left fully rigged to carry torpedoes. A few hours later these torpedoes would be desperately needed.[54]

Other, but not all, CVE skippers did the same thing—some, like the *Petrof Bay*'s Kane and the *Ommaney Bay*'s Young, even making sure that all their Avengers were loaded with torpedoes. Their prescience would turn out to be of great importance on the twenty-fifth.

At 0155 Admiral Kinkaid directed the escort carriers to send out three searches at daybreak. One was to cover the sector between 340° and 030°. Picked for this job was Admiral Stump's group, Stump having received the order at 0430. The *Ommaney Bay* was ordered at 0509 to undertake this task, but in the darkness and on a rain-swept deck, the "Big O" did not finish launching a five-bomber/seven-fighter search for almost two hours.[55] Alas, this search, which could have found Kurita's ships bearing down on Taffy 3, only got off about the same time that the Japanese ships began firing on the "jeeps." Another search, by a PBY the night before, just missed the Center Force before it came out of San Bernardino Strait. These two searches, unfortunately ill-timed, could have made a difference.

Meanwhile, other missions were being readied on the carriers. Operating farthest south, Taffy 1's planes would be sent against the bedraggled remnants of the Southern Force. Next to the north, just east of Leyte Gulf, Taffy 2 would search San Bernardino Strait and provide cover over the gulf. Finally, farthest north and off southern Samar, Taffy 3 (which had been directed to have twelve Avengers armed with torpedoes and twelve more to carry 500-pound SAP bombs) would also cover the strait and Leyte Gulf.[56]

An initial strike force of nine Avengers and four fighters from the *Santee* and two torpedo-laden bombers and six Hellcats from the *Sangamon* was launched at 0545, its mission to find and sink the Surigao Strait survivors. At about 0830 this group of aircraft found Shima's force entering the Mindanao Sea from the strait. Attempting to stay up with these hastily retiring vessels was the battered *Mogami*.

To the attackers it appeared that the leading group of ships was composed of a pair of "*Fuso*-class" battleships with two "new type" destroyers as escorts. Three miles astern was a "*Tone*" cruiser with another destroyer. The identification of the cruiser was not bad—it was the *Mogami*—but the pilots' identification of the two lead ships as *Fuso*-class battleships was woefully inaccurate. These two vessels were the cruisers *Nachi* and *Ashigara*, which needed about 20,000 tons to bring them up to battleship size, although in length and appearance they resembled battleships.

With the fighters leading the way strafing to beat down the anti-aircraft fire, the torpedo planes raced in to drop their "fish" at the two cruisers. The *Santee* Avengers wound up in a poor position for an attack, coming in from dead ahead of the ships, and it is doubtful if they had any success. As they began to jink away, the Japanese flak reached out to disintegrate one of the Avengers, only a bright ball of flame and a black smear of smoke remaining to descend slowly to the water.

Off the leading cruiser's port bow bored in the pair of *Sangamon* Avengers. Despite being bumped around by the flak, both planes were able to drop their torpedoes from about 1,000 yards and escape between the lead cruiser and a destroyer. The two torpedoes ran normally, and the *Sangamon* pilots thought they saw columns of water shoot up alongside the ship. Though the torpedoes may have hit, there is no indication of this in Japanese records.

As he sped between the cruiser and destroyer, Lieutenant (jg) Harry A. Powers's turret gunner sprayed the deck of the "tin can" with a liberal number of .50-caliber shells. This apparently dampened the enemy gunners' enthusiasm enough to enable the Avenger to escape unscathed. The two TBMs rejoined and returned to Tacloban to rearm and refuel.[57]

While the *Santee* and *Sangamon* planes were going after the *Nachi* and *Ashigara*, five Wildcats and six Avengers from the *Ommaney Bay* pounced on the *Mogami*. The fighters went in first in 60-degree dives, strafing to discourage the gunners. Close behind came the TBMs spaced out in trail. As each pilot reached his drop point (approximately 2,000 feet) he salvoed his load of 500-pound SAP and general-purpose (GP) bombs. Splashes surrounded the *Mogami*, and several of the bombs may have hit the cruiser, but the end had not yet come for this well-traveled veteran of the Pacific war. Skidding and swerving to throw off the gunners' aim, the VC-75 planes raced away untouched.[58]

Forty minutes later seventeen planes pounced on the cruiser, and this time there was no escape. Several hits on a *"Fuso"*- or *"Yamato"*-class battleship were claimed by the CVE airmen, but she was only the *Mogami*, almost as indestructible as the *Yamato*. After receiving these hits, she required a torpedo from a screening destroyer to finally sink her three hours later.[59]

Meanwhile, other aircraft from the Taffies were busy on a variety of tasks. One of these proved to be "a most unfortunately timed mission."[60] For the last few days, escort carrier planes had been dropping supplies to the troops as they moved inland. This morning ten of the *Marcus Island*'s Avengers had been loaded with cans of water, boxes of K rations, and rifle ammunition to drop to 96th Division troops. Launched at 0545 for Leyte, just a bit over an hour before Japanese shells began falling about the Taffy 3 carriers, these planes would not return to the *Marcus Island* until 1030, when the Center Force was retiring toward San Bernardino Strait.[61]

By 0530 the carriers of Taffy 3, northernmost of the three CVE units, had launched a TCAP of twelve Wildcats. This was followed by an additional four Avengers and two FM-2s for ASP over the gulf. Other planes were airborne for local CAP and local ASP. Following the launch of these planes, Taffy 3's CVEs secured from general quarters and the ships' crews lined up for breakfast. The sun would be rising at 0630, but few sailors would see it because of overcast skies with numerous squalls and rain showers scudding through the area.

A short time after the sun rose, unseen by most, there came the first indication that this was not going to be an ordinary day. Over the inter–fighter director net came the unmistakable chatter of excited Japanese voices. While the officers and men of Taffy 3 digested this odd happening, they saw bursts of antiaircraft fire about twenty miles to the north. Almost immediately after this, the *Fanshaw Bay*'s radar screens registered "unidentified surface craft" just eighteen and a half miles away.

It was Kurita and his Center Force, and he was getting ready to open fire on the still unsuspecting Taffy 3.

"THEY'RE SHOOTING AT US IN TECHNICOLOR"

THE BURSTS OF antiaircraft fire seen by the men of Taffy 3 had been directed at a lone plane over the Center Force. Ensign Hans L. Jensen's TBM had been launched at 0551 from the *Kadashan Bay* on an ASP mission. About 0630 Jensen's radioman, ARM3c D. G. Lehman, saw on his radarscope a large number of blips north of what he knew were the ships of Taffy 3. Although the contact was outside his search sector, Jensen immediately headed for it through the heavy, damp clouds.

Breaking out of the clouds at 1,800 feet about twenty miles north of Taffy 3, Jensen and his crew found themselves staring in awe and horror at the Center Force as it bore down on the as-yet-unsuspecting carriers. Quickly he radioed he had spotted an enemy force of four battleships and twelve cruisers and destroyers.

The Japanese force was in four columns on a general line of bearing of 60° to 240° and was steering 170° at 20 knots. In the column farthest east was DesRon 10—the light cruiser *Yahagi*, with the destroyers *Urakaze*, *Isokaze*, *Yukikaze*, and *Nowake*. The next column was made up of the heavy cruisers of CruDiv 7—the *Kumano*, *Suzuya*, *Tone*, and *Chikuma*—followed at a distance of a bit over three miles by BatDiv 3—the *Kongo* and *Haruna*. In the third column were the two heavy cruisers of CruDiv 5—the *Haguro* and *Chokai*—followed about three miles back by BatDiv 1—the *Yamato* and *Nagato*. Finally, the last column, and the one farthest west, was composed of the ships of DesRon 2—the light cruiser *Noshiro* and the destroyers *Kishinami*, *Okinami*, *Hayashimo*, *Akishimo*, *Hamanami*, *Fujinami*, and *Shimakaze*.[1]

Seeing the Avenger looking them over, the Japanese gunners let loose an intense but inaccurate barrage. This was the antiaircraft fire seen by Taffy 3. As the Japanese vessels opened fire on the escort carriers, Jensen glided in to drop three 350-pound depth bombs from only 1,200 feet on a heavy cruiser, probably the *Haguro*, close enough to splash water on her deck. As Jensen retreated, his gunner, AMM3c M. M. Soter, lashed out at the cruiser with his guns. The flak continued to be inaccurate until Jensen was almost back in the clouds; then a couple of shells exploded close enough to rock the Avenger violently.

Concealed in the edge of the clouds, Jensen saw one of the battleships launch a Pete floatplane, which soon headed in his direction. Jensen waited until the Pete was almost directly underneath him, then dove out of the clouds to pounce on it. His two .50-caliber wing guns chewed up the floatplane's wings but didn't down it. As he pulled out, Jensen began a roll and found himself upside down over the Pete. In this position Sotar began firing and tallied more hits on the enemy plane. The Pete scooted back to its battleship, which had no time to stop and pick it up amid the day's fast-moving events, so this plane played no further part in the battle. Thus Jensen may have had a two-pronged effect; he sighted the enemy force first, albeit with no time to spare, and he may have prevented the Japanese from using a spotting plane to maximize their gunfire. Later in the day, following a short stay at Tacloban, Jensen would be over the Center Force once more to drop bombs on the enemy ships.[2]

The appearance of Jensen's plane and the inaccurate fire of the Japanese gunners did not please Admiral Kurita. The sinking of his flagship, the *Atago*, in Palawan Passage on 23 October, with his subsequent series of ship changes and the heavy air attacks that sank the *Musashi* the next day, had not been particularly beneficial to Kurita's state of mind. Now it appeared that his force was going to get pounded once again. Kurita was worried.

Suddenly lookouts on the *Yamato*, Kurita's new flagship, reported ships about 30,000 yards to the south. Completely surprised by this sighting, the Japanese variously reported seeing battleships and cruisers in the force and some even insisted that the carriers that could be seen were Japanese.[3] Contributing to this inability to identify the ships was the fact that the Japanese did not have the right photographs of the U.S. escort carriers. Unable to identify the carriers and sorely let down by Japanese air reconnaissance efforts, Kurita believed he had run into units of TF 38.

Just a short time prior to this sighting, Kurita had ordered his force to redeploy from a columnar cruising formation to a circular antiaircraft disposition, this entailing a course change from 170° to 110°. The Center Force was in the process of changing formations when Taffy 3 was sighted. Surprised and shaken by the sudden appearance of U.S. vessels, Kurita gave a disastrous order, "General attack!" Instead of ordering his heavy ships to form a battle line, with the destroyers forging ahead for torpedo attacks, Kurita allowed his ships to enter the battle "every man for himself." Before it had even started, the Japanese attack broke down. The resulting undisciplined charge would be a major factor in the eventual salvation of Taffy 3.

Jensen's report of the Center Force had been directed at the *Natoma Bay,* Taffy 2's flagship. Ziggy Sprague, on his own flagship, the *Fanshaw Bay,* only received a garbled transmission. Then Sprague got a report from the *St. Lo*'s Ensign William C. Brooks, who had seen the Japanese just moments after Jensen and like him also attacked just with depth bombs, dropping them on a cruiser.[4]

Brooks's report, "Enemy surface force of four battleships, seven cruisers, and eleven destroyers sighted 20 miles northwest of your task group and closing in on you at 30 knots!" annoyed Sprague, who believed that the young aviator had seen Halsey's ships.

"Air plot, tell him to check his identification!" Sprague growled over his intercom.

Brooks quickly sent a less-than-reassuring reply: "Identification of enemy force confirmed. Ships have pagoda masts."[5] If further confirmation was needed, lookouts on the CVEs began reporting the distinctive "pagoda" masts of Japanese battleships and cruisers looming on the horizon.

Sprague ordered his ships to change course to 090° and to increase speed to 16 knots. This was quickly followed by an order to make maximum speed, for the CVEs a breathtaking 17–18 knots. At this time the carriers were in a roughly circular formation 2,500 yards in diameter, while the screening destroyers and destroyer escorts were patrolling an outer circle about 6,000 yards from the formation's center. On the easterly course the carriers would be heading almost into the wind, and their planes could be launched without backtracking. More course changes would be made throughout the battle, these describing a rough arc curving to the southwest as Taffy 3 tried to avoid encirclement by the Japanese and also to meet Admiral Oldendorf, who it was hoped would be steaming north to help.

Unfortunately, it would have taken close to three hours for Oldendorf's ships to reach Taffy 3, even *if* he could have gotten them together. Several of his cruisers and a number of destroyers were in

Victor at Samar: Rear Admiral Clifton A. F. Sprague. (National Archives)

Surigao Strait chasing the survivors of the night's slaughter. Additionally, fuel and ammunition were in short supply, items that would be needed if Oldendorf did meet Kurita. In any event, the old battleships played no part in this action.

But these were things that Sprague had no knowledge of. Right now he had more serious concerns. At 0655 Sprague ordered "Stand by to launch all planes for attack on enemy fleet 15 miles astern." This was quickly followed by "Launch all planes as soon as possible."[6] Deck crews working furiously to load and send off their aircraft broke many launch records. A minute after his launch order, Sprague, still harboring the thought that the ships might be American, cautioned his pilots to identify the ships before attacking.

At 0658 the *Yamato* opened fire, the *White Plains* estimating the distance at 29,200 yards.[7] Towering geysers of water sprouted astern of the carriers. Immediately a plain-language call for help went out. To the south the other two Taffies heard the plea and, after securing permission from Admiral Kinkaid, began launching everything that could fly. At this time, though, there weren't many planes to send. A number of Taffy 1's aircraft were attacking the remnants of the Southern Force, while Taffy 2's planes were on missions over Leyte. It would take time before either force could throw its full weight into the fray. Eventually, though, Taffy 2 would contribute the majority of the aircraft sorties in the battle.

Upon receiving Ziggy Sprague's plea for help, Kinkaid sent a plain-language dispatch to Halsey at 0707 informing him of the situation and requesting help. Just a few minutes before, in reply to a query he had made at 0412 asking if TF 34 was guarding San Bernardino Strait, Kinkaid had received from Halsey the shocking news that TF 34 was going north with the fast carriers. Halsey would not receive Kinkaid's entreaty until 0822. Eighteen minutes after his first message, Kinkaid reinforced it with the statement that Oldendorf's battleships were low on ammunition. (This was not completely true. As Morison points out, the battlewagons still had enough armor-piercing and high-capacity ammunition left to inflict a goodly amount of damage, though not enough for a drawn-out action.)[8]

It would take almost two hours, until 0922, for this last message to reach Halsey. Another message, sent at 0727 and received by Halsey at 0900, simply asked, "Where is Lee? Send Lee!" (Lee was Vice Admiral Willis A. Lee, the veteran battleship commander who had been designated to lead TF 34.)

Even Ziggy Sprague got in a message to Halsey at 0735 telling of the attack on his ships by battleships and heavy cruisers. Message after message flowed from Kinkaid to Halsey requesting help and proclaiming the situation critical. But all that Halsey did (still being intent on destroying the Northern Force) was to order Vice Admiral John S. McCain's TG 38.1, then en route to Ulithi for replenishment, to return as quickly as possible. Halsey believed that there

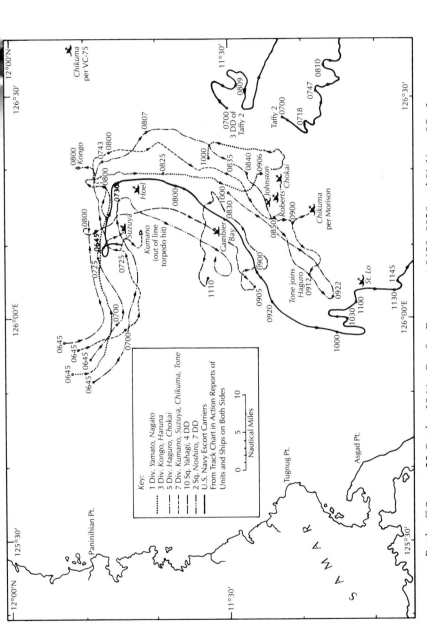

Battle off Samar, 25 October 1944—Gunfire Engagement 0658–0930 and Sinking of St. Lo

Chikuma
per VC-75

11°30'

0700
0809
0700
3 DD of
Taffy 2

0747

Taffy 2
0700
0718

0810

0807

0800
Kongo
0743
0800
0800

0800
0825

1000

Hoel
0730
0835
0840
0906

Johnston
Suzuya
0800
Roberts Chokai
Kumano
(out of line
torpedo hit)
0725

0645
0800
Chikuma
per Morison

0700
0900
Gambier
Bay
1000
0830
0850

Tone joins
Haguro
0912

0700
1110

0905
0900
0922

0645
0645
0645

0920

St. Lo
1145

0645
0645

1130

0700
1030
1100

1000

Key:
1 Div. Yamato, Nagato
3 Div. Kongo, Haruna
5 Div. Haguro, Chokai
7 Div. Kumano, Suzuya, Chikuma, Tone
10 Sq. Yahagi, 4 DD
2 Sq. Noshiro, 7 DD
U.S. Navy Escort Carriers
From Track Chart in Action Reports of
Units and Ships on Both Sides

0   5   10
Nautical Miles

Paninihian Pt.

Tugnug Pt.

Asgad Pt.

S A M A R

were enough planes on the CVEs to hold off Kurita until Oldendorf's battleships arrived. He had no idea, of course, of how poorly
armed some of these aircraft were or at just how close quarters the
battle was being fought.

It would take a message from Nimitz, a message that was misinter-
preted, to change Halsey's mind.

With the enemy shells beginning to creep up on his carriers, at
0701 Sprague ordered his ships to make smoke, which they did with
abandon. Black funnel smoke mingled with the white chemical
smoke from smoke generators. (Some flattops were even using spare
generators taken from aircraft.) The smokescreen trailed behind the
ships, lying low in the hot and heavy air.

Aboard every ship in Taffy 3, officers and men stared northward
with dread at the Japanese fleet. But not everything was doom and
gloom. Aboard the *White Plains* a pair of signalmen watched as the
enemy ships opened fire. "I can't read their signals, but they certainly
send a lot of dashes," said one signalman. "Yeah," his buddy replied
drily, "and they are likely to be periods by the time they get here!"[9]

One of the *White Plains*'s officers began to chew gum in earnest.
The day before, he had bought a carton of gum in the ship's store.
Today he had brought the gum topside, intending to share it with
others. But when the shells started falling about the carrier, he began to pop stick after stick of the gum into his mouth. After the
battle he discovered that the entire carton had been chewed, although he had not shared one stick of gum with anyone else and he
could not recall spitting any out.[10]

On the *Fanshaw Bay* Admiral Sprague's staff was able to smile a bit
as they heard Admiral Stump trying to reassure Sprague over the
TBS (Talk-Between-Ships). "Don't be alarmed, Ziggy," Stump radioed, his voice growing louder and higher-pitched as he spoke. "Remember, we're back of you! Don't get excited! Don't do anything
rash!"[11]

On the flank nearest the Japanese, the *Fanshaw Bay* and *White
Plains* were the first to bear the brunt of their fire. The enemy was
using dye marker to help spot the fall of their shells (the *Yamato*'s
were colored pink and the *Kongo*'s yellow), and gaily-colored plumes
of pink, red, yellow, green, blue, and purple-tinted water began to
rise about the carriers. Cried one sailor on the *White Plains*, "They're
shooting at us in Technicolor!"[12]

This Technicolor shooting came perilously close to the *White
Plains*. Several times she was straddled as she furiously launched
aircraft. At 0704 a salvo "measured the carrier as calipers, diagonally

The Gambier Bay *and a pair of destroyer escorts lay down a smokescreen as the Center Force bears down on Taffy 3. Hank Pyzdrowski's TBM will be catapulted off pilotless. Photo taken from the* Kalinin Bay. *(National Archives)*

from the port quarter to the starboard bow, four shells dropping microscopically close forward and two aft."[13] Water splashed over the ship. One of the shells exploded beneath the surface under the carrier's stern, shaking and twisting her violently and causing Captain Sullivan to report, erroneously, that his ship had been hit.

On the flight deck an FM-2 jumped its chocks, and its spinning propeller chewed three feet off the wing of the fighter ahead. Men were knocked off their feet and loose gear flung about. In the engine rooms the "black gang" (engine-room crew) found themselves in semi-darkness, soot and dust flying around. The most serious casualty was the rupture of the canvas expansion joints in the blower ducts supplying air for the forced draft of number 3 and 4 boilers, this almost causing a loss of steam pressure to the starboard main engine. With quick thinking and hard work, the damage was patched within fifteen minutes. To compensate for the reduced air supply, the fuel pumps were opened wide, which maintained speed on the starboard shaft but also caused huge amounts of black smoke to belch from the flattop's stacks. Of course, at this time this was no real problem because every ship was laying as dense a smokescreen as possible. When the damage was repaired, the ship's crew swore that the ship leaped forward as the forced draft kicked in and maximum speed was attained.[14]

Additionally, the ship lost all electrical power for several minutes, as well as steering control. With the steering loss, the *White Plains* staggered about like a drunk. This may have been a blessing, because the enemy, seeing the carrier seemingly out of control and believing the smoke pouring from her stacks to be caused by the shellfire, shifted their fire to other targets.

Steering control was soon regained and the five remaining undamaged fighters on the flight deck were launched. (The ship had launched four FM-2s earlier for TCAP, one was unavailable on the hangar deck, and two had just been damaged.) Four Avengers that had been loaded with depth bombs had their loads refitted with nose contact fuzes, and these planes were also sent off. Two other Avengers in the hangar were loaded with torpedoes, but almost three hours passed before these planes could be launched.[15]

When the Japanese believed that the *White Plains* was done for, they shifted fire to the *St. Lo.* Two salvos landed dangerously close ahead of the carrier, the first series of four splashes falling in a line beginning 200 yards slightly off her starboard bow, while a second group of four shells landed the same distance off her port bow. In spite of the *Gambier Bay*'s loss later and the *Kalinin Bay*'s ordeal, Japanese gunnery throughout the action was not particularly good, with much water churned around by the tremendous amount of metal being flung at the carriers but surprisingly few hits scored. Perhaps their shooting, in very compact patterns, was too good. A little looser pattern covering a larger area might have brought more hits.[16]

Sprague could see that his force was being overtaken by the enemy. He didn't see how Taffy 3 could last much longer. Then Mother Nature intervened. A heavy rain squall loomed just ahead, and Sprague guided his ships into its dark, wet sanctuary, the ships entering between 0706 and 0715. There, Taffy 3 was afforded almost fifteen minutes of respite. While hiding in the rain, Admiral Sprague ordered a course change from 090° to 110°. This was the first of several course changes that would bring Taffy 3 back to the southwest, heading for help coming, it was hoped, from Leyte Gulf.

As Taffy 3 began its slow turn back to the southwest, Kurita kept his ships heading almost due east. Theoretically, an axis of 110° was maintained until the Center Force was due north of Taffy 3, but practically, because of evasive maneuvers to escape the air and destroyer attacks, most of Kurita's ships were steering almost due east between 0706 and 0750. Because of this divergence in courses, the range opened, and this, coupled with the need for Kurita's ships to resort to radar rangefinding, caused the Japanese gunfire to fall off in volume and accuracy.

While the carriers were in the scant safety of the rain squall, the first attacks by the Taffy 3 planes fell on the enemy. By 0730 the carriers had launched 95 aircraft (not including those already on missions):

Carriers	Aircraft Launched
Gambier Bay	10 FM-2s, 8 TBMs (two with no bombs, three with 2 × 500-lb GP bombs each, two with 2 × 350-lb depth bombs armed only with hydrostatic fuzes, one with a torpedo but only 35 gallons of gas)
Fanshaw Bay	1 FM-2, 11 TBMs (ten with 500-lb SAP bombs, one with 2 × 350-lb. depth bombs)
St. Lo	15 FM-2s, 4 TBMs (two with 8 × 100-lb GP bombs, one with no bombs, one with an unknown loading)
White Plains	5 FM-2s, 4 TBMs (with 350-lb depth bombs armed with contact nose fuzes)
Kalinin Bay	10 FM-2s, 10 TBMs (three with 500-lb GP bombs and 8 × 5-in rockets, six with 10 × 100-lb GP bombs and 8 × 5-in rockets, one with machine gun ammunition only)
Kitkun Bay	11 FM-2s, 6 TBMs (with 4 × 500-lb. SAP bombs each)[17]

More aircraft would be launched after 0730, but these planes, plus the ones already airborne on CAP and ASP, would make the initial air attacks.

By the very nature of the action, these attacks were made piecemeal; one, two, or three aircraft at a time with little coordination between attacks. But not much else could be done; the pilots didn't have time for proper rendezvous, and the suddenness of the onslaught had prevented any planning. Nevertheless, the planes darted in like a swarm of angry bees to sting and sting again.

"Hux" Huxtable had been in the Gambier Bay's wardroom waiting for breakfast when he heard the general alarm. Figuring it was just a warning of another mission into the Sulu Sea, Huxtable waited because he was hungry and was not going anywhere without at least some juice and toast. Suddenly VC-10's personnel officer ran in yelling, "Captain, you better get up to the ready room in a hurry! They are already manning the planes!" Huxtable took off at a full gallop, still unaware of what was going on.

Grabbing his plotting board, Huxtable ran for his plane. As he clambered into his Avenger, he asked his plane captain if the bomber had a load. When informed that the plane was unarmed, he told the man to notify Buzz Borries, the ship's air officer, that he needed a bomb load; he didn't see any use in going anywhere without bombs. Looking up at the island, he saw Borries move forward to talk to

Captain Vieweg. Vieweg made a big sweeping motion with his arm as though to say, "Get 'em off!"

About this time what sounded like a big rifle shot resounded next to Huxtable's left ear. Looking in that direction, he saw large splashes next to the *White Plains*. Now he knew what was so urgent. "I was more than ready to get on the catapult," he said later.[18] Three TBMs were shot off ahead of Huxtable, and then he was launched. As soon as he was airborne he called the *Fanshaw Bay* to ask what his orders were. The reply was short and simple: "Attack immediately."

After the first four Avengers had been catapulted, three more were brought up from the hangar deck. The first one waddled onto the catapult and Lieutenant (jg) William Gallagher and his crew scrambled in. "Wait! Wait! It's got no gas!" screamed the plane captain. Gallagher's plane had only thirty-five gallons in its tanks, far below its 300–500-gallon capacity. But there was no time for it to be fueled. Vieweg signaled a launch. Nodding his head and waving his hand, Gallagher took off, made a left turn, and headed for the Japanese ships.

The next Avenger in line was fully gassed and was carrying a torpedo. Lieutenant (jg) Robert E. Weatherholt and his crew climbed in and waited for the "cat shot." In the cockpit Weatherholt sat, calmly smoking a cigarette. Just before the catapult officer gave the launch signal, Weatherholt took a last drag from his cigarette, flicked it from the cockpit, and grinned at the deck crew as he took off.

Hank Pyzdrowski and his crew were supposed to take the last Avenger, but when the big plane was hooked up to the catapult, there was a delay. Impatient to get going, Pyzdrowski yelled, "She's charged! Let 'er go!" He looked up at the bridge, where Borries was pointing at the ship's ensign. To keep from being hit by the gunfire, Captain Vieweg had changed course, and now there was little wind over the deck.

Jumping from his plane, Pyzdrowski ran to the bridge to plead with Borries to launch him. "Wait" was the only answer. Disgustedly, Pyzdrowski ran back to his plane and ordered his crewmen out. He'd fly this mission alone. But again there was the numbing wait as the shell splashes continued to pop up uncomfortably close to the ship.

Pyzdrowski once more climbed from his cockpit. Avengers had been catapulted in a dead calm before. He could do it now. As he ran up to Borries, the air officer pointed at the catapult. The pilot-less Avenger was being shot off. Looking just like a cat shot should, the big plane rose into the sky and flew for a few seconds. Then it fell off on a wing and went into the sea. It was the *Gambier Bay*'s last launch.

Meanwhile, Huxtable was leading his men against the Center Force. As he broke out of some low clouds, Huxtable saw four cruisers slicing through the water, with four battleships farther back in the gloom. Pulling back up in the soup, he led his small force through the clouds to a point where he figured he would be near the cruisers. His navigation was on the mark. Popping back out of the clouds, Huxtable saw the cruisers dead ahead, his planes approaching from their starboard side.

The sky was filled with the angry red lines of tracers weaving randomly as they sought the planes, punctuated with the sudden swirls of flak bursts, some black, some of various colors. Breaking to the left, Huxtable dove for the trailing cruiser at 190 knots. He pressed in until he was about 2,000 yards from it. Without any bombs and not a kamikaze, Huxtable decided to pull out. He retired to 4,000 yards, figuring the enemy wouldn't waste any shells on him at that distance. That daydream was suddenly shattered when five different-colored flak bursts appeared just 150 yards in front of his Avenger, Huxtable flying through the smoke of the middle burst. During this first attack on the cruisers, Huxtable saw one near miss on the second cruiser in line.

Huxtable radioed Admiral Sprague and informed him that Taffy 3's best course appeared to be south. There was no reply, but Sprague had his hands full. Checking in with the *Gambier Bay*, Huxtable was told to go to Tacloban to rearm. Not sure there were any supplies of worth there, Huxtable returned to making his dummy runs, opening his bomb bay doors to feign torpedo drops, until about 0900, when he finally headed for the beach. These dummy runs by Huxtable and by many other "jeep" pilots proved to be extremely unsettling to the Japanese and were one factor in causing them not to press their attacks.

While Huxtable was preparing to make another run, Bill Gallagher joined him. Gallagher's engine was smoking heavily and his TBM was holed in several places. By this time Gallagher must have been almost out of gas. Nevertheless, he had flown directly for the enemy, dropped his torpedo against a cruiser, and was heading for Tacloban. He didn't make it. When last seen, he was setting his Avenger down in the water. Sadly, this gallant pilot and his equally gallant crew were never recovered.

Lieutenant Henry B. Bassett had been on his squadron commander's wing when he dove on the cruisers, but when Huxtable went for the trailing cruiser, Bassett went for the lead ship, a *Mogami*-class vessel. The cruiser was wiggling and weaving through the water as Bassett was in his dive, red tendrils of flak spouting from all over her superstructure. Just as he dropped his first 500-pounder, his TBM shuddered as gunfire ripped through it. Quickly dropping his second bomb, Bassett beat a fast retreat into the clouds. Both bombs apparently missed. When Bassett came back out of the clouds, he found that his Avenger was sporting a large ragged hole in its starboard horizontal stabilizer. The plane was still flying fine, however, and Bassett headed for the beach, landing at Dulag a bit after 1100.

Launched ahead of Huxtable, Ensigns Robert L. Crocker and William C. Shroyer joined up with the skipper to see what they could do against the Center Force. Crocker couldn't do much, not carrying any bombs either, but his dry runs were effective in drawing fire onto him instead of onto the planes with some heavier armament. When he landed at Dulag he had a hole in his left wing and his instruments had been knocked out. To top his morning off, a fighter ran into his TBM on the ground and damaged its propeller.

Shroyer did have some bombs, two 500-pounders, and he was able to use them to some effect. Because of the low clouds, his first run was just a strafing attack, and he backed off when bracketed by antiaircraft fire. Soon he found himself over a *Tone*-class cruiser. At least a dozen Wildcats were raking the vessel with machine-gun fire. Shroyer pushed over in a shallow glide and dropped his bombs, these landing on the cruiser's stern. A pilot from another squadron confirmed the hits. Sometime later, when headed for Dulag, Shroyer would again pass over this cruiser, by then lying dead in the water.[19]

Other VC-10 fliers were also making their presence known to the Japanese. Lieutenant (jg) Charles J. Dugan had been one of the first fighter pilots to take off, over a 40-mm mount instead of straight up the deck. He wondered why everyone was in such a hurry; then he saw the Japanese ships. Next he wondered where the "rich kids" (the fast carrier pilots) were. "This is their kind of work," he thought. "We haven't been hired to fight the whole Jap fleet by ourselves."

A hunter in his youth, Dugan always went after the biggest game—and today that was the *Yamato*. As he put it, attacking a battleship was on-the-job training because "the books and manuals that [he] had read on how to be a fighter pilot did not anywhere tell you where you should shoot a battleship with .50-caliber machine guns to mortally wound it."

Dugan decided that he had to get something like this monster battleship between the eyes, right in the bridge area. He dove on the

Yamato and began to fire. All about the bridge he could see his shells twinkling like Christmas-tree lights as they hit. At 900 feet he yanked back on his stick, and his Wildcat shot into the air, blacking him out in the process. Dugan figured that he hadn't hit many people on the bridge but he certainly had taken "a lot of paint off their front door."

Several more times he returned to strafe the ships, blacking out each time he pulled up. Antiaircraft fire followed him into the clouds but never hit his plane. Dugan got a little cocky then, saying later, "It made a lot better war of it knowing the bastards couldn't shoot." At last out of ammunition and after making a few dry runs on the ships, he headed for Tacloban.[20]

Many of the pilots, out of ammunition, returned again and again to make dry runs on the Japanese ships, often forcing them to turn away from these attacks and thus keeping them from drawing closer to the "jeeps." But VC-10 didn't have a monopoly on this type of activity today. Virtually every squadron was doing the same thing.

As one Japanese officer said of the harassment that the Center Force was getting, "The attack was almost incessant, but the number of planes at any one instant was few. The bombers and torpedo planes were very aggressive and skillful and the coordination was impressive; even in comparison with the great experience of American attack that we already had, this was the most skillful work of your planes."[21]

The *Fanshaw Bay* launched twelve planes, joined by four more that had been on CAP. Racing ahead, the four CAP fighters immediately began a series of strafing passes on the leading battleships and cruisers. Most attacks were made in 60-degree dives, opening fire at about 4,000 feet and pulling out at 1,000 feet. Heavy antiaircraft fire met the Wildcats, but the gunners were poor deflection shooters and most of their fire exploded well behind the planes.

Lieutenant Ray Anderson sprayed the bridge of a battleship with machine-gun fire. No damage could be seen, but he and his buddies returned again and again to strafe. The lack of any observable damage galled the fighter pilots. "I would have felt much less insignificant," Anderson lamented later, "had I had four 5-inch H.E. [high explosive] rockets on zero length launchers or one or two 250-lb. bombs. As it was, I jettisoned about 450 pounds of gasoline, which I would gladly have traded for the above."[22]

In a few minutes the rest of the VC-68 planes showed up. Dick Rogers, the CO, had led his group first northwest, then north at 8,000 feet through the wet, slate-colored broken clouds. After turning north, Rogers dropped down to a thousand feet to see if he could see the Japanese ships. Through the mist and haze he saw a group of six cruisers and battleships. Quickly he radioed the rest of his planes (which had stayed high) to come down. The time was approximately 0735.

Like most of the early attacks, these attacks were largely uncoordinated (despite the Japanese officer's perceptions) and involved planes striking from every direction. Led by fighters strafing, eight TBMs pounced on a pair of heavy cruisers, probably the *Haguro* and *Chokai*. Black, purple, yellow, and green bursts of flak speckled the sky, but these did not deter the bombers. Although carrying only two depth bombs, Ensign George F. Smith dove on the second cruiser in line. The flak buffeted the Avenger as it screamed down, but could not knock it off course. At 2,000 feet Smith released his depth bombs, then kept diving until he was just above the water. Looking back, Smith saw his bombs explode just off the cruiser's port bow. None of his comrades appeared to have scored, but with all the violent maneuvering by both planes and ships, it was hard to tell.

Seeing a battleship ahead, Smith opened up with his wing guns. As he zipped by the battlewagon, his two crewmen laced its decks with their turret and ventral guns. With nothing left to drop, Smith headed back to his ship to pick up some more bombs. Unable to land on the *Fanshaw Bay*, he homed in on Taffy 2's *Marcus Island*, where he and six other wandering Avengers were taken aboard. In a fast and furious rearming, the TBMs were loaded with torpedoes and sent out again.

While Smith was attacking one cruiser, Lieutenant William J. Slone was picking on another. Slone saw a couple of battleships entering a rain squall, followed by the *Yahagi* and her four destroyers. Before they could fade into the mist, Slone was upon them. Swooping down from 8,000 feet, he began his run. Flak bursts blossomed all around his plane, and when he passed through 4,000 feet, his Avenger was staggered by a hit that almost severed the main wing spar. Nonetheless, Slone pressed on to drop three 500-pounders (one hung up) from 3,000 feet. Although his gunners reported that all three bombs hit the *Yahagi* and another flier said that this ship later sank, it was not the *Yahagi*. She survived to be sunk alongside the *Yamato* in April 1945.

(Many reports of "hits" were no such thing. In the violent and fast-moving action, numerous hits were claimed and several ships were claimed sunk. Not all these claims were true, but that is because so much was taking place at one time that most pilots couldn't be sure of what they saw. However, this work generally describes these attacks just as the pilots saw them because of the impossibility of reconciling their accounts.)

Rogers's other pilots were attacking everything they could see. Lieutenant (jg) Jerry J. Jacoby claimed a 500-pound bomb hit on a cruiser, and Lieutenant (jg) Harvey L. Lively claimed three hits on the same vessel ten minutes later. This ship was probably the *Suzuya*, these attacks causing her to veer away from the CVEs and to reduce speed. Another pilot dropped a bomb on one of the battleships, doing little damage.

By 0805 the VC-68 Avengers had expended all their armament and were on their way back to the carrier to rearm. All of the twenty-odd fighters that were then over the Japanese fleet were directed to make continuous strafing runs on the ships, especially on those closest to the carriers. For about forty minutes, until 0845, the fighters harassed the onrushing vessels, often forcing them to take violent evasive action and consequently slowing their pursuit.[23]

These strafing (and dry) runs throughout the battle had a greater effect on the Japanese than their attackers had expected. The psychological damage to the Japanese was considerably more than the physical damage (though that was great enough) and was taking its toll. Nevertheless, the cruisers creeping up on the "jeeps'" port flank were drawing nearer the vulnerable carriers.

At 0530 the *St. Lo* had launched six planes for both LASP and TASP. Two of these planes, on TASP, never took part in the battle. The other four were in it from the beginning. As mentioned earlier, Bill Brooks had sighted the Center Force shortly after Hans Jensen and had darted in to drop his depth bombs alongside either the *Tone* or *Chikuma*. A short time later the other three pilots on LASP, after a hasty sweep of their sectors, showed up to plant their depth bombs alongside several other ships. Two of the pilots landed on the *Marcus Island* for rearming, one on the *Ommaney Bay*, and the last went to Tacloban.

At 0718, when the *St. Lo* was in the middle of the squall, she began launching four TBMs and fifteen FM-2s. The fighters proceeded to beat up what ships they could with their .50-calibers before finally heading for the beach. Meanwhile, VC-65's skipper, Lieutenant Commander R. M. Jones, claimed three hits on a battleship; Lieutenant (jg) J. R. Gore strung five "centuries" across the deck of a cruiser, then strafed as long as his ammunition lasted; Lieutenant (jg) L. E. Waldrop made eight bombing, strafing, and rocket runs on four cruisers and a destroyer; and Lieutenant (jg) Kash (without bombs or rockets) made several strafing runs until he also ran out of ammunition. Waldrop headed back toward the carriers, while the others turned toward Dulag or Tacloban.[24]

Only five fighters and four TBMs were able to be launched from the *White Plains* when the shells began falling. Four FM-2s and five Avengers had been launched earlier for missions over Leyte. Just as the planes were being sent off, a salvo landed alongside the carrier, causing two fighters to crunch together so they could not be launched.

The fighter pilots did what every other fighter pilot was doing that day—they strafed. As Lieutenant (jg) Solen N. Hales said later, "I couldn't find anything else to do so I made some strafing runs on a battleship." However, as the squadron CO pointed out, "There are no confirmed reports of enemy battleships sinking as a result of these strafing attacks."[25]

Led by Lieutenant (jg) Walter P. Owens, the four VC-4 Avengers attacked what was evidently the *Haguro* as she and the other cruisers were closing in on the CVEs. From 8,000 feet the four planes peeled off in an echelon formation to glide to 6,000 feet preparatory to the final dive. From there, one after another, the TBMs pushed over in 50-degree dives directly for the cruiser. After dropping their bombs, all planes made gut-wrenching pullups and scooted away. Two of the TBM crews eventually wound up on the *St. Lo* in just enough time to have her sunk from under them. All survived and were recovered uninjured.[26]

The *Kalinin Bay*'s contribution to these initial attacks was a launch completed by 0725 of ten FM-2s (three more were launched about twenty-five minutes later) and ten TBMs. Because of the rain and the smokescreen, the rendezvous took a bit longer than usual, actually taking place on the run toward the Japanese ships. Radio failure caused Lieutenant Commander Bill Keighley, VC-3's commander, to turn over the lead of the "torpeckers" to Lieutenant Patsy Capano.

Fifteen minutes after taking off, Capano saw four cruisers, two battleships, and several destroyers churning south at high speed. Immediately he gave the order to attack, the VC-3 planes pouncing on the vessels from out of the broken clouds. Keighley used his Avenger as a dive-bomber, dropping his "centuries" diagonally across a *Tone*-class cruiser. Three of these were claimed as hits, but being so light, probably did little damage. Capano dropped his bombs with unknown results on the leading cruiser of the formation, then joined with Keighley to strafe the cruisers. Keighley and his gunners continued to strafe whatever ships they could see, often joining whoever seemed interested in doing the same thing, until about 1130, when he left for Dulag.

Picking on the *Haruna* was Ensign Richard G. Altman. When he was directly over the battlewagon, he pushed over in a steep dive-bombing attack. First he fired four 5-inch rockets, these hitting the ship amidships. He followed these up with two 500-pound GP bombs. One just nicked the *Haruna*'s bow, while the other exploded off her bow. After he pulled out, Altman looked around for another target and saw a cruiser slicing through the water. From 1,000 feet he fired his last rockets, later claiming two hits on the cruiser's superstructure. Altman also headed for the beach to rearm.

Following behind Keighley's and Capano's group were four more VC-3 TBMs. They attacked the same group of ships at almost the same time, about 0750. Lieutenant Walter D. Crockett made a run on the *Haruna* from astern, dropping his bombs from 2,500 feet. Pulling back up into the clouds, Crockett did not see if his bombs had hit. What he had seen was an Avenger from another squadron suddenly turn into a fiery comet and a second TBM plunge into the water.

The other members of Crockett's division picked out other vessels. First, Lieutenant (jg) Earl L. Archer, Jr. strafed a destroyer, then took on the two leading cruisers. Between 4,500 and 3,000 feet he toggled out his bombs on the second cruiser, continuing his dive toward the lead vessel. He walked his eight rockets up the cruiser's deck and could see pieces of the ship flung into the air by the hits.

Ensigns G. Neilan Smith and James R. Zeitvogel rocketed several ships, and Smith also plunked a couple of 500-pounders alongside a cruiser. Before retiring, they shot off all their ammunition at the weaving and twisting vessels. At 1015 Crockett and Smith landed on the *White Plains*, while Archer and Zeitvogel headed for Tacloban. The next day Archer would become the Dulag LSO, conditions there being so bad that carrier approach techniques were necessary.

VC-3's fighter pilots made pass after pass on the ships, most of these in almost sixty-five-degree dives with pullouts right on the water. With so many aircraft going so many directions, unit cohesion was soon lost, and most of the runs were made alone or by joining whoever was closest.

Although most of this action was plane against ship, the VC-3 fliers did manage to get in some air-to-air combat. Ensigns George A. Heinmiller and Geoffrey B. King each picked off a Val that had stumbled into their paths during this wild and woolly affair. Most of the fighter pilots went to Tacloban, where the increasingly muddy airstrip was becoming more unsafe all the time. Three of the FM-2s crashed on landing and were complete washouts, one Wildcat was lost in a ditching, and four other aircraft were left in various states of disrepair.[27]

On the *Kitkun Bay* flight quarters were sounded "on the double" at 0655. Dick Fowler's men were out of the ready room and into their planes so fast that the first fighter was launched only about a minute later. By the time the last of the Avengers leapt off the flattop's deck, the Technicolor geysers were sprouting all around. The VC-5 airmen had no trouble finding the Center Force: if they made a 180-degree turn and flew for a couple of minutes, there were the Japanese.

The fighters led the way with almost vertical dives on the ships, pulling out at wavetop level, then darting in again to make more passes. Angry red lights that lit up each ship like a pinball machine showed that not all of the exposed gunners had been chopped down by the machine-gun fire. With the heavy cruisers closing in off the *Gambier Bay*'s port quarter, most of the fighter attacks were directed against these vessels. Lieutenant Paul B. Garrison had made twelve firing runs and eight dummy passes when a large-caliber shell tore through his left wing and flipped him on his back. Sensing that his luck might be running out (as well as his gas, which was down to twenty gallons), Garrison turned for Tacloban, landing there about 1000.

Around 0905 the VC-5 Avengers began their attacks. Because of the heavy cloud cover and with flak barrages directed at the holes in the clouds, one of these barrages shooting down one bomber and setting another ablaze, Fowler had needed that long to gather enough aircraft for an organized attack. From above he had watched other planes making, for the most part, well-executed attacks on the *Kongo* and *Haruna*. He was highly displeased, however, that some TBM pilots chose to make horizontal bombing runs from 6,000 feet. With the twisting and turning of the Japanese ships, such runs inevitably failed. These attacks were probably made by the scratch group of six TBMs and twenty fighters that the commander support aircraft, Captain R. F. Whitehead, had gathered from those planes that had been on other missions when the Center Force struck.

Finally Fowler ordered his planes to go in. "The tactics of the glide bombing attack would not be approved by the safety engineers," Fowler said, "as the pilots handled their TBM-1Cs just about like they were dive bombers."[28] Three TBMs, all that had been able to stay with Fowler, followed him down from 8,000 feet. The ship they were diving on was the *Chokai,* which was close enough now to the CVEs to be receiving 5-inch hits from the *White Plains*'s stern "peashooter."

Apparently engrossed with the carriers, the crew of the *Chokai* didn't see the plummeting planes until too late. Of the twelve

500-pound SAP bombs that fell from the Avengers' bomb bays, all but three struck the ship. One hit the cruiser's stern, sending her into a sharp right turn. Smoke billowed from the stricken cruiser and she began to slow. Soon the destroyer *Fujinami* drew alongside to take off her crew and then sink the *Chokai* with a torpedo.

While Fowler's four planes were doing in the *Chokai*, Lieutenant Charlie Lee had his hands full. The antiaircraft burst that had downed his wingman had also set Lee's Avenger ablaze, punctured an oil line, and taken a good-sized chunk out of one of his propeller blades. None of these things helped the TBM's flying capability, but Lee was determined to do his part in the attack. The fire kept going out, then relighting, but that didn't stop Lee from making a glide bombing run on a battleship, which he might have hit, and a "tin can," which he missed. Lee staggered to Tacloban for a safe landing.[29] Fowler landed on the *Manila Bay* about 1000, where he rearmed and prepared to lead a major strike against the then-retiring Center Force.

Back at sea level, when Taffy 3 entered the rain squall between 0706 and 0715, the ships enjoyed a short respite as the Japanese fire slackened. Ziggy Sprague took this opportunity to send his three destroyers into the fray. Asking these *Fletcher*-class ships of but 2,100 tons each to go against the pride of the Japanese Fleet, with ships up to 71,000 tons, was a tremendous gamble, but one that had to be taken. And these destroyers and their smaller cousins, the destroyer escorts, fought such a battle that the words "courage," "gallantry," or "audacity" can only begin to describe their qualities.

At 0716 Sprague ordered his screening vessels to counterattack the big Japanese ships. Actually, one of his destroyers, Commander Ernest E. Evans's *Johnston* ("G.Q. Johnny" to her crew), had already been sniping at the advancing enemy. Her station had been closest to the Japanese, and upon seeing the battleships and cruisers bearing down, Evans had told his crew to prepare to attack. As he did so, on his own initiative he turned toward the Center Force and began to lay a smokescreen. Seeing that Vice Admiral Kazutaka Shiraishi's CruDiv (Cruiser Division) 7 was striding out ahead of the battleships, Evans (still without orders) charged the heavy cruisers.

Under the leaden sky the *Johnston* cut through the water at up to 30 knots, throwing a curling bow wave high into the air. When first seen, the heavy ships were about 18,000 yards away. Evans intended to cut that distance in half. When the Japanese saw the *Johnston* boring in, they opened fire on the doughty destroyer. Perhaps they were surprised by Evans's audacity, for their first salvos were off target. "G.Q. Johnny's" weren't. Operating in rapid-fire, her five 5-inch mounts snapped out at the big ships, the sound of their firing sounding like the yips of a terrier when contrasted with the Great Dane roar of the enemy vessels. She achieved numerous hits on the cruisers, particularly on the *Kumano,* which was leading the way.

By this time Evans had received Sprague's order for a torpedo attack. He was more than ready. When the range dropped to 10,000 yards, Evans loosed his full load of ten "fish," then doubled back into the protection of his own smokescreen. A few minutes later, at 0727, two or three highly satisfying explosions were heard on the *Johnston.* When the "tin can" emerged from the smokescreen moments later, the *Kumano* was burning fiercely. (The Japanese said later that only one torpedo hit the *Kumano,* but this was enough to blow her bow almost completely off.)

The cruiser veered out of column to port and slowed to 14 knots. Shortly, the *Suzuya,* which had already been the recipient of a couple of bombs and was herself slowing down, came alongside her sister ship to take off Admiral Shiraishi and his staff. Both ships were left astern of the rest of the Center Force and were out of the fight.

About three minutes later the *Johnston* was hit hard. Three 14-inch shells, followed by three 6-inch shells, all probably from the *Kongo,* slammed into the destroyer, violently rattling her. Knocked out were the after fire and engine rooms, and power was lost to the steering engine and to all three after 5-inch mounts. Snapped off the mast, the SC radar antenna fell on the bridge, killing three officers. More men were killed below decks. One of the shells blew Evans's clothes off above the waist and severed two fingers of his left hand.

Fortunately, the rain squall that had sheltered the flattops now passed over the *Johnston.* For a vital ten minutes she was able to tend to her wounds and to restore partial power to two of her 5-inch guns. The third 5-incher would have to operate in local control.

By now the *Johnston* was not alone in her battle. The screen flagship, the *Hoel,* commanded by Commander L. S. Kintberger, entered the action with a gunfire duel at 14,000 yards with the *Kongo.* The *Hoel's* 5-inch guns were no match for the *Kongo's* 14-inch guns and armor plating, and at 0725 she took a hit on her bridge. Despite the hit, Kintberger took his ship closer, finally firing a half-salvo of five torpedoes at the battleship from only 9,000 yards. They missed but forced the *Kongo* to turn sharply left out of their way.

Before the *Hoel* could pull away, several large-caliber shells slammed into her, destroying one of her engines and knocking out three guns. Towering geysers erupted all about her, causing Kurita to believe that his ships had blown up a cruiser. But they hadn't blown up anything—yet. For a few frightening moments, the *Hoel* headed directly for the onrushing enemy ships because of a jammed rudder. Her two forward 5-inchers popped away, trying to inflict as much damage as possible.

Fortunately, steering was regained and the destroyer swung away. Alone in these initial counterattacks, the *Hoel* would be joined by the rest of Taffy 3's screen shortly. At 0742 Sprague had ordered a second torpedo attack, the "execute" coming at 0750. Leading this charge would be Commander Amos T. Hathaway's *Heermann*, which had been on the disengaged side of Taffy 3 and thus had been unable to join the *Johnston* and *Hoel* for their attacks.

The *Heermann* raced through the middle of the formation, almost colliding with the DE *Samuel B. Roberts* in the process, to join the *Hoel*. Because of the smoke and mists that cloaked the scene, these varying the visibility anywhere from 100 to 25,000 yards, at 0749 the *Heermann* almost collided with the ship she was to meet, the *Hoel*, and just managed to avoid this embarrassment by backing up at emergency full power.

Shortly afterward the two destroyers began firing their torpedoes at the line of heavy cruisers coming down from the north on a course of 120°. A loss of communications forced the *Hoel* to manually train her torpedoes, but a bit after 0750 she fired her last five torpedoes at the *Haguro* from a distance of about 6,000 yards. All the torpedoes seemed to be running hot and normal, and the *Hoel* reported seeing columns of water erupting about the cruiser. According to the Japanese these torpedoes missed, but since no aircraft were then bombing the cruiser, the cause of these explosions can only be speculated upon. Nevertheless, in evading the torpedoes, the *Haguro* took a 5-inch shell amidships (probably from the *Hoel*) and skittered out of line to begin turning in circles.

Taking aim at the *Haguro* at almost the same time was the *Heermann*, which sent seven torpedoes toward the cruiser, then about 9,000 yards away. All seven missed, to continue into the distance. The *Haguro* saw the *Heermann* and lashed out with fifteen salvos of 8-inch gunfire, which also missed. Not all of the seven torpedoes had been fired when first the *Kongo*, then the *Haruna*, and trailing behind, the *Yamato* and *Nagato* were seen about 9,000 yards to the north off the destroyer's port side. Towering columns of water shot up around the *Heermann* as the battleships took her under fire. But once again Japanese marksmanship was off, and the destroyer was hit by only a few fragments.

At 0800 Hathaway fired his last three torpedoes at the *Haruna*, then just 4,400 yards away, and beat a hasty retreat, followed by a trail of splashes where salvos had landed. As the *Heermann* retired, she laid down more smoke and took the opportunity to shoot at anything Japanese that moved.

Meanwhile, what had happened to the torpedoes that had missed the *Haguro?* They had continued to run, and suddenly the *Yamato* steamed into their path. Trying to "comb" the torpedoes, the *Yamato* turned sixty degrees to port. This didn't seem to be enough so she kept coming around until she was heading almost due north. She did comb the torpedoes, four to starboard and two to port, but this also left her with the torpedoes chasing her from astern. For a vital ten minutes the *Yamato,* dutifully followed by the *Nagato,* raced northward. These torpedoes, which were probably from the *Heermann,* though Samuel Eliot Morison opts for the *Hoel,* may have missed the *Yamato,* but the effect was almost the same as if they had hit.[30] Effectively out of the battle were the *Yamato* and *Nagato.*

When the *Heermann* charged into action, she had just barely missed hitting the *Roberts,* which immediately tagged along behind her. The *Roberts's* skipper, Lt. Commander R. W. Copeland, had been eager to get a piece of the action and, when Sprague ordered a second attack, had asked the screen commander, Commander W. D. Thomas in the *Hoel,* if this included the DEs. At first Thomas said no, but soon reversed himself and told the destroyer escorts to form up for a torpedo attack. This was all Copeland wanted to hear, but instead of joining the other DEs on the far side of the formation, he lit out behind the *Heermann.* Also joining up was the *Johnston,* just emerging from the rain squall.

A short time after the *Hoel* and *Heermann* had fired their torpedoes, the *Roberts,* using the smokescreen with great skill, was able to close to within 4,000 yards—pointblank range—of the cruiser column. Three torpedoes were fired, which missed, and the little DE retired, firing defiantly at a cruiser. Splashes surrounded the gutsy destroyer escort but, amazingly, no shells hit.

While the *Roberts* was dueling with the cruisers, the other destroyer escorts were entering the fray. Like the *Roberts,* the *Raymond,* skippered by Commander A. F. Beyer, took on the enemy fleet all by herself. The *Haguro* began firing at the DE but was never able to hit her. About this time the *Raymond* sighted eight or nine destroyers curving in on the carriers' starboard quarter, but the *Haguro,* being closer, was of greater concern. At 0756 she fired three torpedoes at the cruiser, which was then also under air attack, but they missed astern. With the cruiser just 6,000 yards distant, the *Raymond* turned about and quickly retired, splashes from 8-inch shells trailing in her wake.

Also not waiting for a formal joinup was Lieutenant Commander Samuel Hansen. Upon getting the word to form up, he took his ship, the *Dennis,* to the sound of the gunfire. The *Haguro* (the target of seemingly every "small boy") sprayed her shells about the *Dennis* for almost three minutes but was unable to hit her. The *Dennis* did not expend her torpedoes on the *Haguro.* Instead she fired them at either the *Chokai* or *Tone.* Unfortunately, all missed. For several minutes she traded shots with the cruisers, receiving no hits in the exchange. Then she raced back to join the *Heermann, Johnston,* and *Roberts,* which were headed southwestward to screen the carriers again.

Missing from this group of ships was the *Hoel,* because she was sinking. After freeing her jammed rudder, she had turned southwest for her retirement. She didn't get far. With only one engine working, she was swiftly overtaken by the enemy ships. On her port beam was the *Kongo,* 8,000 yards away, while on her starboard quarter 7,000 yards away was the column of heavy cruisers. The *Hoel* could only keep up with these ships, not pull away from them. Virtually every Japanese ship took their shots at the destroyer and for some time she was able to avoid all they could throw. Then her luck ran out.

A flurry of shells pounded the *Hoel.* Ranging in size from 16-inch to 5-inch, they tore the destroyer apart, maiming and killing her crew. In this massacre, for that was what it was, the *Hoel* took more than forty hits, all of them armor-piercing. She began to slow and then, at 0830, an 8-inch shell took out her remaining engine. Coming to a halt, she began to list to port and settle by the stern. Five minutes later Commander Kintberger told his men to prepare to abandon ship. Almost to the last her forward 5-inch guns kept up their fire. The men went into the water, and at 0855 the *Hoel* capsized and sank. The price her men had paid for their part in the defense of Taffy 3 was terribly high. Of her crew of 353, only 82 would survive, including Commanders Kintberger and Thomas.

By 0820 the "small boys" were racing back to again screen the carriers. The *Heermann,* with a pronounced proclivity for close calls, almost ran into the *Fanshaw Bay* at 0835 (the carriers themselves were maneuvering radically to avoid the Japanese gunfire) and five minutes later just missed the *Johnston* (heading for her last fight), which, because of her damage, was having difficulty steering. As the two ships swept by each other, both crews let out a rousing cheer.

By 0826 the less-harassed *Tone* and *Chikuma* had forged ahead of the *Haguro* and *Chokai* and were closing in on the carriers' port quarter. Ziggy Sprague ordered the DEs on his starboard side to get in between his carriers and the cruisers. At this time the *John C. Butler* and *Dennis* were on that side, and they soon joined the *Raymond*, which had been on the formation's port side and had been taking potshots at the leading cruiser for some time.

Lieutenant Commander J. E. Pace's *Butler* did have her three torpedoes available, but because of the speed and course of the cruisers, she would never get the chance to use them. Nevertheless, the three destroyer escorts sniped at the enemy vessels with their 5-inch guns. At 0842 for some reason the *Chikuma* made a complete circle, the *Tone* taking her place in the lead. All three DEs quickly shifted their fire to this new menace. The *Tone* roared back, sending a shell through the *Dennis*'s deck and out her starboard side. A second hit destroyed a 40-mm gun director, while a third knocked out her No. 1 5-inch gun. Since her No. 2 gun was already inoperative because of a breech problem, Commander Hansen decided to retire under the cover of the *Butler*'s smokescreen.

Four "paintscrapers" fell near the *Butler,* but she was able to niftily sidestep them with little damage. By this time she was nearly out of 5-inch shells; her gunners had been firing almost constantly. At 0918 she ceased firing, whereupon Admiral Sprague ordered her to move up on the disposition's port bow and lay more smoke to provide some concealment for the *Fanshaw Bay*, which was now coming out of the smoke, giving the Japanese a good line on her.

Also sharing in this action had been the *Heermann*. Upon her return, she began firing at the *Chikuma*. For a time the cruiser ignored her, concentrating instead on the *Gambier Bay*, but with the carrier burning and listing, the *Chikuma* shifted her fire to the *Heermann*. Three other ships also took the destroyer under fire. At 0845 a shell hit her pilothouse, killing three men and fatally wounding a fourth. One of those killed was Bucky Dahlen, the VC-10 flier who had been picked up the day before. Dahlen had been assigned to help the gunnery officer spot enemy planes, but since none were present, Dahlen had gone to the bridge to see about getting another job. Just as he entered the pilothouse, the shell landed. His reprieve from death had not lasted even a day.

The other ships began hitting the *Heermann*. One 8-inch shell struck near her bow at the waterline. This hit flooded her forward magazines and destroyed a storage locker containing navy beans. In one of the few amusing incidents this day, the shell stirred the beans into a thick, nauseating paste that was sucked into an uptake and deposited all over the supply officer, who was standing next to the stack.

The destroyer suffered several other hits that were not damaging enough to disable her. Commander Hathaway kept his ship at full speed, even though the hit forward was causing her to take on a great amount of water that threatened to drive her under. Good damage-control work, aided by extra shoring timbers Hathaway had loaded prior to leaving for Leyte, kept her afloat.

When the *Chikuma* came under air attack at 0902, she ceased firing at the *Heermann*. For a time the cruiser's place was taken by the *Tone,* and she and the destroyer traded shots for about three minutes. Planes from Taffy 2 then went after the *Tone,* and at 0920 she and the *Haguro* retired from the battle.

About 0850 the *Roberts* took a shell, which wiped out her No. 1 fireroom and holed her below the waterline. She then began taking hit after hit, including two or three 14-inch shells from the *Kongo* that ripped her open and left the ship abaft the stack a jumbled mass of death and destruction. The little DE went dead in the water, and all power was lost.

Speaking about another battle, Iwo Jima, Admiral Nimitz said, "Uncommon valor was a common virtue." The same statement could easily apply to the sailors and airmen of Taffy 3. A case in point: Although all power on the *Roberts* had been lost, as had the air supply for her guns' gas ejection system, the crew of the No. 2 gun manually loaded, rammed, and fired six charges. They knew very well the danger in this but continued anyway. Their luck ran out with the seventh charge.

Before the breech was closed, the seventh charge cooked off, killing or mortally wounding all but three members of the gun crew. Two of these died later in the rafts. When the first man entered the mount after the explosion, he found the gun captain, GM3c Paul H. Carr, horribly wounded, with his side ripped open from neck to thigh. Nonetheless, he was holding a 54-pound projectile over his head trying to load it into the unrecognizable mass that had once been his gun. Carr pleaded with the man to help him get this round off.

Taking the projectile from Carr, the sailor laid it on the deck and removed another wounded man from the mount. When he returned moments later, Carr was again trying to place the heavy projectile into the loading tray. A few minutes later Carr died, unable to fire his last shell at the enemy.

Commander Copeland had ordered his ship abandoned at 0910, but because of his insistence that the wounded be given first aid and placed on rafts, this was not completed until 0935. Soon the *Roberts* rolled over on her side, then lifted her bow into the air and sank by the stern. It was 1005. Almost half her crew, eighty-four officers and men, would be lost in this action.

Out of torpedoes, Commander Evans didn't have to follow the *Hoel, Heermann,* and *Roberts* back into the maelstrom, but he did, so as to give the other ships as much support as he could. The *Johnston* had gotten out of that scrape relatively unscathed, but she was hurting from the pounding she had received from the *Kongo.* Still, Evans brought her back to screen the carriers as they curved around toward the southwest. The destroyer's 5-inchers were becoming hot as they poured shell after shell into the cruisers.

Suddenly Evans saw a chilling sight. Roaring in from off the carriers' starboard quarter was the light cruiser *Yahagi* leading the four destroyers of DesRon 10, this attack apparently undertaken by Rear Admiral Susumu Kimura on his own volition. Alone, the *Johnston* charged the foe. Initially 10,000 yards, the range quickly dropped to 7,000 yards as the *Johnston* and the enemy ships closed with each other. The *Johnston* almost immediately scored hits on the *Yahagi,* but was also taking her share. Shortly after 0900 the *Yahagi* sheered away, not to escape the *Johnston*'s fire, effective as it was, but to launch torpedoes. At 0915 the destroyers also turned hard right to fire their dreaded Long Lance torpedoes.

The Japanese would claim that three carriers and one "cruiser" were sunk by these torpedoes, but they were mistaken. In fact, the *Johnston* had interfered with DesRon 10's torpedo attack, forcing them to release their torpedoes before they were in optimum position. Although the Long Lances had an outstanding range, they still had some 10,500 yards to run to reach the nearest carrier, which would at the same time be opening the range even more. As these torpedoes neared the flattops they began to slow and porpoise. High above, VC-65's Lieutenant (jg) Waldrop was returning from his bombing attack and saw the torpedoes streaking through the water. Quickly he warned the carriers, then dove to strafe the deadly missiles. At least one of them was blown up by Waldrop's fire, while another was thrown off course by the *Kalinin Bay*'s sharpshooting 5-inch gun crew.

Commander Evans had not waited to see what the torpedoes were going to do. Seeing the destroyers turning away, Evans shifted his fire back to the heavy cruisers. For the next half hour the *Johnston* took on the cruisers, then the ships of DesRon 10, snapping at her heels. This uneven battle could have only an unhappy ending. Under the torrent of shells, "G.Q. Johnny" began to falter. By this time Evans had had to shift his command to the fantail, the bridge having been shattered, and was yelling maneuvering orders down a hatch to the men who had to operate the rudder by hand.

It was soon over. Mangled bodies littered her decks, her last en-

gine was knocked out, and all communications were lost. At 0940 the
Johnston coasted to a stop. Five minutes later Evans gave the order to
abandon ship. Like a flock of vultures the enemy destroyers closed
in, pumping shell after shell into the inert mass of wreckage that was
once a graceful *Fletcher*-class destroyer. Slowly, then faster and
faster, she rolled over, finally sinking at 1010. As one of the Japanese destroyers slid by the survivors, they saw the ship's captain
salute the *Johnston* and her crew.

Only 141 out of the *Johnston*'s complement of 327 men were eventually rescued. Approximately 50 were killed in action, another 45
died of their wounds, and 92, including the gallant and courageous
Commander Evans, died of drowning or shark attacks before rescue
vessels reached them.

This naval version of the Charge of the Light Brigade, though it
didn't stop the enemy force, threw it into confusion and forced the
Japanese to make poorly organized attacks. Also, instead of being
concentrated on the vulnerable CVEs, much of the enemy fire had
to be turned against these snapping and snarling terriers, the DDs
and DEs. Time, valuable time, was bought at terrible cost to these
ships. The *Johnston*—sunk; the *Hoel*—sunk; the *Roberts*—sunk; the
Heermann—damaged; the *Dennis*—damaged. Only the *Raymond* and
Butler escaped this mad tumult virtually unscathed.[31]

Immediately after the sighting of the Center Force shortly before
0700, Sprague had ordered his planes launched and ordered Taffy
3 to head east into a rain squall. From approximately 0705 until
about 0930 the Taffy 3 aircraft attacked the Center Force. Just a few
minutes after his order to launch aircraft, Sprague ordered his destroyers to counterattack. This phase of the battle took place between 0715 and 0855, when the *Hoel* went down. A second counterattack, by the destroyer escorts, was ordered at 0742. These various
counterattacks continued until approximately 0918. After finishing
their attacks, the destroyers and destroyer escorts raced back to
screen the carriers, then heading about 220°.

The *White Plains* and *St. Lo* had had several near misses fall about
them shortly after 0700. The sheltering embrace of the rain squall
saved them for several minutes. At 0723 the ships of Taffy 3 began
to emerge from the mist. While most of the enemy ships were still
steering east, the *Chokai, Haguro, Chikuma,* and *Tone* cut farther
south to flank the CVEs. Upon seeing the powerful unit beginning
to overtake his ships, Sprague sent his "small boys" out for their
counterattack and changed course to 200°. At 0732 he came back to

170°, due south fourteen minutes later, and finally back to 200° by 0800.

While his planes and screening vessels were going after the four cruisers, Sprague had his carriers going all out. Nevertheless, the cruisers continued to close. Some of the carriers were already firing their 5-inchers at the enemy when Sprague radioed at 0735, "Open up with peashooters on stern." He followed this a minute later with, "All Great Danes [carriers] stand by to open up with your guns when range is clear."[32]

On the *Kitkun Bay* Captain Whitney drily told his gunnery officer, "Mr. Kuhn, the enemy is now within range. You may fire the 5-inch at will."[33]

After the DDs and DEs went in for their attacks, Sprague told his carriers to make as much smoke as possible. As the carriers ran ahead of the enemy, their deck crews were frantically fueling and arming those planes still on board. Practically every flattop unceremoniously dumped its highly dangerous napalm bombs into the water. On some ships the communications departments were told to prepare all secret material for quick destruction.[34]

In the distance the gun flashes of the cruisers could be clearly seen. Several moments later there would be a moaning whine as the shells arced in. There would be a *chunk-chunk-chunk* as the salvos hit the sea in beautiful close patterns. Too soon, the salvos began to hit the carriers.

Because of the direction in which Taffy 3 was headed, the wind was blowing the smokescreen away from the trailing carriers, the *Kalinin Bay* and *Gambier Bay*. Clear fields of fire toward these two ships were afforded the cruisers, which were quick to take advantage of them.

First to be hit was the *Kalinin Bay*. Earlier she had launched all but five of her aircraft. About 0750 she was able to get three FM-2s off, but two torpedo-loaded Avengers were stranded because of a catapult malfunction. As the last fighter leaped off the deck, the "K.B." took her first hit. A salvo of very near misses from a battleship flung fragments through the hangar from the starboard side abaft the forward elevator. Almost immediately afterward an 8-inch projectile pierced her hull below the waterline just forward of the engineering spaces. Before the battle ended, the *Kalinin Bay* would be hit fourteen times, mostly by 8-inch shells.

Although these were armor-piercing shells and many tended to go right through the thin-skinned carrier, they still caused tremendous damage. The first 8-inch shell opened a like-sized hole at the waterline, took out an evaporator as it continued, and exploded on

Heavy smoke pours out of the Kalinin Bay's *stack as Japanese shells fall nearby. On the horizon are three enemy ships—one just to the left of the splashes, one just to the right, and a third, smoking, about two thirds of the way toward the funnel smoke. (National Archives)*

an aviation lube oil tank. Another projectile went completely through the ship, leaving only one entrance hole but two exit holes. (The propensity of these shells to break up was noted later. Many of them broke into two or three pieces without detonating.) The shells that did explode wiped out a fresh water tank, knocked out many electrical circuits, twisted and distorted the forward elevator platform so much as to render it useless, and started numerous fires, as well as causing heavy flooding. One shell exploded under the fantail, sending a huge fragment spiraling into the pyrotechnic locker. No fire was started in this highly combustible area, but flooding up to a depth of five feet was caused.

Damage control parties set to with a vengeance to save their ship. In the ship's and aviation armories one fire rekindled three times before being extinguished after a ninety-minute fight. A minor but potentially dangerous fire involved an acetylene bottle. A shell fragment had punctured the bottle, starting an intense blaze. Acetylene and air can form an explosive mixture, but luckily, a five-minute fight extinguished this dangerous blaze.

The damage control parties were sparing in their use of water on the fires that broke out, foam and CO_2 being used to great effect. This was fortunate because the Kaiser-class carriers had very poor drainage on the hangar deck, and too much free water on the hangar deck and elevator pits could cause a drastic reduction in the stability of these vessels, already approaching their limits of stability and longitudinal strength under their usual wartime loadings.

The main thing Captain Williamson wanted to do now was to keep his ship going at full speed. To slow down would be fatal. Thus he had to make sure that the flooding to the forward engine room caused by the first 8-inch shell was controlled. It was nip-and-tuck. Before it was stopped, the flooding rose to the engine room's floor plates, yet the engines never missed a beat.

However, because of the flooding, the *Kalinin Bay* was soon listing seven degrees to port. Some 150 tons of ballast were shifted twenty feet to starboard to bring the ship back upright. Instead, the flattop lurched over to an eight-degree starboard list. This turned out to be a blessing in disguise. Less water was being taken in on the port side, enabling most of the holes to be plugged while pumping reduced the water level in other sections. In fact, within a few hours most spaces were free of water.[35]

Not only had the *Kalinin Bay* been taking hits, she had been dishing them out as well. After firing for several minutes without success at the Japanese vessels, the ship's 5-inch gun crew planted one squarely on the No. 2 turret of one of the heavy cruisers. A great cheer went up as smoke and flames obscured the turret. Surprisingly, considering the length of time the ship was under fire (over an hour) and what damage she incurred, the "K.B.'s" casualties were remarkably few, only five men killed and fifty-five wounded.[36]

The *Kitkun Bay* and *St. Lo* were lucky too. Though almost continuously straddled throughout the action, neither ship was hit, and the *Kitkun Bay* suffered only a few casualties from flying fragments. Also lucky was the *White Plains*, her only damage (which was not serious) happening early on from the "caliper straddle."

The *Fanshaw Bay* was not so lucky. Beginning at 0750 she was struck by four 8-inch projectiles, while two shorts landed just off her starboard bow. As it passed through the ship, one shell blew off a ventilator, which killed an officer and fatally wounded a sailor as it went over the side. A second shell passed under the barrels of a 40-mm gun, tearing off the face of the pointer. Deflected by the 40-mm gun shield, the main portion of the shell ricocheted over the flight deck, while its nose cap ended up in a compartment. The major damage was caused by a shell that smashed the catapult track, then continued on to cause a low-order explosion in the flag office. But even this damage was not great, and the carrier was ready for flight operations in short order. Four small fires that were kindled were soon snuffed out, and minor flooding was quickly controlled. Ship's casualties were four men killed and eighteen wounded. Not willing to stand by and just take it, the flattop's 5-inch gun crew opened up on one of the cruisers. Within a couple of minutes they were right on target, scoring at least five hits on the ship's superstructure.[37]

Unluckiest of all was the *Gambier Bay*. When the CVEs came out of the rain at about 0723, their formation was still neat and tidy. (This would change as the flattops chased salvos and crossed each other's sterns.) Unfortunately for the *Gambier Bay* and *Kalinin Bay,* they were toward the rear of the formation going almost directly downwind and were coming out of the smokescreen.

As the *Gambier Bay* came out of the mist, flurries of shells began falling about her. At first the enemy fire was inaccurate and very slow, almost a minute and a half between salvos. The spread for these salvos was as small as twenty-five yards. As the salvos landed closer and closer, Captain Vieweg began to chase the splashes.

"I maneuvered the ship alternately from one side of the base course to another as I saw that a salvo was about due to hit," he said later. "One could see that the salvos would hit some distance away and gradually creep up closer, and from the spacing on the water could tell that the next one would be on if we did nothing. We would invariably turn into the direction from which the salvos were creeping and, sure enough, the next salvo would land right in the water where we would have been if we hadn't turned. The next few salvos would creep across to the other side and gradually creep back and would repeat the operation. This process lasted for, believe it or not, a half hour, during which the enemy was closing constantly."[38]

At 0741 the fantail 5-incher began firing on a cruiser 17,000 yards on the port quarter, and several hits were claimed. Shortly afterward more shells began to splash about the *Gambier Bay*. A few minutes later three unidentified ships were seen on the horizon off to the south-southwest. (These were destroyers from Taffy 2.) A message was sent to these ships by the 24-inch searchlight, "We are under attack," but the ships pulled away and eventually disappeared.

The *Gambier Bay*'s first hit slammed into her at 0810. This 8-inch shell struck the flight deck about six feet aft of the after elevator, leaving a six-by-eight-foot hole in the deck. When it exploded on the gallery deck, it started several fires, all extinguished in less than five

A Japanese heavy cruiser fires on the Gambier Bay. *(National Archives)*

minutes. Seven minutes later another shell detonated in the carrier's chain locker.

It was the third hit that sealed the ship's fate, though. At 0820 a shell estimated to be anywhere from 14-inch to 16-inch hit the water only a few feet to port of the flattop and exploded about twelve feet below the surface. Its mining effect ruptured plating, and a gush of water shot into the forward engine room. By the time the engine-room personnel were able to secure the boilers, the water was up to their waists and rapidly getting higher. An effort to pump out the engine room was attempted, but the 1,200 GPM (gallons per minute) capacity of the pumps made no headway against the estimated 19,000 GPM inflow. With the loss of the engine room, the *Gambier Bay*'s speed fell off to 11 knots, and the cruisers, making 30 knots, closed in for the kill.

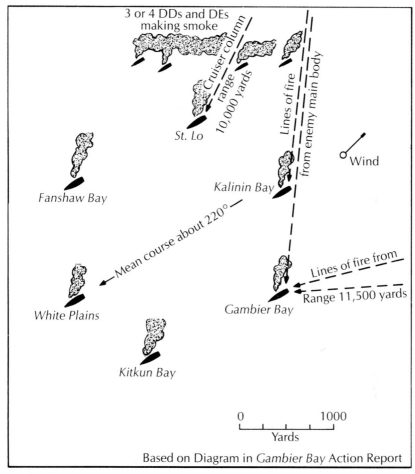

3 or 4 DDs and DEs
making smoke

Cruiser column

range 10,000 yards

St. Lo

Lines of fire

from enemy main body

Wind

Fanshaw Bay

Kalinin Bay

Mean course about 220°

Lines of fire from

Gambier Bay

Range 11,500 yards

White Plains

Kitkun Bay

0   1000

Yards

Based on Diagram in *Gambier Bay* Action Report

Battle off Samar, 25 October 1944—Tactical Situation at 0816–0820

Four minutes after that fatal hit, another shell sliced through the port side a little aft of the spot where the big projectile had exploded. Almost all in a damage-control party trying to plug the leaks in this area were killed, and more of the ship was opened to the sea. Soon a port list developed.

With the carrier slowing down and the cruisers broad on her port beam, the shelling increased in violence and rapidity. Men were being cut down all over the ship. One man's head was taken off, his torso continuing to twitch for what seemed several minutes. Lieutenant Commander Wayne H. Stewart, VC-10's flight surgeon, was killed as he bent over to work on a wounded man. Others were terribly mutilated by the shellfire.

But the *Gambier Bay*'s crew kept working to save their ship. Men plunged into the oily, debris-cluttered water in the lower holds to try to plug holes. On the flight deck a sailor scooped up in his bare hands a red-hot piece of a shell, carried it to the side, and tossed it overboard. Others fought the flames that were springing up all over. These efforts were soon doomed to failure as further hits holed the fire main, causing a loss of pressure.

The lookouts kept on with their jobs. One sailor approached a lookout as he peered out toward the cruisers. "How ya doin'?" the utterly relaxed lookout asked.

"Fine. How're *you* doing?"

"Okay. Pardon me." The lookout spoke into his microphone: "*Tone*-class cruiser bearing 060 now three thousand yards." He turned back to the other man. "What were you saying, pal?"[39]

About 0837 three shells, apparently from both 5.1-inch and 8-inch guns, staggered the carrier. One of these caused extensive flooding in the after engine room; after the boilers were secured, it was abandoned about 0845. The *Gambier Bay* went dead in the water, rocking slightly in the swells and quivering violently as other shells struck her.

After making sure that all classified material was given the "deep six," Captain Vieweg gave the order to abandon ship at 0850. The carrier was listing farther and farther to port and was obviously done for, yet the *Chikuma* and another cruiser continued to rake her with their fire from very close range. A number of men in the water would be killed by this gunfire. About the time the abandon-ship order was given, yet another shell set afire the carrier's last aircraft down on the hangar deck. This explosion wounded many men who were then on their way to their abandon-ship stations. The fire that was started by this shell probably set off the plane's torpedo, which later blew the forward elevator out of the ship.

While his men were abandoning ship, Vieweg and his navigator, Lieutenant Commander George Gellhorn, oversaw the operation from the bridge. At 0855 Gellhorn left the ship via the starboard bridge lifelines. Just as he did so, another shell tore through the island. Vieweg waited a few moments before trying his hand at abandoning ship. He headed down toward the flight deck but found the smoke and hot gases pouring up through the island intolerable and was left in the "embarrassing" position of being stuck between the smoke in the island and the smoke below decks.

At last able to reach the flight deck, Vieweg stumbled aft along the island structure through the choking smoke trying to reach a catwalk. Unable to see in the smoke, he found one the hard way, by falling into it. The smoke was so hot and black that for a moment he thought he had fallen into a stack. Finally he reached for a handhold and pulled himself up and over the edge. Suddenly he found himself falling again, this time some forty feet into the water.

Vieweg was still wearing his helmet tightly secured under his chin, and when he hit the water his helmet almost choked him. Having abandoned ship on the starboard side, Vieweg had to swim aft and around to the port side to get away from his ship, which was being set down upon him.[40]

The men in the water watched the cruisers close to pointblank range and continued pumping their shells into the now-derelict hulk. Vieweg noted that even at that distance, the shooting of the Japanese was not very good, many shells missing the *Gambier Bay*. At 0907 the little "jeep" rolled over on her side; four minutes later she was gone. She had not gone down easily. Between the time of her first hit at 0810 and her abandonment at 0850, the *Gambier Bay* had absorbed fifteen hits ranging in size from 14-inch to 4-inch. These fifteen hits were those for which a specific time was known. In addition, there were at least eleven more hits for which no time could be established before the abandon ship order was given.[41]

As the *Gambier Bay* was being smashed by the cruisers, another threat had appeared on Taffy 3's other flank. This was Admiral Kimura's DesRon 10 pounding down off the carriers' starboard side. As we have seen, because of the *Johnston*'s intervention and, perhaps, because of some poor torpedo work by the Japanese, their attack was a failure. The Americans didn't know this attack would fail, however, and after seeing the cruisers closing in to be followed by the new menace of the destroyers, a *White Plains* radioman commented to an officer, "The situation is getting a little tense, isn't it?"[42]

By 0905, as seen from the *White Plains*, the Japanese ships extended from the starboard quarter around aft to the port quarter, and the cruisers had closed to 11,700 yards. One of the 40-mm battery officers bucked up his men with "Just wait a little longer, boys. We're sucking them in to 40-mm range."[43] At this range the flattop's 5-incher was able to score at least six hits on the *Chokai*, but the real damage to her was done by Fowler's VC-5 pilots, who attacked the cruiser at the same time.

For a while it appeared to be all over for the Taffy 3 carriers. They were being crowded closer and closer to the shores of Samar—

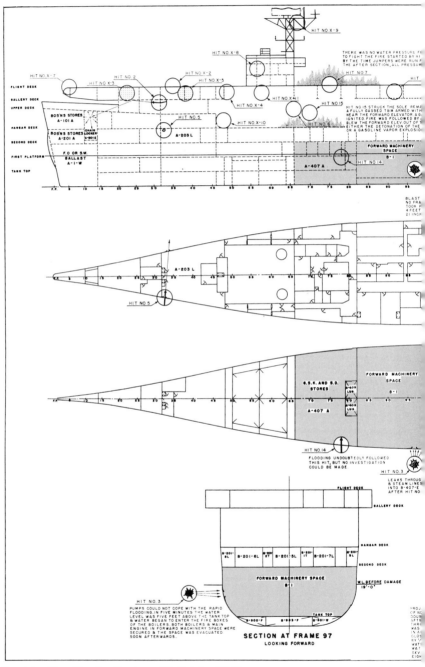

Gambier Bay *Gunfire Damage, 25 October 1944*

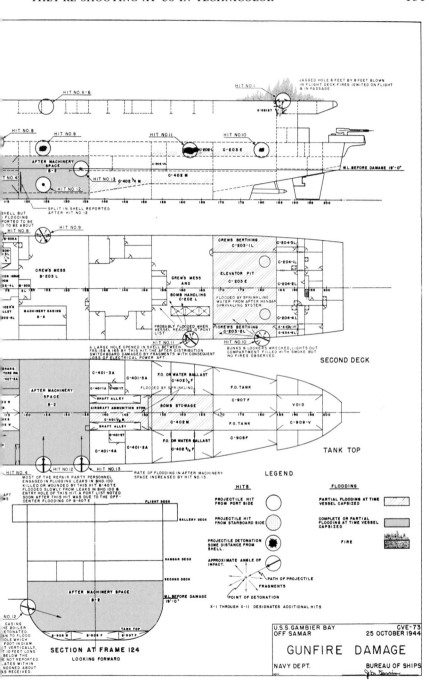

JAGGED HOLE 6 FEET BY 8 FEET BLOWN
IN FLIGHT DECK FIRES IGNITED ON FLIGHT
& IN PASSAGE

HIT NO.I

HIT NO. X-6

HIT NO.8   HIT NO.9   HIT NO.11   HIT NO.10

C-081ST

C-202 L   C-203 E

AFTER MACHINERY
SPACE
B-2

C-303 L

W.L BEFORE DAMAGE 19'-0"

T NO 4   HIT NO.13   C-402 ¾ M

C-402 M

HIT NO.12

SPLIT IN SHELL REPORTED
AFTER HIT NO.12

SHELL BUT
FLOODING
PORTED TO BE
0 TO BE ABOUT

HIT NO.9

HIT NO.8

CREWS BERTHING
C-203-IL   C-204-3L

C-204-IL

CREW'S MESS
B-203 L

ELEVATOR PIT
C-203 E

CREW'S MESS
AND

C-204-EL

BOMB HANDLING
C-202 L

MACHINERY CASING
B-2

FLOODED BY SPRINKLING
WATER FROM AFTER HANGAR
SPRINKLING SYSTEM.

C-204-2L

DER'S
LLEY

PROBABLY FLOODED WHEN
VESSEL REACHED 15° PORT
LIST

CREWS BERTHING
C-203-2L   C-604-1L

HIT NO.11   HIT NO.10

A LARGE HOLE OPENED IN SHELL BETWEEN
FRS.159 & 165 BY THIS HIT THE AFTER DISTRIBUTION
SWITCHBOARD DAMAGED BY FRAGMENTS WITH CONSEQUENT
LOSS OF ELECTRICAL POWER AFT.

BUNKS & LOCKERS WRECKED,LIGHTS OUT
COMPARTMENT FILLED WITH SMOKE BUT
NO FIRES OBSERVED.

SECOND DECK

C-401-3A   C-401-5A   F.O. OR WATER BALLAST
C-402½ F

AFTER MACHINERY
SPACE
B-2

C-401-1A   C-401-1T   FLOODED BY SPRINKLING

F.O. TANK

SHAFT ALLEY

AIRCRAFT AMMUNITION STOW.   BOMB STOWAGE   C-907 F   VOID

C-401½ M

C-402 M   F.O. TANK   C-909-V

SHAFT ALLEY

C-401-5T

F.O. OR WATER BALLAST
C-402 ¾ F

C-905F

C-401-4A   C-401-2A

TANK TOP

HIT NO.4   HIT NO.12   HIT NO.13

RATE OF FLOODING IN AFTER MACHINERY
SPACE INCREASED BY HIT NO.13.

LEGEND

MOST OF THE REPAIR PARTY PERSONNEL
ENGAGED IN PLUGGING LEAKS IN BHD.100
KILLED OR WOUNDED BY THIS HIT B-407E
FLOODED SLOWLY FROM LEAKS IN BHD.100 &
ENTRY HOLE OF THIS HIT.A PORT LIST NOTED
SOON AFTER THIS HIT WAS DUE TO THE OFF-
CENTER FLOODING OF B-407E

HITS   FLOODING

FLIGHT DECK   PROJECTILE HIT
FROM PORT SIDE

PARTIAL FLOODING AT TIME
VESSEL CAPSIZED

GALLERY DECK   PROJECTILE HIT
FROM STARBOARD SIDE

COMPLETE OR PARTIAL
FLOODING AT TIME VESSEL
CAPSIZED

PROJECTILE DETONATION
SOME DISTANCE FROM
SHELL.

FIRE

HANGAR DECK   APPROXIMATE ANGLE OF
IMPACT.

SECOND DECK   PATH OF PROJECTILE

FRAGMENTS

AFTER MACHINERY SPACE
B-2

W.L. BEFORE DAMAGE
19'-0"   POINT OF DETONATION

X-I THROUGH X-II DESIGNATES ADDITIONAL HITS

NO.12

CASING
HE BOILER
ETONATED
AN TO FLOOD
OLE WHICH
FOOT IN DIAM
T VERTICALLY,
T IO FEET LONG
BELOW THE
E NOT REPORTED
ATES WITHIN
NOONED ABOUT
S RECEIVED

TANK TOP

B-905 M   B-905 F   B-907 F

SECTION AT FRAME 124
LOOKING FORWARD

U.S.S.GAMBIER BAY   CVE-73
OFF SAMAR   25 OCTOBER 1944

GUNFIRE DAMAGE

NAVY DEPT.   BUREAU OF SHIPS

at 0905 only thirty miles away—and the enemy ships were drawing ever nearer. Then, suddenly, the cruisers ceased fire and turned back to the north. At the moment they were ready to inflict the maximum damage, they retired.

Kurita, afraid that his ships would enter a Leyte Gulf bereft of ships and be trapped there, and confused and staggered by the intensity of the attacks on his ships by the CVE planes and Taffy 3's screening vessels, plus the defensive fight being put up by the flat-tops themselves, decided it was time to retire. At 0911 he ordered his ships to close on the *Yamato* and head north. A few minutes later the *Haguro* and *Tone* ceased fire and turned away from the carriers. On the other side of Taffy 3 the ships of DesRon 10 completed the destruction of the *Johnston* before they, too, retired.

On the bridge of his flagship, the *Fanshaw Bay*, Ziggy Sprague was worrying about the torpedoes fired his way by DesRon 10 when he heard a signalman yell, "God damn it, boys, they're getting away!"

"I could not believe my eyes," he reported later, "but it looked as if the whole Japanese fleet was indeed retiring. However, it took a whole series of reports from circling planes to convince me. At best, I had expected to be swimming by this time, along with all my crews."[44]

Indeed, the Japanese were getting away. Kurita, beset by the planes swarming around his ships like crazed bees, beset by the DDs and DEs charging in again and again to loose torpedoes and rake his ships with gunfire, beset by doubts that he could force his way into Leyte Gulf and, if he could, to find it empty of ships, finally decided he had to get his ships back together. His force was in terrible disarray, Kurita having lost control of it at the outset of the battle, and the incessant air and surface attacks had created even more chaos.

Initially, Kurita intended to regroup, help those heavy cruisers that were then badly in need of assistance, and rush in once again as an orderly, concentrated force toward Leyte Gulf. But once he had broken off his pursuit of Taffy 3, the reality of his situation settled heavily upon him. Before he had even taken on Sprague's carriers he knew that Shima and Nishimura would be of no help. He was under great pressure, and had been since the *Darter* had sunk his flagship from under his feet on the twenty-third. This pressure and the fear of the unknown were beginning to wear him down. And so he vacillated.

The Center Force had been ordered to rendezvous on the *Yamato* at 0911, the huge battleship turning north as soon as the message was sent. Some minutes later the other ships also turned north. For example, the *Haguro* ceased fire at 0912 and the *Tone* five minutes later. Unknown to Kurita, at the time of the recall these two cruisers were just 10,000 yards—point-blank range—from the carriers. But, obeying orders, these cruisers and all the others (like the destroyers of DesRon 10 that had been snapping at the heels of the CVEs from the other flank) turned to join the *Yamato*. Kurita's chance for victory at Leyte Gulf was now irrevocably gone.

Still, Kurita would dawdle and wander around, heading north until 1055, then taking a variety of courses to the west and southwest (leading the Americans to believe that this time Kurita was going to break into Leyte Gulf), until finally turning back north at 1236. The majority of these course changes were caused by the continual air attacks on his ships while Kurita debated what to do. By 1310, however, the Japanese were obviously leaving the field of battle. Kurita had already notified Admiral Toyoda in Tokyo at 1236 of his intention to abandon his attack on Leyte Gulf. Instead, he would go after some phantom enemy force that had been erroneously reported north of Suluan Island.

When interrogated by U.S. naval officers after the war, Kurita (having intercepted several messages from Taffy 3 and other sources) said that fear of being caught by the expected air reinforcements was one reason why he broke off the engagement. He also stated that he doubted he would have done much good if he had entered the gulf. Yet this was the mission his force had been given, the mission all the other components of SHO-GO had been sacrificed for.

Kurita also told his interrogators that he planned to go north to help Ozawa with night torpedo attacks, and continued, "My intention was not primarily to join Admiral Ozawa but to go north and seek out the enemy. If I failed to find the enemy, . . . my intention was to go north and seek out the enemy but to be able to retire through San Bernardino Strait at dark. . . . Secondarily or overall, I wanted to be at San Bernardino Strait at sunset to get through and as far to the west as possible during the night."[45] It is obvious, even a year after the battle when these interrogations took place, that Kurita's psyche had been handled rather roughly at Leyte Gulf. Any enemy force that was north of the Center Force would be taken care of *only* if it barred the escape route through the strait. The only thing Kurita was interested in on the afternoon of 25 October 1944 was getting away from those pesky, frightful planes and those equally detestable DDs and DEs that would not leave his ships alone.

The surface battle was over. After almost two and a half hours of nearly constant shelling, most of the ships of Taffy 3 had escaped. It was not the end of the battle—not yet. There were still a lot of air attacks to be made on the Center Force, and the dying was not yet over for the CVEs. But the other two Taffies had been making contributions in this battle as well.

Shortly after midnight on the twenty-fifth Admiral Stump had ordered all Taffy 2 carriers to be prepared to load torpedoes on short notice, in anticipation that they would be needed against the cripples fleeing Surigao Strait. Thus, when the Center Force unexpectedly appeared on top of Taffy 3, the planes were ready for their torpedoes.

Between 0500 and 0600 Taffy 2 launched a number of aircraft for CAP, ASP, direct support, and supply drop missions. Armed with the wrong kind of bombs or, as in the case of the supply missions, no bombs at all, these planes would not be available to attack the Center Force until they were rearmed, which would take some time. Nevertheless, Stump had enough planes on hand to give the enemy a severe lashing.

Immediately upon receiving Ensign Jensen's report of Japanese ships, Stump ordered all of Taffy 2's available Avengers to be loaded with torpedoes. Speed records were set as the crews labored to debomb the TBMs and replace the loads with torpedoes. Getting an Avenger loaded with a "fish" was generally a time-consuming job, but today some crews were getting the missile ready and loaded in just one hour. Not just with torpedoes were speed records being broken. On the *Manila Bay* thirty-two rocket motors and bodies were taken from the magazine, assembled, and loaded onto four Avengers along with three 500-pound general-purpose (GP) bombs each in twenty-five minutes. Three other TBMs had their depth bombs removed and replaced with 100-pounders or 500-pound GP bombs in less than fifteen minutes.[46]

Because the wind was from the northeast, Taffy 2 would be steering a converging course with the Japanese ships for some time. But there was no other choice. At 0737 the carriers turned into the wind and began launching the first strike.

On the bridge of his flagship, the *Natoma Bay*, Admiral Stump was talking to his ACI officer, Ben Grosscup, as the launches began. "You know," Stump said, "when I was at the academy as a midshipman we used to talk a lot about the deathless statements of our old naval heroes, and I've often wondered just what sort of deathless statement I would make at the appropriate time. The one that sticks in my mind is that of John Paul Jones, who said, 'No Naval Commander makes a tactical error in laying his ship alongside that of the enemy.' That was in the days of the grappling hook and side-by-side fighting."

Grosscup, who had been watching the carriers, interrupted Stump's musings. "Fox is down on all ships, Admiral." This meant that the launchings had been completed.

With a little sigh Stump acknowledged Grosscup and said, "Grosscup, John Paul Jones to the contrary notwithstanding, the time has come to get the hell out of here. Order flank speed in the opposite direction."[47]

Taffy 2's first strike, consisting of fifteen Avengers with torpedoes and twenty fighters, had taken eight minutes to be launched.[48] Now the ships swung back to the south-southeast, making the best speed they could, a breath-taking 17½ knots. Because he had a bit more time to get his strike organized, Stump was able to give general directives to his pilots on such matters as the rendezvous points for the planes, the unit commanders for the different parts of the strike force, and also the strike commander.

Stump, in the meantime, had been on the air to his carriers, barking out orders and keeping a tight, controlled rein on his force. As Captain Lee remembers him, "He was nothing if not vocal. He spent all of this long period of the battle with his microphone in his hand talking to all of us skippers on his six carriers, giving us all kinds of encouragement, sort of like a football coach running up and down the sidelines shouting to the players on the field."[49]

Before this first strike was launched, Stump told his fliers to go after everything that floated and not just concentrate on one or two ships. This they did with great success.

The planes that had been on CAP were already heading for the enemy when the first strike was launched. Immediately upon arrival over Center Force, the Wildcats began the first of many strafing runs. These first air attacks by the Taffy 2 planes coincided closely with those from Taffy 3.

Because of the low clouds and rain showers passing through the area, the squadrons were unable to join up, and so each unit had to attack piecemeal. These kinds of attacks were probably more effective than the pilots imagined, not necessarily from the standpoint of physical damage but from the standpoint of harassment. Too often the heavy ships had to turn away from the planes, wasting valuable time that the "jeeps" used to their advantage.

Among the first torpedo planes to make runs on the cruisers were four from the *Natoma Bay*. Lieutenant William B. Morton led his comrades against the heavy cruisers. Instead of being in column, two of the cruisers were almost parallel to each other. From 7,000 feet the quartet glided down, building up as much speed as possible. When the planes broke out of the clouds they were bounced around by a hail of gunfire. As the Avengers started their runs, the closer cruiser (the *Tone* or *Chikuma*) began to turn sharply to the right, while the other ship, the *Chokai*, made only a slight left turn.

Morton could see that he would only have a bow shot at the first cruiser, so he roared over that vessel at 1,800 feet and let his gunners rake the ship's decks. Taking aim at the *Chokai*, Morton punched his electric release, followed immediately by a hard yank on the manual release. The Avenger bounced a bit as the ring-tail torpedo dropped and headed straight for the cruiser. Just as he zoomed over the *Chokai*, a 25-mm shell exploded behind Morton's instrument panel, a fragment slicing into his leg. Seconds later Morton's turret gunner let out a whoop as he watched a dirty column of water spring into the air and engulf the cruiser's stern.

Although the turn of the *Tone*-class cruiser had left Morton without a shot, it had given the other three pilots excellent position to make quartering runs. One after another they dropped their torpedoes and scooted away. Lieutenant Wilbur F. Hiser's was seen to hit amidships, and the other two were also thought to have been heading directly for the ship, but whether they hit is unknown.

Upon pullout Hiser's plane was hit by flak, seriously wounding his radioman. To obtain medical attention for his crewman, Hiser headed for the beach and landed at Tacloban. Morton, in the meantime, was on his way back to the *Natoma Bay,* but he knew he wouldn't be able to get his battered "Turkey" aboard. Almost all of his instruments had been knocked out, as had been the hydraulic system. With no hydraulic pressure to lower flaps or close the bombbay doors, Morton nonetheless made an excellent water landing near one of Taffy 2's DEs. He and his crewmen were picked up safely.

VC-21 and VC-27 planes combined to attack the heavy cruisers, which were undergoing as much harassment as they were giving the CVEs. In this all-out attack by anywhere from seven to fifteen TBMs and many fighters, the fliers claimed several hits on the cruisers and one destroyer. One VC-21 pilot disappeared after making a strafing run. Nothing appeared to be wrong with his plane, but he was not seen again.

As his outfit's planes were making their attacks, VC-27's skipper, Lieutenant Commander P. W. Jackson, showed up. He had been launched earlier as an air coordinator for support work over Leyte. Before his group could do anything for the troops, Jackson was told to lead them against the enemy ships. His planes were ill-equipped for bombing ships, most of them carrying bomb loads of "centuries" plus rockets, but they were needed now.

Shortly after 0900 Jackson's planes arrived over the Center Force.

After looking the situation over, he sent his group in. For the moment Jackson remained behind, pondering which ship he would pick for his target. Suddenly a floatplane Jake popped out of the clouds below. Jackson was in excellent position for a tail shot, and he was quick to take advantage of this. His wing guns stuttered for a few seconds and the Jake, completely enveloped in flames, spiraled into the clouds.

Through a break in the clouds Jackson spotted two heavy cruisers cutting through the water. From 7,000 feet he swooped down at a steep angle. At 2,500 feet he began dropping his ten 100-pounders. Most of them missed astern but two landed squarely on a cruiser's stern, starting some small fires. As he jinked away at low altitude, one of Jackson's crewmen reported seeing a submarine just under the surface. Jackson himself picked up the wake of a periscope as he racked his big Avenger into a tight turn. From about 800 yards away he unleashed his full load of eight rockets at the periscope, and most of the rockets exploded around it. Already Jackson had had a pretty eventful day: one Jake shot down, hits on a cruiser, and the possible damaging of a submarine. Yet Jackson was not yet finished.[50]

Before his planes had been launched against the Japanese, Stump sent his three destroyers (the *Haggard, Hailey,* and *Franks*) to the rear of the formation to intercept any possible Japanese thrust against Taffy 2. These were the destroyers seen by the *Gambier Bay* a bit before 0800. The five destroyer escorts were stationed ahead of the carriers for screening purposes. Before long the three destroyers came under the fire of the *Kongo* and *Haruna.* Although the Taffy 3 ships were much closer, the two battleships began shelling Stump's destroyers at very long range. Of course, this helped the battered ships of Taffy 3 but was not appreciated by the three "tin cans."

On the *Natoma Bay* Ham Lokey watched with fascination as the colorful geysers sprang up around the destroyers. There was quiet on the *Natoma Bay*'s bridge as everyone stared at the towering columns, which would collapse and then be replaced by more columns. Turning to Lokey, Captain Morehouse said, "If you have anything in particular that you want to take over the side if we abandon ship, you might step down to your cabin and get it."

Morehouse extended this offer to another officer, and both men ran below. When Lokey returned, he had an extra life jacket, a whistle, a waterproof flashlight, a picture of his wife, a bottle of malted milk tablets, and an aviator's helmet to cover his bald head from the sun. The other man who had gone below returned carrying only a few papers. Lokey asked him what he was taking.

"My original orders," was the reply.

"What in the world do you want with those?"

"I don't know. They just told me in Indoctrination School that if I was ever separated from my ship it was a good thing to have my original orders with me."[51]

Luckily, the *Natoma Bay*'s crew didn't have to abandon ship.

Also involved in these first attacks were some Taffy 1 planes. When the first reports of the enemy force were received, a group of eight FM-2s from the *Petrof Bay* and *Santee* were waiting with six Hellcats, all carrying bombs, from the *Sangamon* and a TBM Air Coordinator from VT-26 over Leyte. Instead of ground targets, the planes were directed against the Center Force. All of the fighters made numerous strafing runs on various ships from the biggest down to the smallest. What damage was inflicted by the Hellcats' 500-pounders is unknown, as the bombs were released at very high speed and the pilots jinked away without looking to see if they hit. The 100-pounders dropped by the Avenger were too light to do any lasting damage but apparently did cut down some exposed gunners on an unidentified ship.

Two VC-76 Wildcats were lost during this action, one to friendly fire at Tacloban and the other to enemy antiaircraft fire. Lieutenant Abe Forsythe had made his runs and was trying to land at Tacloban when what seemed like every gun in the vicinity opened up on him. His plane was hit several times and Forsythe decided it would be a lot safer to ditch than to try to brave the fire (which showed no sign of abating) and land on the airstrip. He plunked his fighter into the water offshore and was quickly picked up by a destroyer.

Also hammered by flak, this time Japanese, was Ensign Jess L. Curtright. Just as he broke out of the clouds to begin his dive, Curtright's fighter was nailed by a burst of flak that tore off almost two feet of his right wing. Nevertheless, he continued his strafing pass, dropping his right wing tank as he zoomed over the ship. Just before he reached the safety of the clouds another shell blew off his engine cowl and cockpit hatch. Almost half of one of the propeller blades was also blown away.

Curtright had to put his plane down in a hurry. Near three Japanese destroyers he landed with a big splash. A loud explosion behind him brought him to his senses. One of the destroyers had blown off half his plane's tail as it wallowed in the water. Another shell slammed into the Wildcat just behind the cockpit as Curtright scrambled out of it. Unable to get his raft out, Curtright had to watch the destroyers set his plane afire as they swept past.

The Japanese weren't done with him yet. Later that morning an enemy plane strafed Curtright four times without hitting him. Without a life raft, Curtright was not in an enviable position, especially when friendly planes flew low over him several times and didn't spot him. But he didn't give up hope, and the next morning the *Tingey*, looking for survivors, saw Curtright and pulled him aboard.[52]

In the meantime, a major strike made up of four FM-2s and six TBMs of VC-76, five F6Fs of VF-37, seven F6Fs of VF-60, five TBMs of VT-60, eight FM-2s of VF-26, and five TBFs/TBMs of VT-26 was launched at 0725. As the planes were rendezvousing, the first kamikazes dove on Taffy 1. (See Chapter 7.) To protect his ships, Tommy Sprague called all the fighters back over the carriers. A few minutes later Sprague released the four VC-76 Wildcats and the seven VF-60 Hellcats to rejoin the Avengers over Dinagat. This going and coming had burned up a lot of fuel, and some of the planes had to turn back before reaching the Japanese fleet.

Finally, about 0910, the strike group started north. The planes reached the vicinity of the battle at about 1000. A smoking, obviously heavily damaged cruiser was crawling away to the northwest. By now the planes had been airborne almost three hours and some pilots were reporting fuel tanks more than half empty. They held a discussion on whether to attack the damaged cruiser, which came to an abrupt halt when Lieutenant Commander James W. McCauley cried out, "To hell with the cruiser! We're after the Japanese Fleet!"[53]

And they found it. Two separate groups were merging on a northwest course when first seen. The planes were coming in head-on toward the ships. Realizing the fuel predicament, Lieutenant Commander T. M. Bennett, the flight leader, ordered an immediate attack. The five VT-26 Avengers were able to make an anvil attack, in which groups of bombers would come in from both sides of the bow, on the *Yamato*, and at least two hits were claimed on the monster ship by the fliers. One Avenger was hit during its approach, causing its wheels to drop and jamming its bomb bay doors before its torpedo could be released; doing only 160 knots, the pilot flew right over the *Yamato*'s bow. All three crewmen got a closeup look at the battleship's bridge before they slipped away. Of the five *Santee* Avengers in this attack, only Commander Bennett's would make it back to a carrier. All of the others would have to set down in the sea out of fuel or damaged.

Several hits on a *Kongo*-class battleship were claimed by the VT-60 Avengers, while four VF-60 Hellcats claimed one hit and three near misses on a destroyer. The VC-76 torpedo planes also went after the *Kongo* and *Haruna,* mistaking them for the *Fuso* and *Yamashiro*. Lieutenant Dick Tacy made two runs on a battleship. His first run was spoiled by a release malfunction so he continued right over the ship, pulled up into the clouds, made a 180-degree turn, and came back in from the opposite side. His torpedo ran straight but the crew, having their hands full as the TBM was bounced around by the flak, did not see whether it hit. With only a few minutes of fuel left, Tacy landed on the *Fanshaw Bay*.

After dropping his torpedo, Lieutenant Alan E. Schwarzwalder flew right down the side of the *"Fuso."* Until the flak shook him from his reverie, the large Japanese flag displayed by the ship "particularly fascinated him and held his attention."[54] Schwarzwalder and another pilot who had dropped on the second battleship landed on the *Ommaney Bay*.

Two other torpedo pilots went after the *Yamato*, with unknown results. One had to ditch within sight of the *Petrof Bay*, but the other just made it back to the flattop. The last VC-76 Avenger pilot, Ensign William E. Niemann, attacked one of the *Kongo*-class battleships. Just as he entered his dive at 8,000 feet, a shell hit his bomb bay, forcing him to pump them open by hand. By the time he got them open, he was rapidly closing with the battleship. From only 900 yards away he dropped his torpedo and watched it start bubbling toward the ship.

Yanking hard on his stick, Niemann shot over the battleship's stern in a tight left turn. He made quick retreat right between two lines of ships, with the enemy gunners probably scoring more hits on each other than they got on the twisting Avenger. Niemann made it back to Taffy 3 and tried to land on the *Fanshaw Bay*, but he had to go around on his first attempt when he couldn't get his landing gear or flaps down. As he was circling for another attempt, the kamikazes struck, leaving Niemann nowhere to go. Almost out of fuel, he splashed north of Taffy 3. The crew had no trouble getting out of their plane, but they would be in their raft for over five hours before the *Dennis* picked them up.[55]

At 0833 Taffy 2 came back to the northeast to launch the second strike and to land six Avengers from Taffy 3. This launch of eight fighters and sixteen torpedo bombers (all with torpedoes) was completed at 0844, and the formation came back to the southeast.[56] A few planes, unable to be launched with the first strike (for various reasons), had also been sent off as they had become available.

Eight of the torpedo planes had come from John Dale's VC-20. Dale led his planes to the west, using the clouds to conceal their approach. The *Kongo* and *Haruna* were picked for VC-20's targets. Telling each pilot his job in this attack was time-consuming, primarily because all radio discipline had broken down by now. Thus, "communication was practically impossible because the air was jammed with pilots' personal problems."[57]

With things finally settled down, Dale led his men into a screaming dive. Four planes headed for the lead battleship, two toward the other, one pilot who had dropped behind went for a cruiser, and an eighth plane got lost and made no attack. Though no fighters were there to protect the lumbering Avengers, Dale didn't hesitate and bored on in. Unfortunately, none of the torpedoes from Dale's group of four planes hit.

Luckier was Ensign Warren Kruck. Kruck and his section leader streaked toward the second battleship. As the leader made his attack, the battlewagon began a turn to the right. This threw off the leader's attack and his torpedo missed, but it left Kruck with almost a full broadside shot. Through an amazing amount of flak, Kruck bored in to drop his torpedo at a range of 1,800 yards. As he pulled out, an antiaircraft shell exploded next to his plane, throwing it into a wild skid.

Kruck decided he had better get on the deck. Between the two battleships, so low that one time Kruck believed he hit the water, the Avenger sped. Looking back over his shoulder, he saw his torpedo hit, a tower of smoke and a huge sheet of flame erupting from the battleship's side. Just then an antiaircraft shell slammed into the plane. It reared and shuddered and burst into flames. Kruck was sure he had had it.

His turret gunner couldn't answer his calls, so Kruck decided to wait and see if things calmed down. They did. The fire died out and the plane's engine kept purring away. At first, seeing the shell splashes moving toward Taffy 2, he had not been too enthusiastic about landing on his ship. To land at Tacloban had been his first thought, but when his gunner regained consciousness, Kruck headed back to the *Kadashan Bay*. A few hours later he was in the air again, chasing the retreating enemy.[58]

Two young VC-81 ensigns missed what they were aiming at but came up winners anyway. George W. Gaiennie and Robert F. Voltz made torpedo runs on a battleship, possibly the *Haruna*, but had to watch in disappointment as the big ship neatly combed their "fish." "How in the hell did we miss that big son-of-a-bitch?" a frustrated voice radioed. But as the pair watched the wake of their torpedoes, their spirits picked up. The torpedoes were headed right for a cruiser. Two explosions blossomed on the ship, one amidships and the other on the fantail. "Banjo's [the *Natoma Bay*] got a cruiser!" came an elated cry. What ship the two fliers drilled (if, in fact, they even did hit the cruiser) is unknown, although the *Suzuya* or *Chokai* are the prime suspects.[59]

Also in on this series of attacks was VC-75. At 0910 Lieutenant (jg) Clark Miller made a single-handed run on the bristling *Kongo*. His torpedo missed, but that was just another example of the extent to which the fliers were protecting their own ships.

Meanwhile, VC-80's Lieutenant (jg) H. D. Bryan almost didn't get to drop his torpedo. Diving toward a battleship, Bryan had to pull out almost immediately. Upon being armed, his torpedo had dropped out of its sling and was now lying on the bomb bay doors. After ducking away to check the situation and to see if the torpedo had started its arming cycle, Bryan returned to make another run. Simply by opening his doors, he released it at a range of 1,400 yards. It is doubtful if the torpedo even ran. Another VC-80 pilot claimed yet another hit on a *Tone*-class cruiser. (All the hits these vessels were reported to have taken should have sunk them long before.[60])

Taffy 2's third strike of twelve Avengers, five of which were carrying torpedoes and the others 500-pounders, and eight fighters went off at 0935. Concerned that this launch would place him dangerously close to the Japanese, Stump catapulted his Avengers into a crosswind. The launch went off without a hitch, but if Stump had only known that at that moment the Center Force was turning back to the north, he could have come into the wind and have had one less worry.

Even though the Japanese were retiring when this group of planes arrived over them, they were in no mood to put up with more unwelcome attention from the TBMs and FM-2s. A furious barrage of antiaircraft fire blackened the sky. One Wildcat was shot down by the flak, though its pilot was able to coax a few miles out of his plane to get away from the enemy. Seen to climb in his raft, he was never found by later search efforts. Several other planes were battered by the very accurate flak, but then, the Japanese had certainly been getting a lot of practice.[61]

VC-68's George Smith had picked up a torpedo from the *Marcus Island* and had been sent out on a second mission. Spotting a cruiser circling another obviously damaged cruiser, Smith spent several minutes planning his strategy. Finally he teamed up with a pair of fighters. The fighters led the way with strafing runs on the cruiser's starboard bow. Occupied with the fighters, the gunners didn't spot Smith until he had dropped his torpedo, and then their fire was inaccurate. Smith's torpedo hit the cruiser about thirty feet from her stern. Immediately she slowed down and careened to starboard, leaving a heavy trail of oil. As Smith left, the cruiser was listing to port and turning in tight circles.[62]

Not once but three times did the *Natoma Bay*'s Ensign John T. Goodwin brave the antiaircraft fire. Because of an arming-lever malfunction, none of his bombs had dropped on his first run. A second pass, with the radioman pulling the arming lever at the proper moment, had the same results. Perhaps thinking the third time would be the charm, Goodwin made yet another attack, his radioman all the while yanking on the lever as hard as he could. It worked. All four bombs tumbled out, hitting close aboard a battleship.

Another VC-81 pilot, Lieutenant (jg) L. S. Conner, made runs on both a battleship and a cruiser, getting one hit on the battlewagon. As he retired, Conner was asked by a VC-20 TBM pilot to give him some cover while he went for a cruiser dead in the water several miles south of the main enemy force. Glad to help, Conner led the way, his wing guns twinkling. The VC-20 pilot's run was good, his torpedo spearing the cruiser amidships. But as he pulled up, his TBM was engulfed in flames and it tumbled into the sea. There were no survivors.[63]

Up until now almost all the air action had been on the American side. Few Japanese planes had been seen, most having been shot down or chased away. Some Japanese planes, however, did break through to open a new and terrifying era of warfare. An unhappy Taffy 3 would once again see death at close range before the day was over, but it was another unit (Taffy 1) that would first meet the new Japanese weapon—the kamikaze.

DEATH FROM THE SKY

In 1281 the Mongol leader Kublai Khan sent a powerful armada to invade and conquer Japan, but his armada was scattered and destroyed by a mighty typhoon. Since then the Japanese people have believed that their nation was saved by the heavenly intervention of a "divine wind"—the *kamikaze*.

Some 663 years later, as the hated Americans closed in on the homeland, the Japanese formed a Special Attack Corps. The mission of the men of that unit was to destroy the Americans by diving their own planes into the enemy ships. The corps was given the name "Kamikaze," for its planes and men were to fall on the enemy like the divine wind.

The idea of diving one's plane into an enemy vessel or other target was not new—Japanese fliers had done it before. But their actions had generally resulted from a spur-of-the moment decision by a flier unable to return to his base, for whatever reason, who wished to make his death meaningful by taking some of the enemy with him. Occidental fliers in similar situations had employed the same suicidal tactic. But what was different about the World War II kamikazes was the tremendous scope of this effort and its meticulous advance planning.

The father of the Special Attack Corps was Vice Admiral Takijiro Onishi, who had only just arrived in the Philippines on 17 October to take command of the First Air Fleet, which (along with the Fourth Air Army) provided the air defense of the Philippines. Onishi discovered he had precious little left to use for defense. Halsey's raids in September had ravaged the air units, over 800 planes being lost. Though reinforcements were flown in and in early October the First Air Fleet and the Fourth Air Army had some 400 aircraft on hand, by the time of the Leyte landings the number had dwindled rapidly. When Onishi reached the Philippines he discovered that only about fifty planes in his command were operational, and that while the Fourth Air Army claimed to have 150 planes operational, many of those had been withdrawn from the Philippines.[1]

But Onishi was no quitter. He was well known in the Imperial Japanese Navy as a firebrand, with a passionate devotion to the theories of air power. For some time Onishi had been considering suicide tactics against U.S. ships. He was not alone; many in the army and navy following the fall of Saipan were groping for something—anything—that could stop the juggernaut sweeping down on Japan from the east. In the Philippines Onishi (with the blessing of his superiors) finally concluded that it was time to implement suicide tactics.

On the evening of 19 October Onishi journeyed to Mabalacat, part of the huge Clark Field complex northwest of Manila. Here, where the 201st Air Group was based, the kamikazes were born. In the quiet of the tropical night Onishi discussed with the 201st's staff what must be done. Gravely the officers listened to Onishi, and when he was done the 201st's staff gathered to consider his remarks. They knew the position their country was in. They knew their position in the Philippines. There was little doubt in their minds about what must be done, although most would have preferred another kind of action.

It was decided. The 201st Air Group would form the first organized kamikaze unit, the Special Attack Corps. Volunteers for this unit were not hard to come by, virtually all of the 201st's pilots stepping forward when told of the new task assigned the group. The commander of the new unit was Lieutenant Yukio Seki. This group was then divided into four units: *Shikishima* (a poetic name for Japan), *Yamato* (Japan's ancient name), *Asahi* (morning sun), and *Yamazakura* (mountain cherry blossoms).

The afternoon of 20 October saw the volunteers of the *Yamato* unit fly south to Cebu to form the nucleus of another kamikaze outfit, this one from the 601st Air Group. News of the formation of the Special Attack Corps had spread rapidly, and more eager volunteers joined at Cebu. In just a short while volunteers were available at all the major air bases in the Philippines. The Americans would soon feel the divine wind.[2]

Despite the eagerness and fervor of the Japanese airmen to hurl themselves into the American vessels, the first few days after the formation of the kamikazes were not propitious for the suicide flights. Poor weather hampered flight operations considerably, while an attack on Lahug by Taffy 1 aircraft on 21 October partially pulled the fangs of the *Yamato* unit by destroying five Zekes as they were warming up for the first kamikaze missions from Cebu.

This situation would change quickly on the twenty-fifth—for the better for the kamikaze pilots; for the worse for the men and ships of Taffies 1 and 3.

Just a short while after the shells from Kurita's ships began falling on Taffy 3, the first organized kamikaze attacks hurtled in on an unsuspecting Taffy 1. From Mabalacat came Lieutenant Seki's *Shikishima* unit of five kamikazes, with an escort of four other Zekes. From Davao came First Flying Petty Officer Keeichi Ueno's *Asahi* planes along with First Flying Petty Officer Toyobumi Kato's *Kikusui* (floating chrysanthemum) unit—six planes with four escorts. (The *Asahi* unit had been sent to Davao earlier to form the nucleus of further kamikaze groups.)[3]

The Davao planes drew first blood. On the morning of the twenty-fifth Taffy 1 was operating about forty miles east of Siargao Island (an outlying island guarding the southeastern approaches to Leyte Gulf) and was about 130 miles south of Taffy 3. At 0545 a Wildcat/Avenger strike force had been launched against the remnants of the Southern Force. Before these aircraft returned, the chilling report that the ships of Taffy 3 were under fire from enemy vessels reached Tommy Sprague. He quickly issued orders to recover and rearm all available aircraft and send them to Taffy 3's aid. While these operations were under way, the Davao kamikazes put in an appearance.

Five Avengers and eight Wildcats had just been launched by the *Santee* when four enemy planes were spotted ducking in and out of the clouds at ten thousand feet, almost directly over the ships. Immediately following this sighting, three of the planes dove on the carriers, the fourth plane stooging around for a time while taking care to select the proper target. It was 0740.

The *Santee* was caught in a very awkward and vulnerable position. On her hangar deck several TBMs were being rearmed and numerous depth bombs and GP bombs were lying on the deck. Neither did her gunners have time to bring their guns to bear on the hurtling plane nor had Captain Blick time to swing his ship out of the way.

With guns blazing, the Zeke swept in from astern to smash into the flight deck on the port side forward and outboard of the aft elevator. The kamikaze continued its violent path through to the hanger deck. As the plane speared through the flight deck, the small bomb it was carrying exploded just under the deck, sending shards of steel whizzing about. Some of these shards struck depth bombs lying on the deck, splitting the casings open. Torpex spilled from

Debris flies through the air as the kamikaze hits the Santee *on 25 October 1944. Note the sailors crouched behind the tractor at the left. (National Archives)*

these bombs to burn and sizzle with great intensity, but did not explode.

Blasted in the flight deck was a long, narrow hole thirty by fifteen feet. Fires started on both the flight and hangar decks, one on the hangar deck close to a stack of 1,000-pound bombs but luckily beaten down before a catastrophe occurred. For that matter, none of the fires were very serious. More serious were the casualties, forty-three total with sixteen of those fatal.[4]

Just seconds after the *Santee* was hit, another kamikaze circled astern of the *Suwannee*. Black puffs of flak sprouted around the Zeke. Some of this antiaircraft fire struck home, staggering the plane. Seeking an easier target, the Zeke pilot spiraled down for a short time, then pushed over in a 45-degree dive toward the *Sangamon*. Again the black puffs surrounded the plane.

The Zeke was heading directly for the forward part of the *Sangamon*'s flight deck, appearing to be a sure hit. Then a 5-inch shell hit the plane, flipping it over to dive into the sea close aboard the flattop's port bow. Fragments of the plane and its bomb flew through the air to wound three men standing on the forecastle, one fatally. The hit that had sent the Zeke into the water had been the only shot fired by the *Suwannee*'s 5-inch gun crew, but it had done the job.[5]

A third Zeke pointed its nose at the *Petrof Bay*. Immediately Captain Joseph L. "Paddy" Kane ordered a series of fishtails for his ship, the maneuverability of the Kaiser-class vessel readily apparent as she swung about in tight turns. The Zeke pilot was having a hard time keeping a bead on the pirouetting ship, and the heavy antiaircraft fire thrown at him didn't help his concentration. As the suicider plummeted down, more and more shells ripped into the Zeke and it began to reel. In seconds the kamikaze was out of control, rolling and tumbling into the sea close enough off the *Petrof Bay*'s starboard side to throw water onto her flight deck.[6]

Kamikazes weren't the only assailants to plague Taffy 1. Unheard and unseen by the screening vessels, Lieutenant Commander Masahiko Morinaga had brought his submarine, the *I-56*, close to Taffy 1. Taking his time, he surveyed the scene and picked his intended victim, the *Santee*. Shortly before 0756 he fired a spread of torpedoes at the carrier.

Five minutes previously, the *Santee*'s crew had finally brought her fires under control and were beginning to clean up the mess left by the kamikaze. At 0756 one of Morinaga's torpedoes struck the flattop's starboard side abreast the after elevator. Fortunately, the hit was a glancing one and the explosion took place some distance from the carrier's side. Nevertheless, plates were sprung and machinery deranged. Some flooding caused a 6-degree list, but by 0935 the *Santee*'s crew had everything under control and her speed was still over 17 knots. Morinaga's intrusion brought a quick response from the destroyer *Trathen*, yet in spite of a heavy and long depth-charging, he was able to escape and make his way back to Japan.[7]

The torpedo explosion caught everyone's attention in Taffy 1 but didn't stop them from keeping their eyes peeled for the fourth plane, which was still wandering. Spotted at 0758 slightly astern of the formation circling in the clouds at 8,000 feet, the Zeke was quickly taken under fire. A puff of smoke, then a thin trail showed that the plane had been hit. But it hadn't been stopped.

Rolling over, the Zeke began a dive on the *Suwannee*. A Hellcat made a pass on the kamikaze, but the enemy plane zipped out of range before the F6F pilot could draw a bead. At a forty-five-degree angle the Zeke roared in, boresighted on the carrier's flight deck. At 0804 the Zeke smacked into the *Suwannee* forty feet forward of the after elevator, ripping a ten-foot hole in her flight deck. Most of the Zeke's fuselage and its bomb continued into the hangar, where the bomb exploded. This explosion and the passage of the kamikaze's engine blew a hole about twenty feet in diameter in the hangar deck, the engine finally coming to rest on the main deck.

A billowing, roiling black and gray cloud of smoke soared into the sky. Only one plane had been parked on the hangar deck, but it was now a mass of flames. Prompt activation of the sprinkler system, along with the use of foam and CO_2, quenched the hangar fire within fifteen minutes. Remarkably, damage to the ship was not extensive, the main casualties being the knocking out of the after elevator and a temporary loss of steering. By 1009 a patch had been placed on the hole in the flight deck and the Suwannee was again conducting flight operations.[8] From her came a defiant message: "All we found of the Jap are bits of his flesh. We're ready for battle again."[9]

This attack was the last kamikaze mission against Taffy 1 on the twenty-fifth. Although the Americans were shocked and appalled at this new manifestation of the horror of war, the Davao kamikazes had not accomplished much. Two carriers had been damaged, but not knocked out of the battle. There had been personnel casualties, but compared with later kamikaze attacks, these were light.

Not fully comprehending the extent and seriousness of this new tactic by the Japanese, several commanders were less than impressed with the attacks, even after the St. Lo was sunk later in the day and the Suwannee badly damaged the next day. One of these skeptics was the Petrof Bay's CO, Paddy Kane. In his action report following the battle, he wrote:

1. A kamikaze attack is a stupid way to attack *because it has less chance of getting home* than other types of bombing. [Italics in original.]
2. The reason it has less chance is that the plane should be shot down between 2,000 and 500 feet when the plane is quite large in the sights and the density of shot required to bring it down decreases with nearness.
3. Keep firing at it until it breaks up, blows up, or crashes. The best chance of stopping it is when it looks like a freight car in your sights.
4. It actually does less damage as a rule than a regularly dropped bomb that reaches the vitals of the ship. It is more spectacular but has less penetrative qualities.
5. It is like the "bayonet charge" of infantry and like enemy infantry it is most surely stopped at close quarters, *so keep shooting!* [Italics in original.][10]

Only time would show how terribly wrong Captain Kane's observations were.

At 0911 Kurita had ordered his ships to rendezvous with the *Yamato*. Less than fifty minutes later, Halsey received a query from Admiral Nimitz: "Where is, repeat, where is TF 34? The world wonders." The latter sentence was padding and is irrelevant, a fact Kinkaid's staff realized when they intercepted the message. But Halsey's decoders made a mistake and left the padding in. When Halsey read the message he became infuriated, cursing and ranting until his chief of staff calmed him down.

Halsey took the message to be criticism, and in a way it was, for Nimitz was implying that TF 34 was not where it was supposed to be. After he calmed down, Halsey spent almost an hour deciding what to do. Finally, at 1055, long after Kurita had started his retirement, he ordered TG 38.2 to join TF 34 and head south for San Bernardino Strait. Characteristically, he took all of the battleships south, leaving none to face the Northern Force. Actually, in what became known as the Battle of Cape Engano, Halsey's other ships took care of the Northern Force. Four carriers and two destroyers were sunk by the fast carrier planes and the light surface forces.

Halsey's decision had come too late. In what became known inelegantly as "the Battle of Bull's Run," the battleships headed south. Fueling of destroyers would slow TF 34 down, and the battleships would accomplish nothing against the Center Force or the Northern Force.

While Halsey pondered what to do, the ships of Taffy 3 came under attack from an unexpected quarter. Upon seeing the Japanese ships turning away, more than one Taffy 3 sailor had heaved a deep sigh of relief that their ordeal was apparently finished. Unknown to them, only the first half of the game was over. Kickoff for the second half was just minutes away.

Following the retirement of the Japanese ships, general quarters had been secured on many of the Taffy 3 ships, and some of the men had finally been given the chance to grab a bite to eat. Few aircraft were still on the carriers. At 1015 a small strike consisting of six Avengers from the *Kitkun Bay* (five carrying torpedoes), two TBMs with torpedoes from the *White Plains*, and two FM-2s from the *St. Lo* was launched. It would be the last strike sent out by the Taffy 3 carriers.

The Taffy 3 planes droned north until they sighted a *Tone*-class cruiser in a high-speed tight circle. Deciding that the cruiser was a tempting target, the flight leader spread out his planes for an anvil attack. Because of a balky engine, one of the VC-5 planes had to break off and head for Tacloban. The remaining seven torpedo planes dove steeply on the cruiser from off both sides of her bow.

Heavy flak greeted the planes but did no damage. Swerving wildly to the right, the cruiser was able to evade most of the torpedoes but left herself open to the "fish" launched from her port side. Two of these slammed into her amidships, causing an immediate list. As these planes pulled away, the crews saw a lone unidentified TBM make a run on the cruiser. One second it was an Avenger thundering toward the ship; the next second it was a ball of red and orange flame arcing into the sea.[11] Afterward, most of the planes were able to land on their own carriers, the kamikaze attack over by the time they returned.

Meanwhile, leaving Mabalacat at 0725 had been the five Zekes of Lieutenant Seki's *Shikishima* unit, plus another four escorting fighters. Hedge-hopping to the southeast, Seki's planes were over Leyte Gulf around 1030. In his search for suitable targets, Seki spotted the ships of Taffy 3 slowly steaming southeast. Seki pointed out the carriers to his companions, then pulled up several thousand feet into the scattered clouds to gain an optimum attack position. Finally satisfied, at 1049 he rocked his wings and peeled off toward the ships. Close behind came the other four kamikazes, the remaining fighters circling overhead to record the results of the attacks.

Two minutes later the Americans discovered the presence of these planes as they snarled out of the sky. Out of position when the kamikazes streaked in, the few airborne Wildcats were unable to get off a shot. Apparently the first to see the suiciders and the first to open fire was the destroyer escort *Raymond,* but the other ships quickly cut loose. By this time, though, the Zekes were right on top of the carriers and their speed helped carry them through most of the flak.

One of the Zekes aimed at the *Kitkun Bay.* Crossing just ahead of the flattop from port to starboard, it zoomed up, followed by a trail of tracers from the "jeep's" guns. As his airspeed dropped off, the pilot pulled his plane over in a dive right at the *Kitkun Bay*'s bridge. Again the antiaircraft fire reached out to tear into the Zeke, the pilot firing back in return. This defensive fire may have wounded or killed the pilot, for he just missed the ship's island. The kamikaze whipped over the island, smashed into the port catwalk (tearing away about fifteen feet of it), and careened into the water just twenty-five yards away. When the kamikaze chopped through the catwalk, the bomb it was carrying exploded, flinging fragments everywhere. Surprisingly, this close call resulted only in the death of one man and the wounding of sixteen others. The ship suffered minor damage.[12]

Close on the heels of this kamikaze came a second, aiming at the *Fanshaw Bay*. Unlike his predecessor, he got nowhere near his target before being splashed. Another Zeke screamed in toward the *White Plains*. To the men on the carrier it appeared that the pilot of this plane "expected to land on the after end of the flight deck," as the Zeke was only about 500 feet high and roaring in from directly astern.[13]

A hail of flak enveloped the kamikaze, yet on it came. Watching intently from the bridge, Captain Sullivan waited until the pilot appeared to have fully committed himself, and then ordered hard left rudder. The ship began to swing and the guns on her after port side chimed in, their shells chewing chunks out of the onrushing Zeke. The kamikaze wove from side to side; then, only a few yards astern, it rolled left and just missed the port catwalk aft of the No. 2 stack. Plane and bomb exploded between the catwalk and the water, showering fragments upon the flight deck. As on the *Kitkun Bay*, damage to ship and crew was light. Only eleven men were wounded, none seriously, and the damage caused by the explosion was cleaned up in a few minutes.[14]

So far in this intense, frantic action Taffy 3's luck had held. Now it ran out. About ten minutes before the kamikazes appeared, the *St. Lo* had taken aboard a Wildcat from the *Kalinin Bay*, two *White Plains* Avengers, and two more of her own TBMs. These planes were struck below to be rearmed and refueled. Two other aircraft were in the hangar but they were inoperable. Four torpedoes had been removed from their stowage racks and were lying on the deck. In addition, four other torpedoes were still in their racks and sixty-four bombs of various sizes were in ready stowage. The planes had been in the process of being fueled, but that was discontinued when the enemy appeared.

A second aircraft had initially dived on the *White Plains*, but when antiaircraft fire started it smoking, it turned toward the *St. Lo*. Though taken under fire by the carrier's guns, the Zeke continued on to make a right turn into the "groove" and swept in at high speed over the ramp. No more than fifty feet high, the plane released a bomb that sliced through the flight deck into the hangar. The plane followed the bomb, crashing into the flight deck a few yards farther on. There was a bright flash followed by a loud clatter as pieces of the plane skittered up the deck and over the bow. Flaming gasoline was flung all around, but caused surprisingly few casualties among those men stationed at the guns or in other exposed areas.

To Captain McKenna, looking down from the bridge, the damage to his ship did not appear to be serious, a little debris on the flight deck and a hole two feet in diameter left in the deck by the bomb being the only evidence of damage. Hoses that were already in place for landing operations were quickly in action to douse the few flames that could be seen lapping about the edges of the hole.

Below decks, however, the situation was very serious. In the hangar "a ball of fire smashed down from the overhead" as the bomb exploded directly above an aircraft that had been gassed and rearmed.[15] Gas from this plane and from other unidentified sources quickly formed a large pool, which burned with flames from eighteen inches to two feet high almost the width of the hangar in that vicinity. Immediately the hanger sprinkling system was turned on, but only the forward water curtain and sprinklers had pressure to deliver water. The sprinklers in the area of the fire could produce just a trickle of water. Of the several fire hoses that were run out, only one had sufficient pressure, and this was lost within a few minutes.

About forty-five seconds after the first explosion, a second occurred in the hangar—another plane blowing up. Out of the hole in the flight deck poured dense black smoke and flames, burning several men in a fire-fighting party who had gathered about the hole. Around the port edge of the flight deck more smoke issued. On the hangar deck the port bomb hatch was lifted from its opening and deposited several feet away. The bomb hatch on the deck below was also lifted from its opening but fell back in almost its original position. Following the first blast, lights on the ship had flickered off, then back on. The second explosion blacked out a major portion of the ship (except for battle lanterns), and the next explosion took care of the rest of the lights.

So far, except for the fire on the hangar deck, damage to the *St. Lo* had been minor. The dense smoke, though, had forced the evacuation of the after engine room, the men reaching the forward messroom safely. Crucial in the crew's attempts to fight the fire had been the lack of water pressure, partially supplied by the aft engine. But the third blast really sealed the carrier's fate.

At about 1055 a very large, very sharp blast accompanied by a bright yellow flash occurred in the hangar, and a glowing fireball framed by clouds of smoke and debris shot into the sky. Some men were blown into the water by this explosion; others were blown to bits. This major detonation was probably caused by a pair of torpex-filled torpedoes that had been lying almost in the center of the fire. Survivors stated later that the after elevator platform blew upward and disappeared. So did much of the after section of the flight deck, some twenty-five feet of it also being folded forward by this eruption. Many bulkheads were caved in and several hatches blown off their hinges. A couple of these hatches caught the after engine-room gang as they sought safety. All but one were killed or fatally wounded by the flying hatches; the one man to escape had luckily gone aft, out over the fantail.

This tremendous explosion also warped the forward elevator and knocked out steering control. Seeing that his men were fighting a losing battle, Captain McKenna told them to prepare to abandon ship. Because most of the communication circuits were out, his order had to be passed by word of mouth or by those few sound-power circuits that were still undamaged. Forced by the flames to leap for their lives or be blown off the ship by the explosions, some men were already in the water.

As the men moved to their abandon ship stations, yet another heavy, sharp explosion took place. The partially warped forward elevator was folded in half. From where the flight deck had once been, flames licked greedily into the air. Huge billows of black and gray smoke floated up and behind the carrier, which was almost dead in the water and listing some three degrees to port.

By this time most of the *St. Lo*'s crew had gathered on the forecastle or on the flight deck forward. McKenna gave the order to abandon ship, and the men began to scramble down lifelines or dive into the water. The wounded men were lowered into the sea, where waiting sailors took them under tow. Watching from the carrier's tiny bridge were McKenna, the air officer, and a bugler. About this time an extremely violent blast rocked the ship. Once again smoke and flames soared upward. Rocket motors stowed in the after part of the hangar were apparently ignited by this blast, for a continuous stream of dazzling white flame squirted from this part of the ship for some time.

While Captain McKenna and his party were leaving the bridge about 1105, a sixth explosion of considerable magnitude took place. This detonation blew out the starboard hangar bulkhead, taking with it a good part of the aft starboard side of the ship. Some of the debris peppered the men in the water, probably killing some and definitely injuring others.

A seventh tremendous explosion was felt and heard by the men in the water, an underwater hammering that injured several more men and knocked the breath from many others. It didn't seem possible that many large blasts could be left in the little carrier, but there was still one big one to go. About five minutes after McKenna entered the water, one last gigantic explosion racked the *St. Lo*. Prior to this time all of the detonations (except perhaps for the next to last) had occurred high in the ship. This one was obviously deep in the bowels of the ship in the area of her bomb magazine. Apparently the ravening fire had finally found its way down through the sprung bomb hatches to the magazine, where hundreds of bombs and rockets were still stowed.

When McKenna entered the water, his carrier had been listing a few degrees to port. Now she began to roll to starboard, her rate slowly accelerating. Within a couple of minutes her flight deck was almost perpendicular to the water. There was a large hole in her bottom between the after stack and elevator. She began sinking by the stern, twisting as she went down, her bow thrust vertically into the air. Then she was gone.

Soon the screening vessels were plucking the *St. Lo*'s men from the water. For over four hours the four escorts crisscrossed the scene, stopping every now and then to gather in survivors. Despite the violence of the carrier's death, her abandonment had been orderly, with the wounded handled especially carefully. The *Heermann* picked up seventy-five stretcher cases. Eventually 784 men were rescued, but another 114 *St. Lo* sailors were lost.

Could the *St. Lo* have been saved? Possibly, if the ship's sprinkler system had worked. The first two explosions did not do much damage to the ship. Water pressure was lost, however, and the hangar deck fire could not be contained. Typical of all the Kaiser vessels, the *St. Lo* had a fire main system made up mostly of cast iron. This material was very susceptible to damage, including that caused by shock, and in this instance the cast-iron fittings fractured and allowed the precious water to escape. This was an example of the deficiencies that plagued the Kaiser designs.[16]

Japanese writers later claimed that Lieutenant Seki had dived into the *St. Lo*. Available evidence indicates that this is not true, one of Seki's comrades being the carrier's executioner. Seki himself went after the *Kalinin Bay* just a few minutes after the *St. Lo* was hit. Though he had led his formation down by 1049, Seki apparently took his time in choosing a target and didn't start his own attack until after 1100.

At 1110 a group of approximately fifteen Judys was sighted by the *Kitkun Bay*.[17] It is not known where these planes came from or even if there were actually that many present—other ships did not see that many, nor do Japanese records mention such a group. At this time Taffy 3's screen was busy rescuing the *St. Lo*'s men, leaving the carriers unprotected, so if fifteen planes were available, it is somewhat surprising that only four more attacks were made on the CVEs.

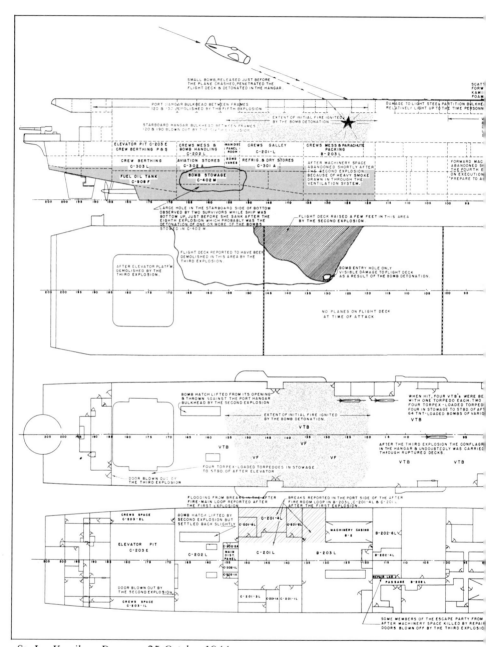

St. Lo Kamikaze Damage, 25 October 1944

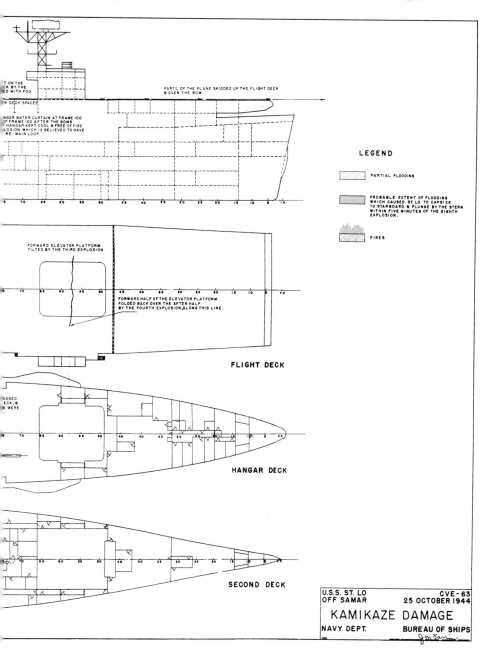

LEGEND

PARTIAL FLOODING

PROBABLE EXTENT OF FLOODING
WHICH CAUSED ST. LO TO CAPSIZE
TO STARBOARD & PLUNGE BY THE STERN
WITHIN FIVE MINUTES OF THE EIGHTH
EXPLOSION.

FIRES

PARTS OF THE PLANE SKIDDED UP THE FLIGHT DECK
& OVER THE BOW.

FORWARD ELEVATOR PLATFORM
TILTED BY THE THIRD EXPLOSION

FORWARD HALF OF THE ELEVATOR PLATFORM
FOLDED BACK OVER THE AFTER HALF
BY THE FOURTH EXPLOSION, ALONG THIS LINE.

FLIGHT DECK

HANGAR DECK

SECOND DECK

U.S.S. ST. LO	CVE- 63
OFF SAMAR	25 OCTOBER 1944
KAMIKAZE DAMAGE	
NAVY DEPT.	BUREAU OF SHIPS

One of these was on the *Kitkun Bay*. Two FM-2s were launched by the ship at 1117 for CAP. Six minutes later a Judy began a run on the "jeep." Taken under fire, the Judy was staggered by the intense flak. A wing suddenly tore off, followed by the other wing, and the Judy plunged into the water about fifty yards off the port bow. Its bomb struck the water on the other side of the ship, throwing a towering column of water into the air and drenching all on that side of the carrier. The *Kitkun Bay* sustained only minor damage.[18]

Not quite so lucky was the *Kalinin Bay*. A pair of Zekes (Lieutenant Seki and his wingman) jumped her about the same time as the attack on the *Kitkun Bay*. When first seen, the planes were several thousand feet up, heading in the opposite direction to that of the ship. Seki's plane began a steep, twisting spiral when abeam the carrier. All guns that could bear took the Zeke under fire, hitting it a number of times. Nevertheless, the Zeke continued to corkscrew until it crossed the *Kalinin Bay*'s starboard quarter to hit the flight deck. A large ball of flame and a column of smoke marked the spot where Seki had done his work. Luckily for the ship, Seki had hit with a glancing blow. Most of the Zeke went skipping up the deck, leaving a deep indentation about eight feet wide, until it went overboard on the port bow. The fires it started were quickly extinguished.

Right behind Seki came his wingman. His dive was very steep, estimated to be 70 degrees, and was at a right angle to the ship's axis. Because all of the guns on the starboard side had clear shots at this kamikaze, it was hit early in its dive and was smoking heavily as it swooped down. At the last moment the Zeke pulled up slightly and crashed into the after port stack, also carrying away the catwalk in that area and demolishing a 20-mm mount. What remained of the Zeke tumbled into the water, where its bomb exploded, rattling the ship.

A third kamikaze also made a pass on the carrier. Not taken under fire, the pilot apparently misjudged his dive. Instead of hitting the *Kalinin Bay*, he went straight into the sea off her port quarter.[19] With this attack the ordeal of Taffy 3 was finally over.

In midafternoon, while Taffy 3 was preparing to leave the area, a small strike of TBMs with torpedoes was launched from the *Kitkun Bay* and *White Plains*, the only "jeeps" still capable of launching aircraft. A torpedo from one of the VC-5 Avengers was reported to have lanced a *Nachi*-class cruiser.[20] That would be the last score for Taffy 3. After recovering as many planes as possible (many were stranded at Tacloban and Dulag and would come back on other carriers days later), Ziggy Sprague led his carriers southeast out of the battle.

The four CVEs sailed alone, Taffy 3's screen having been di-

rected by Sprague to remain in the vicinity of the *St. Lo*'s sinking to
pick up survivors. "This desperate expedient which left the Task
Unit without any screen for the next eight hours was made necessary
by the absence of any rescue effort from other sources," said Admiral Sprague, adding, "We had been through so much by then that it
didn't seem to make any difference whether we had escorts with us
or not."[21]

After pulling the survivors from the sea, the four escorts turned
to rejoin Taffy 3. Because of flooded compartments, the *Heermann*
and *Dennis* could only make 15 knots, so the *Butler* and *Raymond*
forged ahead to rendezvous with the flattops. Upon meeting the
carriers, the two DEs transferred most of the rescued to them and
then turned back into Leyte Gulf to take on fuel and to turn over to
hospital ships the seriously wounded survivors. Meanwhile, the *Heermann* and *Dennis* kept plodding toward the Palaus, eventually reaching Kossol Passage, where repairs could finally be made.

While heading southeast, Taffy 3 made radio contact with strike
groups from the *Hornet* and *Wasp*. These two groups, part of Admiral McCain's TG 38.1, which had been en route to Ulithi for replenishment and was rushing back to join the battle, had been launched
at extreme range and needed to find the shortest heading to the
enemy. Ziggy Sprague was able to furnish this information, and the
two groups went on to attack the Center Force.

At 2000 Taffy 3 at last received some escorts: the destroyers *Spros-
ton*, *Hale*, and *Picking*. These three vessels had been detached from
escorting transports and sent to provide Sprague's carriers with a
comforting presence. Several hours later Taffies 1 and 3 met briefly
to exchange information, Taffy 1 turning back toward Leyte Gulf
soon afterward.

Though slowly drawing away from the battle, the CVEs were still
not safe. At 2237, while Taffy 1 was steaming toward its meeting
with Taffy 3, lookouts on one of its DEs, the *Coolbaugh*, sighted the
feathery wake of a periscope. Immediately the destroyer escort
charged in to deliver a hedgehog attack, the other ships making a
90-degree emergency turn. Just as the turn was completed, two torpedoes swam past the *Petrof Bay*, one twenty yards to port and the
other passing under the overhang on the starboard side. It had been
a close call. The attack by the *Coolbaugh* was unsuccessful, and the
submarine escaped. The *Richard M. Rowell* encountered another sub
and attacked it the next morning, but it also escaped.[22]

Ziggy Sprague's Taffy 3 reached Mios Woendi (one of the
Schouten Islands off northwest New Guinea) on the twenty-ninth,
leaving the next day for Manus.

The running fight of Taffy 3 has gone down in naval history as one of the most courageous actions, but it was just one portion of this massive battle and Taffy 3's departure from Leyte Gulf did not mean the battle was over—far from it. Throughout the twenty-fifth the other Taffies' planes were almost continually in the air to hound the fleeing enemy ships.

Taffy 2's fourth strike, a large one of nineteen fighters and thirty-seven Avengers, only eleven of which were carrying torpedoes, was launched at 1115. (Commander Fowler reports the strike group to be equally mixed, thirty-five fighters and thirty-five bombers.)[23] This was a hodgepodge strike, made up of planes from all Taffies that for various reasons had had to land on the Taffy 2 carriers. Placed in overall command of this strike was VC-5's Dick Fowler. The strike was divided into two attack groups, one led by Fowler and the other by VC-20's John Dale.

As the planes droned north their pilots first saw the mortally wounded *Suzuya*, decks awash, with the destroyer *Okinami* standing by. Fowler told his men to ignore those vessels and to continue on toward the main enemy force. Shortly after 1200 they sighted the Center Force fifteen miles off the middle of Samar on a course of 330° toward San Bernardino Strait. Immediately Fowler sent a contact report. Almost as soon as he had stopped talking, his headphones began to buzz with requests from planes farther away for bearing and distance to the enemy. Since he was then trying to place his own planes in position for the attack, he did not receive these requests kindly.

Fowler directed Lieutenant Commander Dale's planes to attack the right side of the formation, while he led his own planes in on the left side. Using a big cumulus cloud for cover, Fowler's group swooped in from the northwest. Upon seeing the planes streaking toward them, all the Japanese ships started hard left turns. This maneuver just gave the pilots better setups for their bombing runs, allowing them to make lengthwise instead of broadside attacks.

Very heavy antiaircraft fire speckled the sky—the usual black bursts predominated, but there were also red, purple, green, and yellow bursts, and several very unusual ones that resembled bales of cotton flying through the air. When they exploded, a large amount of this "cotton" was scattered, and out of the explosion there appeared an inverted cone of silvery wire strands hanging down almost thirty feet. They were quite spectacular, but as far as is known, did no damage to any plane.[24]

Damage was being done to the enemy, though. Fowler walked three 500-pounders across a battleship's midsection, while the planes following him deluged the ship with near misses and at least one more hit. The ship may have been the *Nagato*, which reported a bomb hit near her bow. (Kurita later said that during this attack his ships suffered little, but this is patently untrue.)

Led by the Wildcats, other Avengers were attacking anything on the water. Carrying the *Savo Island*'s last torpedo, Lieutenant Commander Jackson used it on a battleship, and caught the ship as it was completing a circle. A flash and a column of dirty water obscured the ship's after turret. For that effort Jackson received one small hole in his TBM's fuselage. Other VC-27 pilots claimed hits on another battleship and a cruiser and also took time out to shoot down a Jake that was trapped in the middle of the fight. Three more Jakes were shot down over the Center Force by VC-21 fighters.

John Dale's group also caught the Japanese with beautifully coordinated attacks. The fighters led the way, the glide bombers following, with the torpedo planes dropping just as the last bombs hit. Several bomb hits were scored on various ships and at least one torpedo was believed to have hit. But several planes were also hit, to plunge flaming into the water or blow up. Dale's Avenger took a shell in its engine, which knocked off a cylinder and punctured an oil line, and Dale just made it back to the *Savo Island*.[25]

If Kurita had been harboring even the slightest thought of turning back for Leyte Gulf, this attack certainly changed his mind. At 1236 he radioed Admiral Toyoda of his decision to head back through San Bernardino Strait. He would be hastened on his way by more attacks by CVE aircraft and by the first appearance of fast carrier aircraft, these being from McCain's TG 38.1.

As the planes winged their way back to their carriers (most of the Taffy 3 planes would return to their own ships), the fliers saw survivors in the water. One such group from the *St. Lo* was picked up by some destroyer escorts. When Admiral Stump was notified of the men in the water, he radioed Admiral Kinkaid of their approximate position and assumed that rescue efforts would begin immediately. These efforts, however, were botched from the start (see Chapter 8). The survivors from the *Gambier Bay*, *Hoel*, *Johnston*, and *Roberts* would be in the water longer than was perhaps necessary.

Just as Taffy 2's fourth strike was finishing up, planes from TG 38.1 pounced on the Center Force. They had been launched at extreme range and with only a vague idea of where the enemy was. The flight leaders from that group had probably been the ones to badger Commander Fowler about the position of the Japanese ships. Finally able to break through the chatter, the *Natoma Bay*'s CIC vectored the fast carrier planes to the Center Force. Task Group

38.1's attacks just fueled Kurita's determination to get back through the strait as quickly as possible.

Several of TG 38.1's planes had to land on Taffy 2 carriers following their attacks, much to the disgust of some of the "jeep" sailors. Feeling that their planes had been doing the work and that the fast carrier boys were "Johnny-come-latelys," the CVE men were incensed when they had to push some of their own planes overboard to make room for the visiting Hellcats, Helldivers, and Avengers.

But the men of the *Ommaney Bay* got even, if only in a small way. One more plane had to be jettisoned on their ship, but which one? The VC-75 planes were all decidedly the worse for wear after weathering the flak over the Center Force. But one of the visiting planes was a shiny new Avenger belonging to the exec of a fast carrier squadron. Which plane went? When the exec learned about his plane, he was beside himself with rage, for not only was his plane gone but all his personal gear, including a rifle, extra food for survival, and so on.[26]

Despite the arrival of the TG 38.1 aircraft, Stump and Taffy 2 were not yet ready to call it quits for the day. Two more strikes were launched, the next to the last one being sent off at 1331. Only three VC-75 Avengers were loaded with torpedoes, every other carrier was now out of them, and these were the "Big O's" last ones. The other eight TBMs of this strike had to carry GP bombs. As well as torpedoes, the "jeeps" had run out of SAP bombs. Escorting the bombers were eight fighters.[27]

Because of the inappropriate bomb loads for the situation, this mission brought few results—except by the three VC-75 torpedo planes. The pilots would claim the sinking of a cruiser, and not just any cruiser, but the *Chikuma*. Virtually all accounts of the battle have placed the *scuttling* of the *Chikuma* in the vicinity of 11°21′N, 126° 12′E at about 0930. But the reports of the VC-75 planes indicate a different position.

At about 1400 Snuffy Smith's radioman, ARM2c A. R. Zubik, saw a blip on his radar. It was nothing definite, fading in and out, but Smith thought it was worth taking a look at. As the trio flew through the scattered clouds, the radar return grew stronger. About ten miles from the target Smith began a gradual descent, and within a couple of minutes he could see the cruiser dead in the water, the destroyer *Nowake* standing by.

The three pilots—Smith, Lieutenant R. L. Hogden (the squadron executive officer), and Lieutenant (jg) Clark Miller—made their runs against meager defensive fire from either the cruiser or the destroyer, almost like a training session back home. All three torpedoes hit the cruiser amidships. Within fifteen minutes the *Chikuma* had gone under, this event witnessed by all three crews. The position given by the crews for the cruiser's demise was 11°52′N, 126°36′E.[28]

This position is about thirty-eight nautical miles north of the spot where most histories have placed the *Chikuma*'s sinking. It is this writer's opinion that the *Chikuma* was indeed sunk there by the VC-75 fliers around 1415, for the following reasons:

1. Many squadrons reported seeing a *Tone*-class cruiser (not a *Mogami*-class, like the *Suzuya*) in obvious difficulty lagging behind the main enemy force. These observations were made through the time of Taffy 2's 1331 launch. The *Tone* was never in great difficulty herself, although her steering gear had been temporarily knocked out, and she remained with the main force. Thus, the fliers must have been seeing the *Chikuma*. Unlike the other heavy cruiser classes, the *Tone*-class vessels were easy to identify: all their main 8-inch armament was clustered in four turrets forward of the bridge, and their quarterdecks were flat and barren of turrets and had been intended for the use of several planes.

2. Detailed to rescue the *Chikuma*'s survivors and then scuttle the cruiser had been the *Nowake*. If the destroyer had done her job at 0930 and then spent the next couple of hours picking up survivors, why was she unable to catch up with the rest of Kurita's ships before they started through San Bernardino Strait shortly before 2200? There is no indication that she had suffered any damage that would have slowed her down, and all the milling around by the Center Force until almost 1300 should have given the *Nowake* the opportunity to, if not catch up to, be close behind the Center Force as it headed back through the strait. But the *Nowake* never did catch up and was sunk at 0110 on 26 October by ships of Halsey's TG 34.5 (two battleships, three light cruisers, and eight destroyers), which had finally put in a belated appearance.

3. The reason the destroyer never made it was that when Kurita finally made up his mind to dash for San Bernardino Strait, the *Nowake* had *not even started* to pick up the *Chikuma*'s survivors because there was not yet a need to do so. The cruiser's only need at that time was for a screening vessel. Only after 1400 would the *Nowake* be needed for any rescue attempt.

Kurita's ships began entering the strait at 2140, about nine hours after he set a definite course in that direction. If the *Nowake* had finished rescuing survivors at 1600 and herself started north at the same assumed speed of the rest of the Center Force, she would have arrived off the strait at about 0100, just the time she was discovered and sunk by TG 34.5. Conversely, if she had left the site of the

Chikuma's sinking at noon she should have easily beaten TG 34.5 to the entrance of the strait.

In summary, too many sighting reports extending into the afternoon told of a *Tone*-class cruiser in trouble, and only the *Chikuma* fits that description. Also, the *Nowake* should have been close enough behind the Center Force to escape interception (she did not report any problems) *unless* she was rescuing the cruiser's men in the afternoon, not the morning. So the author concludes that there was no way the *Chikuma* could have sunk in the morning, and that three VC-75 fliers did her in.

For years VC-75 veterans attempted to interview survivors from the *Chikuma*. In all cases they were rebuffed, sometimes at the instigation of Japanese government officials. For the VC-75 veterans the question why will always remain.[29]

Felix Stump had one more strike to throw against the Center Force, a twenty-six-Avenger/twenty-four-Wildcat force launched at 1508.[30] As before, antiaircraft fire was heavy and a couple of planes were shot down. Several hits were claimed but because of the lighter bombs the planes were carrying, they did not inflict much damage. There were other reasons for the lack of success. Some pilots had been in the air almost eight hours and had already flown several missions, and the strain was beginning to show. What would have been hits earlier were now misses. The fliers still pressed home their attacks with the same daring and zeal they had shown throughout the day, but the edge was off their skills, and they knew it.

Planes from Taffy 1 were also in on this last strike. A mixed bag of aircraft from all four carriers took off at 1530. When they arrived over the ships, they picked a *Mogami*-class cruiser as the target. The fighter pilots claimed two 500-pound bomb hits, while the torpedo pilots put in claims for two torpedo hits on the same vessel.[31]

Several Zekes jumped the planes as they retired, only to find themselves retired—permanently. VC-21 pilots destroyed two of the Zekes, while some VC-20 pilots may have downed another.[32] The main air-to-air action, however, took place about twenty-five miles north of Taffy 2.

A short time after the sixth strike was launched, Taffy 2 came back to the west in order not to draw too far away from Leyte, to aid those people who were in the water, and to be in position to send in the destroyers to pick off cripples if any were still around. Stump was even mulling over the idea of one more strike against the Japanese, but this mission was not to be. At 1632 a large bogey was reported seventy miles away and closing fast. The CAP was vectored toward the incoming raid, while another twenty-eight fighters were launched as quickly as possible.

When spotted, the Japanese formation was made up of about eighteen Vals with almost as many Zekes and Tojos providing escort. Tearing into a group of four planes, Ralph Elliott's division suddenly found itself surrounded by sixteen other angry Japanese. Quickly the Americans went into a weave. A Tojo flashed in front of Elliott, and he nailed it with a burst to its engine. There was a big puff and then just pieces of debris through which Elliott and his wingman had to fly. Another Tojo making a run on an FM-2 started a split S when Elliott's tracers zipped by him, but the maneuver came too late. With flames coming from its wing roots, the fighter dove into the ocean.

Elliott's wingman, Ensign Wilton O. Stubbs, also picked off two enemy planes, one in a head-on run. VC-27 pilots downed four more planes in this hot and heavy dogfight. In return, one Wildcat was lost, though its pilot was recovered.[33]

Other pilots also enjoyed some success against this enemy raid. Three VC-80 pilots, plus VC-10's Joe McGraw, found themselves face to face with a gaggle of Vals. The Vals were the only things the FM-2 pilots saw until they were almost on top of them; then several Zekes popped into view. Disregarding the fighters, the Wildcats clawed into the Vals. McGraw sent a Val shooting into the water and followed this by fatally holing a Zeke. One other Val was destroyed by a VC-80 pilot, but the Zekes shot down another Wildcat.

Ensign W. R. Eason jumped a Val, pumped it full of holes, and sent it down in flames. Just as he pulled up over his victim, his engine stopped. He had made his dive while drawing fuel from his wing tanks, and on his pull-up the G forces had caused a loss of suction. As he switched tanks and tried to get his engine restarted, Eason's instrument panel suddenly exploded in his face. A Zeke had caught him napping. Luckily, the Zeke made only one pass, but it had been enough.

Unable to restart his engine, Eason had to ditch. The impact was hard and Eason hit his head on the gunsight, but he was not knocked unconscious. After getting out of his plane with little difficulty, Eason spent the night in his raft and was picked up by a destroyer the next afternoon.[34]

The enemy raid was turned back, the raiders losing sixteen planes, with an additional ten damaged. This was the final battle of what had been a most interesting and exciting day. At last the escort carrier aircrews and ships' crews were allowed to take a breather.

During the day 117 Avengers and 87 Wildcats from Taffy 2 had dropped 49 torpedoes and 76 tons of bombs, and fired 276 rockets plus many, many rounds of ammunition.[35] It had been a tough day for both plane and loading crews.

Taffy 2's last plane was taken aboard at 1831, and Stump set course to the southwest to close with Taffy 1. Initially he had intended to keep heading west toward the area where survivors had been reported, but there had been a report of a special rescue group for that job so he turned to the southwest.[36] His action was unfortunate, because the rescue effort, at least initially, was disorganized and poorly coordinated, and men would die because of that.

Kurita's ships were also getting a breather as they sped back through San Bernardino Strait. Night hid them from further depredations by the CVE planes. By 2140 the first ships were entering the strait, which was again brightly lit for navigational purposes. Straggling behind, the *Nowake* didn't make it. She went down under the guns of TG 34.5's cruisers and destroyers. The big battleships, which might have accomplished something if Halsey had released them earlier or kept them off the strait, accomplished nothing.

And so 25 October 1944 ended. History would record the escort carriers' fight as the Battle off Samar. For the escort carriers there had been many moments of valor and sacrifice prior to 25 October and there would be many after, but this day would stand as their proudest moment. The "jeeps" had taken on the giants and cut them down to size, and in the process had become giants themselves. But one day does not make a war, and the CVEs would be back in action carrying the fight to the enemy on the twenty-sixth.

FINALE AT LEYTE GULF

By THE CLOSE of 25 October the Japanese Fleet was in full retreat. But the battle was still not over. Aircraft from both sides would be out on the twenty-sixth, and both would draw blood. Some of the U.S. planes would come from those muddy fields that were laughingly described as airstrips—Tacloban and Dulag.

All day on the twenty-fifth these mudholes had been a beehive of activity. Planes from almost every carrier had landed, refueled, rearmed, and taken off again to attack the Center Force or fly CAP over the beachhead. (Several enemy planes were shot down during this latter duty.) Not every plane made it off a second time, however. The viscous muck on the airstrips claimed many planes during the day. The army engineers fought a valiant battle to lay down pierced steel matting or dump load after load of coral for a base, but in the end the mud won. Some planes ran into bomb craters on landing or takeoff, others met immovable objects and were totaled, and still more just became stuck and were bulldozed to one side to keep the strips clear.

An Avenger landed at Tacloban that looked as if it had fought the entire war—its fabric control surfaces were just ribbons fluttering in the breeze, bullet holes were everywhere on the fuselage, oil covered the cowling and windscreen, its engine sounded like a worn-out washing machine. Somehow its pilot managed to coax it off the landing strip and park it. Within minutes a large sign was propped up in front of the tired bird, "Buy War Bonds."[1]

Chaos was the order of the day at the two strips. Although most army personnel worked willingly to help the navy airmen get their planes airborne again, there were a few exceptions. A navy lieutenant and an army general got into a heated argument over the pres-

ence of the navy planes. The general wanted to bulldoze all the
Wildcats and Avengers to one side so that his strip could receive the
P-38s that would be arriving the next day. Considering that these
same FM-2s and TBMs were the ones that were helping to protect
the general, his attitude was shortsighted, to say the least. The lieutenant won the argument.[2]

In spite of the commendable efforts of a pair of army officers to
control traffic with a jury-rigged jeep-mounted radio, pilots whose
planes were almost out of fuel landed where they wanted to, sometimes with disastrous consequences. To make the situation even
more uncomfortable, Japanese planes made a few hit-and-run raids
on the fields, keeping the antiaircraft gunners trigger-happy and
willing to shoot at anything that flew overhead. Not a few CVE
planes were holed or even shot down by the gunners. Fed up with
this indiscriminate firing, a VC-10 pilot pulled his .45 on one gun
crew. In vivid terms he told them that if they opened fire on another
plane, they were dead. They didn't do any more firing.[3]

Accidents were commonplace at Tacloban and Dulag, and there
were also a few close calls. VC-10's Charles Dugan came close to
becoming a statistic. He was standing in the cockpit of his fighter
buckling on his parachute when he saw an Avenger in obvious difficulty heading directly for his plane. Quickly he dove over the side of
his plane. Instead of landing in the mud, he found himself hanging
upside down, his parachute caught in the cockpit. Closing his eyes,
he thought, "I hope my mother doesn't find out I died this way,
hung by my ass over the side of my fighter."

After a few seconds Dugan opened his eyes. The TBM, instead of
plowing into his plane, had turned 180 degrees and was tearing off
in the other direction. It hit a fuel truck, dug its nose into the
ground, and came to a stop in a shower of mud. No one was hurt
but one more plane had been wiped out.[4]

With so many aircraft suffering varying amounts of damage from
both the Japanese and the airstrip conditions, some pilots resorted to
"borrowing" whatever planes seemed to be flyable. Others tried val-
iantly to repair the damage themselves, helped whenever possible by
army personnel who wanted the planes to leave. He never said how
he did it, but one VC-65 pilot somehow managed to get a new wing
put on his fighter.[5]

When darkness settled over the area on the evening of 25 October, many CVE fliers were still stuck at the two strips. More than a
few were given a blanket, a carbine, and some ammunition by the
army and told to choose a foxhole and start picking off snipers.
After spending an uncomfortable night in a foxhole, one pilot spoke

for all the CVE fliers when he said that he "did not recommend them for the tired aviator."[6] For most of the airmen their stay on the beach was short, only one night. A few, however, remained stuck on Leyte for several days before they finally returned to their ships.

For one last time the Center Force the next day would feel the sting of the carrier planes. After passing back through San Bernardino Strait, the Center Force was next seen by the Americans shortly after 0800 on the twenty-sixth. Kurita was setting a good pace southward in Tablas Strait just a few miles off Panay's northern tip. With luck he would be out of range of the U.S. carrier planes in a few hours.

His luck didn't hold. About 0830 the first of a series of attacks by planes from Halsey's carriers swept in on Kurita's force. Heavy clouds, heavy antiaircraft fire, and fatigue from many flights in just a few days all contributed to keeping the damage to the Japanese to less than what was wanted. Still, more enemy vessels went down. The light cruiser *Noshiro* was torpedoed, then finished off with a bomb. Her bow blown off, the destroyer *Hayashimo* was run aground, to be used for target practice for the next week. The heavy cruiser *Kumano*, which had been severely damaged by CVE planes on the twenty-fifth, managed to escape until 25 November. Running from island to island in the Phlippines in a vain attempt to escape, she was hounded and harassed continually until fast carrier planes finally sent her under on the twenty-fifth. Several of his other ships were damaged before a badly shaken Kurita was able to lead his depleted force out of range.

Other Japanese forces did not get away unscathed. Army Air Force planes got into the act on the twenty-sixth, sinking the earlier-damaged and barely moving *Abukuma*, late of the lamentable Southern Force. Also scoring were the fliers from the CVEs. After all they had been through, they weren't about to let the Japanese escape without giving them a good-by present.

While the other Japanese forces had been pounded, Vice Admiral Naomasa Sakonju's transport unit of the light cruiser *Kinu*, destroyer *Uranami*, and four transports had stolen into Ormoc Bay on Leyte's western shore to unload 2,000 troops. (One part of Sakonju's command, the heavy cruiser *Aoba*, had been damaged by a torpedo from the submarine *Bream* on the twenty-third and took no further part in the battle.) On the morning of the twenty-sixth the troops were put ashore and Sakonju headed back west into the Visayan Sea. With so many aircraft out searching for fleeing Japanese vessels, it wasn't long before they sighted the transport force.

Upon receipt of the sighting report, a strike group of twenty-three Avengers and twenty-nine fighters was launched by Taffy 2. In addition, Taffy 1 launched thirteen TBMs and fifteen to twenty fighters. Because of the heavy expenditure of torpedoes and bombs the previous day, the Taffy 2 planes carried only 500- and 250-pound GP bombs and rockets; the Taffy 1 Avengers had torpedoes. Shortly after 1000 the CVE planes arrived over Sakonju's ships. With no air cover, the enemy vessels were overwhelmed by the attackers. Two of the transports were quickly sent to the bottom, soon to be joined by their two escorts.

The *Kinu* and *Uranami* threw up a heavy barrage, but this was only able to down a VC-20 Wildcat and a VC-68 Avenger that was flying off the *Petrof Bay*. Seeing the fighter pilot in the water, the *Uranami* charged him. This attack came to an abrupt halt when a couple of bombs, several rockets, and many .50-caliber bullets punched numerous holes in the destroyer. Soon her bow began to settle, and finally nothing remained on the surface of the sea except an oil slick and some bubbles. Both the VC-20 pilot and the VC-68 crew were picked up later.

Sinking the *Kinu* took a bit longer. Like most Japanese cruisers, she was a tough ship, but she received a terrible pounding at the hands of the CVE fliers—at least seven bomb hits, numerous other bombs falling close enough to rip open seams, many rocket hits, and possibly a couple of torpedoes. At 1730, long after the CVE planes had departed, the *Kinu* sank south of Masbate Island. Partial retribution for Taffy 3's ordeal had been achieved by the "jeep" fliers.[7]

While returning to their ships, the airmen spotted near Bantayan Island a "strange-looking" vessel tentatively identified as a battleship of the *Ise* class. An afternoon strike failed to find this ship, so the bombs were used against dock installations at Cebu. Just what the mystery ship was has never been determined.

In addition to the attacks on the fleeing enemy ships, escort carrier planes saw action all day against numerous Japanese planes. Generally, these fights came out in favor of the Wildcats and Hellcats, at least ten of the enemy planes falling to their guns. One Wildcat, but not its pilot, was lost during these combats.

Of more serious concern was the reappearance of the kamikazes. On the morning of the twenty-sixth two groups from the Cebu-based *Yamato* unit were sent to locate and destroy the U.S. ships. One of these groups, two kamikazes with one escort, was jumped by fighters and all shot down.

The second group of three kamikazes and two escorts had better luck.[8] Shortly after noon Taffy 1 was still operating in the same general area as from the start of the invasion, east and slightly south of Leyte. Landing operations were under way, and the planes that had taken part in the attack on the *Kinu* and *Uranami* now returned to their ships.

The incoming kamikazes were picked up on radar about thirty-five miles away and the CAP vectored to intercept them. Although they paid the price with their lives, the three escorts kept the CAP away from the kamikazes, which continued on. One of these, intent on diving on the *Petrof Bay*, was surprised by an Avenger returning from ASP and went down in a mass of flames. The two remaining planes were left alone to pick their victims. It was now about 1238.

One of the kamikazes chose the *Suwannee* as his target and began his last dive. Below him the carrier was landing aircraft. Seven fighters and three Avengers were packed closely together on the forward end of the flight deck, while another ten planes were parked in the hangar. All were fully gassed. As the kamikaze hurtled down, a VT-60 pilot was taxiing his Avenger onto the forward elevator.

The kamikaze's timing was perfect. Before the pilot and his crew could even unstrap, the Zeke plowed into the Avenger. There was a thunderous roar, a flash of flame, and a gush of black smoke. An instant after the suicider smashed into the ship, the bomb he had released at bridge height penetrated the elevator platform and exploded in the hangar. In seconds fires were raging both in the hangar and on deck among the aircraft. Searing heat and choking smoke forced Captain Johnson to order the bridge abandoned and the conn shifted aft.

In the hangar the ship's fire marshal, William S. Brooks, was knocked unconscious and injured by the blast. Nonetheless, upon regaining consciousness, Brooks crawled around and under the planes to the valves controlling the water curtain and forward sprinkler system and opened them. The water gushing from the sprinklers effectively prevented the fire on the forward elevator, which had been smashed down to hangar deck level, from spreading to the gassed planes in the hangar. Just the day before, Brooks had accomplished a similar feat when another kamikaze had struck the *Suwannee*. Brooks's actions helped contain the hangar fire to a manageable level, and it was under control in quick order.

Up on the flight deck it was another story. Nearly all of the gas tanks of the planes parked forward had been ruptured, and an inferno instantly erupted on the forward portion of the flight deck. Burning gasoline flowed across the deck and over the carrier's side. To the men of the *Petrof Bay* watching horrified from nearby, the "fire was a grim and impressive spectacle indeed . . . it was obvious

The kamikaze attack on the Suwannee, *26 October 1944. (National Archives)*

that personnel in the adjacent gunbuckets and walkways were having a poor time of it."[9]

Indeed they were. The blaze forced many from their stations, incinerated others, and trapped still more. In one of the latter instances, a group of men was cut off on the forecastle. Some had been burned or had been wounded by flying shrapnel. Attempts to get medical supplies to them had failed, and one sailor, unable to withstand the wounded's pleas for help, decided to get the supplies himself. Though several men tried to dissuade him, he brushed them away and began climbing through the smoke and flames toward the flight deck.

It seemed that he might just make it when an Avenger in his path blew up. When the smoke cleared, the man could be seen clinging to the edge of the flight deck. One of his legs had been blown off. Unable to maintain his hold, he fell into the water and was never recovered.[10] This man's name was not recorded, but he was typical of many of the Suwannee's men who risked their lives to rescue men trapped in various compartments, particularly those in radio control and on the bridge. Others also risked their lives bringing the fire hoses right into the heart of the fire.

Their task was not made any easier when a second enemy plane sneaked in a few minutes later to drop a bomb that wiped out the catapult machinery room. Fortunately, casualties from this bomb were few. This was lucky, for the Suwannee and her crew had been hurt severely. The explosions and fires forced the evacuation of the forward battle dressing station, causing the doctor, Lieutenant Walter B. Burwell, to move his patients (who were increasing in number) from compartment to compartment until they finally reached safety in the chiefs' quarters.

Captain Johnson took his ship out of formation to head downwind and keep the fire and smoke contained to the forward part of the ship. For a few minutes all power on the ship was lost, and the carrier coasted to a stop. After the power was quickly regained, the Suwannee again took her spot in the formation. Extinguishing the fires took almost an hour. When they were out, the carrier was in sad shape. Fully a third of her deck was charred, some flooding was still encountered, and there was a great deal of blast and fragment damage. Worst of all was her human damage. Over 100 men had been killed or would die of their wounds, and another 170 had been wounded; altogether, nearly a third of her entire complement required some medical care. But she was afloat and would fight again.[11]

In fact, the Suwannee would be back in action sooner than anticipated. Hardly had she started back home than her first lieutenant

A wardroom on the Suwannee *is turned into a makeshift sick bay after the kamikaze attacks, 26 October 1944. (National Archives)*

was flying back to Seattle with photos, diagrams, and reports of her damage. Before the flattop had even tied up at the Puget Sound Navy Yard in late November, many parts had already been built and were ready to install. The shipyard workers needed just thirty-six hours to manufacture a new elevator and begin easing it into place. By early February the *Suwannee* was back at sea preparing for her next operation.[12]

Escaping the fate of the *Suwannee* had been the *Petrof Bay.* Just seconds after the *Suwannee* was hit, another Zeke dove down on "the Mad Russian." Having seen what would happen if they didn't knock it down, the gunners opened up with all they had. The kamikaze screamed down in an almost vertical dive. Captain Kane tried to throw the pilot's aim off with a hard turn to port, but the kamikaze countered with an aileron roll that kept him centered on the carrier's flight deck.

Then suddenly, when only 500 feet in the air, the Zeke's tail was shot off. The Zeke flopped into a flat spin, doing two complete circles before it slammed into the sea just fifty feet astern of the ship. Even when it was apparent that the Zeke was not going to hit the *Petrof Bay,* her guns continued to bark, ripping huge pieces from the erstwhile kamikaze. It had been awfully close.[13]

At last things calmed down. The kamikazes were the enemy's last gasp, and for TG 77.4 the battle was finally over. How busy the CVEs had been can be seen from some extensive statistics compiled by the navy's Air Operations Research Group.

A close study of squadron and ship records indicates that there are some errors, mostly minor, in the above charts. However, they are not enough to invalidate the major thrust of these statistics—that the escort carrier planes were inordinately busy during the period 24–26 October.

Although the Battle for Leyte Gulf was "officially" over, for some men another battle was still raging, one against the sea and the sharks. First to sink on the twenty-fifth had been the *Hoel* at 0855, followed by the *Gambier Bay* at 0907, the *Roberts* at 1005, the *Johnston* at 1010, and the *St. Lo* at 1125. Because of the close-quarters action of the first four ships, rescue efforts for those survivors would be slow in coming. In contrast, most of the *St. Lo*'s men were picked up in relatively short order.

What should have been a fairly routine, although extensive, rescue operation turned into a poorly organized and badly botched effort. After the *St. Lo* sank, Ziggy Sprague stripped his carriers of their screen in order for them to rescue the men of the *St. Lo.* He was in no way ignoring the plight of the other survivors, but his crews had their hands full. He was also under the impression that Kinkaid was already taking measures to rescue the survivors. This same impression was held by Admiral Stump, who had radioed Kinkaid between 1230 and 1300 of the presence of several hundred men in the vicinity of 11°12′N, 126°30′E.

This position was in error, being twenty to forty miles south of where the ships had actually gone down. Still, it should have given Kinkaid's PBYs a starting point for a search effort. But the PBYs didn't even get started. With hundreds of sailors from the sunken ships in the water, the flying boats were being used instead to pluck one, two, or three men at a time from the sea, men from downed aircraft.

Not until after 1530 would the first search and rescue mission—by ships—be ordered, and this would search the wrong spot, another incorrect position near the first reported spot. If aircraft could have been used in conjunction with this effort, the search area would have

Sorties Flown During the Battle for Leyte Gulf

	Strikes Against Japanese Force	Search	Engaging Enemy	Not Engaging Enemy	ASP	Leyte Support	Aborts	Total
24 Oct 1944								
VF	0	0	1	96	0	225	1	323
VT	0	0	0	0	50	84	2	136
25 Oct 1944								
VF	209	0	27	120	0	86	6	448
VT	232	6	0	0	16	16	15	285
26 Oct 1944								
VF	33	20	9	106	0	62	0	230
VT	22	29	0	0	37	29	1	118
Total for Task Group 77.4	496	55	37	322	103	502	25	1540[14]

	ENEMY AIRCRAFT ENGAGED		DESTROYED	
	VB	VF	VB	VF
24 Oct 1944	120	58	52	25
25 Oct 1944	38	92	14	42
26 Oct 1944	11	34	6	23
	169	184	72	90[15]

U.S. AIRCRAFT LOSSES, 24–26 OCTOBER 1944

	LOSSES IN STRIKES ON JAPANESE FLEET			LOSSES IN OTHER ACTION SORTIES			ON OTHER FLIGHTS	NOT IN FLIGHT		TOTAL
	AA fire	Aircraft	Operational	AA fire	Aircraft	Operational		Own Action	Enemy	
24 Oct 1944	0	0	0	0	1	5	1	0	0	7
25 Oct 1944	24	0	24	2	5	7	4	2	6	74
26 Oct 1944	4	0	1	0	1	4	2	2	10	24
	28	0	25	2	7	16	7	4	16	105[16]

NUMBER OF ATTACKS BY SQUADRONS, 25 OCTOBER 1944

		BOMB	ROCKET	TORPEDO	BOMB	ROCKET	TORPEDO
					With at least one hit claimed		
Sangamon	AG 37	13	0	1	1	0	1
Suwannee	AG 60	13	0	9	4	0	5
Petrof Bay	VC-76	2	0	9	0	0	2
Santee	AG 26		Data missing			Data missing	
Kadashan Bay	VC-20	27	10	7	6	5	1
Marcus Island	VC-21	23	11	3	16	7	2
Savo Island	VC-27	20	8	9	11	8	3
Ommaney Bay	VC-75	10	2	11	9	1	3
Manila Bay	VC-80	16	2	6	4	1	2
Natoma Bay	VC-81	38	4	6	7	1	2
Kalinin Bay	VC-3	7	5	1	6	4	1
White Plains	VC-4	5	0	2	5	0	0
Kitkun Bay	VC-5		Data missing			Data missing	
Gambier Bay	VC-10	6	1	2	4	0	0
St. Lo	VC-65	7	2	2	1	0	2
Fanshaw Bay	VC-68		Data missing			Data missing	
		187	45	68	74	27	24[17]

been broadened and, most likely, the men in the water would have been seen. A surprising lack of communication was evident. Perhaps because of the shock of the day's events, both Halsey and Kinkaid were unaware of some vital facts. After the sinking of the *Nowake,* several of Halsey's destroyers made a sweep off Samar. They were unaware that several Seventh Fleet vessels had gone down and, thus, made no effort to look for survivors. And Kinkaid was unaware that some Third Fleet ships were in the general area of the sinkings.

Only two ships, the destroyer escorts *Richard S. Bull* and *Eversole,* took part in the initial search, and because they were given inaccurate positions, they could find nothing. In the meantime, men from the sunken ships were beginning to die. Some had been severely wounded. Others, perhaps so shocked they couldn't think clearly, gave up and floated away.

There was another, terrifying reason—sharks. A wounded *Gambier Bay* officer, who believed that he should take his turn in the water with the other men was ripped to pieces by a shark. Others also fell victim to these ravenous beasts. One gunner's mate from the *Johnston,* however, survived two shark bites, the big fish evidently finding the sailor too tough.

A VC-10 pilot, Ensign Leo P. Zeola, had a close call. Captain Vieweg had directed him to try to keep up the spirits of the men in one raft. Zeola had swum to Vieweg's raft to report and was paddling back to his own raft. He was very tired as he stroked along.

As he passed one raft a sailor leaned over its side. "Mr. Zeola, you'd better hurry."

"Why's that?" Zeola countered.

"Because there's a big shark behind you."

Suddenly not feeling tired, Zeola stroked away with abandon. He reached his raft safely, but it took several minutes for his heart to return from his throat to its proper place.[18]

There would be no rescue for the men of Taffy 3's sunken ships on the twenty-fifth. A cold night would pass, and fewer men would be present when the sun came up the next day. In the meantime, another search effort had gotten under way. Set up by Rear Admiral Daniel E. Barbey, the amphibious force commander, it consisted of two 175-foot-long patrol craft, the *PC-623* and *PC-1119,* and five LCI(R)s (Landing Craft, Infantry [Rocket]). Barbey's own staff surgeon and two pharmacist mates were sent along to help, but they were unable to bring much in the way of medical supplies and even less in blankets and clothing.

At 1835 this little group departed San Pedro Bay. Although Lieutenant Commander J. A. Baxter, the *PC-623*'s CO, had been named

commanding officer of this tiny group, he soon turned command
over to the *LCI(R)-71*'s skipper, Lieutenant Commander R. E. Sargent, who was senior and who had had more experience in handling
groups of ships. Because of their relatively slow speed, not until
0830 on the twenty-sixth did the rescue force reach the supposed
vicinity of the *Gambier Bay*'s sinking. Because it was an inaccurate
position, they of course found nothing.

Forming an approximately east-west line with a mile between
ships, the seven vessels began to comb the water in twenty-five-mile
legs, gradually working to the west. Hour after hour went by. Still
nothing. By noon they were eighteen miles northeast of the *Gambier
Bay*'s actual spot of sinking. By sundown they were about the same
distance southwest of it. The only person sighted was a Japanese
flier clinging to a box; he was brought aboard.

As sundown came and went, the two PCs and the five gunboats
were the only ships actively seeking survivors. At 1725 the *Bull* and
Eversole had been recalled to reinforce Taffy 1's screen. (Sadly, the
Eversole's crew would soon be in the water too. Early on the twenty-
ninth she was torpedoed by a Japanese sub, possibly the *I-45*, and
went down swiftly. Unlike the Taffy 3 survivors, the *Eversole*'s men
were rescued within a few hours. A little over four hours after the
destroyer escort sank, another DE, the *Whitehurst*, caught the submarine and blew her apart with hedgehog attacks.)[19]

In spite of the departure of the two destroyer escorts, the other
little ships were not about to give up the search. Then at 2229 some
Very lights arced into the air about twenty miles to the west. The
PC-623 raced ahead, the other ships trailing behind.

In the darkness the men on the rafts and in the water could hear
a thrumming as the *PC-623* neared. They weren't sure what the
sound was, but were afraid that if it was a ship it might be Japanese.
A voice rang out across the water: "Ahoy, the raft! What ship are
you from?" No one answered. Then a searchlight snapped on to
sweep the water. "Are you American?"

At last there was a babble of voices. "Yes. Yes. We're Americans.
Gambier Bay."[20]

Lieutenant Commander Baxter radioed his find and began haul-
ing the men in. For many of the survivors it was a terrible struggle to
climb aboard; their limbs were numb from the hours in the water.
Others with frightful wounds were gently lifted onto the deck. All
were thirsty, hungry, and utterly fatigued. Transferred to the *PC-
1119* were the most seriously wounded, and before dawn she left the
scene with 183 survivors to be taken to hospital ships.

The other six vessels remained to comb the water for more men.

Here and there the rescuers saw a group of survivors in the slim beam of the searchlight or heard shouting in the inky blackness. By 0335 of the twenty-seventh, over 700 of the *Gambier Bay*'s men had been pulled in. But there were still more to come. At 0745 more rafts were seen, and men from the *Roberts* were recovered. They were followed by more sailors from the *Roberts* and *Hoel* and finally by fifteen men from the *Johnston*. After rescuing close to 1,150 men, the tiny force turned back toward Leyte Gulf.[21]

But not everyone was saved at that time. One small party from the *Gambier Bay* drifted for almost seventy-two hours before being picked up by a PT boat. And there were those who didn't survive, men who had been seen alive in the water and who might have been saved if the search effort had begun earlier and in the right spot. There were at least 116 of them from the three "small boys," including the gallant Commander Evans, who died or just disappeared before rescue came.

For the "jeeps" off Samar their casualties had not been light:

	Killed or Missing	*Wounded*
Taffy 1 Ships' Crews	283	136
Taffy 3 Ships' Crews	792	768
CVE Aviators	43	9
	1118	913[22]

But their operations were almost over at Leyte. Already the Taffy 3 carriers had started back to Manus on the twenty-fifth. On the twenty-seventh the *Suwannee* headed back to the Puget Sound Navy Yard, with the *Santee* leaving for Manus the same day. The next day the *Chenango* and *Saginaw Bay* returned from Morotai with a load of replacement planes and pilots. Disappointed at having missed the main battle, the VF-35 pilots tried to make up for it by downing four enemy fighters during the day.

Over the next few days several other Japanese planes were shot down by the CVE fliers, including one more by the sharpshooting Ralph Elliott, but the action had decidedly cooled down from the excitement of the twenty-fourth through the twenty-sixth. Many pilots who had been stuck ashore finally made it back to a carrier, not necessarily their own. Some, with their planes out of service, hitched rides in whatever Avenger was going their way. Deck crews were astounded when such an Avenger would land and out would tumble ten to fifteen very happy aviators.

At last the rest of the CVEs departed from the waters off Leyte. Early on the thirtieth the *Marcus Island, Savo Island, Kadashan Bay,* and *Manila Bay* were organized as TU 77.4.4 and left for Manus.

The *Sangamon, Chenango, Saginaw Bay, Petrof Bay, Natoma Bay,* and *Ommaney Bay* remained in the vicinity for only a few hours more before they, too, departed for Manus. The Battle for Leyte Gulf was history.[23]

Hardly was this action over than controversy arose, a controversy that has continued until this day. The battle has been dissected over and over again by a multitude of historians. Since this is true, the controversy will be covered only lightly here.

There is no doubt that Leyte Gulf was a great victory for the Americans. After all, the Japanese lost some twenty-six ships totaling 305,710 tons in the main battles, plus several others in peripheral actions, against only six ships (all except one from Taffy 3) totaling some 36,000 tons for the Americans. But the surprising of Taffy 3 and its close brush with disaster was a matter of grave concern to the U.S. high command. Questions about both Halsey's and Kinkaid's handling of the battle began immediately afterward.

In virtually all histories of Leyte Gulf the major blame for the near disaster has fallen on Halsey. A strong believer in carrier power, he was seduced by the bewitching bait Ozawa dangled in front of him—the Japanese carriers. Yet he and his intelligence officers should have been able to count, or at least read between the numbers: to count the aircraft that were *not* seen on the flattops' decks; to count the major naval units that were *not* with Ozawa's force, these being instead with Kurita. If the enemy carrier force had been so important, it would have had more battleships and heavy cruisers attached to it for protection.

In going after Ozawa's ships, Halsey took his entire force north with him, leaving San Bernardino Strait unguarded. His night snoopers from the *Independence* had noted the Center Force heading back east at a good 20 knots, not the speed of a badly mauled force. But Halsey refused to believe that these ships were anything more than stragglers, although why would stragglers be heading east rather than west? For some unknown reason Halsey did not pass this information on to Kinkaid. Even if he had, however, Kinkaid would probably not have done anything, still believing that Halsey's TF 34 was guarding the strait.

At this time Halsey's preparatory battle plan to form TF 34 became its most mischievous. When he had radioed this battle plan to his commander shortly after 1500, Halsey had intended it only as a warning message. Unfortunately, Kinkaid (not one of the addressees) intercepted the message and took it as a fait accompli. *Kinkaid did not query Halsey to see if TF 34 was being formed.* And he did not hear Halsey's clarification a short time later in which Halsey stated that TF 34 would only be formed when directed by him.

Contented that TF 34 had been formed, Kinkaid did not see fit to seek confirmation until 0412 on the morning of the twenty-fifth, when he asked Halsey about the battleships. Halsey's reply came only at 0705 and by that time Kinkaid already had his answer, courtesy of the Japanese.

Leaving San Bernardino Strait unguarded by even one destroyer was probably Halsey's biggest mistake. Granted, he wanted his ships concentrated against what he believed to be the main threat, Ozawa's carriers, but his numerical advantage in ships and planes amounted to more than a little case of overkill.

Concerning the uncovering of San Bernardino Strait, Ziggy Sprague said,

> When the enemy attack by his southern force through Surigao Strait developed, the question of the whereabouts of the enemy northern component [actually the Center Force] became even larger and more formidable. This unit had never been assigned any responsibility for covering the exit of San Bernardino Strait, either by reconnaissance or by force, and in the absence of any information that this exit was no longer blocked, it was logical to assume that our northern flank could not be exposed without ample warning.
>
> Had this T.U. had any reason to suspect that an enemy sortie could be made through San Bernardino Strait undetected by other U.S. forces, a search to the northeast would have been launched from a more easterly position, and it is probable that a direct surface action could have been avoided.[24]

Kinkaid is not blameless. He took too much for granted, particularly where Halsey was concerned. He should have been better informed of what his fellow fleet commander was doing. He let Oldendorf charge down Surigao Strait chasing the fleeing enemy instead of reorganizing, which was asking for trouble since other Japanese units had still not been heard from. His search efforts left something to be desired, although he was obviously expecting Halsey to keep tabs on the other enemy units.

Probably the biggest culprit in this whole action, however, was the divided command structure. There was no clearcut definition of duties for the two fleet commanders; they were just supposed to "cooperate." This cooperation was hamstrung by inadequate communications, caused in part by MacArthur's insistence that all of Kinkaid's messages be routed through the Manus radio facility for retransmission, a time-consuming process.[25] Because of the amorphous command structure, too often Kinkaid and Halsey were making assumptions about the other's plans and/or tactics without checking to see if these assumptions were correct. The situation could have led to tremendous disaster.

That it didn't is a tribute to the officers and men of both the Third and the Seventh Fleets. Especially it is a tribute to the men of Taffy 3. "The high degree of skill, the unflinching courage, the inspired determination to go down fighting, of the officers and men under my command cannot be too highly praised," was how Admiral Sprague saluted his men.[26] And a grateful government would honor the men, squadrons, and ships of Taffy 3 with the Presidential Unit Citation.

Sprague had one more comment about the battle. "The failure," he said, "of the enemy main body and encircling light forces to completely wipe out all vessels of this Task Unit can be attributed to our successful smoke screen, our torpedo counterattack, continuous harassment of enemy by bomb, torpedo, and strafing air attacks, timely maneuvers, and the definite partiality of Almighty God."[27]

DIVINE WIND
—TWO VERSIONS

BACK TO MANUS's Seeadler Harbor came the escort carriers, their crews shaken at the ferocity of the action at Leyte Gulf and horrified at the appearance of the kamikazes. They would get the rest they needed. The carriers' squadrons would get replacement aircraft and aircrews. The ships would be painted, have their engines overhauled, and so on. But although they were now in a so-called "rear area," death was still waiting to claim the unwary, the unlucky, the untrained.

Because so much ordnance had been used up by the ships and aircraft at Leyte, the carriers' magazines were virtually empty when they reached Manus. Waiting to rearm the "jeeps" were several ammunition ships, including the *Mount Hood.*

On 9 November it was the *Natoma Bay*'s turn to send a loading party to the *Mount Hood* to pick up a load of ammunition. One of the members of this party, John Sassano, was not impressed with the job the *Mount Hood*'s crew was doing as they loaded bombs onto landing craft ahead of the *Natoma Bay*'s own boat. In fact, he was more than a little nervous about their nonchalance, sliding bombs down a makeshift wooden ramp from three decks above the landing craft and letting them bounce off the decks and the sides of the boats below. Sassano made sure that his boat had at least some cushioning for the bombs to land on, but it was nerve-racking work. When the working party returned to the *Natoma Bay*, they discovered that the load only half filled the magazines. The men would have to return to the *Mount Hood* the next morning.

Bright and early the next day the crew from the carrier returned to the ammunition ship. This time Sassano made sure that one of the flattop's crew was at the top of the ramp to see that the bombs were eased down the ramp, not heaved. The day before, Sassano had noticed quite a bit of exudate coming from the nose cones of many of the bombs. "Only one spark," he had thought. Finally, a bit before 0800, the *Natoma Bay*'s boat was loaded and by 0830 the bombs were being hoisted aboard the carrier.[1]

While the rearming was under way, men like MoMM2c John Keenan were going about their normal duties. Keenan had just wandered out of the hangar onto the port forward sponson when a thunderous, earsplitting roar drowned out all the other sounds in the harbor. Staring at the *Mount Hood*, Keenan saw her come out of the water, then fall back to be covered by a malevolent cloud of black smoke that spread over everything nearby and mushroomed thousands of feet into the sky. He turned to give an alarm and suddenly found himself in the middle of the hangar, flung there by the force of the explosion.[2]

Also an eyewitness to the *Mount Hood*'s death was the *Ommaney Bay*'s communications officer, Bill Stewart. Crossing the anchorage in a whaleboat on the way to pick up some mail, Stewart was staring at the "beautiful ship" when he saw a small flash of light, followed immediately by the tremendous blast. Although the ammunition ship was over a mile and a half away, debris showered about his small boat, including one large, jagged piece of steel shaped like a Christmas tree that landed less than a hundred yards away. This detritus had hardly stopped falling when Stewart's boat had to ride out a minor tidal wave caused by the explosion. Stewart cut short his trip and hurriedly returned to the "Big O."[3]

When the roar and the smoke at last subsided, there was no sign of the *Mount Hood*. She had virtually been vaporized, the largest remaining piece of her only some sixteen by ten feet. On the harbor floor, approximately nineteen fathoms below the spot where she had been anchored, there was a trench about three hundred feet long, fifty feet wide, and thirty to forty feet deep. The ammunition ship's crew had vanished along with their ship (except for eighteen who had been on the beach at the time). There were other casualties and much damage among the ships clustered about the *Mount Hood*. When these were finally tallied, there were forty-five known dead and another 327 men missing, with 371 more injured. An investigation never officially ascertained the exact cause of this disaster, but John Sassano and his working party knew.[4]

The destruction of the *Mount Hood* provided much scuttlebutt fodder for the CVE sailors, but the biggest scuttlebutt involved just where the "jeeps" would be heading for the next operation and when. In the interim, there were other jobs to do, primarily involv- ing covering the convoys en route to and from Leyte, these convoys being attacked with irritating regularity by aircraft supposedly from Mindanao.

Featured most prominently in these boring but necessary missions were the *Marcus Island, Savo Island, Petrof Bay, Makin Island, Lunga Point, Bismarck Sea,* and *Steamer Bay* (a new arrival in the Southwest Pacific Theater). The job was boring because few enemy aircraft were sighted and none shot down. (The most irritating thing about these convoy support operations was that too many of the bogeys that were intercepted were army planes whose crews apparently did not know how to turn on their IFFs.)[5]

But if those carriers were not experiencing any action, another one was. The *Anzio* was the flagship of a hunter-killer group operat- ing east of the Philippines. Embarked on the carrier was a green squadron, VC-82. The *Anzio* was a new name but not a new ship; she was the ex–*Coral Sea.* A big new carrier was being built and the name *Coral Sea* was to be given to her, so the little "jeep" had to get a new name, and she was christened the *Anzio* on 15 September. This change of name didn't sit too well with her crew. They figured that their ship had earned the right to carry the name of that famous battle and that the new, bigger carrier should look elsewhere for a name.

On 4 November the *Anzio* and her screen of five destroyer escorts left Ulithi bound for her operating area in the Philippine Sea. The group, TG 30.7, had hardly left Ulithi when it was directed to ren- dezvous with the light cruiser *Reno,* which had been torpedoed by the *I-41* off San Bernardino Strait. The next day TG 30.7 met the *Reno,* at which time the *Anzio* delivered needed supplies to the stricken cruiser. For the next two days the carrier provided ASW and CAP over the cruiser as she was towed toward Ulithi by the tug *Zuni.* A nearby typhoon didn't help the *Reno,* but she reached Ulithi safely on 10 November.

Leaving the *Reno* on the eighth, TG 30.7 headed for a new ren- dezvous, this one with TG 30.8, the Logistics Group. As protection for TG 30.8, hunter-killer operations would be carried out in the vicinity of the various fueling areas. For several days there was little excitement, then on the eighteenth—pay-dirt.

On a routine search during the blackness of the early hours, VC- 82's skipper, Lieutenant Commander C. H. Holt, got a radar con- tact. When he neared the object, Holt dropped some flares, where- upon the contact faded from the scope. Calling for help to the

Avenger patrolling the task group's other flank, Holt set about tracking down what was obviously a submarine. The plane dropped float lights and sonobuoys, and soon unmistakable submarine noises could be heard over the sonobuoys.

When the second TBM arrived, it dropped more sonobuoys and made a Fido attack. The homing torpedo missed, so the planes waited for the DEs *Lawrence C. Taylor* and *Melvin R. Nawman* to reach the scene. When they arrived where the two Avengers were circling, the two vessels began their own search. About 0605 the *Taylor* reported gaining contact with the sub and drove in for a hedgehog attack. The missiles missed. The *Taylor* curved around for another hedgehog run; this time one explosion reverberated through the water. Satisfied that the submarine was pinpointed, the *Taylor* raced in for the kill. A final salvo brought forth three explosions, followed by a tremendous blast that rattled the destroyer escort.

Shortly afterward a large mass of diesel oil came to the surface along with pieces of deck planking, cork, and other debris. On the ships' sonars the submarine appeared to be going deeper, and several attacks were made before the contact faded. The sub had indeed been going deeper, but only because it was sinking, ripped open by the hedgehogs. The victim of this well-coordinated action was the *I-26*, the same submarine that had torpedoed the *Saratoga* in August 1942 and sunk the *Juneau* in November of that year. It had taken two years but the navy had tracked her down.[6]

Upon being informed of TG 30.7's success, Admiral Halsey radioed the task group, "Action makes you member of plucking board for Nip submarines. Well done to all hands."[7] This was only the first in a series of sub sinkings that would make the *Anzio*'s group one of the premier sub-killers of the Pacific war.

But if TG 30.7's ships and planes were enjoying success, another CVE/DE hunter-killer group was having a terrible time. Originally employed in the invasion support role, the *Corregidor* was now in the ASW business. Her new captain was Wade McCluskey, who had been the *Enterprise*'s air group commander at Midway. Also new was her squadron, VC-83, and the coming ASW cruise would show that the squadron needed more training.

One of the problems about the *Corregidor*'s first ASW mission was that it was in the real backwater of the war, the shipping lanes between San Francisco and Hawaii. Still, a liberty ship had been sunk by a submarine, and the *Corregidor*'s orders were to find it.

The ship tracked the submarine down, but a series of attacks on it by the VC-83 planes on 2 and 4 November did nothing but disturb the fish. The results of these attacks were not well received at CinC-Pac headquarters. Commenting on this ASW cruise, Nimitz's chief of staff, Admiral C. H. "Soc" McMorris, pointed out that too many of the VC-83's attacks had been needlessly delayed and poorly executed. He recommended that VC-83 be replaced as soon as possible on the *Corregidor* so it could receive additional training.[8]

Following a second unsuccessful ASW cruise in late November and early December, VC-83 went to the beach for some intensive training. The squadron, however, would not make another antisubmarine cruise on any carrier. Replacing VC-83 on the *Corregidor* was VC-42, a veteran squadron from the Atlantic, which had also suffered some teething problems when first operating from the *Croatan* in April.

VC-42 had been one of the pioneer squadrons in night operations off escort carriers and would continue these night missions in the Pacific. Ironically, by the time the squadron boarded the *Corregidor* in December it had regularly been flying at night off the *Croatan* and *Bogue* since the previous April, yet some in the Pacific still didn't believe that CVE aircraft could operate at night. This rather amazing display of ignorance by officers in command positions who should have known better would continue to dog the CVEs throughout the rest of the war, even though the evidence of successful CVE night operations was a matter of record.[9]

The VC-42 fliers discovered that anti-submarine warfare was conducted differently in the Pacific. There were more friendly ships, including submarines, than in the Atlantic, which created identification problems, especially at night. "Under these conditions," the VC-42 history records sarcastically, "a Japanese sub could have surfaced at night practically in the task force and we would have been powerless to attack before carrying on an extended conversation in blinker."[10] The VC-42 fliers saw Pacific ASW operations as defensively oriented compared to the aggressiveness shown in the Atlantic.

One thing to take into account, however, was the radical difference between the types of war being waged in the two oceans. In the Atlantic the war was against the U-boat and for the protection of the convoy lanes, these two indivisible tasks being greatly assisted by the knowledge of enemy intentions gained through the code-breaking efforts called "Ultra." The only invasions of importance in the European area in 1944 were at Anzio and southern France (both in the Mediterranean and with little chance of naval interference) and at Normandy. Thus, naval defense of these targets rested primarily with the U-boats.

The Pacific was different. A large enemy surface fleet, despite the losses at Leyte Gulf, still existed. Assaults against defended shores seemingly were made every month. The power of the U.S. Navy was directed at destroying the enemy's surface fleet and at protecting the invasion forces. Though a serious nuisance, Japanese submarines were not considered so great a threat that much effort should be expended on them. Also, without the marvelous advantage that Enigma presented the Allies in the Atlantic (though the navy was wonderfully served by the efforts of its own cryptanalysts), Japanese submarines were harder to find.

In any event, VC-42's operations from the *Corregidor* (which lasted until May 1945) proved to be singularly lacking in excitement. No submarines were sighted and only a couple of planes were lost in operational accidents. But if the *Corregidor* and VC-42 did not see much action, other "jeeps" got more than their share near an island named Mindoro. The capture of this island was the next step in the retaking of the Philippines.

After months of interservice wrangling, the JCS did not settle the question of whether Luzon or Formosa would be the next target until about three weeks before the landings on Leyte. On 3 October they issued "their last important directive" of World War II.[11] The main points of this directive were: 1) MacArthur would invade Luzon on 20 December, while Nimitz provided the support; 2) Nimitz would invade one or more of the islands in the Bonins-Volcano group on 20 January 1945 and islands in the Ryukyus on 1 March; and 3) The invasion of Formosa, while not canceled, was put on the back burner.

As part of the plan for the landings on Luzon, the island of Mindoro (in the central Philippines) was to be invaded so as to provide airfields from which Army Air Forces planes could operate against Luzon targets and to cover the forthcoming Lingayen landings. Though few Japanese troops were on the island, Mindoro was a gamble. The island was surrounded by enemy airfields, and the nearest American fields, on Leyte, were hardly usable. Even if the fields there had been fully developed, they lay 260 miles away, too far for effective land-based fighter support. In addition, Leyte was on the "rainy" (even for this wet group of islands) side of the Philippines and the rain could shut down the Leyte fields at any time. Air cover for the assault convoys would have to be provided by the navy.[12]

The close quarters of the Philippine waters precluded the use of the fast carriers; thus the work was left to the "jeeps," and it promised to be hard and dirty. The success of the kamikazes at Leyte Gulf still fresh in their minds, the CVE sailors were not particularly enthusiastic about the prospects of this operation.

Commanding the Visayan Attack Force, as the Mindoro assemblage was designated, was Rear Admiral Arthur D. Struble. His force was divided into three groups: the Mindoro Attack Group (the actual assault force, which included destroyer transports, landing craft, minesweepers, and other small craft), the Close Covering Group of one heavy and two light cruisers and seven destroyers, and the Motor Torpedo Group with twenty-three PTs.[13]

In addition, Rear Admiral Theodore D. Ruddock's TG 77.12, the Heavy Covering and Carrier Group, provided the big guns for the operation. Ruddock's force consisted of the following ships:

TASK GROUP 77.12
R. Adm. Theodore D. Ruddock

Task Unit 77.12.1   **R. Adm. Ruddock**
Battleships *West Virginia* (FF), *Colorado, New Mexico*
Light cruisers *Denver, Columbia, Montpelier*
Destroyers *Waller, Renshaw, Conway, Cony, Eaton, Robinson, Conner, Bennion, Sigourney*

Task Unit 77.12.7	**R. Adm. Felix B. Stump** (ComCarDiv 24)
Natoma Bay (F)	Capt. A. K. Morehouse
VC-81 24 FM-2, 9 TBM-1C	Lt. Cdr. R. C. Barnes
Manila Bay	Capt. F. Lee
VC-80 24 FM-2, 9 TBM-1C	Lt. Cdr. H. K. Stubbs
	R. Adm. William D. Sample (ComCarDiv 27)
Marcus Island (F)	Capt. C. F. Greber
VC-21 24 FM-2, 9 TBM-1C	Lt. Cdr. T. O. Murray
Kadashan Bay	Capt. R. N. Hunter
VC-20 24 FM-2, 9 TBM-1C	Lt. Cdr. J. F. McRoberts
Savo Island	Capt. C. E. Ekstrom
VC-27 24 FM-2, 9 TBM-1C	Lt. Cdr. P. W. Jackson
Ommaney Bay	Capt. H. L. Young
VC-75 24 FM-2, 9 TBM-1C	Lt. Cdr. A. W. Smith

Screen: Destroyers *Remey, Mertz, McDermut, Patterson, Haraden, Twiggs, Stembel, Ralph Talbot, Braine*[14]

In late November the carriers began leaving Manus to congregate at Kossol Roads, in the Palaus. Just before the *Kadashan Bay* sailed for the Palaus, her planes were flown aboard from the Ponam airfield, where VC-20 had been stationed during the interim. Several new planes had been obtained from the local Carrier Aircraft Service Unit (CASU) by the squadron, many of these not in much better shape than those replaced. Hans Jensen (the young officer who had first sighted the Center Force bearing down on Taffy 3) was taking off in a replacement Avenger when his engine failed. Retracting his landing gear, he turned toward the shallow water offshore. But because of the way the landing gear and flaps were linked together, his flaps also retracted. The big torpedo plane stalled, hit the water, and flipped over on its back on a small reef, trapping Jensen underwater. Before help could reach him, he had drowned.[15]

It was at Palau that, because of the very real threat of kamikaze attacks, the fighter complement of each carrier was raised from sixteen to twenty-four, and the number of fighter pilots was increased to twenty-eight. Generally, this was accomplished by temporarily assigning men and planes from carriers which at the last moment were deleted from this operation. With the increase in the number of Wildcats, the number of Avengers on each carrier was reduced from twelve to nine.[16]

Before the carriers left Palau for Mindoro, the extra Avengers were put ashore and their crews told to report to the Naval Air Station, Peleliu. When these sixteen crews reported to the Peleliu Air Base Operations, they discovered that there was no NAS, Peleliu, and technically they were in limbo. The marines on the island really didn't want this hodge-podge outfit, but after some wheeling and dealing by Lieutenant (jg) Anthony M. Peyou, the anointed senior officer of the group, they were assigned a couple of tent wards in the field hospital, where they set up operations.

About the only ones who welcomed these cast-ashore navy crews were the island's flight operation officers, who arranged for them to take over the antisubmarine patrol from a marine unit that was relocating. This worked out fine for a time until the Avengers, which mostly had been the ones the squadrons had been wanting to get rid of, began to give out. The crews had been working on the planes themselves, but they had been developing so many bugs that the pilots and crewmen just couldn't handle them. Finally, several mechanics from MAG-11 were obtained. Still, the planes were so worn and parts so hard to come by that the group was lucky if two or three out of the sixteen planes were able to fly on any given day.

The crews left behind on Peleliu weren't sure if they would ever see their carriers again because "each ship had sent the replacements or a few JG's they wanted rid of."[17] But on 18 December, except for one damaged plane left on the island, all of the planes and crews returned to their carriers. Their sojourn had been interesting, if not particularly productive.

The carriers and their escorts remained at Kossol Roads for almost a week; then, on 10 December, they sortied for Mindoro. During the night of 12–13 December the invasion force passed through

The "jeeps" leave Kossol Roads for the Mindoro landings. (Via Natoma Bay *Association)*

Surigao Strait and entered the restricted waters of the Visayas. Up until then things had been quiet, but all hell would soon break loose.

On the morning of the thirteenth the Mindoro Attack Group and the Heavy Covering and Carrier Group were fairly close to each other as they transited the Mindanao Sea. Acting as OTC for TG 77.12 was Admiral Stump. Prior to departing for this mission, he and Admiral Ruddock worked out a plan in which Stump would act as OTC for the task group each day beginning approximately one hour before dawn and continuing until flight operations ended for the day. Ruddock would become OTC during the night. This setup worked well, and it remained in effect until TG 77.12 retired through Surigao Strait on the seventeenth.[18]

Dotting the sky over the Mindanao Sea on the thirteenth were clumps of cumulus clouds, perfect hiding spots for enemy snoopers—and a snooper was hidden in them. About 0900 he sighted the invasion armada, and within a few hours of his report a group of kamikazes with a fighter escort took off from a field on Cebu.

During the morning the CVEs kept a twelve-plane CAP over the two task groups. A further thirty-five Corsairs from the Leyte-based MAG-12 kept an eye on the vulnerable destroyer transports and landing craft.

Around 1500, as the Mindoro Attack Force was about to enter the Sulu Sea around the southern tip of Negros, a Val streaked in from low astern to smash into Admiral Struble's flagship, the *Nashville*. The two bombs the plane was carrying added to the devastation. Fires broke out on the cruiser and ready ammunition began to cook off. Killed in the searing explosions were 133 officers and men, and another 190 were wounded. Included in the list of those killed were Admiral Struble's chief of staff, the chief of staff to Brigadier General William C. Dunckel (commander of the ground forces), and Colonel John T. Murtha, the commander of the 310th Bombardment Wing, whose bomb groups would be based on the Mindoro fields. General Dunckel and several of his staff were wounded.

Prompt and efficient damage control brought the fires under control within ten minutes, but the kamikaze pilot had done his work—the *Nashville* had been knocked out of the operation. Admiral Struble, General Dunckel, and their staffs transferred to the destroyer *Dashiell* before the cruiser returned, escorted by a destroyer, to Leyte Gulf.

Not much later the carrier group came under the kamikazes' sights. To the "jeep" crews this had obviously been just a matter of time. The number of bogeys on the radar scopes had been increasing and the CAP had tangled with enemy planes at various times. While on CAP over the task force at 1430, four VC-27 Wildcats were vectored to make a strike on Dumaguete airfield on southwest Negros. Upon arrival at the field, the planes made one strafing run on what appeared to be mainly inoperational aircraft scattered around the field. However, as they pulled out, they saw seven Oscars flying toward Dumaguete at 3,000 feet. The four FM-2s tore into the enemy planes and a wild low-altitude melee ensued. Lieutenant James L. Naftzger and Lieutenant (jg) Wilton O. Stubbs jumped one Oscar, which evaded them with a violent vertical turn. Two more Oscars popped into view, and Naftzger got the tail of one of the fighters and quickly sent it into the water. Although Stubbs initially overran his target, which was trying to land, he was able to make two more passes on the low and slow fighter. These did the trick, and the plane crashed into the trees bordering the airfield.

Meanwhile, Ensign Thomas S. Mackie and Ensign R. H. Dorman engaged the other Oscars. When the VC-27 planes tore into the Japanese flight, it fell apart, each fighter going its own way. Dorman tacked onto the tail of one of the planes and dispatched it with several bursts. As he pulled up in a wingover, Dorman saw another Oscar stalking Mackie. A head-on pass drove the fighter off in obvious trouble.

One of the enemy planes tried to shoot it out with Mackie in a propeller-to-propeller confrontation but lost and slammed inverted into the sea. Mackie pulled up into the base of the clouds and saw a pair of Oscars starting a Japanese version of the Thach Weave. It didn't work. A long burst of fire shredded the trailing fighter's left wing, and the plane spun into the ground.

Having become separated during the action, Mackie and Dorman finally rejoined and began chasing the last Oscar, then running for safety. At only a hundred feet off the ground the pair followed the fighter as it twisted and turned and tried to use every fold of ground for cover. Both pilots took turns at the Oscar. At last there was a flash, and the fighter's right wing fell off. In a split second it crashed into the trees. In this short action, which took only five or six minutes, only one of the seven Japanese fighters escaped, and he might not have been able to fly for long.[19]

Later, while the *Nashville* was undergoing her ordeal, a *Manila Bay* pilot bagged an Irving and smoked an Oscar. In mid-afternoon the CVE fliers drew more blood. Another sweep of Dumaguete resulted in the destruction of four more airborne Oscars.[20]

Shortly after 1700 the radar screens of Admiral Ruddock's force once again came alive with bogeys, this time closing from the northeast. These blips were the seven kamikazes and three escorts of Sublieutenant Hiroshi Komatsu's No. 2 *Kongo* Unit, which had taken off from Cebu at 1630.[21] While more fighters were readied for launch, the CAP was vectored to meet these intruders. Eventually some thirty FM-2s would be airborne.

About thirteen miles out, the Wildcats tore into the enemy force. VC-81's Ensign Robert H. Mount was a member of a division that had been launched to reinforce the CAP, and they came upon a twin-engined Irving flying right on the deck. (This plane was probably not a member of No. 2 *Kongo*, but a freelancer.) The plane was "tooling along" at about 200 knots, and the Wildcats, doing 220 knots, only slowly gained on it.

Apparently hoping to outrun the Americans, the enemy pilot tried no evasive maneuvers and stayed on the deck. Finally catching the Irving, the first three Wildcats made their passes. These seemed to have no effect, so Mount gave it a try and was able to score numerous hits in the cockpit area. The Irving caught fire, flew into the water, then bounced back into the air and continued to fly for almost a minute before it smashed into the water for good.[22]

VC-75 fliers from the *Ommaney Bay* found some good hunting when they intercepted the bulk of the raid. Sixteen Wildcats had been launched at 1725 to join the four planes already on CAP.

Shortly afterward they spotted an Irving, and six pilots (including one on loan from VC-76) tore after it. The enemy pilot had been making a run on an Avenger, but when he saw the onrushing horde, he broke off and dove for the deck. Every pilot wanted to get in on the act, and a frantic chase ensued. Dropping their wing tanks, the Wildcats raced in from every direction to lace the Irving with .50-caliber bullets. Finally, its right engine burning, the Irving nosed over and crashed.

In the meantime, four other VC-75 pilots spotted a clump of Lilys and Hamps flying some 6,000 feet above them. The Japanese planes stayed in formation as the FM-2s climbed, then broke away to attack when the Americans neared. Ensign T. J. Hill picked out a Hamp making a run on another section and gave it a good .50-caliber hammering. The Hamp flipped on its back and crashed.

Ensign V. E. Logsdon jumped a Lily and started its left engine smoking, but his second run was unsuccessful when he dove too steeply. Zooming back up, Logsdon positioned himself close to the Lily's tail. A long burst into the cockpit and fuselage caused the bomber to dive burning into the sea.

A VC-76 pilot temporarily assigned to VC-75, Lieutenant (jg) Wilbur F. West, cut the last Lily out of the pack with a run from the side. The Lily dove away in a sharp turn, but West stayed with it although three of his guns had jammed. Frustrated by the stoppage, West tried to ram the Lily but missed. For a few moments he flew formation with the Lily as it spiraled down, and he could see its pilot slumped over. At last able to recharge his guns, West dropped back to give the Lily its coup de grâce. The bomber's left engine started to burn and its fuselage began to rip apart; then it crashed from about 500 feet.

Also destroying a Lily was the aptly named Lieutenant Ace Johnson. Coming in fast from astern, Johnson got in three telling blows. Because he was going so fast, Johnson missed a second run, but he did not need to make one. The Lily was already diving straight down.[23]

The VC-75 group was not seeing all the action; VC-20 was getting its share. A VC-20 division was vectored toward a low-flying bogey about ten miles away. When they reached the spot, a quartet of Oscars emerged from clouds to scoot across the water toward the ships. As the Wildcats dropped on the enemy fighters, two of them turned away from the ships. The remaining two pressed on.

All four VC-20 pilots went after the two Oscars that were heading for the ships. Rapidly gaining on the lead plane, all of the Wildcats fired at the same time. Their fire was devastating. The Oscar flew into the water, bounced into the air, then exploded in a greasy ball of smoke and flame. Ensign Franklin W. Pinkerton smoked the second plane but did not see it crash because the intense antiaircraft fire forced him to break away.

Meanwhile, Lieutenant (jg) Kenneth W. Gnuse and Ensign Robert E. Beatty spotted another Oscar off to their left. This one was also down on the deck and really streaking toward the ships. The pair were only able to damage the fighter before the heavy antiaircraft fire drove them off. When last seen, the Oscar was racing for the destroyer *Haraden*.[24]

Though the CAP downed the majority of the attackers, three managed to evade the defenders and make runs on the ships. One of these, obviously the Oscar nicked by the VC-20 Wildcats, dove on the *Haraden*. Intense flak failed to knock the plane off course, and its right wing sheared off the aft and starboard sides of the destroyer's bridge. As the plane careened into the searchlight on the No. 1 stack, its bomb load exploded, blowing the ship's stack overboard. Burning gasoline was hurled all over the after part of the ship, and scalding steam from ruptured lines contributed to the destruction. For a moment the *Haraden* disappeared in a cloud of flame and smoke, but when the smoke lifted she was still afloat, though dead in the water. Good damage control efforts made relatively short work of the fire, and within an hour she was moving again. But like the *Nashville*, the *Haraden* had been knocked out of the operation. She limped back to Leyte Gulf with a casualty list of fourteen dead and twenty-four wounded.[25]

Streaking toward the *Manila Bay* came a second kamikaze, but it never got closer than 1,400 yards from her. A wall of flak turned the plane into a comet whose flames were only extinguished when it crashed into the water. The third plane tried to hit the *West Virginia*, but again the antiaircraft fire was too intense and accurate; the suicider crashed and burned astern the battleship.[26]

This was the last attack of the day. The defending fighters had done a good job in their battles with the enemy planes, claiming eighteen shot down and two more as probables. No U.S. planes had been lost in combat. However, an operational accident on the *Natoma Bay* when a landing aircraft cartwheeled into some parked planes cost the carrier one plane destroyed and two others damaged.[27]

The night of the thirteenth passed uneventfully as the task groups churned westward and then northward through the Sulu Sea. An hour before dawn the *Natoma Bay* launched a twelve-plane CAP to cover the Slow Tow Convoy (a motley collection of tugboats and tows, LCTs (Loading Craft, Tank), a gasoline tanker, destroyers, and destroyer escorts) plodding along behind the main force. Four VC-81 fighters encountered a like number of Zekes intent on attacking the convoy.

The enemy fighters were orbiting the convoy at 1,500 feet in a loose V formation when they were bounced. Apparently surprised, the two closest Zekes didn't have a chance. Both plunged into the water without taking any evasive action. A little harder to bring down were the other two Zekes. Ensign O. J. Miller found his target to be very maneuverable and fast, but by judicious use of flaps he was able to stay with the nimble Zeke. Following the Zeke in a dive, Miller had to use his trim tabs to help him pull out just one hundred feet from the water. The Zeke was not as lucky and went straight in.

Because it was so far ahead of Ensign B. L. Therrel that he couldn't have caught it, the last Zeke should have gotten away. But the enemy pilot wanted to fight and turned back toward Therrel. Both planes barreled in toward each other, firing, until they broke off at five hundred feet. As he swung around, Therrel was able to get in a full deflection shot. The Zeke pilot may have been hit, for as the fighter began a split S, it fell off on one wing and crashed.[28]

Meanwhile, a fighter sweep and a fighter/bomber strike were finding some good targets over Panay and Negros. Though the eight-plane sweep brought down only one airborne plane near San Jose de Buena Vista airfield on Panay, the other strike found many targets. Eight Wildcats and six bomb-laden Avengers from the *Ommaney Bay* had been sent against airfields on Negros, thought to be the source of the attacks of the day before. Though the field at Bacalod was considered a prime target, upon arrival there the fliers found it to be badly cratered, with no planes visible. Continuing north and east, the VC-75 airmen discovered a strip, Dos Hermanos, about five miles east of Talisay. Parked about the field were approximately twenty twin-engined bombers and a number of fighters. A Zeke was in the landing pattern.

The appearance of the American planes caught the Japanese flatfooted. Pounced on by Lieutenant Commander Allen W. "Snuffy" Smith, the squadron's CO, the airborne Zeke was shot down in flames about 200 yards north of the field. With no other airborne defenders to contend with, the VC-75 group concentrated on the airfield. Led by four strafing Wildcats, the sextet of Avengers planted 100-pounders and 350-pound depth bombs (armed with instantaneous nose fuzes) along the edges of the runway and in the dispersal areas. Another division of fighters followed with a strafing; then all planes joined in crisscrossing the field in more strafing runs.

A huge blast marked the destruction of an ammunition dump,

and smoke from burning aircraft smudged the air. Though enemy flak was weak and inaccurate, one shell caught an Avenger and wounded two of its crew. (The pilot landed on the *Manila Bay* to obtain medical attention for his crewmen.) When the Americans turned for home, eight bombers were burning on the field and sixteen other planes had been damaged.[29]

There were sighs of relief from the American commanders told of the destruction of the Japanese planes. Those aircraft would not be taking part in suicide attacks for some time, if at all. If the Americans had known about another Japanese plan that, luckily, misfired, they would have exhaled an even bigger sigh. An enemy force of almost 190 planes had been assembled to attack the Mindoro convoys on the fourteenth. However, taken in by a feint toward Palawan by the invasion force, the morning searches covered the wrong areas and missed the U.S. ships. Then a later attack from the Clark Field complex north of Manila ran afoul of fighter sweeps from TF 38. Two thirds of these planes were shot down and the remainder could not find the convoys.

Yet another attempt by Visayan-based aircraft to attack the convoys in the afternoon was also a bust. Around 1330, as the radars began brightening with an increased number of blips, general quarters was sounded and the CAP sent to intercept. Three Oscars getting ready to push over on the ships—two actually starting to descend—were jumped by four planes from VC-20. When the enemy pilots saw the Wildcats coming, they pulled up and turned toward them. Lieutenant (jg) Oyd L. Dauphin stitched the fuselage and engine of one of the Oscars, its engine belching fire momentarily. The Oscar split-essed for the deck with Dauphin close behind. Twisting and turning, the Oscar tried to escape, but with just one gun working, Dauphin exploded it just above the water.

One of the diving fighters chandelled back past Lieutenant (jg) Doy H. Duncan. Although partially blacked out, Duncan followed him straight up, firing all the while. Rolling out of the chandelle, the Oscar roared back toward Duncan. At that point Duncan didn't have time to spend on that plane because the third Oscar was also making a run on him. After trading ineffectual shots with that plane, Duncan looked about to see what had happened to his original quarry. He finally picked up the Oscar limping toward Panay. Jettisoning his wing tanks (in the excitement he had forgotten to drop them), he hustled after the smoking plane. Duncan was soon joined by another pilot and the pair took turns ventilating the Oscar. There was one final burst and the Oscar cartwheeled into the water.

A very agile Oscar from a second section of three planes gave

Lieutenant (jg) Lester C. Little a lot of trouble. Finally, following a series of wingovers and flipper turns, Little was able to get some good shots off. His aim was true and the fighter "displayed a sharp interest in sea-level conditions, twisting down in a steep spiral."[30] Little had to pull out at one thousand feet to avoid friendly antiaircraft fire, but the Japanese plane corkscrewed on into the water.

Yet another Oscar tangled with Ensign R. S. Cole and Lieutenant (jg) Everett W. Campbell and came out second best. Cole and the Oscar pilot got into a weaving contest in which neither side scored. Fully occupied with Cole, the Japanese didn't realize Campbell was near until too late. As he opened fire, the Oscar broke away and Campbell slid toward his tail. On a 60-degree deflection shot, numerous hits aft of the cockpit and in the wing root caused the fighter to explode. Before this action was over, VC-20 pilots shot down three more planes, while a pair of VC-21 FM-2 jockeys knocked down a Zeke.

Not yet finished with their attacks, the Japanese were back a couple of hours later. Like the earlier ones, these raids were beaten off by the defending fighters. The enemy attacks tapered off, and none of the planes got close enough to be a threat. A few planes remained near the ships the rest of the day but contented themselves with just keeping tabs on the Americans. Once again the "jeep" pilots had a good day. A tally of twenty-four planes, eight on the ground and sixteen in the air, was the claim for this day's action.[31]

Uncle Day, the day of the landings on Mindoro, was 15 December. The troops of the 19th Infantry Regiment and the 503rd Parachute Infantry Regiment (traveling this time by ship instead of by air) encountered little ground opposition, but in the air it was a different story. Though the Japanese had shown little eagerness to close with the U.S. force on the fourteenth, this day they showed no lack of zeal and aggressiveness.

Since 0430 snoopers had been sniffing around the ships, and an hour later they began dropping red and white flares. No attacks developed, but not long afterward close to forty enemy planes (divided equally between kamikazes and escorts) began taking off from Clark Field and Davao.[32]

By 0715 the planes were nearing the battleship/carrier force. A few high-flying aircraft closed with the CVEs at 0722 and were driven off by heavy flak. A Zeke was brought down by VC-21 planes seven minutes later, but more kamikazes were congregating. Army Air Forces planes relieved the escort carriers of their job of covering the invasion force at 0800, and TG 77.12 turned back toward Leyte.

The Japanese didn't care which way TG 77.12 was heading; all they saw were juicy targets of battleships and carriers.

At 0812 the enemy planes made their move. A Kate or Jill trying to reach the carriers ran afoul of the destroyer *Ralph Talbot*. Her guns blew the plane apart, but its speed had been so great that flaming pieces of the wreckage continued on to strike the destroyer.[33]

Ten minutes later the *Marcus Island* received the attention of some very determined Zekes. Initially, lookouts on the carrier had seen three planes off the port quarter flying at about 15,000 feet. One of these planes disappeared into a cloud, while the remaining two turned toward the carrier, one crossing over the ship's stern to the starboard quarter and the other making a steep turn to stay on her port quarter.

The latter did a chandelle, then began its dive on the carrier from astern. It appeared to the men on the "jeep" that the pilot was at first aiming at the forward elevator but shallowed out his dive to aim at a point forward of the elevator. (Before departing on this operation several carriers including the *Marcus Island* and *Natoma Bay*, had darkened the markings on both elevators to blend with the deck color. Then the outline of a dummy elevator was painted midway between the forward elevator and the bow.[34] The Zeke pilot probably was aiming at the dummy elevator. Elevators were both vulnerable and strategically important; they were natural weak points in the deck, and damage to one could make the entire deck unusable.)

Though taken under fire immediately, the kamikaze did not show damage until it was about 1,000 feet away. The 20-mm guns came on target and the plane started to puff smoke. This fire may have wounded or killed the pilot, for his plane just kissed the carrier as it zoomed by. Unhappily, though the flattop's damage was minor, when the Zeke's wingtip glanced off the starboard lookout platform it decapitated one lookout and injured another. A towering column of water only twenty feet off the starboard bow showed where the Zeke crashed.

Just ten seconds later, while the *Marcus Island* was still shuddering from the explosion of the first plane, the second Zeke streaked in. It hurtled toward the carrier from the starboard quarter and also appeared to be aiming at the dummy elevator. As the Zeke passed through 500 feet, it rolled 90 degrees and smashed into the water in this attitude just thirty feet off the port bow. The bomb it was carrying exploded, hurling shrapnel through the air, which wounded six men and caused some minor damage. The two kamikazes had crashed so close to the carrier that the water thrown up by them

A Zeke is taken under fire by Natoma Bay *gunners on 15 December 1944. (National Archives)*

covered the entire ship except for the last twenty yards of the flight deck.

It had been a very close shave for the *Marcus Island,* and the Japanese were not yet finished with her. A few minutes later a Judy attempted a glide-bombing attack on the ship. As the ship twisted and turned, the Judy pilot had a hard time maintaining his aiming point. Sailors on the carrier could see the Judy continually skidding, even as its bomb was released. The bomb missed astern, and the Judy soon followed it into the water.[35]

The defending fighters had been trying their best to keep the kamikazes away from the ships and did have some success. As VC-21 airmen shot down a Tojo, four VC-75 FM-2s met five bomb-toting Zekes twenty miles west of the task group. The enemy planes were flying in a "loose column with no apparent leadership."[36] The Tail-End Charlie of this "formation" broke away by himself with the four Wildcats hot on his tail. By some excellent flying the Japanese evaded the attacks of three of the FM-2s and was able to ventilate "Snuffy" Smith's fighter with a few 20-mm shells. (Smith was a bit unlucky this day. Upon taking off earlier from the *Ommaney Bay,* his own ship had accidentally fired at him and also put some holes in his plane.) The Zeke finally ran out of airspace and was shot down by Ensign J. A. Rouse.[37]

While the VC-75 planes were mixing it up with the Zeke, an Oscar was picked off by VC-27's Ralph Elliott, who was continuing his winning ways. In this encounter Ensign F. L. Moelter disappeared. A friendly fighter was seen to be smoking and its pilot seen to bail out. There had been a lot of flak around, and it is very possible that Moelter's plane had been hit by this fire. Despite a search, Moelter was never found.[38]

For a few minutes the task group radar screens were clear; then another raid approached. Around 0940 a group of planes (variously identified as Vals or Zekes) attacked the carriers. One plane dropped a bomb near a destroyer and scooted away to safety. Another plane was downed by a combination of gunfire from a destroyer and the *Manila Bay,* and a third had its tail shot off by the *Natoma Bay.*

Then a Frances braved the fire of virtually all the ships to make a run on the *Ommaney Bay.* Racing in from the front of the formation, the plane came under fire almost immediately. When the "Big O's" lookouts first saw it, the Frances was approaching the carrier from off the port bow and in a slight dive from 1,500 feet. "Brigham" Young ordered full right rudder, and his carrier swung around until the plane was abeam. At this point every gun on the port side (including the stern 5-incher) zeroed in on the onrushing Frances. When the plane was just four hundred yards away, a sheet of flame streaked back from its wings and fuselage. Roaring by thirty feet over the end of the flight deck, where several planes were parked, the Frances continued until it struck the water in a convulsion of smoke, flame, and foam some four hundred yards away.[39]

This raid was the last on the task group for the day, although numerous bogeys remained nearby until night fell. Not all of the action had been around TG 77.12. Several fighter sweeps had been made on airfields in the vicinity. Though few aircraft were found airborne, a number were caught on the ground (primarily at the Dos Hermanos and Fabrica airfields). At the end of the day the ACI officers tabulated the figures and came up with the following score: five Japanese planes shot down, nine destroyed and eleven probables claimed on the ground, plus at least ten more damaged.[40]

The escort carrier force had intended to retire from the area on the fifteenth; Army Air Forces planes were to take over the job of covering the beachhead. Bad weather on Leyte, though, prevented the army planes from taking off. So at 1950 the CVEs were directed to continue their invasion cover for one more day.[41]

This burning Frances just misses the Ommaney Bay *on 15 December 1944. (National Archives)*

Following the excitement of the day before, the men of the task group were grateful for the relative calm on the sixteenth. As it turned out, the little action that did take place was away from the task group and handled by the FM-2s. Though it was very cloudy, few enemy planes attempted to use the cloud cover to get close to the ships. The one aircraft that did venture near the task group, a Jake, had a quick demise at the hands of some VC-75 pilots. More Jakes were found by VC-27 planes during a sweep of Puerto Princessa, Palawan. Caught roosting on the water, four of the Jakes never had a chance, while a fifth floatplane that was in the air was too slow to escape. The *Savo Island* airmen also destroyed a Judy on the airfield. Over Mindoro VC-81 fighters shot down an Irving and also picked off a Val snooping a convoy.[42]

Shortly after 1300 the carriers and battleships were finally allowed to leave Mindoro and head for Leyte Gulf. For the remainder of the operation army planes would provide the cover. As TG 77.12 retired through the Mindanao Sea, strikes were launched at airfields on Negros, Panay, and Mindanao. Some damaged planes were noted on several of the fields, but this time all of the fields seemed to be inoperative.

Late in the day the task group passed into Leyte Gulf and was on its way to Kossol Roads. The Mindoro operation was over. In covering the convoys and the beachhead, the CVE planes had flown 864 sorties, 770 by the fighters and 94 by the Avengers. Sixty-seven Japanese planes were claimed destroyed, with a further thirteen probably destroyed. United States losses were eight planes operationally, one plane and pilot (VC-27's Moelter) in combat.[43]

For the escort carriers the operation had not been as expensive as planners had feared. Only the *Marcus Island* had incurred any damage at all. To some observers the enemy air attacks were "sporadic and disorganized [which] indicated clearly a general lack of trained pilots and units."[44] Indeed, the attacks at Mindoro had, for the most part, been sporadic and disorganized, mainly because Japanese air power had virtually been destroyed in the Philippines. A new batch of approximately 150 Japanese planes and pilots would arrive in mid-December, too late to use at Mindoro but ready for the next American assaults.[45] Though many of these pilots were ill-trained, at Lingayen they would show, to the distress of the navy, that they were more than willing to sacrifice their lives to stop the American juggernaut.

The kamikaze threat was still real enough for various officers to state their concerns to the higher commands. "For a steep diving suicide plane a ship is practically helpless," Brigham Young commented. "These enemy planes *must* be intercepted by the CAP *before* they can reach any point over a disposition where a *steep* dive can be initiated."[46] (Italics in original.)

Fitzhugh Lee, of the *Manila Bay*, emphasized, "Single suicide attacks can usually be frustrated by heavy antiaircraft fire, especially if *recognized and taken under fire early enough in their approach.*" However, he also stated, "The intent of the plane is not usually recognized soon enough to permit individual effective evasive maneuvers by the ship."[47] (Italics in original.)

Additionally, a number of ideas surfaced concerning types of weapons to use against kamikazes, some far-fetched, some not. The first line of defense still remained the fighters, but heavier antiaircraft armament was needed by the ships. In this regard, one idea was the use of ship-mounted 5-inch rockets. Another novel idea was directional high-powered, high-frequency radio waves to explode attacking planes. Yet another was the use of searchlights to blind the pilots. (This latter idea was used later by some CVEs and may have been, at least partially, effective.)[48] The next few months would give the escort carrier officers and men many more opportunities to study and analyze their foe's tactics and try to come up with a remedy—*any* remedy.

The Mindoro operation had been a unique afffair for the "jeeps." Commenting on the composition of the carrier/battleship force, Captain Lee said,

> It is believed that this is the first time that a "Slow Carrier Task Force" has been operated for any length of time as a unit in the same screen. From the carrier point of view use of the utilization of the OBB's [old battleships] and CVE's together presented no difficulties. The angular rate of turn was almost the same and the turning circles were sufficiently close to cause no problem. (Oddly enough it appeared that the *Cleveland*-class cruiser was the ship which turned the slowest and with the largest turning circle.) The slow acceleration and deceleration of the battleships was noticeable but no handicap. All in all it is considered that the Task Group, within its limits, formed an excellent tactical unit as a striking or covering force. As a defensive force it is to be noted that 144 fighters were carried. Since the FM-2 has a higher rate of climb than the F6F, and since there were six launching decks available, it is probable that a greater number of effective defensive fighters could get into action against an attacking enemy more quickly from this "Slow Carrier Task Group" than from a "Fast Carrier Task Group."[49]

Admiral Ruddock was profuse in his congratulations to the men of the CVEs:

> On our retirement from a dangerous and trying mission outstandingly accomplished, the task group commander wishes to express his pride in your job. He considers it a privilege to have been associated with you in its accomplishment. This group is the first combat team to consist of escort carriers with old battleships, cruisers, and destroyers. Beyond any possibility of doubt, the babies proved themselves the equal of any. To the gunners, the engineers, the communicators and all others but most especially to our superb fliers, a heartfelt *Well Done*.[50]

While Admiral Stump was equally proud of his men, he didn't want them to become complacent.

> Without detracting from [the CVE's] excellent performance, it should be realized that we were lucky. This operation was no test of the possibility of any future operations to be conducted without complete

control of the air. Nothing has been demonstrated that was not known before.

Aircraft carriers, big or little, are very expensive, highly vulnerable, mobile airfields. They take from one to over two years to replace with high expenditures of war productive effort. They are vital to our offensive effort. Therefore, they should not be exposed unnecessarily in confined waters where their own defensive powers are vastly reduced. They should not be used in place of relatively easily obtained airfields.[51]

If Stump had been able to see into the future and the forthcoming Lingayen operation, he might have reiterated his words even more forcefully.

As TG 77.12 returned to the Palaus and thence to Manus, it encountered some heavy weather. Rolls up to 15 degrees were reported by several of the escort carriers, with the consequent problems of plane handling on the tossing decks. If the men on the CVEs of TG 77.12 had only known what the men on some sister ships were encountering hundreds of miles to the northwest, they would have been quite content with 15-degree rolls.

For these other escort carriers were facing the wrath of another divine wind—typhoon! Their battle was just as desperate, just as deadly, and, for some, just as fatal as the battle against the man-made divine wind.

Halsey's Third Fleet (built upon the powerful TF 38) had been pounding airfields on Luzon since the fourteenth. Meant to keep the Japanese planes on Luzon bottled up so they couldn't create havoc with the Mindoro operation, TF 38's raids had been effective, but now the task force needed fuel and replacement aircraft. On hand to supply the planes and fuel was Captain Jasper T. Acuff's At Sea Logistics Service Group, organized as TG 30.8. The following carriers and their screens were part of TG 30.8:

Task Unit 30.8.12	**Capt. H. B. Butterfield**
Nehenta Bay (F)	Capt. Butterfield
Rudyerd Bay	Capt. C. S. Smiley
Screen: Destroyer escorts *Wesson, Swearer*	
Task Unit 30.8.14	**Capt. R. W. Bockius**
Cape Esperance (F)	Capt. Bockius
Altamaha	Capt. A. C. Olney
Kwajalein	Capt. R. C. Warrack
Screen: Destroyer *Hull*, destroyer escorts *Donaldson, Hulbert*	

Providing ASW cover for the At Sea Logistics Group was TG 30.7:

TASK GROUP 30.7
Capt. G. C. Montgomery

Anzio	Capt. Montgomery
VC-82 11 FM-2, 16 TBM-1C	Lt. Cdr. C. H. Holt

Screen: Destroyer escorts *Lawrence C. Taylor, Melvin R. Nawman, Oliver Mitchell, Tabberer, Robert F. Keller*[52]

Early on 17 December the Third Fleet and TG 30.8 rendez-voused. Lying about 300 miles east of Luzon, the rendezvous point was just outside the radius of Japanese fighters. It also lay right in the usual typhoon track.

And a typhoon was chugging right up that track!

No one yet knew, however, that the U.S. Navy's primary striking force was directly in its path. Around 1000 on the seventeenth fuel-ing operations began—or, rather, were attempted. Wind and sea generally making up from the north made fueling very difficult, if not downright dangerous. Winds were clocked up to almost 40 knots, and waves were becoming heavier and higher. Though the big battleships and carriers were riding relatively easy, the "small boys," the destroyers and destroyer escorts, plus the CVEs, were finding the going rough. Hoses kept parting, and keeping station was almost impossible. At 1000 the barometric pressure on the *New Jersey* was 29.85.[53] From that time the pressure kept dropping and the wind kept rising as the typhoon roared closer.

At 1310 Halsey ordered that fueling operations be suspended as soon as possible and the force head northwest for the next morn-ing's rendezvous. Located at 17°N, 128°E, this point was approxi-mately 160 miles northwest of the original rendezvous and would turn out to be about 120 miles north of the typhoon's actual track. Unfortunately, this decision also meant that quite a few of the de-stroyers and destroyer escorts were still critically low on some des-perately needed fuel.

About two hours after his original order to suspend fueling and head for the new rendezvous, Halsey again changed the fueling point, to some 180 miles south of the original spot. In retrospect his choice was disastrous, for it would put Halsey's fleet just fifty-five miles south of the typhoon's actual track.

Yet another, even worse, change in the rendezvous was ordered at 2220. Halsey and his staff were trying to outguess the typhoon, and they were losing. This new position was later plotted as only forty miles north of the typhoon's actual track, and put the Third Fleet in an extremely unsafe spot, in the "dangerous semicircle," the area where the speed of the typhoon's movement would be added to the speed of the wind's counterclockwise rotation.[54]

During the night the typhoon swept in upon the Third Fleet. Halsey and several of his commanders, including Vice Admiral John S. McCain, CTF 38, and Rear Admiral Gerald F. Bogan, CTG 38.2, could not make up their minds just where the storm was, placing it over one hundred miles away in various positions. A series of course changes only aggravated the situation, just moving the force closer to the center of the storm.

(One of the surprising and unsettling features of this entire affair was how many of the junior officers, skippers of the destroyers and destroyer escorts, had a better feel for the storm and its position. This "feel" was noticeably lacking among many of the senior officers.)

A little after 0700 on the eighteenth Admiral McCain tried to do some fueling, but it was no use. By now the waves were monstrous— estimated by one skipper at more than sixty feet high.[55] The wind was slicing off the tops of the waves and driving the spray and rain horizontally through the air. This day was monochromatic: gray ships pounding through gray seas under a gray sky. Only the white foam and spray broke the grayish somberness.

Among the first to realize that a typhoon was approaching had been the escort carriers of Captain Acuff's replenishment group. When fueling operations had been ordered at 0722, the *Nehenta Bay*, *Kwajalein*, and *Rudyerd Bay* came to course 060°. At this time the "jeeps" began to pound heavily, and massive amounts of water were shipped over their forecastles and flight decks.

Captain Butterfield, skipper of the *Nehenta Bay*, reported to Admiral McCain that the escort carriers could not take the pounding and that another course was needed for them. Finally, at 0752 McCain directed the CVEs to set their own course and speed, and Captain Acuff designated Butterfield as their OTC. Accompanied by the destroyer escorts *Wesson* and *Swearer*, the CVEs turned south, but even on this heading the ships were having trouble.

The *Nehenta Bay* was rolling between 30 and 37 degrees. (The maximum righting moment of the Kaiser-class vessels had been figured at 37½ degrees.) Steering control was lost momentarily but swiftly regained. To maintain steerageway, it was necessary to increase speed to 12 knots. This increase didn't help the other two carriers as they lost steerageway and fell behind.

Butterfield decided his ship would ride better if she was brought around to a northwesterly heading. This was better, but not much.

Though the *Nehenta Bay*'s roll steadied at less than 30 degrees, she still pitched heavily. Almost full rudder was required to keep her bow into winds gusting to over 95 knots in the face of heavy swells pushing down from the north. At 1330 the ship registered a barometric pressure reading of 29.117, quite high considering that other ships were recording pressures less than 27.00.[56]

At last, after what seemed an eternity, the storm passed. The winds dropped, the barometer began to rise, and the temperature, which had fallen as the storm neared, also began to climb. The pitching and rolling decreased and the *Nehenta Bay*'s crew was able to move about the ship in relative comfort.

The *Nehenta Bay* had come through the typhoon with light damage. Three planes had gone over the side and another had been blown into a catwalk. A 20-mm gun had been lost overboard when the plane landed in the catwalk. There was additional damage to the carrier, including some to the flight deck, but all in all, she had had a pretty easy time—not comfortable, but fairly easy.[57]

Meanwhile, the *Anzio* was also having her share of problems. For over an hour during the height of the storm she was rolling up to 39 degrees—beyond the supposed maximum righting moment of 37½ degrees. Tremendous waves swept over the edge of her flight deck and occasionally dumped water down her port stacks. Though her planes had been tied down and then retied, two of them were lost overboard.

In the *Anzio*'s hangar, her crew fought a constant battle to keep the aircraft there secure. One plane did break loose to smash against a bulkhead before being secured. The only injury on the ship during the storm, a broken arm, was incurred during the fight to capture the renegade plane.

Like the *Nehenta Bay*, the *Anzio* weathered the typhoon with minor damage. Her forward catwalks and lookout stations were twisted and deformed, several life rafts and one of her whaleboats were carried away, and there was some water damage inside the ship. Two of her escorts, the *Tabberer* and *Nawman*, were dismasted but continued to screen the carrier. Soon the *Tabberer* would be in the right place at the right time to perform almost miraculous rescues of sailors from ships that didn't survive the typhoon's wrath.[58]

Also facing the typhoon was the *Kwajalein*. At 0940 she lost steering control, but with rudder 25 degrees right the ship seemed to ride fairly well. Throughout most of the storm full rudder throw from side to side resulted in no more than a ten-degree change. The action report noted, "With visibility reduced to about 1,000 yards during most of the storm the attending risk of collision caused by this and lack of steering control gave Captain Warrack more gray hairs than the direct hazard of the storm itself."[59]

The *Kwajalein* encountered severe pounding when her flat stern dropped on a rising sea after being lifted clear. "The effect of the resultant working of the flight deck expansion joints," Warrack reported later, "probably exaggerated by the aircraft riding up and down on their landing gears as the ship labored, was startling and wonderful to behold."[60] At one point the carrier rolled 39 degrees to port, a roll that the ship's first lieutenant maintained was impossible even though Captain Warrack had himself watched both the roll and the inclinometer.

At 1300 a Hellcat broke loose to roll across the flight deck and into a gun mount. Under frightful conditions, the deck crew managed to shove the plane overboard. Two more planes were jettisoned at the height of the storm and two others wrecked. When the storm's intensity abated, the *Kwajalein* began to act more like a ship than a block of wood floating on a raging river. Luckily, the ship received only minor damage and, in contrast to the experiences of the two carriers described below, lost few of her aircraft.[61]

One pair of "jeeps" had a lot of problems. As a replenishment carrier, the *Cape Esperance* was carrying thirty-nine planes on her flight deck plus more on the hangar deck. This load was almost her undoing. Captain Bockius had begun battening down his ship on the seventeenth. Aircraft had been secured with manila lines and half-inch wire cable, the forward elevator was dropped to the down position to lower the carrier's center of gravity, and fuel oil, some two hundred tons of it, had been transferred from the starboard tanks to the port tanks. In addition, as a counterbalance the crew was ordered to remain on the ship's port side unless it was absolutely necessary to move about.

At 0952 the *Cape Esperance* began maneuvering independently. Rolls of 36 degrees were common, and an occasional 39-degree roll got everyone's attention. Against the power of the sea the carrier was making little headway as Captain Bockius tried to maneuver her into a position where she could at least hold her own. Worried about the top-heaviness of his ship, Bockius discussed with his executive officer the possibility of the crew jettisoning the planes. They quickly discarded this idea because of the danger to the crew. Then, suddenly, the problem resolved itself. Despite the heavy lines holding them down, one after another the planes tore loose from their moorings. As they ripped loose, Avengers and Hellcats rammed each other and then were flung overboard.

One plane wound up on top of the forward starboard stack and burst into flames. With this blaze threatening the bridge, Bockius ordered all unnecessary personnel out of the area. The *Cape Esperance* seemed in serious trouble. Lady Luck, however, decided to let the carrier off the hook. As the ship pounded up the crest of waves, then plummeted into the troughs, the stuck plane began to move. The carrier shuddered in the raging sea and the plane finally tore loose to fall into the water. The fire had threatened to turn into a full-fledged conflagration was snuffed out by the wind-swept spray and rain.

The loss of the planes was a godsend to the *Cape Esperance*. Each plane lost meant less load on the flight deck and a consequent lowering of her center of gravity. But the carrier was still not out of the woods. About 1600 another plane on the flight deck broke loose to career about and then fall into the forward elevator well, landing on another aircraft. For a few moments another fire seemed in the making, but luckily, no blaze started.

At last the seas and winds began to subside. Several more hours would pass before the *Cape Esperance* was out of the grip of the typhoon, but she had come through. Of the thirty-nine planes that had been on deck, only seven were left, and eight more on the hangar deck had to be stricken later. The carrier had only eleven planes left to deliver to TF 38.[62]

Also having more than her share of problems was the *Altamaha*. She was carrying sixty-five replacement aircraft, most of them on the flight deck. Her troubles began when a following sea swept over her fantail and flooded her after elevator well. Coupled with the water sloshing in over the fantail, a broken fire main helped contribute to a water level of over four feet in the elevator well. A bucket brigade was formed to combat this flooding. This was extremely dangerous work as men slipped, slid, and dodged shifting debris, a misstep quite possibly meaning drowning, but five hours later the flooding was under control.

Initially, Captain Olney ordered an increase in speed to 11 and then 12 knots in an effort to maintain control, but this only resulted in long surfing runs down the swells with tremendous rolls at the end. Olney then attempted various combinations of speed and helm, but an "increase in speed only made the roll worse without getting rudder control and reduction merely allowed the ship to ride in the trough with some danger of broaching."[63]

As the carrier wallowed and rolled in the grip of the sea, a six-ton crane on the hangar deck tore loose from its fittings to rampage through the hangar. Soon it was joined in its crazy path of destruction by a smaller finger lift. Together their battering-ram forays demolished two jeeps and three fueled planes. In turn, this mass of wreckage slid about the hangar creating more havoc.

If this was not enough for the *Altamaha*'s crew, a Hellcat spotted on the catapult tore loose and fell into the forward elevator well. The elevator had been lowered to permit the escape of gasoline fumes collecting in the hangar, but this accident jammed the elevator in the "down" position. A few minutes later a second plane joined the first in the elevator well. Then at 1230 a third plane, which had been partially secured to the searchlight platform after getting adrift, fell over the edge of the well but was prevented from going all the way down by the heavy manila securing lines.

Fortunately no fires were started from these excursions. To prevent such a disaster the hangar deck had been foamed, but the result was a mess, with men slipping and sliding in the gunky mixture as the carrier gyrated in the sea. Also creating problems were a couple of compartments where bottles of ammonia had broken, the acrid odor sickening people nearby. Damage control parties, using rescue breathing appparatus, required some time to clean out these compartments.

Up on the flight deck, meanwhile, planes were being ripped apart by the ferocious wind, well in excess of 100 knots. Parked at the forward end of the flight deck, the propellers of four planes suddenly began windmilling in the gale until the planes were snatched from their moorings and tossed overboard. And the wind continued to shriek. More planes began to leave the carrier, courtesy of the wind and sea, but this helped considerably the *Altamaha*'s ability to ride out the storm.

Finally the carrier edged away from the typhoon's center, her ordeal over. Like the other escort carriers, she had been lucky. But the experience had not been without cost. Of the sixty-four aircraft slated for transfer to the fleet carriers, only a third were left: thirty-one had been flung overboard, twelve more were too badly damaged and had to be jettisoned, and one was intact but needed a structural inspection, leaving only twenty in any shape for delivery to TF 38's carriers. Surprisingly, considering the pounding she had received, only six of the *Altamaha*'s crew had been injured, and they with only minor cuts and bruises. Yes, she had been lucky.[64]

Other vessels had not been. Three destroyers, including two of the unstable *Farragut* class, capsized.[65] Pitifully few survived from these ships.

The first of these survivors was plucked from the tumultuous waters by one of the *Anzio*'s screening vessels, the *Tabberer*, as the destroyer escort hunted not for men but for a course that would give her a reasonably stable ride. In the blackness of night the *Tabberer* rescued a sailor from the capsized *Hull*. His rescue was the first indication that the destroyer had gone down. Immediately this news was radioed to nearby ships, and the little DE began a rescue operation that would last forty-eight hours.

When this gutsy destroyer escort was finally finished with her lifesaving efforts and the *Rudyerd Bay* had relieved her, the *Tabberer* had on board fifty-five very lucky survivors of the *Hull* and *Spence*. Precious few more would join them.[66]

On the twentieth one of the *Anzio's* escorts, the *Swearer*, picked up nine survivors of the *Spence's* sinking. Fourteen more men from the *Hull* were rescued by the *Robert F. Keller* and *Cogswell*. Finally, on the morning of the twenty-first, the *Brown* chanced upon the last twelve survivors of the *Hull*. Less than an hour later the *Brown*, racing to the scene after an escort carrier plane had sighted them, pulled the last men from the sea. There were just six of them, the only survivors from the third destroyer to sink, the *Monaghan*.

After the typhoon had churned its way northwestward and left the Third Fleet behind, the fleet was in disarray. This divine wind had dealt a painful blow. Three destroyers had been sunk; 790 men had been lost; major structural damage had been inflicted on a cruiser, 3 light cruisers, 2 escort carriers, and 3 destroyers; 19 other ships had suffered lesser damage; and 146 planes (including 94 from the CVEs) had been lost or damaged beyond repair.[67]

The Third Fleet was effectively out of action, at least temporarily. A natural divine wind had done what an unnatural one could not. But the Japanese would get another chance to show what they could do at Lingayen.

A COVEY OF KAMIKAZES

GENERAL MACARTHUR'S long-cherished dream of returning to the main Philippine island of Luzon came a step closer to reality with the landings on Mindoro. Initially, the Luzon landings were intended for 20 December, but because the Mindoro assault was delayed until the fifteenth to better assemble the forces, the Luzon landings (to take place at Lingayen Gulf) were pushed back to 9 January 1945.

The delay was welcomed by virtually all involved (except perhaps MacArthur). Some needed rest was afforded the men of TF 38 and Admiral Kinkaid's Seventh Fleet; much-needed rehearsals could be fitted into the schedule; supplies for the operation could be stockpiled further. Of particular importance at this point was a need for more CVEs and more aircraft. The Battle of Leyte Gulf, Mindoro, and the December typhoon had made it difficult to find enough of them for further operations (including training and transport) in spite of their rapid production.

Additionally, the number of aircraft available in the forward areas had fallen below what was considered necessary for full operations. One reason was that although the carriers of CarTransRonPac had been estimated to carry an average of seventy-five planes per ship, in actual practice they could carry only sixty-five. Thus, in November only 506 planes were delivered, whereas about 1,100 were required. To increase the number of CVEs on transport duty, the British were requested to furnish some escort carriers (which they later would), the French carrier *Bearn* was expected to be available for use in February 1945, and the "jeeps" operating in the Atlantic were foreseen to be ready upon the defeat of Germany.[1]

In the meantime, the landing date for Luzon couldn't be put off indefinitely, and the invasion force finally set sail from Huon Gulf, from Sansapor and Aitape, from Manus and Purvis Bay, and from many other points (from which, in most cases, the Japanese had been forcibly ejected earlier). The Luzon operation was on.

As commander of TF 77, Vice Admiral Kinkaid was in overall command, with Vice Admirals Daniel E. Barbey and Theodore Wilkinson in charge of the San Fabian (TF 78) and Lingayen (TF 79) Attack Forces, respectively. In command of TG 77.2, the Bombardment and Fire Support Group, was Vice Admiral Oldendorf, while the Close Covering Group, TG 77.3, was commanded by Rear Admiral Russell S. Berkey. All of these officers had held corresponding positions at Leyte.

The only new name in this command setup was that of Rear Admiral Calvin T. Durgin. Durgin had become a naval aviator in 1920 and had served in various aviation commands since that time. During the North Africa landings he had commanded the *Ranger.* This was followed by a stint as Commander Fleet Air, Quonset NAS, until June 1944, when he became commander of TG 88.2 for the invasion of Southern France. In October he became commander of CarDiv 29, which at that time included the *Makin Island, Lunga Point, Bismarck Sea, Salamaua,* and *Hoggatt Bay.* His combat welcome to the Pacific would be at Lingayen, a very hot welcome indeed.

Durgin took charge of a new CVE command that came into being on 10 December 1944. Part of a reorganization of the escort carriers into three distinct groups, Durgin's command was Escort Carrier Force Pacific Fleet, which had been established to administer the growing number of CVEs in a combat role. The other two groups were the earlier-mentioned Carrier Transport Squadron and the Carrier Training Squadron, which consisted of CarDivs 11 and 12.[2] As ComEsCarForPacFlt, Durgin would be a "type" commander, yet he would also be a "force" or "group" commander, in which capacities he acted at Lingayen.

For the Lingayen operation Durgin commanded TG 77.4, the Escort Carrier Group. His force consisted of no less than eighteen CVEs and their screens:

Task Unit 77.4.1	Lingayen Carrier Group	R. Adm. Durgin (also CTG 77.4 and ComCarDiv 29)
Makin Island (FF)		Capt. W. B. Whaley
VC-84	15 FM-2, 9 TBM-3, 1 TBM-3P	Cdr. W. H. Rogers
Lunga Point		Capt. G. A. T. Washburn
VC-85	14 FM-2, 12 TBM-3	Lt. Cdr. F. C. Heriman
Bismarck Sea		Capt. J. L. Pratt
VC-86	16 FM-2, 12 TBM-3	Lt. B. M. Lakin

Salamaua
  VC-87   14 FM-2, 10 TBM-3
Hoggatt Bay
  VC-88   16 FM-2, 12 TBM-1C

Capt. J. I. Taylor
   Lt. H. N. Heisel
Capt. J. A. Briggs
   Lt. Cdr. E. N. Webb
     (KIA 15 Jan 1945)
   Lt. E. L. Kempf

Screen: Destroyers *Maury, Gridley, Bagley, Helm, Ralph Talbot, McCall, Patterson,* destroyer escorts *Edmonds, Howard F. Clark*

Task Unit 77.4.2   San Fabian Carrier
                    Group

R. Adm. Felix B. Stump
      (ComCarDiv 24)

Natoma Bay (F)
  VC-81   20 FM-2, 12 TBM-1C
Wake Island
  VOC-1   23 FM-2, 6 TBM-3
Savo Island
  VC-27   19 FM-2, 12 TBM-1C
Ommaney Bay
  VC-75   19 FM-2, 10 TBM-1C,
            1 TBM-1CP, 1 TBM-3
Manila Bay
  VC-80   20 FM-2, 12 TBM-1C
Steamer Bay
  VC-90   16 FM-2, 12 TBM-3

Capt. A. K. Morehouse
   Lt. Cdr. R. C. Barnes
Capt. A. V. Magly
   Lt. Cdr. W. F. Bringle
Capt. C. E. Ekstrom
   Lt. Cdr. P. W. Jackson
Capt. H. L. Young
   Lt. Cdr. A. W. Smith

Capt. F. Lee
   Lt. Cdr. H. K. Stubbs
Capt. S. Teller
   Lt. Cdr. R. A. O'Neill

Screen: Destroyers *Hall, Halligan, Abbott, Paul Hamilton, Twiggs, Bell, Burns*

Task Unit 77.4.3   Lingayen Protective
                    Group

R. Adm. Ralph A. Ofstie
      (ComCarDiv 26)

Kitkun Bay (F)
  VC-91   15 FM-2, 1 FM-2P, 10 TBM-3,
            1 TBM-3P

Capt. A. Handly
   Lt. Cdr. B. D. Mack
     (KIA 5 Jan 1945)
   Lt. F. M. Blanchard

Shamrock Bay
  VC-94   20 FM-2, 11 TBM-3, 1 TBM-3P

Capt. F. T. Ward
   Lt. Cdr. J. F. Patterson

Screen: Destroyer escorts *John C. Butler, O'Flaherty*

Task Unit 77.4.4   San Fabian Protective
                    Group

R. Adm. William D. Sample
      (ComCarDiv 27)

Marcus Island (F)
  VC-21   26 FM-2, 9 TBM-1C
Kadashan Bay
  VC-20   22 FM-2, 11 TBM-1C, 1 TBM-1CP

Capt. C. F. Greber
   Lt. Cdr. T. O. Murray
Capt. R. N. Hunter
   Lt. Cdr. J. F. McRoberts

Screen: Destroyer escorts *Richard S. Bull, Richard M. Rowell*

Task Unit 77.4.5   Reinforcement Carrier
                    Group

R. Adm. George R. Henderson (ComCarDiv 28)

Saginaw Bay (F)
  VC-78   20 FM-2, 12 TBM-3
Petrof Bay
  VC-76   20 FM-2, 12 TBM-1C

Capt. F. C. Sutton
   Lt. F. G. Lewis
Capt. R. S. Clarke
   Cdr. J. W. McCauley

Screen: Destroyers *Charrette, Conner*

Task Unit 77.4.6   Close Covering Carrier Group
(Was formed as needed from vessels of Task Units 77.4.3, 77.4.4., and 77.4.5)

Hunter-Killer Group   **Capt. J. C. Cronin**
(Nominally Task Group 77.5, but actually operated as part of Task Unit 77.4.1)

Tulagi   Capt. Cronin
     VC-92   21 FM-2, 12 TBM-3   Lt. J. B. Wallace

Screen: Destroyer escorts *Ulvert M. Moore, William Sieverling, Kendall C. Campbell, Goss, Stafford*[3]

As the above listing shows, several squadrons were making their first combat appearance in the Pacific. Among these was a unique outfit, VOC-1. The primary duty of this squadron was spotting for naval gunfire, although at Lingayen VOC-1 operated in a general support role and flew but one spotting mission during the operation. At the time of the Luzon landings only two such squadrons existed in the navy. VOC-2 was still in training and would not be available until Okinawa.

When initially formed, VOC-1 had been designated VOF-1 (Observation-Fighter Squadron One) and was only the third navy unit to get Corsairs. The idea behind a fighter-equipped observation unit was that the fighters would be more able to take care of themselves over hostile shores than the slow and ill-armed floatplanes usually used for observations. So, led by "Bush" Bringle, VOF-1 trundled off to Fort Sill, Oklahoma, to learn gunfire spotting at the army's artillery school. Hardly had VOF-1 finished the school when its Corsairs were taken away. "Corsairs can't fly off CVEs" was the explanation given the pilots, an explanation that didn't sit too well with the fliers, especially considering that they had had little trouble with the big bird when qualifying aboard the *Charger.*

Having loved the Corsair, the VOF-1 men were not excited about receiving Hellcats. But once again they qualified aboard a "jeep" and were off to war. The squadron didn't head for the Pacific, though, instead taking part in the invasion of southern France. Flying off the *Tulagi,* the VOF-1 pilots performed their spotting duties in a highly efficient manner and along the way also managed to shoot down six German aircraft and destroy many enemy vehicles.

After the job in France was finished, the squadron returned to the United States for a short break, then hopped back on the *Tulagi* to head for the Pacific. Upon its arrival in Hawaii VOF-1 received a nasty surprise. Its Hellcats were going to be replaced by Wildcats, and six Avengers would be added, thus making it a composite squadron. On 24 November VOF-1 faded into history, VOC-1 taking its place.

None of the aircraft changes had been looked on with favor by the squadron pilots, but they had no say in the matter. "Bush" Bringle's outfit, however, was probably one of the most highly trained units in the Pacific. Almost all of his pilots had been carrier qualified in the Corsair, Hellcat, and Wildcat, and most had five hundred hours or more of flying time. The majority of his men were combat-seasoned, and they would see a lot more combat in the Pacific.[4]

Gathered at Manus, the escort carriers had not been affected by the typhoon that had battered Halsey's Third Fleet. In the last days of December 1944 the invasion force began moving out for Luzon. Task Units 77.4.1 and 77.4.2 sortied on the twenty-seventh to rendezvous with TG 77.2 and the Minesweeping and Hydrographic Group (TG 77.6). Two days later TU 77.4.4 left Manus, with TUs 77.4.3 and 77.4.5 following on 31 December and 2 January, respectively. These latter three units were escorting the two transport groups and the reinforcement group.[5]

The voyage from Manus to Leyte Gulf was quiet, but after the invasion force passed through Surigao Strait and entered the Sulu Sea, events deteriorated rapidly. The Japanese had sighted portions of the fleet, and they were preparing an intense kamikaze effort.

An oiler, the *Cowanesque,* from the invasion force's Service Group was the first to feel the hot blast of the divine wind. On 2 January a Val dove on her. Though most of the plane went into the water, parts hammered the oiler's deck. Damage was light but two men were killed.[6] It was only the beginning.

When Admiral Oldendorf's ships entered the Sulu Sea, he placed TU 77.4.1 in the van of the force, with Admiral Durgin's flagship, the *Makin Island,* providing fighter direction for the lead ships. Bringing up the rear was TU 77.4.2, using the *Natoma Bay* as its fighter-director ship.

Tension grew in the invasion force when the bogeys began showing up on 3 January. Most of these were kept at a distance by the CAP, plus the cover of army and marine land-based planes. In the growing darkness, one enemy plane did break through these defenses, but antiaircraft fire splashed him near the *Makin Island* and the Australian heavy cruiser *Shropshire.*[7] This plane was one of almost twenty Japanese aircraft that fell to the flak and defending fighters during this and the next two days. Still, this was only one sixth of the aircraft the Japanese would fling against the invasion force through 7 January.[8]

En route to Lingayen on 1 January 1945. In the left column are the Makin Island, Hoggatt Bay, *and* Tulagi. *The* Ommaney Bay *leads the column to the right, followed by the* Wake Island, Steamer Bay, Manila Bay, *and* Natoma Bay. *The picture was taken from the* Savo Island. *(National Archives)*

General quarters was the order of the day for 4 January, starting at about 0330 when screening vessels fired at a bogey that ventured too close. Nothing major developed—then.

As the ships plodded northward through the Sulu Sea, general quarters was sounded several more times during the day, but again the enemy refused to close. During the forenoon, screening vessels queued up to fuel from accompanying oilers. Fortunately, this period passed quietly. Then, shortly before 1700, as the force was approaching Mindoro Strait and preparing to pass into the South China Sea, a large bogey (estimated at fifteen planes) was picked up at a distance of forty-five miles coming in from the west.

This raid split into two groups, one bypassing the leading ships to head directly for the rear formation. The other came straight in toward the ships in the van. Numerous spurious returns from the

The Lunga Point *passes the* Makin Island *in the Sulu Sea, 4 January 1945.*
(National Archives)

many small islands dotting the area hampered the FDOs in their vectors to the CAP, and the only success for the defending fighters was the shooting down of one of two planes by army P-47s twenty miles northwest of the force. (This success was not reported to the task group until later, and the plane that struck the *Ommaney Bay* was believed to be the second enemy plane, this aircraft having been chased toward the ships by the P-47s.)[9] With no returns showing on the rear disposition's screens, the enemy had apparently retired. Thus, the attack that came swiftly at 1712 was a complete surprise.

Fully aware that kamikaze attacks would be likely during this operation, the *Ommaney Bay*'s Captain Young had made sure that all fire equipment on his ship had been thoroughly tested and that hoses and CO_2 bottles were readily available. He also warned all hands, especially the lookouts, to be particularly alert because radar would not necessarily note the presence of enemy aircraft. Instead of the usual six air lookouts, ten were assigned, and a special sun lookout, equipped with Polaroid glasses, was stationed on the signal platform just above the carrier's open bridge.[10]

Unfortunately, all these measures went for naught.

At 1700 the *Ommaney Bay*'s group shifted into a new disposition as the oilers that had been operating with TU 77.4.2 dropped astern to take up new positions. Below decks on the "jeep," men were in the chow line; the food that afternoon was spaghetti. (Years afterward there would be those who still couldn't stand the sight of spaghetti, which brought back too many memories.) Other men were watching silvery flying fish skim over the blue waters of the Sulu Sea. It was a beautiful, tranquil scene that quickly became hideous.

Suddenly, and seemingly out of nowhere, a twin-engined Frances (which had taken off from a base on Mindanao) dove on the "Big O" at 1712. There had been no warning, and the *New Mexico* was the only vessel to get off even a few rounds. Ricocheting bullets were the first indications to the *Ommaney Bay*'s crew that something was amiss. Glancing up, they saw the bomber barreling in at a 45-degree angle from almost dead ahead, only 1,000 feet high.

Sweeping over the forward part of the open bridge, the plane just missed Young, his executive officer, and the air officer as they all ducked. It sliced through the after part of the bridge, wiping out the signal bridge and its personnel, and collapsing the superstructure onto the flight deck. Continuing, the Frances slammed into the starboard side of the flight deck and its bombs ripped off. One exploded slightly below the hangar deck near the No. 1 boiler uptakes. Where the other bomb exploded was never definitely established; it really didn't matter.[11]

Lloyd E. Beighly was a mechanic and had just finished working on his plane when the kamikaze struck. Hearing the machine-gun fire, he started toward a nearby hatch yelling, "Let's go, boys!" The next thing he knew, he was flying head over heels off the ship. When he sputtered his way back to the surface, he found that the skin on his arms and face was in shreds and he could see only out of his left eye. His life preserver had been blown off. A piece of a kapok life jacket floated by and Beighley grabbed that; then he spotted a piece of wood and also used that for support. Not satisfied with his jury-rigged flotation devices, Beighley sought something better. A life raft floated into view and Beighley swam to it. In the raft lay a shipmate—he was dead. Despite its gruesome cargo, Beighley made himself as comfortable as he could in the raft. After some time the *Ulvert M. Moore* moved in to pluck him from the raft, and his ordeal was over.[12]

The ordeal had just begun for the rest of the "Big O's" crew. Almost immediately after the kamikaze struck, the carrier's trouble started. An Avenger parked aft of the bridge had been hit by the suicider, and the TBM began to blaze, the flames spreading aft on the flight deck. Dense black smoke engulfed the carrier's starboard side.

Some sailors had been knocked off their feet by the crash; others just felt the ship jump. One of the latter was L. J. Britton. Under the weather and on medication, Britton was not in tiptop shape at the time. When the plane hit he felt the ship shudder. Half sitting up in his bunk, he asked his roommate what had happened.

Casually, his roommate replied, "I think we took a torpedo aft."

"Oh," Britton replied and lay back down.

Suddenly realizing what they had just said, both men jumped up and ran into the passageway. They could see flames flickering along its sides, but they were able to avoid the fires and made a round-about trip to safety.[13] Their perilous excursion had to be circuitous because of the damage the ship had received. On the gallery deck VC-75's ready room was demolished. A clipping room was afire and ammunition was popping off, and other clipping rooms were beginning to burn as the fire intensified and spread.

The hangar was a shambles. Planes had not yet been degassed for the night and were still carrying machine-gun ammunition. Several of the aircraft had been destroyed by the bomb, and burning gas from these planes had sprayed throughout the hangar. In seconds the forward part of the hangar was ablaze and ammunition began to explode. Of small comfort to those on the hangar deck was the fact that, though the starboard gasoline line had been broken by the impact, the gasoline system had been purged earlier. Still, the devastation was bad enough. Numerous bulkheads buckled or ruptured. Dense gray smoke enveloped the hangar, followed by a choking mass of black smoke drawn from an oil fire in the forward engine room.

Farther below there was more damage. Many compartments were destroyed. An oil tank had apparently been ripped open, because oil or fuel was noted in various areas and the black smoke looked oily. Boiler and steam lines ruptured in the forward engine room, the fires under the boilers were extinguished by the blast, and the "black gang" was forced to abandon the area. Personnel in the after engine room remained at their posts. Unable to contact the bridge, they kept their engines running until about 1736. At that time the heavy smoke entering the engine room became unbearable and after securing the boilers, they, too, had to leave.

Worst of all in the present situation—the fire main had ruptured. The main had been divided into forward and aft units, and with the break in the line and the loss of the forward engine room (which

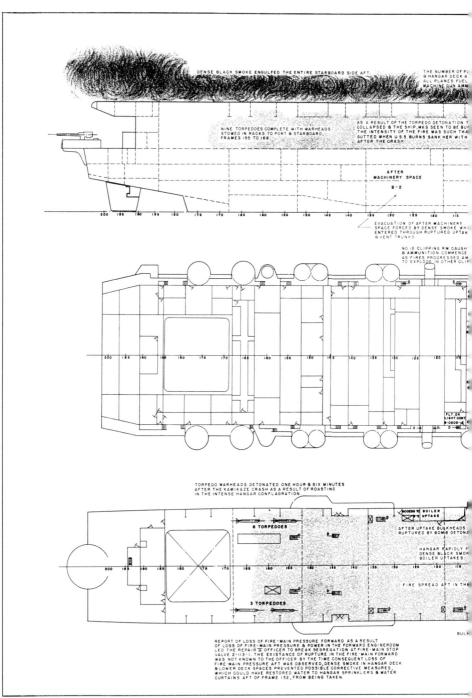

DENSE BLACK SMOKE ENGULFED THE ENTIRE STARBOARD SIDE AFT.

THE NUMBER OF PL
& HANGAR DECK A
ALL PLANES FUEL
MACHINE GUN AMM

NINE TORPEDOES COMPLETE WITH WARHEADS
STOWED IN RACKS TO PORT & STARBOARD,
FRAMES 155 TO 168

AS A RESULT OF THE TORPEDO DETONATION T
COLLAPSED & THE SHIP WAS SEEN TO BE BU
THE INTENSITY OF THE FIRE WAS SUCH THA
GUTTED WHEN U.S.S. BURNS SANK HER WITH
AFTER THE CRASH

AFTER
MACHINERY SPACE
B - 2

EVACUATION OF AFTER MACHINERY
SPACE FORCED BY DENSE SMOKE WH
ENTERED THROUGH RUPTURED UPTAK
& VENT TRUNKS

NO 12 CLIPPING RM CAUGH
& AMMUNITION COMMENCE
AS FIRES PROGRESSED AM
TO EXPLODE IN OTHER CLIP

TORPEDO WARHEADS DETONATED ONE HOUR & SIX MINUTES
AFTER THE KAMIKAZE CRASH AS A RESULT OF ROASTING
IN THE INTENSE HANGAR CONFLAGRATION.

ACCESS TO BOILER
& UPTAKE

6 TORPEDOES

AFTER UPTAKE BULKHEADS
RUPTURED BY BOMB DETONA

HANGAR RAPIDLY F
DENSE BLACK SMOK
BOILER UPTAKES.

FIRE SPREAD AFT IN THE

3 TORPEDOES

BULK

REPORT OF LOSS OF FIRE·MAIN PRESSURE FORWARD AS A RESULT
OF LOSS OF FIRE·MAIN PRESSURE & POWER IN THE FORWARD ENGINEROOM
LED THE REPAIR Ⅱ OFFICER TO BREAK SEGREGATION AT FIRE·MAIN STOP
VALVE 2-113-1. THE EXISTANCE OF RUPTURE IN THE FIRE·MAIN FORWARD
WAS NOT KNOWN TO THE OFFICER BY THE TIME CONSEQUENT LOSS OF
FIRE MAIN PRESSURE AFT WAS OBSERVED, DENSE SMOKE IN HANGAR DECK
& LOWER DECK SPACES PREVENTED POSSIBLE CORRECTIVE MEASURES,
WHICH COULD HAVE RESTORED WATER TO HANGAR SPRINKLERS & WATER
CURTAINS AFT OF FRAME 132, FROM BEING TAKEN.

Ommaney Bay *Kamikaze Damage, 4 January 1945*

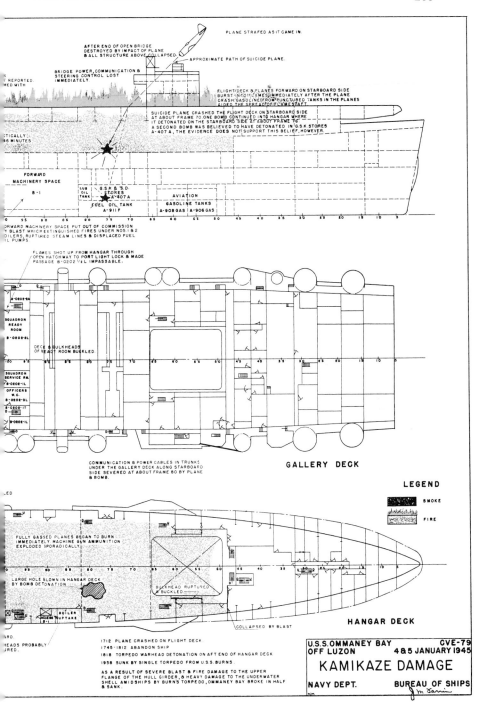

PLANE STRAFED AS IT CAME IN.

AFTER END OF OPEN BRIDGE
DESTROYED BY IMPACT OF PLANE
& ALL STRUCTURE ABOVE COLLAPSED.

APPROXIMATE PATH OF SUICIDE PLANE.

BRIDGE POWER, COMMUNICATION &
STEERING CONTROL LOST
IMMEDIATELY

REPORTED.
MED WITH

FLIGHT DECK & PLANES FORWARD ON STARBOARD SIDE
BURST INTO FLAMES IMMEDIATELY AFTER THE PLANE
CRASH. GASOLINE FROM PUNCTURED TANKS IN THE PLANES
AIDED THE SPREAD OF FLAME.

SUICIDE PLANE CRASHED THE FLIGHT DECK ON STARBOARD SIDE
AT ABOUT FRAME 70. ONE BOMB CONTINUED INTO HANGAR WHERE
IT DETONATED ON THE STARBOARD SIDE AT ABOUT FRAME 76.
A SECOND BOMB WAS BELIEVED TO HAVE DETONATED IN G.S.K. STORES
A-407 A, THE EVIDENCE DOES NOT SUPPORT THIS BELIEF, HOWEVER.

CTICALLY
6 MINUTES

FORWARD
MACHINERY SPACE
B-1

LUB
OIL
TANK

G.S.K & S.D.
STORES
A-407 A

FUEL OIL TANK
A-911 F

AVIATION

GASOLINE TANKS
A-908 GAS | A-906 GAS

ORWARD MACHINERY SPACE PUT OUT OF COMMISSION
BLAST WHICH EXTINGUISHED FIRES UNDER NOS. 1 & 2
OILERS, RUPTURED STEAM LINES & DISPLACED FUEL
L PUMPS.

FLAMES SHOT UP FROM HANGAR THROUGH
OPEN HATCHWAY TO PORT LIGHT LOCK & MADE
PASSAGE B-0202 1/2 L IMPASSABLE.

SQUADRON
READY
ROOM
B-0202-2L

DECK & BULKHEADS
OF READY ROOM BUCKLED.

SQUADRON
SERVICE RM.
B-0202-1L

OFFICERS
W.C.
B-0202-3L

B-0202-1T

B-0202-1L

COMMUNICATION & POWER CABLES IN TRUNKS
UNDER THE GALLERY DECK ALONG STARBOARD
SIDE SEVERED AT ABOUT FRAME 80 BY PLANE
& BOMB.

GALLERY DECK

LEGEND

SMOKE

FIRE

FULLY GASSED PLANES BEGAN TO BURN
IMMEDIATELY. MACHINE GUN AMMUNITION
EXPLODED SPORADICALLY.

LARGE HOLE BLOWN IN HANGAR DECK
BY BOMB DETONATION.

BULKHEAD RUPTURED
& BUCKLED.

BOILER
UPTAKE
B-1

COLLAPSED BY BLAST.

HANGAR DECK

ARD.
HEADS PROBABLY
URED.

1712 PLANE CRASHED ON FLIGHT DECK.
1745-1812 ABANDON SHIP.
1818 TORPEDO WARHEAD DETONATION ON AFT END OF HANGAR DECK.
1958 SUNK BY SINGLE TORPEDO FROM U.S.S. BURNS.

AS A RESULT OF SEVERE BLAST & FIRE DAMAGE TO THE UPPER
FLANGE OF THE HULL GIRDER, & HEAVY DAMAGE TO THE UNDERWATER
SHELL AMIDSHIPS BY BURN'S TORPEDO, OMMANEY BAY BROKE IN HALF
& SANK.

U.S.S. OMMANEY BAY   CVE-79
OFF LUZON   4 & 5 JANUARY 1945

KAMIKAZE DAMAGE

NAVY DEPT.   BUREAU OF SHIPS

supplied the pressure), there was no pressure to the forward unit of the fire main. Unaware of this break, a damage control officer opened a valve to route water from the aft to the forward unit, causing the entire fire main to lose pressure. And CO_2 bottles were not going to knock down the fire that was now raging on the *Ommaney Bay*.

Within seconds of the kamikaze hit, communications, lights, and power failed throughout the ship, though emergency lighting did come on shortly afterward. With no water pressure to fight the fire and with communications drastically limited, Captain Young rapidly realized that his crew was fighting a losing battle.

Destroyers attempting to come alongside to fight the fire were unable to get close enough because of the intense heat. The *Bell* finally came alongside at a right angle to the "Big O's" starboard bow and hoses were run out, but the fire was spreading too fast. Then the *Bell* had to back clear when the carrier drifted down on her, smashing the destroyer's port bridge wing.[14]

Finally, Captain Young decided it was time to get his men off the ship. By then the *Ommaney Bay* was just wallowing. At 1745, a bit over a half hour after the kamikaze struck, the most seriously wounded began to be taken off. With two men escorting each wounded man, the wounded were strapped into cots, covered with kapok life jackets, and lowered into the water. Five minutes later word was passed for the remaining men to abandon ship on her windward side. A number of men had already left the ship, many being forced off the fantail by the tremendous heat. One such group was lucky to find a life net on which to cling. Many injured were among this group but, luckily, a partially burned raft drifted by and its first aid kit was retrieved. Morphine and dressings from this kit were lifesavers for several of the injured.

One of the most seriously wounded was VC-75's skipper, "Snuffy" Smith, who was seen clinging to a 40-mm ammo can by S1c John Mitchell. Mitchell swam out to bring Smith back to the net and found that he was bleeding from a nasty head wound and was almost unconscious. Completely exhausted himself, Mitchell nevertheless dragged Smith back to the net, where his injuries were treated as much as possible. About an hour later the men on the net were picked up by whaleboats sent by the rescue ships. Ironically, Smith recovered from his wounds only to die in a plane crash a few months after his return to the United States.[15]

In another group of survivors a large, burly fellow suddenly panicked and began thrashing the water. "Help! I can't swim!" he kept screaming. Noting that the man had a fully inflated life belt on, an

The destroyer Bell *closes with the* Ommaney Bay *as the carrier's fires rage out of control. (National Archives)*

officer scolded him, "If you can yell that loud, you can swim to the 'can.' " The man settled down and, indeed, did swim to one of the destroyers.

Abandoning ship could be an adventure, as Hank Henderson discovered. Henderson left the ship via a fire hose dangling from the forward starboard catwalk. Going down the hose wasn't easy. First, he was encumbered by a wounded man whom he was carrying across his thighs. Second, when he was about ten feet from the water, he lost his grip on the hose and fell backward. The injured man fell clear and was later rescued, but that didn't solve Henderson's problem. As he had fallen backward, his foot had become entangled in the hose and he was stuck. For almost twenty agonizing minutes he hung upside down by one ankle, trying to get loose from his snare. At last he cut the laces on his boot, pried his foot out of the boot, and fell clear. He had a very sore ankle and a headache, but he was safe.[16]

At 1812, after one last look around, Captain Young was the last man to abandon ship. Six minutes later, as whaleboats from the screening vessels crisscrossed the water picking up survivors, torpedoes stored in the aft end of the hangar blew up with a thunderous roar. The flight deck collapsed and the ravening fire spread throughout the ship. Debris from the explosion rained down, killing two *Eichenberger* sailors in the act of rescuing survivors.

Following a thorough search for more survivors, Admiral Oldendorf ordered the *Burns* to sink the *Ommaney Bay* with a torpedo. Two minutes before 2000, as night enfolded the scene, the torpedo slammed into the burning and gutted hulk. There was a brief flash that illuminated nearby ships; then the "Big O" sank, sizzling and gurgling, into the depths of the Sulu Sea.

Casualties for this sinking were not huge, but they weren't small, either. Ninety-five men were killed or missing and sixty-five wounded. The dying wasn't over for some of the *Ommaney Bay* men. A number of them were transferred to the cruiser *Columbia,* where they helped fill out that undermanned ship's complement. On the sixth the *Columbia* was crashed by two kamikazes, not sinking her but killing and wounding many of her crew. Among the dead were seven who had been saved from the *Ommaney Bay.*[17]

The carrier's loss presented Admiral Stump with some problems. In order to pick up the survivors and then distribute them to other ships of TU 77.4.2, the entire disposition had to stop. This, of course, put the task unit behind schedule, although the timing would be regained later. Also, these survivors had to be retransferred to other ships upon arrival at Lingayen; this had some effect on air operations when the CVEs had to drop out of formation to do these transfers.[18]

Later Captain Young made several pertinent comments on this action. On suicide tactics he noted that "antiaircraft fire lags behind [kamikazes] to a much greater degree than any other targets. The higher speed of enemy planes making diving approaches must be taken into consideration and the fact impressed on A.A. personnel."[19]

Another point he brought out was one that had bothered many CVE captains for some time and was one that was never resolved, having to do with the hangar deck water curtain. The water curtain was basically an overhead sprinkler system that could blanket and separate sections of the hangar. Controls of the curtain were located on the hangar deck, and vital seconds could be lost before someone on that deck opened the water curtain valves. Young recommended that a remote control switch he placed on the bridge for use in those precious seconds when it would be most useful. The Bureau of Ships disagreed, believing control could be lost just as easily on the bridge as on the hangar deck.[20] Actually, in the *Ommaney Bay*'s case it is

The explosion on the Ommaney Bay *as seen from the* Natoma Bay. *(Via* Natoma Bay *Association)*

doubtful, because of the broken fire main, that remote control switches would have made a difference.

Not waiting for any BuShips recommendation, the *Manila Bay*'s Fitzhugh Lee decided to do something about fire protection. Concerned at how quickly the *Ommaney Bay*'s hangar deck seemed to have been engulfed in flames, Lee sought out the "Big O's" hangar deck officer, whom his ship had picked up. From him Lee learned that everything had happened so fast that there had been no time to sound the sprinkler alarm.

With this bit of information Lee gathered his principal officers to concoct a plan to make sure the hangar deck sprinklers were turned on. A special alarm circuit was installed from the bridge to the hangar deck. If Lee believed his ship was about to be hit, he would punch the alarm button and the sprinklers would be turned on *before* the kamikaze struck. And if the kamikaze did miss, some aircraft might be ruined by the deluge of water, but planes were easy to replace and ships were not.[21] Lee didn't realize just how soon his plan would be tested.

The *Ommaney Bay*'s sinking had not been the only excitement on the fourth. Just minutes after she had been hit, the "glint of a silver wing told [the *Lunga Point*'s crew they] were nominated."[22] The *California* and *Portland* opened fire on the fast-moving plane, but their bursts were long. At 4,500 yards the carrier's own guns joined in the clamor and it seemed that they were scoring, but the suicider kept coming. Then there was a flash of flame, and the plane wavered. Streaking over the carrier from stem to stern, the kamikaze left a trail of fabric and light metal to float down onto the *Lunga Point*'s deck. It passed only a hundred feet over her stern to burst into many pieces fifty yards aft of the ship. Flying pieces slightly wounded two men on the flattop.[23]

During the night the task force passed through Mindoro Strait and into the South China Sea. "This is a very historic occasion," one CVE captain told his crew later in the day. "For the first time since the fall of the Philippines, American surface ships are now entering the South China Sea."

Unimpressed, a sailor told a shipmate, "Let's go home and spread the news."[24]

Throughout 5 January Oldendorf's ships drew nearer the main enemy airfields, and the Japanese met the Americans with more air attacks. Reconnaissance planes had been tracking the formation for some time, and the Japanese were sure that Lingayen Gulf was the target. They planned to disrupt the invasion with everything they had.

Since the newly won fields on Mindoro were "socked in" by weather, the Wildcat pilots had to provide the brunt of the air defense on the fifth. Action started early. A heckler tried to close with the formation at 0327 and was shot down by antiaircraft fire for its trouble. Next, at 0837 the CAP tangled with a group of approximately eighteen enemy planes thirty-five miles from the ships. Four VOC-1 Wildcats bounced several yellowish-green-painted Oscars flying at 15,000 feet. Lieutenant M. G. O'Neill had an Oscar dead to rights when he discovered he had neglected to turn on his gun switch. He continued his dive, with the Oscar now on his tail. Reversing course, O'Neill took on the enemy fighter, scoring many damaging hits. The Oscar smoked, bounced about a little, and dove into the water.

O'Neill's wingman, Lieutenant (jg) Fred W. Fenzel, had flamed another fighter in this initial action, the Oscar going straight in.

Seeing three more Oscars to his right and a bit higher, Fenzel whipped his FM-2 around and lit out after them. When he slowed to drop his wing tanks and to switch his fuel, he lost some distance but gained it back with the use of water injection. Fenzel raked one of the Oscar's fuselage and wing roots and saw the plane begin to burn. A report of more bogeys in the area caused him to break off his attack, and he did not see if his target crashed. Ganging up on yet another Oscar, two other VOC-1 pilots had the pleasure of seeing it make a big splash in the ocean.[25] Six more Japanese planes were shot down by defending fighters before the rest ran for home.

Just four hours later the Japanese were back. This time it was the Mabalacat-based *Kongo* Unit No. 19, a group of fifteen kamikazes with two escorts led by Lieutenant Yutaka Aono. They fared about as well as the planes of the previous raid. Augmented by some P-47s, the Wildcats shot down four enemy planes and turned the raid back.[26]

Throughout the day interesting things kept happening around Oldendorf's force. About 1430 an unlucky pair of Japanese destroyers attempting to escape from Manila to Formosa was spotted by a patrolling plane. Sent after them, the destroyer *Bennion* got close enough to engage in a gunnery duel, but no great damage was done to either side. The *Bennion* was finally recalled to help screen the minesweeper group then moving into the area, and it was left up to TU 77.4.1 aircraft to see what they could do. They did pretty well. Twenty-four rocket-carrying Wildcats and sixteen Avengers with torpedoes, bombs, or rockets were sent after the destroyers.

After a short search, the planes found the two destroyers, the 1,262-tonners *Momi* and *Hinoki*, racing back to Manila. The air coordinator, Lieutenant Commander Fred C. Herriman from VC-85, had a hard time controlling the excited fliers, and more than half an hour passed before he could get them calmed down enough to assign targets. While eight Wildcats provided high cover, the rest of the fighters led the way with a tumultuous strafing and rocket attack. The FM-2s alone would fire ninety rockets at the frantically maneuvering vessels. Following the fighters came the corpulent Avengers with seven torpedoes, twenty-nine 500-pound bombs, and eight rockets.

The two destroyers put up a weak and inaccurate defensive fire as the attackers closed in like vultures. Smoke and towering columns of water hid the ships, and it was hard for the airmen to tell if they were really having any effect on the destroyers. They were: several bombs pierced the twisting and turning ships, with other near misses lifting them from the water. Finally a torpedo disembowled the

Momi and she went down in a spasm of spray, smoke, and fire. Lucky for a while was the *Hinoki*. Though damaged, she would escape to Manila, but when she sortied again on the seventh she ran afoul of Admiral Barbey's TF 78. That time there was no escape.[27]

Near the end of the attack a pair of VC-92 pilots saw a burst of flak near the *Bennion*. Turning toward the destroyer, they saw a quartet of Vals with bright yellow sides escorted by two mottled brown and green Zekes. The enemy planes were about 1,500 feet higher than the Wildcats. Lieutenant C. K. Brust, Jr., and his wingman, Ensign W. P. Wells, headed for the Japanese planes. Seeing the Wildcats coming, the Vals ran for safety while the Zekes remained behind to cover the dive-bombers' escape. The Zekes began an up-and-down scissors, and Brust went for the diving Zeke while Wells took the other one.

Brust's first shots, from 600 feet, were on target. Pieces flew from the fighter and it began to smoke slightly. Another burst as the Zeke began a tight left turn apparently killed the pilot, for the Zeke's turn continued to tighten until the fighter stalled and went into the water.

Meanwhile, Wells was chasing his prey in a circle. In his attempts to evade his pursuer, the Zeke pilot made some violent maneuvers, maneuvers so violent that he apparently blacked himself out. When this happened he naturally relaxed the pressure on his controls and the Zeke leveled off. In these instances Wells was able to punch in some telling blows. Finally the Zeke tried to dive away, which gave Wells a great shot. The Zeke began to burn inside, the glow lighting up the canopy. With a final squirt by Wells, the Zeke plunged into the sea.[28]

While the *Tulagi* planes were dispatching the Zekes and the *Momi* was sinking, a large group of enemy aircraft was approaching the task force. Led by Lieutenant Shinichi Kanaya, the sixteen kamikazes, escorted by four fighters, had left Mabalacat at 1557. By 1650 they were closing with Oldendorf's force as it passed about a hundred miles west of Corregidor.

In one fierce battle, VC-84 fighters destroyed six Zekes. VC-27's Ralph Elliott upped his score with two more planes in another fight, but more attackers broke through. Aboard the ships the waiting men swiveled their heads until their necks hurt, stared into the sun until tears came to their eyes. Gun mounts whined as they pivoted back and forth, their barrels looking like snakes as they wove up and down. At 1712 the leading ships came under attack. Full speed and radical maneuvers did not help. Two planes plunged into the sea, but one of these landed so close to the Australian destroyer *Arunta* that she was stopped dead in the water. A third plane passed ahead of the *Lunga Point* and swerved toward the cruiser *Louisville*. Despite a wall of flak, the plane smashed into the cruiser's No. 2 turret. Though a short-lived fire was started, and one man killed and another fifty-nine wounded (including her captain), the "Lady Lou" hardly broke stride and remained in action.

Another suicider got through to plow into the destroyer escort *Stafford*, then screening the *Tulagi*. A gaping hole was torn in her starboard side, causing the flooding of her No. 2 fire and engine rooms. Two sailors were killed and another twelve wounded. Unlike the *Louisville*, the *Stafford* was out of the fight, having to return to Leyte Gulf.[29]

The escort carriers weren't left alone. At 1743 the *New Mexico* reported planes off her starboard bow. Two minutes later many planes came in low out of the sun off the formation's port side. All ships began blasting away. One plane blossomed into flames and fluttered into the water; the others pressed on.

Two Zekes picked the *Manila Bay* as their intended target. Just fifty to a hundred feet above the water, they jinked in until about 1,000 yards away, then pulled up in sharp climbing turns, rolled over on their backs, and dove on the ship from about 800 feet. The first fighter-bomber (both kamikazes were carrying a small bomb) came screeching down, its wings and cowl sparkling as it strafed. Captain Lee quickly ducked, but two men next to him were slower, and machine-gun bullets tore into them. As he dropped to the deck, Lee punched the newly installed sprinkler alarm. Hardly had he touched the alarm button than the Zeke hit at the base of the island. From a distance, noted the action report, "a ball of flame appeared to engulf the entire bridge structure, but when the smoke cleared away the bridge was seen to be still intact."[30]

To the men on the bridge there was a bright yellowish flash that seemed to persist for several seconds, singeing the hair and eyebrows and burning the exposed skin of almost everybody there. Lee suddenly found himself several feet in the air; then he landed heavily on all fours. Also in the air was an aircraft tow bar, flung there by the explosion. Before Lee could stand, this heavy bar landed atop him, knocking him breathless. Lee had been bounced and battered about, but except for some minor singeing and what would become a very sore, black and blue back, was uninjured.

The kamikaze slashed through the flight deck, leaving parts of it strewn about the island, and continued through the CIC and radar rooms, where more parts were left, and into the hangar. Here its bomb exploded. Shrapnel whizzed around the hangar, setting two TBMs afire. The hangar was full of planes, with those parked forward fully gassed in anticipation of further attacks on the two Japanese destroyers. Flames leapt about, but Lee's alarm system proved to be a lifesaver—and a ship-saver. Within a couple of seconds the water curtain and sprinkler systems were operating, inundating the area. By use of these systems and fog and foam hoses, the fire was quickly beaten down.

Fifteen seconds after the first suicider, the second one followed. The pilot of this plane might have been wounded, or the unique use of the forward 24-inch searchlight to blind the pilot might have had an effect. In any event, the Zeke just clipped the carrier. Zooming past the bridge with its wings vertical to the water, it sheared the starboard yardarm off, then careened into the water some thirty-five feet from the ship. The ensuing explosion flipped a wing onto the *Manila Bay*'s fantail.

The first kamikaze had taken out all the communications from the bridge to the rest of the ship. The second kamikaze, though it missed, knocked out the communications from the secondary battle control station at the stern, where the executive officer was stationed. Thus, for a time Lee was left with just a megaphone and a lot of runners to relay messages about the ship.

Fifteen men had been killed and fifty-one more injured. Though the damage caused by the kamikazes initially appeared to be extensive, upon closer examination it was not too bad. No doubt about it, the *Manila Bay* had been hurt, but she was a fighting ship with a fighting crew. While the planes she had airborne were sent to other carriers, her crew began working on the ruptured flight deck. When the *Manila Bay* (codenamed Circus for this operation) finally got her radios working, Lee radioed Admiral Stump, "Circus performance interrupted for a while. Have two rings operating, expect to have third ring operating soon."[31] Within twenty-four hours the *Manila Bay* was conducting limited flight operations and by 10 January was back to a full schedule.

The men cleaning up the mess left by the first kamikaze found some interesting items. "The Jap pilot was thoughtful enough to leave cards," Lee said later. "From the wreckage were recovered his wallet (containing photographs and cards), a small notebook containing compass compensation formulae, and a silk Japanese flag with inscriptions in Japanese."[32]

Later, in reporting on the damage and the structural limitations of the Kaiser-class carriers, Captain Lee made some interesting observations:

These ships were built without direct Navy supervision, in great haste, and using materials and equipment in many instances which are ordinarily below standard in U.S. Navy ships. This resulted in the Navy getting some badly needed aircraft carriers when the need was acute. They' have proved to be very valuable ships. Without disparaging them in the least it is worthwhile recording that a lot of electrical equipment, instruments, gear, and fittings of inferior quality went out of commission from battle shock; standard Navy equipment seemed to withstand the same shock much better. Quality pays.[33]

A few minutes after the attacks on the *Manila Bay*, the *Savo Island* had its turn. An Oscar pulled up sharply and banked toward the carrier. As it pushed over into its dive, the suicider was taken under fire by several vessels, but this didn't deter the enemy pilot. Quickly joining this cacophonous barrage were the *Savo Island*'s port batteries. About eight hundred yards from the ship the Oscar began to trail smoke.

Captain Ekstrom ordered hard right rudder and the CVE began to swing, the pilot trying to follow the maneuver but not quite managing it. As with the *Manila Bay*, the use of the twenty-four-inch searchlight to blind the pilot may have had some effect. It was close but no cigar for the kamikaze. Wobbling and weaving, the plane passed between the ship's mast and the whip antenna just aft of the mast. Its wing clipped the SG radar antenna off its supports, and then the Oscar plopped into the sea.[34]

As the *Savo Island* was having this near miss, the *Natoma Bay* was drawing the unwanted attention of yet another kamikaze. This Zeke came in at water level from the port quarter, then zoomed up to about 1,000 feet trying to line up with the carrier's fore and aft axis. Instead, he overshot as she swung into a turn and had to dive from the starboard quarter. Black puffs of flak bloomed about the plane as the 40-mms opened fire, the forties being quickly joined by the barking of the 20-mms. To crewmen unable to see the action, the sound of the latter guns was a sure sign that something unpleasant was getting close.

Down in the "flag bag" below the gun gallery level, Herb Faulkner was one of those who couldn't see what was going on. Curiosity getting the better of him, Faulkner scurried up a ladder to the flight deck for a look. The first thing he saw was the Zeke boring in. Deciding the view was really better down in "flag bag," he made faster time down the ladder than coming up.[35]

Tracers ripped into the plane, and suddenly its left wing tore off. Spinning crazily into the water, the Zeke crashed virtually under the 5-inch mount on the fantail, pieces of the plane being flung onto the fantail. Burning fuel from the kamikaze lay in the *Natoma Bay*'s wake.[36]

Just a minute later the *Australia* was crashed amidships. The crash killed twenty-five men and wounded thirty.[37] Meanwhile, other kamikazes were attempting to attack the ships, but these had no success. One made the mistake of passing between the *Natoma Bay* and the *West Virginia*. Gunners on the "WeeVee" held their fire because the carrier was in the line of fire, but the *Natoma Bay*'s gunners weren't so cautious. Appraising the accuracy of the "Big NB's" fire, an eyewitness said, "Eighty percent of our shells hit the 'WeeVee' full on. Ten percent hit the water and bounced into the 'WeeVee,' the other ten percent hit the water and bounced over." At least one shell hit the plane, for it crashed just astern of the two vessels. As soon as the enemy plane crashed, the *West Virginia* signaled the carrier, "*Natoma Bay*, cease firing! We surrender!"[38]

Night finally fell, and the kamikazes headed back to their bases. It had been a bad day for the invasion force, but even worse lay ahead. In the meantime, far behind the bombardment and escort carrier groups came Admiral Barbey's San Fabian Task Force (TF 78). Covering this large assemblage of ships were the *Marcus Island* and *Kadashan Bay*.

Japanese planes began observing this force on 2 January, with all eluding the CAP. The next day was different. During the morning two VC-21 Wildcats were vectored toward a bogey seventeen miles from the carriers. Told to descend to 5,000 feet, Lieutenant G. D. Mickelwait and his wingman discovered a rain squall at that altitude and continued descending to fifteen hundred feet. Shortly after leveling off, the pair spotted a Frances crossing a mile ahead. The enemy pilot evidently saw the Wildcats at the same time, because he made a diving turn away from the fighters. Giving chase, Mickelwait and his wingman found themselves losing ground, but by dropping their wing tanks and pushing the throttles to the firewall, the pair slowly began to close the distance. Mickelwait finally got close enough to loose some long-range bursts. (His wingman had dropped behind and was out of the fight.)

On his fourth burst Mickelwait scored a telling hit to the Fran's right engine. It was still another fifteen minutes, during which time he almost became a statistic himself when he momentarily lost control while flying through the Fran's slipstream, before he finally bagged the bomber. There was a flash and pieces began to fall off the Frances. It started a slow turn, then dug its wing into the water and disintegrated in a ball of fire.[39]

During the night of 4–5 January, TF 78 passed through Surigao

Strait, following Oldendorf's previous route. As the task force passed between Negros and Siquijar on the afternoon of the fifth, two midget submarines tried to crash the party. Hank Suerstadt, from the *Marcus Island*'s VC-21, was right on top of one of the runt-sized subs when it raised its periscope for a look around. A depth bomb Suerstadt dropped that landed about sixty feet from the sub didn't contribute to its well-being. After the explosion subsided, the midget submarine was 45 degrees off its original course and seemed to be dead in the water, with a heavy starboard list and well down by the stern. Before Suerstadt could make a rocket pass, the destroyer *Taylor* charged up. She ended the midget's career by depth-charging and ramming it. The other midget submarine escaped.[40]

Following the San Fabian Attack Force was Admiral Wilkinson's Lingayen Attack Force (TF 79). Covering the transports in the force were the *Kitkun Bay* and *Petrof Bay*. Up until now their voyage had been uneventful, but that would only remain true for a few more days.

On 6 January Admiral Oldendorf's ships eased into Lingayen Gulf. The fire support vessels took station off the landing beaches at Lingayen and San Fabian, the minesweepers prepared for their hazardous mission, and Admiral Durgin's carriers moved into their designated operating area northwest of the gulf to begin their part in the invasion. For the sixth, air operations would consist of the usual CAP and ASP missions, plus bombing sorties over the landing area and some gunfire spotting missions.

The Japanese didn't wait long to put in an appearance. Just as the battleships began pounding the shore and the minesweepers moved in to clear channels (as it turned out, there were few mines), about ten enemy planes swept in over the gulf. Three VOC-1 pilots caught a Val as it dove on a destroyer. They made sure the dive ended short, thus receiving a "sincere expression of gratitude" from the ship. Another of the enemy planes was a dark-blue-painted Frances. Lieutenant Commander R. C. Barnes, VC-81's CO, caught the bomber from the side. His fifties stitched the Fran from nose to tail, causing the bomber to fall out of control into the ocean.

Five minutes later Barnes's division spotted some more bogeys. As these were being chased, a Val appeared above in the base of the clouds. Lieutenant (jg) John F. Sargent chased it, and both he and the Val disappeared into the clouds. Just a few seconds later the Val tumbled out of the overcast, a trail of smoke corkscrewing behind it. Meanwhile, the bogeys the other members of the division had been going after turned out to be a wandering TBM and FM-2.

A jubilant Lieutenant Henry Suerstadt tells Rear Admiral William D. Sample of the sinking of a midget sub on 5 January 1945. (National Archives)

A collision in the making? A telephoto lens makes the spacing look closer than it really is between the California *and an escort carrier. (National Archives)*

After regrouping, Barnes's pilots saw another Val diving on the ships. All four gave chase, catching the dive-bomber quickly. Taking turns, the quartet riddled, but could not down, the Val. By then the planes were right on the deck, just a few feet from the water. As Sargent turned to follow the twisting and jinking Val, he dipped his left wing into the ocean. There was a brief flash and his FM-2 fell apart, the wreckage splattering all around. At almost the same moment the Val also splattered itself over the sea.

A subdued threesome once more took up their patrol and shot down another Val a short time later. The destruction of four planes during this action was not enough to ease their grief over the loss of Sargent.[41]

In a morning strike on inland targets, VC-81 aircraft found some remunerative ones, including an ammunition dump which went up in a spectacular fireworks display. They also sunk several small ships. Trying to break up these attacks, the Japanese lost one Zeke to covering Wildcats and an Oscar (which reportedly had white balls instead of the customary red ones for the national insignia) to four TBM gunners who sandwiched it between them.

Although they never realized it, the Japanese did manage to bag one Avenger, however. Lieutenant (jg) Robert F. Voltz was just pulling out of his bombing run when he was jumped by a Zeke that shot off part of the Avenger's tail surfaces, putting the big "Turkey" into a spin. Though he was able to recover, Voltz was a sitting duck because he couldn't maneuver with the mangled tail surfaces. The Zeke made five more passes as Voltz limped out to sea, and on one of these killed Voltz's turret gunner, AMM3c George H. Neese. Another run wounded ARM1c Michael D. Sweeney.

Apparently out of ammunition, the Zeke finally left. The enemy pilot hadn't shot down the TBM, but he had left it in sad shape. When Voltz got back to the *Natoma Bay*, he couldn't lower his tailhook; told not to land, he was given the choice of bailing out or ditching. Voltz decided to ditch, since he believed that Sweeney wouldn't survive a parachute jump. In spite of high swells and a partially lowered landing gear, Voltz set his Avenger down smoothly and was able to get his semiconscious radioman and the life raft out of the plane before it sank. The *Bell* picked up both men, who were transferred back to the *Natoma Bay* a few days later.[42]

Around 1130 another series of raids on the ships in Lingayen Gulf started. Most of these planes were apparently from Clark Field, where *Kongo* Units No. 22 and 23 (made up of twenty aircraft, including escorts) had taken off earlier.[43] This time the CVEs were not bothered, but the other ships took a beating. The destroyer *Richard P. Leary* was brushed by a kamikaze that splashed close aboard; the *Walke* shot down two planes, but a third plowed into her, killing her captain; yet another destroyer, the *Allen M. Sumner*, was hit and had fourteen men killed and twenty-nine wounded.

Bombarding the shore was the battleship *New Mexico*, a prime target because she was unable to maneuver. A kamikaze slammed into the port wing of her navigating bridge, causing grievous damage to the ship's superstructure and inflicting many casualties. Among the dead were Winston Churchill's personal liaison officer at MacArthur's headquarters, Lieutenant General Herbert Lumsden; the *New Mexico*'s commanding officer, Captain R. W. Fleming; and *Time* Magazine correspondent William Chickering.

A bit after noon the minesweeper *Long* was hit by a suicider, and extensive fires were started. A crucial misunderstanding led to a premature abandonment of the ship. Before a salvage party could return, another kamikaze hit her amidships, breaking her back. The *Long* sank the next day. Just after the *Long* was first hit, the destroyer transport *Brooks* was ravaged by another kamikaze.

The divine wind continued to blow over the invasion force. Two Zekes dove on the destroyers *Barton* and *O'Brien*, one just missing the *Barton*, the other exploding in a fireball on the *O'Brien*'s fantail. Luckily the damage was not great. Later that afternoon, when the bombardment group began to retire for the night, five Zekes and one Judy of Sublieutenant Kunitame Nakao's *Kongo* Unit No. 20 put in an appearance. One of these planes streaked in to hit the battleship *California* at the base of her mainmast. The old "Prune Barge" was hurt but remained in action.

Two more planes targeted the light cruiser *Columbia*. The first zipped between her masts, spraying her with gasoline, then crashed close aboard. A few hours later another plane careened into the No. 4 turret, starting numerous fires and flooding several compartments. Seven *Ommaney Bay* survivors were among the dead. Still, the *Columbia* remained on station.

At 1732 the destroyer-minesweeper *Southard* was crash-dived. Two minutes later the *Australia* took another kamikaze. It was her second of the operation; it wouldn't be her last. The *Louisville* was also on the receiving end of a second suicider. This one tore apart the bridge, sky control, and a 40-mm mount. Horribly burned by flaming gasoline, Rear Admiral Theodore E. Chandler had to be coaxed away from the fire hose he was handling to get first aid. It was too late; he died the next day.[44]

The sixth of January had been a terrible day for the Americans (and Australians) at Lingayen. One ship had been sunk, eleven others damaged, and hundreds of men killed or wounded. The outlook for the coming days seemed grim indeed. Escort carrier planes had been up throughout the day, but they had been unable to prevent the kamikazes from breaking through, prompting Admiral Wilkinson to report later, "The outstanding single deficiency in air operations was the inability of escort carriers to provide adequate air defense for an amphibious force during the twilight periods and at night."[45]

Wilkinson's statement is true—however, practically all of the damage by the kamikazes occurred in daylight, not at night. One of the reasons for the "inadequate" air defense was the sinking of the *Ommaney Bay* along with the damage to the *Manila Bay* and, later, the *Kadashan Bay* and *Kitkun Bay*. The loss of aircraft from these ships naturally reduced the number of fighters available. In Admiral Stump's task unit this meant that because of the heavy air support requirements, only eight fighters could be maintained on LCAP. "This is not an adequate combat air patrol," he argued, "to provide an effective air defense against suicide bombers."[46]

Captain Robert Hunter of the *Kadashan Bay* reinforced Stump's argument by declaring, "The Fighter Director Doctrine stating that a defense consisting of 50% the number of planes used by the attacking force is *obsolete* [italics in original] with regard to suicide bombers. The instant such a force is attacked it splits and each plane attempts to make its attack individually. The only air defense is to use an overwhelming number of planes for the interception to make sure that every Jap plane is shot down."[47]

Hunter recommended that Snapper Patrols (visual low-altitude fighter direction) be used more extensively, though Stump thought the Snapper Patrols should be used only when nearby land masses blanked out radar screens. Carrying Hunter's call for an "overwhelming number" of aircraft further, the *Makin Island*'s Whaley wished to see three or four carriers of a task group to carry fighters only, similar to the use of the *Kalinin Bay* at Saipan.[48]

Whaley's idea had some merit but because of the missions given the escort carriers, it proved impracticable to implement. (This is a point that Wilkinson and other planners seemed to have missed. The CVEs at Lingayen, and Mindoro, had been given dichotomous missions—ground support and air defense—and one couldn't be emphasized without causing the other to suffer.) While the large carriers did receive an increase in the numbers of fighters carried (the Hellcat and Corsair both being excellent fighter-bombers), increasing the number of Wildcats on a CVE would reduce the effectiveness of their close support missions, the Wildcat, though adequate, not being a great fighter-bomber.

Another problem facing the defending fighters was the lack of time to intercept the incoming raids. As at Mindoro, the surrounding islands with their high peaks often blanked out ships' radars. Enemy planes were thus able to sneak through the "black holes" caused by these mountain returns. An additional hindrance to effective interceptions was the fact that none of the CVEs had any altitude-determining radar equipment.[49] In his action report, Admiral Stump would remark, "In view of present Jap suicide tactics the importance of having at least one SM or SP radar in each carrier task unit cannot be overemphasized. Maximum efficiency of the combat air patrol cannot be obtained, no matter how large, unless the altitude of the incoming raid can be ascertained."[50]

Finally, when the Wildcats did manage to intercept, they were sometimes outrun by newer Japanese aircraft. "Too much is expected of these escort carriers," Admiral Oldendorf would comment. "They are gamely and courageously led and can be counted on for the last measure of devotion," but for the time being they seemed outclassed.[51]

Yet an engrossing fact about the Wildcat at Lingayen later emerged. At Lingayen the ratio of FM-2 losses to enemy aircraft destroyed was ninety Japanese planes to one Wildcat. During the whole of 1944 the ratio of losses for FM aircraft was thirty-five to one. A corresponding figure for the Hellcat was about twenty-four to one. All in all, despite the obsolescence of their aircraft and considering the qualms some senior officers had about their effectiveness, that was a very good showing by the Wildcat pilots.[52]

In the fighter pilots' defense, the kamikaze attacks at Lingayen took everyone by surprise with their fury and intensity. Groping for a solution, a number of commanders believed that it was possible for the fighters to completely eliminate these suicide activities. It was not. They could destroy many of the attackers, but they could not get all, especially those who were very determined to press their attacks to the fullest. This painful fact was brought out again at Iwo Jima and relearned at Okinawa.

Help was needed at Lingayen, however. "Our CVEs entirely inadequate providing air cover," Oldendorf radioed Kinkaid. "Japanese suicide dive-bombers seem able attack without much interference owing to radar difficulties."[53] (Oldendorf was one who believed the CVE planes should have put up an impregnable defense.) Help was summoned from the Third Fleet, then getting ready to strike Formosa. Swinging back to plaster the Luzon airfields, Halsey's raids helped to keep down the enemy air activity for the next couple of days.

But they didn't halt the Japanese. Early on the seventh a group of planes struck the minesweepers in the gulf and sank the *Hovey* with a torpedo. Following this attack, things quieted down for several hours. There were enemy planes about, to be sure, but most were driven off or shot down before they caused any trouble. More aircraft were discovered on the supposedly unserviceable San Jose strip by an Avenger/Wildcat antisub team. The pair asked permission to attack, but this took some forty-five minutes to obtain. Luckily, none of the enemy planes took off in the interim and the two pilots were able to beat up the field with favorable results, several planes burning on the ground when they left.[54] Obviously, the CVE planes *were* doing their job.

This day saw a VC-92 Avenger run afoul of some Zekes and be shot down. Lieutenant Donald D. Dilly was flying an antisub patrol ten miles west of the *Tulagi* when he reported being attacked by three Zekes. He also radioed that he had a hole in his wing, but his engine was running all right. Following that message nothing more was heard from Dilly, but a few minutes later a plane in an adjacent sector saw tracers being fired at a low-flying plane and then that plane exploding. It was most likely Dilly's Avenger. Despite an extensive search, no survivors were found.[55]

Throughout the day many missions were flown against various targets in back of the beaches. On one of these missions a VC-90 Avenger was shot down, the pilot and one crewman killed. The other crewman was captured by the Japanese; he was never seen again. Another strike by three VC-81 planes showed that the fliers of that squadron had developed awfully good eyesight. A strafing attack on a vehicle park revealed a "1940 Plymouth coupe in good condition." After the attack the "Plymouth" was no longer able to run.[56]

That evening, when the fire support vessels were retiring for the night, the Japanese scored again with a bombing raid that sank the minesweeper *Palmer*. The seventh of January had been a much quieter day, but two more ships still had been sunk.

The eighth was S day minus one, and the escort carriers once again had more excitement than they really wanted. As usual, snoopers had been present during the night but two were shot down by P-61s on night CAP. Shortly before the sun came up, the kamikazes were back to pick on the twice-wounded *Australia*. Lookouts on other ships reported five planes heading for the cruiser. Actually, only the leading plane was a kamikaze, the others being VC-88 Wildcats striving mightily to head off the enemy plane before it did its dirty work.

The FM-2s didn't quite make it. Antiaircraft fire splashed the kamikaze just yards short of the *Australia,* and its remains skidded into the cruiser's side. Also taken under fire were the pursuing Wildcats. All suffered varying degrees of damage, with one being shot down, though the pilot was rescued. Just moments later another kamikaze slid into the *Australia,* blowing a large hole in her side. The cruiser and her crew, though battered and bruised, were tough, and after making repairs, remained with the task force.[57]

In the meantime, the San Fabian and Lingayen Attack Forces were moving into the area, and two of the covering CVEs received a rough welcome to Lingayen Gulf. At 0700, as the sky was brightening rapidly in the east, both the *Marcus Island* and *Kadashan Bay* launched two divisions of fighters. Sixteen minutes later a large bogey was detected fifty miles to the east, which soon separated into three groups.

The CAP was sent to intercept, but when it became obvious that more fighters were needed, another division was launched from the two CVEs. In a fight that would last over thirty minutes, the augmented CAP pounced on the incoming raid. VC-21's Lieutenant (jg) Charles R. Bradford and Ensign Willis N. Penney took out after a Zeke. Quickly catching it, Bradford needed only a few shells to send the Zeke burning into the water. As he pulled out of his run, Bradford discovered that Penney had disappeared.

Although he was now alone, Bradford continued the hunt. Soon he saw another plane, a Tony, going in the opposite direction. Both pilots saw each other at the same time and veered together. This movement quickly settled into a tight merry-go-round as each flier tried to gain the advantage. Finally Bradford broke away, and the Tony didn't follow. Whipping back around, Bradford was on the Tony's tail where he was joined by Lieutenant (jg) Otis A. Hamm from the *Kadashan Bay.* In a long tail chase, Bradford drilled the Tony just forward of its cowl. As his fighter began to roll, the Tony pilot bailed out. At this point a Tojo tried to interfere but Hamm slammed home a solid burst from his four fifties. Like the previous victim, the Tojo's pilot bailed out.

So far the VC-21 and VC-20 fliers had disposed of three Japanese aircraft. Ensign Penney was doing his best to add to this total. After becoming separated from Bradford, Penney took on a Tony diving on him. Pulling up, Penney raked the onrushing fighter in its wings and engine. Passing over Penney, the Tony blossomed into flames; then, completely enveloped by fire, it plowed into the sea. Penney, with only one gun working, next tried to take on another Tony. When this plane was joined by two others, Penney decided discretion was the better part of valor and broke off the combat. These latter two planes were soon shot down by other FM-2s.

Meanwhile, Lieutenant (jg) R. H. Moore's division of VC-20 fighters jumped six Tojos flying in a V of sections. Moore and his wingman dove on the first section from behind. There was a short burst from Moore's .50-calibers, and a Tojo lay burning on the water. Pulling up, Moore began chasing a second Tojo through some violent maneuvers. Each time the Tojo made a quick turn, Moore would overrun him, but when the plane straightened out, Moore would be back behind. At one point the Tojo split-essed from just a thousand feet, but Moore refused to play that game. Instead, he waited for an opening, and when it came he creamed the Tojo with several bursts. Rolling from one hundred feet, the Tojo smacked into the sea.[58]

At 0746 the *Kadashan Bay* finished launching her four FM-2s. As the VC-20 planes struggled for altitude, the pilots saw a plane begin a dive toward the carrier. Too far away to break up the obvious suicide dive, the pilots could only watch as the kamikaze struck with a brilliant flash. Although their ship was in trouble, the VC-20 fliers didn't have time to worry about her. There were still lots of Japanese planes about.

A Tony glided toward the *Kadashan Bay*, and all four pilots jumped it. In a fast battle Lieutenant L. J. Carr drilled the Tony, which wobbled out of control, lost a wing, and smashed into the ocean. Another Tony was chased by a VC-21 Wildcat whose pilot managed to momentarily flame the fighter, but broke off his attack when he overran it. Lieutenant (jg) J. W. Lash took this opportunity to rake the Tony from wingtip to wingtip in a quick pass from 7 o'clock. Again the fire flared momentarily and then went out. It was left up to Lieutenant (jg) H. H. Peoples to finish the job. Closing to just fifty feet from Tony's tail, he held down his trigger for a long burst, which finally sent the fighter, still not burning, into the water.[59]

The plane the VC-20 airmen had seen streaking toward the *Kadashan Bay* had indeed hit the carrier. Shortly after the last group of fighters had been launched, the flattop's crew saw a plane break away from a fight several miles to the east. Seeing the plane aiming for his ship, Captain Hunter ordered full left rudder. All guns that could (including the 5-inch) took the plane under fire, and flashes and puffs of smoke showed that the plane was hit. Still, on it came.

The kamikaze, an Oscar, was aiming directly at the bridge, where everyone tensed and waited for the impact. Suddenly the Oscar began to nose over and slammed into the *Kadashan Bay*'s side at the

The Kadashan Bay *lurches as a kamikaze strikes her, 8 January 1945. (National Archives)*

waterline, tearing a 9-by-17½-foot hole in her hull directly under the island and completely destroying the junior officers' country. This area flooded rapidly because of the heeling of the ship as it turned. On the flight deck several planes were bounced together. A gasoline fire ignited but was quickly extinguished. Though not extensively damaged, the *Kadashan Bay* was through at Lingayen. Her gasoline system had been rendered inoperative and, because of flooding and the fire-fighting efforts, she was down seven feet at the bow.

Surprisingly, the only casualties she suffered were three wounded, one of these being Lieutenant A. F. Buddington, a VC-20 pilot. In his quarters in the junior officers' country, he had been knocked unconscious by the explosion, and the next thing he knew, he was floating in the water without a lifejacket. Apparently, when the compartment filled with water, he was washed out through the hole in the ship's side, miraculously missing its jagged edges. Still more miraculously, the *PC-1600* was passing by and her crew spotted Buddington. He was picked up and returned to the carrier several days later.

On 10 January, after transferring her planes to the *Marcus Island*, the *Kadashan Bay* returned to Leyte Gulf with the first return con-

voy. From Leyte Gulf she headed for San Diego, where she under-
went extensive repairs. Her combat days were over. Upon her return to duty in April, she was assigned to CarTransRonPac, spending the rest of the war as a ferry or training carrier.[60]

It was the *Kitkun Bay*'s turn later that afternoon. She and the
Shamrock Bay were covering TF 79 as it plodded behind TF 78.
Sunset was nearing and the sky was a gorgeous turquoise blue, with
muted oranges and reds beginning to intensify and dominate the
blue. But in contrast with the beauty of the sunset came the kamikazes to add the ugliness of their planes exploding in gouts of vile
redness and billows of foul black.

At 1806 a group of aircraft was reported closing from the southwest twenty miles away. The CAP of eight VC-91 and four VC-94
fighters was vectored to meet this raid. Half of the fighters missed
the attackers, but six *Kitkun Bay* planes were able to make the interception. Lieutenant (jg) J. T. Sippel and Ensign Robert McCollough
were on a Snapper Patrol at 1,500 feet to the rear of the convoy
when they saw a splash to one side of the convoy followed almost
immediately by the sight of a Val diving in front of them. A wingover brought the pair onto the Val's tail. Jinking violently, the Val
escaped most of McCollough's shells. Sippel, however, slid in to fire
a short burst of just twenty-five rounds per gun. The Val flamed,
rolled on its back, and crashed.

The other four VC-91 pilots, meanwhile, saw three more Vals a
few miles farther out. Ensigns Matthew J. Hoff and John N. Metzger
teamed up to blast one of the Vals out of the sky. A second dive-
bomber was a bit more trouble for Lieutenant W. F. Jordan and his
wingman. On the first pass the wingman drew a blank as the Val
banked sharply left, but Jordan slammed home a solid burst into the
plane's engine and wingroot. There was a streak of fire and the Val
dove for the water. At 500 feet its pilot bailed out, his chute
streamed, and he cannonballed into the sea.

The third Val escaped the other VC-91 fighters until Sippel and
McCollough showed up. After just one pass by Sippel, what remained of the Val lay burning on the water. Obviously kamikazes,
none of the Vals had carried a rear gunner.[61] Two more Japanese
planes eluded the CAP, though, to continue toward the ships.

While the kamikazes were taking their time to search for suitable
targets, "Count" Berkey's Close Covering Group of cruisers and destroyers was racing back from TF 78 to beef up TF 79's air defenses.
A few minutes after the dogfight ended, a pilot in the CAP reported, "I see a Zeke. Angels 8. Ten o'clock on the formation. Shall I
intercept?" The fighter director officer on the *Mount Olympus,* the

vessel controlling the CAP, did not reply to that pilot but vectored a *Kitkun Bay* division toward the bogey. While they were heading toward the bogey, the FDO asked the fighter leader (Dexter 51) if he saw it.

Dexter 51 replied that he did not, but asked if he should continue climbing toward it. The FDO, believing there was only one plane, decided to keep the fighters low in anticipation of other attacks. Hardly had he finished talking when the Snapper FDO excitedly broke in. "The Zeke is coming in! In a dive at 9 o'clock! Dexter 51 stay away! Too much gunfire here!"[62]

Having finally found the targets they wanted, the two kamikazes that had escaped the CAP began their dives. It was 1855, eight minutes after the sun had gone down. One of the planes veered off in the face of the intense flak, but the other, most certainly the plane that had been reported at 10 o'clock to the formation, was undeterred. Picking up speed, it plummeted toward the *Kitkun Bay.* Growing darkness and large areas of flak bursts made it hard for the carrier's gunners to zero in on the suicider. Leveling off slightly at 3,000 yards, the plane hurtled in at tremendous speed. (Some observers, in obvious exaggeration, estimated its speed at 500 knots.)

The plane ripped into the flattop's port side at the waterline, blowing a seven-by-fifteen-foot hole in her hull. The explosion of the plane's gas tanks killed four men and started a fire. Luckily, the bombs the plane was carrying were duds. One was later found next to the No. 3 boiler, broken in half, with nose and tail fuzes sheared off, and the other, again with the fuzes sheared away, was found lodged in the machine shop. Fires broke out, all power went off, and the *Kitkun Bay* began rapidly listing to port. In the engine room the men felt the ship quiver violently, followed by a tremendous crash on the port side as the dud bomb arrived. A sheet of fire enveloped the entire port side of the after engine room.

"This was indication enough for me that the situation was beyond control," said the chief engineer. "I gave the order to abandon this engineering compartment, which was done on the double."[63]

Fighting their way through the flames and receiving burns of varying severity in the process, the men in the port side fireroom left via an escape trunk. The remaining men escaped by way of a ladder on the other side of the main engine. When they reached the first platform of the engine room, they found the smoke so heavy and noxious that they had trouble breathing, let alone seeing. In the dense smoke one man climbed the wrong side of a ladder leading to a mess hall and hit his head on the overhead. Dropping back down, he told those gathered about the ladder that the hatch was bolted down. This error was soon straightened out, and the men went up the proper side of the ladder to safety.

To add to the *Kitkun Bay*'s woes, just as the kamikaze hit, a 5-inch shell fired by one of the screening vessels struck the catwalk on the opposite side of the ship. This stray shell alone killed thirteen men and catapulted another sailor into the water, where he was rescued. For a time the situation on the carrier appeared very serious. Smoke filtered throughout the ship. Flooding had caused her to list 13 degrees to port and she was down four feet by the stern. All hands were ordered topside to gather on the ship's starboard side. Aircraft parked on the port side were manhandled over to the other side of the flight deck. About half an hour after the attack, all unnecessary personnel were transferred to the screening vessels. After destroying some secret communications material, Admiral Ofstie and his staff went aboard the destroyer *Smith,* to transfer later to the *Shamrock Bay.*

By 1947 the fleet tug *Chowanoc* was standing by to take the carrier in tow. Shortly afterward the flooding was checked, pumping was reducing her list to 4 degrees, and repair parties were returning to the forward engine room to restore partial power. The *Kitkun Bay* would survive. On the morning of 9 January she was able to cast off her tow and proceed under her own power. All personnel except the wounded returned later in the day, and flight operations were even resumed.

It had been hoped that she would be able to participate in the remainder of the operation, but heavy seas and her doubtful seaworthiness prompted her return to Leyte Gulf. Directed to return to Leyte with a slow convoy on the eleventh, she arrived there on the fifteenth. After stays for temporary repairs at Leyte Gulf, Manus, and Pearl Harbor, she returned to the United States in late February, not to return to the combat zone until July, when she supported Third Fleet operations.[64]

In his report of this action, the *Kitkun Bay*'s executive officer had a few words to say to those (primarily located in the rear areas) who downgraded the effectiveness of kamikaze attacks:

> It has been stated that the suicide attack is the most stupid form of attack because it has the least chance of getting in. This idea does not sell well to people who know better from bitter experience. This form of attack has the following very obvious advantages:
> (a) It is an aerial torpedo with human control all the way in, which enables it to pick the most favorable target and maneuver to the last.
> (b) It offers the biggest return for the least investment.

(c) A one-way trip doubles the range of the plane.
(d) Pilot training probably requires but a fraction of the usual time.
(e) One attacking plane ties up a prohibitive number of defending CAP planes.
(f) *It has terrifying psychological value.* [Italics in original.][65]

The damage to the two carriers put a big crimp in the operations of the CVEs charged with convoy coverage. The six carriers assigned to TUs 77.4.3, 77.4.4., and 77.4.5 were to have operated as TU 77.4.6 to cover the convoys going to and from the beachhead. Instead, the two carriers were going back to Leyte Gulf and the *Shamrock Bay* was transferred to TU 77.4.2 to replace the sunken *Ommaney Bay*. Thus, the *Saginaw Bay*, *Marcus Island*, and *Petrof Bay* had to put in double duty during their tour at Lingayen.[66]

Actually, as it turned out, the day of greatest activity for the "jeeps" had been 8 January, and the busiest carrier had been the *Marcus Island*. With so many Japanese planes skulking about that day, she had been quite energetic. On the eighth she had launched ninety-four planes and recovered ninety-nine (some from the *Kadashan Bay*). This averaged out to a launching or landing every 3.8 minutes of activity, and was believed to be a record for a combat CVE.[67]

The ninth was S day at Lingayen. To support the landings, a special strike group of sixteen fighters and nine bombers, plus an air coordinator, operated in a belt 3,000 to 10,000 yards inland. A regular support group of eight Wildcats and twelve Avengers and an air coordinator operated further inland under the direction of the commander of support aircraft.[68] These groups met little resistance as they bombed and rocketed supply dumps, roads, small craft, and many other targets throughout the day. On many other flights no targets could be found. This led Admiral Durgin to complain, "It is particularly disheartening to work through most of the night breaking out bombs and loading them in aircraft and then have the additional work of unloading those same bombs because no targets were available."[69]

The *Manila Bay*, following her bout with the kamikazes, was back on S day carrying out a "fairly full" schedule, which included sending off forty-two sorties. She still had some major handicaps to put up with. The explosion of the first kamikaze had jammed and bulged the forward elevator upward, so when the aircraft had to fly off, they received a nasty bounce prior to reaching flying speed. For the predawn launches the catapult was used exclusively. Additionally, the barriers had taken a beating in the explosion; it was lucky that they weren't put to the test.

To replace the seven Avengers lost in the attack, the "Manila Maru" received seven from the *Kadashan Bay* and one more from the *Shamrock Bay*. Three replacement fighters were also received from the *Kadashan Bay*. None of the planes were in particularly good shape, but neither were the *Manila Bay*'s own aircraft. Most had received some form of damage from bomb blast, shrapnel, fire, or water. In spite of the intense efforts of the mechanics, the planes never really worked right afterward. Later the loss of an Avenger when its flaps retracted during a catapult shot was believed to be the direct result of the bomb explosion.[70]

By this time in the war the system of replacing aircraft on a combat carrier had become an everyday occurrence. But it could also be complicated, as the *Manila Bay* discovered. For example, the *Manila Bay* took on as a replacement a *Kitkun Bay* FM-2 delivered from the *Shamrock Bay* by a *Kadashan Bay* pilot. This plane was later swapped to the *Steamer Bay* for a *Manila Bay* plane left on the former carrier after the kamikaze attack.[71]

For the escort carriers, except for the support missions, S day was relatively quiet, although VC-81 fighters did shoot down three Zekes near San Fernando. Still around were the kamikazes. One got through to hit the *Australia* for a fifth time, finally forcing this tough and doughty ship to retire for repairs. A tragic accident did mar the day for the *Makin Island* when a 3.5-inch rocket on an Avenger accidentally discharged, blowing a sailor over the side. A search for the man was unsuccessful.[72]

On 10 January TU 77.4.6 (the Close Covering Carrier Group) was formed under the command of Admiral Henderson. Instead of six "jeeps" it had only the *Saginaw Bay, Marcus Island,* and *Petrof Bay,* screened by the destroyers *Charette* and *Conner* and destroyer escorts *Richard S. Bull* and *Richard M. Rowell.*[73]

The tenth saw some VC-94 fighters involved in an unfortunate incident. On patrol over the gulf, a division of FM-2s saw four other planes, three painted green and the other silver, pop out of some clouds and dive on the transports. The FM-2s gave chase and finally overtook the intruders. One pass sent one of the unidentified aircraft into the sea, its pilot bailing out. It was only when the VC-94 fliers were swinging back for another run that they realized the "enemy" planes were actually P-47s. The Thunderbolt pilots had not announced to any of the controlling agencies in the gulf that they were around and, to top it off, had begun rather unfriendly dives on the ships. This error cost them a plane.[74]

Weather turned out to be the major factor in air operations on the tenth. Low clouds scudded through the area and the ocean began kicking up, making "dancing masters" out of the carriers' LSOs and greatly hampering air operations.[75]

Two of the "jeeps," in particular, found the rough weather not to their liking. A little before noon, as the *Natoma Bay* was turning out of the wind, she suddenly rolled 32 degrees to port. At this time fighters were being respotted forward. Two were flipped over on their backs, and the crewmen in the cockpits were injured. A crane brought to the flight deck to right the planes was itself tipped over by another roll. Damaged beyond repair, the planes had to be jettisoned.[76] A similar calamity befell the *Marcus Island*. Later that afternoon, while turning in the heavy seas, she abruptly rolled 14 degrees to starboard. One fighter departed over the side, another landed upside down in a catwalk, a third Wildcat's tailwheel slid into another catwalk, and an Avenger's tail surfaces were damaged. This time there were no injuries.[77]

The rough water at Lingayen brought with it high winds, which were a mixed blessing. As the *Manila Bay* reported somewhat sourly, "The chronic complaint of the escort carriers during the last year of the Pacific War has been the lack of wind in the usual operating areas. . . . The China Sea off the Gulf of Lingayen furnished a feast after the famine with attendant indigestion pains."

The heavy seas contributed to excessive rolling and pitching so "air operations in general were slowed up and it was a tribute to Grumman airplanes, pilots, landing signal officers, and the operating crews of the flight and hangar decks that operations continued almost without interruption from weather," the *Manila Bay* continued. "While the *Casablanca*-class carrier has a bad pitch and roll at times, it does have the characteristic of having comparatively steady periods at short and fairly regular intervals, at which times the planes can be landed quite successfully."[78]

Additionally, the *Natoma Bay* reported that in the roll and pitch conditions the CVEs encountered off Luzon, *twenty-four* men were needed to spot an Avenger to prevent the possibility of damaging or losing the plane.[79]

With the landings assured and with direct support of the landing force winding down, on the tenth Admiral Kinkaid directed that TGs 77.2 (Bombardment and Fire Support Group), 77.3 (Close Covering Group), and 77.4 (Escort Carrier Group) be formed into the Lingayen Defense Fleet under Admiral Oldendorf's command. Usually operating as three units disposed as the points of an equilateral triangle ten miles on a side, on occasion the big ships were divided equally between the two carrier units, thus forming two "Slow Carrier Task Groups."[80] The Lingayen Defense Fleet contin-

On 16 January 1945 the Saginaw Bay *hits rough water in the South China Sea. (National Archives)*

ued to provide assistance as needed to the troops ashore, but was also assigned the task of protecting the shipping from possible enemy surface attack (which never took place).[81]

For the next few days rough seas continued to plague the escort carriers. Nevertheless, air operations continued apace. Those targets that were found were attacked, with generally favorable results.

On one of these missions Lieutenant (jg) Arthur W. Gilkey and his Avenger crew got a closeup view of the Luzon countryside. Taking off from the *Lunga Point* on the eleventh, Gilkey was carrying an army observer as well as his regular crewmen. Though not carrying any bombs, Gilkey was determined to make the best use of his machine guns, and he got the chance when he found some camouflaged tanks. Since tanks had been scarce, Gilkey immediately began a series of strafing runs that soon had the tanks and several nearby trucks blazing, which pleased Gilkey greatly. His pleasure suddenly soured when he saw his engine oil pressure drop to zero and the engine begin to run rough. The big Avenger was not going to fly much longer, so Gilkey looked for a place to land. A nearby rice paddy looked okay and he was able to make a gear-up landing in it with little difficulty and just bumps and bruises for the crew.

Their joy at surviving the landing was momentarily dampened when some thirty men came running out of the underbrush. Luckily, they turned out to be English-speaking guerrillas. So began a ten-day odyssey for the Americans. For the next week and a half the four crewmen were shuttled from place to place, sometimes just ahead of pursuing Japanese. Several times they acted as doctors, using the supplies from their first aid kits to treat the guerrillas' various ailments. Finally, on the twenty-first, Gilkey and his three companions contacted men of the 40th Infantry Division, and their sojourn behind enemy lines was over.[82]

Because of his enforced absence, Gilkey missed the excitement in TU 77.4.1 on the morning of the thirteenth. For the past several days the CVE pilots had seen few enemy planes, and had quickly routed or shot down those they had seen. Lest the Americans become too complacent about enemy air activity, however, every now and then the Japanese would remind them that a kamikaze could be a remarkably efficient instrument of destruction. On the thirteenth it was the escort carriers' turn to be reminded.

For the last two days fueling operations for the carriers had been under way. These had been a trial because the rough seas broke several hoses and caused other problems. Early on the thirteenth the fueling recommenced about eighty miles from Lingayen Gulf. Just after 0900 the *Salamaua* was waiting her turn to come alongside an oiler.

Observing the scene from the "Sal's" forecastle was her first lieutenant, Lieutenant Commander Robert P. Harbold. He wanted to see what lines the carrier ahead was using during her fueling. Suddenly the boatswain standing next to Harbold began punching him in the ribs. Irritated, Harbold turned to the man and found him looking rather sickly. He was trying to say something but no sounds were coming from his mouth. Finally jabbing a finger into the air toward the rear of the ship, the boatswain got Harbold's attention. What Harbold saw was frightening. Plunging almost vertically toward the *Salamaua's* flight deck was a Japanese plane!

With a thunderous crash the kamikaze tore through the carrier's flight deck. A pillar of smoke marked the spot of the pilot's immolation. Admiral Durgin queried the *Salamaua* on the cause of the smoke. "Something just went through our flight deck" was the laconic reply.[83]

The kamikaze and the two bombs it was carrying bit deeply into the carrier's bowels, leaving a hole sixteen by thirty-two feet in the flight deck. Parts of the fuselage and engine wound up on the ship's tank tops. One of the bombs went completely through the ship and out her starboard side near the waterline without detonating. The explosion of the other, near the tank tops, was not too damaging, although fragments whined about the area and the blast buckled a number of bulkheads. If the bomb had exploded a few frames farther aft, it would have gone off right in the middle of the light-cased bomb stowage area.

On both the flight and hangar decks and in the immediate vicinity of the explosion several fires were kindled, but most were quickly knocked down except for one major blaze on the hangar deck. Threatened by this fire were a number of bombs and depth bombs stowed there. But except for the detonation of some hydrostatic fuzes, this situation was soon under control. Within thirty minutes all fires had pretty well been contained. The next major problem was flooding. Water pouring through the twenty-inch exit hole left by the dud bomb flooded the after engine room, and an 8-degree starboard list soon developed. In addition, the starboard engine had been knocked out, and power, communications, and steering temporarily lost. The *Salamaua*'s human cost was fifteen men killed and eighty-eight wounded. Her participation in the rest of the Lingayen operation was over.[84]

The *Salamaua* had not been the only target of a suicider, but the other kamikaze never got close to his intended victim, the *Tulagi*. Heavy antiaircraft fire from that carrier greeted the attacker, and he veered off toward the *Hoggatt Bay*. A proximity-fuzed 5-inch shell ended the kamikaze's career. There was a puff of smoke that completely enveloped the plane, and when next seen, it was fluttering into the water, a mass of flames.[85] That was the end of the action, but once again a CVE had to return to Leyte Gulf ahead of schedule.

The attack on the *Salamaua* was the last successful kamikaze attack in the Philippines. There was a short lull in their general use, but Iwo Jima was just a month off and Okinawa only two and a half months away. The divine wind would blow again.

Strikes on enemy positions on Luzon by CVE planes continued for the next few days, for the most part uneventfully, though a few planes and pilots were lost in these strikes. Occasionally an attack brought some excellent results. On the fourteenth VC-92 planes bombed a group of buildings near San Isidro. "The 'range problem' was generously worked out by the Japs," the squadron reported later, "through their having located the buildings in rows, making a 'lengthwise' attack virtually foolproof."[86] Three bombs were dropped; three holes resulted where three buildings had once stood.

The following day saw even more spectacular results. Some fifty trucks parked on a mountain road were found by VC-92 fliers.

Because of the mountainous terrain and low clouds draping over the peaks, no bomb runs were possible. Instead, strafing and rocket passes did the trick. At least twenty-three trucks were destroyed, including an ammunition truck hit by a rocket, which blew up with such force that the explosion obliterated three other vehicles. The VC-92 fliers discovered that their own handiwork could backfire on them. Debris flung into the air by the ammunition truck explosion damaged two planes and probably caused the loss of another. Crossing back over the coast, this Avenger suddenly lost all oil pressure. The pilot made a successful ditching, and the crew was rescued by a destroyer.[87]

Having more than its share of bad luck on the fifteenth was VC-88. Ensign E. C. Minick was making a steep glide-bomb attack on a target when pieces began to fall off his plane. Suddenly, at about 1,500 feet, the tail of his Avenger came off. After the tail ripped away, Minick was still able to drop three of his four 500-pounders. The TBM leveled off slightly, then pancaked into the ground, leaving a huge mushroom cloud to cover the scene.

VC-88's skipper, Lieutenant Commander E. N. Webb, also had some problems while attacking the same target. Despite several attempts to release it, one of his bombs hung up. He would have to land on the *Hoggatt Bay* still carrying the 500-pounder. Upon his return to the ship, Webb's approach and landing seemed to be nearly perfect. Suddenly, as the Avenger was pulled to a stop by the arresting gear, there was a tremendous blast. Where an instant before there had been an Avenger, now there was just a mass of flame, smoke, and twisted metal. Apparently, the bomb Webb was still carrying had gone off.

Webb and his crew never had a chance. Neither did several plane handlers gathered nearby. When the smoke and flames cleared, Webb, his two crewmen, and seven other sailors were dead, and fourteen others wounded. One more man would die in the firefighting and salvage operation. The *Hoggatt Bay*'s flight deck was temporarily out of commission, but despite a noticeably concave deck, within three hours the flattop had resumed air operations.[88]

On the afternoon of 17 January the USAAF took over responsibility for air activities over Luzon. Admiral Durgin took eight of the CVEs back to Ulithi, while Admiral Stump took charge of a reformed TG 77.4 (the *Natoma Bay, Marcus Island, Savo Island, Steamer Bay, Petrof Bay,* and *Tulagi*). In anticipation of possible enemy forays against the American positions on Mindoro and Luzon, TG 77.4 joined Admiral Berkey's Close Covering Group to operate west of northern Mindoro.[89]

The *Manila Bay*'s trip back to Ulithi was not relaxing, at least for Captain Lee. Because of the flattop's lack of radar, she was placed at the rear of the formation. Normally, stationkeeping at night was done by radar, but this was, of course, impossible in the *Manila Bay*'s case. So, on those dark nights when nothing could be seen, Lee liked to slow up and lag behind the rest of the ships. Lee later recalled that most of the communications between himself and Admiral Durgin tended to be arguments. Lee would signal, "I want to stay behind," and, invariably, Durgin would reply, "No, you've got to stay up because of danger of submarine attack." This dialogue kept up until Lee would almost have preferred to be sunk by a submarine than risk the possibility of a collision with friendly ships. The *Manila Bay*'s luck held, and she finally reached San Francisco for major repairs.[90]

During their stay at Lingayen the escort carriers had been kept busy. A total of 5,971 sorties had been flown by the planes of the three main task units between 6 and 17 January, with nearly a quarter of the sorties—1,416—in direct support of the ground troops. Ninety-two enemy planes had been destroyed by the Wildcats and Avengers. In exchange, fourteen U.S. planes had been lost in combat, and an additional sixty-five planes were operational losses. This high number of operational losses was directly attributable to the suicide attacks. Forty-one planes alone were lost on the *Ommaney Bay* and *Manila Bay*, these being considered operational casualties.[91]

The kamikaze attacks from unneutralized airfields greatly distressed Admiral Durgin. "The original concept for combatant CVE employment in air support missions presumed," he later reported,

A) Prior to the assault, important enemy airfields and installations in the objective area had been neutralized by persistent air attack.
B) Control of the air had been secured over a considerable radius.
C) A means had been established whereby through offensive action, air control could be maintained and the approach of enemy surface forces detected.

Under these general rules, the escort carriers achieved considerable success and effectively played the roles in the amphibious assaults that characterized our westward march.

In the invasion of Luzon this well-tested and proven concept for the employment of CVE's was not followed. Likewise it had not been followed in the preceding operation against Mindoro.[92]

There appears to have been a great deal of confusion among the Seventh Fleet, Third Fleet, and Far East Air Force commands about just who was supposed to neutralize the Japanese airfields. According to Admiral Kinkaid, this task was the responsibility of land-based aircraft and the "escort carriers were assigned the task of furnishing local air support and combat air patrol over ships and operations in the Gulf. They were never expected to provide the offensive combat air patrol necessary to neutralize fields in the target area."[93] On the other hand, Halsey believed that airfields in the Lingayen region (which could include the major fields around Manila) had been re-served for the "jeeps." Finally, MacArthur's headquarters had as-signed, or believed it had assigned, the mission of neutralizing air-fields to FEAF and the Third Fleet.[94]

This confusion probably helped the Japanese to mount more strikes than would have been possible if the tasks of each major command had been better and more closely coordinated. Fortu-nately for the Americans, the Japanese ran out of aircraft before doing any more damage than they had already accomplished.

Lingayen had not been the best place in the Pacific for the escort carriers to be. Nine of the carriers had undergone kamikaze attacks, with the *Ommaney Bay* being sunk and five others receiving varying degrees of damage. Commenting on the damage the CVEs had been absorbing, Admiral Henderson said,

> Consideration of a few CVE figures presents a rather surprising pic-ture. In approximately eleven weeks, twenty-eight ships of the CVE class, Kaiser and *Sangamon* types, have been employed in the opera-tions at Leyte and Lingayen. Of this number thirteen have been sunk or damaged by enemy action, and one damaged by a bomb explosion on deck in connection with an arrested landing. Three ships have been sunk—the remaining eleven have been damaged to an extent necessitating from one to six months' absence for repairs. This ap-pears to be a record for punishment absorption that has never been achieved by any other type over such a short period. The major amount of damage by far has been accomplished by suicide dives.[95]

Leyte and Lingayen had shown that these supposedly tender and vulnerable vessels were capable of taking more punishment than had earlier been thought. Still, thinly protected by screening vessels and not having great defensive firepower themselves, the escort carriers were, in a sense, "out on a limb" in every invasion. In February 1945 the then-Commander Air Force, Pacific Fleet, Vice Admiral George D. Murray, compared the protection afforded a fast carrier with that of an escort carrier. It makes interesting and sobering reading (con-sidering that by the nature of their job, which required the CVEs to sit off hostile shores for a great length of time, they were terribly exposed to potential disaster).

In a normal disposition the relative weighted factors of protection for the two carrier types was approximately

	CV	CVE
Gun Defense	35	2
Day VF Defense	50	7
Night VF	12	0
Speed and Maneuverability	3	1
	100	10[96]

This disparity never grew closer for the rest of the war. An escort carrier group's relative vulnerability remained a gnawing concern of the navy, particularly when an invasion of Japan was expected to be stoutly and fanatically opposed.

The remainder of TG 77.4's stay off Luzon and Mindoro was relatively calm, the heaviest workload occurring on 29 and 30 January, when the CVE planes were used to cover and provide direct support for landings in the Zambales province of Luzon. Meant to seal off Bataan and also hit from the side the Japanese troops slowly retreating toward Manila, these landings were unopposed and did not take too much of the escort carriers' time, TG 77.4 being relieved of this mission on the afternoon of the thirtieth. Departure was delayed twenty-four hours, though, to hunt down an enemy submarine seen by two fighter pilots that afternoon. Despite intensive searches by carrier planes by day, a "Black Cat" night-flying aircraft by night, and surface ships, nothing was found.

However, as the task group began its retirement for Ulithi on the evening of the thirty-first, another contact was made. An attack by a pair of destroyers apparently wounded the submarine, but did not kill it. Because the type carried superior ASW equipment, a destroyer escort was requested. Detached from the *Tulagi*'s screen, the *Ulvert M. Moore* raced to the scene. Upon her arrival, the *Moore* found an oil slick and used this to set up her runs. Making five deliberate hedgehog attacks, the *Moore* scored on every one. But not until the last run did a monstrous underwater explosion shake the DE and the two destroyers. That was the end of the 601-ton *RO-115* and the end of the CVEs' part in this operation.[97]

Task Group 77.4 anchored at Ulithi on 5 February. For the escort carriers the campaign in the Philippines was at last over. It had been tough and debilitating, and they were in need of some rest. But Iwo Jima and a return engagement with the kamikazes was less than three weeks away.

VISIT TO A VILE ISLAND

NOT ALL OF THE action involving the escort carriers in January took place around Lingayen. From 10 to 20 January Halsey's Third Fleet, recovered from its brush with the typhoon, was running rampant in the South China Sea. Halsey had long wanted to enter this sea, and he discovered many juicy targets clustered on or near its shores at Camranh Bay, at Hong Kong, on Hainan, and on Formosa. The TF 38 fliers encountered good hunting as they bombed and strafed surface targets and shot down enemy planes attempting to interfere.

Close behind Halsey's force came Captain Acuff's TG 30.8, with its usual complement of oilers and escort carriers. Among the CVEs was the *Nehenta Bay*, this time providing cover for the vulnerable oilers.

Not wishing the TF 38 fliers to have all the action, a pair of VC-11 pilots got their own chance. At 0710 on the twelfth a bogey was detected sixty-four miles from the carrier and a division of fighters was launched. When the fighters got the first vector, neither division nor section leaders were in contact with the ship. Both wingmen, however, heard it and decided to go after the bogeys themselves. The wingmen were brothers, Lieutenant (jg)s G. L. and A. S. Donnelly.

When the Donnellys were thirteen miles from the *Nehenta Bay*, they sighted a Jake floatplane flying 2,000 feet above them. The Jake tried to dive away but the Donnelly brothers were on its tail. At 3,000 feet the Jake turned right, leaving an opening for G. L. Donnelly to pepper its right side. His brother scored seconds later, getting hits in the floatplane's left fuselage and wing, which began to smoke and sparkle.

The Jake spiraled down to 500 feet, where the Donnellys bracketed it. No matter which way it turned, a Wildcat was in position to punch in more .50-caliber shells. Finally, G. L. Donnelly set the Jake afire and it slipped toward the water. His brother made one more pass, after which the plane did a wingover into the ocean.[1]

Weather in the South China Sea was similar to what the CVEs at Lingayen had been encountering and reminded some who had undergone that ordeal of a minor version of the 18 December typhoon. Rough seas, with waves up to thirty feet high, hampered fueling operations considerably on 17 January. The *Nehenta Bay*, in particular, had a rough time. Around 1930 several heavy waves broke over her flight deck, collapsing the steel supports under its forward portion and buckling other steel members farther aft. The flight deck bent down to rest on the forecastle, putting the catapult out of commission. Though her planes could still be flown off and the carrier continued to operate, missions for the Avengers were reduced because without the catapult they had to carry a much smaller load. A survey of the damage indicated that the 18 December typhoon had weakened many structural members and the ship had just taken too many more rough seas. Still, the *Nehenta Bay* carried on with her mission until it was completed, then returned to port for repairs.[2]

Their job over in the Philippines, the escort carriers immediately began planning for the next operation—the invasion of Iwo Jima. There was little time for any rest and relaxation, particularly for the men who returned with Admiral Stump to Ulithi on 5 February. On the tenth most of his carriers, but not Stump, who remained at Ulithi, sortied again. Once more commanding the CVEs was Rear Admiral Durgin, his force this time composed as follows:

TASK GROUP 52.2   SUPPORT CARRIER GROUP
R. Adm. Calvin T. Durgin

Task Unit 52.2.1	R. Adm. C. A. F. Sprague (ComCarDiv 26)
Natoma Bay (F)	Capt. A. K. Morehouse (to 1 March)
	Capt. B. B. Nichol
VC-81 20 FM-2, 10 TBM-1C, 2 TBM-3	Lt. Cdr. W. B. Morton
Wake Island	Capt. A. V. Magly
VOC-1 28 FM-2, 6 TBM-3	Lt. Cdr. W. F. Bringle
Petrof Bay	Capt. R. S. Clarke
VC-76 20 FM-2, 12 TBM-1C	Cdr. J. W. McCauley
Sargent Bay	Capt. W. T. Rassieur (to 15 March)
	Capt. R. M. Oliver
VC-83 20 FM-2, 12 TBM-1C	Lt. Cdr. B. V. Gates
Steamer Bay	Capt. J. B. Paschal, Jr.
VC-90 16 FM-2, 12 TBM-3	Lt. Cdr. R. A. O'Neill

Screen: Destroyers *Daly, Ralph Talbot;* destroyer escorts *Grady, Richard S. Bull, Richard M. Rowell, O'Flaherty*

Task Unit 52.2.2	R. Adm. Durgin (ComCarDiv 29)
Makin Island(FF)	Capt. W. B. Whaley
VC-84 20 FM-2, 12 TBM-3	Lt. Cdr. D. K. English
Lunga Point	Capt. G. A. T. Washburn
VC-85 18 FM-2, 11 TBM-3,	Lt. Cdr. F. C. Heriman
1 TBM-3P	
Bismarck Sea	Capt. J. L. Pratt
VC-86 19 FM-2, 12 TBM-3	Lt. B. M. Lakin

Screen: Destroyers *Hutchins, Helm, Bagley*

Task Unit 52.2.3	R. Adm. G. R. Henderson (ComCarDiv 25)
Saginaw Bay (F)	Capt. F. C. Sutton
VC-88 20 FM-2, 12 TBM-3	Lt. F. G. Lewis
Rudyerd Bay	Capt. J. G. Foster
VC-77 15 FM-2, 11 TBM-1C,	Lt. Cdr. F. J. Peterson
1 TBM-1CP	(KIA 19 Feb)
	Lt. R. W. Newell

Screen: Destroyers *Stockton, Patterson,* destroyer escorts *J.C. Butler, Edmonds*

Task Unit 52.2.4	Capt. L. A. Moebus
(attached 21 February)	
Saratoga (F)	Capt. Moebus
Alaska	Capt. K. H. Noble

Screen: Destroyers *McGowan, Melvin, McNair*

In addition, two other escort carriers were assigned specific anti-submarine duty, though they often operated with the vessels of the other task units. They were:

Task Unit 50.7.1	Capt. G. C. Montgomery
Anzio	Capt. Montgomery
VC-82 12 FM-2, 14 TBM-1C	Lt. Cdr. C. H. Holt

Screen: Destroyer escorts *Oliver Mitchell, Lawrence C. Taylor, Robert F. Keller, Melvin R. Nawman*

Task Unit 50.7.3	Capt. J. C. Cronin
Tulagi	Capt. Cronin
VC-92 19 FM-2, 12 TBM-3	Lt. Cdr. J. B. Wallace

Screen: Destroyer escorts *William Seiverling, Kendall C. Campbell, Ulvert M. Moore, Goss*[3]

Iwo Jima, one of the volcanic islands that make up the Bonins-Volcano (or Nanpo Shoto) chain and located almost halfway between Saipan and Tokyo, was a very desirable acquisition. Enemy fighters harassing the B-29s en route to Japan would be eliminated, and U.S. fighters would be able to use the Iwo airfields as bases for bomber escort or fighter sweeps over Japan. Also, the Superfortresses flying the long route between the Marianas and Japan would be able to use the island as a safe haven after battling the flak and fighters over the targets.

Violence was apparently Iwo Jima's destiny. The island was born less than a century earlier in a volcanic eruption that thrust lava and volcanic dust into the atmosphere to form a scabrous piece of terrain with hardly enough plant life to be called vegetation, and this violent birth was still evident in 1945. Iwo Jima's ground was torn and ragged; heat radiated from the ground in many spots; here and there sulfur vents spewed their fumes into the sky and steam hung hotly over the vents. Now to the natural violence of Iwo Jima would come man's violence.

Leaving Ulithi on 10 February (minus the *Anzio*, which came from Eniwetok, and the *Tulagi*, which left Ulithi on the nineteenth), TG 52.2 reached Saipan on the twelfth, where rehearsals were held that day and the next and more supplies were loaded. Task Units 52.2.1 and 52.2.2 then headed for Iwo Jima with the gunfire support vessels, TU 52.2.3 leaving Saipan on the sixteenth and providing air cover over the transports carrying the 4th and 5th Marine Divisions.

On the evening of the fifteenth the two lead task units were in position off Iwo, and operations began early the next day. Despite poor weather (rough seas, low clouds, rain, and fog), weather that would remain much the same throughout the operation, the CVE pilots were out in force bombing and spotting positions on the island. VOC-1's pilots found out early that the low ceilings severely handicapped them in their spotting chores. Nearby Chichi Jima also received its share of attention to make sure enemy troops there didn't get too rambunctious.

Before long the airmen discovered that despite the limited area of Iwo Jima (which in a way simplified their job), the terrain and the numerous underground defenses required many more support missions and much higher accuracy than they had previously been used to. Additionally, the low clouds forced them to fly spotting missions at lower than normal altitudes, increasing the vulnerability of the FM-2s to enemy ground fire. At Iwo Jima VOC-1 would have twenty planes damaged by flak and three more shot down.[4]

The CVE fliers quickly learned how treacherous the weather around Iwo Jima could be. On the first day of operations, the sixteenth, the *Natoma Bay* launched an LCAP mission about an hour before dawn. With light rain dripping from a heavy overcast, the coming of dawn was marked by the night's darkness seeping into an ashy gray, rather than by a burst of the sun's rays on the horizon.

Climbing through this weather, one pilot didn't realize that strong winds were blowing him far afield. When he finally realized his predicament, he radioed the *Natoma Bay* for a vector. Compounding his problem, however, were an inoperative IFF and a weak VHF radio. He contacted the ship, and was given a vector toward the carrier—but the plane the radar operators were tracking was not the lost Wildcat. Eventually they told the pilot to let down through the overcast, where he should find the *Natoma Bay* just a few miles ahead. Instead the pilot descended into a severe storm, where he remained for four hours before he finally had to ditch, over one hundred miles southwest of the *Natoma Bay*. After spending two and a half days in his tiny raft, he was sighted by an *Anzio* Avenger, which dropped him a larger raft. A few hours later a floatplane picked the pilot up and returned him to his carrier.[5]

For the first few days at Iwo enemy air activity was minimal, but antiaircraft fire from the island defenses was hot and heavy. It hit many planes, but most were able to return to their ships. One of the first planes to be shot down this way was a *Lunga Point* fighter early on the sixteenth, the pilot being rescued.

Makin Island planes made up for this loss later that morning. Returning from an aborted fighter sweep of Chichi Jima and Haha Jima, the VC-84 fighters came across a pair of luggers chugging toward Iwo, packed with troops. A vicious rocket and strafing attack made sure the ships didn't reach Iwo. As the luggers began to sink, the troops that were still alive went over their sides. One of the Japanese soldiers tried to launch a small boat, but a well-aimed empty wing tank dropped by Lieutenant (jg) M. J. Simpson stopped him by capsizing the boat. There appeared to be few survivors of this massacre.[6]

A slight improvement in the weather on the seventeenth allowed a full complement of strikes and spotting missions to be flown against the islands in the area. Also showing an improvement was the shooting of the Japanese troops. At Chichi Jima the airfield was strafed and bombed, though the few planes noted there did not burn. In addition, several small craft were sunk or damaged there and at Haha Jima. One of these small vessels, apparently carrying ammunition, blew up with such force that it damaged the fighter attacking it.

At Iwo a flight of VC-81 Avengers found the defensive fire to be highly accurate. Eight torpedo planes were attacking gun positions between Motoyama Airfields No. 1 and No. 2 when they were caught in a heavy crossfire. The squadron skipper's plane was hit in the wing, rupturing the spar, but with some very delicate flying, Lieutenant Commander W. B. Morton was able to nurse his plane back to the *Natoma Bay*. An inspection showed that the TBM was not

A moment of tranquility for the Natoma Bay *off Iwo Jima. (Via* Natoma Bay *Association)*

worth repairing and it was jettisoned. Two other Avengers were well shot up by the flak, but like Morton, they made it back to the ship.

Not quite as lucky was Ensign James J. McMahon. A shell smashed into his plane's bomb bay, just missing the five bombs nestled there, then ricocheted into the middle cockpit, where it exploded. Luckily, no one was injured. However, a second shell hit and ignited a smoke bomb, which in turn set the radioman's clothing, backpack, and parachute afire. Though able to extinguish the fires, the radioman was severely burned. Yet another hit ripped most of the fabric off the Avenger's tail surfaces. McMahon was also greatly concerned that the enemy fire had knocked out his plane's hydraulic system, meaning that he would have to make a water landing. Still carrying the five bombs, McMahon ditched safely near the *Bull,* and all three crewman were quickly picked up.[7]

VOC-1 planes also took a beating over Iwo. While spotting for the battleship *Idaho,* Lieutenant (jg) Thomas L. Murphy's Wildcat disappeared. Whether because of flak, the weather, or some other reason, he never returned to the *Wake Island*. Ensign William H. Bethea did, though the damage to his plane by the flak was so extensive "as to raise doubt as to [his fighter's wings'] ability to support the aircraft."[8] Both of the FM-2's wings had to be replaced. There was one more wing change on the *Wake Island* that day. Upon landing, a flak-damaged FM-2 rolled into a catwalk. After pulling the plane from its resting place, the airedales found that it needed not just a new wing, but replacement of its landing gear, propeller, and engine, too.[9] The seventeenth was a busy day for both the ship and her squadron.

One other plane was lost on the seventeenth, a *Petrof Bay* Avenger hit by flak. The pilot was able to ditch his plane near a destroyer, and the three men hardly got wet before being rescued by the ship.[10]

Unfavorable weather conditions continued on the eighteenth, low clouds again hanging moistly over the area. Still, many sorties were launched, most of the missions concentrating on positions flanking the landing beaches. Not yet beaten down, intense antiaircraft fire holed a number of planes and knocked down a *Makin Island* Avenger.

The napalm bomb was the weapon of the day. Both fighters and bombers carried this weapon, which was very effective against the deeply dug-in and camouflaged positions when they worked. Too often at Iwo, however, the napalm bombs turned out to be duds and wouldn't burn even when struck by .50-caliber bullets. One of these bombs came close to causing a disaster on the *Lunga Point*. It had failed to release from a Wildcat, and after much deliberation, the fighter was taken aboard. As the plane landed, the bomb was jarred loose to skid along the flight deck, crewmen ducking out of the way as it bounced and rattled past the island. Luckily, the bomb didn't ignite and a couple of brave sailors quickly disarmed it and pushed it over the side.[11]

Busy once again were the VOC-1 pilots. They would stay busy throughout the entire battle, logging 892 spotting sorties and 2,375.5 flying hours before leaving for Ulithi on 11 March. At Iwo Jima, two, even three, missions a day were common for the squadron's pilots. Their main task was spotting for the gunnery ships offshore, but they did not accomplish this unarmed. A normal load would be a full ammunition loading plus six rockets, with the addition at times of a couple of bombs. Generally, a mission could last up to four hours, three spent in spotting and one hour looking for their own targets.

Upon arrival on station, the spotter would contact the ship with which he was to work. This process could be maddening. Often a ship would not answer when first contacted, leading the pilot to believe his radios were not working. Then, sometimes up to an hour later, the ship would come up on frequency wondering why all the delay. Communications would be the big bugaboo of the spotters. The FM-2s were equipped with a ten-channel VHF set and a two-channel MHF set, but the MHF was primarily used. The use of the smaller capacity unit by the planes, the Shore Fire Control Party (SFCP), and the ships led to the overloading of frequencies, especially when some sixteen planes were trying to contact sixteen ships, as were the SFCPs (units of which were attached to the individual marine battalions).

Bringle vehemently pleaded for more VHF sets, which were underutilized, as well as much more reliable units. Disregarding long-standing complaints about the reliability of the MHF sets, the higher commands turned down his requests. Their reasoning was, first, that the system worked just fine (which was untrue), and, second, more logically, that since the SFCPs had only MHF sets, it would be too much trouble to change everyone over. These complaints would resurface at Okinawa, but the war would be over before anything was done about the problem.

As to the actual communications procedures, the VOC-1 pilots occasionally tended to be a bit more colorful than precise in their spotting instructions. This sometimes irked the marines, who would have rather heard "Up one hundred, left one hundred" than "Up just a hair." Still, the job got done; as Bringle reported, "For a man of war to repeat verbatim and apply a spot given as 'left a teeny weeny bit' may not be in keeping with the virility of its appearance but is indicative of the cooperation given."[12]

Some feathers were also ruffled by the spotters' technique of "firing the ship." This technique had been briefed prior to this operation and had been included in the operations plan, yet some ships' captains took offense that a mere ensign was ordering his ship to fire. The technique was really very simple. Being on top of his target, the spotter was in the best position to see where and when to fire. Adopted was the army expression "Fire at my command," the spotter being the controlling factor, thus "firing the ship." Several ships, however, refused to fire when told to; some others agreed to comply and then fired when they got good and ready. The consequence was that some good targets were missed and several Wildcats were almost blown out of the air by unexpected salvos from their own ships.

To Bringle those ships that had worked with fighter-type spotters at Normandy and southern France appeared to have less difficulty understanding the requirements and procedures of the VOC-1 pilots than those ships that had not. It took time, but by Okinawa this type of gunnery spotting was working very well.

Finally, the use of a fighter squadron for spotting was still looked on as an experiment. The Shore Fire Control Party had priority on gunfire missions even when the air spotters had a better view of the target. Nevertheless, in most cases coordination between the VOC-1 planes, the specific SFCP, and the ships (notwithstanding the communications foulups) was accomplished with no ill feeling over who was doing the spotting or calling in the fire.[13]

Especially high in praise of the squadron was the 5th Marine Division. In its action report the division commented, "The only complaint that could possibly be made against the VOF spotting planes is that there were not enough of them. This division would want one with every spotter if they were available. Missions conducted by VOF were many, quick, precise, and devastating to the Japanese. Even their very presence overhead decreased the enemy's freedom of movement."[14]

As dawn broke at Iwo Jima on the nineteenth, the *Saginaw Bay* and *Rudyerd Bay* slid into position off the island, their job of covering the transports finished. Later in the day Admiral Henderson would assume tactical command of both TUs 52.2.2 and 52.2.3, in essence forming one unit. It was D day, 19 February. In contrast to the preceding days, the nineteenth was marked by fair weather and a light breeze that hardly stirred the surface of a tranquil sea. At 0640 the big naval guns opened up for the prelanding bombardment. More ships joined in the shelling at 0730, making the island quake with the ferocity of the cannonade. Between 0805 and 0825, 120 planes from TGs 58.2 and 58.3 struck the landing beaches and the flanking areas.

By now familiar with the island, CVE pilots acted as target coordinators for the fast carrier strikes and also flew marine observers looking the situation over. For the *Rudyerd Bay* its first observer mission ended unhappily. VC-77's skipper, Lieutenant Commander Frank J. Peterson, was carrying a 5th Marine Division observer over the landing beaches when a shell ripped into the Avenger, instantly turning it into a fireball. The first troops had ground ashore at 0902, and the invasion was only twelve minutes old when VC-77 lost its CO and his crew.[15]

Acting as target coordinators was not the only thing the "jeep" fliers were doing. They flew many strikes against positions on Iwo and also on Chichi Jima, where a pair of Rufe floatplanes were caught in Futani Harbor and destroyed. Also flown were ASP and

CAP, naval gunfire spotting, tactical air observation, artillery spotting with marine observers, smoker, and photo missions. Propaganda leaflets were dropped, with predictably poor results. One plane even carried cameramen to take color movies of the landings. All in all, it was a busy day.

The nineteenth saw another group of escort carriers appear off Iwo. These were from the Logistic Support Group (TG 50.8). Four CVEs, the *Bougainville, Admiralty Islands, Attu,* and *Windham Bay,* were delivering replacement planes and aircrews to the fast carriers, while the *Makassar Strait* and *Shamrock Bay* provided the air cover for the deliveries. Aircraft went first to TGs 58.1, 58.4, and 58.5 on the nineteenth, with further shipments to TGs 58.2 and 58.3 the next day and more deliveries on the twenty-third to all the task groups except TG 58.5. The transport carriers remained in the vicinity to send a few more planes to TF 58 until 1 March, when they packed up to head for Ulithi. For the transport carriers and their crews it was just another several days' work, but the figures show just how important these logistics operations were to the process of keeping the pressure on the enemy. At Iwo Jima 254 aircraft and 65 pilots and crews were delivered to the fast carriers, a number almost equal to the contents of three *Essex*-class carriers.[16]

Though CVE planes were out in force on the twentieth, bad weather hampered their activities considerably. In the morning flying was curtailed and was completely stopped in the afternoon by the low clouds and rainshowers.

During the missions that were flown on this day, enemy flak continued to be accurate, as VC-88's Lieutenant C. L. Herbster found out. Herbster was attacking gun emplacements north of Airfield No. 2 when he saw a "bright red flash" just ahead of his Avenger. Gas fumes then filled the cockpit, causing him to believe his plane's gas tanks had been holed. They had, but with no real danger to the crew. Herbster hurried back to the *Saginaw Bay,* only to find the carrier launching planes and unable to take him aboard. While waiting, Herbster began to circle. When he tried to straighten out, he found that he couldn't—both ailerons had gone spongy and were useless. Too low to bail out, Herbster had to ditch his TBM with its left wing down. The plane hit hard but didn't cartwheel and all three crewmen were soon picked up. But the Japanese antiaircraft fire had claimed one more CVE plane.[17]

Weather again improved on the twenty-first, and Japanese planes appeared at Iwo—and made the most of it. That afternoon the veteran *Saratoga* was steaming about thirty miles northeast of the island. Previously operating as a night-flying carrier with TF 58, the

"Sara" had been released from that duty in the morning to provide night cover over the assault force and to operate as part of TU 52.2.4 in conjunction with Admiral Durgin's escort carriers.

At 1628 a group of bogeys was reported approaching from seventy-five miles away. Initially identified as "friendlies," they were, in fact, a mixed bag of twelve Judys and eight Jills, escorted by twelve Zekes. These planes made up Lieutenant Hiroshi Murakawa's *Mitate* Unit No. 2. All of the Judys were carrying bombs, while the Jills were evenly split, half with bombs and the other half carrying torpedoes. Murakawa's planes had left Katori airfield near Yokosuka at 0800, staged through the tiny island of Hachijo, and were now bearing down on the Americans off Iwo.[18]

A few minutes later this attacking force split into two groups, one heading straight for the *Saratoga,* and the "Sara's" CAP was vectored out to investigate them. The Hellcat pilots splashed two of the intruders, but at 1659 six more popped out of the overcast to dive on the not particularly maneuverable *Saratoga.* One was shot down by the flattop's alert gunners, but two others skipped across the water into the "Sara's" side, their bombs detonating deep inside her. Another plane dropped a bomb that exploded on the anchor windlass. A fifth plane crashed into the port catapult. The last kamikaze smashed into an aircraft crane, leaving parts of the plane strewn over the deck and sending its right wing blazing into the No. 1 gallery, wiping it out. Three minutes was all this attack had taken.

Though she was severely hurt, the "Sara's" power plant was still putting out and her fires were gradually being controlled. Her flight deck was unserviceable, however, and her airborne planes were directed to land on the CVEs. Then, at 1846, as night was beginning to fall, three more kamikazes jumped the *Saratoga.* Two of these were shot down right away. To the CVE crews watching the action at a distance, the battlecruiser *Alaska,* covering the carrier, was putting up "such a barrage that she appeared to be in flames herself."[19] Just before it crashed the flight deck, the third plane dropped a bomb. The plane itself, which bounced over the side, did little damage, but the bomb blew a twenty-five-foot hole in the flight deck and caused more destruction below decks.

The *Saratoga* had been knocked out of the ring, suffering 123 men killed and 192 wounded and grievous material damage. Nevertheless, by 2015 she was able to recover, but not launch, planes. Five of her own fighters were taken aboard, plus a wandering Wildcat from the *Makin Island.* Not too sure of where he was, this last pilot climbed out of his fighter and remarked to an airedale, "Gee, I'm glad I'm not on the old 'Sara.' All hell's broken out there!" The deckhand stared at the pilot for a moment, then replied wearily, "Take a good look around, brother. This *is* hell!"[20]

Operating south of the *Saratoga*'s group, the escort carriers did not escape the kamikazes. Thirty miles southwest of Iwo Jima was TU 52.2.1, which would leave for the fueling area at 1822 and take no part in the ensuing fight. Cruising together thirty miles east of the island and about thirty-five miles south of TU 52.2.4 were TUs 52.2.2 and 52.2.3. Bogeys were first detected closing with the CVEs at 1653, but neither a division of *Lunga Point* fighters nor a division from the *Makin Island* found anything in the clouds. At 1707, the radio signal "Flash Red–Control Yellow" (enemy aircraft in area, attack imminent) was broadcast, followed a minute later by general quarters. Eleven divisions of fighters were ordered scrambled at 1710. Including those CAP aircraft returning from Iwo, at least 65 fighters were airborne.

For a time nothing happened; then the *Bismarck Sea* was ordered to scramble an additional eight fighters, this being accomplished at 1730. Fifteen minutes later *Saginaw Bay* planes saw a Jill north of Minami Iwo Jima but were unable to catch the fast-moving aircraft, which dove on a group of LSTs and hit either the net cargo ship *Keokuk* or the *LST-477*.[21] By 1800 all screens were clear of bogeys and the planes scrambled earlier were told to land, followed by the LCAP.

Except for one three-plane division from the *Makin Island*, by 1825 all of the CAP was down. About this time another contact developed and the three Wildcats vectored toward it. Though the plots of the defending fighters and the bogey merged at twelve miles, the enemy was missed in the half-light. The time was now about 1845, and the sun had set at 1833. On the horizon was the burning *Saratoga*.

Earlier the "jeeps" had moved into an air defense formation. They were still in this circular formation—five of them in a circle of 2,500 yards' radius centered on the *Saginaw Bay*. Northernmost of the carriers was the *Lunga Point*, the *Bismarck Sea* bearing 072 degrees from the center. The formation was steaming on a course of 040 degrees. Suddenly five or six planes streaked in from the northeast, low on the water. All ships opened fire, and the tracers from their guns formed a bright and colorful filigree in the darkening sky.

Braving this fire, the planes (identified as Jills) darted in. Their target was the *Lunga Point*. At about 700 yards the first plane dropped a torpedo, then flew into a 5-inch burst from the carrier's gun. As it flipped over, the 40-mms and 20-mms finished it off, the

Jill blossoming into petals of flame and tumbling into the water 200 yards from the ship. The Jill's torpedo cut through the water about 50 to 100 yards ahead of the carrier and sped off into the darkness.

Another Jill, hot on the heels of the first, also dropped a torpedo, which missed ahead. Concentrating on the first plane, the gunners didn't take this Jill under fire, and it crossed only fifteen feet over the fantail and escaped. A third plane, hit at point-blank range by the *Lunga Point*'s five-incher, just fell apart.

One last plane (actually the third in sequence) came much too close for the comfort of the *Lunga Point*'s crew. Though taken under fire at about one thousand yards, it kept boring in from the starboard side. At six hundred yards a torpedo fell from the Jill to skim just ten or fifteen yards past the carrier's stern.

A few seconds before it reached the *Lunga Point,* the Jill began to burn. Its pilot was obviously attempting to hit the flattop's island, and in this he was partially successful. Just before hitting the carrier, the plane's gas tanks exploded in a fearsome flash of flames that struck the after end of the island, the Jill's right wing shearing off upon impact. As the plane careened on, its landing gear tore loose and flew into a catwalk. The rest of the plane continued its fiery path across the flight deck, over the catwalk, between two 20-mm guns, and off the port side.

Flaming gasoline was scattered over the after end of the island, the flight deck, and catwalks on both sides of the ship, yet the damage from this spectacular crash was remarkably light. The fire on the flight deck took only about three minutes to extinguish, and fires on the signal platform and after end of the island were under control in another two minutes. Several antennas were damaged or destroyed, the flight deck was scorched and propeller marks scarred its surface, but all in all, the damage was minor.

Personnel casualties were also minor, primarily because the carrier's crew had been wearing flashproof clothing, until then considered a nuisance. Following this close call "everyone now wears flashproof gear willingly; it is no longer a hot, uncomfortable contraption the Captain makes us wear."[22]

The *Lunga Point* had been very lucky. By 0600 the next day she was back in full operation.[23] At that same time, however, there was one less carrier with the task unit. That carrier was the *Bismarck Sea*.

When the CVEs recovered the planes that had been scrambled at 1710 and 1730, the *Bismarck Sea* became crowded with aircraft. Besides her normal complement, she took aboard a pair of TBMs transferring passengers from the *Natoma Bay* and *Wake Island,* and a *Saratoga* fighter that had been on a message drop. This brought the

A kamikaze scorches the Lunga Point. *(National Archives)*

number of planes on the carrier to one F6F, 19 FM-2s, 15 TBMs, and 2 OY-1s (a marine spotting plane). To make room for the extra torpedo planes, four Wildcats, not yet degassed, had to be sent to the hangar deck, completely filling that space.[24]

All the ships opened fire during the attack on the escort carriers. A few seconds after the *Bismarck Sea* ceased fire on the first of the Jills attacking the *Lunga Point,* her lookouts saw another plane boring in only twenty-five feet above the water and aiming directly at their ship. The after starboard guns opened fire as soon as the plane was clearly seen, at about 1,000 yards. Tracers sliced through the plane, but on it charged. Desperately the gunners kept firing until they couldn't depress their guns any further.

Smashing into the ship abeam the after elevator, the kamikaze's engine ripped loose to come to rest in the after elevator well. The elevator had been on its way up and almost to the flight deck when the suicider struck; its cables were cut and it fell to the hangar deck with a tremendous thud. Torpedoes were knocked loose from their stowage racks to roll around on the deck. Steering control was lost and the *Bismarck Sea*'s TBS was knocked out.

In the vicinity of the crash, fires immediately broke out and the crew discovered that the after sprinkler system and water curtain were inoperative. Quickly they ran hoses from the forward end of the hangar, and for a while it appeared that the fires could be controlled. Then, just two minutes after the first kamikaze struck, a second came out of nowhere to dive vertically into the *Bismarck Sea* just forward of her burning after elevator.

A hole a bit larger than the size of the plane's fuselage was torn in the flight deck. Part of a wing was ripped off, to lie on the flight deck near the island. Landing in the midst of the four Wildcats that had not been degassed, the kamikaze exploded with a colossal blast, blowing out the entire rear of the hangar and knocking overboard all hands on the fantail. Killed by the explosion were most of the firefighters, as were the men of Repair 3 stationed directly beneath the hangar deck at the center of the blast. B lkheads as far forward as amidships were smashed in. Fires intensi and quickly became uncontrollable. Ammunition from the clipping rooms above the hangar deck began to fall through ripped decks, and soon this ammunition was going off, making the hangar a death trap.[25]

The after part of the ship became a raging inferno, with flames shooting high into the darkening sky through the hole in the deck left by the second kamikaze, the elevator opening, and the sundered sides of the hangar deck. Aboard the *Saginaw Bay* a sailor watching the fires on both the *Bismarck Sea* and *Lunga Point* thought the scene was like "Broadway and 42nd Street on New Year's Eve."[26] But there was no celebrating on the *Bismarck Sea*. At 1900 the flattop's crew was ordered to go to their abandon ship stations. In the engine rooms the "black gang" secured the boilers and stopped the engines. Little smoke was noted in the engineering spaces when they were abandoned.

At 1905 Captain John L. Pratt ordered his men to abandon ship. Taking life rafts from the planes, the men began to pass them over the side. As this was taking place, a huge eruption rocked the carrier. Probably caused by the detonation of one or more of the torpedoes lying on the hangar deck, the explosion blew out both sides of the after end of the hangar as well as tearing the after section of the flight deck apart. The carrier began to list to starboard.

For about an hour the *Bismarck Sea*'s crew continued to leave their ship. One of the more spectacular departures was an eighty-foot swan dive by a lookout from a searchlight platform into the cold, choppy water. He survived. The carrier continued to list, stopping temporarily at 20 degrees and then increasing at a faster rate. On the screening vessels surrounding the stricken carrier, men could

The Bismarck Sea *explodes, as seen from the* Saginaw Bay. *(National Archives)*

hear loud crashing as machinery ripped loose or aircraft snapped their lines to ram into each other, then fall into the water.

Around 2007 the *Bismarck Sea* lurched sharply to starboard to hang at an angle of 80 degrees for what seemed an eternity, but was actually only about thirty seconds. Her island broke away and disappeared beneath the water. A few seconds later she rolled completely over. By 2015 she had disappeared stern first. No explosion marked her passing, just a great mass of steam left floating over the water.[27]

Leaving the ship did not mean the ordeal was over for the carrier's crew. The sea was rough; the water temperature was cool (about 70 degrees F); it was dark; many men did not have lifejackets; and a Japanese plane strafed the men in the water, killing some. Crisscrossing the area, marked with the dim light of a buoy as a reference point, three destroyers and three destroyer escorts pulled waterlogged and shivering men from the sea.

Rescue efforts continued until the next morning, 625 men eventually being recovered. Unfortunately, this left 318 casualties for the *Bismarck Sea*. It was later estimated that approximately 125 men lost their lives in the violent explosions aboard ship; an undetermined number were killed by portions of the ship falling on them or by the

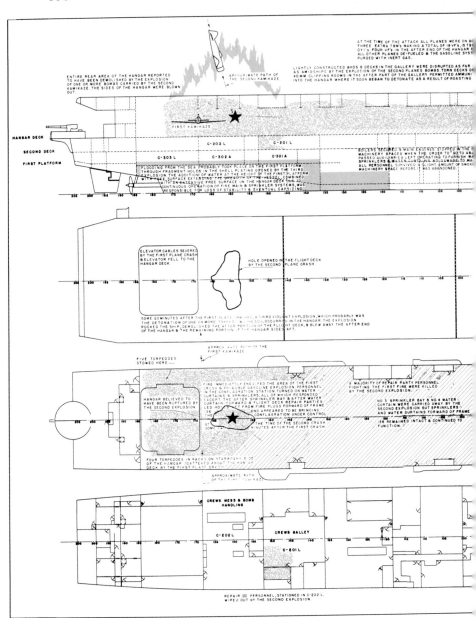

Bismarck Sea *Kamikaze Damage, 21 February 1945*

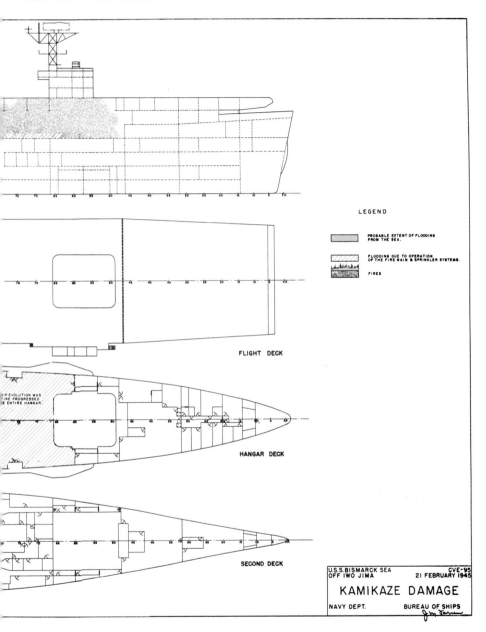

LEGEND

PROBABLE EXTENT OF FLOODING
FROM THE SEA.

FLOODING DUE TO OPERATION
OF THE FIRE MAIN & SPRINKLER SYSTEMS.

FIRES

FLIGHT DECK

HANGAR DECK

SECOND DECK

U.S.S. BISMARCK SEA   CVE-95
OFF IWO JIMA   21 FEBRUARY 1945

KAMIKAZE DAMAGE

NAVY DEPT.   BUREAU OF SHIPS

strafing; and sadly, over 100 more men drowned as a result of the rough and chilly water and a "lack of confidence in themselves."[28]

Standing nearby as the *Bismarck Sea* sank was the *Anzio*. For the men on that carrier the sinking brought out a sick feeling of "please, not again." Almost a year and three months earlier they had watched the *Liscome Bay* blown apart. They had seen the first escort carrier go down and now, though they did not know it, they had seen the last one sink.

At last the remaining enemy planes disappeared off the screens. Quiet should have returned to the area, but this was not to be, at least not yet. There were still several *Saratoga* planes in the air waiting for a chance to land, but the ships' gunners were naturally trigger-happy and were quick to fire as these planes attempted to land. At least one pilot had to ditch because he ran out of fuel after trying several passes at a carrier. Another pilot made three attempts at a landing before the gunners left him alone.[29]

Most of the *Saratoga* planes were finally directed to the beach, though nine of her planes did land on the CVEs. Five of the latter took refuge on the *Makin Island*. The first four came aboard with no problem, but the fifth pilot had a close shave. After forgetting to lower his tail hook, he dove for the deck, hit hard, and bounced into the air to land upside down in the barriers. Luckily, there were no injuries, but two Hellcats had to be written off.[30]

At 2040 the *Saratoga* was detached to proceed to Eniwetok and thence to the United States for extensive repair work. Aboard the big carrier thirty-six aircraft had been lost, including those that had to be jettisoned to reduce the fire hazard. Another thirty-seven planes had been lost when the *Bismarck Sea* went down.[31]

With the *Saratoga* limping eastward, Admiral Durgin recalled the *Wake Island, Petrof Bay,* and three escorts from TU 52.2.1, which was then heading for the fueling area. Taking the *Saratoga*'s place off Iwo was the *Enterprise*. When the "Sara" had left TF 58 to take up her duties with the escort carriers, the "Big E's" crew had been openly derisive, calling the *Saratoga* the "Queen of the Jeeps" and some other, unprintable names. Now they found that their ship had inherited that title—and gained another appellation as well, perhaps not as stirring as the "Big E," but apt. Operating with so many carriers named after bays, she was soon being called the "*Enterprise Bay*."[32]

These kamikaze and torpedo attacks would be the last of the "jeeps" off Iwo Jima. That was all right with the CVE sailors because they had their hands full just doing their jobs. As Admiral Durgin said later, "The strenuous tempo at which the CVEs, along with the other units of the Fleet, have been operating the last six months far exceeds anything thought possible earlier in the war. In this operation, the CVEs were 30 to 40 miles off Iwo for a period of twenty-two days, and except for one day out for fueling, provided air support the whole time. For a part of this time, this Task Group had planes in the air for 172 consecutive hours, flying both day support missions and night antisubmarine patrols."[33]

Iwo wasn't easy for the CVE pilots. Bombing was especially difficult because of the continual low clouds that blanketed the island. VC-81's skipper, Lieutenant Commander W. B. Morton, called the type of bombing his men had to use "dip bombing." "The bomber, under the overcast," he said, "dips his nose to pick up the target, then quickly pulls up his nose obscuring the target. At the same time he releases a string of bombs hoping one will be in range."[34]

Another problem encountered by all squadrons was a lack of coordination between the strike groups. During the Iwo Jima operation it was common for aircraft from various squadrons to operate in one "gaggle." This prompted Morton to remark, "It is almost unbelievable to watch the confusion in a single attack with eight VF and eight VT from different carriers."[35]

An example of the confusion and poor coordination or cooperation that sometimes occurred appears in a report from VC-82 of a close support mission on 7 March. The flight leader was from another squadron and he could not locate the target, a fortified ridge with a concrete blockhouse. White phosphorus was fired on the target and the planes made their runs. "Flight leader," VC-82 would say, "claimed that in spite of the assurance of SAC [Support Air Commander] and CASCU [Commander Air Support Control Units] to the contrary, our attack was landing too close to the ground forces." At the request of the flight leader, more white phosphorus was placed on the target, and while this was being done he "conducted a long 16-plane tail chase over the island instead of orbiting the target area." When he returned, he was told that the strike had been canceled and to orbit nearby. Deciding he wanted to return to his carrier instead, the flight leader said "so long" and left.

Lieutenant Commander Holt, VC-82's skipper, was astonished and disgusted at this incident. "This was the most unsatisfactory and fouled-up hop our men have been on," he would complain. "The target was evident at all times to the other pilots who were anxious to attack. The flight leader was garrulous, argumentative and unwilling to conduct an attack over an area after both the SAC and CASCU had approved the dummy run."[36]

This incident was a relatively rare case of poor leadership, but

the difficulties of running mixed formation attacks remained at
Iwo Jima. By Okinawa these problems would, for the most part, be
resolved.

A concomitant problem was congestion over the target area. According to VC-92, the following hectic and dangerous traffic jam
could be encountered almost any time: "Six VOF spotters, two or
three artillery spotters, three or four Cubs and several seaplanes, in
addition to the support groups buzzing over the island at a single
moment, all intent on their own missions, without regard for other
aircraft. Add to this the crisscross of mortar, naval and artillery
trajectories over the objective, and it becomes clear that the occupational hazards of direct air support are not entirely of the enemy's
making."[37]

Also, it is doubtful if there was one operation during the war in
which radio discipline wasn't a problem. Iwo Jima was no different.
Considered a general rule, not an exception, was the following exchange that cluttered the airwaves in one short period.

> "Squeaky, this is Wally. Damn it, you have been high and fast on
> the last three passes! Now, come down and slow her up!"
>
> "Number Two, you are lagging way behind. Get in here and stay
> with me!"
>
> "Gadget Two, this is Gadget Base. Prep Charlie. Over."
>
> "Gadget Two, this is Gamecock Ten. Prep Charlie. Acknowledge.
> Over."
>
> "Gadget Two, this is Gadget Two Three. Gamecock Ten is calling
> you on channel ten for Prep Charlie."
>
> "Hell, Gamecock Ten, this is Gadget Two. Sorry, I was still on CAP
> circuit. I am on channel one now. Besides, I am in the traffic pattern
> now. Wilco. Out."[38]

On the twenty-third the *Tulagi*, carrying twenty-seven fighters on
her hangar deck, thirty-four Avengers and another thirteen Wildcats on her flight deck, plus spare pilots, joined Admiral Durgin's
force. Over half of these planes were delivered to the other flattops.
Proud of their ship, Captain Cronin's crew made sure there would
be no disparaging comments (which would reflect on them) about
the condition of the aircraft they were delivering.

For once the planes had been in reasonable shape when they were
taken aboard the *Tulagi*, but the ship's crew fine-tuned them to
make them combat-ready. However, "after arrival at the rendezvous," Cronin said, "the big problem became selling our wares. Naturally we were anxious to become operational and practically resorted to high-pressure methods to peddle our commodity, spare
planes and spare pilots."[39] Cronin's high-pressure methods worked,

with several skippers remarking favorably on the condition of the planes they had received.[40]

Now free to function offensively, on the twenty-fifth the *Tulagi* began combat operations. Along with the *Anzio,* she would be most active in an antisubmarine role, but both would also undertake close support missions.

Both carriers were active on the twenty-sixth trying to ferret out any unwelcome undersea visitors. The *Tulagi*'s planes assisted the destroyer escort *Finnegan* in searching for a suspected sub, but in actuality the DE had already destroyed that boat (the *I-370*) several hours earlier.[41] Planes from the *Anzio* had better luck. Just after midnight on 26 February Lieutenant (jg) W. J. Wilson was launched to relieve another aircraft that had been scouring an area where the *Bennion* had made a sonar contact. Up until 0220 Wilson was just boring holes in the sky; then a blip blossomed on his plane's scope. Passing over the surfaced target, Wilson took the black shape on the water to be a destroyer. A second pass showed Wilson he was wrong. The black shape was a sub and it was diving!

Racking his Avenger around, Wilson started an attack. When Wilson reached an attack position the sub had disappeared, but a faint patch of phosphorescence marked the swirl left by its submergence. He dropped a Fido from 150 feet; it landed about 150 yards ahead of the swirl. Following close behind the Fido were a pair of sonobuoys. Listening to the sonobuoys, Wilson's radioman heard a "roaring noise which died to zero."[42]

Wilson continued his search until relieved a couple of hours later, when a quartet of destroyers and destroyer escorts took over. They could find no sign of a submarine because no submarine was left. At daylight a large oil slick covered the surface, all that remained of the *RO-43.*[43]

There were more enemy subs lurking about, and twenty-four hours later another *Anzio* pilot pounced on one. Lieutenant (jg) F. M. Fay was on a routine search early on the twenty-seventh when his radar picked up the presence of a surface target. Fay closed fast with the target. A sub, completely surfaced and practically dead in the water, lay ahead. At 280 knots, Fay was going too fast, and he zipped right past it. When he was able to slow down and return to the spot where the sub had been, it had disappeared. He dropped a float light to mark the spot, followed by a sonobuoy pattern.

No sound came from the sonobuoys, but at 0338 a conning tower broke the surface near the float light. The sub went back down quickly, with Fay right on top of it. A Fido speared the water a hundred yards ahead of the sub's swirl. Over the sonobuoys came loud propeller beats, these continuing until a loud explosion stopped them. A 30-foot geyser of water broke from the surface of the ocean.

Soon another VC-82 plane joined Fay, and the two aircraft continued to monitor the sonobuoys, over which unusual noises were heard but not identified. Another Fido was dropped but apparently missed. However, a short time later numerous air bubbles rose to the surface, followed by a large amount of oil. Though the two Avenger crews believed a submarine had sunk, they couldn't be sure. Later in the day a pair of DEs combed the area but were unable to dredge up anything.

It was only after the war that Fay discovered he had indeed sunk a submarine. It had been the big *I-368*, which carried *Kaiten* (human torpedoes).[44] Another Japanese submarine, the *I-58*, had also tried to break through the antisubmarine defenses around Iwo Jima, but the *Tulagi* and *Anzio* so harassed her that she was finally recalled without accomplishing anything.[45]

For the "jeeps," operations at Iwo Jima settled down into the monotonous and somewhat frustrating regularity of ground-support missions daily, shipping and harassment strikes on Haha Jima and Chichi Jima, and the usual CAP and ASW patrols. The CVE aircraft were shot at and shot back. Napalm and standard bombs were dropped, occasionally with some effect.

On one mission a group of CVE fliers took out their frustration on the Japanese in a big way. Eight VC-77 planes with a like number from another squadron were attacking cave positions in a cliff. Several passes had been made when the marine ground observer controlling the mission radioed, "Wait! Hold it! They are waving a white flag!"

Almost immediately a pilot shot back, "The hell with that! Let's bomb the s—— out of them!" In an instant all sixteen pilots were diving on the target, using the flag as an aiming point. Luckily, in this wild melee there were no collisions. The target was blanketed with bombs.[46]

Even DDT was used at Iwo. Because of a rapid increase in the number of flies on the island, probably caused by the number of bodies left unburied, a special DDT-spraying flight was made by two *Makin Island* Avengers on 28 February. Results were good and the spraying was repeated on 4 March.[47]

Losses continued throughout this period of repetitious missions. Though most were operational, some happened in combat. For example, on 1 March a VC-85 Avenger was shot down over Iwo Jima and all aboard were killed. Two days later, while on a strafing mis-

Hit by flak over Iwo Jima and with his right aileron useless, VC-90's skipper, Lieutenant Commander Robert O'Neill, lands aboard the Steamer Bay *on 23 February 1945. Saying "I know where it is and I'm going after it!," O'Neill hopped out of his damaged plane and into another FM-2 and went back to hit the antiaircraft position that had gotten him. (National Archives)*

sion at Chichi Jima, a VC-81 Wildcat was hit by flak. The pilot was apparently killed or stunned by the hit, for his plane immediately went into a 45-degree dive and crashed into the water.

Then, on the sixth, VC-88's Ensign R. P. Provost was attacking positions in Iwo's northern portion when a large shell tore through the underside of his Avenger and through the radio compartment. Smoke began to pour from the wounded plane. Believing his radioman to be seriously wounded and in need of assistance, Provost dove for Airfield No. 1. The enemy shell had knocked out the aircraft's hydraulic system, a fact Provost discovered when he couldn't get his landing gear down. Nevertheless, he bellied in his plane with little damage to the plane, but discovered his prompt actions had been in vain. His radioman was dead.

On the seventh the "hot spot" of the Bonins, Chichi Jima, claimed another victim. A group of VC-82 and VC-88 fighters accompanied by a guide TBM struck airfields and harbor installations on the island. Because of the usual cloudy weather that hung about the island, VC-82 had developed the technique of doing wingovers into the clouds, then diving out of them for the runs. The pilot lost this day had a tendency to fly a very loose formation, and when his division began its wingover into the broken clouds, he became separated from the other planes and was never seen again. He might have become disoriented.

On this same mission a VC-88 flier had a close call when flak tore a gaping three-by-six-foot hole in his left wing. Barely able to control his fighter, he made it back to Iwo Jima, where he had to use both the north/south and east/west runways before bringing his plane to a stop.[48]

In small compensation for these losses, on 1 March four VC-81 fighters caught a Frances heading for the carriers. One pilot set the bomber's right engine aflame and a second exploded its gas tanks. Ten seconds later there was just a pool of flame lying atop the water.[49]

By the first week of March CVE operations finally began tapering off. On 2 March a 4,000-foot runway was ready for fighter operations on Iwo and proved to be a lifesaver to more than one CVE pilot. Two days later a damaged B-29 made an emergency landing on the strip, the first of many B-29s that would seek the haven of the island. On the sixth army fighters flew in to take over the CAP from the CVEs. They were followed on the eighth by marine squadrons, which took over the responsibility for antisubmarine patrol.

With the arrival of the army and marine planes, the escort carriers' job was finished at Iwo Jima. One of the last missions for a "jeep" pilot was to act as air coordinator for a group of P-51s attacking positions in the constantly dwindling target area.

On the afternoon of the eighth VC-84's skipper, Doug English, was given the job of guiding the army fighters to their targets. English "decided very wisely and modestly that his TBM-3 with everything forward to the firewall might have some slight difficulty in keeping ahead of the P-51s," so after marking the target, he pulled off to one side to observe the runs by the fighters. English thought that, considering they were army pilots, they had done a very good job.[50]

On the seventh the *Anzio* and *Steamer Bay* proceeded to Leyte. The next day the *Makin Island, Natoma Bay, Petrof Bay, Lunga Point, Rudyerd Bay,* and their escorts were detached to head for Ulithi. Task

Unit 52.2.3 (the *Saginaw Bay, Wake Island, Tulagi,* and escorts) remained until 11 March when it, too, departed for Ulithi.

En route to Ulithi the *Makin Island* was involved in a neat ship-to-ship personnel transfer. Normally this type of transfer was an everyday occurrence, but this was a little different, involving the transfer of a sailor suffering from appendicitis from a submarine to the carrier. Rendezvous was effected between the two vessels and the stricken seaman transferred via stretcher along the lines that "tied" the ships together. Just as the transfer was completed, a petty officer on the sub fell overboard, and the lines were disconnected while the sub searched for its man. When he was finally recovered, he was found to have been seriously injured. Once more the lines were rigged and the injured man was taken aboard the carrier. Unfortunately, the *Makin Island's* doctor was unable to save him, although the sailor with appendicitis recovered nicely. What made this ship-to-ship transfer outstanding was that, except for the time the sub turned on its searchlight to look for the petty officer, virtually the entire operation had been conducted in almost complete blackness.[51]

For the escort carriers and their squadrons, Iwo had been a reasonably good operation, if not from the losses suffered, at least from the amount and quality of ground support given the marines. Over 8,000 sorties had been flown, approximately 400 tons of bombs and 150 napalm tanks dropped, and 9,000 rockets fired.[52] As an example of the intensity of this operation, when the *Lunga Point* returned to Ulithi, she had only six bombs left in her magazines, having dropped 596 during the battle.[53]

In general the marines were satisfied with this support, some saying that it was excellent and much improved over past operations.[54] Others, however, were disappointed in the CVE effort, citing a lack of heavy bombs and claiming the "better" pilots came from the fast carriers; "better" obviously meant the marine airmen that were flying off the *Essex, Wasp, Bennington,* and *Bunker Hill.*[55] This condemnation of the "jeep" fliers is surprising, considering that many of them had much greater experience at close support than their fast carrier brethren.

The activity at Iwo Jima had not been without cost. Counting those aircraft that went down with the *Bismarck Sea,* the CVEs lost eighty-three aircraft, many of these operationally. In return, one enemy plane was shot down by VC-81 and eleven by ships' gunfire.[56]

A serious blow had been the loss of the *Bismarck Sea.* The other carriers, particularly the *Anzio* and *Tulagi,* had had to take up the slack. At Iwo these two carriers had to work both sides of the street—operating day and night in both the ground support and antisubmarine roles. This demanding schedule taxed the ships' crews and pilots greatly.

On the *Anzio* some pilots (and their crewmen) flew for seven consecutive nights, and six to seven hours of flying each night was not unusual for the ship. It didn't take long before the airmen became irritable and began to voice numerous vague complaints and to have trouble sleeping. The skippers and squadron commanders realized that the dual duties imposed upon their men were straining them to the limit, and performing these duties any longer would have degraded the missions greatly.[57] Before higher commands could really do anything about these complaints, the war ended.

On 11 March the first group of escort carriers anchored at Ulithi; the last group sailed in on the fourteenth. Since Palau the "jeeps" had been operating almost constantly, with only a couple of weeks' break between each operation. It was no different this time. There was just enough time for the crews to spend a few hours on Mog Mog, Ulithi's recreation island, before getting back to work. In less than three weeks marine and army troops would be landing on Okinawa, and the escort carriers would be in the thick of the battle again.

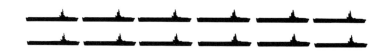

THE LONGEST BATTLE

IF THE "jeep" sailors thought their stay at Ulithi would be restful and without excitement, they were rudely jolted out of that thought. Hardly had the first escort carriers returning from Iwo Jima dropped their anchors at Ulithi on 11 March than a kamikaze that had flown all the way from Kanoya, Japan, sneaked in to smash into the fast carrier *Randolph*. Damage turned out to be light, and the carrier was able to sail a few days later with TF 58 for strikes on Japan and Okinawa. Nonetheless, the fires on the flattop and another explosion and fire on a nearby island as a second suicider mistook it for a warship caused several CVE skippers to rearrange their mooring spots hastily.[1]

Next for the American forces pounding their way closer to the Japanese homeland was Okinawa. Lying about 450 miles south and a bit west of Kyushu, it was the largest of the approximately 140 islands that curve in a gentle arc almost 800 miles long between Kyushu and Formosa. These islands make up the Nansei Shoto, or Ryukyus. Okinawa had not been the original target of the American planners; for some time Admiral King favored an assault on Formosa. Objections to such an assault came from a variety of sources, including Admiral Spruance; Lieutenant General Robert C. Richardson, Jr., commanding general of the United States Army Forces Pacific Ocean Areas; and Lieutenant General Millard F. Harmon, commanding general of the Army Air Forces Pacific Ocean Areas. Most of the objections revolved around the amount of men and matériel that would be needed to take even a portion of the island, the disadvantages of Formosa as a base for air operations against Japan (it was virtually the same distance from Japan as the Marianas, and B-29s could be much more easily tracked flying from Formosa than from the Marianas), and the fear that an assault on Formosa would lead to nothing but a dead end.

Finally, in October 1944 Iwo Jima and Okinawa were chosen in place of Formosa. Initially the Okinawa landings were to take place on 1 March 1945. This date, however, depended on how well things went at Iwo Jima as well as at Luzon, availability of shipping and fire and air support units being a critical factor. Ultimately, the landings would not take place until 1 April. Okinawa was important to the Japanese and would be just as valuable to the Americans. It was to be used as a staging base for the proposed invasion of Japan. Also, its size meant that a number of airfields could be built on the island: some for fighters to escort the B-29s, and some for additional bombers (B-24s, B-25s, and so forth) to add their weight to the bombing campaign.

Gathered for this assault was the largest force yet assembled in the Pacific. For the amphibious phase some 1,213 vessels of all types and sizes were assigned; TF 58 added another eighty-eight ships; the Royal Navy's TF 57 (which would have a major role in the operation) contributed twenty-two; the logistics and service forces would have almost two-hundred more. Finally, the assault troops of the marine corps, army, and navy gathered under Lieutenant General Simon B. Buckner's Tenth Army totaled over 180,000 men—a magnificent assemblage.[2]

The number of escort carriers working at one time or another during "Iceberg," as the Okinawa operation was named, would be greater than for the Leyte invasion. The following ships were assigned to Iceberg for the initial phase (ships were shuffled freely between units during the long stay at Okinawa, and other CVEs and escorts, as noted later, were active off the island in May and June):

TASK GROUP 52.1   SUPPORT CARRIER GROUP
R. Adm. Calvin T. Durgin

Task Unit 52.1.1	**R. Adm. C. A. F. Sprague** **(ComCarDiv 26), to 7 April** **R. Adm. E. W. Litch** **(ComCarDiv 26),** **to 9 May, 17–24 May** **R. Adm. G. R. Henderson** **(ComCarDiv 25), to 17 May** **R. Adm. H. M. Martin** **(ComCarDiv 23)**
Makin Island (FF)	Capt. W. B. Whaley, to 16 June Capt. Ira E. Hobbs
VC-84 16FM-2, 11 TBM-3	Lt. Cdr. D. K. English

Fanshaw Bay (F) VOC-2 24 FM-2, 6 TBM-3	Capt. M. E. Arnold Lt. Cdr. R. M. Allison
Lunga Point VC-85 18 FM-2, 11 TBM-3, 1 TBM-3P	Capt. G. A. T. Washburn Lt. Cdr. F. C. Herriman
Natoma Bay VC-9 18 FM-2, 12 TBM-3	Capt. B. B. Nichol Lt. J. O. Kay
Savo Island VC-91 20 FM-2, 12 TBM-3	Capt. W. D. Anderson Lt. F. M. Blanchard
Steamer Bay VC-90 20 FM-2, 13 TBM-3	Capt. J. B. Paschal Lt. Cdr. R. A. O'Neill
Anzio (ASW) VC-13 12 FM-2, 14 TBM-1C	Capt. G. C. Montgomery Lt. R. P. Williams

Screen: Destroyers *Ingraham, Patterson, Bagley, Hart, Lowry,* destroyer escorts *Lawrence C. Taylor, Melvin R. Nawman, Oliver Mitchell, Robert F. Keller, Tabberer, Richard M. Rowell, Richard S. Bull, Dennis, O'Flaherty*

Task Unit 52.1.2	**R. Adm. Felix B. Stump** **(ComCarDiv 24)**
Marcus Island (F) VC-87 20 FM-2, 11 TBM-3, 1 TBM-3P	Capt. H. V. Hopkins Lt. H. N. Heisel
Saginaw Bay (F) (ComCarDiv 25) VC-88 19 FM-2, 11 TBM-3, 1 TBM-3P	Capt. R. Goldthwaite Lt. E. L. Kempf
Sargent Bay VC-83 18 FM-2, 10 TBM-1C, 3 TBM-3	Capt. R. M. Oliver Lt. Cdr. B. V. Gates (KIA 22 April) Lt. M. S. Worley
Petrof Bay VC-93 18 FM-2, 12 TBM-3	Capt. R. S. Clarke Lt. Cdr. C. P. Smith
Rudyerd Bay VC-96 17 FM-2, 12 TBM-3	Capt. J. G. Foster, Jr. Lt. Cdr. W. S. Woollen
Wake Island VOC-1 28 FM-2, 6 TBM-3	Capt. A. V. Magly Lt. Cdr. W. F. Bringle
Tulagi (ASW)	Capt. J. C. Cronin, to 8 May Capt. W. V. Davis
VC-92 20 FM-2, 12 TBM-3	Lt. Cdr. J. B. Wallace

Screen: Destroyers *Capps, Evans, John D. Henley, Bradford, Boyd,* destroyer escorts *William Seiverling, Ulvert M. Moore, Kendall C. Campbell, Goss, Fleming, Sederstrom*

Task Unit 52.1.3	**R. Adm. William D. Sample** **(ComCarDiv 22)**
Suwannee (F) Air Group (CVEG) 40	Capt. D. S. Cornwell Lt. Cdr. R. D. Sampson (KIA 4 April) Lt. Cdr. Sampson Lt. Cdr. J. C. Longino (CAG 5 April on)
VF-40 19 F6F-5	
VT-40 11 TBM-3, 1 TBM-3P	Lt. Cdr. Longino Lt. C. R. Campbell

Sangamon	Capt. A. I. Malstrom
CVEG 33	Cdr. F. B. Gilkeson
VF-33 16 F6F-5E, 8 F6F-5N,	Lt. Cdr. P. C. Rooney
1 F6F-5P	
VT-33 6 TBM-3E	Cdr. Gilkeson
Chenango	Capt. G. van Deurs (to 2 May)
	Capt. H. D. Felt
CVEG 25	Lt. Cdr. R. W. Robinson
	(KIA 8 April)
VF-25 18 F6F-5, 1 F6F-5P	Lt. B. Phillips
	(CAG 8 Apr–5 May)
VT-25 11 TBM-3, 1 TBM-3P	Lt. Cdr. P. M. Paul
	(CAG 5 May on)
Santee	Capt. J. V. Peterson
CVEG 24	Lt. Cdr. R. J. Ostrom
	(KIA 10 April)
VF-24 18 F6F-5	Lt. Cdr. Ostrom
	Lt. Charbonnet
	(also CAG 10 April on)
VT-24	Lt. D. W. Cooper

Screen: Destroyers *Metcalf, Drexler, Fullam, Guest, Massey,* destroyer escorts *Edmonds, John C. Butler, Bebas, Tisdale, Eisele*

SPECIAL ESCORT CARRIER GROUP
Capt. C. L. Lee

Hollandia	Capt. Lee
White Plains	Capt. D. J. Sullivan
	(to 20 May)
	Capt. F. Funke
Sitkoh Bay	Capt. J. P. Walker
Breton	Capt. F. Obeirne

Screen: Destroyer transports *Kilty, Manley, George E. Badger, Greene*

(The carriers of this group transported Marine Air Groups 31 and 33, with 192 F4Us and 30 F6Fs, to Okinawa, arriving 6 April.)

TASK GROUP 50.8   LOGISTICS SUPPORT GROUP
R. Adm. Donald B. Beary

Task Unit 50.8.13

Shamrock Bay	Capt. F. T. Ward (to 20 May)
	Capt. J. E. Leeper
VC-94 18 FM-2, 12 TBM-3	Lt. Cdr. J. F. Patterson
	(KIA 9 April)
	Lt. L. E. Terry

Screen: Destroyers *Dewey, Aylwin*

Task Unit 50.8.23

Makassar Strait	Capt. H. D. Riley
VC-97 16 FM-2, 12 TBM-3	Lt. Cdr. M. T. Whittier

Screen: Destroyers *Dale, Farragut*

(These ships provided CAP and ASP for TG 50.8 and later were assigned to Task Group 52.1 for support operations.)

Task Unit 50.8.4   CVE Plane Transport Unit

Attu   Capt. H. F. MacComsey
Admiralty Islands   Capt. M. E. A. Gouin
Bougainville   Capt. C. A. Bond
Windham Bay   Capt. G. T. Mundorff

Screen: Destroyer escorts *Greiner, Sanders, Lovering, Wyman*

(These carriers transported replacement aircraft and pilots to both the fast carriers and the CVEs operating off Okinawa.)[3]

The Okinawa landings were set for 1 April, but before that island was assaulted, another group of islands just fifteen miles west of Okinawa had to be taken. They were known as the Kerama Retto, and in their sheltered waters a good-sized fleet could anchor. In retrospect, the decision to take these islands first was a godsend to the invaders.

The Kerama Retto had been intended as a place for fueling and replenishment. In this it would excel, but it would also be a place of succor, for the kamikazes would be in full cry at Okinawa. But even the Kerama Retto would not be left alone by the enemy, earning the sobriquet of "Bogey Gulch" or "Suicide Gulch" for the many attacks on the anchorage. Following the Kerama Retto landings, the Americans discovered that another suicide threat to the invasion fleet had been forestalled. The islands were the sites of many suicide boat installations. Hundreds of these small boats, each carrying two 250-pound depth charges, were to be used in suicide attacks against U.S. vessels, but the capture of the islands nullified these plans.

After too short a stay at Ulithi (and other anchorages), the invasion forces began moving out on 21 March for the last big battle. Three days later, the escort carriers entered their operating areas south of the Kerama Retto. That evening just after dusk, an accident occurred, which, fortunately, was not as serious as it could have been. A Hellcat night fighter from the *Sangamon* (then operating with TU 52.1.1) was in the landing pattern when, for some reason, it crossed over the *Natoma Bay*'s flight deck and struck her mainmast. Cartwheeling into the sea, the plane sank almost immediately, taking the pilot with it. For the most part, damage to the carrier was confined to communications and radar antennas, and most were repaired in a short time.[4]

Such accidents perhaps should not have happened. By this time in the war the squadrons reaching the combat zone were thought to be highly trained and qualified for combat carrier operations. In many instances this was true, but not always. For the *Chenango* it was not. "Several of the pilots, including the Air Group Commander, had

Rear Admiral Calvin T. Durgin aboard his flagship off Okinawa. (National Archives)

made only a total of eight carrier landings when they came aboard," the flattop reported later.

> The Group had never made a proper carrier rendezvous or join-up. Training in these fundamentals was conducted daily from San Francisco to Tulagi, but the operational losses of aircraft was high as a result of the group's inexperience.
>
> Since it is much easier to replace wrecked aircraft on the West Coast than at sea off Okinawa, it is believed that every effort should be made to give newly-formed groups more carrier experience before they depart in a combat carrier for active operations.[5]

Similarly, the *Breton* (engaged in ferrying planes and pilots to the combat carriers) would report, "Not one pilot of the 64 embarked has ever been catapulted."[6]

Despite comments like these, Durgin later stated, "The pilots received as replacements during this operation were far better trained than any received during previous operations. Evidently the program initiated by Commander Air Forces, Pacific, for training of pool pilots has produced excellent results."[7]

On the twenty-fifth the escort carriers began softening up the Kerama Retto for the landings. Numerous strikes were flown against targets at both the Kerama Retto and Okinawa, and several planes damaged by defending fire.

Results of these attacks were difficult to analyze, but the outcome of a tangle that day between Wildcats and enemy planes was easier to calculate. Shortly before 1800 a large bogey reported to be between five and fifteen aircraft was detected about forty miles from TU 52.1.1. As it continued to close with the force, a division of VC-92 fighters was vectored to intercept it. At 1813 the quartet saw the enemy, one Tojo and four Frans. The FM-2s, in good position for a bounce 1,500 feet above the Japanese, made a deadly attack. The Tojo went into the water first. Seeing their escort turn into a ball of flame, the bombers dove for the deck, but this didn't help. Two of the bombers were dispatched quickly and a third damaged. Even though damaged, this aircraft and the remaining Frances were able to outrun the Wildcats.[8]

About forty minutes later an Avenger pilot spotted five more Frans crossing in front of TU 52.1.2. Though taken under fire by the ships, this group scooted away unscathed into the growing darkness. There had been one loss to the defending fighters. Lieutenant James M. Alston, from VOC-1, had to ditch while returning from the CAP and was not recovered. In August 1944 Alston had been shot down behind German lines while flying with VOF-1 during the invasion of southern France. That time he had been lucky and had evaded capture to return to the squadron. On 25 March his luck ran out.

The next day the Army's 77th Division landed on several of the islands in the Kerama Retto. They encountered minimal resistance on the ground, and by the twenty-eighth the entire group of islands was declared secure. For the CVE fliers, covering these landings had been a fairly simple job, with only meager flak to contend with. An *Anzio* Avenger was lost, though this may have been caused by "friendly" forces; the pilot's last words were that he was being fired on by surface forces. A Tony was bagged by a *Makin Island* fighter but another enemy plane escaped.[9]

The twenty-sixth also saw the arrival of the first kamikazes. These initial forays were weak, caused in great part by the devastating raids

TF 58 had thrown against the Kyushu airfields on 19–20 March and another raid on the twenty-ninth. Also contributing to the destruction were B-29 attacks on the Kyushu fields on 27 and 31 March. These various attacks had the extremely important effect of delaying the concentrated air attack, named Operation TEN-GO, which the Japanese had been planning to inflict on the forces off Okinawa.

Meanwhile, on the night of the twenty-sixth both the *Anzio* and *Tulagi* left their respective units to operate independently in the antisubmarine role. As at Iwo Jima, this pattern of daytime support missions and nighttime antisubmarine operations was a fairly regular, and very tiring, feature of both carriers' work at Okinawa.

Of course, antisubmarine work was nothing new to the *Anzio*'s VC-13. While aboard the *Core* and *Guadalcanal* in the Atlantic, the squadron had sunk six U-boats. Still, more ASW operations were "discouraging" to the VC-13 airmen. The opportunity to participate in support missions and CAPs (which in one case would turn out quite to the squadron's liking) helped alleviate the monotony of the antisubmarine patrols.[10]

The morning of the twenty-seventh saw a minor clash between VC-9 TBMs and Japanese Vals. Orbiting about five miles north of the small island of Tokashiki, the crews of the four Avengers saw a pair of Vals streaking toward a fire support group that included the cruiser *Indianapolis*. Intent on crashing one of the ships and apparently not noticing the Avengers, the two Vals passed just two-thousand feet from the bombers. All turret gunners blasted away, and their fire appeared to hit both planes. Breaking away from the others, Lieutenant (jg) Peter H. Hazard gave chase in his lumbering Avenger. As pursuer and pursued dropped out of the sky they were enveloped by flak. Hazard's plane smashed into the sea, leaving no survivors. Seconds later one of the Vals nicked the destroyer escort *Foreman*'s bow, carrying away a lifeline and knocking a man off his feet. It had been close.

Some *Makin Island* Wildcats also tangled with a Val that morning. Chasing the kamikaze through the flak-filled sky, they were able to shoot the dive-bomber down, but not before one of the fighters was hit by the flak and disintegrated. Though the pilot was thrown clear, his parachute streamed and he was killed.[11]

With little opposition in the Kerama Retto, the CVE planes spent the last days of March hitting targets on Okinawa. They made special efforts, particularly on the twenty-ninth, to make the Okinawan fields untenable to enemy aircraft. On one such mission a pair of *Marcus Island* pilots observed a bomb-laden Oscar heading west. As they gave chase, they saw the enemy pilot rock his wings, jettison his bombs, and then turn back toward Yontan Airfield. The VC-87 pilots teamed up to air-condition the Oscar considerably but couldn't bring it down. Breaking off their attacks, the pair watched the Oscar spiral slowly down over Yontan to finally crash-land off the runway.[12]

The previous day the Yontan Strip had been devoid of aircraft. Today, however, VC-84 pilots found a wealth of targets—an estimated 20–30 Vals, Oscars, Tonys, Zekes, Nicks, and one Sally—sitting around the field. In a series of passes virtually at ground level lasting almost forty-five minutes, eight Wildcats beat up the field. When they left the scene twelve planes were burning and eight others had been damaged. In addition, another quartet of VC-84 fighters raided the Kadena field, south of Yontan. In this attack three Jills were claimed destroyed and four other planes damaged.[13]

Low clouds and rain in the target area on the twenty-ninth and thirtieth hampered considerably the fliers' efforts and made already dangerous missions even more so. On a mission on the thirtieth VC-84 and VC-93 pilots found themselves playing an unwanted game of "chicken" as the squadrons came at each other head on in the mist. Most planes were able to avoid one another, but two didn't. The prop of the Wildcat of VC-84's Ensign Henry Wardenga chewed into Ensign Gordon A. Collipriest's FM-2, ripping it apart. Just four hundred feet off the ground, the VC-93 pilot had no chance. Amazingly, Wardenga, trapped in his smashed cockpit and suffering agonizing injuries, was able to coax his battered fighter back to a safe landing on the *Makin Island,* where he had to be pried out of his cockpit.[14]

At dawn on 1 April a light overcast covered the Okinawa area. The air was slightly cool, but most of the marines and soldiers preparing to land probably took no note of the temperature. It was Love-day, the day of the landings. It was also April Fool's Day and Easter Sunday. The Japanese pulled an April Fool's joke on the Americans, but in return, the only Easter eggs delivered to the Japanese were those fired from the guns of the support ships offshore or laid by those predatory birds soaring overhead.

The April Fool's joke surprised the invaders. Expecting fierce resistance on the beaches, instead the assault troops walked ashore almost unopposed. The Japanese commander, Lieutenant General Mitsuru Ushijima, had left only small forces near the landing beaches to delay the invaders, massing the greater portion of his troops in the southern part of the island. A smaller force was also ensconced in the wild hills of the Motobu Peninsula.

Though the landings were easy, the Americans would soon find out that conquering the rest of the island would be a bloody task. Before the battle was over, Okinawa would be turned into a vast slaughterhouse. Still, the first few days on Okinawa went well for the invaders, the vitally important airfields, located at the spot of the landings, being taken with few casualties.

The planes from the escort carriers were busy from the outset, and the pace of these operations was such that the aircraft attrition rate began to soar. Thus, on the first the *Windham Bay* from the Plane Transport Unit made the first of what would become many deliveries of replacement aircraft to the combat CVEs.[15] Also from the outset the CVEs used the Kerama Retto roadstead on a rotating basis. When detached from their task units, the carriers and their escorts would proceed to the Kerama Retto, where they would spend the day taking on bombs and ammunition, then return to their unit. This system proved to be an efficient and swift method for keeping an optimum number of carriers on station. In the Kerama Retto ships' crews could not relax, however. The sight of the many ships anchored there was too tempting to the Japanese. Many attacks, both routine and kamikaze, were made on the anchorage during this operation, sinking a number of ships.

From the start of Iceberg enemy aircraft had been active, though not in the numbers they soon would be. Fighters from the fast carriers got most of the glory (and the planes), but the CVE squadrons also saw their share of air-to-air combat. On the first the CAP bagged a Tony west of the Kerama Retto, and the next day *Tulagi* planes caught some "easy meat," two Vals, and blasted both from the sky.[16] And better hunting was in the future—along with some bitter days, for the kamikazes were just warming up.

Not everything went the Americans' way, and several planes were shot down on the first two days of the invasion, although more often losses were not enemy-caused. Operational accidents were always the bane of carrier operations, and Okinawa was no different. For example, on 2 April a *Chenango* F6F landing on the *Sangamon* went through two barriers, badly damaging that fighter and another *Chenango* plane. Just an hour later another fighter took out the remaining barriers, in the process wrecking that F6F and causing major damage to three other Hellcats and three Avengers. Two of the fighters later had to be jettisoned.[17]

Action began to heat up for the escort carriers on the second. Anchored in the Kerama Retto were the *Lunga Point* and *Saginaw Bay,* both ships loading ammunition. Shortly before 0900 a Zeke popped out of some clouds to make a run on the *Saginaw Bay.* Heavy flak turned the Zeke toward an LST. This fire was clearly effective, because the Zeke began to wobble and lurch through the sky, finally falling into the water a few hundred feet from the LST. Discussing this attack, Captain Washburn said, "The thrill value of this attack was in no way lessened, however, by the timely demise of the Jap even though it was unorthodox from his point of view."[18]

Though this attack was unsuccessful, it served to keep the "jeep" crews on edge. That evening more attacks were thrown against the *Lunga Point* and other nearby units as they were returning to TU 52.1.1. No planes came close to the *Lunga Point*, but several transports were hit, and one, the destroyer transport *Dickerson*, had to be scuttled.[19]

From the first day, the planes of VOC-1 and VOC-2 had been busy providing gunfire spotting for the ships offshore. Okinawa was VOC-1's third operation in the Pacific, although only its second in a full-fledged spotting role. VOC-2 was making its first appearance in combat. Both squadrons were bedeviled by communication problems, most of these revolving around the much-disliked MHF radio sets, which were still the primary radios used in gunfire spotting. Despite protestations from such as Admiral Durgin about the inadequacy of these sets, they would be used until the end of the war. As at Iwo Jima, these spotting missions could 'e downright dangerous, VOC-1 losing five pilots on them. Nevertheless, this didn't stop either squadron from exerting every effort to do their jobs, even if this meant flying just fifty feet above the ground, an altitude that was not uncommon.

For VOC-2, a mission on 2 April was the "perfect example of air-ground and Army-Navy cooperation." That morning Lieutenant (jg) Richard A. Spindler was beginning his mission when he saw a trio of U.S. infantrymen, heavily burdened by their packs, trudging up a road. A few hundred yards away, unseen by the soldiers but visible to Spindler, a Japanese horse grazed. By zooming near the horse, Spindler was able to herd it toward the soldiers. When they finally saw the horse, they were able to corral it. As Spindler flew away he could see that one soldier "was stroking [the horse's] nose, another was slipping a rope over its head, and a third was lashing their combat packs on its back."[20]

The next day, heavy seas surged through the area. These didn't particularly hamper flight operations but did lead to some exciting moments. In the morning, while changing course, the *Lunga Point* rolled 23 degrees, flinging an FM-2 over the side and causing a lookout in the path of the plane to make a hasty, if unplanned, departure from the ship. It is claimed that, being a conscientious lookout, in mid-air on his forty-foot jump he took off his phones and reported, "Control. Lookout 3 going off the line." He was re-covered unhurt.[21]

The same day the *Steamer Bay* lost a sailor overboard when a railing broke. Unlike the *Lunga Point* seaman, he was not recovered. There was a sad irony in the loss of the sailor. Not happy aboard a CVE, for weeks he had been offering anyone one hundred dollars for a way to get off the *Steamer Bay*.[22]

Of greater import than the weather this day was the appearance of kamikazes near the CVEs. Shortly after 1700, bogeys congregated around TU 52.1.2. One raid slowly closed with the ships, then disap-peared. *Sargent Bay* fighters bounced a second raid of two Zekes or Judys and downed one of the enemy planes. The other escaped to press on toward the ships, but didn't last long; the destroyer *Capps* blew it out of the sky before it got too close.

As this plane burned on the water, two other planes surprised the *Wake Island*. The men on the flattop were still recovering from a violent roll the ship had taken just minutes before. Two Wildcats (with plane captains in their cockpits) rolled over the side; two other fighters were flipped on their backs; and four more fighters were thrown together and damaged. Luckily, there was no fire and the two plane captains were recovered.

The adrenalin had hardly stopped flowing when the Japanese planes caused it to start again. When first seen at 1743, the enemy aircraft were at about one thousand feet, rushing up from astern. The leading plane went into a steep dive and crashed into the water a hundred yards off the flattop's port bow. Already halfway into its dive when the first kamikaze splattered into many pieces, the second plane also missed the *Wake Island*, but not by much. It crashed along-side the carrier's starboard side just forward of the island. A plume of water shot high into the air and the *Wake Island* shuddered.

As the carrier's hull flexed from stem to stern, men were knocked off their feet. A hole 18 by 45 feet was ripped in her side, and soon she was listing about 5 degrees. No fires were started, and damage control parties quickly had the flooding under control. A full inspec-tion required a trip to the Kerama Retto, where it was discovered that the severe hull flexing had caused damage that could not be repaired there. After the hole in her side was shored up, the *Wake Island* left for Guam and repairs. She would be back.

Left behind when she went to Guam was her squadron, VOC-1. Although the men in the squadron believed they needed a rest, the higher echelons needed their spotting services more. Grumbling and griping, VOC-1 moved over to the *Marcus Island*, while that ship's VC-87 returned with the *Wake Island*.[23]

Following the attack on the *Wake Island*, Japanese aircraft remained near the ships, but declined to close. Finally, *Rudyerd Bay* fighters bagged one last Zeke, and the enemy planes departed around sunset. Because of their late departure, it was necessary for most of the CAP to land after dark. For the *Rudyerd Bay* it was a trying experience. Eight of her pilots had to make night landings. Unfortunately, none of the VC-96 fliers had been night-qualified, and it showed. The ensuing landings demolished two FM-2s and one Avenger and seriously damaged four other planes.

Watching this performance from his flagship, Admiral Stump was not impressed. Later, in "strongly" recommending that all pilots be night-qualified, Stump added, "We can rest assured that the time will come sooner or later when they [the pilots] will have to land after dark!"[24]

The next few days were fairly calm for the escort carriers. That changed on 6 April. Since March the Japanese had been husbanding their steadily dwindling supply of aircraft for a massed attack by both conventional and kamikaze planes. The raids by TF 58 in the last half of March had put a dent in these plans, named Operation TEN-GO, but had in no way curtailed them.

By the sixth the Japanese were ready to execute TEN-GO. Some 735 aircraft (303 of them kamikazes) were available for use on 6 and 7 April.[25] This was far short of the 4,500 aircraft the Japanese had been planning to use, but it was more than enough to wreak tremendous havoc on the U.S. fleet encircling Okinawa. Eventually, ten massed attacks, named *kikusui* or floating chrysanthemums, would fall upon the fleet.

The first attack howled in on the afternoon of 6 April. The day was cloudy and fairly cool, but many men would find themselves sweating profusely before it ended. After the morning's relative calm, the afternoon seemed to be one attack after another. Hardest hit were the destroyers and destroyer escorts, most acting as radar pickets. Though their planes were busy all afternoon, the CVEs weren't bothered by the kamikazes this day.

That afternoon things almost literally heated up on the *Anzio*. As a Wildcat was being catapulted, the napalm bomb it was carrying broke loose, splashing some of its liquid on members of the catapult crew. They were not seriously injured, but the bomb's fuze was burning and could explode at any moment. Disregarding the danger, ACOM R. D. Gipson straddled the bomb and carefully removed its detonator and fuze. Gipson then threw both over the side while the *Anzio*'s crew let out a big sigh of relief. During his exertions Gipson suffered slight burns, but was fit for duty in a few days.[26]

While another TBM waits its turn, a VC-9 photo Avenger gets ready to be catapulted from the Natoma Bay. *(Via* Natoma Bay *Association)*

Shortly after the napalm bomb incident, four more VC-13 FM-2s were launched for a support mission on Okinawa. About 1700 the quartet was still waiting for a target assignment when they received an urgent call to report to "Helpmate"—the destroyer *Colhoun,* which, with her sister ship, the *Bush,* was in serious trouble.

Earlier in the day the two destroyers had already beaten off several raids, but in the afternoon more than forty kamikazes ganged up on the two ships. The *Bush* knocked down several of the furiously attacking planes, but one got through to smash into the "tin can" and stop her dead in the water. Patrolling the next radar picket station, the *Colhoun* hurried to the *Bush*'s aid. She, however, would run afoul of the kamikazes' malevolence herself. Though the CAP downed many planes before they got near the ships, about fifteen Japanese aircraft broke through to pick on the mortally wounded *Bush* and the *Colhoun.*

At about this time, 1700, the VC-13 Wildcats arrived to observe a frantic scene. While the *LCS-64* was rescuing the *Bush*'s crew, the *Colhoun* was rapidly circling about them, her guns firing continuously. Darting in from every direction were Japanese planes. The four fighters immediately waded into the fight. Lieutenant (jg) Douglas R. Hagood saw a Val boring in off the *Colhoun*'s starboard bow. Ignoring the heavy flak, Hagood jumped the Val. The dive-bomber dropped a bomb, which missed the destroyer's bow, and as it zoomed up over her stern, Hagood got in a burst that sent the plane into the sea off the *Colhoun*'s fantail.

Spotting another Val making a run on the destroyer's port side just twenty feet off the water was Lieutenant (jg) Thomas N. Blanks. He also saw another plane streaking in on the starboard beam, with most of the "tin can's" guns blasting away at it. A solid burst from Blank's guns into the Val's cockpit caused it to half-roll, begin to blaze, and finally career into the water. As he pulled up over the *Colhoun,* Blanks saw the second enemy plane crunch into the destroyer with a tremendous explosion.

Meanwhile, Lieutenant (jg) William E. Davis pounced on a Zeke, with good results. The Zeke burst into flames and flew into the water just yards short of the destroyer. Looking around for other prey, Davis spotted a Val, but the heavy antiaircraft fire forced him to break off his attack. Said the action report, "By this time F6Fs and F4Us were on the scene and the competition for Japs was growing keen."[27] Though Davis's first Val had gotten away from him, a second was not so lucky. A Hellcat had just made a pass on this plane with apparently no results and was circling for another run when Davis arrived. Overtaking the Val as it made a slow turn, Davis raked its fuselage with his shells. The ex-kamikaze plunged into the sea.

Both Blanks and Hagood were still busy. Blanks saw a Val being chased by Hellcats. When the Val passed over the *Colhoun,* the F6Fs pulled away, but Blanks was waiting. Some .50-caliber shells sent it tumbling into the water, left wing first. In the meantime, Hagood was looking for a reported bogey somewhat east of the main action. A Zeke popped out of the clouds and Hagood gave chase. The Zeke did a slow roll and was in the middle of a second when Hagood let him have it. The fighter never finished the roll; it just spun slowly into the ocean.

High scorer for the VC-13 foursome was Ensign Eugene D. Pargh. His first victim was a Zeke that he chased over the *Colhoun* before finally planting it in the water. Pargh's next kill was a slow-moving Val that he shot down with several long-range bursts. Another Val was Pargh's last score. Beating two Hellcats to it, he fired from astern and sent it blazing into the water.

Because of low fuel and dwindling ammunition, the quartet had to leave the fracas. They had been impressed with the courageous fight put up by the *Colhoun,* but courage had not been enough. Despite the help of the defending fighters and their own guns, both the *Colhoun* and *Bush* went down the tremendous onslaught by an overwhelming number of kamikazes.[28]

VC-13 had not been the only escort carrier squadron to score big this day. Six enemy planes, the first airborne aircraft seen by any VC-93 pilot, had been destroyed by four squadron pilots in less than twenty minutes.[29] Four Vals went down quickly under the guns of VC-96 Wildcats.[30] In brawls with two groups of enemy aircraft, the *Lunga Point's* VC-85 bagged eight. Not a bad score, but the VC-85 fliers did not feel like celebrating. Following the last fight, one of the pilots radioed that he was low on fuel and was heading for Yontan. He never made it; two days later his body was found floating offshore.[31]

While the air battles were going on, the *Tulagi* was getting a close look at the kamikazes. Moored inside the southern entrance to the Kerama Retto roadstead, she was busy loading ammunition from three nearby Victory ships now serving as ammunition ships. At 1627, while this activity was under way, the *kikusui* attacks spilled over to the Kerama Retto.

The *Tulagi's* crew sighted a Zeke approaching very low from the port quarter and took it under fire. As the plane began to burn, it turned toward the nearest target, the *LST-447.* Despite more hits on the kamikaze from the LST's guns, the plane continued on to smack into the landing vessel just above her waterline. Within minutes an uncontrollable fire was raging, which burned for almost twenty-four hours before the LST sank.

More Japanese planes were attempting to penetrate the anchorage, one ducking behind a small island. Figuring that the plane would continue on its course, the *Tulagi's* gunners concentrated their fire at the other end of the island. Sure enough, the plane appeared where the flattop's fire was directed and went down, leaving a heavy trail of smoke.

Captain Cronin had been trying to get more fighters into the air to help the CAP and finally received permission from the senior officer present afloat (SOPA) to launch two FM-2s. All the ships in the roadstead were informed of the impending launch. This didn't do much good. Taken under fire by "friendly" ships just after being catapulted, one of the fighters was shot down, its pilot bailing out safely.

At last able to finish loading ammunition, the *Tulagi* weighed anchor and left the Kerama Retto. Her crew was very happy to leave for "safer" waters, for besides the *LST-447,* two of the nearby Victory ships had also been hit, burning and exploding for hours before they finally sank.[32] (The loss of the two vessels was a serious blow to the ground troops. Both had been loaded with the major portion of the 81-mm mortar shells in the United States. Because of their loss, there was a severe shortage of this ammunition during the rest of the battle, a shortage only partially alleviated by flying in more ammunition.)[33]

The sixth of April had been a horrendous day for the U.S. Navy off Okinawa. Besides the cargo ships and the LST, the *Bush* and *Colhoun* had been sunk. Ten other vessels suffered major damage and many casualties during this, the first and greatest of the *kikusui* attacks.

The *kikusui* attacks continued into 7 April, but these, though causing considerable damage, were not as severe as the previous day. Coming within a hundred yards of becoming a damaged vessel, though, was the *Sitkoh Bay*. She was part of the Special Escort Carrier Group bringing MAGs 31 and 33 to Okinawa. This group reached the Okinawa area on the sixth, at which time the *Hollandia* and *White Plains* were directed to postpone their launchings for several days because the LST transporting their marine squadrons' equipment and maintenance personnel had been bombed and much gear lost.[34] The *Sitkoh Bay* and *Breton* pressed on until they were sixty miles southeast of Okinawa.

About noon of the seventh they began launching brand-new 20-mm cannon-armed F4U-4Cs for Yontan. Eight Corsairs had just been launched as a CAP and the decks were being respotted when a twin-engined Lily put in an appearance. Five VMF-311 pilots jumped the Lily, ripping huge holes in its fuselage with their 20-mm fire. Though burning, the Lily charged on directly for the *Sitkoh Bay*'s bridge. Antiaircraft fire now began to tear into the kamikaze and it started to wobble. Then, just one hundred years from the carrier, the Lily slammed into the water to leave a funeral pyre blazing on the surface. VMF-311's Lieutenant John J. Doherty was given credit for the kill, but the *Breton*'s crew believed that at least a half credit should have gone to the *Sitkoh Bay*'s gunners.[35]

Two days later the *White Plains* and *Hollandia* sent the planes of MAG-33 to Kadena airfield, where they began combat operations almost immediately. One of MAG-33's squadrons, VMF-323 "Death Rattlers," would become the highest-scoring unit on Okinawa with 124½ enemy planes claimed.[36]

The seventh saw the first of a number of changes in the composition of the task units during the Okinawa battle. The *Savo Island* left TU 52.1.1 to trade places with the *Shamrock Bay*, then covering the ships of TG 50.8. A similar trade was made by TU 52.1.2's *Sargent Bay* and TG 50.8's *Makassar Strait*.[37] These temporary tours with the Logistics Group were welcomed by the carriers. They enabled the crews to get some rest, receive mail, and even watch some movies following the punishing routine of daily missions and alerts. They also enabled the mechanics to put in some much-needed work on the by now well-worn aircraft.

In the meantime, air support missions for the CVEs continued apace. One such mission on the eighth proved to be more exciting to a *Lunga Point* Avenger crew than they really wanted. Low clouds were hindering the attackers as they bombed enemy positions, forcing them to use shallower dives than normal. Making his first dive under these conditions was VC-85's Lieutenant (jg) Robert H. Cron. Just as he fired a salvo of rockets and began his pullout, Cron's TBM shuddered and its engine began to belch smoke. Oil splattered the windscreen, completely covering it. To find a place to set his plane down, Cron had to lean out of his cockpit.

Cron saw a level field and banked toward it. Skimming over a small village, he made a wheels-up landing. The Avenger skidded along for a short distance, then slid into a large mound, where it stopped abruptly. Flames swept back from the engine, threatening to trap the three crewmen. Hastily they jumped from the plane to race for a ditch 150 yards away. Just as they dove into the ditch, the Avenger's bomb load went off in a colossal blast, completely obliterating the plane and digging a crater a hundred feet in diameter.

For the moment the three men were safe, but they were in a perilous spot because American lines were two and a half miles to the north. Closer, but still almost a mile away, was Yonabaru Wan, a small bay on the eastern coast. That was where they would head, hoping to reach the beach and turn north. Their prospects were none too good, for they knew the Japanese were taking no prisoners.

Off they set. Frequently they had to dive for cover as U.S. artillery shells landed near them. Once they almost walked up to a camouflaged Japanese tank, but at the last moment they saw it and beat a speedy retreat. At last they reached the shore of Yonabaru Wan and started north along the beach.

So far their luck had held. Now it ran out. Every few moments the turret gunner, AOM2c Kenneth C. Orcutt, had been glancing back, covering their rear. Suddenly he gave a strangled cry. The other two men spun around. Pounding up from behind was a pair of riflecarrying Japanese soldiers, only a hundred yards away!

As rifle bullets whizzed past them, the trio began to run. Seeing a break in the seawall, Cron ducked through it and back inland. His two crewmen followed. This side of the seawall offered no cover either, and the two Japanese were soon taking potshots at them again. The only chance for the three Americans was the sea. Leading the way, Cron scrambled over the seawall and dashed toward the water. His radioman followed, but as Orcutt attempted to vault the wall, he cried out and fell, wounded or dead, on the landward side of the wall. The others couldn't stop to see what had happened to their companion but plunged on into the surf and inched their way out to sea.

Content just to watch and wait, the soldiers did not fire at the Americans. Cron and his radioman, ARM2c Rual W. Melton, found a coral ledge to stand on, but walking on it was very tiring, so they decided to move into shallower water. As soon as they tried this, though, the two soldiers began yelling and shooting at them again. Resigned to the fact that they were stuck on their coral ledge, the fliers looked about for salvation.

It came in the guise of an artillery observation plane. On a spotting mission, the pilot of the OY-1 saw the men still wearing their bright yellow Mae Wests. He dropped a raft which, unluckily, fell too close to the Japanese. Then, waggling his wings, he left, but not before contacting other units. Within ten minutes an Avenger showed up to circle Cron and Melton, followed a short time later by a pair of fighters. Then at 1300 two OS2U floatplanes landed, taxied up to the coral ledge under the watchful eyes of the fighters, and gathered Cron and Melton in. The time from when they had been shot down until they were rescued had been a little over four hours. One week later they were back aboard the *Lunga Point*.[38]

On the same day as Cron's and Melton's adventure, VOC-2's Lieutenant Irving M. Applebaum was spotting for a light cruiser in Nakagusuka Wan (a larger body of water of which Yonabaru Wan was a part). Suddenly he saw the telltale streak of a torpedo feathering through the water toward the cruiser. Quickly radioing this piece of news to the cruiser, he then attempted to destroy the torpedo by strafing it. He was unsuccessful, but the torpedo did become erratic and soon sank. Looking closely at the shoreline, Applebaum found the launching site, a set of tracks leading from a cave about 100 yards inland. After a pounding by the cruiser's guns and VOC-2 planes, no more torpedoes came from that cave.[39]

The eighth also saw Admiral Durgin's carriers take on a new task, that of trying to neutralize the Sakishima Gunto (a group of islands between Okinawa and Formosa) airfields. The Royal Navy's contribution to Iceberg, TF 57, had been covering these islands, which had been showing very energetic aerial activity. Because its ships were somewhat short-legged, TF 57 had to retire every few days for fuel. Thus, on the eighth the "big" CVEs of TU 52.1.3 initiated the "jeep's" participation in beating down any activity in the Sakishima

Gunto. This participation by various CVEs would continue through June.

The CVE fliers discovered that the Japanese on these islands were full of vim and vigor and were pretty good shots as well, much better than their compatriots on Okinawa. Nor did they scrimp on ammunition. The Sakishima Gunto, particularly the major islands of Ishigaki and Miyako, quickly earned the title of "Flak Alley." It remained a hot spot throughout the entire campaign; the Sakishima Gunto gunners would down planes until the end.

On the first day of the escort carrier attacks, Air Group 25's skipper, Lieutenant Commander Richard W. Robinson, was shot down over Ishigaki. Though he made a successful ditching five miles south of the island, a PBM Dumbo took five hours to reach the scene, and by that time Robinson had drowned. This episode left a bitter taste in the mouths of the TU 52.1.3 fliers, many calling the delay in the arrival of the Dumbo "inexcusable when a plane goes down almost every day."[40] The Ishigaki gunners would also get Air Group 24's commander, Lieutenant Commander Rexford J. Ostrom. Hit while on a strafing run, Ostrom bailed out, but his parachute failed to open.

But the biggest losses suffered by the escort carriers while engaged at the Sakishima Gunto were not caused by the enemy. Once again an operational accident was the culprit, the *Chenango* the victim. At midday on the ninth, Captain George van Deurs's ship was routinely recovering aircraft. The day was bright and warm and would be even warmer in just a few minutes.

A Hellcat had just landed and was taxiing ahead to join the closely packed planes gathered forward. Behind the fighter the barriers snapped back up in readiness for the next landing. Another fighter touched down hard and bounced, its tailhook grabbing the arresting wire. But this time there would be no solid thump as the wire brought the plane to a quick stop. Instead, there was a "twang" as the plane's tailhook broke and, unfettered, the fighter hurtled over the barriers.

The crash alarm yowled through the air, and plane handlers working on the planes forward glanced aft. Seeing the Hellcat bowling toward them, they ran, stumbled, or leaped toward safety. Caught in his cockpit, the pilot of the first fighter could only watch as the men suddenly disappeared from view. It was the last thing he would ever see.

"Like a giant auger," the propeller of the rogue plane chewed into the first Hellcat and its unfortunate pilot.[41] Jumbled together, what were once two aircraft rumbled ahead to crunch into the parked

An accident about to happen. A Hellcat bounces over the Chenango's barriers prior to smashing into the planes parked forward. (National Archives)

The Chenango's *senior flight deck CPO drags a plane away from the raging fire. Note the men with fire hoses under the plane's tail. (National Archives)*

planes. There was a dull boom, followed by a flash of flame. Black smoke billowed up and swept aft down the deck, enveloping the *Chenango*'s bridge in the dense, oily cloud.

Amid the burning planes, ammunition began to cook off, one rocket zooming aft through the smoke, others firing straight down through the flight deck. The initial explosion had ripped off the hatch leading from the forecastle into the officers' country. At his battle station there was a corpsman, Richard J. Seyler. When the explosions began, Seyler rushed forward to render aid. As he stepped through the torn hatchway, he almost tripped over the body of the *Chenango*'s first lieutenant. He had been scalped and was bleeding profusely.

All Seyler was carrying was his first aid pouch, but he immediately began working to save the grievously wounded officer. Noting no holes in the man's skull, Seyler carefully replaced his scalp, then wrapped yards of bandage about his head, leaving only small openings through which the man could see and breathe. Able to locate a stretcher, Seyler got his patient back to the sick bay. His prompt work saved the officer; in fact, the man would be left with only a small scar as a reminder of his close call.[42]

On the flight deck the pilot of the rogue plane somehow managed to stagger out of the flames. His flight suit did not appear even to be scorched, yet he was suffering from near-fatal burns. He was rushed to the sick bay. Captain van Deurs had ordered his ship swung out of the wind, and as the *Chenango* turned, the smoke shifted to flow over the carrier's port side so it would not be much of a factor.

Jumping onto one of the little tugs used to tow aircraft, the flight deck's senior chief petty officer quickly attached a tow-bar to one of the as-yet-undamaged planes. Then, ducking as machine gun bullets zipped past him, he pulled the plane to safety. He was able to return one more time to save another plane, but that was all. The fire was raging too fiercely to save any more.

In the gun tub just underneath the flight deck, a group of men were trapped. But they had fire hoses and for hours they were able to cool themselves and a loose 500-pound bomb teetering ominously just above them. Below these men, on the forecastle, corpsman Seyler and others were wading ankle-deep in gasoline. Suddenly it ignited in a big flash, engulfing the men in flames. Quick work in turning hoses on each other prevented many serious injuries, although Seyler's hair was burned off and he suffered other burns. So, like the first lieutenant, Seyler found himself in sick bay with his own head wrapped up like a mummy's. He still felt good enough to continue dressing others' wounds and burns.

The *Chenango* eased out of formation while her battle with the flames continued. After about four hours, the flattop's men won the battle. There was still some danger: the 500-pounder, now cooked to well-done but still very tender, lay menacingly at the forward end of the flight deck. The hazardous job of disposing of this threat was turned over to a specially selected crew. Unable to lift or roll it, they had to slide it inch by inch across the charred deck, using jury-rigged chocks to hold the bomb steady. After some time they reached the edge of the deck and, with a line, dumped the bomb into the ocean. It never exploded.

With the fire out at last, the crew could take a short breather. In the middle of the battle against the flames from the beginning had been the executive officer. He had seen and inhaled enough smoke to last a lifetime, but the first thing he said when he reported to van Deurs on the bridge was, "Gee, is the smoking lamp lit up here? I sure need a cigarette."[43]

The *Chenango* had been seriously hurt. Twelve aircraft were now just rubble, and her flight deck was charred but usable. A number of men had been injured and three killed. Because the remains of those who died had to be identified, Seyler, who "couldn't smell too well through [his] nose and being smelly [himself]," was elected to do the identifications using dental charts.[44] The following day the three men were buried at sea with full military honors. A tough ship, the *Chenango* was operating again with TU 52.1.3 within forty-eight hours.[45]

Over the next few days, routine strike missions were flown by all task units, but fighting again warmed up on the twelfth. Baying loudly around Okinawa that day were the kamikazes. The second wave of the *kikusui* attacks began on the twelfth, carrying over to the next day. Approximately 185 kamikazes, plus another 150 fighters and 45 torpedo planes, would be involved in this orgy of destruction.[46]

Bogeys began testing the radar pickets around 0600. For the rest of the day these dangerous pests hovered near the ships. The main attacks came after 1300. On picket duty 72 miles northwest of the landing beaches, the destroyer *Mannert L. Abele* was on the receiving end of the first *Oka* (a rocket-propelled suicider) to be seen by the Americans. Known as "cherry blossom" to the Japanese, the *Oka* soon received the epithet "*Baka*" (foolish) from the Americans. But there was nothing foolish about the speed and striking power of this new kamikaze type. Though she had been struck by another kami-kaze, it was the explosion of the little one-way terror that doomed the destroyer. The *Abele*'s midsection virtually disintegrated upon this impact and she sank like a stone. Fortunately, she was the only major vessel lost on the twelfth.[47]

(The crew of the *Makin Island* might have seen an *Oka* earlier in the day. Around 0500 a bogey had been tracked on radar, a bogey that suddenly split into two parts—probably indicating the separation of the rocket from its mother ship. A couple of minutes later an "object" whizzed past the carrier's bow to splash a thousand yards away. It had been moving so fast that in all probability it was a *Baka*, in this case a mis-guided missile.)[48]

Out in force all day trying to break up the *kikusui* attacks, and doing a good job of it, were the fighters from the "jeeps." Around 0915 CVEG-40's skipper, Lieutenant Commander J. C. Longino, caught a bomb-toting Myrt fifteen miles ahead of the task group. His first shots set the Myrt's left wing afire, and the plane began to wobble. A second burst exploded its gas tanks and it lurched into the sea, leaving three parachutes—one of normal size and two others much smaller—to descend slowly into the patch of wreckage burning on the water.[49] The real air battles didn't begin until 1300, however.

In a hard-charging fight north of Okinawa that afternoon, eight VC-93 FM-2s had a field day. One group of four planes was orbiting about fifteen miles north of Okinawa, the destroyer *Stanly* acting as fighter director. Soon the destroyer vectored Lieutenant (jg) R. C. Sullivan's division toward some bogeys headed south. They turned out to be four Vals strung out in a column and flying at 5,000 feet.

If the Val pilots took notice of the Wildcats barreling in toward them from the side, they gave no indication, continuing straight ahead. Picking the third Val in line as his target, Lieutenant R. E. Friedrich began firing as he approached from the side and continued as he mushed around on the Val's tail. On target almost immediately, his shells ripped the dive-bomber to pieces. The Val slowly tilted forward, then spun into the water. Sullivan took the second Val and closed to within fifty feet before opening fire from directly astern. The impact of his four fifties was deadly. The Val seemed to stop in mid-air, then fell away.

The next victim of the VC-93 fliers was the fourth Val in line. Like the previous two, this pilot refused to do any evasive maneuvers, just turning back to the north at his original speed. His first shots short, Ensign R. R. Parsons kept firing until he could see his tracers chewing into the Val's fuselage. Suddenly there was a puff of smoke, a flash of flame, and the aircraft was a fireball curving into the water.

So far none of the enemy fliers had shown any inclination to get away from their pursuers. This was not the case with the last pilot:

he threw his plane all over the sky. Some of Sullivan's shells hit the wildly gyrating Val, but most missed. Then the Val pilot started a climbing turn, leaving a small opening that Sullivan took advantage of. A short burst shattered the Val's canopy. The pilot obviously dead, the Val fell off on one wing and smashed into the water.

Not yet finished was the foursome. As the division rejoined at 3,000 feet, a pair of planes was seen headed their way at 1,000 feet. When these planes drew closer, they could be seen to be a Val escorted by an Oscar. The Val didn't last long. Making a flat side run, Friedrich was able to explode the bomber with three bursts. When he saw what happened to his cohort, the Oscar pilot began to run to the east, jinking violently all the while. Because of these maneuvers, Ensign Parsons had a hard time getting hits. Finally, after seven long bursts, Parsons was delighted to see the Oscar start burning and spin into the sea.

Hardly had the division rejoined once more than a Zeke was seen diving on an LCI. On his tail immediately was Friedrich, who disposed of this kamikaze in just a few seconds. Yet another plane, a Val, was spotted about 3,000 yards away and the four Wildcats tore after it. All four pilots took turns raking the dive bomber, but it was left to Lieutenant (jg) H. Foster to finish it off.

Foster was actually an Avenger pilot who had been recently indoctrinated into fighters tactics and the Wildcat, and was serving as an additional FM-2 pilot when needed. Obviously he was needed today and, equally obvious, his training had taken very well. After disposing of the Val, Foster saw an Oscar diving on a destroyer. By using water injection, Foster was able to get on the enemy's tail. Despite heavy flak, Foster stayed in this position. His fire took effect and the Oscar tumbled lazily out of the sky.

About five minutes later Foster saw a Zeke at 3,000 feet being chased by a Corsair. When the Zeke made a diving turn toward a ship, the Corsair overran, but Foster took its place. Again braving the antiaircraft fire (bursts of which would appear in his gun camera film), Foster scored some damaging hits. Nosing down, the Zeke splashed about 400 feet off the destroyer's port bow.

This division's work was done at last. In an outstanding action the four pilots had destroyed six Vals, two Zekes, and two Oscars. In the meantime, the other VC-93 division had also encountered enemy planes, but this time they wound up with the short end of the stick. The four Wildcats were orbiting at 18,000 feet several miles west of the other division when a Tojo was seen under attack by several Corsairs. The nimble Tojo was continually forcing its pursuers to overrun.

Finally, Lieutenant L. V. Lieb and his wingman, Lieutenant (jg) R. M. Reid, decided to show the Corsair pilots how it was done. Lieb made a head-on pass, and he could see his tracers entering the Tojo's engine and fuselage. As Lieb zoomed past the fighter, Reid took over with a high side run that killed the pilot. Flipping onto its back, the Tojo went into an inverted spin into the water.

While Lieb and Reid attacked that Tojo, Ensigns C. J. Janson and P. B. Baumgartner saw two others. These Tojos were also being attacked, unsuccessfully, by Corsairs. Both men dove to the attack. Seeing more trouble, the Tojos turned to meet the Wildcats. One of the enemy fighters tried to take out Janson with a tail pass, but Baumgartner discouraged him with several shots that started the Tojo smoking. When last seen, the Tojo was diving away, an F4U hot in pursuit.

Looking back at the remaining Tojo, Baumgartner saw Janson and a Corsair making simultaneous runs from 8 and 4 o'clock. Suddenly the Tojo turned and the FM-2 and F4U collided. Wings from both planes ripped off, and the wreckage tumbled out of the sky. One parachute blossomed, not Janson's, and Baumgartner watched it float downward.

His attention on the chute and where it would land, Baumgartner was unaware that the second Tojo had crept up behind him until his windscreen and instrument panel shattered under a hail of bullets. Fortunately, the Tojo pilot was not very aggressive and Baumgartner was able to chase him off in spite of an engine that was on its last legs. Seeing a pair of destroyers, Baumgartner intended to ditch alongside them. This plan came to an abrupt halt when both ships began firing on him, completing the job started by the Tojo. He had to ditch immediately and was picked up uninjured by another destroyer ninety minutes later.[50] Despite the loss of one pilot and two planes, the eight VC-93 pilots had fought a good battle, which resulted in a substantial reduction of aircraft in the enemy stockpile.

But they had not been the only CVE pilots to score this eventful day. Also picking off a pair of the obsolete Vals were some VOC-1 Wildcats. Yet another Val was destroyed by a *Lunga Point* Avenger. Seeing the dive-bomber crossing in front of him, the TBM pilot gave chase and, although an Avenger was not usually used as a fighter, engaged the Val in a short dogfight. At times the two planes got so low their propwash left a wake in the water. It was an uneven battle, and the dive-bomber was last seen burning in an Okinawan ravine. (Surprisingly, a *Makin Island* Avenger crew also claimed this plane, saying that the VC-85 TBM had chased the Val into their guns.)[51]

More Vals fell prey to other fliers. Four of the vulnerable planes

A VC-88 pilot shot down this Val on 12 April 1945, just one of many that fell to Wildcat guns that day. (National Archives)

fell to a quartet of VC-84 fighters, while two more, along with a Nate, were bagged by the spotters of VOC-2.[52]

Additional Japanese planes fell to escort carrier aircraft the next day. The big scorers were from VF-40. Led by the group commander, Lieutenant Commander J. C. Longino, four Hellcats were orbiting ninety miles northwest of Okinawa when at 1720 their picket destroyer vectored them toward an incoming bogey. At 1740 they spotted a Sonia (a fixed-gear reconnaissance aircraft similar in appearance to a Val) at 5,000 feet. Boxed in, the Sonia lasted only a couple of minutes.

Just minutes after returning to their station, the VF-40 planes were vectored toward some more bogeys. This time four Sonias were seen droning southward. This action was not really a fight, but more like an execution. Two of the enemy planes went down under the guns of Longino, while Lieutenant (jg) L. Monteau flamed the remaining pair. Like so many of their comrades before and so many to come, the Sonia pilots refused to maneuver, seemingly resigned to their fate.[53]

The thirteenth also saw TU 52.1.2 take over responsibility for the neutralization of the Sakishima Gunto airfields, a job that would last for three days. Determined to keep their airfields operational for the planes trying to stage through the islands, the Japanese threw up heavy volumes of antiaircraft fire. This flak downed two *Tulagi* planes and a *Marcus Island* fighter, with the loss of all these crews. Luckier were the pilots (one of which was VC-93's skipper) of two *Petrof Bay* fighters that were brought down by the flak. Dumbos picked up both fliers after just a few minutes in the water.[54] Losses were not one-sided. A number of enemy planes attempting to use the airfields were caught on the ground and destroyed.

Until the end Ishigaki would remain a tough target. On the fourteenth a fighter from the *Makassar Strait*'s VC-97 was shot down, although its pilot was able to induce his plane to stagger a few miles before ditching south of the island. VOC-1 planes covered the downed flier, but the Dumbo sent to rescue him ran low on fuel before a pickup could be made. To prevent the Japanese from sending a boat to capture the pilot, Bush Bringle and his wingman stayed around until darkness fell. Before returning to the *Marcus Island,* the pair made several impromptu strafing runs on Ishigaki installations, burning buildings reflecting the effectiveness of their attacks. The next day the Dumbo showed up to rescue the VC-97 airman.[55]

The four carriers of TU 52.1.3 returned to the Sakishima Gunto on the eighteenth, spending the rest of the month trying to keep the airfields inoperative. The *Sangamon,* with a contingent of night fighters, drew the job of sending night intruder and heckling missions over the islands. Generally these missions were without excitement, only serving to keep the enemy stirred up.

On the eighteenth, the first night of operations, a VF-33 pilot got in some productive target practice. Ensign John V. Delaney and another pilot had been launched at 2030 to conduct an intruder mission. The other pilot went to beat up the Miyako airfield; Delaney did the same to the Ishigaki strip and then droned around keeping the Japanese awake. Shortly he saw a plane circling the field and flashing a white light. After making sure it wasn't his partner, Delaney began to stalk the enemy plane, a twin-engined Nick. From about 200 feet Delaney loosed a couple of bursts. The Nick burst into flames, rolled on its back, and crashed near the field with a violent explosion. A large fire started and was spreading when the night fighters left to return to the *Sangamon.*[56]

This mission and others flown over the Sakishima Gunto could be exciting. Most, however, were not particularly entertaining for the airmen. As the *Chenango* put it, "The morale of the pilots and ship's company was not improved by the apparent lack of imagination displayed in continually cratering six airfields at Sakishima."[57]

Before TU 52.1.3 returned to action, *kikusui* No. 3, a collection of

The pilot of this VT-40 Avenger braces himself for a "cat shot" from the Suwannee, *21 April 1945. (National Archives)*

almost 400 kamikazes and escorts, swarmed in over Okinawa on 16 April. On the same day, elements of the 77th Infantry Division landed on Ie Shima, a small island just three and a half miles from Okinawa's Motobu Peninsula. To subdue the enemy would take five days of hard fighting. Among the casualties of this bitter fight was the famed war correspondent Ernie Pyle.

These *kikusui* attacks did not especially bother the escort carriers, the destroyers on radar picket duty around Okinawa once again bearing the brunt of the kamikaze attacks. Only the destroyer *Pringle* was sunk in these raids, but several other vessels (including the destroyer *Laffey*, which fought a magnificent battle against twenty-two of the one-way fliers) were seriously damaged.

If the kamikazes didn't bother the CVEs, CVE planes certainly

A division of VC-84 FM-2s over Okinawa on 15 April 1945. (National Archives)

bothered the kamikazes. In one action on the sixteenth, after working over enemy positions on Ie Shima, four VOC-1 fighters were
returning to the *Marcus Island.* Hearing that bogeys were approaching from the north, the four pilots began peering about trying to
spot the intruders. Soon they saw a pair of low-flying Kates. Lieutenant (jg) Edward W. Olszewski pounced on one of the green-painted
Kates. He closed in until he was only about 100 feet behind the
plane, then opened fire. Flames came from the Kate's engine as it
rolled to the left and plowed into the water. The Kate was added to
Olszewski's scorecard of two Ju 52s shot down over southern France
in August 1944. The second Kate didn't escape. All four pilots took
turns blasting it out of the sky.[58]

Besides kamikazes, there was another danger that the escort carriers had to face at Okinawa: floating mines. Hardly a day went by
without several of these mines being sighted and having to be destroyed by the carriers or their screening vessels. It is possible that
some of the mines were duds, but the resounding explosions of
many as they were detonated by gunfire showed that no chances
could be taken.

With so many mines seen daily, everyone on the *Chenango* could
only manage a weak smile at Admiral Sample's remark, "It's a good
thing there aren't any mines out here after dark."[59]

New targets were hit on the eighteenth. The tiny islands of Minami Daito and Kita Daito, lying almost 200 miles east of Okinawa,

received the attention of twelve *Marcus Island* Wildcats. It was no picnic for the attackers. Antiaircraft fire was extremely heavy, holing several planes and swatting two others out of the sky. One of the latter pilots was rescued by a Dumbo, but the other was killed.

Almost lost himself at Kita Daito was Bush Bringle. Flak slashed through his FM-2, cutting his throttle linkage. The fighter's 1,350-horsepower Wright Cyclone stopped cold. Bringle was getting ready for a water landing when, just a few feet from the water, the Cyclone caught hold again. It was barely ticking over and Bringle had no throttle or prop control, but at least the Wildcat was flying. In this condition 170 knots was the speed at which the FM-2 was going to fly. For the time being Bringle was just along for the ride.

It took him about an hour to get back to the *Marcus Island*. Bringle had plenty of time to figure out how he was going to land. Now he would see if he had figured right. He could get his wheels down, but his flaps were inoperative and, of course, he had no throttle control. A waveoff was out of the question. Lining up with the flattop's deck, Bringle made a flat approach. To control his speed, he had to flip his magneto switch on and off, an interesting and delicate procedure in these circumstances. Just as if it were an everyday occurrence, he planted his fighter down in what Captain H. V. Hopkins later termed an "extraordinarily excellent landing."[60]

By this time at Okinawa the CVEs had settled down into a monotonous cycle of daily strikes, photo missions, CAPs, and so forth. Targets were attacked with, usually, few observable results. It was frustrating, boring work; work, however, that could end in sudden, painful death. On one of these strike missions VC-83's skipper, Lieutenant Commander Billy V. Gates, collided with another plane strafing the target. Neither pilot was able to escape before their planes smashed into the ground.[61]

Day after day, though, the fliers went out to do their jobs. Also doing their jobs were the ships crews, and their routine too could be monotonous and frustrating. Complained the *Chenango*, "The multitude of daily and special reports required kept one officer busy collecting and checking information most of the time. It sometimes seemed more difficult to get out the required reports on time after a strike than to prepare the flight."[62] Escaping, at least for a short while, from this monotomy of strikes and reports, more strikes and more reports, was the *Natoma Bay*. For some time she had been bothered by engine problems, and these finally became too much. On the seventeenth she left for Guam, where her balky engines were repaired. The flattop would return to Okinawa in enough time to see a lot more action.[63]

Another frustrating mission for the "jeeps," in particular the *Anzio* and *Tulagi*, was hunting submarines. This vital job was usually without excitement, the fliers spending many hours boring holes in the sky and never seeing anything but blue seas and whitecaps. Then there would be that moment when a submarine was sighted. The resulting attack might or might not be successful, but it certainly got the adrenalin pumping.

For the *Anzio* one of these moments came on 24 April. The flattop had been detached from TU 52.1.1 (where she had been operating primarily as a close support carrier) a day earlier to look for a reported sub east of Okinawa. On the afternoon of the twenty-fourth one of the carrier's pilots saw a surfaced submarine. His attack was unsuccessful, however, and despite the efforts of this TBM crew, relieving Avengers' crews, and a pair of DEs, efforts that continued until the twenty-seventh, the submarine escaped.

Following this unproductive mission, the *Anzio* headed for Ulithi for a bit of rest and a lot of maintenance. At Ulithi her dazzle pattern camouflage was replaced with a fresh coat of navy gray. Also replaced were VC-13's TBM-1Cs, their place being taken by TBM-3Es with improved radars. In late May the *Anzio* returned to Okinawa.[64]

Luckier than the *Anzio* in the quest for enemy submarines was the *Tulagi*. VC-92 planes came close on 25 April when sonobuoys dropped near an oil slick radioed indications of a submarine. Several Fido attacks were made, but the underwater noises continued to be heard until they finally faded away. The Avenger crews were disappointed that no kill had been made, but their kill would come soon enough.

Launched from the *Tulagi* at 1418 on the twenty-ninth, Lieutenant (jg) Donald L. Davis was on the first leg of his search pattern when he saw a fully surfaced submarine heading east. From 4,000 feet Davis swept down on his quarry. Seeing the Avenger screaming in, the sub's captain began maneuvering his vessel violently, yet at first he did not try to submerge. Finally the sub swung around toward the TBM and began to dive. When Davis reached his drop point, the sub's conning tower was still visible, though getting lower in the water. He toggled out one depth bomb from 800 feet, and the bomb exploded a few feet to the right of the conning tower.

Davis racked his "Turkey" around in a tight turn, dropping his flaps and slowing to 110 knots at the same time. The turn took only thirty seconds, and as he roared in from directly astern, Davis could see water "boiling from the craft's screw's." He dropped a Fido from one-hundred feet, landing smack in the middle of the swirl.

A hunter-killer carrier—the Tulagi. *(National Archives)*

For about half a minute nothing happened; then suddenly the sea seemed to bulge, and green dye from the Fido's internal marker stained the water. Davis dropped several sonobuoys, and over them came "loud crunching and cracking sounds," the death throes of a submarine. Soon an oil slick began to coat the ocean's surface, gradually becoming larger. Davis was joined by more planes and a pair of destroyer escorts, but there was no need for this increased activity. Now lying at the bottom of the sea, the *I-44* would never surface again.[65]

While the *Tulagi* planes were hunting, and finding, a submarine, VOC-1 fliers were hunting, and finding, a covey of Vals near Okinawa. *Kikusui* No. 4, consisting of 120 navy and 45 army planes, only 59 of which were kamikazes, was thrown against the U.S. fleet on 28 April.[66] That afternoon a division of FM-2s led by Bush Bringle was vectored toward some bogeys by a radar picket destroyer. The bogeys the VOC-1 team flushed were a pair of Vals.

Bringle flamed the first Val almost immediately and it fell out of control. The second Val was a bit tougher. The entire division was needed to bring it down, with Bringle almost getting hit himself when he flew in front of his wingman, who was then firing at the dive-bomber. Partially enveloped in flames, the Val still tried to make a fight of it but was torn apart by a torrent of .50-caliber slugs.

About an hour later, another division of VOC-1 fighters encountered a quartet of Vals northwest of Okinawa. When first seen, the leading three aircraft were flying in a loose V. Seeing the Americans at the same time, the Japanese leader waggled his wings and his wingmen opened out and down. This maneuver just made the Vals more vulnerable.

Lieutenant (jg) T. H. McManus opened up on the right-hand Val with no discernible effect. Passing over that plane, McManus fired on the Val to the left. Gas began to stream from the bomber's left wing tank. McManus was joined by Lieutenant F. S. Schauffler, and the pair took turns shooting at the seemingly indestructible Val. This indestructibility lasted just a few moments longer, the plane suddenly skidding off to one side, digging a wing into the water, and breaking into many pieces.

The right-hand Val escaped McManus but did not escape Lieutenant (jg) R. V. B. Yentzer. As Yentzer's four fifties hammered the Val, a streak of crimson flowed back from its right wing root. This quickly spread until the entire right side of the fuselage was covered. Twisting and tumbling, the Val crashed.

Rather spectacular was the demise of the leading Val. From directly astern, Lieutenant (jg) W. A. Foley opened fire. The bomber began to blaze, then broke apart. Trying to get out of his dying aircraft, the enemy pilot was flung into the air as the .50-calibers ripped into him. Left shimmering in the air as the Val fell in two parts were hundreds of thin silvery discs, possibly "window."

As Yentzer and Foley finished their work, another Val stumbled onto the scene. He didn't last long. Both pilots filled the plane full of holes; it caught fire and spun into the ocean.[67] Three more of the obsolete Vals fell to the guns of the TU 52.1.2 fliers, bringing the total to nine. Enough kamikazes got through the defensive screen thrown up by the CVE, land-based, and TF 58 planes, however, to damage nine ships, including the easily identifiable hospital ship *Comfort.*

In late April a major change for the escort carriers off Okinawa took place. Land-based aircraft were taking over more of the ground support duties, and it was finally possible to reduce the number of CVEs at Okinawa. Thus, on the twenty-ninth TU 52.1.2 was dissolved, with some flattops heading back to Guam for a short rest or back to the United States and major refits. The general organization for Durgin's force was now seven CVEs in TU 52.1.1 and four in TU 52.1.3 for direct support missions, one in TU 50.7.3 for ASW work, and two in TU 50.8.13 for Logistics Group protection.[68]

Leaving on the twenty-ninth were the *Savo Island, Marcus Island,* and *Saginaw Bay,* taking with them Admirals Stump and Henderson. (Henderson would return to command TU 52.1.1 for a short period in May.) Durgin later stated that Stump had been "by far the best of all the Escort Carrier Division Commanders" under Durgin's com-

It was a long, tiring battle for the "jeeps" off Okinawa. Here some of the flight deck crew try to get some shut-eye on the Suwannee. *(National Archives)*

mand.[69] But Stump, having been in action since the fall of 1943, badly needed some rest. Some of the squadrons would not be going back with their ships. Swapped with the *Makin Island*'s VC-84 was the *Savo Island*'s VC-91. In another trade, the unlucky fliers of VOC-1 only got a couple of weeks' rest before reembarking on their original flattop, the *Wake Island,* which returned to action in late May.[70]

There was one other change of note during this period, one with amusing overtones. On 8 April Captain Harry D. Felt reported aboard the *Chenango* with orders to relieve George van Deurs as the ship's skipper. This surprised and angered van Deurs, as he had not received his own orders. He told Felt, "Well, that's nice, but I haven't got any orders to go anywhere. Sit down and have a cup of coffee and make yourself at home. I'm not turning over."[71]

So Felt sat and watched while van Deurs ran the ship until he received his own orders. It took almost a month, but Felt finally took command of the *Chenango* on 2 May, van Deurs becoming a commodore and moving up to become chief of staff to Admiral Oldendorf.

There must have been something about the *Chenango* that instilled in her captains an intense pride in their ship, because a similar incident had occurred when van Deurs himself had reported in August 1944 to relieve Dixie Ketcham. Ketcham would not relinquish command until he reached the proper port for the change of command ceremonies. Needless to say, it took several days before van Deurs was at last in command.[72]

Though there were fewer escort carriers off Okinawa now, there was no relaxation in the pounding of the enemy on that island or in the Sakishima Gunto. On 3 May the Japanese did some pounding of their own. The next kamikaze attacks, *kikusui* No. 5, began that day and succeeded in sinking a destroyer and an LSM (Landing Ship, Medium) and damaging four other vessels. Another destroyer was attacked by three Judys, the kamikazes themselves being jumped by four VC-96 Wildcats, which drove off two of the raiders. The remaining suicider continued on, but the destroyer's accurate gunfire blasted it out of the sky before it got too close. Her gunfire was perhaps too accurate, for it also shot down one of the pursuing FM-2s. After but four minutes in the water the pilot was picked up unhurt by an LCS (Landing Craft, Support).[73]

The following day was even worse for the Americans. One of the unfortunate recipients of the kamikazes' attention was the *Sangamon*. The fourth was very cloudy, and the clouds provided excellent hiding spots for the kamikazes. Shortly before dawn the *Sangamon* and her two escorts slipped into the Kerama Retto to take on ammunition and supplies. During her stay there, general quarters was sounded three times, slowing the replenishment process. And had it not been for the late arrival of some aviation lubricating oil, she would have left the anchorage earlier. This delay may have turned a routine day into a disastrous day.

At 1830 the *Sangamon* finally got under way, heading south to rejoin TU 52.1.3. Low cumulus clouds hung heavily and wetly in the sky, particularly to the west, where a setting sun painted the clouds with brilliant splashes of reds, oranges, and pinks. The ocean, initially colored a beautiful clear blue, gradually turned to a slate gray as the sun went down. Most of the ammunition that had been taken on earlier had been struck below. Only some boxes containing 5-inch rocket bodies and a like number of rocket warheads were still stacked in the hangar when a large raid was reported closing from the southwest.

Marine Corsairs shot down four of the planes in this raid, but the remainder kept on. At 1902 a plane identified as a Tony was seen circling left very fast to a position off the *Sangamon*'s port quarter. Watching the plane closely, Captain Malstrom ordered a hard left turn as well as ordering his gunners to open fire. Joining in were the

The Shamrock Bay *leaves the Kerama Retto on 4 May 1945. In the foreground the* Sangamon *prepares to leave. (National Archives)*

flattop's escorts, the *Dennis* and *Fullam,* as well as a passerby, the minesweeper *Spear.*

The Tony made a wide arc, then barreled in from astern. Antiaircraft fire hit the kamikaze, but it wasn't stopping it. Suddenly smoke began to stream from the Tony and it rolled to the left. Only a few hundred yards from the *Sangamon,* the plane seemed to be upon the carrier in an instant. Luck was on the *Sangamon*'s side. Apparently out of control, the Tony, wings in a vertical position, slashed into the water just twenty-five feet off the starboard quarter.

As a towering plume of water shot into the air, the carrier quivered all over. Luckily, considering the proximity of the explosion, only one antenna was sheared off. Three sailors, seeing the Tony seemingly about to land in their laps, dove overboard, but were soon picked up by the *Spear.*[74]

Relative quiet reigned for the next half hour, enabling ordnancemen to finish sending the rockets stowed on the hangar deck down the recently installed bomb elevator to the magazines and closing its hatch. The sun set at 1903, and a few minutes later two night fighters were catapulted for night CAP. They were hardly airborne when they were vectored toward a bogey twelve miles away. Nothing was found, and the Hellcats returned to circle the ships.

At 1925 the *Fullam* reported another bogey, also twelve miles

A Tony zeroes in on the Sangamon . . . *(National Archives)*

away. Vectored out again at 2,500 feet, the two night fighters just missed the enemy plane, which had apparently come in very low. As the suicider broke through some clouds three miles away, it was taken under fire. It ducked back into a heavy black cloud aft of the *Sangamon,* and all firing was checked. Moments later the plane, now identified as a twin-engined Nick, plunged out of the cloud heading right at the carrier. Intense flak that lit up the darkening sky ripped into the Nick but did not knock it off its fatal course. Roaring in from astern at over 350 knots, the Nick leveled off slightly for a moment, then nosed over again in a shallower dive. About 600 yards away, its left engine began to blaze. Yet on it came. Just before the Nick slammed into the carrier, it dropped a bomb that penetrated the flight deck to explode in the hangar. A fraction of a second later

. . . and just misses. (National Archives)

the kamikaze followed its bomb through the flight deck just a few yards farther on. Most of the plane, including its engines and heavily armored wing sections, wound up in the hangar.

A "tremendous, blinding, gaseous explosion" rocked the ship.[75] Both of the *Sangamon*'s elevators (each weighing twenty-six tons) were blown out of their wells. The after elevator was deposited, upside down, on the edge of its well, and the forward elevator was canted and thrown onto the flight deck. Between the elevators the flight deck itself was buckled upward, a hole twenty by ten feet in the center.

All over the carrier, men were knocked off their feet. Shrapnel sliced through thin steel and men with impartiality, cutting men down in the code room, the clipping rooms along both catwalks, and in the midships pump room. Luckily it was standard operating procedure on the *Sangamon* for personnel on the hangar deck to clear that area when the guns started firing, and no one was in the hangar when the Nick hit.

Orange tongues of flame licked at the bridge and black clouds of smoke swirled about it. Captain Malstrom ordered everyone off the bridge except for himself, his orderly, the navigator, and the helmsman. The flattop had been hit at 1933. Communications remained intact for a while, and Malstrom was able to order a turn out of the wind. By 1955, though, all communications from the bridge had been lost, and the *Sangamon* began an uncontrolled turn. Steering was finally assumed aft, steadying the ship on a southerly course. Because of the heat from the fire and the choking smoke, the bridge was abandoned at 2025, Malstrom establishing a command post at the forward end of the flight deck.

Below, in the hangar, an inferno was raging. Eleven planes were in the hangar. All had been degassed, but this didn't stop the fire from spreading wildly. Some men had already been blown off the ship, and the mounting flames forced more to leap for safety. The fire effectively split the ship into two sections, and it was fought from both ends with no coordination between the firefighting parties. A great impediment to the firefighters was the failure of the hangar deck water curtains and sprinkler system, caused by damaged risers and the isolation of water valves by the fire. After a lot of hard work by repair parties on the risers and by finally reaching some of the valves, most of the sprinkler system was activated.

As the men ran hoses from each end of the hangar, another danger became evident. Though the planes had been degassed, they had not been dearmed. This ammunition, and that in the clipping rooms, began to go off. Fifty-caliber and 20-mm shells whizzed through the air and out the thin sides of the ship. Moving his hose forward to fight the blaze, AMM3c Ted Mann caught one of these wild shells in his helmet and was knocked cold. Waking up a few minutes later with a splitting headache, Mann continued to fight the fire.[76]

Other individuals were fighting their own battles with the conflagration. As he inched forward against the blistering heat, one man said, "Hell, this is just like fire school only they didn't have all that damn .50-caliber and 20-mm ammunition exploding. Wonder if that damn stuff is dangerous."[77]

Lieutenant John McDuell and another man teamed up to crawl onto the smoldering hangar deck using a foam nozzle to beat down the fire. Others soaked them constantly with a stream of water to keep them from being burned by the fiery debris from above. The use of foam and water did not always prove so compatible. When one group would get a burning plane liberally coated with foam, their handiwork would promptly be washed off by others following with a stream of water. At one point the firefighters were temporarily driven back by what was thought to be another bomb explosion but turned out to be a bursting arresting gear accumulator.

Not just on the hangar deck were the *Sangamon*'s men fighting to save their ship. Crewmen on the flight deck were manhandling those planes yet unburned out of the way of a number of planes set afire. The only place to push the aircraft was over the side. A runner went forward to seek permission to jettison the unburned planes; by the time he was able to fight his way through the chaos amidships and return with the permission, the planes were already overboard.

Meanwhile, a number of vessels closed with the *Sangamon* (now dead in the water) to render assistance. The *LCI-61* fought the hangar deck fire from the port side. While attempting to do the same, the *LCI-13* had her superstructure damaged extensively when the carrier swung into her. On the starboard side the destroyer *Hudson* was supplying water through eight hoses, but like the *LCI-13*, she suffered heavy topside damage. She was lucky, too. While she was alongside the flattop, a burning plane fell from the flight deck onto her depth charges. Before these exploded, her crew pushed the burning remains of the plane overboard.

By 2130 it was possible to move back and forth along the flight deck. In another half hour all fires were reported under control. Malstrom later said, "Again it has been proved that firefighting school is worth all the man days it requires."[78] The *Sangamon* was not a pretty sight. Her flight deck was broken and charred; heaps of ash and metal marked the remains of aircraft, of which only one was left undamaged; the island was scorched and unusable; the hangar was completely gutted, with roller curtains blown out and bulkheads bent outward; her steel sides were riddled and torn; seventeen men were dead or dying and many others wounded. But she was still afloat. That was amazing. No other escort carrier faced with a hangar fire of such magnitude had survived. And some fleet carriers, notably the *Franklin*, had been hard pressed in their battles with such fires.

The Bureau of Ships noted several factors that led to the *Sangamon*'s survival. Her planes had been degassed; all hangar personnel had cleared the hangar, reducing casualties there; and *all* hands had been thoroughly trained in firefighting techniques.

There were two other factors that gave the *Sangamon*-class ships an advantage over other carriers in overcoming a hangar fire. Loss of stability due to the large volumes of firefighting water sloshing about

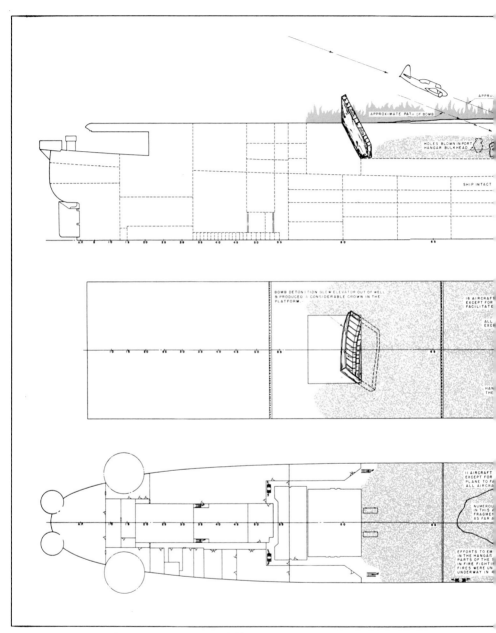

Sangamon *Kamikaze Damage, 4 May 1945*

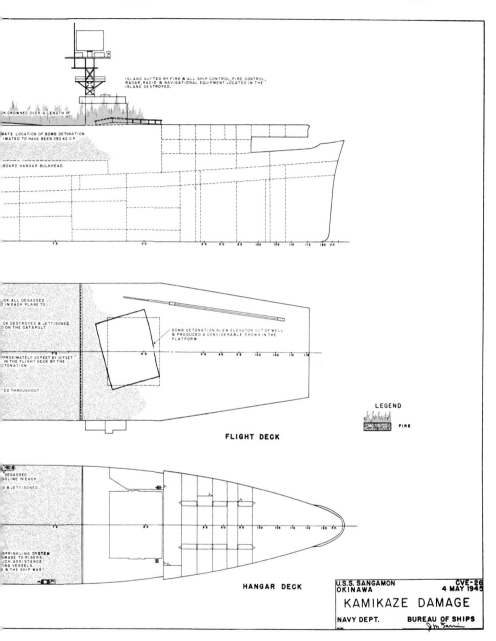

ISLAND GUTTED BY FIRE & ALL SHIP CONTROL, FIRE CONTROL,
RADAR, RADIO & NAVIGATIONAL EQUIPMENT LOCATED IN THE
ISLAND DESTROYED.

K CROWNED OVER A LENGTH OF

ATE LOCATION OF BOMB DETONATION
IMATED TO HAVE BEEN 250 KG G P

BOARD HANGAR BULKHEAD.

CK ALL DEGASSED
IN EACH PLANE TO

CK DESTROYED & JETTISONED
ON THE CATAPULT

BOMB DETONATION BLEW ELEVATOR OUT OF WELL
& PRODUCED A CONSIDERABLE CROWN IN THE
PLATFORM.

PPROXIMATELY 20 FEET BY 10 FEET
IN THE FLIGHT DECK BY THE
TONATION.

ED THROUGHOUT

LEGEND

FIRE

FLIGHT DECK

DEGASSED
OLINE IN EACH

D & JETTISONED.

SPRINKLING SYSTEM
AMAGE TO RISERS.
UCH ASSISTANCE
NG VESSELS.
B THE SHIP WAS

HANGAR DECK

U.S.S. SANGAMON	CVE-26
OKINAWA	4 MAY 1945

KAMIKAZE DAMAGE

NAVY DEPT.   BUREAU OF SHIPS

high in the ship, such as occurred on the *Franklin* and *Gambier Bay*, was eliminated by the open main deck under the hangar. Also, again in contrast to the *Franklin* and the *Ommaney Bay*, the *Sangamon*'s machinery spaces were aft of the hangar and were able to function relatively normally throughout the fire. An amidships type of engineering plant would have had serious problems.[79]

At 2320 the *Sangamon* was under way again. An Aldis lamp borrowed from the *LCI-13* and a VHF radio from her sole remaining aircraft were her only means of communications with her two escorts. Shortly after dawn she rendezvoused with TU 52.1.3. In her battered state she made a great contrast to her sisters, the *Suwannee*, *Santee*, and *Chenago*. And there was a newcomer also steaming gracefully with the other carriers—the *Block Island*, one of the new *Commencement Bay*–class vessels that had been specifically designed as an escort carrier. Her design owed much to the *Sangamon*.

After cruising with TU 52.1.3 all day, the *Sangamon* departed on a long journey back to Norfolk. She had been in the war from North Africa to Okinawa, and she and her crew had fought well. Now she would fight no more.[80]

The fourth of May had been a terrible and bloody day for the U.S. Navy at Okinawa. Besides the *Sangamon*, sixteen other ships had been damaged by the kamikazes, and the fury of these attacks had sunk four more vessels. Yes, it had been a day of great slaughter, but the ships and crews never wavered and the navy remained at Okinawa.

The kamikaze that struck the carrier had not been deterred by the *Sangamon*'s firepower. This lack of stopping power had first been seen at Leyte Gulf. The single 20-mm mounts that made up the majority of the guns on the *Sangamon*- and *Casablanca*-class carriers took the brunt of the complaints. Though effective against normal air attacks, the 20-mms were just too light to stop the determined attacks of the kamikazes.

The replacement of the single 20-mm mount with double mounts, not much heavier, had been seriously considered, but the fitting of these new mounts had started on very few ships when the war ended. There were other proposals. At least one recommendation was for the installation of rocket batteries; another concerned the use of some unspecified "death ray."

Several of the CVE captains took things into their own hands, installing .50-caliber guns in various positions on their ships. The *Hoggatt Bay* carried eighteen such weapons on tripod mounts, while the *Natoma Bay* had several fifties mounted on her forecastle. Captain Nichol of the latter ship believed these guns served only as morale builders. It is hard to see how the smaller machine guns could have much effect, being shorter-ranged with shells of lighter weight. Only in volume of fire would the .50-caliber be useful on the escort carriers.

There was one interesting example of an experimental installation of some machine guns on an escort carrier. In early 1945 the *Cape Gloucester* was fitted with four of the army's Mark 31 quadruple .50-caliber mounts. They had a tremendous rate of fire and were devastating at short range, as German soldiers often discovered to their grief. But because of their weight, relatively short range, and complexity, these quad mounts were dispensed with following the war.

In addition to the above armament limitations, the escort carriers had a concomitant problem, a lack of screening vessels. Escort carriers were generally screened by destroyer escorts, and few of them. The newer destroyers went to TFs 58/38, more were assigned shore gunnery missions, still more destroyers and destroyer escorts were guarding convoys around the world. Still, it seemed that CVE groups, which were involved in vital invasion support operations, were often given the leftovers.

Captain Robert Goldthwaite of the *Saginaw Bay* earnestly presented the problem in his action report. "No target is so vulnerable to attack and total destruction as the CVE Task Unit as presently constituted," he reported.

Forced to remain within a restricted area close to the objective for protracted periods, it is readily located and the enemy can bide his time to avail himself of the most favorable time and conditions for attack. Composed of 5, 6, or 7 CVE and an average of not over 8 DE-DD screen vessels, disposed in a comparatively widespread formation for launching and recovery of aircraft, lacking altitude computing radar and possessing the inadequate AA battery now installed in CVE and in the DE which comprise a large part of its screen, it presents the most vulnerable target, protected by the weakest AA defense, of any available objective of comparable importance.

This weakness of AA defense could not be overlooked by anyone who went through the past operation [Okinawa]. It was a cause for serious concern at all times, and especially during the dusk and dawn periods and on bright moonlight nights, when the only real means of defense, the CAP, is ineffective. This concern does not indicate any lack of courage, determination, or willingness to accept these conditions on the part of the personnel if nothing can be done about it or if other military considerations warrant such risk. However, if the air effort made available at the objective by the CVE Task Units is of sufficient importance to warrant the expenditure of the time, money, personnel and material required to build, train, equip and operate the CVE, then it would appear that such a unit is sufficiently important to warrant reasonably adequate protection against sure destruction whenever the enemy decides to make it the objective and attack in strength.[81]

The newcomer that the *Sangamon's* crew had seen, the *Block Island,* was carrying a unique air group—MCVG-1 (Marine Carrier Air Group One). Fearful of having its air units left in the backwash of the war, for some time the Marine Corps had been agitating to get its squadrons aboard carriers. Finally, in mid-1944 the navy and marines worked out a plan that would put marine squadrons on CVEs. (Actually, the kamikaze threat forced the use of marine squadrons on the *Essex*-class carriers before their use on the escort carriers.)

On 21 October 1944, a Marine Carrier Groups, Aircraft, Fleet Marine Force, Pacific was formed at Santa Barbara, California. Its commanding officer was Colonel Albert D. Cooley. Under his command were two Marine Air Support Groups (MASG), with four carrier air groups (MCVG) making up an MASG. Each MCVG would be composed of an eighteen-plane fighter squadron, VMF-(CVS), and a 12-plane bomber squadron, VMTB(CVS).

For ships, an MASG was to have four "jeeps" with marine squadrons and two CVEs with navy squadrons. The navy planes were to be used for CAP, ASW, ASP, etc., while the marine planes were to be used for close air support. In addition, marine ground crews and administrative personnel were organized into Marine Carrier Aircraft Service Detachments (CASD). The CASDs would be a unit of the MASGs until on ship, when they would become part of the ships' complement.[82]

Training began immediately for the marines, and they quickly found that flying a big Corsair (a fighter only starting to be based on the big carriers) off the CVEs was no easy task. Eight carrier landings were required for qualification, a number that was just too few for most of the marines, but the majority of the fliers made it through the program. They were lucky, though, to be doing their qualifications on the bigger *Commencement Bay*-class flattops instead of a smaller escort carrier.

At last, on 3 February 1945, MASG-48 (which Colonel Cooley also commanded) got its first carrier, the *Block Island.* Attached to the carrier was Lieutenant Colonel John F. Dobbin's MCVG-1, consisting of VMF-511, VMTB-233, and CASD-1. Thereafter, at approximately one-month intervals, three other carriers were assigned. The *Gilbert*

Islands received Lieutenant Colonel William R. Campbell's MCVG-2 (VMF-512, VMTB-143, CASD-2); Major Royce W. Coln's MCVG-3 (VMF-513, VMTB-234, CASD-3) was attached to the *Vella Gulf;* the *Cape Gloucester* got Lieutenant Colonel Donald K. Yost's MCVG-4 (VMF-351, VMTB-132, CASD-4). To round out this organization the *Kula Gulf* and *Siboney* were to be added later. All six carriers would form CarDiv 27 under Rear Admiral Dixwell Ketcham, the *Chenango's* skipper earlier in the war. Before CarDiv 27 could operate as a unit, the war ended.[83]

All of the above flattops were of a new class of escort carrier, the *Commencement Bay* class. These ships reflected the operational experienced gained by all types of CVEs so far in the war, and the navy's preference for the *Sangamon* class of escort carrier. Fifteen ships, CVEs 105–119, were ordered on 23 January 1943, followed later by a further eight ships, CVEs 120–127, all being built at the Todd-Pacific shipyards in Tacoma, Washington. Several of the latter vessels were never finished, and were broken up while still on the slips.

In many ways these new carriers were just upgraded *Sangamon*s, but were improved tremendously over the former oilers and, of course, were designed as escort carriers. The primary improvement of the design was the separation of the engine rooms to reduce the possibility of losing both to just one hit. Geared turbines of increased horsepower driving two shafts gave these ships a slightly higher speed than other CVEs. Heavier aircraft could be carried on the stronger flight deck, the elevators were faster, and two catapults were fitted. Dimensions of the *Sangamon*s and these new CVEs were generally similar, their beams being the same but the newer vessels being about four feet longer. The flight deck of the *Commencement Bay* ships was only one foot shorter than that of the *Sangamon*s but was five feet narrower. However, the hangar deck was almost twenty feet longer, which meant that these new vessels could carry more aircraft.

Rising above the flight deck was a new and larger island similar to that on the *Saipan*-class light carriers. There were a number of other design improvements, but probably of most importance to the sailors fighting the kamikazes was the increase in firepower. Two 5-inch/.38-calibers were mounted aft, with two quad-forty mounts in between on the fantail. Another quad-forty mount was on the forecastle. Eight additional twin 40-mm mounts were located forward and about amidships, with twenty 20-mm guns rounding out the armament.[84]

The first of the new flattops to see action was the *Block Island.* Commissioned on 30 December 1944, by April she was on her way west to join the fighting at Okinawa. Her skipper was Captain Francis M. Hughes, who had commanded the old *Block Island* when she had been sunk by a U-boat in May 1944. Now he and close to seven-hundred other men from that carrier were manning the new carrier and hoping to square accounts with the enemy.[85]

On board the carrier were the eight F4U-1Ds, eight F6F-5(N)s, two F6F-5(P)s, and twelve TBM-3s of MCVG-1. Joining TU 52.1.3 on 5 May, the flattop spent the next few days getting acquainted with the situation around Okinawa. On the tenth the first missions were flown, the initial strike composed of four Avengers hitting positions on southern Okinawa. Later that day a group of eight Avengers, four Corsairs, and four Hellcats hit Hirara and Nobara fields on Miyako in the Sakishima Gunto. These attacks were costly to the marines. The usual heavy flak knocked down one Avenger, with the loss of its crew, and another TMB's hydraulic system was shot out. This latter plane ditched alongside the carrier, and its crew was recovered quickly.[86]

For the marines and the *Block Island,* these strikes were just the beginning of what would become a busy time. When the carrier retired to Leyte on 16 June, the marines had flown 1,100 combat sorties, half of these being target sorties over Okinawa and the Sakishima Gunto. Four fighter pilots, two Avenger pilots, and four crewmen had been killed.[87] One of those lost was VMF-511's CO, Major R. C. Maze. He and his wingman had already made one pass at the Ishigaki airfield on 27 May and were returning to rocket some vessels lying off the Ishigaki pier. With the enemy fully aroused, this was not a very good idea, and Maze paid for it. As the wingman pulled out of his rocket pass, he saw Maze's Corsair plow into the sea in a welter of flame, smoke, and muddy water.[88]

These initial operations of marine squadrons operating from CVEs had been reasonably successful. The Corsair was a "highly efficient small carrier airplane," much more so (in the *Block Island's* opinion) than the Hellcat. This was primarily because of wing-folding differences—the Hellcat's was manual, the Corsair's hydraulic—and maintenance problems with the F6F.[89] It is possible that these problems were caused more by the last-minute arrival on the carrier of the night fighter Hellcats, which didn't give maintenance personnel enough time to get used to them. Still, having four different types of aircraft on board complicated matters more than was really necessary.

An additional problem involving the Corsair/Hellcat mix was that the Hellcats were not supposed to be flown on ground support missions, only used as night interceptors. Though the F6Fs did, in fact,

VMTB-233 TBMs from the Block Island *off Kadena Airfield on 20 May 1945.*
(National Archives)

fly some strike sorties, the Corsairs and their pilots had to fly the
majority of the missions with no relief because the Corsair and Hellcat pilots were not cross-trained.[90]

Joining TU 52.1.3 on 21 May was a second marine carrier, Captain L. K. Rice's *Gilbert Islands*. Initially the only losses suffered by
MCVG-2 were operational ones, but on 3 June a VMTB-143
Avenger was shot down at Ishigaki. Two of the crew were able to get
out of their fatally holed plane and were rescued by a PBM making a
hazardous pickup under fire.[91]

There were other losses. During a mission over Iriomote Island, a
VMF-512 FG-1D Corsair went into a violent spin and shed many
pieces before crashing. Four days later, while attacking Nobara airfield, an Avenger was hit while in its bomb run. A large part of its
right wing was ripped off and it tumbled from the sky. When the
plane plowed into the ground, its bombs exploded with a blinding
flash that sent a cloud of smoke into the sky.[92]

On the twelfth, planes from the *Gilbert Islands, Block Island, Santee,*
and *Suwannee* took part in a mission that, had it worked, would have
been a first for CVE fliers—a strike on the homeland island of
Kyushu. Taking off from their ships at 0500, the CVE aircraft flew

to Kadena for refueling and last-minute instructions, then took off
again for Kyushu. When the airmen reached Kyushu, they found it
completely socked in (not an uncommon occurrence in the area).
Unable to bomb the primary target, the fliers returned to bomb a
seaplane base on Amami O Shima. They then returned to Kadena,
refueled, and flew back to their carriers.[93]

Before the *Gilbert Islands* left Okinawa in mid-June, her squadrons
flew almost 750 missions and knocked down one enemy plane. Returning to Leyte, she joined the *Block Island* and *Suwannee* in support
of the landings at Balikpapen, Borneo.

Making brief appearances in the western Pacific in July and August were the remaining two marine carriers. The *Cape Gloucester*
joined other "jeeps" in an interesting sojourn into the South China
Sea. The *Vella Gulf* arrived at Guam on 20 July, and her planes
raided the much-bombed islands of Pagan and Rota on the twenty-
fourth and twenty-sixth. She arrived at Okinawa on 9 August, coin-
cident with the dropping of the second atomic bomb, and her next
assignment was covering the occupation of Japan.[94]

The operations of the Marine CVE squadrons had been mixed
blessings. Though the fliers had been specifically trained for close
support, the only opportunities they had been given to function in
this role were eight days of missions for the *Block Island* and five days
for the *Gilbert Islands*. They had spent the rest of the time cratering
the Sakishima Gunto airfields. It was a sad misuse of these specially
trained fliers.

According to Robert Sherrod, one of the reasons was the apparent antipathy of Admiral Durgin to the use of the marines in the
close support role. Sherrod has said that Durgin believed that anyone could do close support and that the rapport between marine
fliers and ground troops was a myth. After the war it was finally
decided that the marines would concentrate on the close support
role.[95]

By this point in the war, however, Durgin had had plenty of
opportunity to see how his fliers had fared in the area of close
support. They had done remarkably well, and Durgin was justifiably
proud of them. He saw no need to break up a winning combination
just to satisfy marine aspirations. Neither Durgin's belief that "anyone can do close support" nor the converse—"marines were the only
ones able to provide effective close support"—is true.

Meanwhile, the fighting on Okinawa continued, bitter and intense. By the first week of May, U.S. troops had completed the
conquest of the northern portion of the island, although guerrilla

activity remained a threat for some time. To the south the Tenth
Army was coming up against the main Japanese def ses. The Japanese were being compressed into an area less tha ｣ a quarter of the
size of the island. But it was in this area that they had made their
major preparations and where the bloodiest fighting would take
place.

Most of the escort carriers that had been around Okinawa since
the start were still there. But now some newer, fresher faces were
showing up, faces like the *Shamrock Bay, Steamer Bay, Makassar Straits,
Shipley Bay, Hoggatt Bay,* and *Nehenta Bay.* With the arrival of these
new vessels, many of the other carriers could be replaced. Some
would only be going back to Guam or Ulithi for a short rest. Others
would be going all the way back to the United States.

One of the latter vessels was the *Petrof Bay.* At Okinawa "the Mad
Russian's" squadron, VC-93, had lost four Wildcats in combat and
six operationally, plus another four Avengers operationally. These
losses had cost the lives of two pilots and one crewman. The squadron had bagged seventeen enemy planes in the air and claimed one
more as a probable. Many other planes on the ground were also
claimed as destroyed or damaged. To alleviate the heavy workload
that the fighter pilots had to endure at Okinawa, six of the VC-93
torpedo pilots had been checked out as fighter pilots. As it turned
out, one of these "hybrids" would become VC-93's leading scorer,
with four Japanese planes to his credit.[96]

Along with the coming and going of various CVEs, there were
two events worthy of note in May. Early on the eighth, word came
that Germany had surrendered. Although relieved that one of the
Axis partners had been knocked out of the war, most soldiers and
sailors realized that a lot of fighting and dying was still happening
on Okinawa, and that there would probably be a lot more before
Japan surrendered.

The second event occurred on 28 May. More cosmetic than sub-
stantive, it was Admiral Halsey's relief of Admiral Spruance. With
this change the Fifth Fleet became the Third Fleet, and all subordi-
nate units also changed numbers (TU 52.1.1 became TU 32.1.1, and
so on).

With new TBM-3Es and a fresh coat of paint, the *Anzio* returned
to replace the *Tulagi* in the antisubmarine role and the *Tulagi* began
another period of close support. It wasn't long before the *Anzio's*
planes hit paydirt. On the twenty-eighth the carrier and her four
screening DEs received word from a minesweeper of a possible submarine contact. When the hunter-killer force reached the site of the

initial contact, the flattop's aircraft began a series of searches, as did the destroyer escorts. But nothing was found until the morning of the thirty-first.

Early that day Lieutenant (jg) Sam L. Stovall was on the last leg of what up to then had been a very boring five-hour search. At 0436 his radar operator picked up a blip on his screen that appeared to be more solid than the rain squalls also dotting the screen. Stovall made an approach but the blip kept fading off the scope. At last the blip held steady, and Stovall headed for it.

Popping out of some clouds at 2,000 feet, Stovall saw a fully surfaced submarine heading toward him just three miles away. In the half-light of dawn (sunrise was thirty-six minutes away), the submarine "looked black and as big as a DE." Immediately Stovall began a rocket run on the sub's port beam. He fired four rockets, the last two appearing to hit just short of the sub's conning tower.

As Stovall circled for another run, the submarine began to dive. Stovall's second attack was a failure because he had forgotten to switch from "RP" (rocket projectile) to "Bomb-Torpedo" on his armament selector. Circling back again, he was able to drop his Fido by using the emergency release.

Two hundred feet ahead of the diving submarine's telltale swirl, the Fido sliced into the water. The emergency release also sent all six of Stovall's sonobuoys into the water. Within two minutes submarine noises could be heard over the sonobuoys. In another few minutes the radioman suddenly heard a violent hissing sound that became so painfully loud he had to yank off his earphones. This sound slowly faded and was replaced by noises like "tin cans being crunched."

An Avenger crew hurrying to help Stovall heard an explosion over one of the sonobuoy frequencies, and the *Oliver Mitchell,* then fifteen miles from the contact, felt a heavy shock shortly after the Fido entered the water. As the sun rose it was apparent that this submarine had made her last voyage. A heavy oil slick coated the water for hundreds of yards. Splintered planking, chunks of cork, rolls of toilet paper, wood with Japanese characters stamped on it, and bits of human flesh were picked up by two DEs scouring the area.

There was no doubt. Stovall had sunk the *kaiten*-carrying *I-361.* VC-13 was carrying on in the Pacific its success against submarines that it had so ably begun in the Atlantic.[97] Quick to praise the *Anzio*'s group were Admirals Halsey and Beary. "A rousing well done to you and your gang," Halsey radioed, "for pulling the plug on that Nip for the last time." Admiral Beary added, "Congratulations on the haul of monkey meat. Keep up the good work."[98]

The carrier and her escorts continued with their hunter-killer operations, chasing down several contacts with no success. Then, on 11 June, when the *Anzio* was taking on aviation fuel from the oiler *Caliente,* a pair of fuel tanks ruptured, spilling fuel into the flattop's voids and cofferdam. Because of this accident, the *Anzio*'s participation in continued ASW operations was out of the question. For the remainder of her time on station the carrier conducted a radio deception operation. Task Force 38 had been hitting Japan but now was retiring for replenishment under radio silence. Using a radioman from Halsey's staff, the *Anzio* began sending the deception traffic on the eleventh. This chicanery was intended to keep the Japanese on edge and fearful of the presence of TF 38. It continued until 17 June, when the carrier set course for Leyte and repairs. As they headed for port, the *Anzio*'s crew claimed that theirs was the "only ship to relieve the entire Task Force 38."[99]

Though land-based aircraft had taken over more and more of the support role by now, the CVE planes (especially those of VOC-1 and VOC-2) were kept busy. After the *kikusui* attack that damaged the *Sangamon* on 4 May, there were three more of these suicide missions in May. These didn't bother the "jeeps" too much, except to provide more hunting for the FM-2s, but they did sink and damage many other ships. Okinawa had become a very bloody place for the U.S. Navy.

Still, the Americans were dishing out more than they were taking. For example, while spotting for a destroyer VOC-2's Lieutenant (jg) John V. Canterbury saw artillery fire coming from a ravine parallel to the beach. Unable to get his ship into position because of shallow water, Canterbury used his Aldis lamp to contact two nearby LCI(G) gunboats. When they came up on his radio frequency, he was able to coach them into a position where they could take the enemy artillery under fire. The LCI(G)s soon destroyed the guns.[100]

Enemy planes also continued to fall to the guns of the CVE fliers, three of the obsolete Vals being destroyed by VF-40 pilots on the fifteenth. Enemy troops were not safe from the attention of the fliers, either. Aloft as an air coordinator for the *Nehenta Bay* on 31 May was VC-8's skipper, Lieutenant Norman D. Hodson. Hodson was a veteran of the early fighting in the Pacific, having flown with VF-6 from the start of the war until after Midway. Later he moved to the Atlantic, joining VC-1 and helping to sink a couple of U-boats. Next he took command of VC-8 and was its commanding officer when, flying from the *Guadalcanal,* the squadron took part in one of the most dramatic actions in that ocean—the capture of the *U-505.* On 31 May Hodson had dispatched several planes on what was known as "organized confusion" strikes (attacks where the planes came in close on one another's heels and from different directions). With no other missions to coordinate for a while, Hodson sought out some action on his own. Flying at 150 feet about four miles south of Naha, Okinawa's largest city, Hodson saw a rare sight: Japanese soldiers out in the open. There were only two of them, but that was two more than most pilots had seen. The pair was walking along a road and Hodson came strafing straight up the road. The action report commented, "The Japanese soldiers did not leave the road but merely crouched down in the center. For them this was unfortunate."[101]

June came, and with it came a sense of déjà vu for the sailors of Halsey's Third Fleet. In December many of them had ridden through a killer typhoon. On 5 June they found themselves in another. In a remarkably similar set of circumstances, Halsey led his fleet into the path of the typhoon. This time, though, it was the larger vessels that suffered the major damage, not the smaller ships as in December. That is not to say that these smaller ships, including some escort carriers, had an easy time—far from it.

Part of Rear Admiral Donald B. Beary's TG 30.8, the Logistics Group, the CVEs received a ride their crews would not soon forget. During the early hours of 5 June the storm roared in on the Third Fleet. Unable to get a clear picture of the situation and the direction the storm was taking, Halsey's force backed and filled across the track of the typhoon. Beary was sure the course his group was on (300 degrees) would run it back into the storm and so reported to Halsey at 0245. He was right, but after several other courses proved too much for the escort carriers, the course was returned to 300 degrees at 0310. Not quite an hour later all CVEs were directed to proceed independently.[102]

At the height of the typhoon the *Salamaua* lost steering control and fell off into the trough of the mountainous seas. On the "Sal's" bridge Captain J. I. Taylor could look up at the waves towering over his ship. The carrier was rolling and pitching so much that men on the bridge had to hold on to anything they could to keep from being thrown about. Green water in massive amounts broke over her flight deck and poured in sheets down an open ventilation tube into the steering room. On the bridge a pane of glass broke, sending shards flying about. Slowly and carefully, the men removed the rest of the panes. Other parts of the flattop began to rip off. Carried away were her forward starboard lookout platform and gallery walkway, the No. 1 40-mm gun mount, and the aircraft handling boom. The pounding seas lifted the leading edge of the flight deck, rupturing the catapult supports and several bulkheads.

To the men below it seemed as though they were in a huge oil can constantly being squeezed. Some vowed that they saw bulkheads move. Up on the flight deck an Avenger tore loose from its moorings to run wild among the other parked aircraft, wrecking them all and killing one man. All this damage had taken just ten minutes, from the moment the *Salamaua* flopped into the trough until she regained steerageway.[103]

In similar straits was Captain G. T. Mundorff's *Windham Bay*. By 0300 the aircraft on her hangar deck were beginning to work loose from their moorings. A few minutes later "the bottom appeared to fall out of the glass and the pressure dropped at an alarming rate."[104] Water swept over the flight deck, and though the forward elevator was up, it poured through the cracks between the elevator edges and the flight deck in a "solid sheet," eventually filling the elevator well to a depth of four feet.

Unable to gauge the wind accurately because the wind-measuring equipment had blown away, the *Windham Bay* estimated the peak wind to be 127 knots plus gusts, and the mountainous seas to be 75 feet from trough to crest. "The ship was pitching violently and the bow would alternately plunge deeply with screws clear of the water, racing madly, and then rise to extraordinary heights before plunging again."[105] Then, at 0355, as the carrier's bow crashed down with a particularly thunderous shudder, the forward lookout platform and Nos. 1 and 2 40-mm gun sponsons ripped loose. This was followed by the collapse onto the forecastle of the entire portion of the flight deck.[106]

During this frenzied maelstrom the risk of collision was always present. The CVE that came closest to having an unwanted meeting was the *Attu*. At 0400 some flags tore loose to wrap themselves around the SG antenna, thus knocking out the PPI (Plan Position Indicator) radarscope. With so many ships nearby almost out of control themselves, it was a terrible time to be without a piece of equipment essential for stationkeeping. "As ships of this class will win any leeway race," the *Attu* reported later, "our apprehension was justified by the after lookout reporting ship close aboard on starboard quarter. We cleared this tanker by ahead full both engines and drifted across his bow clearing by several hundred feet. About ten minutes later we had a repeat performance with another tanker looming up close aboard on starboard bow. By backing full we cleared, but until it was an accomplished fact it was not believed possible. Our bow and tanker's stern could not have cleared by more than 50 feet."[107]

Like the other carriers, the *Attu* had several planes blown over the side and many others wrecked or damaged. There was a short interlude when the *Attu* lurched into the eye of the storm. The seas were still huge, still heavy and pounding, but the winds subsided enough that the crew could do a quick cleanup and unfoul the SG antenna. In the eye several birds were flying in a "confused manner," but the birds probably weren't any more confused than the *Attu*'s crew.

The respite in the eye didn't last long, and "the second half of the storm hit with a crescendo of wind which soon reached a familiar whine, and the granddaddy of all waves."[108] This portion of the storm was just as wild as the first part, but at least with the SG operating, collision was not as great a threat.

A few hours later TG 30.8 passed through the typhoon and was finally into calmer waters. The CVEs were not pretty sights, with planes in tangled masses and structural damage evident. Substantial losses had been suffered by the transport carriers; forty-six planes had been lost overboard or wrecked, twenty-seven on the *Bougainville* alone. Nevertheless, the next day the carriers (except for the *Bougainville,* which had planes stuck on the hangar deck because of inoperative elevators) launched seventy-three combat-ready aircraft for TF 38 and received forty-three flyable duds.

That the carriers were able to deliver the replacement aircraft is a tribute to both the CVEs and the crews that manned them. Their mission was a vital task, and not even a typhoon would prevent them from completing it. At Okinawa the carriers of the Logistics Group delivered a total of 968 planes and 220 aircrew to the various task groups. Among the aircraft delivered were several Kingfisher floatplanes, lowered into the water from the carrier by crane and taxied to the cruiser *Detroit,* where they were catapulted from that ship for further delivery.[109] The job of the transport carriers was, for the most part, unknown and unsung during the war, but without them the teeth of TFs 58/38 would have been pulled.

Two times through a typhoon was too much for the navy to stomach, and the two storms almost cost Admiral Halsey his job. In effect, they did cost Vice Admiral John S. McCain, TF 38's commander, his job, though not until after the war was over. Given his status as a popular hero, Halsey retained his command but was closely watched thereafter.

The escort carriers of Admiral Durgin's force evaded the typhoon, but they could not evade the kamikazes. By 1 June the *kikusui* attacks were dwindling. Only two more massed attacks would be made, between 3–7 June and 21–22 June, and these would involve only about ninety-five kamikazes. But these attacks, plus the individ ual raids in between, showed that the kamikaze was still a deadly weapon and hard to stop.

On the morning of 7 June TU 32.1.1 was operating some sixty miles east of the Sakishima Gunto. Throughout the early morning hours a number of bogeys had been reported but none had neared the ships. At 0515 the CAPs were launched, with fighters stacked from three-thousand to eighteen-thousand feet. Fifteen minutes later the strike missions went to hit the already well-pounded airfields in the Sakishima Gunto.

For an hour the force's radar screens remained clear of bogeys and were still clear at 0635 when a lookout sighted an aircraft broad on the *Natoma Bay*'s port quarter only about seven-hundred yards away. Identified as a Zeke, the plane was flying at five-hundred feet and speeding directly toward the carrier. It made a sharp left turn and glided in over the *Natoma Bay*'s stern, strafing as it came. When it was abreast of the bridge and flying at that level, the kamikaze pushed over sharply and smashed into the flight deck just abaft the ramp and between the ship's centerline and the catapult track.

When the suicider hit, it felt to the ship's crew that the carrier had been pushed straight down into the water. A ball of fire erupted from the flight deck, followed by a soaring mushroom-shaped cloud of smoke. Disintegrating upon impact, the Zeke's wings and bits of fuselage bounced over the bow while its engine and bomb pierced the flight deck. Actually, the Zeke pilot had picked a poor spot for his demise because the major force of the impact and blast was absorbed by the anchor windlass. Still, one man was killed and four others wounded.

The impact did blow a hole approximately thirteen by twenty-eight feet in the flight deck. A Wildcat that had been spotted on the catapult was holed by shrapnel and its gas tanks set afire, the burning gasoline spreading to the carrier's forecastle. To get rid of the blazing fighter, it was catapulted off the ship. A few minutes later all fires were under control.

As soon as the fires were extinguished, repairs of the flight deck began. Large timbers and sheets of plywood and steel were used to cover the hole. Large pipe stanchions supported this entire assembly. Not damaged had been the catapult, and even before repairs had been completed to the hole, aircraft were being catapulted. By 1500 repairs to the deck were good enough to permit normal deck launchings.[110]

A couple of minutes after the *Natoma Bay* was hit, five other planes were seen about three-thousand yards away. The leading

Repairs are still under way on the hole left by the kamikaze while the first plane to take off after the attack is catapulted from the Natoma Bay. *(Via* Natoma Bay *Association)*

plane was identified as a Wildcat, and all hands relaxed. Just then the trailing plane in the rather loose formation peeled off to dive on the *Natoma Bay*. Every gun on the carrier's port side took the now obviously enemy plane under fire.

Seen to be an Oscar, the plane closed with the flattop until it was 1,000 yards away. At this point it turned to parallel the ship's course. Antiaircraft fire, mainly 20-mm, stitched the plane yet did not knock it down. The intense flak finally took effect as the Oscar veered toward another carrier, nosed up, did a wingover, and plunged into the sea just fifty yards off the *Hoggatt Bay*'s starboard bow.[111]

As mentioned earlier, a lack of stopping power by the 20-mms was evident. "The fire power of this class CVE [Kaiser] is entirely inadequate," the *Hoggatt Bay* would report, "and in particular it is considered that the probability of hits from all the 20-mm guns is practically nil . . ."[112] Only the coming of the end of the war solved this problem for the escort carriers.

At last, after a bitter eighty-two-day battle, organized resistance ended on Okinawa on 21 June, though not until 2 July would the campaign be declared officially closed. For the CVEs the campaign had been tiring, conducted at a high level of activity. Direct air support, spotting, and photo missions had been the carriers' major missions. In addition, however, numerous other "housekeeping chores" were assigned, such as beach observation, artillery observation, courier flights, night and day antisubmarine patrols, DDT spray missions, air delivery of supplies, dropping propaganda leaflets, and search flights. In the course of these missions some 18,133 sorties were flown, almost 2,000 tons of bombs dropped, and 30,000 rockets fired. Many ground targets were destroyed and 280 enemy aircraft were claimed shot down by the "jeep" fliers. In return the escort carriers lost sixty-five planes, thirty-two of these operational losses.[113]

Everyone was tired, particularly the fliers of VOC-1, who had been active during almost the entire campaign. Their spirits soared when the following message was received from Admiral Durgin, who had in some way been involved with the squadron since it had been formed as VOF-1 in 1943: "This is my Op Plan 1-45. Code name is Double Trouble. Advance agents have completed arrangements for beach house, gulls, swimming hole, beer, sand, sun, squaws. VOC-1 will provide other accessories, including steaks. Hour is established as 1300 King, Sunday. Agents will sweep channels. As approach air support by staff. Spotting by Admiral. Target and rendezvous details will follow."

Durgin quickly received a reply: "Your Double Trouble not understood. This squadron has completed its tour of combat duty. However, in view of critical situation, VOC-1 will comply. Logistics as requested. Please furnish advanced photo interpretation on all squaws."[114] Thus VOC-1's long war came to an end.

The men of VOC-1 must have been relieved to be leaving the scene of such bloodletting. Okinawa had been a campaign of unmitigated malevolence. Japanese military and Okinawa civilian losses had been tremendous, estimated to be over 150,000 dead. But the invaders had suffered grievously, too—almost 75,000 casualties of all kinds. For the navy's part, thirty ships had been sunk (most by kamikazes) and another 368 damaged, and almost 9,800 sailors had been killed or wounded. These losses were the worst yet endured by the United States Navy in the war.[115]

Okinawa was still just another battle, however, and the escort carriers were not yet finished with their part in the Pacific war. Far to the south of Okinawa, in the Netherlands East Indies, lay Borneo. For the Americans, compared to operations like Iwo Jima and Okinawa, Borneo was just a sideshow. But this island, the world's third-largest, was a treasure trove of oil, rubber, diamonds, and rare woods, and the British and Dutch wanted to regain control of Borneo before the Japanese could destroy the refineries and oilfields.

MacArthur's headquarters drew up a plan for three landings on Borneo. The infantry troops to be used would be Australian, the naval forces mainly American. On 1 May the first landings took place at Tarakan (a large island just off Borneo's northeastern tip). The second, at Brunei Bay on Borneo's northwest coast, occurred on 10 June. Balikpapen, on the southeast coast, was the site of the final landings.

Because of distance and weather problems at the few airfields that were in range of Balikpapen, three escort carriers provided air support. On hand for the landings was Rear Admiral Sample's TU 78.4.1, consisting of the *Suwanee*, *Block Island*, *Gilbert Islands*, one destroyer, and five destroyer escorts. For the CVEs this operation was a snap.

Few Japanese aircraft were present, so the main job of the carriers was close support. Arriving off Balikpapen on 30 June, the CVEs began operations the next day, D day, with strikes against motor pools, troop concentrations, and many buildings. Though these attacks were generally successful, in one instance *Suwanee* planes bombed and rocketed buildings the Australians had already captured, causing some casualties. After this incident the CVE planes spent their time attacking targets farther afield.

One such target was a large vehicle and supply pool discovered thirty miles inland. Forty-eight planes ganged up to demolish this gathering and to disperse the survivors into the jungle. While strafing some trucks, a VMF-512 Hellcat was hit by ground fire. At treetop level, the pilot had no chance to get out as his plane dove into the trees.[116]

The early hours of 3 July saw the only air battle of the operation. First Lieutenant Bruce J. Reuter had been launched from the *Block Island* late on the second for a night CAP. Shortly after midnight the ship's radar picked up a bogey about fifty miles away. Vectored toward the bogey, Reuter had the target on his own scope when he had closed to three and a half miles. A visual on the bogey showed it to be an unsuspecting Jake floatplane. Easing in behind the Jake, Reuter squeezed his trigger and saw his tracers bite into the plane's fuselage. There was a spurt of fire, then a solid sheet of flame and the floatplane spun in.[117]

With the Australians advancing rapidly and targets becoming scarce, the carriers were released. On the third they pulled out to head back to Leyte Gulf.

Meanwhile, up north the *Anzio* had returned to action in her hunter-killer role. Leaving Leyte Gulf on 6 July, she rendezvoused with a refueling force that included the *Kitkun Bay* and *Admiralty Islands* on the fourteenth. Then she headed for her operating area off the coast of Honshu.

Two days later her planes hit paydirt. Lieutenant (jg) William M. McLane was flying a flank search when his radarman picked up a fluctuating radar return that became steady when he turned toward it. At 0737 the broadside silhouette of a surfaced submarine appeared ten miles away. Using the clouds for cover, McLane was able to get the jump on the sub.

Diving out of a small cloud, he raked the slowly moving vessel with his .50-caliber wing guns, followed with a quartet of rockets, two fired at 600 yards and two at 400 yards. They were right on target. One struck the sub's waterline just below the conning tower, while the other three hit about fifteen feet short of the submarine in line with the conning tower.

As the Avenger zoomed past the submarine, McLane's gunner got off some shots. The boat began to dive but at such a shallow angle that it appeared to be going down on an even keel. Returning, McLane dropped two depth bombs which missed by a good margin, then dropped a sonobuoy and tried to release his Fido. However, in his excitement he had failed to switch his armament selector and the homing torpedo didn't drop.

A second try was successful, and the Fido speared the water 200 feet ahead of the telltale swirl left by the now invisible sub. The Fido may have damaged the boat, for an oil slick began to coat the water, but as McLane watched, the slick started to move, first one way, then another. Over the sonobuoy, cavitation noises from the sub's screws could be heard until these stopped twenty minutes later.

Shortly before 0900 another Avenger joined the search, followed twenty minutes later by a third TBM. More sonobuoys were dropped and screw noises heard again. Very loud cavitations were heard over two of the sonobuoys, and moving between them was the oil slick. At 1000, when the slick was midway between the two buoys, Lieutenant Rex W. Nelson dropped a Fido 500 feet ahead of the slick's apex. For ninety seconds nothing happened; then over the buoys came a sound like "the dull roar of a depth charge explosion" or "a hissing which grew louder, then faded." The slick stopped moving and the screw noises died away. A number of small, flat white objects of unknown significance floated to the surface.

It appeared that the VC-13 fliers had gotten the sub, but at 1120 the oil slick (heavier than before) began to inch eastward. Now approaching the scene at full speed were the destroyer escorts *Lawrence C. Taylor* and *Robert F. Keller*. At the spot where he figured the submarine lay, Nelson dropped a smokelight. Using the light and her own sonar indications, the *Taylor* let fly a full hedgehog pattern at 1140, and within a minute several small explosions were felt aboard the DE. Then two violent explosions rocked the *Taylor*, knocking out power to her sonar gear and causing some engine-room damage. A thousand feet above the spot, Nelson and his crew could feel the force of the blast. Looking down, they saw a ripple of water like that caused by a stone dropped into a pond racing outward.

Though the *Keller* followed with another hedgehog attack, it wasn't necessary. The big *I-13*, flagship of SubDiv 1, was making her last dive. Evidence of this soon floated to the surface—pieces of planking and cork, a photograph of a Japanese family, magazines, and bundles of letters.[118] Again Halsey was quick to praise the efforts of the hunter-killer group, radioing, "Violent explosion emanating from Nip subs are music to all ears. Well done."[119]

This sinking (shared with the *Taylor*) was VC-13's last of the war. In the Atlantic the squadron had sunk six U-boats and had added two more in the Pacific, thus ranking VC-13 second behind the nine U-boats bagged by VC-9. It had been a long war for both squadrons, but now the end of the war was approaching rapidly.

For the rest of July through the cessation of hostilities on 15 August, the *Anzio* continued antisubmarine operations off Honshu. She encountered no more submarines, and the *Anzio*'s last skirmish of the war was with bad weather rather than the enemy.

One final combat operation was in store for the escort carriers. On 1 August, after covering a battleship/cruiser force on an antishipping and minesweeping mission west of Okinawa, the *Lunga Point, Makin Island,* and *Cape Gloucester* sortied to screen another antishipping sweep, this one off the coast of China near Shanghai. In this relatively unexciting operation, some enemy aircraft were evident, but they were few and far between. For those that did show up, they didn't return to tell of what they saw. On 4 August a *Cape Gloucester* marine downed a Tabby. The next day three Frans stumbled into the path of the task group.

At 1430 a division of VC-41 planes from the *Makin Island* was vectored to investigate a bogey. Soon two Frances bombers were seen a couple of thousand feet above the Wildcats, the enemy seeing the FM-2s at the same time and diving away. Only one of the VC-41 pilots, Ensign Frank Yates, was able to drop both his wing tanks. Leaving the others struggling behind, Yates lit out after the enemy.

One of the Frans escaped, but Yates caught the other from behind at sea level. His first shells started the left engine burning; his next burst ripped open the fuselage; the third and fourth bursts smashed the Fran's other engine. The Frances tumbled into the sea.

A short time later Lieutenant Colonel Don Yost, a veteran of the Guadalcanal fighting and now MCVG-4's commanding officer, bagged another Frances. Then, at 1710, yet another intruder was detected. This time a division of VC-98 wildcats from the *Lunga Point* did the honors. In a hundred mile chase the four pilots took turns filling the Frances full of holes, one pilot even getting so close that he tried to saw off the bomber's tail with the propeller of his Wildcat. Finally Lieutenant E. R. Beckwith set the enemy plane afire, and it spiraled down to splatter into many pieces. Beckwith's kill was the last of the war for the Wildcat and the CVE fliers. The record achieved by plane and pilot in the Pacific was outstanding, with some 422 Japanese aircraft credited to CVE FM-2s in 1944 and 1945.[120] To this figure should be added another fifteen to twenty-five aircraft shot down by the F4Fs from the three "Old Indispensables" while they were active in the Solomons in 1943. A very good record indeed, for what in essence was an obsolete aircraft.

Though the Frances was the last plane shot down by escort carrier aircraft, they still weren't finished with the shooting war. On the sixth six Corsairs and two Hellcats from the *Cape Gloucester,* eight FM-2s from the *Lunga Point,* and another seven *Makin Island* Wildcats made a fighter sweep of shipping installations at Tinghai Harbor, southeast of Shanghai, and the adjacent airfield. A low ceiling, along with intense and accurate flak, hampered the attackers, but they were still able to sink or damage several small vessels.

There was one loss, the last combat loss for the escort carriers in the war. While making a strafing run, the plane of VC-41's commander was struck. Lieutenant G. V. Knudsen was able to bail out, but because of the heavy gunfire and because he landed too close to shore, the Dumbos were unable to pick him up and Knudsen was never seen again.

With few attractive targets in the area, further attacks were deemed unnecessary, and the force returned to Okinawa on 7 August.[121]

The day before the CVEs returned to Okinawa from off the China coast, a fearsome weapon exploded over Hiroshima. Four days later a second atomic bomb devastated Nagasaki. Faced with the possibility of more of these weapons being dropped on their homeland and the very real threat of the Russian Army then rampaging through Manchuria, the Japanese sued for peace. The Allies

EPILOGUE

THE WAR was over but the job of the escort carriers was not. With their cavernous hangar spaces, the "jeeps" (along with their big sisters) were ideally suited for transporting large numbers of people. And they would be doing just this task for the next several months.

The Recovery of Allied Military Personnel (RAMP) had first priority. Virtually all of these individuals had been prisoners of the Japanese, and many were in poor health. Detailed to take part in this operation were a number of escort carriers. Besides carrying most of the RAMPs, the flattops were to provide air cover in case some recalcitrant Japanese decided to resist, although in fact no resistance was noted.

Among the first of the CVEs to be involved in the RAMP operation were the *Block Island* and *Santee*. They covered the forces involved in the liberation of prisoners from Formosa on 5–6 September. A total of 474 ex-POWs were taken aboard the *Block Island,* while the *Santee* took aboard another 477. Most of these men had been captured at Singapore or in the Philippines and were in terrible shape, primarily because of malnutrition but also because of a veritable textbook of various diseases.[1]

This first mission set the tone for the rest of the recovery operations—cover flights to make sure there was no treachery, and then the embarkation of the pitifully emaciated and ill POWs. At Nagasaki the *Chenango* and *Cape Gloucester* were the carriers involved, while the *Makin Island* and *Santee* took part in the POW evacuation at Wakayama. Farther north the *Kitkun Bay, Hoggatt Bay, Manila Bay,* and *Nehenta Bay* were present at Mutsu Wan on Honshu as Vice Admiral Frank Jack Fletcher, Commander North Pacific, received the formal surrender of those Japanese troops in northern Honshu

A pair of floatplanes greet the Nehenta Bay *and another escort carrier as they approach Adak on 18 August 1945. (National Archives)*

The war is over but the Santee *still has work to do at Formosa, 18 September 1945. (National Archives)*

On 24 September 1945 the Hoggatt Bay *enters Ominato. The other carriers, in no particular order, are the* Kitkun Bay, Manila Bay, *and* Nehenta Bay. *(National Archives)*

and Hokkaido on 6 September. These ships had the distinct pleasure of recovering many survivors of the heroic defense of Wake, including the newly promoted Lieutenant Colonel James Devereux, commander of the marines on that island.[2]

While undertaking these various operations, the escort carriers took on the sad job of looking for the missing aircraft of Rear Admiral William D. Sample, CarDiv 27's commander at Leyte Gulf and later ComCarDiv 22. Despite an intensive search in very poor weather, the plane and all aboard were never found. The navy and the escort carriers had lost a valuable officer.

Only a handful of escort carriers were involved in the RAMP program, but a total of forty-six would be included in Magic Carpet. The sudden surrender of the Japanese caught both the armed ser vices and the politicians short. Quick to judge the temper of their constituents, however, the politicians were soon raising the cry "Bring our boys home!" Thus Magic Carpet, the operation to deliver the soldiers and sailors back to the United States, was born.

The results of this trooplift were remarkable, considering the lack of time for planning, but the virtual denuding of several vital areas because of the political and private pressure would be costly some five years later when the Korean War broke out.[3]

On 9 September 1945 Rear Admiral H. S. Kendall, ComCarDiv 24, was designated commander of TG 16.12 and placed in charge of Magic Carpet. By the end of the month he had 107 ships under his command. Task Group 16.12 got off to a slow start in September, transporting only 8,241 men out of a total of 259,856. War Shipping Administration ships carried the remainder. By December, though, TG 16.12 had hit its stride, carrying 370,596 persons out of a total of 695,486.[4]

Generally, Magic Carpet went smoothly. But every now and then something cropped up to complicate things. In the *Chenango*'s case it was one of those minor typhoons that gave Harry Felt his nickname of "Typhoon Harry." The flattop was returning to the United States from Okinawa with a full load of army troops. Although the ship had no aircraft boarded, a lot of aircraft equipment, including tires, was still stored in racks on the hangar sides. Bunks three layers high filled the hangar deck space. A GI sleeping on a top bunk was about ten feet off the deck.

Shortly after leaving Okinawa, the *Chenango* began to encounter heavy swells, the forerunners of the typhoon. The carrier began to pitch and roll, and many of the soldiers became ill. But the worst was yet to come.

Suddenly the *Chenango* fell off into a deep trough and rolled 30 degrees. All the equipment that had been stored in the racks came loose and began flying about. The GIs, most of whom were seasick and could hardly move, tried to take cover under the bunks. Aircraft tires, bouncing ten to fifteen feet in the air, landed in top bunks upon soldiers too weak to move or bounded down the aisles between the bunks, seemingly chasing those who had the strength to flee.

At last the carrier was spit out by the typhoon and came upon calmer seas. The ship itself had not suffered too much damage, but the soldiers—and some sailors—were very much the worse for wear. Injuries were many, fortunately none serious. The worst part of the whole ordeal was the cleaning up of the mess, both human- and typhoon-caused, on the hangar deck. It took fire hoses, followed by a large sweeper detail, to make that space livable again.[5]

But such episodes were few. As 1946 started, the efforts of TG 16.12 slackened. Nevertheless, the escort carriers were carrying people all over the Pacific. For example, during January a number of CVEs were still operating with TG 16.12—eleven in the Marianas, thirteen in the United States, five in Japan, and the remainder at Okinawa, Pearl Harbor, the Philippines, the Marshalls, and China.[6] Truly, Magic Carpet was a tremendous logistical effort.

Demand for the services of TG 16.12 dropped rapidly after the start of the year, and on 15 March 1946 CarDiv 24 was dissolved. During its existence as TG 16.12, Admiral Kendall's force had carried 1,307,859 persons.[7] Taking over the job was Vice Admiral Oscar W. Badger, Commander Service Force, who would continue Magic Carpet until it was effectively ended on 1 September 1946.

With the end of the war and the spooling down of Magic Carpet, there was little need for escort carriers. Many of the earlier carriers were held for a time in the mothball fleet and then broken up or returned to service as merchant ships. Notable among the *Bogue*-class vessels for service after the war were the *Card, Core,* and *Breton,* reactivated in the late 1950s as aircraft transports, a mission that continued into the 1970s. In fact, while performing this service the *Card* met another enemy, being mined and sunk at a Saigon pier in 1964. Raised and repaired, she was finally withdrawn from service in 1970.[8]

The Kaiser-class carriers were generally placed in mothballs much sooner than the later *Commencement Bay* ships because they had never been more than a stopgap measure and were ill-suited for the newer aircraft and equipment. Carriers of the *Commencement Bay* class soldiered on into the 1970s, some being converted to aircraft transports, some to amphibious assault carriers, and one (the *Gilbert Islands*) to a major communications relay ship.

Most of the escort carriers have now been broken up. A very few can still be seen, mothballed and forlorn.

And what of the navy's first escort carrier, the *Long Island?* Following several Magic Carpet trips, she was decommissioned at the Puget Sound Naval Shipyard on 26 March 1946. She escaped scrapping when she was reconverted into the merchant ship *Nelly.* As the *Nelly* she plied the waters of the world until 1953, when she received another name change. Renamed the *Seven Seas,* she spent much of her time as a floating university. Finally, in 1968 she was anchored permanently in Rotterdam, to serve her last days as a floating dormitory for University of Rotterdam medical students.[9]

The escort carriers never got the recognition that their big sisters, the fast carriers, received. But they probably were involved in a wider variety of tasks. As flagships of hunter-killer groups, they hunted submarines; as support carriers, they provided the ground troops with the necessary air support during those first critical days of the invasion, and often longer; as transport carriers they moved a vast amount of men and material all over the Pacific, and kept the fast carriers operating; as training carriers, they qualified the pilots who would fly not just off the "jeeps" but off the fast carriers as well. Without the superior performance of the escort carriers in these last two tasks, the operations of the fast carriers would have been greatly diminished, if not brought to a halt for extended periods. And last but not least, no crewman of a fast carrier could boast that he had stood toe to toe with the cream of the Japanese surface fleet and come out a winner.

Now the CVEs are just a memory, but to their crews that memory is still fresh. Each year men of the "jeeps" gather at various reunions to remember—to remember the kamikazes, the typhoons, the good COs, the bad COs, the good sailors, the bad sailors, and those they shared these times with. Some, like the men of the *Gambier Bay*, have traveled far to place wreaths on the now-placid waters of the Pacific in such spots as Leyte Gulf.

And they remember their ships, the "little giants" that took on every job tossed their way and performed it with a verve and distinction that belied their size and helped win the war against Japan.

APPENDIX:
U.S. ESCORT CARRIERS

The following table lists the escort carriers built for the U.S. Navy in World War II. The type designation uses the later CVE nomenclature for all ships. An asterisk (*) indicates vessels that served little or no time in the Pacific. Recommissioning dates for the vessels that were brought out of mothballs in the 1950s and 1960s have been omitted.

Hull No.	Name	Launched	Commissioned	Decommissioned
CVE 1	Long Island	11 Jan 40	2 Jun 41	26 Mar 46
CVE 9	*Bogue	15 Jan 42	26 Sep 42	30 Nov 46
CVE 11	*Card	21 Feb 42	8 Nov 42	13 May 46
CVE 12	Copahee	21 Oct 41	15 Jun 42	5 Jul 46
CVE 13	*Core	15 May 42	10 Dec 42	4 Oct 46
CVE 16	Nassau	4 Apr 42	20 Aug 42	28 Oct 46
CVE 18	Altamaha	22 May 42	15 Sep 42	27 Sep 46
CVE 20	Barnes	22 May 42	20 Feb 43	29 Aug 46
CVE 21	*Block Island	6 Jun 42	8 Mar 43	Sunk 29 May 44
CVE 23	Breton	27 Jun 42	12 Apr 43	30 Aug 46
CVE 25	*Croatan	1 Aug 42	28 Apr 43	20 May 46
CVE 26	Sangamon	4 Nov 39	25 Aug 42	24 Oct 45
CVE 27	Suwannee	4 Mar 39	24 Sep 42	28 Oct 46
CVE 28	Chenango	4 Jan 39	19 Sep 42	14 Aug 46
CVE 29	Santee	4 Mar 39	24 Aug 42	21 Oct 46
CVE 30	*Charger	1 Mar 41	3 Mar 42	15 Mar 46
CVE 31	Prince William	23 Aug 42	9 Apr 43	29 Aug 46
CVE 55	Casablanca	5 Apr 43	8 Jul 43	10 Jun 46

Hull No.	Name	Launched	Commissioned	Decommissioned
CVE 56	Liscome Bay	19 Apr 43	7 Aug 43	Sunk 24 Nov 43
CVE 57	Coral Sea/Anzio	1 May 43	27 Aug 43	5 Aug 46
CVE 58	Corregidor	12 May 43	31 Aug 43	30 Jul 46
CVE 59	*Mission Bay	26 May 43	13 Sep 43	21 Feb 47
CVE 60	*Guadalcanal	5 Jun 43	25 Sep 43	15 Jul 46
CVE 61	Manila Bay	10 Jul 43	5 Oct 43	31 Jul 46
CVE 62	Natoma Bay	20 Jul 43	14 Oct 43	20 May 46
CVE 63	Midway/St. Lo	17 Aug 43	23 Oct 43	Sunk 25 Oct 44
CVE 64	*Tripoli	2 Sep 43	31 Oct 43	22 May 46
CVE 65	Wake Island	15 Sep 43	7 Nov 43	5 Apr 46
CVE 66	White Plains	27 Sep 43	15 Nov 43	10 Jul 46
CVE 67	*Solomons	6 Oct 43	21 Nov 43	15 May 46
CVE 68	Kalinin Bay	15 Oct 43	27 Nov 43	15 May 46
CVE 69	Kasaan Bay	24 Oct 43	4 Dec 43	6 Jul 46
CVE 70	Fanshaw Bay	1 Nov 43	9 Dec 43	14 Aug 46
CVE 71	Kitkun Bay	8 Nov 43	15 Dec 43	19 Apr 46
CVE 72	Tulagi	15 Nov 43	21 Dec 43	30 Apr 46
CVE 73	Gambier Bay	22 Nov 43	28 Dec 43	Sunk 25 Oct 44
CVE 74	Nehenta Bay	28 Nov 43	3 Jan 44	15 May 46
CVE 75	Hoggatt Bay	4 Dec 43	11 Jan 44	20 Jul 46
CVE 76	Kadashan Bay	11 Dec 43	18 Jan 44	14 Jun 46
CVE 77	Marcus Island	16 Dec 43	26 Jan 44	12 Dec 46
CVE 78	Savo Island	22 Dec 43	3 Feb 44	12 Dec 46
CVE 79	Ommaney Bay	29 Dec 43	11 Feb 44	Sunk 4 Jan 45
CVE 80	Petrof Bay	5 Jan 44	18 Feb 44	31 Jul 46
CVE 81	Rudyerd Bay	12 Jan 44	25 Feb 44	11 Jun 46
CVE 82	Saginaw Bay	19 Jan 44	2 Mar 44	19 Jun 46
CVE 83	Sargent Bay	31 Jan 44	9 Mar 44	23 Jul 46
CVE 84	Shamrock Bay	4 Feb 44	15 Mar 44	6 Jul 46
CVE 85	Shipley Bay	12 Feb 44	21 Mar 44	28 Jun 46
CVE 86	Sitkoh Bay	19 Feb 44	28 Mar 44	30 Nov 46
CVE 87	Steamer Bay	26 Feb 44	4 Apr 44	1 Jul 46
CVE 88	Cape Esperance	3 Mar 44	9 Apr 44	22 Aug 46
CVE 89	Takanis Bay	10 Mar 44	15 Apr 44	1 May 46
CVE 90	Thetis Bay	16 Mar 44	21 Apr 44	7 Aug 46
CVE 91	Makassar Strait	22 Mar 44	27 Apr 44	9 Aug 46
CVE 92	Windham Bay	29 Mar 44	3 May 44	? Jan 47
CVE 93	Makin Island	5 Apr 44	9 May 44	19 Apr 46
CVE 94	Lunga Point	11 Apr 44	14 May 44	24 Oct 46
CVE 95	Bismarck Sea	17 Apr 44	20 May 44	Sunk 21 Feb 45
CVE 96	Salamaua	22 Apr 44	26 May 44	9 May 46
CVE 97	Hollandia	28 Apr 44	1 Jun 44	17 Jan 47

Hull No.	Name	Launched	Commissioned	Decommissioned
CVE 98	Kwajalein	4 May 44	7 Jun 44	16 Aug 46
CVE 99	Admiralty Islands	10 May 44	13 Jun 44	26 Apr 46
CVE 100	Bougainville	16 May 44	18 Jun 44	3 Nov 46
CVE 101	Matanikau	22 May 44	24 Jun 44	11 Oct 46
CVE 102	Attu	27 May 44	30 Jun 44	8 Jun 46
CVE 103	Roi	2 Jun 44	6 Jul 44	9 May 46
CVE 104	Munda	8 Jun 44	8 Jul 44	13 Sep 46
CVE 105	Commencement Bay	4 May 44	27 Nov 44	30 Nov 46
CVE 106	Block Island	10 Jun 44	30 Dec 44	28 May 46
CVE 107	Gilbert Islands	20 Jul 44	5 Feb 45	21 May 46
CVE 108	*Kula Gulf	15 Aug 44	12 May 45	3 July 46
CVE 109	Cape Gloucester	12 Sep 44	5 Mar 45	5 Nov 46
CVE 110	*Salerno Bay	29 Sep 44	19 May 45	4 Oct 47
CVE 111	Vella Gulf	19 Oct 44	9 Apr 45	9 Aug 46
CVE 112	*Siboney	9 Nov 44	14 May 45	? Nov 47
CVE 113	*Puget Sound	30 Nov 44	18 Jun 45	18 Oct 46
CVE 114	*Rendova	28 Dec 44	22 Oct 45	27 Jan 50
CVE 115	*Bairoko	25 Jan 45	16 Jul 45	14 Apr 50
CVE 116	*Badoeng Strait	15 Feb 45	14 Nov 45	20 Apr 46
CVE 117	*Saidor	17 Mar 45	4 Sep 45	12 Sep 47
CVE 118	*Sicily	14 Apr 45	27 Feb 46	5 Jul 54
CVE 119	*Point Cruz	18 May 45	16 Oct 45	30 Jun 47
CVE 120	*Mindoro	27 Jun 45	4 Dec 45	4 Aug 55
CVE 121	*Rabaul	14 Jul 45	30 Aug 46	30 Aug 46
CVE 122	*Palau	6 Aug 45	15 Jan 46	15 Jun 54
CVE 123	*Tinian	5 Sep 45	30 Jul 46	30 Jul 46

(Construction of CVEs 124–127 was suspended on 12 Aug 45 and their hulls were broken up on the slips; construction of CVEs 128–139 was canceled on 11 Aug 45.)

NOTES

Many entries in this section have been abbreviated. Full source information for them can be found in the Bibliography. The following abbreviations are used: AR (Action Report); WD (War Diary); ACA (Air Combat Action Report); ASW (Antisubmarine Warfare Report).

Prologue

1. "Loss of Liscome Bay," Bureau of Ships War Damage Report No. 45 (hereafter cited as BuShips No. 45), pp. 3, 11.

2. Samuel Eliot Morison, *History of United States Naval Operations in World War II* (hereafter cited as Morison), Vol. VII, *Aleutians, Gilberts and Marshalls*, pp. 139–40.

3. "History of the U.S.S. *Liscome Bay*," p. 2.

4. CTG 52.13 Report of Loss of U.S.S. *Liscome Bay*, Enclosure F1, and Enclosure F2, p. 2.

5. Ibid., p. 4.

6. "Loss of *Liscome Bay*," ComInCh Serial 002903, p. 1.

7. BuShips No. 45, pp. 6–7.

8. Ibid., pp. 5–6.

9. Ibid., p. 5; *Liscome Bay* history, p. 2.

10. *Liscome Bay* AR, Serial 0053, 16 December 1943, p. 4; BuShips No. 45, pp. 7–8.

11. *Corregidor* AR, Serial 004, 5 December 1943, Enclosure C.

12. Marshall U. Beebe, "Sis—*Liscome Bay* and Toko-Ri," p. 62.

13. *Liscome Bay* history, p. 3; Robert L. Schwartz, "The Sinking of the *Liscome Bay*," p. 7; BuShips No. 45, p. 4; Beebe, pp. 63–64.

14. Schwartz, p. 7.

15. Ibid.

16. Ibid., p. 8; CTG 52.13 Report of Loss, Enclosure F6, p. 6; Beebe, p. 64.

17. *Liscome Bay* history, pp. 2–3; Schwartz, p. 8.
18. Schwartz, pp. 7–8.
19. Morison VII, p. 141.
20. CTG 52.13 Report of Loss, Enclosure F6, p. 5.

1. Learning the Ropes

1. Norman Friedman, *U.S. Aircraft Carriers*, pp. 161–62.
2. Ibid., p. 162.
3. R. N. Willis correspondence; Friedman, p. 162; Robert J. Cressman, "The President's Escort Carrier," pp. 21–22.
4. Cressman, p. 23; Friedman, p. 162.
5. Cressman, p. 23.
6. Ibid., p. 24.
7. Ibid.
8. Ibid., p. 25.
9. Ibid.
10. R. S. Rogers correspondence.
11. Morison IV, *Coral Sea, Midway and Submarine Actions*, pp. 82–83; Cressman, p. 27.
12. Robert Sherrod, *History of Marine Corps Aviation in World War II*, p. 73.
13. Ibid., pp. 77–79; *Long Island* AR, Serial 009, 3 September 1942, p. 1; Cressman, pp. 28–29.
14. Sherrod, pp. 96, 103.
15. *Long Island* AR, Serial 009, pp. 1–2; Cressman, p. 29.
16. William T. Y'Blood, *Hunter-Killer*, p. 6; Friedman, pp. 169, 173, 406.
17. Y'Blood, pp. 8–9; Friedman, pp. 173, 407.
18. "History of U.S.S. *Suwannee*," Serial 488, 5 November 1945, p. 2; "History of the U.S.S. *Sangamon*," Serial 075, 3 October 1945, p. 2.
19. "War History of U.S.S. *Chenango*," Serial 011, 31 January 1946, pp. 8–9.
20. Morison V, *The Struggle for Guadalcanal*, p. 353.
21. Office of Naval Intelligence, "Japanese Evacuation of Guadalcanal," p. 29.
22. CinCPac Report of Operations, Serial 00172, 17 April 1943, p. 14.
23. CTF 18 AR, Serial 0010, p. 2.
24. Office of Naval Intelligence, "Japanese Evacuation of Guadalcanal," p. 29.
25. CinCPac Report of Operations, Serial 00172, p. 6.
26. Office of Naval Intelligence, "Japanese Evacuation of Guadalcanal," p. 37.
27. Ibid., pp. 26–43; *Chenango* AR, Serial 045, 14 February 1943, pp. 1–4; Morison V, pp. 354–363.
28. *Chenango* AR, Serial 045, p. 5.
29. *Chenango* war history, p. 10.
30. VT-27 WD, March–April 1943, Serial 50674, 16 April 1943 reports.

31. "History of VF-27," p. 2–3.

32. Morison VI, *Breaking the Bismarcks Barrier*, pp. 118–27.

33. *Chenango* Air Operations Summary, no serial, 30 April 1943; Car-Div 22 WDs, Serial 009, 8 April 1943, p. 1, and Serial 0011, 30 April 1943, p. 3.

34. *Chenango* AR, Serial 063, 30 June 1943.

35. CarDiv 22 VF Reports, 18 July and 21 July 1943.

36. "History of the U.S.S. *Nassau*," Serial 018, 27 November 1945, p. 5.

37. Ibid., pp. 7–9.

38. *Nassau* AR, Serial 00371, 5 June 1943, p. 5; Sherrod, p. 219.

39. Sherrod, p. 219.

40. Brian Garfield, *The Thousand-Mile War*, p. 209.

41. *Nassau* AR, Serial 00371, p. 1.

42. Office of Naval Intelligence, "The Aleutians Campaign," p. 86.

43. *Nassau* AR, Serial 00371, p. 6.

44. VC-21 ACA, no number, 14 May 1943.

45. *Nassau* AR, Serial 00371, p. 2; Sherrod, p. 219.

46. Garfield, p. 233; VC-21 ACA, no number, 16 May 1943.

47. Office of Naval Intelligence, "The Aleutians Campaign," p. 93.

48. *Nassau* AR, Serial 00371, p. 6.

49. Ibid., p. 7; Office of Naval Intelligence, "The Aleutians Campaign," pp. 84–85.

50. CTF 51 AR, Serial 00100, 8 July 1943, Annex B, p. 13.

51. Ibid.

2. The Quickening Pace

1. *Nassau* AR, Serial 00371, p. 14.

2. Hamilton Lokey, manuscript.

3. Friedman, pp. 175–76; Y'Blood, *Hunter-Killer*, p. 10; "A History of the U.S.S. *Marcus Island*," p. 50.

4. Philip A. Crowl and Edmund G. Love, *Seizure of the Gilberts and Marshalls*, pp. 12–24.

5. Morison VII, p. 338; Bureau of Aeronautics, "Weekly Location of United States Naval Aircraft" (hereafter cited as "Weekly Location"); records of ships concerned.

6. Morison VII, p. 337; "Weekly Location"; records of ships concerned.

7. "Corregidor—'Saga of the Mighty "C," ' " p. 3.

8. Green Peyton, *5,000 Miles Towards Tokyo*, pp. 39–40.

9. "Saga of the *Sangamon*," p. 3–4.

10. Jeter A. Isely and Philip A. Crowl, *The U.S. Marines and Amphibious War*, p. 224.

11. Morison VII, p. 139.

12. *Nassau* history, p. 17.

13. "History of the U.S.S. *Anzio*," Serial 0152, 21 November 1945, p. 5.

14. Crowl and Love, p. 161.

15. *Liscome Bay* AR, Serial 0054, 8 December 1943, p. 5.

16. *Corregidor* AR, Serial 004, Enclosure C; *Anzio* history, p. 6; CarDiv 24 History, p. 2.

17. Frank Morris, "Overnight Guest," p. 53.

18. CarDiv 24 history, p. 2.

19. Ibid.

20. CarDiv 24 AR, no serial, 8 December 1943, p. 11, Fourth Endorsement.

21. *Anzio* history, p. 7.

22. "Saga of the Sangamon," p. 4; *Chenango* war history, p. 12.

23. *Nassau* history, p. 17.

24. Ibid.

25. "History of the U.S.S. *White Plains*," no serial, 8 October 1945, pp. 15–17; ComAirPac history, p. 56.

26. "History of the U.S.S. *Kalinin Bay*," no serial, no date, p. 2.

27. Sherrod, pp. 228–30.

28. *Kalinin Bay* history, pp. 2–3.

29. Lokey manuscript.

30. *Nassau* history, pp. 19–20; CinCPac Dispatch 091401, 9 February 1944.

31. *Natoma Bay* WD, Serial 022, 13 March 1944, pp. 1, 3; "History of the U.S.S. *Natoma Bay*," Serial 00001, October 1945, p. 8.

32. Morison VII, p. 346; Action Reports of ships concerned.

33. "Saga of the *Sangamon*," p. 5; CTG 53.6 AR, Serial 054, 1 March 1944, p. 2; Office of Naval Intelligence, "The Assault on Kwajalein and Majuro," p. 20.

34. *Sangamon* Report of Collision with U.S.S. *Suwannee,* Serial 003, 10 February 1944, pp. 2–3, and Serial 004, 11 February 1944; Peyton, pp. 63–65; Office of Naval Intelligence, "Assault on Kwajalein," p. 20.

35. Peyton, p. 67.

36. Morison VII, pp. 344–45; CarDiv 24 WD, January 1944.

37. *Manila Bay* AR, Serial 014, 18 February 1944, pp. 2–3.

38. CTG 52.9 AR, Serial 0019, 18 February 1944, p. 3.

39. CTG 53.6 AR, Serial 054, Enclosures B and C; Peyton, pp. 76–77.

40. CTF 53 AR, Serial 0028, 23 February 1944, Enclosure C; Robert D. Heinl and John A. Crown, *The Marshalls: Increasing the Tempo,* pp. 67–68.

41. Air Operations Memorandum No. 21, Serial 0410, 5 February 1944; *Manila Bay* AR, Serial 014, pp. 3–5, 7.

42. CominCh, "Eniwetok," pp. 70–76.

43. *Anzio* history, narrative, p. 10.

44. Morison VII, pp. 286–87; "Saga of the *Sangamon*," pp. 5–6; *Chenango* war history, p. 13.

45. Clark G. Reynolds, *The Fast Carriers,* p. 139.

46. CominCh, "Eniwetok," p. 70-26.

47. Supplementary Report on Carrier Operations of 30 January–24 February 1944, ComAirForPacFlt, Serial 00395, 20 April 1944, p. 13.

48. CTG 52.9 AR, Serial 0019, p. 9.
49. Reynolds, *The Fast Carriers*, p. 133.

3. Moving West

1. CinCPac Report of Operations, Serial 002135, 23 July 1944, p. 11; VC-66 ASW Nos. 1 and 2, 4 April 1944.
2. History, Commander Air Force Pacific Fleet (hereafter cited as Com-AirPac history), p. 57.
3. History and Accomplishment of Carrier Transport Squadron, Pacific Fleet, p. 1.
4. Ibid., Enclosure F.
5. Ibid., p. 2.
6. Ibid., p. 6.
7. ComAirPac history, p. 58.
8. Morison VIII, *New Guinea and the Marianas*, pp. 409–11, 420; Reports of carriers involved; "Weekly Location."
9. VC-68 Operational Notes for Hunter-Killer Employment, no serial, 6 May 1944, pp. 4–5.
10. William R. McClendon correspondence.
11. *Kalinin Bay* history, p. 6.
12. Morison VIII, p. 420; Report of carriers involved; "Weekly Location."
13. "*Kitkun Bay* War History," Serial 900, 17 November 1945, Chapter 6, p. 2.
14. Ibid., p. 3.
15. John Stewart narrative, supplied by Henry Pyzdrowski.
16. Suwannee AR, Serial 069, 2 October 1944, pp. 4–5; CVEG-60 ACA No. 1-44, 15 June 1944.
17. *Fanshaw Bay* AR, Serial 002, 10 July 1944, pp. 1–2; *White Plains* history, p. 22.
18. VC-68 ACA No. 2, 15 June 1944.
19. CarDiv 24 AR, Serial 0004, 1 July 1944, pp. 3–4.
20. *Suwannee* AR, Serial 069, pp. 4–5.
21. William T. Y'Blood, *Red Sun Setting*, p. 16.
22. Ibid., p. 80.
23. Huxtable correspondence.
24. *Gambier Bay* AR, Serial 046, 4 July 1944, 17 June Action, pp. 3–4; Edwin P. Hoyt, *The Men of the Gambier Bay*, p. 107.
25. *Corregidor* AR, Serial 0004, 28 June 1944, Enclosure B.
26. Ibid., p. 5; *Anzio* history, pp. 19–20.
27. "*Kitkun Bay* War History," Chapter 6, p. 5.
28. VC-65 ACA No. 6-44, 17 June 1944.
29. Faulkner interview.
30. *White Plains* AR, Serial 062, 1 July 1944, pp. 2–3.
31. "Escort Carriers' Gunfire, Bomb and Kamikaze Damages and Losses during World War II," Bureau of Ships War Damage Report No. 60 (hereafter cited as BuShips No. 60), pp. 108–10.

32. *Fanshaw Bay* AR, Serial 001, 10 July 1944, First Endorsement, p. 2.
33. Gerald F. Bogan oral history, p. 74.
34. Ibid., p. 79.
35. *Fanshaw Bay* AR, Serial 001, A/A Action Report, p. 3.
36. *White Plains* AR, Serial 062, p. 3; *White Plains* history, p. 24; Robert F. Johnson correspondence.
37. *Kalinin Bay* history, pp. 19–20.
38. Bogan oral history, p. 77; *Kalinin Bay* WD, June 1944, Serial 062, 1 July 1944, pp. 6–8.
39. Huxtable correspondence; Hoyt, *Men of the Gambier Bay*, p. 110.
40. VC-33 ACA Nos. 4 and 6, 18 and 20 June 1944.
41. VC-33 ACA No. 5, 18 June 1944; VC-5 ACA No. 7, 18 June 1944.
42. "*Kitkun Bay* War History," Chapter 6, pp. 6–7; Hoyt, *Men of Gambier Bay*, p. 113.
43. *Gambier Bay* AR, Serial 046, 18 June Action, p. 5.
44. McClendon correspondence.
45. *Gambier Bay* AR, Serial 046, 18 June Action, p. 5.
46. Ibid., pp. 1–8; *Corregidor* AR, Serial 0004, pp. 5–7; *Anzio* history, pp. 20–21; CarDiv 24 AR, Serial 0004, p. 6; McClendon correspondence.
47. *Corregidor* AR, Serial 0004, pp. 7–8; "*Kitkun Bay* War History," Chapter 6, p. 7; *Anzio* history, p. 21; *Gambier Bay* AR, Serial 046, 19 June Action.
48. CarDiv 24 AR, Serial 0004, p. 7; VC-33 ACA No. 4, 20 June 1944.
49. Hoyt, *Men of the Gambier Bay*, p. 119.
50. McClendon correspondence; Hoyt, *Men of the Gambier Bay*, pp. 119–20.
51. VT-60 ASW No. 1-44, 19 June 1944.
52. *Suwannee* AR, Serial 069, p. 5; Peyton, p. 108.
53. *Chenango* AR, Serial 0138, 10 September 1944; *Chenango* Air Operations Summary, 12 May to 4 August 1944, no serial, 22 August 1944, pp. 1–2.
54. Philip A. Crowl, *Campaign in the Marianas*, pp. 314–15.
55. CarDiv 24 AR, Serial 0004, pp. 8, 11, 13.
56. CVEG-37 ACA No. 2, 24 June 1944.
57. *Sangamon* ACA Reports Summary, Serial 039, 6 July 1944, p. 2; *Suwannee* AR, Serial 069, p. 5.
58. *Suwannee* AR, Serial 069, p. 6; "History of the U.S.S. *Sangamon*," p. 6.
59. *White Plains* history, p. 25; Analysis of Pacific Air Operations (Marianas Operations, 11–30 June 1944), Serial 001224, 20 September 1944, p. 38.
60. *Kalinin Bay* history, p. 6; VC-68 history, p. 3; VC-4 history, p. 10.
61. Clive Howard and Joe Whitley, *One Damned Island After Another*, pp. 218–19.
62. Lokey manuscript.
63. Herb Faulkner interview.
64. *Manila Bay* AR, Serial 063, 26 June 1944; *Natoma Bay* WD, Serial 057, 11 July 1944, pp. 9–10; Howard and Whitley, pp. 223–24.

65. Edward J. Huxtable correspondence.
66. Ibid.
67. Isely and Crowl, p. 334; Crowl, p. 132; CVEG-60 history, pp. IIh/2–3.
68. CTG 52.14 Report of Strafing, Serial 0015, 8 July 1944.
69. Ibid.
70. *Hoggatt Bay* AR, Serial 0107, 18 August 1944, pp. 1–2; *ASW Bulletin,* September 1944, p. 29.
71. *Hoggatt Bay* AR, Serial 0107, p. 2; Theodore Roscoe, *United States Destroyer Operations in World War II,* p. 411.
72. CTF 52 AR, Serial 0232, 24 August 1944, p.4; *White Plains* history, p. 25.
73. CTF 52 AR, Serial 0232, p. 105.
74. Huxtable correspondence; Morison VIII, pp. 361–62.
75. Stewart narrative; Hoyt, *Men of the Gambier Bay,* p. 137.
76. VC-11 ACA Nos. 1 (24 July 1944), 2 (25 July 1944), and 5 (30 July 1944).
77. CTF 52 AR, Serial 0232, p. 112.
78. Isely and Crowl, p. 363.
79. Carl W. Hoffman, *The Seizure of Tinian,* p. 128.
80. CarDiv 24 AR, Serial 0006, 16 July 1944.
81. *Chenango* Air Operations Summary, 22 August 1944, p. 3; Reynolds, *The Fast Carriers,* p. 329; O. R. Lodge, *The Recapture of Guam,* p. 95.
82. CTF 53 AR, Serial 00224, 10 August 1944, p. 22C.
83. Lodge, p. 168.
84. CTF 53 AR, Serial 00224, p. 22C.
85. *Santee* AR, Serial 056, 31 August 1944, p. 1.

4. Approach to the Philippines

1. *Natoma Bay* AR, Serial 029, 21 March 1944, p. 2; CarDiv 24 AR, Serial 0028, 21 March 1944.
2. Lokey manuscript.
3. Ibid.
4. *Corregidor* AR, Serial 009, 15 April 1944, p. 3; *Anzio* history, p. 13.
5. *Chenango* war history, pp. 13–14.
6. Robert Ross Smith, *The Approach to the Philippines,* pp. 20, 23.
7. *Chenango* war history, p. 5.
8. Morison VIII, p. 405; reports of carriers involved; "Weekly Location."
9. Lokey manuscript.
10. Ibid.
11. CVEG-37 ACA No. 1, 30 April 1944.
12. *Chenango* war history, p. 14.
13. *Anzio* history, p. 15.
14. CarDiv 24 history, p. 3.
15. McClendon correspondence.

16. *Anzio* history, p. 16.
17. Jess U. Fritter correspondence.
18. *Anzio* history, p. 17; *Natoma Bay* history, pp. 10–11.
19. *Hoggatt Bay* AR, Serial 0030, 27 July 1944, pp. 2–3; *Red Sun Setting*, pp. 21–24.
20. *Hoggatt Bay* AR, Serial 0030, pp. 3–4; *ASW Bulletin*, September 1944, pp. 28–29.
21. Reports of carriers involved; "Weekly Location."
22. Smith, *The Approach to the Philippines*, pp. 487, 489.
23. *Santee* AR, Serial 069, 9 October 1944, Enclosure C; Bulkley, pp. 368–70; CVEG-37 ACA No. 32, 16 September 1944; Suwannee AR, Serial 073, 2 October 1944; Peyton, pp. 123–26; Morison XII, *Leyte*, pp. 26–27.
24. CVEG-37 ACA No. 32, 16 September 1944.
25. VT-35 ACA No. 1, 21 September 1944.
26. *Midway* AR, Serial 006, 7 October 1944, p. 11.
27. *Fanshaw Bay* AR, Serial 0151, p. 5; Morison XII, pp. 27–28; Clay Blair, Jr., *Silent Victory*, pp. 736–37.
28. Reports of carriers involved; "Weekly Location."
29. Morison XII, pp. 75–76.
30. *Sitkoh Bay* AR, Serial 001, 26 November 1944, p. 2.
31. *Tulagi* AR, Serial 007, 14 March 1945, p. 26.
32. Ibid., p. 27.
33. *Sitkoh Bay* AR, Serial 001, p. 3.
34. VC-20 Squadron Commander's Report, no serial, 10 October 1944, p. 3.
35. *Tulagi* AR, Serial 007, p. 27.
36. *Sitkoh Bay* AR, Serial 001, p. 2.
37. Hoyt, *Men of the Gambier Bay*, pp. 146–47.
38. Morison VII, p. 253.
39. "A News History of the U.S.S. *Hoggatt Bay*," p. 2.
40. Air Analysis, Palau Operations, Serial 001809, no date, p. 7.
41. VC-21 ACA No. 14, 15 September 1944.
42. *Marcus Island* AR, Serial 006, 3 October 1944, p. 3; *Petrof Bay* AR, Serial 049, 2 October 1944, p. 6; Huxtable correspondence; George W. Garand and Truman R. Strobridge, *Western Pacific Operations*, pp. 122–24.
43. Air Analysis, Palau Operations, p. 7.
44. CTU 32.7.1 AR, Serial 0013, 5 October 1944, p. 9.
45. Garand and Strobridge, p. 103.
46. Ibid., pp. 172, 283.
47. VC-20 VF Air Support and Carrier Operations during the Palau Landings, no serial, 3 October 1944, p. 1.
48. Ibid.
49. CTG 32.7 AR, Serial 00011, 10 October 1944, Part V, p. 1.
50. Ibid., Part V, p. 2.
51. Air Analysis, Palau Operations, pp. 7–8.

52. *Hoggatt Bay* AR, Serial 0055, 11 October 1944, pp. 3–4; Roscoe, pp. 435–36.

53. *Sangamon* history, p. 7.

5. The Return

1. Morison XII, p. 7.

2. Ibid., pp. 9–12.

3. Ibid., pp. 13–15.

4. Ibid., p. 113.

5. Ibid., pp. 420–21, 428; reports of carriers involved; "Weekly Location."

6. George van Deurs oral history, pp. 484–85.

7. Alexander G. Booth correspondence.

8. Morison XII, pp. 116, 416, 418–19.

9. Lokey manuscript.

10. *Manila Bay* AR, Serial 0103, 2 November 1944, p. 3; "Saga of the *Sangamon*," p. 9; *Chenango* AR, Serial 0324, 5 November 1944, p. 1.

11. Richard W. Bates, *The Battle for Leyte Gulf, October 1944, Strategical and Tactical Analysis*, Vol. II, p. 159.

12. *Suwannee* AR, Serial 008, 6 November 1944, p. 4; Bates, Vol. II, p. 159.

13. *Chenango* AR, Serial 0324, Mailgram 300647 of October; *Chenango* Air Operations Summary No. 6, 1 November 1944, pp. 6–7.

14. VC-3 ACA No. 99, 18 October 1944; Bates, Vol. II, pp. 159–60.

15. CVEG-60 ACA No. 37–44, 18 October 1944.

16. CTU 77.4.2 AR, Serial 00114, 2 November 1944, p. 5.

17. Bates, Vol. II, p. 279.

18. CVEG-37 ACA No. 39, 19 October 1944.

19. *Chenango* AR, Serial 0324, Mailgram 300647; *Chenango* Air Operations Summary No. 6, p. 7.

20. *Chenango* AR, Serial 0324, Mailgrams 300645 and 300647.

21. Air Analysis, Carrier Operations in Support of the Leyte Campaign, Serial 00233, 4 February 1945, p. 8.

22. CVEG-37 ACA No. 40, 20 October 1944.

23. "Saga of the *Sangamon*," p. 10.

24. BuShips No. 60, p. 116.

25. *Santee* AR, Serial 0018, 5 November 1944, Part II, p. 1; *Sangamon* AR, Serial 065, 5 November 1944, Enclosure A, pp. 2, 7, 17, Enclosure D; *Suwannee* AR, Serial 008, p. 4; "Saga of the *Sangamon*," pp. 10–11.

26. *Marcus Island* AR, Serial 053, 1 November 1944, p. 4; VC-21 ACA No. 51, 20 October 1944; VC-21 history, p. 18.

27. Bates, Vol. III, Part 1, p. 23.

28. Ibid., pp. 25–26.

29. Ibid., p. 304; Denis Warner and Peggy Warner, *The Sacred Warriors*, p. 93.

30. Bates, Vol. III, Part 1, pp. 305–6.

31. Ibid., p. 306; *Manila Bay* AR, Serial 103, p. 11.

32. *Savo Island* AR, Serial 074, 3 November 1944, p. 6.

33. William S. Stewart correspondence.

34. Bates, Vol. III, Part 2, pp. 537–39.

35. Ibid., p. 745.

36. Ibid., p. 744; *Suwannee* AR, Serial 008, p. 5.

37. Air Analysis, Carrier Operations in Support of the Leyte Campaign, pp. 8, 10.

38. Bates, Vol. V, Part 1, p. 92.

39. VC-10 ACA, no number, 24 October 1944.

40. VC-27 ACA No. 20, 24 October 1944.

41. VC-5 ACA No. 53, 24 October 1944.

42. VC-3 ACA No. 110, 24 October 1944.

43. VF-26 ACA Nos. 20 and 22, 24 October 1944.

44. VF-37 ACA No. 48, 24 October 1944.

45. Hoyt, *Men of the Gambier Bay,* p. 170.

46. Bates, Vol. V, Part 1, pp. 127–28.

47. VC-27 ACA No. 21, 24 October 1944.

48. VC-68 ACA No. 14, 24 October 1944.

49. Bates, Vol. V, Part 1, pp. 128–29.

50. VC-21 ACA No. 63, 24 October 1944.

51. McClendon correspondence.

52. Bates, Vol. V, Part 1, pp. 129–30.

53. Edward W. Reed correspondence.

54. *Gambier Bay* AR, Serial 002, 27 November 1944, Enclosure A, p. 3; W. V. R. Vieweg narrative, p. 3.

55. *Ommaney Bay* AR, Serial 0018, 3 November 1944, p. 13.

56. *Fanshaw Bay* AR, Serial 0160, 2 November 1944, p. 4.

57. CVEG-37 ACA No. 44, Supplement, 25 October 1944.

58. VC-75 ACA No. 47, 25 October 1944.

59. *Sangamon* AR, Serial 065, Enclosure A, p. 3; *Suwannee* AR, Serial 008, p. 5; VC-80 ACA Nos. 6 and 7, 25 October 1944; VC-4 ACA No. 60, 25 October 1944.

60. "A History of the U.S.S. *Marcus Island*," p. 15.

61. *Marcus Island* AR, Serial 053, pp. 8–9.

6. "They're Shooting at Us in Technicolor"

1. Adrian Stewart, *The Battle of Leyte Gulf,* p. 149; Morison XII, pp. 247–48.

2. VC-20 ACA No. 69, 25 October 1944; "War History of the U.S.S. *Kadashan Bay,*" Serial 065, 28 November 1945, pp. 8–9.

3. Morison XII, p. 248.

4. VC-65 ACA No. 65, 25 October 1944.

5. Sprague, pp. 40–41.

6. CTU 77.4.3 AR, Serial 00100, 29 October 1944, TBS Log, p. 2.

7. *White Plains* AR, Serial 001, 27 October 1944, p. 1.

8. Morison XII, p. 295.
9. *White Plains* AR, Serial 001, p. 6.
10. Robert F. Johnson correspondence.
11. Morison XII, p. 252.
12. *White Plains* AR, Serial 001, p. 6.
13. Ibid., Enclosure A, p. 2.
14. *White Plains* history, p. 31.
15. *White Plains* AR, Serial 001, Enclosure H, pp. 1–2.
16. Ibid., p. 5.
17. Reports of carriers involved.
18. Huxtable correspondence.
19. Hoyt, *Men of the Gambier Bay,* pp. 188–96.
20. C. J. Dugan correspondence.
21. U.S. Strategic Bombing Survey (Pacific), *Interrogations of Japanese Officials* (hereafter cited as *Interrogations*), Vol. 1, p. 174.
22. VC-68 ACA No. 20, 25 October 1944.
23. VC-68 ACA Nos. 20 to 36, 25 October 1944.
24. VC-65 ACA Nos. 30-44 and 31-44, 25 October 1944.
25. VC-4 ACA No. 62, 25 October 1944.
26. VC-4 ACA Nos. 62 to 66, 25 October 1944.
27. VC-3 ACA No. 113, 25 October 1944.
28. VC-5 ACA No. 56, 25 October 1944.
29. VC-5 ACA Nos. 56 and 60, 25 October 1944; VC-5 History, p. 25; *Kitkun Bay* AR, Serial 005, 28 October 1944, Enclosure H, pp. 1–4.
30. Morison XII, p. 260n.
31. Morison XII, pp. 255–75; Roscoe, pp. 425–31; Stewart, pp. 156–57, 161–71.
32. *White Plains* AR, Serial 001, TBS Log.
33. "*Kitkun Bay* War History," Chapter 10, p. 3.
34. *Kitkun Bay* AR, Serial 005, Enclosure B, p. 1.
35. BuShips No. 60, pp. 17–24; *Kalinin Bay* AR, Serial 094, 30 October 1944, pp. 4–7.
36. *Kalinin Bay* AR, Serial 094, p. 8.
37. BuShips No. 60, pp. 111–13; *Fanshaw Bay* AR, Serial 0160, pp. 7, 15–19, 21.
38. Vieweg narrative, p. 6.
39. Hoyt, *Men of the Gambier Bay,* p. 203.
40. Vieweg narrative, pp. 8–9.
41. *Gambier Bay* AR, Serial 002; BuShips No. 60, pp. 11–17; Hoyt, *Men of the Gambier Bay,* pp. 198–216.
42. *White Plains* AR, Serial 001, p. 6.
43. Ibid.
44. C. A. F. Sprague, "The Japs Had Us on the Ropes," p. 116.
45. *Interrogations,* Vol. 1, p. 46.
46. *Manila Bay* AR, Serial 0103, Part V, Section A, p. 8.
47. Lokey manuscript.

48. CTU 77.4.2 AR, Serial 00114, p. 14.

49. Fitzhugh Lee oral history, p. 7.

50. VC-81 ACA No. 16, 25 October 1944; VC-21 ACA No. 65, 25 October 1944; VC-27 ACA Nos. 25 and 26, 25 October 1944.

51. Lokey manuscript.

52. VC-76 ACA No. 70, 25 October 1944.

53. John D. Ahlstrom, "Leyte Gulf Remembered," p. 49.

54. VC-76 ACA No. 71, 25 October 1944.

55. Ibid.

56. CTU 77.4.2 AR, Serial 00114, p. 15.

57. VC-20 Amplifying Report to ACA Nos. 71 and 73, 25 October 1944.

58. Suggested news release for Kruck in VC-20 ACA Reports.

59. VC-81 ACA No. 17, 25 October 1944.

60. VC-75 ACA Nos. 48 to 50, 25 October 1944; VC-80 ACA No. 8, 25 October 1944.

61. CTU 77.4.2 AR, Serial 00114, p. 16.

62. VC-68 ACA No. 23, 25 October 1944.

63. VC-81 ACA No. 18, 25 October 1944.

7. Death from the Sky

1. Field, pp. 15, 17, 61.

2. Warner and Warner, pp. 85–94; Inoguchi and Nakajima, pp. 3–44.

3. Warner and Warner, p. 103.

4. *Santee* AR, Serial 0018, Part II, p. 2; BuShips No. 60, pp. 65–66; Morison XII, pp. 300–301.

5. *Sangamon* AR, Serial 065, Enclosure A, p. 4, Enclosure D; Morison XII, p. 301.

6. *Petrof Bay* AR, Serial 052, 2 November 1944, p. 3; Ahlstrom, p. 48.

7. *Santee* AR, Serial 0018, Part II, p. 2; BuShips No. 60, pp. 66–67; Morison XII, p. 301.

8. *Suwannee* AR, Serial 008, p. 6; BuShips No. 60, pp. 61–62.

9. "Saga of the *Sangamon*," p. 13.

10. *Petrof Bay* AR, Serial 052, p. 11.

11. VC-65 ACA No. 57 and VC-4 ACA No. 61, both 25 October 1944.

12. *Kitkun Bay* AR, Serial 005, Enclosure B, p. 2; *Kitkun Bay* history, Chapter 10, pp. 7–8; BuShips No. 60, p. 114.

13. *White Plains* AR, Serial 001, Enclosure A, p. 11.

14. Ibid.

15. *St. Lo* AR, no serial, 25 November 1944, Annex J, p. 1.

16. Ibid., pp. 5–6, Navigator's Report, pp. 3–7, Annex J, pp. 1–6; BuShips No. 60, pp. 90–99; Warner and Warner, p. 108; C. Vann Woodward, *The Battle for Leyte Gulf*, pp. 210–11.

17. *Kitkun Bay* AR, Serial 005, Enclosure B, p. 3.

18. Ibid.; "*Kitkun Bay* History," Chapter 10, p. 8.

19. *Kalinin Bay* AR, Serial 094, Enclosure A, p. 3; BuShips No. 60, pp. 19–20; Warner and Warner, pp. 108–9.

20. CTU 77.4.3 AR, Serial 00100, Enclosure C, p. 3; VC-5 ACA No. 59, 25 October 1944.
21. "They Ran . . . But Won," p. 4.
22. Morison XII, pp. 303–5; *Petrof Bay* history, p. 7.
23. CTU 77.4.2 AR, Serial 00114, p. 17; *Kitkun Bay* AR, Serial 005, Enclosure I, p. 5.
24. VC-81 ACA No. 19, 25 October 1944.
25. VC-80 ACA No. 10; VC-27 ACA No. 29; VC-5 ACA Nos. 58 and 60; VC-21 ACA No. 66, all 25 October 1944.
26. Stewart correspondence; Henry H. Henderson correspondence.
27. CTU 77.4.2 AR, Serial 00114, p. 18.
28. VC-75 ACA No. 51, 25 October 1944; A. R. Zubik correspondence; *Ommaney Bay* history, pp. 59–61; *Ommaney Bay* AR, Serial 0018, p. 16.
29. Zubik correspondence.
30. CTU 77.4.2 AR, Serial 00114, p. 18.
31. Ahlstrom, p. 52.
32. VC-20 ACA No. 74; VC-21 ACA No. 67, both 25 October 1944.
33. VC-27 ACA No. 31, 25 October 1944.
34. VC-80 ACA No. 12, 25 October 1944.
35. CTU 77.4.2 AR, Serial 00114, p. 20.
36. Ibid., p. 19.

8. Finale at Leyte Gulf

1. Dugan correspondence.
2. Jack Turner interview.
3. Ibid.
4. Dugan correspondence.
5. VC-65 ACA No. 31-44, 25 October 1944.
6. VC-65 ACA No. 32-44, 25 October 1944.
7. Stewart, p. 208; *Natoma Bay* AR, Serial 00041, 1 November 1944, pp. 12–13; VC-21 ACA No. 68; VC-20 ACA No. 75; VC-27 ACA No. 32; VC-76 ACA Nos. 73 and 74; CVEG-60 ACA No. 48-44, all 26 October 1944.
8. Warner and Warner, p. 111.
9. *Petrof Bay* AR, Serial 052, Enclosure B, p. 2.
10. *Suwannee* AR, Serial 008, Enclosure F, p. 2.
11. Ibid., pp. 6–7, Enclosure D; BuShips No. 60, pp. 62–65.
12. *Suwannee* history, pp. 8–9.
13. *Petrof Bay* AR, Serial 052, Enclosure B, p. 2.
14. "Carrier Aircraft in Battle for Leyte Gulf," p. 53.
15. Ibid., p. 55.
16. Ibid., p. 56.
17. Ibid., p. 20.
18. Hoyt, *Men of the Gambier Bay,* p. 229.
19. Morison XII, pp. 306–7.
20. Hoyt, *Men of the Gambier Bay,* p. 234.

21. Leon Fletcher, "Rescue of the *Gambier Bay*, CVE-73," pp. 29–37, 73; Morison XII, pp. 313–16.

22. Morison XII, p. 316.

23. Air Analysis, Carrier Operations in Support of the Leyte Campaign, pp. 12–13.

24. CTU 77.4.3 AR, Serial 00100, Enclosure B, p. 1.

25. E. B. Potter, *Bull Halsey*, p. 302.

26. CTU 77.4.3 AR, Serial 00100, p. 1.

27. Ibid., Enclosure B, p. 2.

9. Divine Wind—Two Versions

1. *Natoma Bay* Association, *Logbook*, "Recollections," p. 5.

2. Ibid., "Recollections," p. 10.

3. Stewart correspondence.

4. *Natoma Bay* Association, *Logbook*, "Recollections," p. 6.

5. *Petrof Bay* AR, Serial 055, 28 November 1944, pp. 1–3.

6. *Anzio* AR, Serial 0001, 28 November 1944, Enclosure A, pp. 1–2; Roscoe, p. 441.

7. *Anzio* history, p. 29.

8. VC-83 ACA Nos. 1 and 2, 4 November 1944.

9. See Y'Blood, *Hunter-Killer*, for night operations in the Atlantic.

10. "VC-42 History," p. 104.

11. Morison XIII, *The Liberation of the Philippines*, p. 5.

12. Ibid., pp. 3–11, 18.

13. Ibid., p. 19.

14. *Manila Bay* AR, Serial 0093, 23 December 1944, Part I, pp. 1–2; "Weekly Location."

15. *Kadashan Bay* war history, p. 12.

16. VC-75 Squadron Commander's AR, no serial, 18 December 1944, p. 2; "History of VC-81," p. 24; Morison XIII, p. 21.

17. Henderson correspondence.

18. CarDiv 24 AR, Serial 00130, 25 December 1944, p. 6.

19. VC-27 ACA No. 3, 13 December 1944.

20. *Manila Bay* AR, Serial 0093, Part II, p. 5; CarDiv 24 AR, Serial 00130, p. 7.

21. Warner and Warner, p. 139.

22. VC-81 ACA No. 38, 13 December 1944.

23. VC-75 ACA No. 57, 13 December 1944.

24. VC-20 ACA No. 79, 13 December 1944.

25. Morison XIII, p. 24.

26. *Natoma Bay* AR, Serial 00059, 23 December 1944, pp. 3–4; *Natoma Bay* WD, Serial 20005, 1 January 1945, pp. 4–5; *Manila Bay* AR, Serial 0093, Part II, pp. 5–6; *Ommaney Bay* AR, Serial 077, 19 December 1944, pp. 4–5; Morison XIII, pp. 23–25.

27. CarDiv 24 AR, Serial 00130, p. 5; *Natoma Bay* WD, Serial 20005, p. 4.

28. VC-81 ACA No. 29, 14 December 1944.

29. VC-75 ACA No. 58, 14 December 1944.

30. Air Operations Memo, 19 January 1945, p. 7.

31. VC-20 ACA No. 80; VC-21 ACA No. 72, both 14 December 1944.

32. Morison XIII, p. 29.

33. Ibid.

34. *Marcus Island* AR, Serial 080, 19 December 1944, p. 8.

35. Ibid., pp. 3–4.

36. VC-75 ACA No. 60, 15 December 1944.

37. Ibid.

38. VC-27 ACA No. 5, 15 December 1944.

39. *Ommaney Bay* AR, Serial 077, pp. 8, 11, 20–21; *Natoma Bay* WD, Serial 20005, p. 8.

40. CarDiv 24 AR, Serial 00130, p. 5; VC-21 ACA No. 74; VC-81 ACA No. 30, both 15 December 1944.

41. Morison XIII, p. 29.

42. VC-75 ACA No. 62, 16 December 1944; *Savo Island* AR, Serial 008, p. 9.

43. CarDiv 24 AR, Serial 00130, pp. 3, 5.

44. *Ommaney Bay* AR, Serial 077, p. 21.

45. Warner and Warner, p. 148.

46. *Ommaney Bay* AR, Serial 077, pp. 21–22.

47. Air Operations Memo, 19 January 1945, p. 3.

48. *Savo Island* AR, Serial 008, p. 16.

49. *Manila Bay* AR, Serial 0093, Part V, Section D, p. 2.

50. *Natoma Bay* WD, Serial 00005, p. 11.

51. CarDiv 24 AR, Serial 00130, p. 14.

52. C. Raymond Calhoun, *Typhoon: The Other Enemy,* p. 215; reports of carriers involved.

53. Calhoun, p. 32.

54. Ibid., p. 38.

55. Ibid., p. 52.

56. Ibid., p. 65.

57. *Nehenta Bay,* Report of Typhoon, Serial 087, 24 December 1944.

58. *Anzio* history, Serial 0152, pp. 30–31.

59. *Kwajalein* AR, Serial 072, 13 February 1945, p. 1.

60. Ibid.

61. Ibid.

62. *Cape Esperance* AR, Serial 009, 26 December 1944, pp. 5, 8–11; Hans Christian Adamson and George Francis Kosco, *Halsey's Typhoons,* pp. 108–113.

63. *Altamaha,* Encounter with Typhoon, Serial 004, 20 December 1944, pp. 2–3.

64. Ibid.; also *Altamaha* Serial 005, 20 December 1944; Calhoun, pp. 91–93; Adamson and Kosco, pp. 74–79.

65. See Calhoun, pp. 3–8, 155–201 for a lively discussion on the stability problems.

66. Calhoun, pp. 109–15.
67. Ibid., pp. 118–19.

10. A Covey of Kamikazes

1. ComAirPac history, pp. 58–59.
2. Ibid., p. 59.
3. Analysis of Air Operations: CVE Operations, January 1945 (hereafter cited as CVE Operations), pp. 1–2; Morison XIII, pp. 304–6; reports of carriers involved; "Weekly Location."
4. Y'Blood, *Hunter-Killer*, pp. 198, 202, 204–5, 207–9; Barrett Tillman, *The Wildcat in W W II*, pp. 241–42.
5. CVE Operations, pp. 2–3.
6. Morison XIII, p. 98.
7. *Manila Bay* AR, Serial 001, 23 January 1945, Part II, p. 4.
8. Morison XIII, p. 99.
9. CarDiv 24 AR, Serial 001, 18 January 1945, p. 17.
10. *Ommaney Bay* AR, Serial 001, 4 February 1945, Enclosure A, pp. 3–4.
11. BuShips No. 60, p. 40.
12. *U.S.S. Ommaney Bay (CVE-79) and Composite Squadron VC-75 History,* pp. 37–39.
13. Ibid., p. 55.
14. Ibid., p. 23.
15. Ibid., pp. 40–41.
16. Henderson correspondence.
17. *Ommaney Bay* ARs, Serial 001, Enclosure A, pp. 1–2, 4–9, and Serial 002, 3 February 1945; Buships No. 60, pp. 35–43; *Ommaney Bay* and VC-75 history, pp. 37–45; Morison XIII, pp. 101, 108.
18. CarDiv 24 AR, Serial 001, p. 18.
19. *Ommaney Bay* AR, Serial 001, Enclosure A, p. 9.
20. Ibid., pp. 9–10; BuShips No. 60, p. 43.
21. Lee oral history, p. 131.
22. *Lunga Point* AR, Serial 010, 23 January 1945, Enclosure A, p. 4.
23. Ibid., Enclosure C.
24. Price Gilbert, *The Escort Carriers in Action*, p. 89.
25. VOC-1 ACA No. 2, 5 January 1945.
26. Morison XIII, p. 102; Warner and Warner, p. 152.
27. Morison XIII, p. 102; CVE Operations, p. 3; *Tulagi* AR, Serial 001, 3 February 1945, pp. 4–5; ACAs of VC-84, VC-85, VC-86, VC-87, VC-88, VC-92.
28. VC-92 ACA No. 1, 5 January 1945.
29. Morison XIII, pp. 103–4.
30. *Natoma Bay* AR, Serial 00003, 30 January 1945, p. 10.
31. Lee oral history, p. 138.
32. *Manila Bay* AR, Serial 001, Part I, p. 2, also Part II, pp. 10–11, Part IV, pp. 3–5, Part V, Section D, pp. 1–2; Lee oral history, pp. 131–40.
33. *Manila Bay* AR, Serial 001, Part V, Section D, p. 2.

34. *Savo Island* AR, Serial 003, 19 January 1945, p. 6; BuShips No. 60, p. 121.

35. Faulkner interview.

36. *Natoma Bay* AR, Serial 00003, p. 10.

37. Ibid., p. 11; Morison XIII, p. 103.

38. *Natoma Bay* Association, *Logbook*, "Recollections," p. 9.

39. VC-21 ACA No. 76, 3 January 1945.

40. VC-21 ASW No. 1, 5 January 1945; Morison XIII, p. 115; Roscoe, p. 455.

41. VOC-1 ACA No. 3; VC-81 ACA No. 33, both 6 January 1945.

42. VC-81 ACA No. 34, 6 January 1944.

43. Warner and Warner, p. 155.

44. Morison XIII, pp. 105–9.

45. CVE Operations, p. 13.

46. CarDiv 24 AR, Serial 001, p. 17.

47. *Kadashan Bay* AR, Serial 01, 14 January 1945, p. 25.

48. Ibid.; CarDiv 24 AR, Serial 001, p. 19; *Makin Island* AR, Serial 001, 25 January 1945, p. 42.

49. CVE Operations, p. 16.

50. CarDiv 24 AR, Serial 001, p. 18.

51. Morison XIII, p. 110.

52. CVE Operations, pp. 10–11.

53. Walter Karig, *Battle Report*, Vol. V., *Victory in the Pacific*, p. 174.

54. VC-91 ACA No. 1; VC-94 ACA No. 1, both 7 January 1945.

55. *Tulagi* AR, Serial 01, p. 6.

56. VC-81 ACA No. 37, 7 January 1945; VC-90 History, p. 20.

57. Morison XIII, p. 113.

58. VC-21 ACA No. 77, 8 January 1945.

59. VC-20 ACA 81, 8 January 1945.

60. *Kadashan Bay* AR, Serial 01; *Kadashan Bay* war history, pp. 17–18, 20–22; BuShips No. 60, pp. 122–24; Morison XIII, pp. 116–17.

61. VC-91 ACA No. 3, 8 January 1945.

62. *Shamrock Bay* AR, Serial 001, 26 January 1945, pp. 2–3.

63. *Kitkun Bay* AR, Serial 00101, 22 January 1945, Enclosure J, p. 1.

64. Ibid., all enclosures; "*Kitkun Bay* War History," Chapter 13, pp. 5–7; BuShips No. 60, pp. 125–27.

65. *Kitkun Bay* AR, Serial 00101, Enclosure H, p. 1.

66. CVE Operations, p. 4.

67. Ibid., p. 5.

68. Ibid., p. 8.

69. Ibid., p. 6.

70. *Manila Bay* AR, Serial 001, Part V, Section A, pp. 3–4.

71. Ibid., p. 4.

72. *Makin Island* AR, Serial 001, 25 January 1945, p. 14.

73. *Petrof Bay* AR, Serial 16, 27 January 1945, p. 2.

74. *Shamrock Bay* AR, Serial 001, p. 5.

75. *Lunga Point* AR, Serial 01, Enclosure A, p. 8.
76. *Natoma Bay* AR, Serial 00003, p. 17.
77. *Marcus Island* AR, Serial 04, 3 February 1945, p. 12.
78. *Manila Bay* AR, Serial 001, Part I, pp. 3–4.
79. *Natoma Bay* AR, Serial 00003, p. 37.
80. Ibid., p. 17.
81. *Manila Bay* AR, Serial 001, Part I, p. 3.
82. Smith, *Lunga Point,* pp. 156–61.
83. Harbold correspondence.
84. BuShips No. 60, pp. 128–30; Morison XIII, p. 152.
85. *Tulagi* AR, Serial 001, p. 9; *Hoggatt Bay* AR, Serial 004, 23 January 1945, p. II-5.
86. VC-92 ACA No. 11, 14 January 1945.
87. *Tulagi* AR, Serial 001, p. 11.
88. *Hoggatt Bay* AR, Serial 004, Enclosure A; VC-88 ACA No. 25, 15 January 1945.
89. CVE Operations, p. 12; CarDiv 24 AR, Serial 044, 15 February 1945, p. 1.
90. Lee oral history, p. 139.
91. CVE Operations, pp. 10–11.
92. CTU 77.4.1 AR, Serial 00161, 27 January 1945, p. 6.
93. *Luzon Campaign,* p. 238.
94. Ibid.
95. CVE Operations, p. 14.
96. ComAirPac history, pp. 116–17.
97. CVE Operations, pp. 12–13; Roscoe, p. 453; *Tulagi* AR, Serial 002, 5 February 1945, p. 1.

11. Visit to a Vile Island

1. VC-11 ACA No. 6, 12 January 1945.
2. *Nehenta Bay* Damage Report, Serial 001, 24 January 1945.
3. Reports of carriers involved; "Weekly Location."
4. Special Report of Participation of VOC-1 in Iwo Jima Operation, no serial, 13 March 1945, p. 9.
5. *Natoma Bay* AR, Serial 20034, 20 March 1945, Part III, p. 8, and Part V, pp. 8–9.
6. VC-84 ACA No. 22, 16 February 1945.
7. VC-81 ACA No. 48, 17 February 1945.
8. VOC-1 ACA No. 27, 17 February 1945.
9. VOC-1 ACA No. 28, 17 February 1945.
10. *Petrof Bay* AR, Serial 64, 13 March 1945, Enclosure A, p. 1.
11. *Lunga Point* AR, Serial 020, 11 March 1945, Enclosure C, p. 2.
12. VOC-1 Special Report, p. 4.
13. Ibid., pp. 2–10.
14. Analysis of Air Operations, Iwo Jima, p. 33.
15. "History of VC-77," p. 4.

16. ComServRon Six Logistics Analysis—Detachment Operation, Serial 0029, 8 March 1945, p. 6; CTG 50.8 AR, Serial 0028, 3 March 1945; *Windham Bay* AR, Serial 0011, 28 March 1945.

17. VC-88 ACA No. 29, 20 February 1945.

18. Warner and Warner, pp. 173–74; Morison XIV, *Victory in the Pacific*, pp. 52–53.

19. "History of the U.S.S. *Makin Island*," p. 18.

20. Morison XIV, p. 54; *Makin Island* AR, Serial 002, p. 17; Analysis of Air Operations, Iwo Jima, pp. 17–20.

21. Morison XIV, pp. 55–56.

22. *Lunga Point* AR, Serial 020, Enclosure H.

23. Ibid., Enclosure D, pp. 2–4, Enclosure E, pp. 1–2; BuShips No. 60, pp. 131–32.

24. *Bismarck Sea* AR, Serial 001, 25 February 1945, p. 1.

25. BuShips No. 60, p. 101.

26. "The History of the *Saginaw Bay*," Enclosure A, p. 19.

27. BuShips No. 60, pp. 102–3.

28. *Bismarck Sea* AR, Serial 001, p. 10; BuShips No. 60, pp. 99–106.

29. *Makin Island* AR, Serial 002, pp. 58–59.

30. Ibid., p. 51.

31. Analysis of Air Operations, Iwo Jima, pp. 19–21.

32. Morison XIV, pp. 56–57; Gilbert, p. 87.

33. CTG 52.2 AR, Serial 0028, 21 April 1945, p. 8.

34. *Natoma Bay* AR, Serial 20034, Part V, p. 9.

35. Ibid., Part V, p. 8.

36. VC-82 ACA No. 18, 6 March 1945.

37. VC-92 ACA No. 31, 3 March 1945.

38. *Natoma Bay* AR, Serial 20034, Part V, p. 10.

39. *Tulagi* AR, Serial 007, 14 March 1945, p. 26.

40. *Wake Island* AR, Serial 041, 13 March 1945, p. 12.

41. Morison XIV, p. 18; *Tulagi* AR, Serial 007, p. 5.

42. *Anzio* AR, Serial 004, 10 March 1945, Enclosure C.

43. Ibid.; VC-82 ASW No. 2, 27 February 1945; Morison XIV, p. 18.

44. *Anzio* AR, Serial 004, Enclosure C; VC-82 ASW No. 3, 27 February 1945; Morison XIV, p. 18.

45. Morison XIV, p. 19.

46. VC-77 history, p. 6.

47. *Makin Island* AR, Serial 002, pp. 23, 27.

48. *Lunga Point* AR, Serial 020, Enclosure C, p. 6; *Natoma Bay* AR, Serial 20034, Part III, p. 23; VC-88 ACA Nos. 59 and 63, 6 and 7 March 1945; VC-82 ACA No. 22, 7 March 1945.

49. *Natoma Bay* AR, Serial 20034, Part III, p. 23.

50. VC-84 ACA No. 92, 8 March 1945.

51. Fritter correspondence.

52. Analysis of Air Operations, Iwo Jima, p. 3.

53. *Lunga Point* AR, Serial 020, Enclosure C, p. 8, Enclosure D, p. 5.

54. Whitman S. Bartley, *Iwo Jima: Amphibious Epic*, p. 206.
55. Isely and Crowl, pp. 472, 507.
56. Analysis of Air Operations, Iwo Jima, p. 3.
57. *Anzio* AR, Serial 004, pp. 14–16; *Tulagi* AR, Serial 007, Part V, p. A-6.

12. The Longest Battle

1. "History of the U.S.S. *Natoma Bay*," p. 29.
2. Morison XIV, pp. 108–9.
3. Ibid., pp. 373–74, 386; reports of carriers involved; "Weekly Location."
4. *Natoma Bay* AR, Serial 20077, 30 June 1945, Part III, p. 5; *Sangamon* AR, Serial 044, 20 May 1945, Part VI, p. 17.
5. *Chenango* AR, Serial 0130, 4 July 1945, p. 6.
6. Analysis of Air Operations, Okinawa, p. 27.
7. Ibid.
8. *Tulagi* AR, Serial 0006, 6 June 1945, p. 76.
9. *Anzio* AR, Serial 00013, 29 July 1945, p. 4; *Makin Island* AR, Serial 005, 5 June 1945, Part III, p. 5.
10. "VC-13 History," Part II, p. 18.
11. VC-9 ACA No. 9; VC-84 ACA No. 102, both 27 March 1945.
12. *Marcus Island* AR, Serial 044, 2 May 1945, p. 3.
13. *Makin Island* AR, Serial 005, Part III, pp. 12–13.
14. *Petrof Bay* AR, Serial 229, 31 May 1945, p. 6; *Makin Island* AR, Serial 005, Part III, pp. 15–16; Fritter correspondence.
15. Morison XIV, p. 161.
16. *Lunga Point* AR, Serial 081, 27 June 1945, Enclosure C, p. 4; *Tulagi* AR, Serial 0006, p. 6.
17. *Sangamon* AR, Serial 044, Part III, p. 3.
18. *Lunga Point* AR, Serial 081, Enclosure D, p. 3.
19. Ibid., Enclosure C, pp. 4–5; Morison XIV, pp. 176–77.
20. VOC-2 history, 20 August 1945, p. 7.
21. S. Linton Smith, *U.S.S. Lunga Point*, p. 97; *Lunga Point* AR, Serial 081, Enclosure C, p. 5.
22. Anderson interview.
23. *Wake Island* AR, Serial 064, 8 April 1945; BuShips No. 60, pp. 133–35; *Marcus Island* AR, Serial 044, pp. 7–8.
24. CarDiv 24 AR, Serial 0028, 2 May 1945, p. 40.
25. Warner and Warner, p. 196.
26. *Anzio* AR, Serial 00013, p. 8.
27. VC-13 ACA No. 17, 6 April 1945.
28. Ibid.; Morison XIV, pp. 186–91; Roscoe, pp. 474–76.
29. VC-93 ACA No. 29, 6 April 1945.
30. VC-96 No. 32, 6 April 1945.
31. VC-85 ACA Nos. 133 and 134, both 6 April 1945.
32. Morison XIV, pp. 195–96; *Tulagi* AR, Serial 0006, pp. 8, 77–78.

33. Nichols and Shaw, p. 85.
34. *White Plains* history, p. 45.
35. *Breton* AR, Serial 035, 1 May 1945, pp. 1–3; Sherrod, p. 379.
36. *White Plains* history, p. 42; Sherrod, p. 412.
37. *Savo Island* AR, Serial 037, 7 May 1945, p. 3; CarDiv 24 history, p. 15.
38. Smith, *U.S.S. Lunga Point*, pp. 169–71; *Lunga Point* AR, Serial 081, p. 7.
39. VOC-2 ACA No. 58, 8 April 1945.
40. *Chenango* AR, Serial 0130, p. 3; *Santee* AR, Serial 050-45, 19 June 1945, Part V-A-5, p. 9.
41. George van Deurs, "Two-Block Fox," p. 304.
42. Richard J. Seyler correspondence.
43. Van Deurs oral history, p. 520.
44. Seyler correspondence.
45. Van Deurs, "Two-Block Fox," pp. 301–305; *Chenango* history, p. 33.
46. Morison XIV, p. 222.
47. Ibid., pp. 223–24.
48. *Makin Island* AR, Serial 005, Part III, pp. 25–26.
49. VF-40 ACA No. 4, 12 April 1945.
50. VC-93 ACA No. 37, 12 April 1945.
51. VOC-1 ACA No. 101; VC-85 ACA No. 156, both 12 April 1945; *Makin Island* AR, Serial 005, Part III, p. 26.
52. *Makin Island* AR, Serial 005, Part III, p. 26; VOC-2 ACA No. 74, 12 April 1945.
53. VF-40 ACA No. 5, 13 April 1945.
54. *Tulagi* AR, Serial 0006, p. 10; *Petrof Bay* AR, Serial 229, p. 10.
55. VOC-1 ACA No. 106, 15 April 1945; CarDiv 24 AR, Serial 0028, p. 35.
56. VF-33 ACA No. 32, 18 April 1945.
57. *Chenango* war history, p. 19.
58. VOC-1 ACA No. 104, 16 April 1945.
59. *Chenango* war history, p. 33.
60. *Marcus Island* AR, Serial 044, p. 17; VOC-1 ACA No. 103, 18 April 1945; Tillman, *The Wildcat in W W II*, p. 244.
61. *Sargent Bay* AR, Serial 032, 28 June 1945, p. 10.
62. *Chenango* AR, Serial 0130, p. 10.
63. *Natoma Bay* AR, Serial 20077, p. 33.
64. *Anzio* AR, Serial 00013, Appendix 6, also pp. 16–17; *Anzio* history, p. 39.
65. VC-92 ASW No. 4, 29 April 1945; *Tulagi* AR, Serial 0006, p. 19.
66. Warner and Warner, p. 231.
67. VOC-1 ACA Nos. 109 and 110, both 28 April 1945; *Marcus Island* AR, Serial 004, pp. 26–28.
68. *Petrof Bay* AR, Serial 229, p. 3.
69. Durgin letter to V. Adm. A. W. Fitch, 6 May 1945.

70. CarDiv 24 AR, Serial 0028, p. 23; *Makin Island* AR, Serial 005, p. 39; *Marcus Island* history, pp. 43–44.

71. Van Deurs oral history, p. 522.

72. Ibid.; Brooke Hindle, unpublished manuscript, "*Chenango* Never Called Herself a Queen," p. 10.

73. VC-96 ACA Nos. 61 and 62, both 3 May 1945.

74. *Sangamon* AR, Serial 044, Part III, p. 12; Report on Battle Action Aboard U.S.S. *Sangamon*, 4 May 1945, no serial, 11 May 1945, Enclosure A, pp. 1–2.

75. *Sangamon* Battle Action, Enclosure B, p. 2.

76. Ibid., Enclosure B, pp. 2–3, Enclosure H, pp. 1–2.

77. Ibid., Enclosure D, p. 4.

78. *Sangamon* AR, Serial 044, Part VIII, p. 4.

79. BuShips No. 60, pp. 72–73.

80. *Sangamon* AR, Serial 044; *Sangamon* Battle Action; BuShips No. 60, pp. 69–73; "Saga of the *Sangamon*," pp. 21–24.

81. Friedman, p. 152; *Hoggatt Bay* AR, Serial 069, 24 June 1945, Part III, p. 3; *Natoma Bay* AR, Serial 20077, Part IV, p. 1; *Saginaw Bay* AR, Serial 0142, 3 May 1945, Addendum One, p. 6.

82. Sherrod, p. 329.

83. Ibid., pp. 330–31.

84. Friedman, pp. 195, 199; Stefan Terzibaschitsch, *Escort Carriers and Aviation Support Ships of the U.S. Navy*, p. 128.

85. "*Block Island* Unit History," p. 2.

86. *Block Island* AR, Serial 065, 24 June 1945, Part III, p. 6.

87. Ibid., Part III, p. 14; John A. DeChant, *Devilbirds*, p. 247; VMF 511 WD, May 1945.

88. *Block Island* AR, Serial 065, Part III, p. 8; VMF-511 WD, May 1945.

89. *Block Island* AR, Serial 065, Part VI, pp. 5–6.

90. Ibid., Part VI, pp. 10–11, Part VIII, pp. 1–2.

91. *Gilbert Islands* AR, Serial 006, 24 June 1945, p. 14.

92. Ibid.; VMF-512 ACA No. 16, 8 June 1945; VMTB-143 ACA No. 20, 12 June 1945.

93. VMTB-143 ACA No. 29, 16 June 1945.

94. Sherrod, p. 397; DeChant, pp. 247–48.

95. Sherrod, p. 397.

96. *Petrof Bay* AR, Serial 229, pp. 19–20.

97. VC-13 ASW No. 18, 31 May 1945.

98. *Anzio* history, p. 41, Appendix I, p. 1.

99. Ibid., pp. 41–42.

100. VOC-2 ACA No. 177, 23 May 1945.

101. VC-8 ACA No. 4-45, 31 May 1945.

102. CTG 30.8 AR, Serial 0081, 14 June 1945, p. 2.

103. Adamson and Kosco, p. 180; Robert P. Harbold correspondence.

104. *Windham Bay*, Report of Typhoon of 4–5 June 1945, Serial 0028, 14 June 1945, p. 3.

105. Ibid., p. 4.

106. Ibid.

107. *Attu,* Encounter with Typhoon of 4–5 June 1945, Serial 0018, 12 June 1945, p. 2.

108. Ibid., p. 4.

109. ComServRon Six Logistics Analysis, Okinawa Operation, Serial 0072, 31 May 1945, pp. 9–10; CTG 30.8 AR, Serial 0093, 1 July 1945, Appendix I, pp. 2–4.

110. *Natoma Bay* AR, Serial 00033, 30 June 1945, Part III, p. 14, Part IV, pp. 1–2; BuShips No. 60, pp. 136–37.

111. *Natoma Bay* AR, Serial 00033, Part III, p. 15; *Hoggatt Bay* AR, Serial 069, 24 June 1945, Part V, p. 8.

112. *Hoggatt Bay* AR, Serial 069, Part III, p. 1.

113. Analysis of Air Operations, Okinawa, pp. 26–28.

114. VOC-1 history, p. 13.

115. Morison XIV, p. 282; James H. Belote and William H. Belote, *Typhoon of Steel,* p. 310.

116. Sherrod, p. 416; *Gilbert Islands* AR, Serial 007, 8 July 1945, p. 6.

117. VMF-511 WD, July 1945; *Block Island* AR, Serial 074, 11 July 1945, Part III, p. 6, Part VI, p. 2.

118. VC-13 ASW No. 19, 16 July 1945; Roscoe, p. 519; Morison XIV, p. 314.

119. *Anzio* history, p. 43.

120. Tillman, *The Wildcat in W W II,* p. 236.

121. Ibid., pp. 245–46; *Lunga Point* AR, Serial 0112, 7 August 1945; *Makin Island* AR, Serial 008-45, 9 August 1945; *Cape Gloucester* AR, Serial 079, 9 August 1945.

Epilogue

1. *Block Island* AR, Serial 097, 9 September 1945; *Santee* AR, Serial 094-45, 9 September 1945.

2. ComEsCarFor AR, Serial 0778, 10 November 1945; *Makin Island* AR, Serial 087-45, 15 Ocotber 1945; "*Kitkun Bay* War History," Chapter 20, pp. 2–4; Morison XV, *Supplement and General Index,* p. 8.

3. Morison XV, p. 17.

4. Ibid.; CarDiv 24 WD, December 1945.

5. Seyler correspondence.

6. TG 16.12 AR, Serial S1, 1 January 1946.

7. TG 16.12 AR, Serial 07, 15 March 1946, pp. 1, 4.

8. Terzibaschitsch, p. 42.

9. Cressman, p. 30.

BIBLIOGRAPHY

Official Records

Action Reports and War Diaries

For the carriers *Anzio* (ex-*Coral Sea*), *Barnes, Bismarck Sea, Block Island, Breton, Cape Esperance, Cape Gloucester, Chenango, Corregidor, Fanshaw Bay, Gambier Bay, Gilbert Islands, Hoggatt Bay, Kadashan Bay, Kalinin Bay, Kasaan Bay, Kitkun Bay, Kwajalein, Liscome Bay, Long Island, Lunga Point, Makin Island, Manila Bay, Marcus Island, Nassau, Natoma Bay, Nehenta Bay, Ommaney Bay, Petrof Bay, Roi, Rudyerd Bay, St. Lo* (ex-*Midway*), *Saginaw Bay, Sangamon, Santee, Sargent Bay, Savo Island, Shamrock Bay, Sitkoh Bay, Steamer Bay, Suwannee, Tulagi, Wake Island, White Plains, Windham Bay*. Various serials and dates.

Other Carrier Records

Altamaha, Encounter with Typhoon, 18 December 1944, Serial 004, 20 December 1944.

Attu Encounter with Typhoon of 4–5 June 1945, Serial 0018, 12 June 1945.

Chenango Air Operations Summaries. Various serials and dates.

———, Operations of Air Group at Guadalcanal, 10 March to 22 April 1943, no serial, 30 April 1943.

Hoggatt Bay, Comments on Antisubmarine Warfare, Serial 0020, 19 June 1944.

Nehenta Bay, Report of Typhoon of 18 December 1944, Serial 087, 24 December 1944.

———, Damage Report, Serial 001, 24 January 1945.

Sangamon, Report of Collision with U.S.S. *Suwannee,* Serial 003, 10 February 1944; Serial 004, 11 February 1944.

———, Report of Battle Action Aboard, no serial, 11 May 1945.

———, Aircraft Action Reports Summary, Serial 055, 30 September 1944.

Windham Bay, Report of Typhoon of 4–5 June 1945, Serial 0028, 14 June 1945.

Carrier Histories Held in Office of Naval Records
All carriers listed above under Action Reports.

Other Carrier Histories
"History of the U.S.S. *Anzio*," Serial 0152, 21 November 1945.
"*Block Island* Unit History," Serial 929, 28 November 1945.
"War History of U.S.S. *Chenango*," Serial 011, 31 January 1946.
"Corregidor—'Saga of the Mighty "C," ' " no serial, no date.
"A History of the U.S.S. *Fanshaw Bay*," Lt. H. B. Herbert, USNR.
"A News History of the U.S.S. *Hoggatt Bay*," Serial 39731, 18 October 1945.
"War History of the U.S.S. *Kadashan Bay*," Serial 065, 28 November 1945.
"History of the U.S.S. *Kalinin Bay*," no serial, no date.
"*Kassan Bay* Ship's History": Authorization to 1 July 1945, with supplement
    for third quarter 1945, no serial, no date.
Kasaan Bay, "A Brief History of an Active Small Carrier," no serial, no date.
"*Kitkun Bay* War History," Serial 900, 17 November 1945.
"Factual History of the U.S.S. *Lunga Point*," no serial, no date.
"History of the U.S.S. *Makin Island*," 9 May 1944–2 September 1945, no
    serial, no date.
"A History of the U.S.S. *Marcus Island* from the Period 16 December 1943 to
    31 August 1945," no serial, no date.
"History of the U.S.S. *Nassau*," Serial 018, 27 November 1945.
"History of the U.S.S. *Natoma Bay*," Serial 00001, October 1945.
"The History of the *Saginaw Bay*," Serial 0251, 9 October 1945.
"History of the U.S.S. *Sangamon*," Serial 075, 3 October 1945.
"Saga of the *Sangamon*."
"A History of the U.S.S. *Sargent Bay*," Lt. Walter E. Tremain, USNR.
"*Savo Island* Ship's History," Serial 112, 29 February 1946.
"War History U.S.S. *Shamrock Bay*," Serial 378, 1 December 1945.
"*Steamer Bay* War History," Serial 579, 1 December 1945.
"History of the U.S.S. *Suwannee*," Serial 488, 5 November 1945.

Squadron ACA and/or ASW Reports
CVEG-35, CVEG-37, CVEG-60, VF/VT-24, VF-26, VF-33, VF/VT-35, VF/
    VT-37, VF/VT-40, VT-60, VOC-1, VOC-2, VC-3, VC-4, VC-5, VC-8,
    VC-9, VC-11, VC-13, VC-20, VC-21, VC-27, VC-33, VC-41, VC-42, VC-
    63, VC-65, VC-66, VC-68, VC-75, VC-76, VC-77, VC-81, VC-82, VC-84,
    VC-85, VC-88, VC-90, VC-91, VC-92, VC-93, VC-94, VC-96, VC-97,
    VMF-512, VMTB-143; also War Diaries for VGF/VGS/VT-27, VMF-511,
    VMTB-233.
Various serials and dates.

Squadron Histories
"History of Air Group 26," Serial 28, 1 November 1945.
"History of Air Group 35," no serial, no date.
"History of Air Group 37," no serial, no date.

"History of Air Group 60," Serial 04, 1 March 1945.
"History of VF-27," no serial, no date.
"History of VOC-1," Serial 66, 10 July 1945.
"VOC-2 History," no serials, 8 January 1945, 1 March 1945, 20 August 1945.
"Porthole History of VC-3," Serial 133, 20 October 1945.
"History of VC-4," no serial, 16 October 1945.
"The Life and Times of VC-5 or The Odyssey of the Old Crow."
"History of VC-11," no serials, 23 January 1945, 20 September 1945.
"VC-13 History," no serials, 22 June 1945, 24 September 1945.
"History of VC-20," Serial 14-45, 12 February 1945.
"History of VC-21 30 October 1943–31 January 1945," no serial, no date.
"History of VC-27," Serial 04, 10 March 1945.
"VC-42 History," no serial, 26 May 1945.
"VC-63 Squadron History 20 May 1943 to 13 October 1945," Serial 125, 16 October 1945.
"History of VC-68," Serial 012, 11 November 1944.
"History of VC-76," no serial, 10 March 1945.
"History of VC-77," no serial, 24 March 1945.
"History of VC-81," Serial 03517, 24 September 1945.
"History of VC-84 6 January 1944 to 23 May 1945," no serial, 25 August 1945.
"History of VC-85," Serial 018, 7 June 1945.
"VC-90 History," Serial 187, 15 March 1945.

Carrier Division Action Reports and War Diaries
CarDivs 22, 23, 24, 26. Various serials and dates.

Other Carrier Division Records
CarDiv 22: Employment of *Sangamon* Class ACV, Serial 0010, 18 February 1943.
CarDiv 22: VF Action Reports, 18 and 21 July 1943, no serials.
History of Carrier Division 24, Serial 0141, 6 June 1945.

Task Force, Task Group, Task Unit Records
CTF 18 Action Report, Serial 0010, 19 February 1943.
CTF 51 Action Report, Serial 00100, 8 July 1943.
CTF 52 Action Report, Serial 0232, 24 August 1944.
CTF 53 Action Reports, various serials and dates.
CTG 16.12 Action Reports, various serials and dates.
CTG 30.8/50.8 Action Reports, various serials and dates.
CTG 32.7 Action Report, Serial 00011, 10 October 1944.
CTG 51.2 Action Report, Serial 0044, 15 February 1944.
CTG 52.13 Report of Loss of U.S.S. *Liscome Bay*, Serial 0034, 11 December 1943.
CTG 52.14 Report of Strafing of Friendly Troops, Serial 0015, 8 July 1944.

CTG 52.2 Action Report, Serial 0028, 21 April 1945.
CTG 52.9 Action Report, Serial 0019, 18 February 1944.
CTG 53.6 Action Report, Serial 054, 1 March 1944.
CTU 32.7.1 Action Report, Serial 0013, 5 October 1944.
CTU 53.7.2 Action Report, Serial 0105, 8 August 1944.
CTU 77.4.1 Action Report, Serial 00161, 27 January 1945.
CTU 77.4.2 Action Report, Serial 00114, 2 November 1944.
CTU 77.4.3 Action Report, Serial 0030A, 14 November 1944.

Commander, Air Force Pacific Fleet Records

History, Commander Air Force Pacific Fleet, Serial 002238, 3 December 1945.
Analysis of Pacific Air Operations. Various serials and dates.
Air Operations Memorandums. Various serials and dates.
Air Analysis, Supplementary Report of Carrier Operations of 30 January–24 February 1944, Serial 00395, 20 April 1944.
Air Analysis, Palau Operations, September 1944, Serial 001809, no date.
Air Analysis, Carrier Operations in the Philippines, September 1944, Serial 00231, 4 February 1945.
Air Analysis, Carrier Operations in Support of the Leyte Campaign, 17–31 October 1944, Serial 00233, 4 February 1945.
Analysis of Air Operations, CVE Operations, January 1945, Serial 00887, 23 April 1945.
Analysis of Air Operations, Iwo Jima, February–March 1945, Serial 001452, 21 June 1945.
Analysis of Air Operations, Okinawa Carrier Operations, March–June 1945, Serial 002144, 28 September 1945.

Other Documents

"Loss of *Liscome Bay*," CominCh Serial 002903, 30 December 1943.
CominCh *Battle Experience* Series:

> "Assault and Occupation of Attu Island, May 1943." Secret Information Bulletin No. 9.
> "Supporting Operations Before and During the Occupation of the Gilbert Islands, November 1943." Secret Information Bulletin No. 15.
> "Eniwetok, February 1944." Secret Information Bulletin No. 17.
> "Battle for Leyte Gulf, 23–27 October 1944." Secret Information Bulletin No. 22.

United States Fleet Antisubmarine Bulletin. Various monthly dates.
Bureau of Aeronautics, "Weekly Location of United States Naval Aircraft."
"Loss of *Liscome Bay*," Bureau of Ships War Damage Report No. 45, 10 March 1944.
"Escort Carriers' Gunfire, Bomb and Kamikaze Damages and Losses During World War II," Bureau of Ships War Damage Report No. 60, 31 July 1948.

Office of Naval Intelligence *Combat Narratives:*

"The Aleutians Campaign, June 1942–August 1943." (1945)
"Japanese Evacuation of Guadalcanal, 29 January–8 February 1943."
(1944)
"The Assault on Kwajalein and Majuro (Part One)." (1945)
CinCPac Dispatches. Various dates.
CinCPac Report of Operations in the Pacific Ocean Areas. Various serials
and dates.
History of Escort Carrier Force, Pacific Fleet, Serial 618, 12 November
1945.
Commander Escort Carrier Force Action Report, Serial 0778, 10 November
1945.
History and Accomplishment of Carrier Transport Squadron, Pacific Fleet,
1 June 1944 through August 1945, Serial 1078, 29 October 1945.
Commander Service Squadron Six Action Reports and Logistics Analysis
Reports, various serials and dates.
"Carrier Aircraft in Battle for Leyte Gulf, 24–26 October 1944." Air Opera-
tions Research Group Report No. 18, 10 April 1945.
Commo. Richard W. Bates, USN (Ret.). *The Battle for Leyte Gulf, October
1944. Strategical and Tactical Analysis.* (5 vol.) Naval War College. (1957–
58)
In Samuel E. Morison files at Operational Archives, Washington Navy Yard:

Anti-Suicide Action Summary August 1945, Cominch P.0011, Ref.
Series II, Vol. XIV, No. 2; Action Record of Kamikaze Attack Forces,
Ref. Series III, Vol. XIV, No. 24; Statistical Information on World
War II Carrier Experience, Aviation History Section, DCNO (Air),
October 1950, Ref. Series IV, Box 111.

V. Adm. Calvin T. Durgin correspondence and records files at Operational
Archives, Washington Navy Yard.
Luzon Campaign (Vol. I), Air Evaluation Board, SWPA, 2 May 1946.

Narratives at Operational Archives, Washington Navy Yard

Capt. W. V. R. Vieweg, 18 December 1944.
Capt. H. L. Young, 3 March 1945.

Oral Histories at Operational Archives, Washington Navy Yard

V. Adm. Gerald F. Bogan.
V. Adm. Fitzhugh Lee.
Adm. Felix B. Stump.
R. Adm. George van Deurs.

Correspondence and Interviews

John J. Eberle—*Altamaha;* R. Adm. George van Deurs, USN (Ret.), Alexander G. Booth, Dr. Brooke Hindle, Richard J. Seyler—*Chenango;* Capt.

R. S. Rogers, USN (Ret.) (VC-68), Bill Hewson—*Fanshaw Bay;* R. Adm. William R. McClendon, USN (Ret.), Capt. Edward J. Huxtable, USN (Ret.) (VC-10), Jack Turner (VC-10), C. J. Dugan (VC-10), Henry A. Pyzdrowski (VC-10), S. J. Johnson—*Gambier Bay;* Theodore H. Gardner—*Kalinin Bay;* R. N. Willis—*Long Island;* Fred A. Chelemedos—*Lunga Point;* Jess U. Fritter—*Makin Island;* Cdr. Stanley E. Sykes, USN (Ret.)— *Manila Bay;* Herb Faulkner, Hamilton Lokey—*Natoma Bay;* Henry H. Henderson (VC-75), A. R. Zubik (VC-75), William S. Stewart, Charles Rudolph—*Ommaney Bay;* Capt. John D. Ahlstrom, USNR (Ret.), Carl Gable—*Petrof Bay;* Robert P. Harbold—*Salamaua;* George E. Treneer— *Sangamon;* Maury Anderson—*Steamer Bay;* Father Zachary Callahan— *Thetis Bay;* Judge Robert F. Johnson, Edward W. Reed—*White Plains.* (Mr. Harbold and Mr. Lokey both provided copies of their unpublished memoirs; Dr. Hindle provided a draft of a book he is writing on the *Chenango;* and Mr. Pyzdrowski provided narratives by Morris Montgomery, John Stewart, and Lawrence O. Chapman.)

Books

Adamson, Col. Hans Christian, USAF (Ret.), and Capt. George Francis Kosco, USN (Ret.). *Halsey's Typhoons.* New York: Crown Publishers, 1967.

Bartley, Lt. Col. Whitman S., USMC. *Iwo Jima: Amphibious Epic.* Washington: Historical Branch, Headquarters, U.S. Marine Corps, 1954.

Belote, James H., and William H. Belote. *Typhoon of Steel: The Battle for Okinawa.* New York: Harper and Row, 1970.

Blair, Clay, Jr. *Silent Victory.* Philadelphia: Lippincott, 1975.

Bulkley, Capt. Robert J., Jr., USNR (Ret.). *At Close Quarters.* Washington: Naval History Division, 1962.

Calhoun, Capt. C. Raymond, USN (Ret.). *Typhoon: The Other Enemy.* Annapolis: Naval Institute Press, 1981.

Crowl, Philip A. *Campaign in the Marianas.* Washington: Office of the Chief of Military History, Department of the Army, 1960.

Crowl, Philip A., and Edmund G. Love. *Seizure of the Gilberts and Marshalls.* Washington: Office of the Chief of Military History, Department of the Army, 1955.

DeChant, John A. *Devilbirds.* New York: Harper and Brothers, 1947.

Dull, Paul S. *A Battle History of the Imperial Japanese Navy (1941–1945).* Annapolis: Naval Institute Press, 1978.

Field, James A., Jr. *The Japanese at Leyte Gulf.* Princeton: Princeton University Press, 1947.

Friedman, Norman. *U.S. Aircraft Carriers.* Annapolis: Naval Institute Press, 1983.

Garand, George W., and Truman R. Strobridge. *Western Pacific Operations.* Washington: Historical Division, Headquarters, U.S. Marine Corps, 1971.

Garfield, Brian. *The Thousand-Mile War.* Garden City, N.Y.: Doubleday, 1969.

Gilbert, Cdr. Price, Jr., USNR, editor. *The Escort Carriers in Action.* Atlanta: Ruralist Press, 1946.

Heinl, Lt. Col. Robert D., Jr., USMC, and Lt. Col. John A. Crown, USMC. *The Marshalls: Increasing the Tempo.* Washington: Historical Branch, Headquarters, U.S. Marine Corps, 1954.

Hoffman, Maj. Carl W., USMC. *The Seizure of Tinian.* Washington: Historical Division, Headquarters, U.S. Marine Corps, 1951.

Hough, Maj. Frank O., USMC. *The Assault on Peleliu.* Washington: Historical Division, Headquarters, U.S. Marine Corps, 1950.

Howard, Clive, and Joe Whitley. *One Damned Island After Another.* Chapel Hill: University of North Carolina Press, 1946.

Hoyt, Edwin P. *The Battle of Leyte Gulf.* New York: Weybright and Talley, 1972.

———. *The Men of the Gambier Bay.* Middlebury, Vt.: Paul S. Eriksson, 1979.

Inoguchi, Capt. Rikihei, IJN, and Cdr. Tadashi Nakajima, IJN, and Roger Pineau. *The Divine Wind.* Annapolis: United States Naval Institute, 1958.

Isely, Jeter A., and Philip A. Crowl. *The U.S. Marines and Amphibious War.* Princeton: Princeton University Press, 1951.

Ives, Almon B., and Ben A. Meginniss, editors. *The Chenanigan, Victory Edition 1942–1945.* Los Angeles: Kater Engraving Co., 1946.

Karig, Capt. Walter, USNR, et al. *Battle Report.* Vol V. *Victory in the Pacific.* New York: Rinehart, 1949.

Lodge, Maj. O. R., USMC. *The Recapture of Guam.* Washington: Historical Branch, Headquarters, U.S. Marine Corps, 1954.

Morison, Samuel Eliot. *History of United States Naval Operations in World War II.* Vol. IV, *Coral Sea, Midway and Submarine Actions.* Vol. V, *The Struggle for Guadalcanal.* Vol. VI, *Breaking the Bismarcks Barrier.* Vol. VII, *Aleutians, Gilberts and Marshalls.* Vol. VIII, *New Guinea and the Marianas.* Vol. XII, *Leyte.* Vol. XIII, *The Liberation of the Philippines.* Vol. XIV, *Victory in the Pacific.* Vol. XV, *Supplement and General Index.* Boston: Atlantic–Little, Brown, 1949–1962.

Natoma Bay Association, *Logbook.* Privately printed, no date.

Nichols, Maj. Charles S., Jr., USMC, and Henry I. Shaw, Jr. *Okinawa: Victory in the Pacific.* Washington: Historical Branch, Headquarters, U.S. Marine Corps, 1955.

U.S.S. Ommaney Bay (CVE-79) and Composite Squadron VC-75 History. Ommaney Bay Association. Privately printed, no date.

Peyton, Green. *5,000 Miles Towards Tokyo.* Norman: University of Oklahoma Press, 1945.

Potter, E. B. *Bull Halsey.* Annapolis: Naval Institute Press, 1985.

Reynolds, Clark G. *The Fast Carriers.* New York: McGraw-Hill, 1968.

Roscoe, Theodore. *United States Destroyer Operations in World War II.* Annapolis: United States Naval Institute, 1953.

Sherrod, Robert. *History of Marine Corps Aviation in World War II.* Washington: Combat Forces Press, 1952.

Smith, Robert Ross. *The Approach to the Philippines*. Washington: Office of the Chief of Military History, Department of the Army, 1953.

Smith, Lt. S. Linton, USNR. *U.S.S. Lunga Point, CVE-94*. Raleigh: Edwards and Broughton, 1946.

Stewart, Adrian. *The Battle of Leyte Gulf*. New York: Scribner's, 1980.

Terzibaschitsch, Stefan. *Escort Carriers and Aviation Support Ships of the U.S. Navy*. Annapolis: Naval Institute Press, 1981.

Tillman, Barrett. *Avenger at War*. New York: Scribner's, 1980.

————. *The Wildcat in W W II*. Annapolis: Nautical and Aviation Publishing Co., 1983.

U.S. Strategic Bombing Survey (Pacific). *The Campaigns of the Pacific War*. Washington: Government Printing Office, 1946.

————. *Interrogations of Japanese Officials*, two volumes. Washington, Government Printing Office, 1946.

Warner, Denis, and Peggy Warner. *The Sacred Warriors*. New York: Avon, 1984.

Woodward, C. Vann. *The Battle for Leyte Gulf*. New York: Macmillan, 1947.

Y'Blood, William T. *Red Sun Setting*. Annapolis: Naval Institute Press, 1981.

————. *Hunter-Killer*. Annapolis: Naval Institute Press, 1983.

Articles

Ahlstrom, Capt. John D., USNR (Ret.). "Leyte Gulf Remembered." United States Naval Institute *Proceedings*, August 1984.

Beebe, Capt. Marshall U., USN (Ret.). "Sis—*Liscome Bay* and Toko-Ri." Naval Aviation Museum Foundation, Inc., *Foundation*, Spring 1984.

Cressman, Robert J. "The President's Escort Carrier." *The Hook*, Spring 1984.

Deac, Wilfred P. "The Battle off Samar." *American Heritage*, December 1966.

Dickinson, Cdr. C. E., USN, with Boyden Sparkes. "Plug That Last Rat Hole!" *Saturday Evening Post*, 27 January 1945.

Fletcher, Lt. Cdr. Leon, USNR (Ret.). "Rescue of the *Gambier Bay*, CVE-73." *Sea Classics*, May 1981.

Hathaway, Cdr. Amos Townsend, USN. "The Battle as I Saw It." *American Magazine*, April 1945.

Lee, Capt. Fitzhugh, USN. "Shock and Flame—The Kamikazes Strike." *New York Times Magazine*, 1 July 1945.

Morris, Frank. "Overnight Guest." *Colliers*, 2 September 1944.

Reynolds, Quentin, et al. "America's Greatest Naval Battle." *Colliers*, 13–27 January 1945.

Schwartz, Y2c Robert L. "The Sinking of the *Liscome Bay*." *Yank* (Southwest Pacific Edition), 28 July 1944.

Sprague, R. Adm. C. A. F., USN, as told to Lt. Philip H. Gustafson, USNR. "The Japs Had Us on the Ropes." *American Magazine*, April 1945.

"They Ran . . . But Won," *All Hands*, January 1945.

Van Deurs, R. Adm. George, USN (Ret.). "Two-Block Fox." Naval Institute *Proceedings*, March 1955.

White, Lt. Robb, USNR. "Life on an 'Oil-Slick'." *Flying*, July 1945.

INDEX

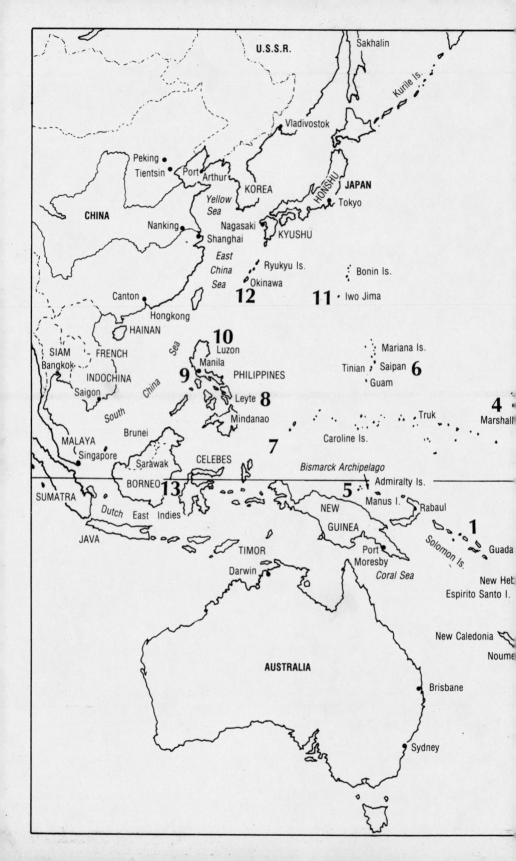